D0679240

Comparative Economic Systems

MODELS and CASES

THE IRWIN SERIES IN ECONOMICS

Consulting Editor
LLOYD G. REYNOLDS
Yale University

AMES *Soviet Economic Processes*
ANDERSON, GITLOW, & DIAMOND (eds.) *General Economics: A Book of Readings* rev. ed.
BALASSA *The Theory of Economic Integration*
BEAL & WICKERSHAM *The Practice of Collective Bargaining* 3d ed.
BLAUG *Economic Theory in Retrospect* rev. ed.
BORNSTEIN (ed.) *Comparative Economic Systems: Models and Cases* rev. ed.
BORNSTEIN & FUSFELD (eds.) *The Soviet Economy: A Book of Readings* rev. ed.
BUCHANAN *The Public Finances* rev. ed.
CARTTER *Theory of Wages and Employment*
CARTTER & MARSHALL *Labor Economics: Wages, Employment, and Trade Unionism*
DAVIDSON, SMITH, & WILEY *Economics: An Analytical Approach* rev. ed.
DAVIS, HUGHES, & MCDOUGALL *American Economic History: The Development of a National Economy* rev. ed.
DOLL, RHODES, & WEST *Economics of Agricultural Production, Markets, and Policy*
DRUMMOND *The Canadian Economy: Organization and Development*
DUE *Government Finance: Economics of the Public Sector* 4th ed.
DUE & CLOWER *Intermediate Economic Analysis* 5th ed.
FELLNER *Probability and Profit: A Study of Economic Behavior along Bayesian Lines*
FERGUSON *Microeconomic Theory*

GAMBS & KOMISAR *Economics and Man* 3d ed.

GORDON *The Investment Financing and Valuation of the Corporation*

GRAMPP & WEILER (eds.) *Economic Policy: Readings in Political Economy* 3d ed.

GROSSMAN, HANSEN, HENDRIKSEN, MCALLISTER, OKUDA, & WOLMAN (eds.) *Readings in Current Economics* rev. ed.

GUTHRIE *Statistical Methods in Economics*

GUTHRIE & WALLACE *Economics* 4th ed.

HAGEN *The Economics of Development*

HARRISS *The American Economy: Principles, Practices, and Policies* 6th ed.

HERBER *Modern Public Finance*

HIGGINS *United Nations and U.S. Foreign Economic Policy*

JOME *Principles of Money and Banking*

KINDLEBERGER *International Economics* 4th ed.

KUHLMAN & SKINNER *The Economic System* rev. ed.

LEE *Macroeconomics: Fluctuations, Growth, and Stability* 4th ed.

LLOYD *Microeconomic Analysis*

LOCKLIN *Economics of Transportation* 6th ed.

MEYERS *Economics of Labor Relations*

PEGRUM *Public Regulation of Business* rev. ed.

PEGRUM *Transportation: Economics and Public Policy* rev. ed.

PHILLIPS *The Economics of Regulation: Theory and Practice in the Transportation and Public Utility Industries*

REYNOLDS *Economics: A General Introduction* rev. ed.

RIMA *Development of Economic Analysis*

SCITOVSKY *Welfare and Competition: The Economics of a Fully Employed Economy*

SIEGEL *Aggregate Economics and Public Policy* rev. ed.

SIRKIN *Introduction to Macroeconomic Theory* rev. ed.

SMITH & TEIGEN (eds.) *Readings in Money, National Income, and Stabilization Policy*

SNIDER *Introduction to International Economics* 4th ed.

SPENCER *Managerial Economics: Text, Problems, and Short Cases* 3d ed.

VANEK *International Trade: Theory and Economic Policy*

WILCOX *Public Policies toward Business* 3d ed.

Comparative Economic Systems

MODELS and CASES

Edited by

MORRIS BORNSTEIN
Professor of Economics
The University of Michigan

Revised Edition
1969

Richard D. Irwin, Inc., Homewood, Illinois
Irwin-Dorsey Limited, Nobleton, Ontario

Revised Edition
First Printing, February, 1969

Library of Congress Catalog Card No. 68–56873
Printed in the United States of America

PREFACE

THIS BOOK is about the organization, operation, and performance of economic systems, both in theory and in practice. It deals with alternative methods of determining the bill of goods to be produced, the allocation of resources to produce it, and the distribution of the resulting income. These are some of the most vital questions of our time—urgent issues for all living economies, both non-Communist and Communist, both developed and underdeveloped. This book explores various alternative answers by analyzing different economic systems and comparing them with each other.

This collection of readings is primarily intended for use in college courses in comparative economic systems. It is somewhat unorthodox because it is specifically designed to serve either as collateral reading in conjunction with one of the textbooks in the field, or as the core around which a comparative economic systems course can be organized. With the latter purpose in mind, I have prepared editorial notes for each division, section, and article in the book which integrate the various parts and selections and which place them in an overall conceptual framework. With few exceptions, the selections are articles reprinted in their entirety, rather than isolated excerpts. As a result, they present the author's full argument and at the same time are of an appropriate length for student reading assignments.

The selections in this volume are the fruit of an extensive search of the literature over a number of years in connection with my courses in comparative economic systems at The University of Michigan. They include "classic" articles by the most distinguished figures in the field, as well as lesser known, often overlooked articles by other authors. In many cases, the articles are reprinted from out-of-print volumes or less accessible journals. All of them can be read with understanding and profit by students with a good grasp of the principles of economics. The book is designed for use in courses in comparative economic systems which require only a year's work in economics as a prerequisite. In a few instances, very technical passages, references to foreign language sources, or supplementary statistical tables have been omitted.

This book covers the principal topics included in most college courses in comparative economic systems, although it is impossible in a volume of reasonable size to include all of the topics treated by different instructors in a field as broadly defined as comparative economic systems. The book excludes certain topics which are covered by relatively few instructors, for example primitive economies, as well as other topics on which a considerable variety of material is readily available in inexpensive paperback form, such as Marxism.

The various topics in this volume are presented in the order I have found most satisfactory in my courses in comparative economic systems at The University of Michigan. Part I provides a conceptual framework for the rest of the book by explaining the criteria by which the performance of an economy may be judged. Part II presents theoretical models of the three most important economic systems—the capitalist market economy, the socialist market economy, and central planning. In Part III these models are illustrated by a number of case studies, including the United States, France, Yugoslavia, the Soviet Union, Eastern Europe, and Mainland China. The selections in Part IV compare economic systems from different standpoints, including the nature of management and the economic system as an instrument of economic development. The concluding selections summarize some of the main points of the book by examining the proposition that Western market and Communist planned economies are becoming more alike.

Although the material is presented in this order, the articles are chosen and the book is constructed so that the selections can logically and conveniently be assigned in several different orders and combinations, to fit the particular instructor's approach to the subject. For example, the case studies in Part III can be assigned immediately after the theoretical models in Part II which they illustrate. Some instructors will prefer to consider the intermediate case of the socialist market economy after presenting the more extreme cases of the capitalist market economy and central planning. Others may find it desirable to use the selection on management in Part IV in conjunction with the discussion of central planning in Parts II and III. Other suggestions for the use of this volume, in conjunction with existing textbooks or as a core book, are offered in the *Teacher's Manual* to accompany the book.

Almost half of the selections in this edition did not appear in the first edition. I wish to thank the many users of the first edition who kindly made suggestions for the new edition. I also wish to express my appreciation to the authors and publishers who granted permission to reprint the selections included in this book. Finally, I am grateful to my wife, Reva, for her encouragement and forbearance during its preparation.

Ann Arbor, Michigan
February, 1969

MORRIS BORNSTEIN

TABLE OF CONTENTS

PART I. PERFORMANCE CRITERIA

PART II. MODELS OF ECONOMIC SYSTEMS

Capitalist Market Economy

Socialist Market Economy

Centrally Planned Economy

PART III. CASE STUDIES OF ECONOMIC SYSTEMS

Regulated Capitalism

Market Socialism

PART I

Performance Criteria

An analytical framework for comparing economic systems is essential in the study of comparative economic systems—both economic models and living economies. The most common bases of comparison are (1) the ownership of the means of production and (2) the method of resource allocation. The means of production may be owned privately (individually), as in capitalism, or publicly (collectively), as in socialism. In turn, resources may be allocated by markets through the use of prices, as in a decentralized market economy, or by administrative commands expressed in real (physical) terms, as in a centrally planned economy. And there are various combinations of institutions and instruments; for example, market socialism combines public ownership with the use of markets and prices for decentralized resource allocation decisions. The nature and problems of capitalist and socialist, and market and centrally planned, economies are analyzed in detail in Parts II and III of this book.

In addition to studying similarities and differences in economic institutions and instruments, it is useful also to compare economic systems in terms of some common criteria which may be regarded as "performance" or "success" indicators. This is the approach of the following selection.

1. SUCCESS CRITERIA FOR ECONOMIC SYSTEMS*

Bela A. Balassa

How can the performance of economic systems —either models or actual cases—be compared? Balassa suggests that this can be done by (1) evaluating an economic system in terms of a number of criteria or "success indicators" and (2) combining the resulting "scores" according to a preference scale which expresses the relative importance of the various indicators. He distinguishes and analyzes five success indicators: static efficiency, dynamic efficiency, growth, consumer satisfaction, and income distribution. Some of these indicators are mutually supporting, while others are mutually conflicting. He compares a capitalist market economy and a socialist planned economy in regard to each indicator, showing the difficulty of reaching a clear-cut conclusion about the superiority of one economic blueprint over the other.

The relative importance of these success indicators, and thus the evaluation of an economic system, will, however, depend on whose preferences or scale of values are considered. For example, the preferences of households, expressed through consumer sovereignty in a market economy, are likely to be very different from those of a central planning authority. Balassa points out the shortcomings of both unlimited consumer sovereignty and authoritarian planning as preference systems. (In Selection No. 8, Jan Drewnowski argues that individual and state preferences can and must be combined into a "dual" preference system.)

---

* Reprinted, with permission, from *The Hungarian Experience in Economic Planning* (New Haven: Yale University Press, 1959), pp. 5–24. Bela A. Balassa is Professor of Political Economy at the Johns Hopkins University.

1. Success Criteria for Economic Systems

ECONOMISTS have long been concerned with the definition of an economic optimum and with the ways it can be achieved. In the first decade of this century V. Pareto defined an optimum (efficient) position by the requirement that there should not exist any possible reallocation of resources which could make anybody better off without making somebody worse off.[1] One of the conditions of a Pareto optimum is that there should be no possibility of increasing the production of one commodity without reducing the production of another. It has been pointed out that this Pareto optimum is not a single point, that there are many possible positions fulfilling the above criteria. All these optima are positions of general equilibrium.

Pareto optima indicate efficient allocation of resources among alternative uses. It can be shown that—within certain simplifying assumptions—efficient allocation of resources is achieved in pure competition, where the so-called marginal equivalences are fulfilled.[2] But the distribution of income resulting from pure competition may not be considered desirable. It is conventionally assumed that the distribution of income can be changed without impairing efficiency by so-called lump-sum redistributions.[3]

In a static system the fulfillment of the conditions for Pareto optima would supply us with a test of efficiency on the basis of which the performance of different economic systems could be evaluated. Since we do not live in a static world, such a test would not lead us very far. Whereas under static conditions the only variable considered is the efficient allocation of resources at a given point of time, in a dynamic world we have to consider more variables than mere static efficiency; next to it, the dynamic efficiency of the system, the growth rate, consumer satisfaction, and the distribution of income are those of basic importance.[4] Considering these variables as success indicators, the evaluation of different economic systems requires the following:

1. *Success Indicators.* We have to extend the meaning of "efficiency test," since efficiency (static and dynamic) does not exhaust the list of variables on the basis of which a conclusion with regard to different economic systems should be reached. We can assume that different values[5]

---

[1] *Manuel d'économie politique* (Paris, 1909), chap. 6.

[2] For a good exposition of the necessary marginal conditions for an optimum see K. E. Boulding's "Welfare Economics," in *A Survey of Contemporary Economics* (2 vols.; Homewood, Ill.: Richard D. Irwin, Inc., 1948–52), Vol. 2 (ed. B. F. Haley, 1952), pp. 14–23.

[3] Lump-sum redistribution means a system of taxes and subsidies which, not being anticipated, do not affect the individual's effort and risk-taking.

[4] These concepts will be defined and examined in the next section.

[5] By values we mean higher or lower levels of any success indicator, some of which are quantitatively measurable (for example, growth by the percentage rate of increase of national income). Some of these, on the other hand, are not measurable quantitatively (for example, static or dynamic efficiency); for them only ordinal ranking can be used.

of our success indicators can be achieved under conditions postulated in various economic systems. Some of the variables are partly cumulative, in the sense that an increase in *A* leads to an increase in *B* (for example, an improvement in dynamic efficiency leads to an increase of the growth rate); some are competitive in the sense that an increase in the value of *C* leads to a reduction in the value of *D* (for example, an equal distribution of income is likely to lead to less efficient resource allocation, or a higher growth rate requires restriction of present consumption). Naturally, even for partly cumulative variables there must be at least one other variable which serves as a restraint, that is, the reduction of which is needed for a further increase of the former variable. In technical terms, for any economic system there is a maximum value of any one variable attainable, given the values of the other variables. The maximum values of the success indicators obtained in this way show the performance of the system. For example, an economic system may achieve a higher degree of static efficiency and more equitable income distribution than another system with a higher degree of dynamic efficiency and a higher growth rate.

2. *Scale of Preferences.* There is only one case where there is no difficulty in choosing between two economic systems. That is when in system Z a higher value of all five success indicators can be achieved than in system *W*. If some of the success indicators show a higher value in one, some in another system, we need additional criteria in order to choose between the systems. One has to decide which success indicators are of greater importance, which have higher priority; in other words, a scale of preferences is needed. The choice between different economic systems should be made on the basis of their proficiency in the various fields enumerated above, given a certain scale of preferences with regard to the success indicators.

We face two questions here: Can we determine theoretically the workings of different economic systems with regard to our success indicators, and can we construct some kind of preference scale on the basis of which the importance of different values of the success indicators can be evaluated? Only if we are able to answer both questions in the affirmative is it possible to present the economist's case with regard to the choice between different systems. But even if this decision can be made, we face the further problem whether these systems can be realized in the real world in their theoretical purity.[6]

[6] In technical terms we have to devise a possibility function for the various economic systems, indicating the maximum achievable value of any success indicator given the values of the other variables. Furthermore, a social welfare function is needed to indicate the society's preferences for the various success indicators. That system would be judged to be superior the possibility function of which is tangent to the highest social welfare function.

THE SUCCESS INDICATORS

STATIC EFFICIENCY IN THE ALLOCATION OF RESOURCES

Static efficiency may be defined as production conforming to the preferences of the community[7] when there is no possibility of increasing the production of one commodity without reducing the production of another. It has been pointed out in the last section that static efficiency can be achieved in an economic system organized according to the rules of competition. Consequently, with regard to static efficiency, the real difference is not between a free enterprise and a socialist system but between, on the one hand, free enterprise and the socialist market solution, and on the other, centralized physical planning.

From the analytical point of view the workings of a purely competitive system and of the market solution for socialism, and the results they lead to, are essentially the same. Nevertheless, some analytical differences have already been noted; in addition, two more factors should be considered.

Socialist writers neglect the importance of the cost of information in the socialist market solution. Whereas in pure competition the information needed to reach equilibrium is possessed by the decision-making units, here it must be collected by the Planning Board, and its collection is time-consuming and costly. Although this disadvantage of the socialist market solution is not relevant in its Yugoslav form, the problem of incentives does arise there also. It can be argued that in a static world the profit motive as incentive leads to a more efficient allocation of resources in a free enterprise system than is possible in the competition of socialist firms.[8]

Centralized planning based on the physical allocation of resources dispenses with the price mechanism in resource allocation. Prices do not express relative scarcities in this system but serve only accounting purposes. Consequently, efficient allocation of resources cannot be achieved. On the other hand, the use of pricing in resource allocation would make centralized planning similar to the socialist market solution.

With regard to static efficiency pure competition appears to be superior to centralized planning on the physical level. Nevertheless, there are two

---

[7] "The preferences of the community" may mean either individual preferences or the authoritative decision of the Planning Board with regard to the final bill of goods (goods destined for ultimate consumption or investment). Efficiency as here defined corresponds to the concept of productive efficiency used by T. C. Koopmans, *Three Essays on the State of Economic Science* (New York: McGraw-Hill Book Co., Inc., 1957), p. 84.

[8] For some further problems concerning the operation of the socialist market solution see F. A. Hayek, "Socialist Calculation: The Competitive 'Solution,'" *Economica*, New Series, Vol. VII, No. 26 (May, 1940), pp. 125–49 [reprinted in this volume as Selection 6, pp. 77–97].

types of "market failure"[9] which impair the efficiency of a competitive system: those existing in a static world with perfect information and foresight, and those connected with imperfect information and uncertain expectations.

The first type contains the following factors:

1. Under conditions of increasing returns competition will break down, partly because monopolies will be formed, partly because an optimum position may be reached only if enterprises producing under increasing returns minimize rather than maximize profit.[10]

2. Direct interaction between producers, between consumers, or between producers and consumers which is unaccounted for in market valuations, also impairs the efficiency of the system. A standard example for these external effects between producers is the apple-grower whose orchard blossoms provide food free of charge for the bees of the nearby beekeeper. Although the social productivity of apple-growing is therefore higher than its private productivity, the farmer's production decisions are based on the latter only; hence apple-growing stops short of the social optimum. A classic example of diseconomies in production is smoke nuisance.

3. Market valuation is no better guide in the case of collective goods either. Roads, education, and defense may be mentioned as examples. Proposed solutions are voting or decision by elected authoritative bodies.[11]

The second type of market failure comprises uncertainty and inconsistency of expectations, inertia and resistance to change, and imperfect information. These phenomena have dynamic implications; hence they will be dealt with in connection with dynamic efficiency, below. One further point needs mentioning here, however. Uncertainty and inconsistency of expectations will bring about fluctuations in the employment of resources. In other words, a purely competitive economy will work at least part of the time with less than full utilization of existing resources. Since static efficiency presupposes full resource use, this factor will result in inefficiencies. On the other hand, in a socialist system this form of unemployment may be avoided. Thus the shortcomings of a socialist system so far as static efficiency is concerned are (partly) counteracted by the full utilization of resources.

One final remark: in our discussion the hypothetical conditions of pure

[9] To use the convenient expression coined by F. M. Bator in "The Anatomy of Market Failure," *Quarterly Journal of Economics*, Vol. LXXII, No. 3 (August, 1958), pp. 351–88. It should be noted that Bator subsumes all factors belonging to the first type of market failure under the heading "externalities."

[10] See P. A. Samuelson, *Foundations of Economic Analysis* (Cambridge, Mass.: Harvard University Press, 1955), p. 232.

[11] For a solution based on individual preferences see P. A. Samuelson, "Public Expenditure: A Diagrammatic Exposition," *Review of Economics and Statistics*, Vol. XXXVII, No. 4 (November, 1955), pp. 350–56.

competition have been considered and we have disregarded monopolistic elements that impair static efficiency achievable in the blueprint of pure competition. Similarly, possible deviations of actual socialist systems from the theoretical blueprints have been left out of account.

Dynamic Efficiency

Static efficiency is concerned with efficient resource allocation at a given point in time; an economic system may exhibit static efficiency even if production is unchanged from year to year. Dynamic efficiency, on the other hand, is concerned with the growth possibilities of an economy. Dynamic efficiency can be indicated by the hypothetical growth rate of national income achievable in different economic systems under identical resource use[12] and saving ratio.[13] (As with static efficiency, we do not require that production conform to individual preferences—it may as well correspond to the preferences of the planners.) The distinction between static and dynamic efficiency has been forcefully expressed in Schumpeter's classical words: "A system—any system, economic or other—that at *every* point of time fully utilizes its possibilities to the best advantage may yet in the long run be inferior to a system that does so at *no* given point of time, because the latter's failure to do so may be a condition for the level or speed of long-run performance."[14]

There is much disagreement on the question whether a free enterprise or a socialist economy is superior with regard to dynamic efficiency. According to Hayek, a higher growth rate could be secured in a free enterprise system "if we assumed that the same restriction of consumption, which has actually taken place [in Russia], had been caused by taxation, the proceeds of which had been lent to competitive industry for investment purposes."[15] The contrary conclusion is reached by, for example, Dobb[16] and Sweezy.[17] Bergson also inclines toward the latter view: "One may imagine that in a highly dynamic economy a Centralist allocation of investment might lead to fewer and smaller errors than a Competitive

[12] The term "identical resource use" is employed here as a shorthand expression for identical initial resources and the use of identical amounts of human labor.

[13] In technical terms, whereas static efficiency means that the economy operates on its production-possibility frontier, dynamic efficiency can be represented by the movement of this frontier in northeast direction. For a rigorous treatment of dynamic efficiency under the assumption of constant returns to scale, absence of technological change, and the knowledge of current rates of price changes on the side of the producers, see R. Dorfman, P. A. Samuelson, and R. M. Solow, *Linear Programming and Economic Analysis* (New York: McGraw-Hill Book Co., Inc., 1958), chap. 12.

[14] J. A. Schumpeter, *Capitalism, Socialism, and Democracy* (New York: Harper & Bros., 1942), p. 83. Italics in original.

[15] F. A. Hayek (ed.), *Collectivist Economic Planning* (London: Routledge and Kegan Paul, 1935), p. 205.

[16] Maurice Dobb, *On Economic Theory and Socialism* (New York: International Publishers, 1955), pp. 41–54.

[17] Paul M. Sweezy, *Socialism* (New York: McGraw-Hill Book Co., Inc., 1949), pp. 234–36.

allocation."[18] Although his remarks were addressed to the competitive (market) solution in a socialist economy, they may apply to free enterprise as well.

Some arguments of primary importance with regard to dynamic efficiency in a free enterprise system and in socialism are the following:

1. No conclusive argument can be offered as far as technical progress is concerned. It is widely held that a free enterprise system is more conductive to technical progress than a socialist economy, since both the endeavor to survive and the profit motive greatly contribute to the introduction of new production methods. On the other hand, it has been argued that under conditions of pure competition productive units are too small and the risk of introducing innovations of considerable importance is too great to permit revolutionary changes in technical methods.[19] If so, monopolistic market structures in a free enterprise economy or centralized direction of investments in a socialist system may achieve a higher rate of technical progress. However, a free enterprise economy with competing large production units could combine the advantages of the profit motive with possession of considerable means to finance innovating activity. Yet Schumpeter emphasizes that in large production units technological progress becomes automatic, "innovation itself being reduced to routine."[20] If this is true, the frequently used objection against the socialist system, that salaried employees are not interested in technical progress, loses much of its force.

Although technological change may come about sooner in a free enterprise economy than under socialism, technological progress can be smoother in a planned economy. Under free enterprise, when innovations are made by individual concerns, other firms may offer resistance; or secrecy, patents, etc. may delay the spreading of new production methods.

2. Primarily in underdeveloped countries a dynamic form of external effects is relevant. Investments in transportation facilities or public utilities are frequently unprofitable for the private producer although "profitable" from the viewpoint of social productivity. Investments of this sort, the so-called social overhead, facilitate the establishment of industrial enterprises. Here centralized decision-making has clear advantages. Nevertheless, one could object that central planning should be restricted to the provision for social overhead only and let private initiative do the rest.

---

[18] Abram Bergson, "Socialist Economics," *A Survey of Contemporary Economics*, Vol. 1 (ed. Howard S. Ellis) (Homewood, Ill.: Richard D. Irwin, Inc., 1948), p. 443.

[19] It should be added here that, according to William Fellner, in the absence of uncertainty and incomplete foresight and under the assumption of perfect rationality, technological progress would proceed in the same way under both pure competition and monopoly: "The Influence of Market Structure on Technological Progress," in *Readings in Industrial Organization and Public Policy* (Homewood, Ill.: Richard D. Irwin, Inc., 1958), p. 294.

[20] Schumpeter, *op. cit.*, p. 132.

3. Uncertainty and inconsistency of expectations in a free enterprise framework are frequently mentioned as a serious drag on dynamic efficiency.[21] Under competition, decisions to increase capacity are made separately by each firm, and these plans are coordinated *ex post facto* only, through the market mechanism. The lack of information on investment decisions of other entrepreneurs and the uncertainty of expectations may lead to a slowing down of investment activity because of excessive cautiousness. Furthermore, decisions with regard to the future are likely to clash, resulting in too much or too little investment in a particular field. It seems that the greater the dynamism of a free enterprise system, the higher the possible waste. On the other hand, the Planning Board (or the monopolist) has more information about investment decisions made, and can thereby avoid overlapping. Also, the planning authority may organize and co-ordinate investment activity well in advance. Nevertheless, this argument is not so conclusive as it seems. Thinking in terms of waste, people are liable to forget that waste may be a necessary corollary to progress. The path of growth may be smoother in a socialist economy, but a dynamic free enterprise system may achieve a higher rate of growth even at the expense of greater fluctuations. This is possible if the endeavor to survive and the profit motive overcompensate for the uncertainty and inconsistency of expectations. Moreover, the expectation that innovations will be made by others may act as a compelling rather than a restricting force.

These arguments and counterarguments suggest that the economist cannot make a conclusive judgment on the dynamic efficiency of the blueprints of different economic systems. It should be added that psychological and sociological factors and differences between the blueprint and its actual realization can also be of decisive importance.

Growth Rate of National Income

Distinction should be made between dynamic efficiency and the actual growth rate of national income.[22] It will be recalled that dynamic effi-

---

[21] Tibor Scitovsky, *Welfare and Competition* (Homewood, Ill.: Richard D. Irwin, Inc., 1951), pp. 233–41.

[22] Two difficulties should be mentioned here in regard to the estimation of the growth rate, although no attempt will be made to evaluate them. First, there is a conceptual problem: the definition of national income. Our results will be different depending on whether we use, for example, the Soviet concept of national income, which is equivalent to the value of material production, or a Western concept, which includes services. Second, there is the problem of measurement: no unequivocal measure of the growth rate can be found. Changes in the proportion of goods with decreasing costs, structural changes in production, new commodities, and quality changes—all make the measurement of the growth rate and the comparison of growth rates in different countries to a considerable degree inconclusive. For an extensive treatment of the problem of measurement see G. W. Nutter, "On Measuring Economic Growth," *Journal of Political Economy*, Vol. LXV, No. 1 (February, 1957), pp. 51–63. Also, "Comment" by H. S. Levine, "Reply" by Nutter, and "Rejoinder" by Levine, in the same journal, Vol. LXVI, No. 4 (August, 1958), pp. 357–63.

ciency was defined as the hypothetical growth rate of national income achievable in different economic systems under identical resource use and saving ratio. The actual growth rate is affected not only by the dynamic efficiency of the system but also by the central authority's action overruling individual preferences in regard to saving versus spending and work versus leisure. Despite dynamic inefficiencies, an economic system may achieve a higher growth rate through an increase in the saving ratio or through an involuntary increase in the amount of labor.

Recently more and more emphasis has been placed on the growth rate. One has the impression that in the eyes of many people the rate of growth is the *sole* success indicator. Much of the recent writing on economic growth as well as a host of political speeches convey the same impression. The dissenting voices—like that of J. K. Galbraith, who contends that "our concern for production is traditional and irrational"[23]—are comparatively few. It is not our concern here to appraise the importance of the growth rate as a success indicator. We shall rather restrict our discussion to the examination of various factors which affect the rate of growth.

In a free enterprise economy, saving is determined by the preferences of the individuals and by corporate saving. In a socialist economy, the central authorities decide what part of national income will be used for investment purposes. The possibility of enforcement of a higher saving ratio in a socialist state makes a higher rate of growth feasible. To quote Fellner: "A totalitarian government, if it could establish itself in a country such as the United States, might not find it difficult to operate the economy at a level of consumption 20 to 25 per cent lower than our present consumption level, and then let consumption rise slowly with the rise of aggregate output. By such a policy, the present American net capital formation could be *more than doubled*, and it is quite likely that the annual economic growth rate of the United States could be *almost* doubled."[24]

The disadvantage of a free enterprise system with regard to the proportion of national income invested can be offset by taxation, the proceeds of which could be lent to individuals for investment purposes, as envisaged by Hayek. But would Hayek really advocate such a policy; would he plead for encroachment upon the individual's freedom to consume or save at will? In view of his doctrine implying the undesirability of forced saving,[25] this is not very likely. But we should not forget that many representatives of "bourgeois" economics have regarded forced saving, brought about by having wage increases lag behind price rises, as a necessary condition for capitalist development.[26]

---

[23] J. K. Galbraith, *The Affluent Society* (Boston: Houghton Mifflin Co., 1958), p. 132.

[24] William Fellner, *Trends and Cycles in Economic Activity* (New York: Holt, Rinehart & Winston, Inc., 1956), p. 73. Italics in original.

[25] See his *Prices and Production* (London: Routledge and Kegan Paul, 1931).

[26] For example, J. M. Keynes, *A Treatise on Money* (2 vols.; New York: Harcourt, Brace & Co., 1930), Vol. 2, pp. 152–63.

We should deal here also with a frequent misunderstanding according to which an enforced increase in saving constitutes a sacrifice on the part of the present generation, the beneficiaries of which will be our descendants only. This is not necessarily true. It can be shown that under certain assumptions the centrally determined increase in saving will lead to an increase in the well-being of the present generation not accounted for in the individual saver's decision. Savings, if invested, may have a "complementarity effect" on wages that is not foreseen by the individual saver. Let us assume that there is sufficient technological change to counteract the fall of the interest rate that would result from an increase in the stock of capital under unchanged technology. Such being the case, the wage rate will rise (because of the increase in capital stock) with interest rate unchanged. Consequently, as soon as the addition to the capital stock has been completed, the savers will enjoy an additional—and at the time of saving unexpected—benefit in the form of wage increases. This complementarity effect appears as an argument for interference with the amount of saving based on individual preferences.

It is another question if we assume that the amounts invested will be used less productively in a centrally planned economy. Such a situation might arise from bureaucratic mismanagement or from the absence of a sufficient guide—in the form of the interest rate—for the comparison of investment alternatives. But even if this assumption is made, our problems would still not be solved. Let us assume the following hypothetical situation: in a socialist economy the saving ratio is 20 per cent, one-fourth of investment is "wasted" (because of the above-mentioned factors), and the growth rate is 6 per cent. Now in a free enterprise economy let us postulate a saving ratio of 10 per cent, no waste in investment, and a 4 per cent growth rate. How are we to decide the merits and demerits of these two hypothetical economies? We need some kind of "preference scale" to evaluate them, and Hayek's preference scale will surely differ from Dobb's.

The central authority may also overrule individual preferences in regard to work and leisure. It can enforce an increase in the amount of work performed: by forced labor, by an enforced extension of labor-hours, or by indirect pressure through the reduction of real wages to raise the number of workers per family. Such practices will lead to a higher growth rate at the expense of leisure.

Consumer Satisfaction

In discussing the three success indicators examined above, we have postulated that production should correspond to the preferences of the community, which may mean individual preferences as well as those of the planners. In other words, in evaluating these indicators no distinction has been made between a system based on consumer sovereignty and one based on autocratic decisions. We have disregarded the problem of *who* decides the goals of the economy and considered only *how* and *whether* these goals are attained. It can be said that the first three indicators are free from value judgments. Advancing consumer satisfaction as the fourth indicator, we introduce the possibility of making value judgments in evaluating the performance of various economic systems. It should be noted, however, that the above duality of the success indicators (individuals' or planners' preferences) can be further retained: although consumer satisfaction may serve as an indicator, the planners will assign zero value to it if they decide to disregard it completely. On the other hand, this indicator makes it possible to differentiate between the performance of economic systems based on consumer sovereignty and those based on autocratic decisions. If two economic systems achieve the same degree of static and dynamic efficiency and the same growth rate, the one based on consumer sovereignty will be judged as more desirable if consumer satisfaction is regarded as an objective. Three factors can be said to contribute to consumer satisfaction: (1) correspondence of production targets to individual preferences, (2) correspondence of the actual saving ratio to the saving ratio desired by individuals, and (3) correspondence of actual work performed to individuals' preferences for work versus leisure.

Consumer satisfaction in its last-mentioned two forms does not affect static and dynamic efficiency but can be regarded as a constraint to the growth rate. We have seen that, given the dynamic efficiency of an economy, the rate of growth can be increased only by overruling individual preferences with regard to saving versus spending and work versus leisure. Such a decision entails a diminution of consumer satisfaction. In other words, given dynamic efficiency, an increase in the growth rate of national income requires loss of satisfaction on the part of the individuals. In the von Neumann model maximization of the growth rate presupposes that the population is being held on the subsistence level: the portion of national income above the amount necessary for subsistence is reinvested.[27] In this study we consider the direct or indirect pressure on the part of the central authority to increase the work performed as a further factor that increases the growth rate and reduces consumer satisfaction.

The level of consumer satisfaction reached can be indicated by the living standards of the population. In appraising this we have to take into account whether the goods produced are those desired by individuals, and also have to consider leisure. For a longer period, the temporal change in living standards should be considered. In this connection it should be noted that over a period sufficiently long to enable the population to enjoy the results of investment activity, a high growth rate may raise future consumption. Yet this is not necessarily so: if, for example, the planners regard the increase of military capacity as their primary objective, a high growth rate will be accompanied by a permanent restriction in consumption.

[27] See Dorfman *et al.*, *op. cit.*, p. 296.

Distribution of Income

In the works of economists following Pareto, income distribution has been said not to affect efficiency. It is assumed that once an efficient allocation of resources has been reached, income distribution can be changed at will, without impairing efficiency, by the use of lump-sum redistribution. But this is far from being true. Lump-sum redistribution is not only impractical; in a dynamic economy even lump-sum measures will affect efficiency. Lump-sum taxes and subsidies altering income distribution in one period will affect the amount of work supplied and risk-taking in the succeeding periods, which, in turn, will affect the dynamic efficiency of the economy.

Consequently, income distribution in its impact on effort and risk-taking has considerable effect on the other success indicators and primarily on the efficiency of the system. It can rightly be assumed that if risk-taking and superior performance are not properly rewarded, the efficiency of the economic system will suffer. On the other hand, income distribution is not only one of the factors affecting other success indicators but a success indicator in itself. The distinguishing characteristic of this indicator is that we need a value judgment in determining what kind of income distribution is desirable and how different distributions are valued. *A* may prefer an equal distribution of income, *B* may give priority to distribution on the basis of productivity, the problem of unearned incomes enters the picture, natural scarcities complicate the issue, etc.[28] The economist can hardly do more than state the fact that income distribution is one of the success indicators which influence the other variables in the economic system, when evaluation of the desirability of different income distributions cannot be made without invoking value judgments.

WHOSE PREFERENCES?

We have now examined the five success indicators which would provide a way to measure the performance of different economic systems. Let us assume for the moment that the values and relationships of these variables for various economic systems are known. As has been seen, we then face the problem of devising some kind of perference scale on the basis of which the values of the success indicators can be rated. The question arises, whose preferences should be relied upon? Two extreme cases may be mentioned: we may say that the decisions of individuals should be considered, or we may rely on a paternalistic authority whose decisions overrule consumers' preferences.

[28] For conflicting interpretations of the concept "just distribution" cf. T. J. B. Hoff, *Economic Calculation in the Socialist Society* (London: Hodge, 1949), pp. 34 ff.

THE CASE FOR AND AGAINST CONSUMER SOVEREIGNTY

Consumer sovereignty may mean two things: (*a*) Consumers are free to choose among the commodities available, or (*b*) Consumers are able to guide production decisions via their demand for consumer goods. The first alternative must be rejected, since it is compatible with central determination of quantities produced of various consumer goods; here the consumer market is only a rationing device to distribute the given amount of goods among consumers. On the other hand, the second alternative means that consumer decisions should regulate the allocation of resources among alternative uses.

If we unconditionally accept consumer sovereignty as the guiding rule, there is no problem of evaluating the various success indicators, since a free enterprise economy with no government intervention would result in such values of these variables that correspond to the individuals' wishes. But are consumers' preferences a reliable guide? Consumer sovereignty has been exalted by many exponents of free enterprise as a measure of freedom. Nevertheless, free consumers' choice can be ensured in a socialist economy as well; the proponents of the market solution also favor consumer sovereignty and reject the authoritative decision-making of the Planning Board with regard to consumer goods.[29]

The doctrine of consumer sovereignty is based on two assumptions. First, it is maintained that it is morally right that the consumer decide what should be produced and what proportion of national income should be saved, and the consumer's decision is realized on the market by "voting," where money serves as a "ballot"; second, it is assumed that there is no interaction in consumption, and consumer demand is determined by factors independent of production. The following qualifications are intended to show the inadequacies in these assumptions and the limitations of the doctrine of consumer sovereignty.[30]

1. It has been pointed out by many that the existing distribution of wealth and income cannot be regarded as desirable. The "ballots" in the possession of the individuals are only partly the result of one's own productive activity. In Knut Wicksell's words: "There is one inequality from which we can never abstract, without making a serious mistake, namely social differences and the unequal distribution of property."[31] If this is so, state intervention is needed to change the quantity of "ballots" in the hands of some individuals.

---

[29] Cf. A. P. Lerner, "Economic Theory and Socialist Economy," *Review of Economic Studies*, Vol. II, No. 1 (October, 1934), pp. 53–54; Oskar Lange, "On the Economic Theory of Socialism," in Benjamin E. Lippincott (ed.), *On the Economic Theory of Socialism* (Minneapolis: University of Minnesota Press, 1938), pp. 93–95.

[30] Market imperfections on the production side have already been dealt with above.

[31] Knut Wicksell, *Lectures on Political Economy* (2 vols.; London: Routledge and Kegan Paul, 1934), Vol. I, p. 77.

2. Against the assumption that consumer wants are independent of production, the social determination of individual tastes and wants has been argued. To quote Samuelson: "Individual tastes and wants are socially conditioned by advertising and custom so that they can hardly be said to belong to him in any ultimate sense."[32] Galbraith uses the analogy of the squirrel wheel: the squirrel (production) moves upward but the wheel turns—that is, individuals, acquiring new tastes, consume the newly produced goods.[33]

Consumption being, in part, socially determined (either by advertising or by the consumption of others), it cannot be said that consumer demand is an independent factor; one can even argue that state intervention may be needed to correct socially conditioned consumer wants.

3. Collective consumption presents similar problems. It has been noted before that a considerable part of national income is spent on goods which are consumed not individually but by the society. Education, road construction, defense, and internal security are the most conspicuous examples. The market mechanism cannot be used to determine the quantity of goods collectively consumed. Galbraith remarks that there is a tendency in the present-day United States to belittle the importance of collective consumption, which is partly due to the conditioning of demand for private goods by advertising.[34] The need for a proper balance between private and collective goods has been emphasized by James Tobin: "Government dollars spent for such things as fire and police protection, education, postal service, highways, parks, hospitals, libraries, sanitation and flood control, need have no inferiority complex with respect to private dollars spent for steaks, television, freezers, alcohol, horse racing, gasoline, comic books, and golf."[35] The need for collective consumption arises from indivisibilities; another form of interpersonal relations appears in the external effects of consumption. One person's consumption may increase the satisfaction of another person (an increase in the telephone network is a good example), or may reduce someone else's well-being (for example, boisterous behavior caused by excessive drinking).

4. Another qualification is connected with the problem of time horizon. Forming their plans, individuals consider time periods of differing lengths for which plans are made. The implications of the clash of individual decisions on time horizon and on investments have been explored by Jan Graaf, who maintains that "these are not decisions which households, acting separately, are equipped to make . . . Politics—or paternalism—is involved."[36]

---

[32] Samuelson, *op. cit.*, p. 224.

[33] Galbraith, *op. cit.*, p. 156.

[34] *Ibid.*, chap. 18.

[35] James Tobin, "The Eisenhower Economy and National Security: Two Views. I. Defense, Dollars and Doctrine," *Yale Review*, Vol. XLVII, No. 3 (March, 1958), p. 329.

[36] Jan Graaf, *Theoretical Welfare Economics* (Cambridge, Eng.: Cambridge University Press, 1957), chap. 6.

5. A. C. Pigou contends that preference for present goods does not imply that the utility of present consumption is greater than the utility of future consumption. In his opinion mankind's "telescopic faculty" is perverted in the sense that, apart from the fact that we do not attach sufficient importance to the welfare of future generations, we are unable to size up our future satisfactions from future goods. In Pigou's words: "the aggregate amount of economic satisfaction which people in fact enjoy is much less than it would be if their telescopic faculty were not perverted, but equal (certain) satisfactions were desired with equal intensity whatever the period at which they are destined to emerge."[37] Consequently Pigou advocates state intervention in saving, since "economic welfare could be increased by some rightly chosen degree of differentiation *in favour* of saving."[38] The idea of man's telescopic faculty crops up also in the writings of some socialist authors, for example in the works of Dobb.[39] Reference should also be made to the previously mentioned complementarity effect, which is independent of man's telescopic faculty.

6. Another argument is that we are inconsiderately using up coal and other scarce natural resources; hence state intervention is needed to preserve such resources. This argument certainly has importance, for example in the case of forests. In other cases it appears to be somewhat overrated: Jevons' fears about the exhaustion of coal reserves have not been realized, because of the substitution of other sources of energy for coal.

On the basis of all these arguments one comes to the conclusion that consumer sovereignty in its pure form cannot serve as a guiding rule in evaluating different economic systems. We turn now to its very opposite: the paternalistic solution.

The Paternalistic Solution

The unconditional acceptance of consumer sovereignty lurks behind advocacy of complete freedom from state intervention. At the other extreme, it is asserted that the planning authority knows the individuals' and the community's needs better than the individuals themselves. The central authority appears, according to this view, to be omniscient and omnipotent. A typical expression of this view can be found in the *History of the Communist Party of the Soviet Union:* "The power of the Marxist-Leninist theory lies in the fact that it enables the party to find the orientation in any situation, to understand the inner connection of current events, to foresee their course and to perceive not only how and in what

[37] A. C. Pigou, *The Economics of Welfare* (London: Macmillan, 1932), p. 26.

[38] *Ibid.*, p. 29. Italics in original.

[39] Maurice Dobb, *Political Economy and Capitalism* (New York: International Publishers, 1945), p. 309.

direction they are developing in the present, but how and in what direction they are bound to develop in the future."[40]

If this is so, why do we need individual preferences? Can't we leave everything to be determined by the infallible authority—the Party? Some Western socialists adhering to the centralist solution put the manner more mildly, calling authoritarian decisionmaking "a diet prescribed by a doctor to a patient."[41] On the other hand, for those who rightly reject totalitarian schemes and the idea of the infallible central authority assistance is furnished by proponents of the socialist market solution. Lange writes, on the abrogation of consumer sovereignty: "Mr. Lerner has sufficiently shown the undemocratic character of such a system and its incompatibility with the ideals of the socialist movement. Such a system would scarcely be tolerated by any civilized people."[42]

A Compromise?

We have attempted to find criteria on the basis of which the relative importance of our success indicators could be evaluated and the merits and demerits of different economic systems judged. We have seen that this evaluation can be made either by unconditionally accepting consumer sovereignty or by letting a central authority decide the issues. In the first case the market would automatically supply the answer; in the second case a central authority would make the decision. But these extreme cases do not stand up to searching criticism. It may be suggested that in some form or other we should rank and weigh individual preferences in regard to the success indicators. *A* may think that the efficient allocation of resources is the measure of success for an economic system, *B* may give priority to the growth rate, *C* may favor an equal distribution of income; but is it possible to strike an average of supposedly widely differing opinions? Can we construct a preference scale for the whole community based on individual preferences? The answer is in the negative. It would require a "superman" to compare and rank the preferences of individuals; hence the community's preference scale in regard to the success indicators cannot be devised.

CONCLUSION

We can conclude, then, that economic arguments are not sufficient to make a choice between economic systems—in the present case between the blueprints of a free enterprise and of a socialist system. Two reasons have

[40] (New York: International Publishers, 1939), p. 355. This book was officially ascribed to Stalin and until recently was regarded as one of the holy books in the Communist orbit.

[41] Dobb, *Political Economy and Capitalism, op. cit.*, pp. 307–14.

[42] Lange, *op. cit.*, p. 95. Cf. Lerner, *op. cit.*, pp. 51–61.

been established: we cannot determine the performance of the various blueprints with regard to the five success indicators, and we are unable to construct a scale of preferences which would give the ranking of different values of the success criteria. Moreover, even if the relative merits and demerits of the blueprints of various economic systems could be judged, their actual realization shows substantial deviations from the theoretical construction. Also as a result of sociological and psychological factors, a free enterprise blueprint may work better in one and worse in another country. Similar considerations are relevant with regard to a socialist blueprint.

Not only do noneconomic factors influence the workings of an economic system, but noneconomic objectives may also modify any results reached by the use of our success indicators. The planners may set targets that are in no way connected with the economic performance of a system. A dictator may be interested exclusively in increasing his power and may disregard economic considerations. Political objectives may exclude the use of efficiency prices if the central authorities do not want to disseminate information on the relative valuation of military and consumer goods. Furthermore, the objective of centralization in decision-making for fear of sabotage on lower levels may hinder the decentralization of production decisions. In all these cases, noneconomic "success indicators" would appear on the scene. Nevertheless, we do not include these indicators in our model, since they are not amenable to evaluation by economic tools and would bring a considerable degree of vagueness into the discussion.

Although our success indicators do not give much help in evaluating the blueprints of various economic systems, they can be useful in appraising the performance of real-world economies. In the examination of any economy two questions can be raised: How does the actual working of the economy differ from the blueprint? How does the economy under consideration "score" in terms of our success indicators?

PART II

Models of Economic Systems

Models of economic systems offer blueprints of schemes of economic organization and control intended to answer the fundamental questions of what, how much, how, and for whom to produce. These models are, necessarily and desirably, simplified abstractions from the complex reality of actual national economies. For that very reason, models enable us to distinguish and compare the basic characteristics and problems of different economic systems. They illuminate in sharp relief alternative answers to the fundamental questions of economic organization, and they provide essential tools for the analysis of living economies, such as the cases studied in Part III of this book.

There are various possible classifications of theoretical economic systems, of which the most basic are capitalist versus socialist economies, and decentralized market versus centrally planned economies. The most common combinations, from these two schemes, are (1) the capitalist decentralized market model and (2) the socialist central planning model. However, other important combinations are (3) market socialism and (4) the detailed central planning within a formally capitalist framework that characterizes fascism. Finally, it is possible, in theoretical models as in actual cases, to find "mixed" economies combining, for example, public and private ownership or centralized and decentralized allocation of resources. It is noteworthy that virtually all the following selections do in fact envision some such combinations, that is, some sort of "mixed" economy. This feature reflects the intention of theory to elucidate reality, not to escape it.

The selections that follow analyze in turn (1) the capitalist market model, (2) the socialist market model, and (3) central planning in a capitalist as well as a socialist institutional framework. The case studies in Part III then provide examples of living economies which approximate each of the theoretical models.

Capitalist Market Economy

The basic characteristics of a capitalist economic system are (1) private ownership of, and private enterprise with, the means of production; (2) the predominance of economic gain as the guiding force in production decisions; and (3) reliance on markets and prices to allocate resources and distribute income.

Two types of capitalism may be distinguished. In "laissez faire" capitalism, government intervention in the economy is absent or negligible. In "regulated" or "mixed" capitalism, there is a substantial amount of government intervention—intended for the most part to improve or bolster the private enterprise market system, rather than to curtail or replace it. There are few advocates of a 100 percent laissez faire economic system with no government intervention, and none exists today, except perhaps in very primitive economies. Rather, the issue, for both theory and policy, is the nature, extent, and success of government intervention in the regulated capitalist economy.

The following selections examine the nature, strengths, and weaknesses of a capitalist economy. The first shows how the decentralized price system ideally assembles and coordinates the available knowledge of the economy in order to allocate resources and distribute income efficiently. The second analyzes the shortcomings of the private enterprise market economy and explains the efforts of government to correct them in a regulated capitalist economy.

2. THE PRICE SYSTEM AS A MECHANISM FOR USING KNOWLEDGE*

Friedrich A. Hayek

Efficiency in resource allocation requires full use of knowledge of the opportunities of supply and demand in the economy. Hayek argues that decentralized decisions in response to prices determined by market forces can utilize this knowledge much better than central planning, which is unable to assemble all the detailed information needed for sound decisions. Market prices can serve as proper guides to economic decisions because they are "rates of equivalence" which embody the whole end-means structure of the economic system. At the same time, the price system achieves "economy of knowledge" by concentrating in simple and unambiguous signals for action the information relevant for each participant in the economic process. On the basis of these price signals, decentralized decisions can be made that are consistent with the activity of the economic system as a whole.

I

WHAT IS the problem we wish to solve when we try to construct a rational economic order?

On certain familiar assumptions the answer is simple enough. *If* we possess all the relevant information, *if* we can start out from a given sys-

* Reprinted, with permission, from *American Economic Review,* Vol. XXXV, No. 4 (September, 1945), pp. 519–30. Originally published under the title, "The Use of Knowledge in Society." Friedrich A. Hayek, who formerly taught at the University of London and the University of Chicago, is now Professor of Economics at the University of Freiburg, Germany.

tem of preferences and *if* we command complete knowledge of available means, the problem which remains is purely one of logic. That is, the answer to the question of what is the best use of the available means is implicit in our assumptions. The conditions which the solution of this optimum problem must satisfy have been fully worked out and can be stated best in mathematical form: put at their briefest, they are that the marginal rates of substitution between any two commodities or factors must be the same in all their different uses.

This, however, is emphatically *not* the economic problem which society faces. And the economic calculus which we have developed to solve this logical problem, though an important step toward the solution of the economic problem of society, does not yet provide an answer to it. The reason for this is that the "data" from which the economic calculus starts are never for the whole society "given" to a single mind which could work out the implications, and can never be so given.

The peculiar character of the problem of a rational economic order is determined precisely by the fact that the knowledge of the circumstances of which we must make use never exists in concentrated or integrated form, but solely as the dispersed bits of incomplete and frequently contradictory knowledge which all the separate individuals possess. The economic problem of society is thus not merely a problem of how to allocate "given" resources—if "given" is taken to mean given to a single mind which deliberately solves the problem set by these "data." It is rather a problem of how to secure the best use of resources known to any of the members of society, for ends whose relative importance only these individuals know. Or, to put it briefly, it is a problem of the utilization of knowledge not given to anyone in its totality.

This character of the fundamental problem has, I am afraid, been rather obscured than illuminated by many of the recent refinements of economic theory, particularly by many of the uses made of mathematics. Though the problem with which I want primarily to deal in this paper is the problem of a rational economic organization, I shall in its course be led again and again to point to its close connections with certain methodological questions. Many of the points I wish to make are indeed conclusions toward which diverse paths of reasoning have unexpectedly converged. But as I now see these problems, this is no accident. It seems to me that many of the current disputes with regard to both economic theory and economic policy have their common origin in a misconception about the nature of the economic problem of society. This misconception in turn is due to an erroneous transfer to social phenomena of the habits of thought we have developed in dealing with the phenomena of nature.

II

In ordinary language we describe by the word "planning" the complex of interrelated decisions about the allocation of our available resources. All economic activity is in this sense planning; and in any society in which many people collaborate, this planning, whoever does it, will in some measure have to be based on knowledge which, in the first instance, is not given to the planner but to somebody else, which somehow will have to be conveyed to the planner. The various ways in which the knowledge on which people base their plans is communicated to them is the crucial problem for any theory explaining the economic process. And the problem of what is the best way of utilizing knowledge initially dispersed among all the people is at least one of the main problems of economic policy—or of designing an efficient economic system.

The answer to this question is closely connected with that other question which arises here, that of *who* is to do the planning. It is about this question that all the dispute about "economic planning" centers. This is not a dispute about whether planning is to be done or not. It is a dispute as to whether planning is to be done centrally, by one authority for the whole economic system, or is to be divided among many individuals. Planning in the specific sense in which the term is used in contemporary controversy necessarily means central planning—direction of the whole economic system according to one unified plan. Competition, on the other hand, means decentralized planning by many separate persons. The half-way house between the two, about which many people talk but which few like when they see it, is the delegation of planning to organized industries, or, in other words, monopoly.

Which of these systems is likely to be more efficient depends mainly on the question under which of them we can expect that fuller use will be made of the existing knowledge. And this, in turn, depends on whether we are more likely to succeed in putting at the disposal of a single central authority all the knowledge which ought to be used but which is initially dispersed among many different individuals, or in conveying to the individuals such additional knowledge as they need in order to enable them to fit their plans in with those of others.

III

It will at once be evident that on this point the position will be different with respect to different kinds of knowledge; and the answer to our question will therefore largely turn on the relative importance of the different kinds of knowledge; those more likely to be at the disposal of particular individuals and those which we should with greater confidence expect to find in the possession of an authority made up of suitably chosen experts. If it is today so widely assumed that the latter will be in a better position, this is because one kind of knowledge, namely, scientific knowledge, occupies now so prominent a place in public imagination that we tend to forget that it is not the only kind that is relevant. It may be admitted that, so far as scientific knowledge is concerned, a body of suitably chosen experts may be in the best position to command all the best knowledge available—though this is of course merely shifting the difficulty to the problem of selecting the experts. What I wish to point out is that, even assuming that this problem can be readily solved, it is only a small part of the wider problem.

Today it is almost heresy to suggest that scientific knowledge is not the sum of all knowledge. But a little reflection will show that there is beyond question a body of very important but unorganized knowledge which cannot possibly be called scientific in the sense of knowledge of general rules: the knowledge of the particular circumstances of time and place. It is with respect to this that practically every individual has some advantage over all others in that he possesses unique information of which beneficial use might be made, but of which use can be made only if the decisions depending on it are left to him or are made with his active coöperation. We need to remember only how much we have to learn in any occupation after we have completed our theoretical training, how big a part of our working life we spend learning particular jobs, and how valuable an asset in all walks of life is knowledge of people, of local conditions, and special circumstances. To know of and put to use a machine not fully employed, or somebody's skill which could be better utilized, or to be aware of a surplus stock which can be drawn upon during an interruption of supplies, is socially quite as useful as the knowledge of better alternative techniques. And the shipper who earns his living from using otherwise empty or half-filled journeys of tramp-steamers, or the estate agent whose whole knowledge is almost exclusively one of temporary opportunities, or the *arbitrageur* who gains from local differences of commodity prices, are all performing eminently useful functions based on special knowledge of circumstances of the fleeting moment not known to others.

It is a curious fact that this sort of knowledge should today be generally regarded with a kind of contempt, and that anyone who by such knowledge gains an advantage over somebody better equipped with theoretical or technical knowledge is thought to have acted almost disreputably. To gain an advantage from better knowledge of facilities of communication or transport is sometimes regarded as almost dishonest, although it is quite as important that society make use of the best opportunities in this respect as in using the latest scientific discoveries. This prejudice has in a considerable measure affected the attitude toward commerce in general compared with that toward production. Even economists who regard themselves as definitely above the crude materialist fallacies of the past constantly commit the same mistake where activities directed toward the acquisition of such practical knowledge are concerned—apparently because in their scheme of things all such knowledge is supposed to be "given." The common idea now seems to be that all such knowledge should as a matter of course be readily at the command of everybody, and the reproach of irrationality leveled against the existing economic order is frequently based on the fact that it is not so available. This view disregards the fact that the method by which such knowledge can be made as widely available as possible is precisely the problem to which we have to find an answer.

IV

If it is fashionable today to minimize the importance of the knowledge of the particular circumstances of time and place, this is closely connected with the smaller importance which is now attached to change as such. Indeed, there are few points on which the assumptions made (usually only implicitly) by the "planners" differ from those of their opponents as much as with regard to the significance and frequency of changes which will make substantial alterations of production plans necessary. Of course, if detailed economic plans could be laid down for fairly long periods in advance and then closely adhered to, so that no further economic decisions of importance would be required, the task of drawing up a comprehensive plan governing all economic activity would appear much less formidable.

It is, perhaps, worth stressing that economic problems arise always and only in consequence of change. So long as things continue as before, or at least as they were expected to, there arise no new problems requiring a decision, no need to form a new plan. The belief that changes, or at least day-to-day adjustments, have become less important in modern times implies the contention that economic problems also have become less important. This belief in the decreasing importance of change is, for that reason, usually held by the same people who argue that the importance of economic considerations has been driven into the background by the growing importance of technological knowledge.

Is it true that, with the elaborate apparatus of modern production, economic decisions are required only at long intervals, as when a new factory is to be erected or a new process to be introduced? Is it true that, once a plant has been built, the rest is all more or less mechanical, determined by the character of the plant, and leaving little to be changed in adapting to the ever-changing circumstances of the moment?

The fairly widespread belief in the affirmative is not, so far as I can ascertain, borne out by the practical experience of the business man. In a competitive industry at any rate—and such an industry alone can serve as a test—the task of keeping cost from rising requires constant struggle, absorbing a great part of the energy of the manager. How easy it is for an inefficient manager to dissipate the differentials on which profitability rests, and that it is possible, with the same technical facilities, to produce with a great variety of costs, are among the commonplaces of business experience which do not seem to be equally familiar in the study of the economist. The very strength of the desire, constantly voiced by producers and engineers, to be able to proceed untrammeled by considerations of money costs, is eloquent testimony to the extent to which these factors enter into their daily work.

One reason why economists are increasingly apt to forget about the constant small changes which make up the whole economic picture is probably their growing preoccupation with statistical aggregates, which show a very much greater stability than the movements of the detail. The comparative stability of the aggregates cannot, however, be accounted for—as the statisticians seem occasionally to be inclined to do—by the "law of large numbers" or the mutual compensation of random changes. The number of elements with which we have to deal is not large enough for such accidental forces to produce stability. The continuous flow of goods and services is maintained by constant deliberate adjustments, by new dispositions made every day in the light of circumstances not known the day before, by *B* stepping in at once when *A* fails to deliver. Even the large and highly mechanized plant keeps going largely because of an environment upon which it can draw for all sorts of unexpected needs; tiles for its roof, stationery for its forms, and all the thousand and one kinds of equipment in which it cannot be self-contained and which the plans for the operation of the plant require to be readily available in the market.

This is, perhaps, also the point where I should briefly mention the fact that the sort of knowledge with which I have been concerned is knowledge of the kind which by its nature cannot enter into statistics and therefore cannot be conveyed to any central authority in statistical form. The statistics which such a central authority would have to use would have to be arrived at precisely by abstracting from minor differences between the things, by lumping together, as resources of one kind, items which differ as regards location, quality, and other particulars, in a way which may be very significant for the specific decision. It follows from this that central planning based on statistical information by its nature cannot take direct account of these circumstances of time and place, and that the central planner will have to find some way or other in which the decisions depending on them can be left to the "man on the spot."

V

If we can agree that the economic problem of society is mainly one of rapid adaptation to changes in the particular circumstances of time and place, it would seem to follow that the ultimate decisions must be left to the people who are familiar with these circumstances, who know directly of the relevant changes and of the resources immediately available to meet them. We cannot expect that this problem will be solved by first communicating all this knowledge to a central board which, after integrating *all* knowledge, issues its orders. We must solve it by some form of decentralization. But this answers only part of our problem. We need decentralization because only thus can we ensure that the knowledge of the particular circumstances of time and place will be promptly used. But the "man on the spot" cannot decide solely on the basis of his limited but intimate knowledge of the facts of his immediate surroundings. There still remains the problem of communicating to him such further information as he needs to fit his decisions into the whole pattern of changes of the larger economic system.

How much knowledge does he need to do so successfully? Which of the events which happen beyond the horizon of his immediate knowledge are of relevance to his immediate decision, and how much of them need he know?

There is hardly anything that happens anywhere in the world that *might* not have an effect on the decision he ought to make. But he need not know of these events as such, nor of *all* their effects. It does not matter for him *why* at the particular moment more screws of one size than of another are wanted, *why* paper bags are more readily available than canvas bags, or *why* skilled labor, or particular machine tools, have for the moment become more difficult to acquire. All that is significant for him is *how much more or less* difficult to procure they have become compared with other things with which he is also concerned, or how much more or less urgently wanted are the alternative things he produces or uses. It is always a question of the relative importance of the particular things with which he is concerned, and the causes which alter their relative importance are of no interest to him beyond the effect on those concrete things of his own environment.

It is in this connection that what I have called the economic calculus proper helps us, at least by analogy, to see how this problem can be solved, and in fact is being solved, by the price system. Even the single controlling mind, in possession of all the data for some small, self-contained economic system, would not—every time some small adjustment in the allocation of resources had to be made—go explicitly through all the relations between ends and means which might possibly be affected. It is indeed the great contribution of the pure logic of choice that it has demonstrated conclusively that even such a single mind could solve this kind of problem only by constructing and constantly using rates of equivalence (or "values," or "marginal rates of substitution"), *i.e.*, by attaching to each kind of scarce resource a numerical index which cannot be derived from any property possessed by that particular thing, but which reflects, or in which is condensed, its significance in view of the whole means-end structure. In any small change he will have to consider only these quantitative indices (or "values") in which all the relevant information is concentrated; and by adjusting the quantities one by one, he can appropriately rearrange his dispositions without having to solve the whole puzzle *ab initio*, or without needing at any stage to survey it at once in all its ramifications.

Fundamentally, in a system where the knowledge of the relevant facts is dispersed among many people, prices can act to coördinate the separate actions of different people in the same way as subjective values help the individual to coördinate the parts of his plan. It is worth contemplating for a moment a very simple and commonplace instance of the action of the price system to see what precisely it accomplishes. Assume that somewhere in the world a new opportunity for the use of some raw material, say tin, has arisen, or that one of the sources of supply of tin has been eliminated. It does not matter for our purpose—and it is very significant that it does not matter—which of these two causes has made tin more scarce. All that the users of tin need to know is that some of the tin they used to consume is now more profitably employed elsewhere, and that in consequence they must economize tin. There is no need for the great majority of them even to know where the more urgent need has arisen, or in favor of what other needs they ought to husband the supply. If only some of them know directly of the new demand, and switch resources over to it, and if the people who are aware of the new gap thus created in turn fill it from still other sources, the effect will rapidly spread throughout the whole economic system and influence not only all the uses of tin, but also those of its substitutes and the substitutes of these substitutes, the supply of all the things made of tin, and their substitutes, and so on; and all this without the great majority of those instrumental in bringing about these substitutions knowing anything at all about the original cause of these changes. The whole acts as one market, not because any of its members survey the whole field, but because their limited individual fields of vision sufficiently overlap so that through many intermediaries the relevant information is communicated to all. The mere fact that there is one price for any commodity—or rather that local prices are connected in a manner determined by the cost of transport, etc.—brings about the solution which (it is just conceptually possible) might have been arrived at by one single mind possessing all the information which is in fact dispersed among all the people involved in the process.

VI

We must look at the price system as such a mechanism for communicating information if we want to understand its real function—a function which, of course, it fulfills less perfectly as prices grow more rigid. (Even when quoted prices have become quite rigid, however, the forces which would operate through changes in price still operate to a considerable extent through changes in the other terms of the contract.) The most significant fact about this system is the economy of knowledge with which it operates, or how little the individual participants need to know in order to be able to take the right action. In abbreviated form, by a kind of symbol, only the most essential information is passed on, and passed on only to those concerned. It is more than a metaphor to describe the price system as a kind of machinery for registering change, or a system of telecommunications which enables individual producers to watch merely the movement of a few pointers, as an engineer might watch the hands of a few dials, in order to adjust their activities to changes of which they may never know more than is reflected in the price movement.

Of course, these adjustments are probably never "perfect" in the sense in which the economist conceives of them in his equilibrium analysis. But I fear that our theoretical habits of approaching the problem with the assumption of more or less perfect knowledge on the part of almost everyone has made us somewhat blind to the true function of the price mechanism and led us to apply rather misleading standards in judging its efficiency. The marvel is that in a case like that of a scarcity of one raw material, without an order being issued, without more than perhaps a handful of people knowing the cause, tens of thousands of people whose identity could not be ascertained by months of investigation, are made to use the material or its products more sparingly; *i.e.*, they move in the right direction. This is enough of a marvel even if, in a constantly changing world, not all will hit it off so perfectly that their profit rates will always be maintained at the same constant or "normal" level.

I have deliberately used the word "marvel" to shock the reader out of the complacency with which we often take the working of this mechanism for granted. I am convinced that if it were the result of deliberate human design, and if the people guided by the price changes understood that their decisions have significance far beyond their immediate aim, this mechanism would have been acclaimed as one of the greatest triumphs of the human mind. Its misfortune is the double one that it is not the product of human design and that the people guided by it usually do not know why they are made to do what they do. But those who clamor for "conscious direction"—and who cannot believe that anything which has evolved without design (and even without our understanding it) should solve problems which we should not be able to solve consciously—should remember this: The problem is precisely how to extend the span of our utilization of resources beyond the span of the control of any one mind; and, therefore, how to dispense with the need of conscious control and how to provide inducements which will make the individuals do the desirable things without anyone having to tell them what to do.

The problem which we meet here is by no means peculiar to economics but arises in connection with nearly all truly social phenomena, with language and most of our cultural inheritance, and constitutes really the central theoretical problem of all social science. As Alfred Whitehead has said in another connection, "It is a profoundly erroneous truism, repeated by all copy-books and by eminent people when they are making speeches, that we should cultivate the habit of thinking what we are doing. The precise opposite is the case. Civilization advances by extending the number of important operations which we can perform without thinking about them." This is of profound significance in the social field. We make constant use of formulas, symbols and rules whose meaning we do not understand and through the use of which we avail ourselves of the assistance of knowledge which individually we do not possess. We have developed these practices and institutions by building upon habits and institutions which have proved successful in their own sphere and which have in turn become the foundation of the civilization we have built up.

The price system is just one of those formations which man has learned to use (though he is still very far from having learned to make the best use of it) after he had stumbled upon it without understanding it. Through it not only a division of labor but also a coördinated utilization of resources based on an equally divided knowledge has become possible. The people who like to deride any suggestion that this may be so usually distort the argument by insinuating that it asserts that by some miracle just that sort of system has spontaneously grown up which is best suited to modern civilization. It is the other way round: man has been able to develop that division of labor on which our civilization is based because he happened to stumble upon a method which made it possible. Had he not done so he might still have developed some other, altogether different, type of civilization, something like the "state" of the termite ants, or some other altogther unimaginable type. All that we can say is that nobody has yet succeeded in designing an alternative system in which certain features of the existing one can be preserved which are dear even to those who most violently assail it—such as particularly the extent to which the individual can choose his pursuits and consequently freely use his own knowledge and skill.

VII

It is in many ways fortunate that the dispute about the indispensability of the price system for any rational calculation in a complex society is now no longer conducted entirely between camps holding different political views. The thesis that without the price system we could not preserve a society based on such extensive division of labor as ours was greeted with a howl of derision when it was first advanced by von Mises twenty-five years ago. Today the difficulties which some still find in accepting it are no longer mainly political, and this makes for an atmosphere much more conducive to reasonable discussion. When we find Leon Trotsky arguing that "economic accounting is unthinkable without market relations"; when Professor Oscar Lange promises Professor von Mises a statue in the marble halls of the future Central Planning Board; and when Professor Abba P. Lerner rediscovers Adam Smith and emphasizes that the essential utility of the price system consists in inducing the individual, while seeking his own interest, to do what is in the general interest, the differences can indeed no longer be ascribed to political prejudice. The remaining dissent seems clearly to be due to purely intellectual, and more particularly methodological, differences.

A recent statement by Professor Joseph Schumpeter in his *Capitalism,*

Socialism, and Democracy provides a clear illustration of one of the methodological differences which I have in mind. Its author is preeminent among those economists who approach economic phenomena in the light of a certain branch of positivism. To him these phenomena accordingly appear as objectively given quantities of commodities impinging directly upon each other, almost, it would seem, without any intervention of human minds. Only against this background can I account for the following (to me startling) pronouncement. Professor Schumpeter argues that the possibility of a rational calculation in the absence of markets for the factors of production follows for the theorist "from the elementary proposition that consumers in evaluating ('demanding') consumers' goods *ipso facto* also evaluate the means of production which enter into the production of these goods."[1]

Taken literally, this statement is simply untrue. The consumers do nothing of the kind. What Professor Schumpeter's "*ipso facto*" presumably means is that the valuation of the factors of production is implied in, or follows necessarily from, the valuation of consumers' goods. But this, too, is not correct. Implication is a logical relationship which can be meaningfully asserted only of propositions simultaneously present to one and the same mind. It is evident, however, that the values of the factors of production do not depend solely on the valuation of the consumers' goods but also on the conditions of supply of the various factors of production. Only to a mind to which all these facts were simultaneously known would the answer necessarily follow from the facts given to it. The practical problem, however, arises precisely because these facts are never so given to a single mind, and because, in consequence, it is necessary that in the solution of the problem knowledge should be used that is dispersed among many people.

The problem is thus in no way solved if we can show that all the facts, *if* they were known to a single mind (as we hypothetically assume them to be given to the observing economist), would uniquely determine the solution; instead we must show how a solution is produced by the interactions of people each of whom possesses only partial knowledge. To assume all the knowledge to be given to a single mind in the same manner

[1] J. Schumpeter, *Capitalism, Socialism, and Democracy* (New York, Harper & Bros., 1942), p. 175. Professor Schumpeter is, I believe, also the original author of the myth that Pareto and Barone have "solved" the problem of socialist calculation. What they, and many others, did was merely to state the conditions which a rational allocation of resources would have to satisfy, and to point out that these were essentially the same as the conditions of equilibrium of a competitive market. This is something altogether different from showing how the allocation of resources satisfying these conditions can be found in practice. Pareto himself (from whom Barone has taken practically everything he has to say), far from claiming to have solved the practical problem, in fact explicitly denies that it can be solved without the help of the market. See his *Manuel d'économie pure* (2d ed., 1927), pp. 233–34. The relevant passage is quoted in an English translation at the beginning of my article on "Socialist Calculation: The Competitive 'Solution,'" in *Economica*, New Series, Vol. VII, No. 26 (May, 1940), pp. 125–49 [reprinted in this volume as Selection 6, pp. 77–97].

in which we assume it to be given to us as the explaining economists is to assume the problem away and to disregard everything that is important and significant in the real world.

That an economist of Professor Schumpeter's standing should thus have fallen into a trap which the ambiguity of the term "datum" sets to the unwary can hardly be explained as a simple error. It suggests rather than there is something fundamentally wrong with an approach which habitually disregards an essential part of the pehnomena with which we have to deal: the unavoidable imperfection of man's knowledge and the consequent need for a process by which knowledge is constantly communicated and acquired. Any approach, such as that of much of mathematical economics with its simultaneous equations, which in effect starts from the assumption that people's *knowledge* corresponds with the objective *facts* of the situation, systematically leaves out what is our main task to explain. I am far from denying that in our system equilibrium analysis has a useful function to perform. But when it comes to the point where it misleads some of our leading thinkers into believing that the situation which it describes has direct relevance to the solution of practical problems, it is time that we remember that it does not deal with the social process at all and that it is no more than a useful preliminary to the study of the main problem.

3. GOVERNMENT AND THE MARKET*

Procter Thomson

What is the proper role of government in a capitalist market economy? Procter Thomson distinguishes two necessary types of government intervention in economic life, both of which are intended to assist, improve, and supplement the private enterprise market economy. Through its "framework activities" the government affects the environment in which the private economy operates. The government's "allocative activities," on the other hand, involve the use of resources for public purposes, modify the distribution of income, or influence the level and rate of growth of economic activity. In contrast to these desirable forms of government activity, there are more questionable types of government intervention which interfere with, or displace, the private market economy, such as price-fixing and public enterprise.

THE DIVISION OF LABOR BETWEEN GOVERNMENT AND THE MARKET

MOST OF the great problems of social policy in this century involve the division of labor between government and the market. The conditions of freedom and equity, of order, efficiency, and progress depend upon our answer to the question: What things should be done by group decision operating through the political process, and what things should be done by individual decisions mediated by the mechanism of the market? The line which divides these processes is neither intuitively obvious nor eternally

* Reprinted, with permission, from *Federal Expenditure Policy for Economic Growth and Stability* (Papers Submitted by Panelists Appearing before the Subcommittee on Fiscal Policy, Joint Economic Committee, 85th Cong., 1st sess.) (Washington, D.C.: U.S. Government Printing Office, 1957), pp. 130–52. Procter Thomson is John C. Lincoln Professor of Economics and Administration at Claremont Men's College.

fixed; it must be decided by free discussion among the responsible citizens of a free society; it changes according to the circumstances of the times, the understanding of the citizenry, and the capabilities of the Government. Nevertheless, there are some general principles which can, or should, guide rational discussion of this great problem.[1]

What are the peculiar characteristics of these two processes? What ends do they seek? How can they work together to achieve these ends?

The Political Process

In any society, the political process is concerned with the allocation of power. In a democratic society that process is designed to secure a group consensus on specific issues of social policy. The consensus is always subject to discussion and modification, but, while it remains in effect, the rules of the game compel individual dissent to be subordinated to group decision. An importer of Swiss watches, for example, may doubt the wisdom of protective tariffs, but, so long as these duties stand on the schedules, he foots the bill and harbors his questions till the next election.

If we take a broad and cursory view of the political process, we find that the scene is occupied by the following groups of actors:[2] First, the electorate, the citizens, who exercise the franchise in the light of their values, their information, and their interests; second, the political parties, who propose issues to the electorate; third, the legislature or parliament, who are selected by the electorate, from the parties, to represent their interests and to transplant the general consensus into specific laws; fourth, the executive, who translates both the laws of the legislature and the consensus of the body politic into specific acts of policy; fifth, the permanent bureaucracy, who carry out the details of executive policy and perform the routine tasks of government; sixth, the judiciary, who interpret the law and adjudicate disputes.

The role-structure of the political process is extraordinarily complex. Equally complex are the functions carried on within this structure. For, in

---

[1] For background, see Frank H. Knight, "The Ethics of Competition," *The Ethics of Competition and Other Essays* (reprint ed., London: George Allen & Unwin, 1936), especially pp. 49–58. Classical discussion of the problem can be found in Adam Smith, *Wealth of Nations*, book V, ch. i, "Of the Expenses of the Sovereign or Commonwealth," and John Stuart Mill, *Principles of Political Economy*, book V, ch. i, "Of the Functions of Government"; ch. xi, "Of the Grounds and Limits of the Laissez-Faire or Non-Interference Principle."

For a summary of current economic thought, see Fritz Machlup, "The Division of Labor Between Government and Private Enterprise," *American Economic Review*, Vol. XXXIII, No. 1 (March, 1943), pp. 87–104. For a sociological treatment, see Max Weber, *The Theory of Social and Economic Organization*, trans. by A. M. Henderson and Talcott Parsons (New York: Oxford University Press, 1947), ch. ii. Also consult Henry C. Simons, *A Positive Program for Laissez-Faire: Economic Policy for a Free Society* (Chicago: The University of Chicago Press, 1948).

[2] This is an expanded version of the list given in Ernest Barker, *The Parliamentary System of Government, Essays on Government* (2d ed.; Oxford: The Clarendon Press, 1951).

all its variety and complexity, the political process represents the most characteristic activity of organized society; namely, problem solving according to specified rules, under given conditions, in an environment of uncertainty. Despite the humbug and chicanery, the oratory and ideologies which lend color and interest to the process, political choice in a democratic society is the solution of common problems through group discussion. Discussion is the essence of democracy. And since the solution of the problem cannot be known before hand, the outcome of the process is indeterminant; it cannot be predicted from given conditions. In this respect it differs radically from the market process in which the given conditions of consumer preferences, industrial technology, and available resources dictate the outcome within tolerable limits of accuracy.

Another outstanding feature of decisions made through political discussion is their uniformity. They must be, so to speak, the same for everyone—everyone, that is, whose circumstances are similar. By contrast with the market mechanism, individual differences are not taken into account save through the ad hoc device of administrative discretion. For example, if the political process determined the disposition of goods among consumers, every household might have an annual dividend of 4 pairs of shoes and 5 quarts of whisky, even though a barefoot teetotaler would find these goods superfluous. On distribution day he would truck them to the public square and barter them for something else, a costly and annoying expedient which the price system renders unnecessary.

Despite the indeterminancy of the political process in general, the roles of some of the actors can be identified and tentative predictions ventured. The individual citizen, in his capacity as a voter, a lobbyist, and a political persuader, acts to maximize the satisfactions he receives from his government. Representatives act to maximize their terms of office. Political parties act to maximize the power they command which, under democratic conditions, is equivalent to maximizing the votes they receive.[3] In this connection, political parties act as entrepreneurs and innovators. Just as entrepreneurs in the market economy design and offer for sale the commodities among which consumers choose, so political parties package the issues on which elections are decided. But the range of choices is much narrower for the American voter than for the American consumer. The voter, therefore, is confronted with a "tie-in purchase." To buy a box of apples, he must take a peck of leeks. To get a labor and taxation policy he likes, he may have to swallow a foreign policy he abominates.

The differences between voting and purchasing also call for brief comment. In democratic societies, the rule is, "One citizen, one vote"—except for juveniles, prisoners, and migrants across political boundaries unable to establish legal residence before the election. In the market, the

---

[3] Anthony Downs, *An Economic Theory of Democracy* (New York: Harper & Bros., 1957).

rule is "Purchases are made with money, and money income is distributed among people in accord with inheritance, effort, and the chances of life." Though public policy must ultimately be ratified by votes, voting is by no means the crucial nexus of the political process, and the formal equality of the ballot box is countervailed a hundred times over by inequalities of power and ability which made themselves felt in the strategy of decision. Given its initial inequality in the distribution of wealth and income, the democracy of the market consists in the fact that one man's dollar is the equal of another man's dollar. Neither race, religion, nor prejudice can stay these instruments from their appointed ends—to guide production and govern the allocation of resources. Finally, the voting mechanism accomplishes its results indirectly and by remote control, as it were; the vote does not immediately call forth that which was voted for. Purchasing, on the other hand, both indicates a preference and accomplishes possession of the thing preferred.[4]

Problem solving through the political process is a necessary consequence of the existence of uncertainty. The degree of uncertainty faced by the society exercises a profound influence on the structure and function of its institutions: The greater the degree of uncertainty, the higher is the cost of acquiring information on issues of public policy. The ordinary citizen being unwilling to bear the costs of acquainting himself with the issues, society specializes the function of detailed policy decisions in a small group of elected representatives. But, again, the greater the uncertainty, the greater the likelihood of error. Thus, the necessity of checks and balances to hold legislative folly within tolerable limits. Political parties are another byproduct of uncertainty; they specify the issues to which voters react, and conduct exploratory expeditions to sample the consensus of the body politic. The normal administrative work of the bureaucracy represents still another aspect of society's unending struggle to routinize the unexpected.

If uncertainty were to vanish, by far the greater part of the apparatus of government would be altogether superfluous. No uncertainty, no problems; no problems, no politics. For in a world without uncertainty the costs of acquiring information about the future are reduced from infinity to zero; the consensus of the body politic is formulated and made known without doubt or delay. Therefore "representative" government and political parties would be obsolescent. Administrative decisions would be reduced to repetitive routine so that the executive arm of the Government would consist of tax collectors and producers of public services. Given perfect certainty, both the verdict of justice and the balance sheet of power are intuitively obvious so that neither adjudication nor a trial of strength are necessary. Order follows inevitably. For disorder arises ei-

---

[4] For further comment, see James M. Buchanan, "Social Choice, Democracy, and Free Markets," *Journal of Political Economy*, Vol. LXII, No. 2 (April, 1954), pp. 114–23.

ther from fraud or from an appeal to force; the first is impossible when concealment is impossible and the second is superfluous when the outcome is inevitable. In this event a society which shared a common pattern of values and which was not plagued with fundamental conflicts of interest has no use for a central authority to maintain order. A society divided into contending interest groups but united by a common standard of justice would decide differences by rational compromise in order to establish equity and preserve stability. In both cases the reserves of force are impounded in a common bank and need never pass into active circulation. (Only the uncertain society needs a central authority to collect and, on occasion, spend these reserves of force.) But a divided society without common standards of justice would impose order in the interests of the strongest.[5]

The Market Mechanism

The market mechanism is concerned with the allocation of resources. It is designed to answer the questions: (1) What things shall be produced? (2) How shall they be produced? (3) How shall the output be distributed among the agents who, jointly, produce it? (4) How shall society provide for maintenance and progress?

In an individualistic social order characterized by free exchange, private property, and personal responsibility these decisions are initiated by individual consumers and individual producers; but the market is a device for making these multitudes of choices mutually consistent, for translating individual decisions about bread, houses, and automobiles into social decisions about prices and outputs. For the buyer, prices are costs which provide both a signal and an incentive to cut back on his use of things that are dear and push forward on his use of things that are cheap. For the seller, prices are returns which provide both signal and incentive to make more of the things that are expensive and less of those that are cheap. For the system as a whole, prices settle at the level which clears the market. The prices of productive services, together with the pattern of ownership of resources, determine the distribution of income among persons and families; and the income of resource owners represents the costs of producers, while the expenditures of resource owners—as consumers of goods and services—represents the income of producers.

The broad and general case for the free market is simply this: Left to their own devices owners of resources will be guided by the signals of the market to put scarce agencies to the most productive uses. Given freedom of maneuver plus reasonable knowledge of the facts, resources will be channeled into the areas where demand is brisk and returns are high and diverted from the uses where demand is slack and returns are low. And the

[5] In the uncertain society, as Thomas Hobbes argued in his *Leviathan* (1651), preservation of order is the elementary task of civilized government. But whatever the degree of uncertainty, order without equity is tyranny.

attempt of each economic agent to maximize his net returns leads, under free competition, to equal returns at the margin for agents of equal capacity. Finally, equal returns at the margin means maximum returns for the community as a whole.

But even if the system of the market worked with perfect efficiency, the ends it secures are no better and no worse than the initial distribution of resource ownership on which it is based. Allocative efficiency does not mean distributive justice. Further, the sovereign consumer whom the market serves may command it to perform services which are, at best, frivolous and, at worst, subversive of higher esthetic and moral values.[6] Consumer sovereignty is no guaranty of individual integrity.

These, however, are evils easier indicted than remedied. For, in addition to the democratic presumption of individual responsibility which forbids arbitrary interference with the means he commands and the ends he chooses, we encounter the political dilemma that public intervention can scarcely be expected to rise above the private standards of the citizens who sanction it. It would be a rare thing, indeed, if citizens displayed more wisdom at the polls than in the market.

Still further, one of the notorious facts of economic and social life is that not all individuals have effective power to exercise their formal freedoms. Freedom without power is illusory. The faith, the presumption, or the hope that the individual is the best judge of his own interests is altogether untrue if his abilities are limited or his understanding corrupted. Here again, however, democracy faces one of its critical dilemmas: How do we detect significant aberrations from rational self-interest and how do we intervene to correct them? Above and beyond the limits of individual ability are the subtle barriers to formal freedoms erected by prejudice, by custom, and by overt coalitions that narrow his range of effective action.

The market, like the political process, is powerfully affected by the degree of uncertainty which the society faces. Economic knowledge is a scarce commodity; and actual adjustments of the market are bound to diverge from the ideal because of the intrusion of the unexpected into the affairs of both producers and consumers. Chance creates both windfall gains and losses in the lifetime income stream of the individual. Uncertainty also takes its toll on the income stream of the society in the form of periodic fluctuations in income, employment, and prices. The market creates an elaborate series of adjustments to handle the problem of uncertainty. The major adjustment consists of a division of labor between those who receive relatively fixed returns (sellers of labor and renters of capital) and those who receive fluctuating returns (stockholders or owners) based on the fortunes of the enterprise. In this picture, the business entrepreneur bundles together the risks which a specific firm is designed to exploit and sells pieces of these chances to owners (or to himself) who pledge their capital to the firm.

---

[6] Knight, *op. cit.*

In the absence of uncertainty, most of economic life would be reduced to repetitive routine. Entrepreneurship would vanish; administration and decisionmaking would become unnecessary. The business cycle would cease to trouble us. The economic problems remaining would be the age old ones of scarcity and poverty in—I might add—an environment of unrelieved monotony.

FRAMEWORK ACTIVITIES OF GOVERNMENT

In discussing the various grounds on which government participates in economic activity, I have divided the normative role of the state into two broad categories. The first covers the "framework" or regulatory activities of government, the second the "allocative" activities. Framework activities establish the structure within which the market functions. They alter or help to establish the "given conditions"—the tastes, resources, and technology—which govern the equilibrium of market forces. Though framework activities involve some use of resources, this aspect of the problem is relatively trivial; the chief issue is the substantive content of the rules and orders which government establishes. Allocative activities, on the other hand, involve substantial use of resources, or modify the distribution of income, or affect the level of economic activity. As we shall see presently, there is some overlap in these categories.

In this and the section following I have attempted to say what government should do; i.e., to extract from the existing body of doctrine in political economy some normative criteria for the economic role of the state. But Leviathan has an insatiable appetite; in the effort to satisfy the political temper of the times, parties often propose and enact measures of doubtful—doubtful, I say, not negative—economic value. These dubious expedients are briefly treated under the catchall heading of "Price Fixing and Government Enterprise."

Rules of the Game

In democratic societies, standards of behavior can be regarded as a series of overlapping circles: The circle of broadest compass is the mores, values, and norms of the society. Inside this is the domain of the common law, based on judicial recognition of social mores. Inside this is basic or constitutional law plus judicial interpretation of constitutional provisions. Still narrower in scope but more detailed in form is statutory law. At the final and smallest of the circles we find administrative law and administrative custom.[7]

Government, then, codifies and administers the common rules of the market as part of this set of overlapping sanctions. It does in two different ways.

[7] The breadth of the circles does not indicate legal priority. Constitutions and statutes can, to be sure, set aside the common law, and the evolution of judicial decisions which modify the common law need not parallel the evolution of the mores. I am indebted to my colleague Prof. Winston M. Fick for this formulation.

1. Standards and norms: The State is the agency which standardizes practices. The great body of doctrine which defines the "law of contract," establishes the meaning of "private property," or implements "the rule of reason" represents the standardizing activities of government as the articulate instrument of custom. This body of rules governs the legal qualities of money, the procedures for buying and selling, the liabilities of partners and stockholders, the means for collecting debts, and the paths to be followed in going into bankruptcy. Law and administrative decisions also guide the process of taking out a trademark, of conducting collective bargaining, of selling stocks and bonds, and of passing on an inheritance.

These positive rules implement order and stability in commercial interchange. In economic terms, they are part of the definition of "resources." For an agent of production is not just a technological datum, for example, so many acres of land or man-hours of labor; it is that plus an invisible penumbra of rights and duties embodied in the law of contract and other parts of the framework.[8]

2. Prevention of force and fraud: Government exercises a monopoly of force in order to prevent fraud and forestall the use of force by private parties. Private force must be held in check, because its use is subversive of both public order and justice. So far as the market is concerned, the reservoir of force at the disposal of the State is employed to uphold contracts and prevent "taxation" of one private citizen by another.

Though illegal use of force almost always involves fraud or concealment, prevention of fraud per se rests on different grounds than does prevention of force. In the long run the fraudulent merchant, the vendor of stocks in nonexistent oil wells, or the manufacturer of tainted foods would be forced into bankruptcy by a free and informed market. But in the meantime the costs of detecting fraud through trial and error involve extraordinary burdens on those who are short-changed, fleeced, or poisoned. It is cheaper all around, therefore, to rule these practices illegal and provide the machinery for enforcing these rules. At the Federal level the Pure Food and Drug Act or the activities of the Securities and Exchange Commission are notable examples of this practice.

Defining the Group Whose Welfare Is to Be Maximized

Part of the exercise of national sovereignty consists in defining the limits of the social body whose welfare is to be maximized. In practice this ordinarily means the ethnic and racial groups who occupy the territory of the state. This object is implemented by a simple but enormously important device—the restriction of immigration.

The broad outlines of social policy on immigration are very largely a closed issue in most nations of the Western World, though they may be

[8] The "institution of the contract" is discussed in Émile Durkheim, *On the Division of Labor in Society*, translated by G. Simpson (New York: The Macmillan Co., 1933).

reopened for review by changes in the balance of power or by shifts in population structure. Barriers to migration raise the income of labor competitive to potential immigrants and lower the earnings of specialized resources that are complementary to poetential migrants. If no restraints are imposed on exports of capital or imports of commodities, neither the rate of interest nor the relative price of internationally traded goods will be much affected by these barriers.

Freedom of Entry

Given a framework of rules and a definition of the group to be served, the case for freedom of entry is overwhelming on both economic and political grounds. Freedom of access is both an implication of political democracy and a necessary condition for economic efficiency.

So far as economic efficiency is concerned, barriers to entry result in the production of less of the restricted commodities and more of all other things than the economy either wants or could have if the barriers were broken down. How do these restrictions arise and how should the State move to demolish them? In the absence of public intervention, the degree of restraint on the free movement of resources would be established by the balance of two contrary tendencies: On the one hand, there is a clear and obvious gain from combining to restrict competition and raise prices—as, for example, a coalition of bakers or of housebuilders in a particular locality or a cartel of metal fabricators or a syndicate of truckdrivers in the country at large. (These gains are greater the smaller the possibility of securing substitutes for the commodity or service the coalition controls.)[9] On the other hand the costs of coordinating the coalition plus the restless forces of competition act to erode these gains away.

The State should, and in some cases does, aid the market in restraining the growth of coalitions. As a minimum it ought not to countenance nor encourage these barriers by law and administrative decisions that create a favorable climate for suspending competition. At the maximum it ought to seek out and break up trusts, combines, and syndicates. This is no easy matter as the complex history of law and court procedures under antitrust clearly demonstrates. However the existence of the Sherman and Clayton Acts plus the activities of the Federal Trade Commission have exercised a profound influence on our economic structure and have helped to prevent the growth of cartelized inefficiency on the European model.

Restrictive practices by trade unions represent still another example of barriers to free entry. The union need not ration entry to the trade or occupation by direct controls such as membership quotas, elaborate ap-

---

[9] For discussion of the underlying economic issues see Alfred Marshall, *Principles of Economics* (8th ed.; London: Macmillan & Co., 1920), book V, ch. vi; as modified by J. R. Hicks, *The Theory of Wages* (reprint ed.; New York: Peter Smith, 1948), pp. 241–47. Further see George J. Stigler, *The Theory of Price* (rev. ed.; New York: The Macmillan Co., 1952), p. 208.

prenticeship requirements, or high membership dues. The same result can be accomplished indirectly by persuading the buyer of labor services not to offer employment below some stipulated wage. The wage rations entry. Unlike producer coalitions, unions have very low overhead costs and can proliferate indefinitely without running into diseconomies of scale.

Regulation of Natural Monopoly

Natural monopoly is an obvious candidate for public regulation. Monopoly creates economic inefficiency by distorting the pattern of production. The price of monopolized articles is higher, the output lower, and the output of all other things is greater than would be the case if monopoly were conducted in the public interest.[10]

Natural monopoly ordinarily arises when the advantages of large-scale production plus the conditions of demand are such that one producer engrosses the entire market for a commodity. And competition in the industry will be imperfect if production and demand conditions are such that a small number of firms dominate the scene. For either pure monopoly or "competition among the few," the individual producer occupies a large enough share of the market so that variations in his output exert an appreciable influence on the price of the goods. In the effort to maximize returns producers will jack up prices above the incremental costs of production.

Given the definition of "the commodity," the degree of monopoly power depends on the extent of substitution in both production and consumption. Everyone has a bit of a monopoly on something: The unctuous manners of a neighborhood grocery-store proprietor may earn him a preferred position over his quarrelsome competitors, but if he attempts to capitalize this dividend into his prices he will merely increase the business of the chainstore down the block. A rutabaga monopoly would be of small avail so long as potatoes, lima beans, and squash could readily be had. A monopoly on gas or electric power in a particular town is a somewhat more serious matter, however, because of the unavailability of close substitutes. Most State and local regulation of monopoly lies in the field of public utilities, and the Federal Power Commission exercises jurisdiction over interstate movements of natural gas and hydroelectric power. A monopoly over a factor of production such as aluminum would also raise questions of public policy even though a host of other metals compete with it for its various purposes.

Now given the economic indictment of monopoly, regulation ought to be designed to encourage efficient use of resources; that is, to force the monopoly to price at its incremental cost of production. But this criterion

---

[10] Melvin W. Reder, *Studies in the Theory of Welfare Economics* (New York: Columbia University Press, 1947), ch. iv, "An Obstacle to the Attainment of Maximum Welfare: Monopoly."

raises a host of technical issues which it is inappropriate to pursue here.[11]

In some instances the public may elect to take over and run the monopoly. In principle, both regulation and operation should arrive at the same end, but since the latter involves government ownership and allocation of resources it will be briefly treated under another heading.

External Economies and Diseconomies

In allocating resources by the market, private welfare is synonymous with public welfare so long as prices reflect the full costs or the full benefits of economic activity. But this reflection is often imperfect, and some of these imperfections raise important issues of policy. A famous illustrative example concerns the manufacture of a commodity which creates smoke or noxious vapors that pollute the surrounding air. The "private cost" to the manufacturer is the expense of labor, raw materials, wear and tear on the plant, et cetera, incurred in producing the article. The "social cost" is that plus the inconvenience and danger which pollution creates for the inhabitants roundabout.[12] For an inhabitant of southern California this is no trivial example, I might add. (In the long run with free choice of places of residence no one would put up with the nuisance unless he felt that other advantages of the locale compensated for it; and thus the place affected would have to offer lower rents or a higher dividend of conveniences in order to be of equal attractiveness with other places. Thus, the long-run cost of the nuisance would be the distortion it created in regard to choice of residence.)

This case illustrates an external diseconomy—external because it operates outside the price system and diseconomy because it creates a cost for someone. In general an external economy (or diseconomy) is created whenever the consumption or production of some commodity or service by one agent creates benefits (or costs) for other persons not covered in the price. There are four categories of these external effects: (1) between consumers, (2) between producers, (3) from producers to consumers, and (4) from consumers to producers.[13] In order to push forward on the production and consumption of things which create external economies and to cut back on those that create diseconomies, public intervention in the interests of economic efficiency is required if the effects are important enough to be worth bothering about. In some instances laws and regulation alone will suffice; in others—to be discussed under the second of our major headings—public resources must be expended.

---

[11] For a summary of these issues see Nancy Ruggles, "The Welfare Basis of the Marginal Cost Pricing Principle and Recent Developments in the Theory of Marginal Cost Pricing," *Review of Economic Studies*, Vol. XVII (1949–50), No. 42, pp. 29–46, and No. 43, pp. 107–26.

[12] A. C. Pigou, *The Economics of Welfare* (4th ed.; London: Macmillan & Co., 1932), part II, ch. ix.

[13] Tibor Scitovsky, "Two Concepts of External Economies," *Journal of Political Economy*, Vol. LXII, No. 2 (April, 1954), pp. 143–51.

For the smoke nuisance case, as an example, zoning regulations and requirements concerning manufacturing processes, private incinerators, and perhaps automobile exhausts seem the appropriate remedy, though—as the Los Angeles case again demonstrates—considerable research, financed by public money, will be needed before precise correctives are discovered.

Most of the important cases where regulation is appropriate involve external diseconomies between producers, or between producers and consumers. Many of these instances also involve the conservation of resources.

An important instance where intervention can improve allocation is presented by external diseconomies between lumbering and farming. Cutting timber increases the rate at which water drains off the surface and exposes farmlands downhill or downstream to the likelihood of flood and erosion. Various remedies have been proposed: one is a requirement that lumber companies replant as they cut (some of them find this profitable to do on their own); another is that they modify the cutting pattern so as to leave undergrowth and small trees standing.

External diseconomies between producers in the same industry are exemplified by the extraction of crude oil from a particular deposit or pool. If drilling rights are owned by a variety of operators, each will seek to pump the deposit as rapidly as possible with the result that pressure of natural gas inside the dome will fall and cut down the yield of the pool. Each producer creates external diseconomies for the others. But production could be maximized if ownership were unified so that external burdens would be transformed into internal costs. If one producer cannot buy out the others—because it is too troublesome or requires more capital than he can lay his hands on—unified extraction can be achieved by public regulation, providing the rules are enforceable and technologically feasible.[14]

The fisheries case is another instance of producer diseconomies, with one additional complication—the economic opportunity, the fishing ground, cannot be owned. Given certain biological variables, which are but imperfectly known at present, the annual rate of take will exert an influence on the total population of certain species of ocean fish. But the individual fisherman does not consider changes in the underlying stock of resources when he voyages out to make his catch. Each one, consequently, creates diseconomies for the others; rational management of the fish population goes by default and is left to chance.[15] The remedy would appear to include some sort of international licensing organization.

Still another aspect of producer diseconomies is found in activities whose unregulated pursuit would clutter up the city streets or create

[14] Clair Wilcox, *Public Policies toward Business* (Homewood, Ill.: Richard D. Irwin, Inc., 1955), pp. 363–66.

[15] Anthony Scott, "The Fishery: The Objectives of Sole Ownership," *Journal of Political Economy*, Vol. LXIII, No. 2 (April, 1955), pp. 116–24.

chaos through unlimited exploitation of limited facilities. An interesting, but somewhat trivial, example is taxicabs in metropolitan areas. In the interests of holding down the burden on other forms of traffic, the number of licenses granted to cabdrivers is limited, the number being decided by a rough estimate of the advantages of service to the consumer versus the disadvantages of cabs to other drivers. Taverns and liquor stores are similarly limited on the presumption, no doubt, that a plethora of such facilities would lower the character and quality of the region. A much more important example is Federal licensing of radio and TV broadcasting in order to prevent dual exploitation of a single channel. Now, whatever the grounds on which such limits are fixed, the license to exploit the facility represents a partial patent of monopoly. Public authority may place hedges on the license; for example, the Federal Communications Commission in granting TV licenses seeks to disperse control over the channels of mass communication. But other things the same, it is surely contrary to either policy or economy to give these prerequisites away. They should be sold on the open market to the highest bidder—providing the applicant meets the other conditions which policy imposes. This criterion most certainly applies to radio and television franchises.

Economies in Pursuing Interests and Acquiring Knowledge

The case for the free market presumes that the individual knows his own interests and is aware of economic alternatives. Common observation suggests that departures in practice from these conditions are as pervasive as they are regrettable. Individual conduct shows many instances of obstinate attachment to "irrational" objectives; the costs of acquiring knowledge of the market are frequently so high that, in the absence of outside help, the sensible man decides that it is more efficient to remain ignorant.

Now the paternalistic role of the state in democratic societies, intervention to improve behavior or combat ignorance, is capable of infinite abuse and must be severely limited. The following represent some of the steps that may be taken on this ground.

Some transactions are restricted or altogether prohibited—e. g., sale of habit-forming drugs, gambling, and the practice of the world's oldest profession. While dope addiction and other aberrations work some hardships on persons outside the transaction, i. e., create external diseconomies, the primary reason for their prohibition is that they do violence to the self.

On a somewhat different level, the state requires the individual to maintain ownership in himself; he may offer his services for rent but cannot sell himself in bondage. Nor can individual citizens sell their electoral franchise. Clearly, however, these actions are prohibited because of their adverse external effects since, if widely practiced, they would subvert the whole climate of freedom.

An intrusion of the state which is widely accepted in practice but still debated in principle is compulsory saving under the Social Security Act. Although the actuarial value of the pension exceeds the accumulated worth of the contributions, the compulsory portion of old-age and survivors insurance is founded on the theory that the ordinary worker shortchanges his future, i. e., discounts future income at a higher rate of interest than he ought rationally to employ.

A still different set of interventions, directed, I think, against the effects of ignorance of market alternatives is licensing of professional practitioners such as doctors, lawyers, and pharmacists. A free market with exact knowledge makes licensing unnecessary, for the self-interest of the buyer rewards the seller according to his worth, and the incompetent can find no customers. But in the absence of exact knowledge the license testifies, when properly administered, to some minimum level of competence and saves the time and cost of determining whether the practitioner deserves his title. For law or medicine these costs would be high. I doubt whether the same is true, however, for barbers, beauticians, and others who need a public certificate to set up shop.

ALLOCATIVE ACTIVITIES OF GOVERNMENT

"Allocative" activities of Government employ resources, influence the distribution of income, or affect the level of national output. Despite their great variety and complexity and despite the even greater complexity of that incredible document, the Federal Budget, which authorizes them, the grounds or reasons for undertaking them are relatively few in number.

Indivisible Services

Among its other functions, market price is a rationing device which governs the volume of goods or services at the disposal of the user. No price, no service. But many activities that are "in the highest degree necessary" cannot be rationed by price and must be available to everyone if they are available to anyone. An example which conveys the essence of the case: lighthouses.[16]

In some cases an indivisible activity could easily be carried on by a voluntary agency which supported itself by fees charged to the user. Shipowners, conceivably, might band together in an association to build lighthouses, or the residents of a river valley might embark on a joint operation to control floods—another indivisible activity which Government ordinarily performs—but the difficulties of promoting and administering the agency, the trouble involved in collecting fees from unwilling beneficiaries, etc., would render the prospect of such associations dubious. In this connection, however, Government may be regarded as a holding company for a group of associations rendering a variety of indivisible

[16] J. S. Mill, *Principles,* Book V, ch. xi, sec. 15.

services to the citizenry.[17] While Government can more readily promote and finance such associations, the holding company is likely to be somewhat larger than optimum size (and not always responsive to the needs of its customers).

Headed by national defense, the dominant function of central governments under existing conditions, the major indivisible services may be listed as follows:

1. National defense and related functions.
2. Police protection.
3. Foreign aid and development.
4. Public health.
5. Pure research.
6. Navigational aids and flood control.
7. Streets and highways—with exceptions as noted below.
8. Wildlife preservation.
9. Public monuments, buildings, and parks—with exceptions.

Comments on selected items:

(2) Individuals can and do hire private watchmen and carry arms to fend off marauders but prevention, detection, and punishment of crime are public offices.

(3) Foreign aid is a function of political and military policy, but long range economic development probably depends on exports of private capital.

(5) Pure research is undertaken both by government and by private nonprofit agencies, such as universities and foundations.

(6) Navigational aids and flood control on inland waterways are often conducted jointly with power production and irrigation which can be rationed by prices.

(7) Save for limited access roads and bridges, highways are indivisible services in the first instance but can be financed by taxes on cars and gasoline in joint demand with highways. These taxes represent user charges whose yield provides a clue to the optimum size of the highway network.

(9) Imposing public edifices and parks, to the extent they have esthetic value, are an indivisible service for the public in general. But visiting a national park, hunting on a game preserve, and using a public recreation facility should, if practicable, be rationed by admission charges or licences in order to prevent overcrowding and cover the costs of operation.[18]

How should indivisible services be produced? Both economic efficiency and political liberty require that Government use the signals and incentives of the price system in acquiring and combining the resources which

[17] Paul A. Samuelson, "The Pure Theory of Public Expenditures," *Review of Economics and Statistics,* Vol. XXXVI, No. 4 (November, 1954), pp. 387–89.

[18] Procter Thomson, "Prices versus Taxes in the Allocation of Public Resources," *Proceedings of the 48th Annual Conference of the National Tax Association* (Sacramento, Calif.: National Tax Association, 1956), pp. 140–57.

supply these services. The market for indivisibles is blind on the demand side, but the supply side should use prices to the fullest extent possible. This clearly implies (1) that Government should pay market prices for the resources it hires, (2) that, whenever possible, Government should contract with private producers to perform services instead of supplying them directly. For, to amplify the second of these criteria, the optimum size of government from the standpoint of political policy may exceed the optimum for purposes of managerial efficiency. If public bodies can contract out or delegate the task of management to private enterprise, they may both reduce the costs and improve the quality of operations.

To exemplify: Highways, public buildings, and dams can be, and normally are, built by private contractors rather than by public employees. The complex weapons and devices needed for military preparedness in the postatomic age are manufactured by private concerns rather than by Government arsenals. The thousands of different items used in the daily operation of government are ordinarily purchased from private dealers. To these statements there are some exceptions. Highway departments sometimes build their own roads; the Military Establishment does manufacture some of its own weapons; and Government agencies sometimes fabricate their own supplies. These exceptions ought to be rigorously and carefully scrutinized. In all too many cases the waste and malfeasance which there occurs would be incompatible with survival under private auspices. But the details of this topic belong elsewhere.

Requisition of military manpower represents one important area where Government ignores the signals of the price system though, to be sure, the ground rules for the draft vary from time to time and coercion is sweetened by persuasion. As a result, it is impossible to ascertain the real costs of defense, i. e., the costs in terms of the value of manpower in other uses. Cheap military manpower secured via the draft is, moreover, an expensive bargain in the long run. In an age where the soldier must command a formidable arsenal of technical weapons, these reluctant defenders are scarcely the equal of a seasoned cadre of professionals recruited by voluntary inducements. At a time, moreover, where potential annihilation lurks in the dark of night for those who stay at home as well as those who go to war, no great premium would be necessary to hire all the permanent staff of our forces or to pay, if need be, for short periods of duty followed by transfer to the Reserves. In a mature and responsible society, finally, a mercenary army of professional soldiers poses no great threat to our democratic freedoms.

External Economies and Diseconomies

As was argued above, prices sometimes fail to reflect the full costs and benefits of particular activities, with the result that the private market produces too few of the things that create external economies and too many of those that create diseconomies. In many cases these departures from optimum can be handled by public regulation and involve no direct use of resources. Particularly is this true of external diseconomies, e. g., the smoke-nuisance case and the oil-well case. But where the activity creates benefits for persons other than the producer or customer, a subsidy is needed to stimulate its production. From the standpoint of public resources, education represents by far the most important example of this principle.

The education of individual A produces, of course, a direct and immediate benefit to A himself; and self-interest alone would induce him, or his parents acting for him, to build up his capital of ability. But A's education also confers advantages on B, and C, and D. For in a democratic society with a universal franchise, education is a necessary condition for wise and responsible exercise of political freedoms. A, if uninstructed and ignorant, could not exercise his franchise wisely and an illiterate electorate would imperil the whole future of democracy. Further, cultural interchange and all the amenities of civilized society demand individual sensitivity to values, ideas, and the world about us. But if left to its own devices, family A might not purchase as much schooling as B, C, and D would like to see them buy. This important instance of external economies in consumption justifies public subsidy for education.

The school government, in this context, is a corporation that implements the interest of each in the education of others. For, to be sure, B's concern for A (and A's for B, etc.) could be implemented by a series of private gifts. But these interests would be better served by a mutual compact among families A, B, C, and D stipulating that each would match—or meet in some agreed ratio—the contributions of the other. A community referendum on school taxes and expenditures assumes precisely this sort of mutual compact. Because of external economies, families A, B, C, and D would elect to expend a greater amount per child than would have resulted from individual purchases plus private philanthropy.

Public subsidies for schools could be expended in a number of ways. Government could subsidize private schools; it could dispense certificates to the family, who could spend the certificate at an accredited school of their choice; or it could operate schools as a department of government. For political and other reasons, current practice favors the latter alternative.

External economies are a pervasive feature of human life but most of them are too trivial to be worth bothering about as subjects of public intervention. Examples are the householder whose well-kept lawn beautifies the neighborhood, or the merchant whose store windows gladden the eye of passing pedestrians.

An analytical curiosity which puzzles and intrigues economists but may or may not be of great practical importance is the possibility of "increasing returns to scale" for a particular industry. In this form of external economy, expansion of production by the firm lowers costs for the industry because optimum size for the exploitation of some common facility has not yet been achieved.[19] These cases, when identified, are appropriate candidates for subsidy. But possibilities for such economies appear to be rather limited, and, in any event, no one seems able to identify these curiosities in practice.[20]

Operation of Natural Monopolies

Monopoly, as already argued, represents an obvious threat to efficiency. The case for controlling it by public intervention is equally obvious. The choice between regulation or public operation turns upon some difficult issues of politics, economics, and administration whose solution varies according to circumstances. Regulation may tempt an alert and aggressive monopoly to befuddle or bribe the regulators. Operation involves the possibility of aggravated bureaucratic waste.

Monopolies in power, water, gas, and transport are often operated by municipalities. The Post Office Department is a monopoly operated by the Federal Government. How should these monopolies be conducted? On the one hand, optimum efficiency is achieved when the price of the service covers the cost of producing the last unit of that service. On the other hand optimum efficiency requires that total sales receipts cover total costs of producing the service; for taxes to finance subsidies inevitably warp the pattern of economic alternatives; moreover equity (equal treatment of equals) is violated when nonusers subsidize users—except in special cases where nonusers receive benefits that are not reflected in the structure of prices. These criteria conflict when the demand schedule for the service intersects the schedule of incremental (or marginal) costs at a point which lies below the schedule of average costs.[21]

If pricing on the basis of incremental costs involves subsidizing the monopoly from the Public Treasury, the governing authority has a number of strings to its bow which it can employ in important special cases. It can vary the quality of the product. By reducing the cost and quality of its services it can eventually come to rest at a point where demand price, incremental cost, and average cost coincide, and where incremental pricing, therefore, just covers total expenses.[22]

---

[19] Allyn Young, "Increasing Returns and Economic Progress," *Economic Journal*, Vol. XXXVIII, No. 152 (December, 1928), pp. 527–42.

[20] Scitovsky, *op. cit.*

[21] For background and further exposition see the articles of Nancy Ruggles cited in footnote 11. Roughly, however, when average cost (total cost divided by number of units) falls as output rises, because of economies of scale, the expenses of producing the last increment of the service are bound to be lower than the average cost of the entire range of output. (For instance if a batter who is hitting .250 before a particular game, pulls his average down, his "incremental" performance that day was less than 1 out of 4.) It follows as a matter of simple arithmetic that incremental cost times number of units sold falls short of total cost.

[22] The existence of an equilibrium at this intersection can be shown as follows: Given an enterprise where incremental cost and demand schedules intersect at any

For the post office, a Federal monopoly which chronically runs at a substantial deficit, these technical considerations are relevant and important.[23] Under existing practices and rates, the postal deficit subsidizes advertisers, book publishers, magazines, other departments of government, and inhabitants of rural areas. (Due to the vagaries of Government accounting, the post office does not bear the full cost of contributions to pensions for employees; on the other hand it is, or was, used as a vehicle for delivering handsome subsidies to private transport agencies such as airlines.) Subsidy in general is justified by the presence of a substantial degree of external economies. In the remote past subventions to publishers might have been justified as a contribution to literacy and education. Surely this presumption is of negligible worth at the present juncture. Surely, also, the diseconomies of high taxes render the postal deficit, and the additional taxation thereto attached, an enterprise devoutly to be liquidated.

Through what steps can the postal service be induced to balance its budget? First, put it on notice that it must balance its accounts. Second, unscramble the records so that it bears the full costs, but no more than the full costs, of its operation; this implies payment by other departments for use of postal buildings and delivery of Government mail and payment of overhead and retirement costs by the post office. Third, and most important, let it set its own rates and establish a defensible system of mail classification. Under this dispensation the postal service would be a quasi-independent corporation free to use the methods of the market, save for the stipulation that (having no stockholders) surpluses, if any, must be plowed into additional facilities. Deficits, when they occurred, would be financed by postal bonds sold to the private market.

If these three steps were taken, might it not be possible to contemplate a fourth and more radical proposal, namely opening the postal business to private enterprise? The quaint and antiquated devices by which, it is

---

point, each increase (or decrease) in quality will raise (or lower) the cost schedules and raise (or lower) the demand schedule. Given diminishing returns to investment in quality of service, each rise in quality will raise the demand price (for a given output) by less than the cost price; each fall in quality will lower the demand price by less than the cost price. Eventually the average cost schedule can be made to overtake the demand schedule where the former crosses the schedule of incremental costs.

By similar reasoning, a monopoly that earns a surplus in the first instance is in the happy position of being able to achieve balance by raising its level of service.

If, now, increasing returns to investment in quality prevail over the relevant range, a public monopoly that incurs a deficit in the first instance should raise rather than lower the quality of its service.

What do variations in "quality" entail? For a city transport system obviously, or for the Federal Post Office (as argued below) many such variations in convenience, promptness, and comfort can be undertaken. For municipal gas, water, and electricity, technical possibilities of variation are much more limited. Installing and repairing facilities, and billing customers would appear to exhaust the range.

[23] Jane Kennedy, "Structure and Policy in Postal Rates," *Journal of Political Economy*, Vol. LXV, No. 3 (June, 1957), pp. 185–208.

sometimes alleged, the post office conducts operations would be put to the test of the market, while prospects of private monopoly would be counteracted by public competition.

EQUALITY

A free and open market tends to pay productive agents the value of what they produce. The income of individuals depends on the unit price of productive services times the number of units which they own—including both capital goods and their own labor power. The number of units of productive services which they own, or have embodied in them, depends on inheritance, effort, and luck. For reasons too obvious to enumerate, the benefits of inheritance, effort, and luck are not equally distributed in the existing social order and are not likely to be so distributed in any conceivable scheme of social organization.

But inevitability does not justify inequality. More accurately speaking, inequality of wealth and income can be modified by social policy; and a democratic social order is powerfully determined to undertake that policy. Equality, or mitigation of gross inequalities, is both an end value of the democratic community and a means to other ends.

In this context the happiest exercise of the power of the state is to promote equality by removing the barriers which restrict opportunity; barriers founded on caste or prejudice, barriers heightened by the presence of ignorance, and barriers which the market itself would sweep away if given scope to do so—all this is a necessary exercise of democratic public power.[24]

The state also intervenes to purchase equality, or mitigate inequity, through the tax-expenditure mechanism. Depending on the schedule of taxes and the imputation of benefits to individuals, the balance of benefits bestowed minus taxes collected is generally positive for the lower income groups and negative for higher income groups.[25] Despite opportunities for evasion, the sawtooth monster embodied in present income and inheritance tax schedules has cut down significantly on the relative share of upper income groups in the national dividend over the past quarter century.[26] Approach toward equality, then, is both a valid aim and a real accomplishment of our democratic fiscal system.

Given the conditions of economic life, a tax-expenditure system which promotes equality conflicts, after a certain point, with other end values of the community. Specifically it conflicts, after some specified point, with

---

[24] Allan G. B. Fisher, "Alternative Techniques for Promoting Equality in a Capitalist Society," *American Economic Review*, Vol. XL, No. 2 (May, 1950), pp. 356–68.

[25] James M. Buchanan, "The Pure Theory of Government Finance: A Suggested Approach," *Journal of Political Economy*, Vol. LVII, No. 6 (December, 1949), pp. 496–505, refers to this balance—with the sign reversed, however—as the "fiscal residuum."

[26] Simon Kuznets, *Shares of Upper Income Groups in Income and Savings* (New York: National Bureau of Economic Research, 1952).

productivity. In full perspective, the relation between equality and productivity doubtless runs as follows: If wealth and income were very unequally distributed, there is a range over which the community could probably achieve both higher output and more equality by redistributing resources from rich to poor. If redistribution continued, a point of maximum productivity and moderate equality would be reached. Thereafter, additional degrees of equality could be purchased only at the expense of some sacrifice of productivity. These sacrifices would be small at first, but would increase steadily till, at the limit, complete equality—the same income for everyone—would be reached only by a very considerable sacrifice of total output.

Now why must equality and productivity be competitive values beyond a certain point? Answer No. 1 is to be found in the adverse incentive effect of progressive taxation on initiative, risk taking, and enterprise. Answer No. 2 rests on the adverse incentive effect of receiving income without expending effort. (Up to a point, of course, the latter effect would be counterbalanced by improvements in ability and standard of living created by subsidies to low-income families.)

To continue: So long as society can get more of both values, both more equality and more income (from a given body of resources), it would be wasteful not to do so. But the problem of choice arises when the two values cannot increase simultaneously, when, that is, additional equality can be purchased only by some sacrifice of productivity and progress. Because we are, or may be, faced with this kind of choice is, of course, no reason for adjuring additional equality. We may judge it worth the price. But in so judging we must take account of the terms of trade between equality and productivity. Here, in brief, is a central problem of democratic government—how much more (or less) equality do we want in terms of the sacrifice (or gain) in productivity involved in moving toward it.

Finally, equality is not achieved by any one activity of government. It is a byproduct and an end product of the whole system of government finance.

Humanitarianism

The market is an impersonal agency. It takes no account of need unless signalized by price and recognizes virtues only when they are marketable. In larger perspective, however, "no man is an island," or, in the language of economics rather than literature, one man's utility function may contain a term for the welfare of another. Humanitarian activities are thus an important special case of external effects between consumers.

Humanitarian objectives can be undertaken by voluntary nonprofit agencies to which individuals contribute in accord with their means and desires. (In the division of labor between government and the market these institutions share some of the elements of both.) Citizen X, however, might be more willing to support some humanitarian activity if assured that Y and Z would follow suit. Accordingly he makes a compact with them under which each is to vote on the amount that all will contribute. Before voting, they decide that the total will be allocated between them in accord with their means. In this way each dollar that X contributes will be accompanied by, say, half a dollar from Y and two from Z. When the vote is taken, therefore, the tax each levies on himself exceeds the amount he would have contributed on his own. Government philanthropy, then, can be regarded as a device to administer such a compact for the community as a whole, voting, of course, being conducted by representatives rather than by the entire electorate.

Humanitarian activities of government include a series of transfer payments for assistance to dependent children, aid to the aged, compensation of the unemployed, and general relief for the indigent and unfortunate.

Economic Stability

An economic environment of individual decisions, mutual interdependence, and uncertain prospects is inevitably subject to fluctuations in income, employment, and prices. While these erratic movements are, in some sense, a concomitant of progress, the business cycle generates a train of evils which no responsible society will passively endure. (1) Uncertainty itself creates costs; elaborate and expensive adjustments must be undertaken by individuals in order to cope with it. (2) Both inflation and depression generate diseconomies in the form of overexpansion of certain sectors of the economy during a runaway boom and underutilization of resources during a slump. (3) The incidence of the cycle is inequitably distributed between individuals. (4) Aggravated uncertainty of the system plus waste and inequity generate political pressures which threaten the stability of democracy.

From the individual point of view the cycle appears as a capital levy of arbitrary amount, levied without announcement or compensation. If the cycle cannot be tamed but must be accepted as an act of providence, social policy, as a bare minimum, ought to share its burdens more equitably.

Under modern conditions, the cycle can, or some of its components can, be mitigated, though not completely controlled, by fiscal and monetary policy. Government can stabilize certain elements of the budget and these in turn can exert a tranquillizing effect upon the market; it can stabilize the level of expenditures over the cycle; it can fix the rates, though not the yield, of the tax system; it can stabilize the quantity of money but not, of course, the number of times that money circulates during the period.

Government can also intervene to stabilize several important variables for the market as a whole. It can, if needed, fix the price of particular things though not the quality and quantity of goods exchanged at this price; it can fix the rate of interest; it can stabilize the general level of prices; and it can stabilize the level of employment.

Under modern conditions, however, the chief problems of fiscal policy are conflict among objectives and inadequacy of means. Regarding conflict, the Government may not be able simultaneously to stabilize the level of prices and the volume of employment. Full employment at forced draft spells inflation, although the terms of trade between more inflation and more employment vary erratically over the course of the cycle. Regarding means, stabilizing either employment or prices or some selected combination of the two can be attempted either through automatic devices or through forecasting and administrative action. Automatic devices or built-in stabilizers take time to operate; forecasting is subject to error, and administrative action may involve both error and delay.

In any event economists know appallingly little about the cure of the cycle and still less about its causes. The situation counsels humility, caution—and more resources for basic research.

MISCELLANEOUS ACTIVITIES: PRICE FIXING AND GOVERNMENT ENTERPRISE

Price Fixing

On an ad hoc basis, the Central Government intervenes to regulate the prices of particular goods and services. In most instances save the control of prices during wartime, these interventions establish minimum prices and redound to the advantage of particular producers.

Primary instances of these activities are farm price supports, tariffs, transportation prices, and minimum wage legislation.

In the short run, parity prices and production quotas on basic agricultural commodities sold in the private market represent an income subsidy to wealthy farmers financed by a sales tax on low income city consumers. For the rise in price is equivalent to a levy on consumption; the larger the farmer's output (or acreage) the greater is the extent of the subsidy which this rise in prices (or soil bank payments) confers upon him; and the wheat, cotton, corn, and tobacco which this program covers are staples of the city worker's budget. (The portion of the crop sequestered in storage by the Commodity Credit Corporation and its equivalents is paid for from general revenues, though a portion of the cost may be recovered if the commodity is later sold or dumped abroad.)

In the long run, the portion of the subsidy that finds its way into income of farm labor tends to retard the migration of workers to the city and slow down the rate of urban economic development. The portion imputed to land bids up the price of farms.[27] In addition to the income

[27] For general discussion see T. W. Schultz, *Agriculture in an Unstable Economy* (New York: McGraw-Hill Book Co., Inc., 1945).

subsidy, the stability of agricultural prices which the program administers enables farmers to employ resources more effectively.[28]

Tariffs and import quotas subsidize producers at the expense of consumers in the short run, while in the long run they draw more resources into the protected trades than would otherwise be the case and lower the national dividend by cutting us off from the advantages of international specialization. In addition, tariff hampers exports, fosters domestic monopoly, and creates political pressures for subsidies to foreign governments. Tariff, however, prevents deterioration in the economic position of workers and investors who are threatened by foreign competition and who can raise enough leverage to secure protection.

The legal minimum wage raises the price but reduces the volume of employment for workers in the trades it protects. For no tendency in economics is more certain or definite than the principle that states: the higher the price of something, other things the same, the less the volume of purchases. This principle, unfortunately, applies to the hiring of unskilled workers in sweated industries. An effective floor on wages which raises costs of production will diminish employment because, first, employers substitute capital for labor and, second, consumers substitute other goods for those produced by the protected trades. If demand for unskilled labor is elastic the minimum wage also reduces the total wages bill and purchasing power placed in the hands of the protected workers.

Benefits of minimum wages are secured by those who gain employment under its provisions. Costs are borne, first, by the workers whom it prices out of the market, second, by consumers who buy the products of protected industries, and third, by resources which are complementary to unskilled labor.

Government Enterprises

In addition to operating natural monopolies which sell to the general public, Government also produces a great variety of supplies and services; for many, but not all of these, Government itself is the sole customer. The Defense Department operates a galaxy of establishments which manufacture arms, build ships, and produce supplies. The Government operates a railroad in Alaska and in Panama; it has turned its hand to the production of rum and molasses in the Virgin Islands; it lends money to farmers (the Farmers' Home Administration), to small-business men (the Small Business Administration), and to importers and exporters (the Export-Import Bank). It builds and owns ships which are leased to private concerns. Finally, Government is the landlord of 400 millions of acres within the 48 States.

What issues of principle and practice are raised by these activities? In

---

[28] D. Gale Johnson, *Forward Prices for Agriculture* (Chicago: The University of Chicago Press, 1947).

general, as suggested above, Government is a most indifferent manager of enterprises. Why? Because Government employees are stupid and lazy? Not at all; here, as elsewhere, the servant is worthy of his hire. Because the civil service, while an admirable device for preventing corruption, tends to protect mediocrity and inhibit initiative? Perhaps; but too much cannot be made of this argument. Because Government is immune from the discipline of the competitive market? In part, yes, but large sections of corporate bureaucracy also enjoy some relative immunity. The ineffectiveness of Government management arises from its diseconomies of scale. Government is too large for maximum efficiency. Or, put a bit more carefully, Government may be no larger than necessary in order to discharge the functions which it alone must command, but if some activity which the market could have performed is added to its structure, that activity will, in general, be conducted less effectively than it could have been conducted by the market. Not only that; but the addition of this activity will dilute the managerial capacity of the top echelon, and existing activities will suffer in consequence.

Now, of course, this general presumption must be modified in particular cases. Many old-line Government bureaus (such as the Forestry Service) and many quasi-public corporations (such as the TVA) have great dedication and initiative with high esprit de corps amongst their staff and are fully the equal of comparable sectors of private enterprise. But the general presumption against Government enterprise should not lightly be cast aside. Government ought not be duplicate the efforts of the market and when it has done so, because of some temporary expediency, it should withdraw as gracefully and rapidly as possible. Exceptions require very strong proof indeed.

Unfortunately, once Government is embroiled in one of these ventures, the cost of disentanglement is high. In some cases no private firms are willing to take the thing off the Government's hands save at bargain-basement prices. Or—as in the case of loans to farmers and small-business men—the activity involves a concealed subsidy which the political power of the beneficiaries is mobilized to retain. Or an arsenal, a manufacturing plant, and an insurance agency become symbols of empire and all the massive power and artful devices of entrenched bureaucracy are arrayed in their defense.

RATIONAL CHOICE IN BUDGETARY POLICY

Given the grounds which sanction Government activities, how should we decide how much of our resources to devote to public purposes? Since the market cannot register the demand for these services, the political process must answer this question for us.

To economize on the labor of decision-making, elected representatives review policy and decide the details of public expenditure. In this, however, they do but reflect the ultimate consensus of the body politic so far as it lies within their power to determine it. Let us inquire, therefore, how the rational society would determine expenditures if the people themselves, after due investigation and debate, held a mass referendum on budgetary policy.

The decision could be made in two separate stages. The first order of business would be determination of the system of taxes, i. e., the array of rates for collecting any given amount of revenue from various income groups. To simplify exposition let us suppose that the revenue is to be collected by a universal tax on personal income. For each amount of revenue some sets of rates promise more equality, and some less; some would exact a smaller sacrifice in productivity, others a greater sacrifice. Indeed each set of rates would yield a specific combination of equality and productivity. The rational voter would select the rates that corresponded to his preferences as a citizen and his interests as a producer.

The society as a whole, let us say, decides to accept some rough average of the systems of rates for which its members voted. This being decided, the taxes levied upon members of each income class for each different amount of revenue are ascertained and announced.

Our citizen-taxpayers repair to the polls again to vote for the level of expenditures. Let us suppose that they are to cast a separate vote for each of the major categories: national defense, health and welfare, conservation, and so forth. How does the rational taxpayer cast his vote? He is aware that, say, expenditures of $10 billion of the community entail $100 in personal taxes, $15 billions, $150 and so on. Given his income and the structure of taxes, each extra dollar levied on him is accompanied by an additional $100 million from the community at large. (These accompanying amounts, of course, vary from one income group to another and from one expenditure level to another.) As a rational citizen-taxpayer he assesses the technical results of these expenditures and evaluates the personal satisfactions they create for him. For each class of activities, he votes for the level of public expenditures where the satisfactions created through Government by the outlay which necessarily accompanies the last dollar in personal taxes equal the satisfactions he would have secured from a dollar of private expenditure. He equalizes at the margin the satisfactions secured from alternative avenues of expenditure.

Depending on their income, their preferences, and the structure of the tax system, each individual selects some different level of expenditures in each category of the budget. The community, let us suppose, balances off these votes by compromising at the median, by taking, that is, the level which slices the votes in half; 50 percent voted for some higher level, 50 percent for some lower amount.

The result, inevitably, satisfies no one perfectly and dissatisfies some exceedingly. First, the tax system appears arbitrary when viewed by citizens who hold different preferences for the terms of trade between equality and productivity. Second, the degree of freedom the voter exercises depends on the number of expenditure categories arrayed for his decision. Third, the optimum for which he votes is surrounded by a margin of doubt. For his choice on "national defense" is bound to be affected by public expenditures and personal taxes for "conservation." But he votes for each in ignorance of the amount the community will determine for the other. Fourth, the community—under the median rule or any other rule—is not likely to satisfy his preferences precisely (unless, by accident, he was the median voter). If, for instance, the community chooses $10 billion, those who wanted more will feel shortchanged, while those who selected less may fancy themselves abused.

What role does representative government play in rational budgetary policy? The variety and complexity of government are beyond the scope of the ordinary citizen, nor would it be at all sensible for him to spend any large fraction of his time and his fortune in public business. That task is entrusted to elected agents who both accumulate knowledge of public affairs and serve as middlemen between the body politic and its government. Even the most dedicated of these agents can form no more than a rough estimate of the issues at stake, and can collect only the most cursory of samples of the true state of public opinion. But given their limits and their commitments, the role of the legislator is to vote as the citizens would have voted if they knew as much as he knows.

Socialist Market Economy

Market socialism (sometimes called "democratic" or "liberal" socialism) seeks to combine the socialist principles of (1) public ownership and (2) limited inequality in income distribution with (3) the use of markets and prices to allocate resources and goods. (In contrast, authoritarian socialism combines public ownership with central planning and allocation by administrative orders.)

In the socialist market model, households have freedom of choice of occupation, as differential wages in the labor market allocate the labor force among jobs. The resulting income differences are reduced by a social dividend paid on a uniform basis unrelated to occupation or wages. Households also have consumer choice in the expenditure of income, as well as a large measure of consumer sovereignty. The latter, however, is abridged but not superseded by the intervention of the Central Planning Board (CPB) in the economy to affect the rate of investment in order to achieve stability and growth.

Two principal solutions to the problem of pricing and resource allocation in market socialism have been suggested. In the solution advocated by Oskar Lange, the prices of consumer goods and labor services are determined by market forces, while the CPB attempts by trial and error to fix prices for producer goods which equate supply and demand. Given these "parametric" prices and some very broad rules for managerial behavior, individual enterprise managers determine the level and composition of their output and their use of inputs. An alternative solution, advanced by Abba Lerner and others, proposes that the prices of producer goods be determined by the interplay of the supply and demand of socialist firms in a market for capital goods.

These blueprints for market socialism originated in response to the argument of various prominent economists in the 1920s that rational economic calculation and efficient allocation of resources were in principle impossible in a socialist economy. The most famous member of this school is Ludwig von Mises, whose views are summarized in the first of the following three selections. To refute this conclusion, Oskar Lange developed the model of market socialism presented in the next selection. Lange's solution to the problem, in turn, has been challenged by Hayek (in the last selection) on the ground that, while perhaps conceivable in theory, it cannot be successfully applied in practice.

4. ECONOMIC CALCULATION IN SOCIALISM*

Ludwig von Mises

Mises denies the possibility of economic calculation and rational resource allocation in socialism. He argues that economic calculation can take place only by means of money prices established in a market for producer goods resting on private ownership of the means of production. Because such markets cannot, by definition, exist in socialism, he concludes that a socialist economy cannot achieve efficient allocation of resources. "Artificial" markets in socialism cannot successfully replace the true markets of capitalism in pricing producer goods so as to use them most effectively.

WITHOUT calculation, economic activity is impossible. Since under Socialism economic calculation is impossible, under Socialism there can be no economic activity in our sense of the word. In small and insignificant things rational action might still persist. But, for the most part, it would no longer be possible to speak of rational production. In the absence of criteria of rationality, production could not be consciously economical.

For some time possibly the accumulated tradition of thousands of years of economic freedom would preserve the art of economic administration from complete disintegration. Men would preserve the old processes not because they were rational, but because they were sanctified by tradition. In the meantime, however, changing conditions would make them irrational. They would become uneconomical as the result of changes brought about by the general decline of economic thought. It is true that production would no longer be "anarchical." The command of a supreme au-

*Reprinted, with permission, from *Socialism: An Economic and Sociological Analysis* (New Haven: Yale University Press, 1951), pp. 119–22, 137–42. This volume is an expanded translation of *Die Gemeinwirtschaft,* originally published in 1922. Ludwig von Mises was Professor of Economics at the University of Vienna.

thority would govern the business of supply. Instead of the economy of "anarchical" production the senseless order of an irrational machine would be supreme. The wheels would go round, but to no effect.

Let us try to imagine the position of a socialist community. There will be hundreds and thousands of establishments in which work is going on. A minority of these will produce goods ready for use. The majority will produce capital goods and semi-manufactures. All these establishments will be closely connected. Each commodity produced will pass through a whole series of such establishments before it is ready for consumption. Yet in the incessant press of all these processes the economic administration will have no real sense of direction. It will have no means of ascertaining whether a given piece of work is really necessary, whether labor and material are not being wasted in completing it. How would it discover which of two processes was the more satisfactory? At best, it could compare the quantity of ultimate products. But only rarely could it compare the expenditure incurred in their production. It would know exactly—or it would imagine it knew—what it wanted to produce. It ought therefore to set about obtaining the desired results with the smallest possible expenditure. But to do this it would have to be able to make calculations. And such calculations must be calculations of value. They could not be merely "technical," they could not be calculations of the objective use-value of goods and services. This is so obvious that it needs no further demonstration.

Under a system based upon private ownership in the means of production, the scale of values is the outcome of the actions of every independent member of society. Everyone plays a two-fold part in its establishment first as a consumer, secondly as producer. As consumer, he establishes the valuation of goods ready for consumption. As producer, he guides production-goods into those uses in which they yield the highest product. In this way all goods of higher orders[1] also are graded in the way appropriate to them under the existing conditions of production and the demands of society. The interplay of these two processes ensures that the economic principle is observed in both consumption and production. And, in this way, arises the exactly graded system of prices which enables everyone to frame his demand on economic lines.

Under Socialism, all this must necessarily be lacking. The economic administration may indeed know exactly what commodities are needed most urgently. But this is only half the problem. The other half, the valuation of the means of production, it cannot solve. It can ascertain the value of the totality of such instruments. That is obviously equal to the value of the satisfactions they afford. If it calculates the loss that would be incurred by withdrawing them, it can also ascertain the value of single instruments of production. But it cannot assimilate them to a common price denominator, as can be done under a system of economic freedom and money prices.

[1] [Producer goods.—EDITOR.]

It is not necessary that Socialism should dispense altogether with money. It is possible to conceive arrangements permitting the use of money for the exchange of consumers goods. But since the prices of the various factors of production (including labor) could not be expressed in money, money could play no part in economic calculations.

Suppose, for instance, that the socialist commonwealth was contemplating a new railway line. Would a new railway line be a good thing? If so, which of many possible routes should it cover? Under a system of private ownership we could use money calculations to decide these questions. The new line would cheapen the transportation of certain articles, and, on this basis, we could estimate whether the reduction in transport charges would be great enough to counterweigh the expenditure which the building and running of the line would involve. Such a calculation could be made only in money. We could not do it by comparing various classes of expenditure and savings in kind. If it is out of the question to reduce to a common unit the quantities of various kinds of skilled and unskilled labor, iron, coal, building materials of different kinds, machinery and the other things which the building and upkeep of railways necessitate, then it is impossible to make them the subject of economic calculation. We can make systematic economic plans only when all the commodities which we have to take into account can be assimilated to money. True, money calculations are incomplete. True, they have profound deficiencies. But we have nothing better to put in their place. And under sound monetary conditions they suffice for practical purposes. If we abandon them, economic calculation becomes absolutely impossible.

This is not to say that the socialist community would be entirely at a loss. It would decide for or against the proposed undertaking and issue an edict. But, at best, such a decision would be based on vague valuations. It could not be based on exact calculations of value.

A stationary society could, indeed, dispense with these calculations. For there, economic operations merely repeat themselves. So that, if we assume that the socialist system of production were based upon the last state of the system of economic freedom which it superseded, and that no changes were to take place in the future, we could indeed conceive a rational and economic Socialism. But only in theory. A stationary economic system can never exist. Things are continually changing, and the stationary state, although necessary as an aid to speculation, is a theoretical assumption to which there is no counterpart in reality. And, quite apart from this, the maintenance of such a connection with the last state of the exchange economy would be out of the question, since the transition to Socialism with its equalization of incomes would necessarily transform the whole "set" of consumption and production. And then we have a socialist community which must cross the whole ocean of possible and imaginable economic permutations without the compass of economic calculation.

All economic change, therefore, would involve operations the value of which could neither be predicted beforehand nor ascertained after they had taken place. Everything would be a leap in the dark. Socialism is the renunciation of rational economy.

* * * *

Some of the younger socialists believe that the socialist community could solve the problem of economic calculation by the creation of an artificial market for the means of production. They admit that it was an error on the part of the older socialists to have sought to realize Socialism through the suspension of the market and the abolition of pricing for goods of higher orders; they hold that it was an error to have seen in the suppression of the market and of the price system the essence of the socialistic ideal. And they contend that if it is not to degenerate into a meaningless chaos in which the whole of our civilization would disappear, the socialist community equally with the capitalistic community, must create a market in which all goods and services may be priced. On the basis of such arrangements, they think, the socialist community will be able to make its calculations as easily as the capitalist entrepreneurs.

Unfortunately the supporters of such proposals do not see (or perhaps *will* not see) that it is not possible to divorce the market and its functions in regard to the formation of prices from the working of a society which is based on private property in the means of production and in which, subject to the rules of such a society, the landlords, capitalists, and entrepreneurs can dispose of their property as they think fit. For the motive force of the whole process which gives rise to market prices for the factors of production is the ceaseless search on the part of the capitalists and the entrepreneurs to maximize their profits by serving the consumers' wishes. Without the striving of the entrepreneurs (including the shareholders) for profit, of the landlords for rent, of the capitalists for interest and the laborers for wages, the successful functioning of the whole mechanism is not to be thought of. It is only the prospect of profit which directs production into those channels in which the demands of the consumer are best satisfied at least cost. If the prospect of profit disappears the mechanism of the market loses its mainspring, for it is only this prospect which sets it in motion and maintains it in operation. The market is thus the focal point of the capitalist order of society; it is the essence of Capitalism. Only under Capitalism, therefore, is it possible; it cannot be "artificially" imitated under Socialism.

The advocates of the artificial market, however, are of the opinion that an artificial market can be created by instructing the controllers of the different industrial units to act *as if* they were entrepreneurs in a capitalistic state. They argue that even under Capitalism the managers of joint stock companies work not for themselves but for the companies, that is to say, for the shareholders. Under Socialism, therefore, it would be possible for them to act in exactly the same way as before, with the same circumspection and devotion to duty. The only difference would be that under Socialism the product of the manager's labors would go to the community rather than to the shareholders. In such a way, in contrast to all socialists who have written on the subject hitherto, especially the Marxians, they think it would be possible to construct a decentralized, as opposed to a centralized, Socialism.

In order to judge properly such proposals, it is necessary in the first place to realize that these controllers of individual industrial units would have to be appointed. Under Capitalism the managers of the joint stock companies are appointed either directly or indirectly by the shareholders. In so far as the shareholders give to the managers power to produce by the means of the company's (i.e. the stockholders') stock they are risking their own property or a part of their own property. The speculation (for it is necessarily a speculation) may succeed and bring profit; it may, however, misfire and bring about the loss of the whole or a part of the capital concerned. This committing of one's own capital to a business whose outcome is uncertain and to men whose future ability is still a matter of conjecture whatever one may know of their past, is the essence of joint stock company enterprise.

Now it is a complete fallacy to suppose that the problem of economic calculation in a socialist community relates solely to matters which fall into the sphere of the daily business routine of managers of joint stock companies. It is clear that such a belief can only arise from exclusive concentration on the idea of a stationary economic system—a conception which no doubt is useful for the solution of many theoretical problems but which has no counterpart in fact and which, if exclusively regarded, can even be positively misleading. It is clear that under stationary conditions the problem of economic calculation does not really arise. When we think of the stationary society, we think of an economy in which all the factors of production are already used in such a way as, under the given conditions, to provide the maximum of the things which are demanded by consumers. That is to say, under stationary conditions there no longer exists a problem for economic calculation to solve. The essential function of economic calculation has *by hypothesis* already been performed. There is no need for an apparatus of calculation. To use a popular but not altogether satisfactory terminology we can say that the problem of economic calculation is of economic dynamics: it is no problem of economic statics.

The problem of economic calculation is a problem which arises in an economy which is perpetually subject to change, an economy which every day is confronted with new problems which have to be solved. Now in order to solve such problems it is above all necessary that capital should be withdrawn from particular lines of production, from particular undertakings and concerns and should be applied in other lines of production, in other undertakings and concerns. This is not a matter for the managers of joint stock companies, it is essentially a matter for the capitalists—the capitalists who buy and sell stocks and shares, who make loans and recover them, who make deposits in the banks and draw them out of the banks again, who speculate in all kinds of commodities. It is these operations of speculative capitalists which create those conditions of the money market, the stock exchanges and the wholesale markets which have to be taken for granted by the manager of the joint stock company, who, according to the socialist writers we are considering, is to be conceived as nothing but the reliable and conscientious servant of the company. It is the speculative capitalists who create the data to which he has to adjust his business and which therefore gives direction to his trading operations.

It follows therefore that it is a fundamental deficiency of all these socialistic constructions which invoke the "artificial market" and artificial competition as a way out of the problem of economic calculation, that they rest on the belief that the market for factors of production is affected only by producers buying and selling commodities. It is not possible to eliminate from such markets the influence of the supply of capital from the capitalists and the demand for capital by the entrepreneurs, without destroying the mechanism itself.

Faced with this difficulty, the socialist is likely to propose that the socialist state as owner of all capital and all means of production should simply direct capital to those undertakings which promise the highest return. The available capital, he will contend, should go to those undertakings which offer the highest rate of profit. But such a state of affairs would simply mean that those managers who were less cautious and more optimistic would receive capital to enlarge their undertakings while more cautious and more sceptical managers would go away empty-handed. Under Capitalism, the capitalist decides to whom he will entrust *his own* capital. The beliefs of the managers of joint stock companies regarding the future prospects of their undertakings and the hopes of project-makers regarding the profitability of their plans are not in any way decisive. The mechanism of the money market and the capital market decides. This indeed is its main task: to serve the economic system as a whole, to judge the profitability of alternative openings and not blindly to follow what the managers of particular concerns, limited by the narrow horizon of their own undertakings, are tempted to propose.

To understand this completely, it is essential to realize that the capitalist does not just invest his capital in those undertakings which offer high interest or high profit; he attempts rather to strike a balance between his desire for profit and his estimate of the risk of loss. He must exercise foresight. If he does not do so then he suffers losses—losses that bring it about that his disposition over the factors of production is transferred to the hands of others who know better how to weigh the risks and the prospects of business speculation.

Now if it is to remain socialistic, the socialist State cannot leave to other hands that disposition over capital which permits the enlargement of existing undertakings, the contraction of others and the bringing into being of undertakings that are completely new. And it is scarcely to be assumed that socialists of whatever persuasion would seriously propose that this function should be made over to some group of people who would "simply" have the business of doing what capitalists and speculators do under capitalistic conditions, the only difference being that the product of their foresight should not belong to them but to the community. Proposals of this sort may well be made concerning the managers of joint stock companies. They can never be extended to capitalists and speculators, for no socialist would dispute that the function which capitalists and speculators perform under Capitalism, namely directing the use of capital goods into that direction in which they best serve the demands of the consumer, is only performed because they are under the incentive to preserve their property and to make profits which increase it or at least allow them to live without diminishing their capital.

It follows therefore that the socialist community can do nothing but place the disposition over capital in the hands of the State or to be exact in the hands of the men who, as the governing authority, carry out the business of the State. And that signifies elimination of the market, which indeed is the fundamental aim of Socialism, for the guidance of economic activity by the market implies organization of production and a distribution of the product according to that disposition of the spending power of individual members of society which makes itself felt on the market; that is to say, it implies precisely that which it is the goal of Socialism to eliminate.

If the socialists attempt to belittle the significance of the problem of economic calculation in the Socialist community, on the ground that the forces of the market do not lead to ethically justifiable arrangements, they simply show that they do not understand the real nature of the problem. It is not a question of whether there shall be produced cannons or clothes, dwelling houses or churches, luxuries or subsistence. In any social order, even under Socialism, it can very easily be decided which kind and what number of consumption goods should be produced. No one has ever denied that. But once this decision has been made, there still remains the problem of ascertaining how the existing means of production can be used most effectively to produce these goods in question. In order to solve this problem it is necessary that there should be economic calculation. And economic calculation can only take place by means of money prices established in the market for production goods in a society resting on private property in the means of production. That is to say, there must exist money prices of land, raw materials, semi-manufactures; that is to say, there must be money wages and interest rates.

Thus the alternative is still *either* Socialism or a market economy.

5. ON THE ECONOMIC THEORY OF SOCIALISM*

Oskar Lange

In Lange's model of market socialism, households, the Central Planning Board (CPB), and socialist managers share in the decisions which guide the economy. Consumer preferences, expressed in a market for consumer goods, decide the goods to be produced. Prices of consumer goods and labor services are determined by the interplay in the market of the supply and demand of households and socialist firms. The CPB, by trial and error, sets the prices of producer goods so as to equate the supply and demand for each good. Given these "parametric" prices, the managers of socialist enterprises and industries determine their inputs and outputs according to two broad rules. First, they must combine factors of production so as to minimize the average cost of production for any output. Second, they must fix output at the level where marginal cost equals the price. In combination, these two rules secure the most economical production of the optimum output.

The CPB distributes a social dividend to households which reduces the inequality of income resulting from market-determined wages. It also decides the rate of investment and then sets an interest rate on capital which equates the demand for capital, on the part of socialist managers, to the amount available.

In order to discuss the method of allocating resources in a socialist economy we have to state what kind of socialist society we have in mind. The fact of public ownership of the means of production does not in itself

* From *On the Economic Theory of Socialism*, by Oskar Lange and Fred M. Taylor, ed. Benjamin E. Lippincott (Minneapolis: University of Minnesota Press,

determine the system of distributing consumers' goods and of allocating people to various occupations, nor the principles guiding the production of commodities. Let us now assume that freedom of choice in consumption and freedom of choice of occupation are maintained and that the preferences of consumers, as expressed by their demand prices, are the guiding criteria in production and in the allocation of resources. . . .

In the socialist system as described we have a genuine market (in the institutional sense of the word) for consumers' goods and for the services of labor. But there is no market for capital goods and productive resources outside of labor.[1] The prices of capital goods and productive resources outside of labor are thus prices in the generalized sense, i.e., mere indices of alternatives available, fixed for accounting purposes. Let us see how economic equilibrium is determined in such a system. Just as in a competitive individualist regime, the determination of equilibrium consists of two parts. (*A*) On the basis of *given* indices of alternatives (which are market prices in the case of consumers' goods and the services of labor and accounting prices in all other cases) both the individuals participating in the economic system as consumers and as owners of the services of labor and the managers of production and of the ultimate resources outside of labor (i.e., of capital and of natural resources) make decisions according to certain principles. These managers are assumed to be public officials. (*B*) The prices (whether market or accounting) are determined by the condition that the quantity of each commodity demanded is equal to the quantity supplied. The conditions determining the decisions under *A* form the *subjective*, while that under *B* is the *objective*, equilibrium condition. Finally, we have also a condition *C*, expressing the social organization of the economic system. As the productive resources outside of labor are public property, the incomes of the consumers are divorced from the ownership of those resources and the form of condition *C* (social organization) is determined by the *principles of income formation adopted.*

The possibility of determining condition *C* in different ways gives to a socialist society considerable freedom in matters of distribution of income. But the necessity of maintaining freedom in the choice of occupation limits the arbitrary use of this freedom, for there must be some connection between the income of a consumer and the services of labor performed by him. It seems, therefore, convenient to regard the income of consumers as composed of two parts: one part being the receipts for the labor services

---

1938), pp. 72–86. Originally published in *Review of Economic Studies*, Vol. IV, No. 1 (October, 1936), pp. 60–66. Reprinted with the permission of the *Review of Economic Studies* and the University of Minnesota Press. Oskar Lange was Professor of Economics at the University of Chicago and Professor of Political Economy at Warsaw University.

[1] To simplify the problem we assume that all means of production are public property. Needless to say, in any actual socialist community there must be a large number of means of production privately owned (e.g., by farmers, artisans, and small-scale entrepreneurs). But this does not introduce any new theoretical problem.

performed and the other part being a social dividend constituting the individual's share in the income derived from the capital and the natural resources owned by society. We assume that the distribution of the social dividend is based on certain principles, reserving the content of those principles for later discussion. Thus condition *C* is determinate and determines the incomes of the consumers in terms of prices of the services of labor and social dividend, which, in turn, may be regarded as determined by the total yield of capital and of the natural resources and by the principles adopted in distributing this yield.[2]

A. Let us consider the subjective equilibrium condition in a socialist economy:

1. Freedom of choice in consumption being assumed,[3] this part of the subjective equilibrium condition of a competitive market applies also to the market for consumers' goods in a socialist economy. The incomes of the consumers and the prices of consumers' goods being given, the demand for consumers' goods is determined.

2. The decisions of the managers of production are no longer guided by the aim of maximizing profit. Instead, certain rules are imposed on them by the Central Planning Board which aim at satisfying consumers' preferences in the best way possible. These rules determine the combination of factors of production and the scale of output.

One rule must impose the choice of the combination of factors which minimizes the average cost of production. This rule leads to the factors being combined in such proportion that the marginal productivity of that amount of each factor which is worth a unit of money is the same for all factors. This rule is addressed to whoever makes decisions involving the problem of the optimum combination of factors, i.e., to managers responsible for running existing plants and to those engaged in building new plants. A second rule determines the scale of output by stating that output has to be fixed so that marginal cost is equal to the price of the product. This rule is addressed to two kinds of persons. First of all, it is addressed to the managers of plants and thus determines the scale of output of each plant and, together with the first rule, its demand for factors of production. The first rule, to whomever addressed, and the second rule when addressed to the managers of plants perform the same function that in a

[2] In formulating condition *C* capital accumulation has to be taken into account. Capital accumulation may be done either "corporately" by deducting a certain part of the national income before the social dividend is distributed, or it may be left to the savings of individuals, or both methods may be combined. But "corporate" accumulation must certainly be the dominant form of capital formation in a socialist economy.

[3] Of course there may be also a sector of socialized consumption the cost of which is met by taxation. Such a sector exists also in capitalist society and comprises the provision not only of collective wants, in Cassel's sense, but also of other wants whose social importance is too great to be left to the free choice of individuals (for instance, free hospital service and free education). But this problem does not represent any theoretical difficulty and we may disregard it.

competitive system is carried out by the private producer's aiming to maximize his profit, when the prices of factors and of the product are independent of the amount of each factor used by him and of his scale of output.

The total output of an industry has yet to be determined. This is done by addressing the second rule also to the managers of a whole industry (e.g., to the directors of the National Coal Trust) as a principle to guide them in deciding whether an industry ought to be expanded (by building new plants or enlarging old ones) or contracted (by not replacing plants which are wearing out). Thus each industry has to produce exactly as much of a commodity as can be sold or "accounted for" to other industries at a price which equals the marginal cost incurred *by the industry* in producing this amount. The marginal cost incurred by an industry is the cost to that industry (not to a particular plant) of doing whatever is necessary to produce an additional unit of output, the optimum combination of factors being used. This may include the cost of building new plants or enlarging old ones.[4]

Addressed to the managers of an industry, the second rule performs the function which under free competition is carried out by the free entry of firms into an industry or their exodus from it: i.e., it determines the output of an industry.[5] The second rule, however, has to be carried out irrespective of whether average cost is covered or not, even if it should involve plants or whole industries in losses.

Both rules can be put in the form of the simple request to use always the method of production (i.e., combination of factors) which minimizes average cost and to produce as much of each service or commodity as will equalize marginal cost and the price of the product, this request being

[4] Since in practice such marginal cost is not a continuous function of output we have to compare the cost of each additional *indivisible input* with the receipts expected from the additional output thus secured. For instance, in a railway system as long as there are unused carriages the cost of putting them into use has to be compared with the additional receipts which may be obtained by doing so. When all the carriages available are used up to capacity, the cost of building and running additional carriages (and locomotives) has to be compared with the additional receipts expected to arise from such action. Finally, the question of building new tracks is decided upon the same principle. Cf. A. P. Lerner, "Statics and Dynamics in Socialist Economics," *Economic Journal*, Vol. XLVII, No. 186 (June, 1937), pp. 263–67.

[5] The result, however, of following this rule coincides with the result obtained under free competition only in the case of constant returns to the industry (i.e., a homogeneous production function of the first degree). In this case marginal cost incurred by the industry equals average cost. In all other cases the results diverge, for under free competition the output of an industry is such that average cost equals the price of the product, while according to our rule it is marginal cost (incurred by the industry) that ought to be equal to the price. This difference results in profits being made by the industries whose marginal cost exceeds average cost, whereas the industries in which the opposite is the case incur losses. These profits and losses correspond to the taxes and bounties proposed by Professor Pigou in order to bring about under free competition the equality of private and social marginal net product. See A. C. Pigou, *The Economics of Welfare* (3rd ed.; London: Macmillan, 1929), pp. 223–27.

addressed to whoever is responsible for the particular decision to be taken. Thus the output of each plant and industry and the total demand for factors of production by each industry are determined. To enable the managers of production to follow these rules the prices of the factors and of the products must, of course, be given. In the case of consumers' goods and services of labor they are determined on a market; in all other cases they are fixed by the Central Planning Board. Those prices being given, the supply of products and the demand for factors are determined.

The reasons for adopting the two rules mentioned are obvious. Since prices are indices of terms on which alternatives are offered, that method of production which will minimize average cost will also minimize the alternatives sacrificed. Thus the first rule means simply that each commodity must be produced with a minimum sacrifice of alternatives. The second rule is a necessary consequence of following consumers' preferences. It means that the marginal significance of each preference which is satisfied has to be equal to the marginal significance of the alternative preferences the satisfaction of which is sacrificed. If the second rule was not observed certain lower preferences would be satisfied while preferences higher up on the scale would be left unsatisfied.

3. Freedom of choice of occupation being assumed, laborers offer their services to the industry or occupation paying the highest wages. For the publicly owned capital and natural resources a price has to be fixed by the Central Planning Board with the provision that these resources can be directed only to industries which are able to "pay," or rather to "account for," this price. This is a consequence of following the consumers' preferences. The prices of the services of the ultimate productive resources being given, their distribution between the different industries is also determined.

B. The subjective equilibrium condition can be carried out only when prices are *given*. This is also true of the decisions of the managers of production and of the productive resources in public ownership. Only when prices are given can the combination of factors which minimizes average cost, the output which equalizes marginal cost and the price of the product, and the best allocation of the ultimate productive resources be determined. But if there is no market (in the institutional sense of the word) for capital goods or for the ultimate productive resources outside of labor, can their prices be determined objectively? Must not the prices fixed by the Central Planning Board necessarily be quite arbitrary? If so, their arbitrary character would deprive them of any economic significance as indices of the terms on which alternatives are offered. This is, indeed, the opinion of Professor Mises.[6] And the view is shared by Mr. Cole, who says: "A planless economy, in which each entrepreneur takes

[6] "Economic Calculation in the Socialist Commonwealth," reprinted in F. A. Hayek (ed.), *Collectivist Economic Planning* (London: Routledge and Kegan Paul, 1935), p. 112.

his decisions apart from the rest, obviously confronts each entrepreneur with a broadly given structure of costs, represented by the current level of wages, rent, and interest. . . . In a planned socialist economy there can be no objective structure of costs. Costs can be imputed to any desired extent. . . . But these imputed costs are not objective, but *fiat* costs determined by the public policy of the State."[7] This view, however, is easily refuted by recalling the very elements of price theory.

Why is there an objective price structure in a competitive market? Because, as a result of the parametric function of prices, there is generally only *one* set of prices which satisfies the objective equilibrium condition, i.e., equalizes demand and supply of each commodity. The same objective price structure can be obtained in a socialist economy if the *parametric function of prices* is retained. On a competitive market the parametric function of prices results from the number of competing individuals being too large to enable any one to influence prices by his own action. In a socialist economy, production and ownership of the productive resources outside of labor being centralized, the managers certainly can and do influence prices by their decisions. Therefore, the parametric function of prices must be imposed on them by the Central Planning Board as an *accounting rule*. All accounting has to be done *as if* prices were independent of the decisions taken. For purposes of accounting, prices must be treated as constant, as they are treated by entrepreneurs on a competitive market.

The technique of attaining this end is very simple: the Central Planning Board has to fix prices and see to it that all managers of plants, industries, and resources do their accounting on the basis of the prices fixed by the Central Planning Board, and not tolerate any use of other accounting. Once the parametric function of prices is adopted as an accounting rule, the price structure is established by the objective equilibrium condition. For each set of prices and consumers' incomes a definite amount of each commodity is supplied and demanded. Condition *C* determines the incomes of the consumers by the prices of the services of ultimate productive resources and the principles adopted for the distribution of the social dividend. With those principles given, prices alone are the variables determining the demand and supply of commodities.

The condition that the quantity demanded and supplied has to be equal for each commodity serves to select the equilibrium prices which alone assure the compatibility of all decisions taken. *Any price different from the equilibrium price would show at the end of the accounting period a surplus or a shortage of the commodity in question.* Thus the accounting prices in a socialist economy, far from being arbitrary, have quite the same objective character as the market prices in a regime of competition. Any mistake made by the Central Planning Board in fixing prices would an-

---

[7] G. D. H. Cole, *Economic Planning* (New York: Knopf, 1935), pp. 183–84.

nounce itself in a very objective way—by a physical shortage or surplus of the quantity of the commodity or resources in question—and would have to be corrected in order to keep production running smoothly. As there is generally only one set of prices which satisfies the objective equilibrium condition, both the prices of products and costs[8] are uniquely determined.[9]

Our study of the determination of equilibrium prices in a socialist economy has shown that the process of price determination is quite analogous to that in a competitive market. The Central Planning Board performs the functions of the market. It establishes the rules for combining factors of production and choosing the scale of output of a plant, for determining the output of an industry, for the allocation of resources, and for the parametric use of prices in accounting. Finally, it fixes the prices so as to balance the quantity supplied and demanded of each commodity. It follows that a substitution of planning for the functions of the market is quite possible and workable.

Two problems deserve some special attention. The first relates to the determination of the best distribution of the social dividend. Freedom of choice of occupation assumed, the distribution of the social dividend may affect the amount of services of labor offered to different industries. If certain occupations received a larger social dividend than others, labor would be diverted into the occupations receiving a larger dividend. Therefore, the distribution of the social dividend must be such as not to interfere with the optimum distribution of labor services between the different industries and occupations. The optimum distribution is that which makes the differences of the value of the marginal product of the services of labor in different industries and occupations equal to the differences in the marginal disutility[10] of working in those industries or

[8] Hayek maintains that it would be impossible to determine the value of durable instruments of production because, in consequence of changes, "the value of most of the more durable instruments of production has little or no connection with the costs which have been incurred in their production" (*Collectivist Economic Planning*, p. 227). It is quite true that the value of such durable instruments is essentially a capitalized quasi-rent and therefore can be determined only after the price which will be obtained for the product is known (cf. *ibid.*, p. 228). But there is no reason why the price of the product should be any less determinate in a socialist economy than on a competitive market. The managers of the industrial plant in question have simply to take the price fixed by the Central Planning Board as the basis of their calculation. The Central Planning Board would fix this price so as to satisfy the objective equilibrium condition, just as a competitive market does.

[9] However, in certain cases there may be a multiple solution.

[10] It is only the *relative* disutility of different occupations that counts. The absolute disutility may be zero or even negative. By putting leisure, safety, agreeableness of work, etc., into the preference scales, all labor costs may be expressed as opportunity costs. If such a device is adopted each industry or occupation may be regarded as producing a joint product: the commodity or service in question *and* leisure, safety, agreeableness of work, etc. The services of labor have to be allocated so that the value of this marginal *joint* product is the same in all industries and occupations.

occupations.[11] This distribution of the services of labor arises automatically whenever wages are the only source of income. *Therefore, the social dividend must be distributed so as to have no influence whatever on the choice of occupation.* The social dividend paid to an individual must be entirely independent of his choice of occupation. For instance, it can be divided equally per head of population, or distributed according to age or size of family or any other principle which does not affect the choice of occupation.

The other problem is the determination of the rate of interest. We have to distinguish between a short-period and a long-period solution of the problem. For the former the amount of capital is regarded as constant, and the rate of interest is simply determined by the condition that the demand for capital is equal to the amount available. When the rate of interest is set too low the socialized banking system would be unable to meet the demand of industries for capital; when the interest rate is set too high there would be a surplus of capital available for investment. However, in the long period the amount of capital can be increased by accumulation. If the accumulation of capital is performed "corporately" before distributing the social dividend to the individuals, the rate of accumulation can be determined by the Central Planning Board *arbitrarily*. The Central Planning Board will probably aim at accumulating enough to make the marginal *net* productivity of capital zero,[12] this aim being never attained because of technical progress (new labor-saving devices), increase of population, the discovery of new natural resources, and, possibly, because of the shift of demand toward commodities produced by more capital-intensive methods.[13] But the rate, i.e., the *speed,* at which accumulation progresses is arbitrary.

The arbitrariness of the rate of capital accumulation "corporately" performed means simply that the decision regarding the rate of accumulation reflects how the Central Planning Board, and not the consumers, evaluate the optimum time-shape of the income stream. One may argue, of course, that this involves a diminution of consumers' welfare. This difficulty could be overcome only by leaving all accumulation to the saving of

---

[11] If the total amount of labor performed is not limited by legislation or custom regulating the hours of work, etc., the value of the marginal product of the services of labor in each occupation has to be *equal* to the marginal disutility. If any limitational factors are used, it is the marginal *net* product of the services of labor (obtained by deducting from the marginal product the marginal expenditure for the limitational factors) which has to satisfy the condition in the text.

[12] Cf. Knut Wicksell, "Professor Cassel's System of Economics," reprinted in his *Lectures on Political Economy* (L. Robbins, ed.; 2 vols.; London: Routledge and Kegan Paul, 1934), Vol. I, p. 241.

[13] These changes, however, if very frequent, may act also in the opposite direction and diminish the marginal *net* productivity of capital because of the risk of obsolescence due to them. This is pointed out by A. P. Lerner in "A Note on Socialist Economics," *Review of Economic Studies,* Vol. IV, No. 1 (October, 1936), p. 72.

individuals.[14] But this is scarcely compatible with the organization of a socialist society.[15] . . .

Having treated the theoretical determination of economic equilibrium in a socialist society, let us see how equilibrium can be determined by a method of *trial and error* similar to that in a competitive market. This method of trial and error is based on the *parametric function of prices.* Let the Central Planning Board start with a given set of prices chosen *at random.* All decisions of the managers of production and of the productive resources in public ownership and also all decisions of individuals as consumers and as suppliers of labor are made on the basis of these prices. As a result of these decisions the quantity demanded and supplied of each commodity is determined. If the quantity demanded of a commodity is not equal to the quantity supplied, the price of that commodity has to be changed. It has to be raised if demand exceeds supply and lowered if the reverse is the case. Thus the Central Planning Board fixes a new set of prices which serves as a basis for new decisions, and which results in a new set of quantities demanded and supplied. Through this process of trial and error equilibrium prices are finally determined. Actually the process of trial and error would, of course, proceed on the basis of the prices *historically given.* Relatively small adjustments of those prices would constantly be made, and there would be no necessity of building up an entirely new price system.

[14] This method has been advocated by Barone in "The Ministry of Production in the Collectivist State," *Collectivist Economic Planning*, pp. 278–79.

[15] Of course, the consumers remain free to save as much as they want out of the income which is actually paid out to them, and the socialized banks could pay interest on savings. As a matter of fact, in order to prevent hoarding they would have to do so. But *this* rate of interest would not have any necessary connection with the marginal *net* productivity of capital. It would be quite arbitrary.

6. SOCIALIST CALCULATION: THE COMPETITIVE "SOLUTION"*

Friedrich A. Hayek

In this article, Hayek criticizes weaknesses and omissions in the market socialist blueprints of Oskar Lange and H. D. Dickinson. For several reasons, Hayek doubts that the "parametric" prices set by the Central Planning Board can in fact be market-clearing prices which equalize supply and demand. He questions whether managers will be able to apply the rules for input and output decisions set forth by Lange. And he points out problems of managerial responsibility, initiative, and incentives not resolved in the market socialist blueprints. Hayek concludes that much more detailed central planning and control would be involved in market socialism than its advocates acknowledge. As a result, the difference between market socialism and authoritarian socialism, and the superiority of the former over the latter, is much less than market socialists claim.

I

Two CHAPTERS in the discussion of the economics of socialism may now be regarded as closed. The first deals with the belief that socialism will dispense entirely with calculation in terms of value and will replace it with some sort of calculation *in natura* based on units of energy or of some other physical magnitude. Although this view is not yet extinct and is still held by some scientists and engineers, it has been definitely abandoned by

* Reprinted, with permission, from *Economica*, New Series, Vol. VII, No. 26 (May, 1940), pp. 125–49.

economists. The second closed chapter deals with the proposal that values, instead of being left to be determined by competition, should be found by a process of calculations carried out by the planning authority which would use the technique of mathematical economics. With regard to this suggestion, V. Pareto (who, curiously enough, is sometimes quoted as holding this view) has already said what probably will remain the final word. After showing how a system of simultaneous equations can be used to explain what determines prices on a market he adds:

> It may be mentioned here that this determination has by no means the purpose to arrive at a numerical calculation of prices. Let us make the most favorable assumption for such a calculation, let us assume that we have triumphed over all the difficulties of finding the data of the problem and that we know the *ophélimités* of all the different commodities for each individual, and all the conditions of production of all the commodities, etc. This is already an absurd hypothesis to make. Yet it is not sufficient to make the solution of the problem possible. We have seen that in the case of 100 persons and 700 commodities there will be 70,699 conditions (actually a great number of circumstances which we have so far neglected will still increase that number); we shall therefore have to solve a system of 70,699 equations. This exceeds practically the power of algebraic analysis, and this is even more true if one contemplates the fabulous number of equations which one obtains for a population of forty millions and several thousand commodities. In this case the rôles would be changed: it would not be mathematics which would assist political economy, but political economy would assist mathematics. In other words, if one really could know all these equations, the only means to solve them which is available to human powers is to observe the practical solution given by the market.[1]

In the present article we shall be mainly concerned with a third stage in this discussion, for which the issue has now been clearly defined by the elaboration of proposals for a competitive socialism by Professor Lange and Dr. Dickinson.[2] Since, however, the significance of the result of the past discussions is not infrequently represented in a way which comes very near to an inversion of the truth, and as at least one of the two books to be discussed is not quite free from this tendency, a few further remarks on the real significance of the past development seem not unnecessary.

The first point is connected with the nature of the original criticism directed against the more primitive conceptions of the working of a socialist economy which were current up to about 1920. The idea then current (and still advocated, e.g. by Dr. O. Neurath) is well expressed by F. Engels in his *Anti-Dühring*, when he says that the social plan of production "will be settled very simply, without the intervention of the

---

[1] V. Pareto, *Manuel d'économie politique* (2nd ed., 1927), pp. 233–34.

[2] The two recent books with which this article is mainly concerned are Oskar Lange and Fred M. Taylor, *On the Economic Theory of Socialism*, edited by B. E. Lippincott (Minneapolis: University of Minnesota Press, 1938), and H. D. Dickinson, *Economics of Socialism* (Oxford: Oxford University Press, 1939).

famous 'value'." It was against this generally held belief that N. G. Pierson, L. v. Mises, and others pointed out that if the socialist community wanted to act rationally its calculation would have to be guided by the same *formal* laws which applied to a capitalist society. It seems necessary especially to underline the fact that this was a point made by the critics of the socialist plans, since Professor Lange and particularly his editor[3] now seem inclined to suggest that the demonstration that the formal principles of economic theory apply to a socialist economy provides an answer to these critics. The fact is that it has never been denied by anybody, except socialists, that these formal principles *ought* to apply to a socialist society, and the question raised by Professor Mises and others was not whether they ought to apply but whether they could in practice be applied in the absence of a market. It is therefore entirely beside the point when Professor Lange and others quote Pareto and Barone as having shown that values in a socialist society would depend on essentially the same factors as in a competitive society. This of course had been shown long before, particularly by Wieser. But none of these authors has made an attempt to show how these values, which a socialist society ought to use if it wanted to act rationally, could be found, and Pareto, as we have seen, expressly denied that they could be determined by calculation.

It seems then that, on this point, the criticisms of the earlier socialist schemes have been so successful that the defenders, with few exceptions,[4] have felt compelled to appropriate the argument of their critics, and have been forced to construct entirely new schemes of which nobody thought before. While against the older ideas that it was possible to plan rationally without calculation in terms of value it could be justly argued that they were logically impossible, the newer proposals designed to determine values by some process other than competition based on private property raise a problem of a different sort. But it is surely unfair to say, as Professor Lange does, that the critics, because they deal in a new way with the new schemes evolved to meet the original criticism, "have given up the essential point" and "retreated to a second line of defence." Is this not rather a case of covering up their own retreat by creating confusion about the issue?

There is a second point on which Professor Lange's presentation of the present state of the debate is seriously misleading. The reader of his study can hardly avoid the impression that the idea that values should and could be determined by using the technique of mathematical economics, i.e. by solving millions of equations, is a malicious invention of the critics, intended to throw ridicule on the efforts of modern socialist writers. The fact, which cannot be unknown to Professor Lange, is of course that this

[3] See B. E. Lippincott, *op. cit.*, p. 7.

[4] The most notable exception is Dr. M. Dobb. See his *Political Economy and Capitalism* (London: G. Routledge & Sons, Ltd., 1937), chap. viii.

procedure has more than once been seriously suggested by socialist writers as a solution of the difficulty—among others by Dr. Dickinson, who now, however, expressly withdraws this earlier suggestion.[5]

II

A third stage in the debate has now been reached with the proposal to solve the problems of determining values by the re-introduction of competition. When five years ago the present author tried to appraise the significance of these attempts[6] it was necessary to rely on what could be gathered from oral discussion among socialist economists, since no systematic exposition of the theoretical bases of competitive socialism was then available. This gap has now been filled by the two books here to be discussed. The first contains a reprint of an essay by Professor Lange, originally published in 1936 and 1937, together with an older article by the late Professor Taylor (dating from 1928) and an introduction by the editor, Professor B. E. Lippincott, which in addition to a quite unnecessary restatement of Professor Lange's argument in cruder terms, does much by the unmeasured praise he bestows on this argument and the extravagant claims he advances for it,[7] to prejudice the reader against the essentially scholarly piece of work that follows. Although written in a lively style and confining itself to the outlines of the subject, it does seriously grapple with some of the main difficulties in the field.

Dr. H. D. Dickinson's more recent book is a far more comprehensive survey of the field, proposing essentially the same solution.[8] It is unquestionably a book of great distinction, well organized, lucid and concise, and should rapidly establish itself as the standard work on its subject. To the economist, the reading of the book provides indeed the rare pleasure of feeling that recent advances of economic theory have not been in vain and have even helped to reduce political differences to points which can be rationally discussed. Dr. Dickinson himself would probably agree that he shares all his economics with—and indeed has learnt most of it from—non-socialist economists, and that in his essential conclusions on the desirable economic policy of a socialist community he differs much more from most of his socialist colleagues than from "orthodox" economists. This, together with the open-mindedness with which the author takes up and considers the arguments advanced by his opponents, makes discussion of his views a real pleasure. If the socialists, like the economists, are ready to accept his

[5] *Op. cit.*, p. 104.

[6] In *Collectivist Economic Planning* (London: Routledge and Kegan Paul, 1935), essay on "The Present State of the Debate."

[7] Dr. Lange's essay is described as the "first writing to mark an advance on Barone's contribution" and to show by "irrefutable" argument the "evident feasibility and superiority" of a socialist system (pp. 13, 24, 37).

[8] It is a curious fact that Dr. Dickinson nowhere in his book (except in the bibliography) refers to Professor Lange's work.

book, as the most up-to-date general treatment of the economics of socialism from the socialist point of view, it should provide the basis for much fruitful further discussion.

As has already been mentioned, the main outlines of the solution offered by the two authors are essentially the same. They both rely to some extent on the competitive mechanism for the determination of relative prices. But they both refuse to let prices be determined directly in the market and propose instead a system of price-fixing by a central authority, where the state of the market of a particular commodity, i.e. the relation of demand to supply, merely serves as an indication to the authority whether the prescribed prices ought to be raised or lowered. Neither of the two authors explains why he refuses to go the whole hog and to restore the price mechanism in full. But as I happen to agree (although probably for different reasons) that this would be impracticable in a socialist community, we can leave this question aside for the moment and shall take it for granted that in such a society competition cannot play quite the same rôle as it does in a society based on private property, and that, in particular, the rates at which commodities will be exchanged by the parties in the market will have to be decreed by the authority.

We shall leave the details of the proposed organization for later consideration and first consider the general significance of this solution under three aspects. We shall ask firstly how far this kind of socialist system still conforms to the hopes that were placed on the substitution of a planned socialist system for the chaos of competition; secondly, how far the proposed procedure is an answer to the main difficulty, and, finally, how far it is applicable.

The first and most general point can be dealt with fairly briefly, although it is not unimportant if one wants to see these new proposals in their proper light. It is merely a reminder of how much of the original claim for the superiority of planning over competition is abandoned if the planned society is now to rely for the direction of its industries to a large extent on competition. Until quite recently, at least, planning and competition used to be regarded as opposites, and this is unquestionably still true of nearly all planners except a few economists among them. I fear that the schemes of Professor Lange and Dr. Dickinson will bitterly disappoint all those scientific planners who, in the recent words of Professor B. M. S. Blackett, believe that "the object of planning is largely to overcome the results of competition."[9] This would be even more true if it were really possible to reduce the arbitrary elements in a competitive socialist system as much as is believed by Dr. Dickinson, who hopes that his "libertarian socialism" "may establish, for the first time in human history, an effective individualism." Unfortunately, as we shall see, this is not likely to be the case.

---

[9] See Sir Daniel Hall and others, *The Frustration of Science* (London: Allen & Unwin, 1935), p. 142.

III

The second general question we must consider is how far the proposed method of centralized price fixing, while leaving it to individual firms and consumers to adjust demand and supply to the given prices, is likely to solve the problem which admittedly cannot be solved by mathematical calculation. Here, I am afraid, I find it exceedingly difficult to understand the grounds on which such a claim is made. Professor Lange as well as Dr. Dickinson asserts that even if the initial system of prices were chosen entirely at random, it would be possible by such a process of trial and error gradually to approach to the appropriate system. This seems to be much the same thing as if it were suggested that a system of equations which was too complex to be solved by calculation within reasonable time and whose values were constantly changing could be effectively tackled by arbitrarily inserting tentative values and then trying about till the proper solution was found. Or, to change the metaphor, the difference between such a system of regimented prices and a system of prices determined by the market seems to be about the same as that between an attacking army where every unit and every man could only move by special command and by the exact distance ordered by headquarters and an army where every unit and every man can take advantage of every opportunity offered to them. There is of course no *logical impossibility* of conceiving a directing organ of the collective economy which is not only "omnipresent and omniscient" as Dr. Dickinson conceives it, but also omnipotent and which therefore would be in a position to change without delay every price by just the amount that is required. When, however, one proceeds to consider the actual apparatus by which this sort of adjustment is to be brought about one begins to wonder whether anyone should really be prepared to suggest that, within the domain of practical possibility, such a system will ever even distantly approach the efficiency of a system where the required changes are brought about by the spontaneous action of the persons immediately concerned.

We shall later, when we consider the proposed institutional setting, come back to the question how this sort of mechanism is likely to function in practice. In so far as the general question is concerned, however, it is difficult to suppress the suspicion that this particular proposal has been born out of an excessive pre-occupation with problems of the pure theory of stationary equilibrium. If in the real world we had to deal with approximately constant data, that is, if the problem were, to find a price system which then could be left more or less unchanged for long periods, then the proposal under consideration would not be so entirely unreasonable. With given and constant data such a state of equilibrium could indeed be approached by the method of trial and error. But this is far from being the situation in the real world, where constant change is the rule. Whether and how far anything approaching the desirable equilibrium is ever reached depends entirely on the speed with which the adjustments can be made. The practical problem is not whether a particular method would eventually lead to a hypothetical equilibrium, but which method will secure the more rapid and complete adjustment to the daily changing conditions in different places and different industries. How great the difference in this respect would be between a method where prices are currently agreed upon by the parties of the market and a method where these prices are decreed from above is of course a matter of practical judgment. But I find it difficult to believe that anybody should doubt that in this respect the inferiority of the second method would be very great indeed.

The third general point is also one where I believe that preoccupation with concepts of pure economic theory has seriously misled both our authors. In this case it is the concept of perfect competition which apparently has made them overlook a very important field to which their method appears to be simply inapplicable. Wherever we have a market for a fairly standardized commodity it is at least conceivable that all prices should be decreed in advance from above for a certain period. The situation is however very different with respect to commodities which cannot be standardized, and particularly for those which to-day are produced on individual orders, perhaps after invitation for tenders. A large part of the product of the "heavy industries," which of course would be the first to be socialized, belongs to this category. Much machinery, most buildings and ships and many parts of other products are hardly ever produced for a market, but only on special contract. This does not mean that there may not be intense competition in the market for the products of these industries, although it may not be "perfect competition" in the sense of pure theory; the fact is simply that identical products are rarely produced twice in short intervals; and the circle of producers who will compete for the services of a particular plant will differ from week to week. What basis is there in all these cases for fixing prices of the product so as "to equalize demand and supply"? If prices are here to be fixed by the central authority, they will have to be fixed in every individual case and on the basis of an examination by that authority of the calculations of all potential suppliers and all potential purchasers. It is hardly necessary to point out the various complications that will arise according as the prices are fixed before or after the prospective buyer has decided on the particular piece of machinery or building which he wants. Presumably it will be the estimates of the producer which, before they are submitted to the prospective customer, will have to be approved by the authority. Is it not clear that in all these cases, unless the authority in effect takes all the functions of the entrepreneur on itself (i.e. unless the proposed system is abandoned and one of complete central direction substituted), the process of price fixing would either become exceedingly cumbersome and the cause of infinite delay, or a pure formality?

IV

All these considerations appear to be relevant whatever particular form of organization is chosen. Before we go further, however, it becomes necessary to consider somewhat more in detail the concrete apparatus of industrial control which the two authors propose. The sketches they provide of the organization are fairly similar, although in this respect Professor Lange gives us somewhat more information than Dr. Dickinson, who, for most of the problems of economic organization, refers us to the works of Mr. and Mrs. Webb and Mr. G. D. H. Cole.

Both authors contemplate a socialist system in which the choice of occupation would be free and regulated mainly by the price mechanism (i.e. by the wage system) and in which the consumers also would be free to spend their incomes as they chose. Apparently both authors also want prices of consumers' goods to be fixed by the ordinary market processes (although Dr. Dickinson does not seem to be quite decided on this point), and also to leave the determination of wages to the bargaining between the parties concerned. Both also agree that for various reasons not the whole of industry should be socialized, but that, besides the socialized there should also remain a private sector, consisting of small enterprises run on essentially capitalistic lines. I find it difficult to agree with their belief that the existence of such a private sector parallel with the socialized sector creates no special difficulties. But as it would be difficult within the space of this article to deal adequately with this problem, we shall, for the purposes of this discussion, disregard the existence of the private sector and assume that the whole of industry is socialized.

The determination of all prices, other than those of consumers' goods and of wages, is the main task of the central economic authority, Professor Lange's Central Planning Board or Dr. Dickinson's Supreme Economic Council. (We shall, following Dr. Dickinson, henceforth refer to this body as the S.E.C.) As regards the technique of how particular prices are announced and changed we get more information, although by no means enough, from Professor Lange, while Dr. Dickinson goes more fully into the question by what considerations the S.E.C. should be guided in the fixing of prices. Both questions have a special importance and they must be considered separately.

According to Professor Lange, the S.E.C. would from time to time issue what, following Professor Taylor, he calls "factor valuation tables," that is, comprehensive lists of prices of all means of production (except labor). These prices would have to serve as the sole basis for all transactions between different enterprises and the whole calculation of all the industries and plants during the period of their validity and the managers must treat these prices as constant. What we are not told, however, either by Professor Lange or by Dr. Dickinson, is for what period these prices are to be fixed. This is one of the more serious obscurities in the exposition of both authors, a gap in their exposition which makes one almost doubt whether they have made a real effort to visualize their system at work. Are prices to be fixed for a definite period in advance, or are they to be changed whenever it seems desirable? F. M. Taylor seemed to suggest the former alternative when he wrote that the appropriateness of particular prices would show itself at the end of the "productive period"; and Professor Lange, on at least one occasion, gives the same impression when he says that "any price different from the equilibrium price would show at the end of the accounting period a surplus or shortage of the commodity in question." But on another occasion he says that "adjustments of those prices would be constantly made," while Dr. Dickinson confines himself to stating that after, "by a process of successive approximation," "a set of prices can ultimately be established in consonance with the principles of scarcity and substitution," "small adjustments will be sufficient to keep the system in equilibrium except in the case of major technical innovations or of big changes in consumers' tastes." Could the failure to understand the true function of the price mechanism, caused by the modern preoccupation with stationary equilibrium, be better illustrated?

While Dr. Dickinson is very uninformative on the mechanism of bringing price changes into effect, he goes much more fully than Professor Lange into the considerations on which the S.E.C. would have to base their decisions. Unlike Professor Lange, Dr. Dickinson is not satisfied with the S.E.C. merely watching the market and adjusting prices when an excess of demand or supply appears, and then trying to find by experimentation a new equilibrium level. He rather wants the S.E.C. to use statistically established demand and supply schedules as a guide to determine the equilibrium prices. This is evidently a residue of his earlier belief in the possibility of solving the whole problem by the method of simultaneous equations. But although he has now abandoned this idea (not because he regards it as impossible, since he still believes it could be done by solving merely "two or three thousand simultaneous equations," but because he realizes that "the data themselves, which would have to be fed into the equation-machine, are continually changing"), he still believes that the statistical determination of demand schedules would be useful as an aid to, if not as a substitute for, the method of trial and error, and that it would be well worth while to try and establish the numerical values of the constants (*sic*) in the Walrasian system of equilibrium.

V

Whatever the method by which the S.E.C. fixes prices, and particularly whatever the periods at which and for which prices are announced, there are two points about which there can be little question: the changes will occur later than they would if prices were determined by the market parties, and there will be less differentiation between prices of commodities according to differences of quality and the circumstances of time and place. While with real competition price changes occur when the parties immediately concerned know that conditions have changed, the S.E.C. will be able to act only after the parties have reported, the reports have been verified, contradictions cleared up, etc.; and the new prices will become effective only after all the parties concerned have been notified, that is, either a date will have to be fixed in advance at which the new prices will become effective, or the accounting will have to include an elaborate system by which every manager of production is constantly notified of the new prices upon which he has to base his calculations. Since in fact every manager would have to be informed constantly on many more prices than those of the commodities which he is actually using (at least of those of all possible substitutes), some sort of periodic publication of complete lists of all prices would be necessary. It is clear that while economic efficiency demands that prices should be changed as promptly as possible, practicability would confine actual changes to intervals of fair length.

That the price fixing process will be confined to establishing uniform prices for classes of goods and that therefore distinctions based on the special circumstances of time, place and quality will find no expression in prices is probably obvious. Without some such simplification the number of different commodities for which separate prices would have to be fixed would be practically infinite. This means, however, that the managers of production will have no inducement and even no real possibility to make use of special opportunities, special bargains and all the little advantages offered by their special local conditions, since all these things could not enter into their calculations. It would also mean, to give only one other instance of the consequences, that it would never be practicable to incur extra costs to remedy a sudden scarcity quickly, since a local or temporary scarcity could not affect prices until the official machinery had acted.

For both these reasons, because prices would have to be fixed for periods and because they would have to be fixed generically for categories of goods, a great many prices would be at most times in such a system substantially different from what they would be in a free system. This is very important for the functioning of the system. Professor Lange makes great play with the fact that prices act merely as "indices of terms on which alternatives are offered" and that this "parametric function of prices" by which prices are guiding the action of individual managers without being directly determined by them, will be fully preserved under such a system where prices are fixed. As he himself points out, "the determinateness of the accounting prices holds, however, only if all discrepancies between demand and supply of a commodity are met by an appropriate change of price," and for this reason "rationing has to be excluded" and "the rule to produce at the minimum average cost has no significance unless prices represent the relative scarcity of the factors of production." In other words, prices will provide a basis for rational accounting only if they are such that at the ruling prices anyone can always sell as much or buy as much as he wishes, or that anyone should be free to buy as cheaply or to sell as dearly as is made possible by the existence of a willing partner. If I cannot buy more of a factor so long as it is worth more to me than the price, and if I cannot sell a thing as soon as it is worth less to me than the price which somebody else would be willing to pay for it, prices are no longer indices of alternative opportunities.

We shall see the significance of this more clearly when we consider the action of the managers of the socialist industries. But before we can consider their action we must see who these people are and with what functions they are invested.

VI

The nature of the industrial unit under separate management and the factors which determine its size and the selection of its management are other points on which both our authors are deplorably vague. Professor Lange seems to contemplate the organization of the different industries in the form of national trusts, although this important point is only just touched upon once when the National Coal Trust is mentioned as an example. The very important and relevant question of what is *one* industry is nowhere discussed, but he apparently assumes that the various "managers of production" will have monopolistic control of the particular commodities with which they are concerned. In general Professor Lange uses the term "managers of production" exceedingly vaguely, leaving it obscure whether the directors of a whole "industry" or of a single unit are meant; but at critical points a distinction between the managers of plant and the managers of a whole industry appears without any clear limitation of their function. Dr. Dickinson is even more vague when he speaks of economic activities being "decentralized and carried on by a large number of separate organs of collective economy" which will have "their own nominal capital and their own profit and loss account and will be managed very much as separate enterprises under capitalism."

Whoever these managers of production are, their main function would appear to be to decide how much and how to produce on the basis of the prices fixed by the S.E.C. (and the prices of consumers' goods and the wages determined by the market). They would be instructed by the S.E.C. to produce at the lowest possible average costs and to expand production of the individual plants till marginal costs are equal to price.

According to Professor Lange the directors of the industries (as distinguished from the managers of individual plants) would have also the further task of seeing that the amount of equipment in the industry as a whole is so adjusted that "the marginal cost incurred by the industry" in producing an output which "can be sold or 'accounted for' at a price which equals marginal cost" is the lowest possible.

In this connection a special problem arises which unfortunately cannot be discussed here as it raises questions of such difficulty and complexity that a separate article would be required. It concerns the case of decreasing marginal costs where, according to both our authors, the socialist industries would act differently from capitalist industry by expanding production till prices are equal, not to average, but to marginal costs. Although the argument employed possesses a certain specious plausibility it can hardly be said even that the problem is adequately stated in either of the two books, still less that the conclusions drawn are convincing. Within the space available on this occasion however we can do no more than seriously question Dr. Dickinson's assertion that "under modern technical conditions, diminishing costs are far commoner than increasing costs"—a statement which in the context in which it occurs clearly refers to marginal costs.

Here we shall confine ourselves to considering one question arising out of this part of the proposal, the question how the S.E.C. will ensure that the principle that prices are equalized to the lowest marginal cost at which the quantity concerned can be produced, is actually put into force. The question which arises here is not "merely" one of the loyalty or capacity of the socialist managers. For the purpose of this argument it may be granted that they will be as capable and as anxious to produce as cheaply as the average capitalist entrepreneur. The problem arises because one of the most important forces which in a truly competitive economy brings about the reduction of costs to the minimum discoverable will be absent, namely, price competition. In the discussion of this sort of problem, as in the discussion of so much of economic theory at the present time, the question is frequently treated as if the cost curves were objectively given facts. What is forgotten here is that the method which under given conditions is the cheapest is a thing which has to be discovered, and to be discovered anew sometimes almost from day to day, by the entrepreneur, and that, in spite of the strong inducement, it is by no means regularly the established entrepreneur, the man in charge of the existing plant, who will discover what is the best method. The force which in a competitive society brings about the reduction of price to the lowest cost at which the quantity saleable at that cost can be produced is the opportunity for anybody who knows a cheaper method to come in at his own risk and to attract customers by underbidding the other producers. But if prices are fixed by the authority this method is excluded. Any improvement, any adjustment of the technique of production to changed conditions will be dependent on convincing the S.E.C. that the commodity in question can be produced cheaper and that therefore the price ought to be lowered. Since the man with the new idea will have no possibility of establishing himself by undercutting, the new idea cannot be proved by experiment till he has convinced the S.E.C. that his way of producing the thing is cheaper. Or, in other words, every calculation by an outsider who believes that he can do better will have to be examined and approved by the authority, which in this connection will have to take over all the functions of the entrepreneur.

VII

Let us briefly consider a few of the problems arising out of the relations between the "socialist managers of production" (whether of a plant or an industry) and the S.E.C. The manager's task is, as we have seen, to order production in such a way that his marginal costs are as low as possible and equal to price. How is he to do this and how is the fact of his success to be verified? He has to take prices as given. This turns him into what has recently been called a pure "quantity adjuster," i.e. his decision is confined to the quantities of factors of production and the combination in which he uses them. But as he has no means of inducing his suppliers to offer more, or to induce his purchasers to buy more, than they want to at the prescribed price, he will frequently be simply unable to carry out his instructions; or at least, if he cannot get more of a material required at the prescribed price, the only way for him, e.g., to expand production so as to make his cost equal to price, would be to use inferior substitutes or to employ other uneconomic methods; and when he cannot sell at the prescribed price and until the price is lowered by decree, he will have to stop production where under true competition he would have lowered his prices.

Another great difficulty arising out of the periodic price changes by decree is the problem of anticipations of future price movements. Professor Lange, somewhat too bravely, cuts this Gordian knot by prescribing that "for purposes of accounting, prices must be treated as constant, as they are treated by entrepreneurs on a competitive market" (!). Does that mean that the managers, although they know for certain that a particular price will have to be raised or lowered, must act as if they did not know? Clearly this won't do. But if they are free to meet expected price movements by anticipatory action, are they to be allowed to take advantage of the administrative delays in making price changes effective? And who is to be responsible for losses caused by wrongly timed or wrongly directed price changes?

Closely connected with this problem is another one, to which we also get no answer. Both our authors speak about "marginal costs" as if they were independent of the period for which the manager can plan. Clearly actual costs depend in many instances as much as on anything on buying at the right time. And in no sense can costs during any period be said to depend solely on prices during that period. They depend as much on whether these prices have been correctly foreseen as on the views that are held about future prices. Even in the very short run costs will depend on the effects which current decisions will have on future productivity. Whether it is economical to run a machine hard or to economize in lubricants, whether to make major adjustments to a given change in demand or to carry on as well as possible with the existing organization, in fact almost every decision on how to produce now depends at least in part on the views held about the future. But while the manager clearly must hold some views on these questions, he can hardly be held responsible for anticipating future changes correctly if these changes depend entirely on the decision of the authority.

Not only, however, will the success of the individual manager depend to a large extent on the action of the planning authority. He will also have to satisfy the same authority that he has done as well as was possible. Either beforehand, or more likely retrospectively, all his calculations will have to be examined and approved by the authority. This will not be a perfunctory auditing directed to find out whether his costs have actually been what he says they have been. It will have to establish whether they have been the lowest possible ones. This means that the control will have to consider not only what he actually did but also what he might have done and ought to have done. And from the point of view of the manager it will be much more important that he should always be able to prove that in the light of the knowledge which he possessed the decision actually taken was the right one than that he should prove to be right in the end. If this must not lead to the worst forms of bureaucracy I do not know what would.

This brings us to the general question of the responsibility of the managers. Dr. Dickinson clearly sees that "responsibility means in practice financial responsibility" and that unless the manager "bears responsibility for losses as well as for profits he will be tempted to embark upon all sorts of risky experiments on the bare chance that one of them will turn out successful." This is a difficult problem with managers who have no property of their own. Dr. Dickinson hopes to solve it by a system of bonuses. This may indeed be sufficient to prevent managers from taking too great risks. But is not the real problem the opposite one, that managers will be afraid of taking risks if, when the venture does not come off, it will be somebody else who will afterwards decide whether they have been justified in embarking on it? As Dr. Dickinson himself points out, the principle would be that "although the making of profits is not necessarily a sign of success, the making of losses is a sign of failure." Need one say more about the effects of such a system on all activities involving risk? It is difficult to conceive that under these circumstances any of the necessary speculative activities involving risk-bearing could be left to managerial initiative. But the alternative is to fall back for them on that system of strict central planning to avoid which the whole system has been evolved.

VIII

All this is even more true when we turn to the whole problem of new investments, that is, to all the questions which involve changes in the size (i.e. the capital) of the managerial units, whether they involve net changes in the total supply of capital or not. Up to a point it is possible to divide this problem into two parts, the decisions about the distribution of the available capital supply and the decisions about the rate at which capital is to be accumulated, although it is dangerous to carry this division too far, since the decision about how much is to be saved is necessarily also a decision about which needs for capital are to be satisfied and which are not. Both our authors agree that, as regards the problem of the distribution of capital between industries and plants, the interest mechanism should as far as possible be retained, but that the decision of how much to save and invest would necessarily have to be arbitrary.

Now however strong the desire may be to rely on the interest mechanism for the distribution of capital, it is fairly obvious that the market for capital can in no sense be a free market. And while for Professor Lange the rate of interest is also "simply determined by the condition that the demand for capital is equal to the amount available," Dr. Dickinson takes great pains to show how the S.E.C. will, on the basis of the alternative plans of activity drawn up by the different undertakings, construct an aggregate demand schedule for capital which will enable it to determine that rate of interest at which the demand for capital will equal supply. The ingenuity and the astounding trust in the practicability of even the most complicated constructions which he displays in this connection may be illustrated by his statement that in a certain case "it will be necessary to establish a provisional rate of interest, then to allow the different organs of collective economy to re-contract with each other on the basis of this provisional rate, and so to draw up their final demand schedule for capital."

All this, however, does not meet the main difficulty. If indeed it were possible to accept at their face value the statements of all the individual managers and would-be managers about how much capital they could with advantage use at various rates of interest, some such scheme as such might appear feasible. It cannot be too often repeated, however, that the planning authority cannot be conceived "simply as a kind of super-bank which lends the available funds to the highest bidder. It would lend to persons who have no property of their own. It would therefore bear all the risk and would have no claim for a definite amount of money as a bank has. It would simply have rights of ownership over all real resources. Nor can its decisions be confined to the redistribution of free capital in the form of money, and perhaps of land. It would have to decide whether a particular plant or piece of machinery should be left further to the entrepreneur who has used it in the past, at his valuation, or whether it should be transferred to another who promises a higher return for it."

These sentences are taken from the essay where the present author discussed five years ago the "possibility of real competition under socialism."[10] At that time such systems had only been vaguely discussed and one could hope to find an answer when systematic expositions of the new ideas should become available. But it is most disappointing to find no answer whatever to these problems in the two books now under discussion. While throughout the two works claims are made about how beneficial the control of investment activity would be in many respects, no indication is given of how this control is to be exercised and of how the responsibilities are to be divided between the planning authorities and the managers of the "competing" industrial units. Such statements as we find, as for instance that "because the managers of socialist industry will be governed in some choices by the direction laid down by the planning authority, it does not follow that they will have no choice at all," are singularly unhelpful. All that seems to be fairly clear is that the planning authority will be able to exercise its function of controlling and directing investment only if it is in a position to check and repeat all the calculations of the entrepreneur.

It seems that here the two writers are unconsciously led to fall back on the earlier beliefs in the superiority of a centrally directed system over a competitive system and to console themselves with the hope that the "omnipresent, omniscient organ of the collective economy" will possess at least as much knowledge as the individual entrepreneurs and will therefore be in as good if not in a better position to make the decisions as the entrepreneurs are. As I have tried to show on another occasion, it is the main merit of real competition that through it use is made of knowledge divided between many persons which, if it were to be used in a centrally directed economy, would have all to enter the single plan.[11] To assume that all this knowledge would be automatically in the possession of the planning authority seems to me to be to miss the main point. It is not quite clear whether Professor Lange means to assert that the planning authority will have all this information when he says that "the administrators of a socialist economy will have exactly the same knowledge, or lack of knowledge, of the production functions as the capitalist entrepreneurs have." If the "administrators of a socialist economy" here means merely all the managers of the units as well as of the central organization taken together, the statement can of course be readily ac-

[10] *Collectivist Economic Planning*, pp. 232–37.

[11] See the article on "Economics and Knowledge," *Economica*, New Series, Vol. IV, No. 13 (February, 1937), pp. 33–54.

cepted, but does in no way solve the problem. But if it is intended to convey that all this knowledge can be effectively used by the planning authority in drawing up the plan, it is merely begging the whole question and seems to be based on the "fallacy of composition."[12]

On this whole all-important question of the direction of new investment and all that it involves, the two studies do not really give any new information. The problem remains where it was five years ago and I can confine myself on this point to repeating what I said then: "The decision about the amount of capital to be given to an individual entrepreneur and the decisions thereby involved concerning the size of the individual firm under a single control are in effect decisions about the most appropriate combination of resources. It will rest with the central authority to decide whether one plant located at one place should expand rather than another plant situated elsewhere. All this involves planning on the part of the central authority on much the same scale as if it were actually running the enterprise. And while the individual entrepreneur would in all probability be given some definite contractual tenure for managing the plant entrusted to him, all new investments will be necessarily centrally directed. This division in the disposition over the resources would then simply have the effect that neither the entrepreneur nor the central authority would be really in a position to plan, and that it would be impossible to assess the responsibility for mistakes. To assume that it is possible to create conditions of full competition without making those who are responsible for the decisions pay for their mistakes seems to be pure illusion. It will be at best a system of quasi-competition where the persons really responsible will not be the entrepreneur but the official who approves his decisions and where in consequence all the difficulties will arise in connection with freedom of initiative and the assessment of responsibility which are usually associated with bureaucracy."[13]

IX

The question how far a socialist system can avoid extensive central direction of economic activity is of great importance quite apart from its relation to economic efficiency: it is crucial for the question of how much personal and political freedom can be preserved in such a system. Both authors show a reassuring awareness of the dangers to personal freedom which a centrally planned system would involve and seem to have evolved

[12] Another and even worse instance of this fallacy occurs in Professor Lippincott's introduction to the essays of Professors Lange and Taylor, when he argues that "there can be no doubt that the Central Planning Board would exercise great power, but would it be any greater than that exercised collectively by private boards of directors? Because the decisions of private boards are made here and there, this does not mean that the consumer does not feel their collective impact, even though it may take a depression to make him aware of it."

[13] *Collectivist Economic Planning*, p. 237.

their competitive socialism partly in order to meet this danger. Dr. Dickinson even goes so far as to say that "capitalist planning can exist only on the basis of fascism" and that in the hands of an irresponsible controller even socialist planning "*could* be made the greatest tyranny the world has ever seen." But he and Professor Lange believe that their competitive socialism will avoid this danger.

Now if competitive socialism could really rely for the direction of production largely on the effects of consumers' choice as reflected in the price system and if the cases where the authority will have to decide what is to be produced and how were made the exception rather than the rule, this claim would be to a large extent substantiated. How far is this really the case? We have already seen that with the retention of the control over investment the central authority wields most extensive powers over the direction of production, much more extensive indeed than is easily possible to show without making this discussion unduly long. To this have yet to be added however a further number of arbitrary elements of which Dr. Dickinson himself gives a quite substantial although by no means complete list. There is in the first instance the "allocation of resources between present and future consumption" which, as we have already seen, always involves a decision about what particular needs will be satisfied and which needs will not be satisfied. There is, secondly, the need for arbitrary decision in respect to the "allocation of resources between communal and individual consumption" which, in view of the great extension of the "division of communal consumption" which he envisages means that another very large part of the resources of the society is put outside the control of the price mechanism and subject to purely authoritarian decision. Dr. Dickinson expressly adds to this only "the choice between work and leisure" and the "geographical planning and the pricing of land," but at other points of his exposition further questions emerge on which he wants effective planning in order to correct the results of the market. But although he (and still more so Professor Lange) frequently hint at the possibilities of "correcting" the results of the price mechanism by judicious interference, this part of the program is nowhere clearly worked out.

What our authors here have in mind perhaps comes out clearest in Dr. Dickinson's attitude towards the problem of wage changes: "If wages are too low in any one industry, it is the duty of the planning organ to adjust prices and quantities produced, so as to yield equal wages to work of equal skill, responsibility, and difficulty in every industry." Apparently here the price mechanism and the free choice of occupation are not to be relied upon. Later we learn that although "unemployment in any particular job affords a prima facie case for lowering the standard wage," a lowering of wages is objectionable "on social grounds, because a lowering in wages . . . causes discontent; on economic grounds, because it perpetuates an uneconomic allocation of labor to different occupations."

(How?) Therefore, "as invention and improved organization make less labor necessary to satisfy human wants, society should set itself to discover new wants to satisfy." "The powerful engine of propaganda and advertisement, employed by public organs of education and enlightenment instead of by the hucksters and panders of private profit-making industry, could divert demand into socially desirable directions while preserving the subjective impression (*sic*) of free choice."

When we add to this and many other similar points where Dr. Dickinson wants his S.E.C. to exercise a paternalistic control,[14] the fact that it will be necessary to co-ordinate national production "with a general plan of exports and imports," since free trade "is inconsistent with the principles of collectivism," it becomes fairly evident that there will be precious little economic activity which will not be more or less immediately guided by arbitrary decisions. In fact, Dr. Dickinson expressly contemplates a situation where "the state, through a definite planning organ, makes itself responsible for the consideration of economic activity as a whole" and even adds that this destroys the "illusion" maintained in a capitalist society "that the division of the product is governed by forces as impersonal and inevitable as those which govern the weather." This can only mean that, with most other planners, he himself thinks of production in his system as one which is largely directed by conscious and arbitrary decisions. Yet in spite of this extensive rôle which arbitrary decisions are to play in his system, he is confident (and the same applies to Professor Lange) that his system will not degenerate into an authoritarian despotism.

Dr. Dickinson just mentions the argument that "even if a socialist planner wished to realize freedom he could not do so and remain a planner," yet the answer he gives makes one doubt whether he has quite seen on what considerations this argument is based. His answer is merely that "a plan can always be changed." But this is not the point. The difficulty is that, in order to plan at all on an extensive scale, a much more extensive agreement among the members of the society about the relative importance of the various needs is required than will normally exist, and that in consequence this agreement will have to be brought about and a common scale of values will have to be imposed by force and propaganda. I have developed this argument at length elsewhere and I have not space here to restate it.[15] And the thesis I have developed there, that socialism is bound to become totalitarian, now seems to receive support from the most unexpected quarters. This at least appears to be the meaning when Mr. Max Eastman, in a recent book on Russia, states that "Stalinism

---

[14] Cf. for instance the passage where Dr. Dickinson speaks about the "people who will not pay voluntarily beforehand for what they are only too glad to have once they have it."

[15] See *Freedom and the Economic System* (Public Policy Pamphlet, No. 29) (Chicago: University of Chicago Press, 1939).

is socialism, in the sense of being an inevitable, although unforeseen, political and cultural accompaniment."[16]

In fact, although he does not seem to see it, Dr. Dickinson himself, in the concluding passages of his book, makes a statement which comes very much to the same thing. "In a socialist society," he says, "the distinction, always artificial, between economics and politics will break down; the economic and the political machinery of society will fuse into one." This is of course precisely the authoritarian doctrine preached by Nazis and Fascists. The distinction breaks down because in a planned system all economic questions become political questions, because it is no longer a question of reconciling as far as possible individual views and desires, but one of imposing a single scale of values, the "social goal" of which socialists ever since the time of Saint-Simon have been dreaming. In this respect it seems that the schemes of an authoritarian socialist, from those of Professor Hogben and Mr. Lewis Mumford, whom Dr. Dickinson mentions as an example, to those of Stalin and Hitler, are much more realistic and consistent than the beautiful and idyllic picture of the "libertarian socialism" in which Dr. Dickinson believes.

X

There can be no better testimony of the intellectual quality of the two books under discussion than that after having written about them at such length one is conscious of having only just scratched on the surface of the problems raised by them. But an examination in greater detail would clearly exceed the scope of an article; and since many of the doubts which are left with the reader concern points which are not answered in the two books, an adequate treatment of the subject would require another book even longer than those discussed. There are however also important problems which are discussed at some length, particularly in Dr. Dickinson's book, which we have scarcely been able to mention. This applies not only to the difficult problem of the combination of a private sector with the socialized sector, which both authors propose, but also to such important problems as the international relations of a socialist community and to the problems of monetary policy, to which Dr. Dickinson devotes a very brief, and on the whole the least satisfactory, section.

A fuller discussion would also have to point out various passages in the argument of both authors where apparently residues of earlier beliefs or views which are purely matters of political creed creep in and strike one as curiously inconsistent with the plane of the rest of the discussion. This applies for instance to Dr. Dickinson's repeated references to class-conflict and exploitation or his gibes at the wastes of competition, and

[16] Max Eastman, *Stalin's Russia and the Crisis in Socialism* (New York: Norton, 1940). As the book is not yet available in this country, the quotation is taken from a review that appeared in the American press.

to much of Professor Lange's interesting section on the "economist's case for socialism," where he seems to employ arguments of somewhat questionable validity.

These, however, are minor points. On the whole the books are so thoroughly unorthodox from a socialist point of view that one rather wonders whether their authors have not retained too little of the traditional trappings of socialist argument to make their proposals acceptable to socialists who are not economists. As courageous attempts to face the real difficulties and completely to remold socialist doctrine to meet them they deserve our gratitude and respect. Whether the solution offered will appear particularly practicable, even to socialists, may perhaps be doubted. To those who, with Dr. Dickinson, wish to create "for the first time in human history, an effective individualism," a different path will probably appear more promising.

Centrally Planned Economy

Central planning may take place in a capitalist or a socialist institutional framework. In a capitalist economy in wartime, there is likely to be a large amount of central planning, as the government mobilizes and deploys the nation's resources for the war effort. Fascism preserves the outward forms of the capitalist institutions of private property and enterprise, but it subjects them to comprehensive regulation in the interests of the state as defined by the supreme leader at the head of the totalitarian government. Authoritarian socialism combines central planning with public ownership.

Whatever the ownership of the means of production, central planning has two main features. (1) *There is comprehensive and detailed planning and control of almost all phases of economic life, in response to planners', rather than consumers', sovereignty.* (2) *Resources are allocated primarily by administrative "commands" in real* (*physical*) *terms—such as production targets, allocation orders, and rationing—rather than chiefly by markets and prices.*

The selections that follow analyze the characteristics and problems of central planning in different institutional contexts. The first presents a concise summary of the main features of a centrally planned economy. In the second, Jan Drewnowski considers different combinations of planners' and consumers' sovereignty which are possible in a centrally planned economy. In the next, Walter Eucken analyzes the centrally administered economy in operation, as illustrated by fascist Germany, comparing it with the market economy. In the last article, Oskar Lange, acknowledging the disadvantages of excessive centralization, proposes a combination of central planning and the market mechanism to guide the economy.

7. BASIC FEATURES OF A CENTRALLY PLANNED ECONOMY*

Alan A. Brown and Egon Neuberger

The authors provide a concise systematic summary of the key features of a centrally planned economy. They discuss in turn its objectives, the planning mechanisms to achieve these objectives, desired effects from the operation of these mechanisms, undesired consequences, and adjustment mechanisms to deal with undesired consequences. The article thus constitutes a brief but comprehensive sketch of a centrally planned economy in operation.

WE MAY identify the basic features of a centrally planned economy (CPE) in terms of its objectives and modi operandi.[1] Let us consider these in sequence under five major headings: objectives and key elements, planning mechanism, desired effects, undesired consequences, and adjustment mechanisms.[2]

---

* Reprinted by permission from *International Trade and Central Planning: An Analysis of Economic Interactions,* ed. Alan A. Brown and Egon Neuberger (Berkeley: University of California Press, 1968), pp. 405–14, with the omission of some footnotes and source references. Alan A. Brown is Associate Professor of Economics at the University of Southern California, and Egon Neuberger is Professor of Economics at the State University of New York (Stony Brook).

[1] As a cautionary note, we may add that this conceptual model attempts to illuminate only the traditional CPE; it does not deal with recent changes resulting from economic reforms.

[2] The sketch of the closed CPE which follows was inspired by Professor David Granick's imaginative organizational model of Soviet planning (David Granick, "An Organizational Model of Soviet Industrial Planning," *Journal of Political Economy,* Vol. LXVII, No. 2 [April, 1959], pp. 109–30). An increasing number of Western economists have also constructed models of CPE's, and only a few of these can be listed here. Professor Bergson, in one of his recent works, presents an analytical framework of the Soviet economy within which he interprets Soviet behavior patterns and assesses economic efficiency (Abram Bergson, *The Economics of Soviet Planning* [New Haven: Yale University Press, 1964]). Professor Montias, in his appraisal of the Polish experience, provides a thorough introduction to the theory of central planning (John Michael Montias, *Central Planning in Poland* [New Haven: Yale University Press, 1962]). Professors Balassa (Bela A. Balassa, *The Hungarian Experience in Economic Planning* [New Haven: Yale University Press, 1959]) and Kornai (János Kornai, *Overcentralization in Economic Administration: A Critical Analysis Based on Experience in Hungarian Light Industry,* translated by John Knapp [London: Oxford University Press, 1959]) both use theoretical models of central planning to

OBJECTIVES AND KEY ELEMENTS

Objectives[3]

Rapid Growth and Industrialization. Planners in traditional CPE's aim at a very high rate of economic growth, as a rule much higher than the rate maintained in market-type economies (MTE's). Not all economic sectors, however, are promoted equally; the result is unbalanced growth. Expansion of industrial sectors is stressed—more specifically, producers' goods and particularly certain heavy industries, such as mining, metallurgy, and machinery production. Attempts to satisfy an ever-increasing demand for industrial inputs lead to a chronic neglect of agriculture, a trend enhanced by the planners' ideological orientation (i.e., their mistrust and fear of the peasantry). Unbalanced industrial growth is generally pursued without regard for the relative resource endowment of individual CPE's.

Centralization. This term is a shorthand expression that includes both *centralized planning* and *centralized control* of economic activities. Thus, centralization means, on the one hand, that important planning decisions are reserved to the system's directors (to use Professor Bergson's expression), and, on the other, that decisions are communicated to operational units by direct commands or directives. This implies a set of institutional mechanisms whose function is to assure the fulfillment of commands. Centralization, it may be added, is at once an important policy objective and a modus operandi of the system (via certain mechanisms to be discussed below). The planners have a revealed preference for centralization per se, pursuing it even at the expense of growth.

Key Elements

The basic goals of rapid growth and centralization give direction and shape to the system. The following six key elements represent a relatively complete shorthand description of the CPE.

---

analyze economic planning in Hungary. A very comprehensive treatment of different models of CPE's and of some alternative Communist economic systems appears in a book by Professor Wiles (*The Political Economy of Communism* [Cambridge: Harvard University Press, 1962]). The fruits of a collective undertaking on various aspects of planning in the Soviet Union and in East Europe have been published in a volume edited by Professor Grossman; the editor's Introduction contains not only a summary of the other contributions but also a succinct model of CPE's (Gregory Grossman [ed.], *Value and Plan: Economic Calculation and Organization in Eastern Europe* [Berkeley: University of California Press, 1960]). Also, an article by Professor Grossman serves as a useful theoretical frame of reference for Soviet-type systems ("Notes for a Theory of the Command Economy," *Soviet Studies*, Vol. XV, No. 2 [October, 1963], pp. 101–23). In a *Festschrift* honoring Professor Gerschenkron, there are several models of Soviet planning (Henry Rosovsky [ed.], *Industrialization in Two Systems: Essays in Honor of Alexander Gerschenkron* [New York: John Wiley, 1966]). Attention will be called, as we proceed, to other contributions relating to specific features of CPE's.

[3] Although preference functions are obviously multidimensional, we attempt to call attention here only to those goals that have been explicitly and strongly stressed by the planners.

Socialist Economy (or *Social Ownership*). According to Western economic terminology, public ownership of the means of production. (While this is one of the independent goals, it is also a means of achieving the goal of centralization, and to some extent the goal of rapid growth.)

Command Economy. Centralized bureaucratic management of the economy, with detailed physical planning and supply.

Pressure Economy. Emphasis on a high rate of forced savings at the macro-level; and on taut planning of outputs, inputs, and inventories at the micro-level.

Priority Economy. Planning based on priorities, reflecting the dominance of political and ideological criteria over economic considerations in the overall formulation of economic policy; e.g., primacy of industry over agriculture, of producers' goods over consumers' goods, and of material goods over services—except for high priority of education, especially technical education of the labor force.

Extensive Development.[4] Output-oriented planning, with stress on ever-increasing quantities of output, achieved with massive infusions of labor and capital inputs.

Closed Economy. Primacy of domestic economic considerations over the exigencies of foreign trade, foreign trade plans being merely addenda to domestic plans. (This is again an independent goal, as well as a means of achieving the goal of centralization.)

PLANNING MECHANISMS

Every economic system requires certain mechanisms, or institutional devices, to achieve its basic goals. In a CPE the planning mechanisms are designed to foster rapid economic growth (particularly in the high-priority sectors) and to safeguard centralization. We may identify three primary mechanisms (vertical coordination and control, system of material balances, and taut planning) and three secondary mechanisms (discontinuous planning, discontinuous incentives, and multiple criteria).

PRIMARY PLANNING MECHANISMS

Vertical coordination and control[5] means a predominant reliance on vertical channels of coordination and control as a basic method of centralization. This emphasis on the "vertical connections" in economy (i.e., direct orders from above) reflects an effort by the planners to reduce

---

[4] This term has gained wide acceptance in Eastern Europe as a descriptive reference to the policies followed under the Stalinist system; we are adapting it to describe the specific feature described below.

[5] János Kornai in his "Model of Economic Mechanisms" distinguishes between vertical connections ("a matter of authority and subordination") and horizontal connections (which "involve contacts [of an enterprise] with other enterprises . . . [all] having equal legal rights and standing") (*op. cit.*, pp. 191 ff.).

their dependence on the "horizontal connections" (i.e., spontaneous, immediate contacts among operational units).[6] This mechanism manifests itself in a threefold separation of economic activities: (*a*) among different sectors of the economy (*intersectoral separation*), (*b*) among the enterprises in given sectors (*interfirm separation*), and (*c*) among departments within given administrative or producing units, as within a ministry or firm (*interdepartmental separation*).

System of material balances is a technique to achieve consistency among the various plans. It has two important aspects: (*a*) *physical planning*, the balancing of equations in physical units to assure a flow of supplies mainly to high-priority sectors, and (*b*) *sequential planning*, the use of successive approximations rather than simultaneous equations to facilitate the planning process.

Taut planning aims at the swiftest possible central mobilization of all available resources—by means of continual sellers' markets—to facilitate rapid growth. It also serves as a technique to motivate operational units. We may distinguish three aspects of taut planning: (*a*) *output* (*target*) *maximization*, (*b*) *input* (*or input coefficient*) *minimization*, and (*c*) *inventory minimization*.

Secondary Planning Mechanisms

Discontinuous planning may be viewed as an elongation of the Robertsonian "planning day" (or Hicksian "week"), i.e., the period during which plans are supposed to remain unchanged.[7] This is also a device to facilitate central planning, since the planners attempt to keep relatively long "planning days" (they sanction interrelated plan revisions only infrequently or discontinuously) so as to minimize the burden of planning.

Discontinuous incentives imply a sharp line of demarcation in the incentive system between success and failure. The purpose is to encourage fulfillment of a centrally specified output pattern. To achieve this purpose, the incentive system is designed to offer rewards if the plans are fulfilled 100 percent (particularly, the physical output plan); failure is defined as falling short of the established quotas. Consequently, little attention is paid to differences of degree.[8]

Multiple criteria mean the absence of a single common standard of value, whether in the planning process (e.g., prices) or in the control mechanism (e.g., profits). The tendency to postulate output targets and

[6] Kornai says, ". . . these vertical connexions are the dominant ones . . . . The influences which result from direct contacts between enterprises are dwarfed by those which reach them from the centre" (*op. cit.*, p. 194).

[7] J. R. Hicks says, "I shall define a week as that period of time during which variations in prices can be neglected. For theoretical purposes this means that prices will be supposed to change, not continuously, but at short intervals" (*Value and Capital* [2d ed.; Oxford: Clarendon Press, 1946], pp. 122–23).

[8] Castigating the practice of "turning '100 percent' into a fetish," Kornai says, "premiums are not paid until the degree of fulfillment of the relevant plan index reaches 100 percent" (*op. cit.*, p. 128).

inputs norms in non-additive, heterogeneous units is functionally related to the system of material balances (i.e., to physical planning). Multiple criteria are also used in assessing the fulfillment of plans, i.e., in measuring the performance of operational units. Thus, multiple criteria and the corresponding proliferation of instructions are means of safeguarding central control, although they often do not accomplish this purpose satisfactorily.[9]

DESIRED EFFECTS[10]

The CPE is able, at least theoretically, to produce certain effects that, given the preferences of the system's directors, are considered desirable. It should be noted that, in practice, some of these effects are attenuated or altogether negated for reasons to be discussed as we proceed.

Socioeconomic Reorganization

Formation of a New Elite. The system is able to orient the whole country toward the goal of economic development, replacing those uninterested in or hostile to rapid growth and centralization with a new elite of greater reliability. The new cadres are fully committed to the fundamental objectives of the system. This is accomplished by substituting a new ruling ideology for the old, and shifting power to adherents of the new ideology. The change is aided by the key elements cited above, especially social ownership, the pressure economy, and the command economy.

Income Distribution. Social ownership makes economic development possible without resort to a highly unequal income distribution, a precondition usually considered necessary to attain a sufficiently high level of investment from private voluntary saving. In practice, however, the wage differentials needed for incentive purposes and the lack of progressive taxes combine to widen the dispersion of disposable incomes in CPE's.

Population Policy. The CPE, by focusing on economic development and giving power to a new elite imbued with a development ideology, should be in a strong position to deal with one of the most crucial issues facing underdeveloped countries—the problem of population growth. But none of the key elements of the system deals directly with this question, and none of the countries that have adopted such a system has developed a consistent long-term population policy.[11]

---

[9] Kornai writes that "excessive centralization inevitably leads to an undue proliferation of instructions" (*op. cit.*, p. 204). "The more instructions are given, the greater the tendency of ministries and other highly placed authorities to 'dictate' and to rely on ordering people about" (*op. cit.*, p. 203).

[10] The most comprehensive treatment may be found in Wiles, *op. cit.*, pp. 253–63, where many of the points listed below are discussed at length.

[11] An excellent discussion of the ramifications of this omission may be found in Oleg Hoeffding, "State Planning and Forced Industrialization," *Problems of Communism*, Vol. VIII, No. 6 (November–December, 1959), pp. 38–46.

Mobilization of Inputs

Capital Formation. The elements of social ownership, the pressure economy, and the command economy are used to impose very high rates of forced saving and investment, with the corollary effect of greater capital formation than under alternative economic systems.

Labor Recruitment. Extensive development, the priority economy, and the socialist economy facilitate the utilization of relatively abundant agricultural labor and unemployed urban labor, as well as the recruitment of women into the labor force.

Labor Training. Another desirable effect is the improvement of the educational levels and vocational skills of the population, a goal promoted by both the priority economy and social ownership (since education becomes a more important avenue of social mobility).

Acceleration and Channeling of Economic Development

Growth of GNP. The pressure economy, the priority economy, and extensive development are jointly utilized to achieve a rapid increase of the gross national product, although not necessarily of the standard of living.

Direction of Development. An important function of the priority economy, the command economy, and social ownership is the ability to concentrate on high-priority objectives (e.g., giving the lion's share of investment funds to industry, especially to its favored branches) and to bring about a rapid structural transformation of the economy.

Regional Development. Attempts to bring the less-developed regions of the country to the more-developed level—together with a corollary tendency toward greater sociopolitical cohesiveness—are also promoted by the priority economy, the command economy, and social ownership.

Alleviation of Market Imperfections

Externalities. The ability to internalize external economies and diseconomies, while clearly a theoretical effect of the CPE—particularly of the command economy, the priority economy, and social ownership—is not easily realized in practice, since central planning organs are not monolithic units and do not have the necessary data and tools to assess externalities accurately.

Restrictive Influences. Social ownership, the pressure economy, and the command economy can be used, with at least partial success, to reduce monopolistic misallocation of resources and organizational slacks by tightly controlling managerial power and severely limiting trade-union interference.

Technological Progress. Control over management and labor and the absence of artificial monopolies based on patents foster a more rapid diffusion of existing technological knowledge. This desirable effect is related to social ownership and certain features of the command economy. Other elements of the system, however—such as the pressure economy, the closed economy, and extensive development—tend to work in the opposite direction.

Promotion of Economic Stability

Price-Wage Stabilization. Elements of the CPE (the command economy and the closed economy) enable the system's directors to control undesirable price and wage fluctuations. If severe inflationary pressures do build up periodically, as has happened in the past, they can be prevented from affecting resource allocation in part by controlling the wage-price spiral.

Insulation from International Business Cycles. CPE's also have more power than MTE's to prevent, at least for a time, external cyclical pressures and disturbances in the balance of payments from dominating domestic economic policies; this is a primary effect not only of the closed economy but also of the command economy. The system's directors do not feel the need to engage in a stop-go policy of investment and growth, nor have the banks the authority to insist on it.

UNDESIRED CONSEQUENCES

We turn now to various undesired consequences of CPE's, rooted in the objectives, key elements, and specific features of the planning system.[12] Although these undesired consequences are interrelated, we may separate them for analytical purposes into four major categories: administrative inefficiencies, unreliable valuation criteria, microeconomic inefficiencies, and macroeconomic problems.

Administrative Inefficiencies

Formal Organization. In its traditional form, the CPE is hypercentralized (i.e., its centralization interferes with economic efficiency) and rigidly organized. Its features, which are embedded in the bureaucratic framework of the command economy, lead to various macroeconomic maladjustments. The absence of flexibility pervades all sectors of the economy, from the Central Planning Board to every subordinate level. It presents serious problems, periodically, in the supply system (where cumulative shortages can arise because of the unavailability of crucial inputs through legal channels, regardless of prices that firms may be willing to pay) and particularly in foreign trade (where potential gains depend on flexible responses to ephemeral changes). First among the

[12] Operationally, it would be difficult to determine whether the emphasis on growth or that on centralization was fundamentally more responsible for the undesired consequences. Although in practice they are joint products, Professor Levine has recently tried to separate the causes analytically, assigning most of the blame to pressure in the system. (Rosovsky, *op. cit.*, especially pp. 269 ff.).

specific problems is an overemphasis on vertical coordination and control channels (and a corresponding neglect of horizontal links among the enterprises), which increases the need for more information in the formulation and implementation of plans. This, along with discontinuities in planning, leads to (*a*) lags in administrative response, (*b*) the neglect of special requirements or atypical conditions, and (*c*) cumulative shortages, which are rendered particularly acute by taut planning (e.g., efforts to keep reserves as low as possible). Thus, the planning mechanisms not only create initial bottlenecks but also generate further repercussions.

Informal Bargaining. On close inspection, it appears that the CPE, in spite of its highly centralized formal organization, is not a system of rational decision making by an omniscient and monolithic unit. Although vertical command channels are overemphasized officially, the formulation and implementation of plans are pervaded at all levels by bargaining. Results more often reflect the power of individuals than the intrinsic strength of their case, and our attempts to explain or predict the behavior of CPE's may be better served at times by tools of game theory than by traditional economic theories of rational resource allocation.

Unreliable Valuation Criteria

Domestic Prices. There are nonsystematic aberrations of domestic prices both from prevailing scarcity ratios and from planners' preferences, primarily because several features of the system tend to immobilize the market mechanism.[13] Without a trial-and-error method, it would be difficult to establish a set of economically meaningful prices for even a handful of basic commodities (e.g., to derive synthetic or shadow prices by means of mathematical programming); and, in any case, the problem of the lack of price flexibility would remain. In a centralized economic system, interrelated price adjustments or general price reforms are too costly and can be undertaken only at infrequent intervals. Several key elements of the system—the command economy, the priority economy, and the closed economy—militate against rational pricing in a CPE. The inability of the planners to formulate economically meaningful and sufficiently flexible prices may also be directly attributed to certain specific planning mechanisms. First, the emphasis on vertical channels and the corresponding neglect of horizontal connections among operational units slow the transmission and reduce the reliability of information. Second, material balancing, with its stress on quota fulfillment in physical terms,

---

[13] Other fundamental problems include ideological mistrust and a lack of intellectual appreciation of the market mechanism, but the desire for centralization and the use of centralized devices of the system are probably the most important reasons for the irrationality of the prices. As Professor Grossman has expressed it: "But most important, to be workable, a market mechanism would require a dispersion of power and a degree of slack in the economy that the regime may be unwilling to grant" (Grossman, *Value and Plan*, pp. 9–10).

delegates financial accounting to a subsidiary role in the planning process. Third, taut planning and its corollary, periodic supply shortages, inhibit equilibrium pricing.

Exchange Rates. Closely connected with irrational domestic prices is the system of generally arbitrary exchange rates. Both the command economy and the priority economy are to blame, although the closed-economy element is chiefly responsible. While foreign trade decisions are not made primarily on the basis of official exchange rates, the lack of reliable and explicit comparisons between external prices and internal costs tends to interfere with planning as well as with control. Arbitrary exchange rates, like irrational domestic prices, are a contributory cause of macro- and microeconomic inefficiencies.

Microeconomic Inefficiencies

Incentive System. Within the pressure economy and the command economy, multiple criteria and discontinuous incentives give rise to a series of problems at the microeconomic level. Both of these aspects of the planning system tend to make incentives dysfunctional: (*a*) multiple criteria lead to uncertainties, or *ambiguous motivation;* and (*b*) discontinuous incentives lead to an exaggerated schism between success and failure, or *dichotomous motivation.* The final consequence is an all-or-nothing philosophy. First, up to a point, there are strong incentives for *simulation* (a familiar manifestation of this is the "assortment problem," the willful misclassification of commodities to show favorable results) and *storming* (regular seasonal spurts in production to fulfill the quota). Second, when simulation is not likely to help, the performance of enterprises tends to suffer more than necessary because of temporary lethargy and (especially) illicit *hoarding*, which occurs to facilitate plan fulfillment in subsequent periods.

Productivity. Extensive development, the pressure economy, the closed economy, and the command economy are jointly responsible for various microeconomic inefficiencies: slow rate of technological and product innovation, poor quality of output, and low productivity of labor and capital (long gestation period, inefficient choice of investment or its location, low-capacity utilization because of supply bottlenecks, and inadequate charges for capital use). At the same time, excessive inventories of unneeded inputs and unsold outputs accumulate.

Firm Size and Specialization. Elements of the command economy, the pressure economy, the priority economy, and the closed economy lead to a pattern of interfirm relationships with: (*a*) a bias toward giant plants with high transport costs and unused capacity, as well as an absence of smaller enterprises needed to provide forward and backward linkages; and (*b*) the presence of nonspecialized enterprises, aiming at narrow self-sufficiency, producing many commodities in small series, and engaging in subcontracting as little as possible.

Macroeconomic Problems

Consumer Satisfaction. The priority economy, the command economy, and social ownership tend to keep consumer satisfactions at relatively low levels because of the high rates of forced saving, the low priority of agriculture and consumer goods industries, and the neglect of service industries (which in turn lead to such corollary problems as the wrong assortment of products in terms of type, size, and style, and the unavailability of products in certain localities).

Agriculture. The past collectivization of agriculture and the low priority assigned to it subsequently (keeping agricultural incomes low and making life miserable for peasants)—the consequences of social ownership and the priority economy—have caused an exodus of the best workers from agriculture. While this neglect of agriculture makes extensive development possible and allows increases in industrial output, it nonetheless debilitates long-term agricultural performance, increases social problems in overcrowded cities, reduces—as mentioned above—the level of consumer satisfaction, and contributes to balance-of-payments problems.

International Specialization. The closed economy, the command economy, and the priority economy are responsible for the relative neglect of traditional export industries and the failure to develop new specialized export industries based on present or prospective comparative advantage. As a result, CPE's become dependent on the exportation of commodities that happen to be in temporary excess of domestic needs. Similarly, the lack of an optimal long-term import policy leads to the importation of commodities in temporary short supply, rather than those in which the country has a comparative disadvantage.

ADJUSTMENT MECHANISMS

CPE's employ certain adjustment mechanisms in an attempt to deal with the undesirable consequences discussed above. These mechanisms may be divided into external and internal safety valves. The *external safety valves*, or *ad hoc* imports, . . . are often used to alleviate planning errors or unforeseen disturbances. . . .[14] By *domestic safety valves* is meant the semilegal mechanisms whose function is to introduce a measure of flexibility—by means of informal decentralization—into the rigidly centralized system. Two allied devices, selective violation of instructions and priority planning, are also used to cope with some of the undesired consequences.

Selective Violation of Instructions. Informally, planning authorities

[14] See Alan A. Brown, "Towards a Theory of Centrally Planned Foreign Trade," in Alan A. Brown and Egon Neuberger (eds.), *International Trade and Central Planning: An Analysis of Economic Interactions* (Berkeley: University of California Press, 1968), pp. 57–93.

are inclined to overlook a case of the neglect of certain instructions by enterprises so long as the more important instructions are observed (chiefly, the fulfillment of physical output plans). There is, as it were, a hierarchy among instructions, the more important ones being safeguarded at the expense of the less important.[15]

Priority Planning. There is a similar hierarchy among various branches of production, i.e., among products of different industries. Thus, priority planning is a means of assuring fulfillments, or overfulfillments, of high-priority output targets—ranking high in the preferences of the system's directors. This occurs at the expense of low-priority goods—commodities that the directors consider to be more expendable, at least in the short run (traditionally, agricultural products and consumer goods).

---

[15] Let us once again cite Kornai: "According to what their consequences are, some instructions have much 'authority' and 'weight,' and are very effective, while others are of more or less formal importance only, having their existence only on paper. Thus, a definite order of the importance of the tasks which arise in the course of the economic process is formed" (*op. cit.*, p. 122).

8. THE ECONOMIC THEORY OF SOCIALISM: A SUGGESTION FOR RECONSIDERATION*

Jan Drewnowski[1]

Drewnowski points out that Lange's model of decentralized market socialism, in which consumer sovereignty is largely preserved, is not applicable to the centralized socialist economies of the Communist countries, in which planners' sovereignty predominates. Drewnowski undertakes to formulate a model of socialism relevant to these countries by analyzing how state and individual preferences can combine to guide the economy.

In socialism (and also in capitalism), two systems of preferences must be distinguished: the multiple system of individual preference functions of consumers, and the single state preference function. The latter embodies the state's economic policy, as formulated by the government and as revealed by its economic activities. In contemporary centrally planned socialist economies, state preferences determine the distribution of resources among consumption, military programs, and investment, as well as the compo-

* Reprinted from *Journal of Political Economy*, Vol. LXIX, No. 4 (August, 1961), pp. 341–54, by permission of The University of Chicago Press. Copyright 1961 by The University of Chicago Press. Jan Drewnowski is Program Director of the United Nations Research Institute for Social Development.

[1] When this was written I was a guest of the Center for International Studies, Massachusetts Institute of Technology, as a Ford Foundation exchange professor. I wish, therefore, to express my thanks to the Foundation, which made my work possible, and to all those economists in Cambridge, Massachusetts, with whom I had the opportunity to discuss many problems relevant to the subject of this paper. As it is impossible to give all their names here, I shall only say that my greatest debt is to Professor Paul N. Rosenstein-Rodan, from whom I received constant help and encouragement during my stay at M.I.T.

sition of military and investment output. However, a dual preference system exists in the sphere of consumer goods production, where state and individual preferences jointly decide the allocation of resources and distribution of goods.

Drewnowski distinguishes three possible combinations of state (planners') and individual (consumers') preferences, with increasing degrees of influence for the latter. In the "first-degree market economy," households possess only consumer choice in the purchase of consumer goods, the quantities of which are fixed by the planners. In the "second-degree market economy," consumer preferences also influence which goods are to be produced, with the resources allocated by the planners, by the existing plants producing consumer goods. In the "third-degree market economy," the pattern of new investments in plants producing consumer goods also responds to consumer demand. Even in the last case, however, planners' preferences determine the overall magnitude of consumption (its share in national product) and the amount of investment devoted to consumer goods industries. As Drewnowski notes, most of the Communist countries are now in transition from a "first-degree market economy" to a "second-degree market economy," extending the sphere of influence of individual preferences somewhat.

I. INTRODUCTION: PRESENT STATE OF THE DEBATE

THERE are queer traits in what is recognized today as the economic theory of socialism. Not only has it remained for a number of years in a stationary state which contrasts strangely with the dynamic growth in the number of descriptive works on socialist and particularly soviet economies, but also it takes an approach that is far from realistic and might even be termed utopian.[2] Incredible as it may seem, the convictions of the authors, rather than the realities of socialist economics, are taken as the basis for theories.

[2] A theory may be termed utopian if it can be shown not only that it is normative but that the system it regards as ideal cannot possibly work in practice. I believe it could be proved that the recognized theory of socialism is utopian, but I do not propose to prove it here. The fact that the theory is explicitly normative and remote from reality is a sufficient ground for criticism.

It can, of course, easily be explained why the economic theory of socialism started that way. When Pareto and, later, Barone discussed the working of the socialist state, no such state existed.[3] They solved a theoretical problem and that was all they could do. Mises, as everybody agrees now, was wrong in his main contention that economic calculation under socialism is theoretically impossible, but he may be forgiven for not taking into account the realities of socialist economics, as he certainly could not have possessed sufficient data at that time about the actual economic problems of the Soviet Union and how they were being solved in practice.[4]

But strangely enough when the discussion of the problem was resumed in the thirties it continued along the same lines. In replying to the arguments of Hayek and Robbins concerning the practical impossibility of economic calculation in socialism, Lange put forward his celebrated proposal for the application of the trial and error procedure in socialist economics.[5] This is a "decentralized decisions" approach which is an alternative to the "centralized decisions" approach of Pareto and Barone. Lange's solution was intended as an answer to criticism based on practical considerations, but in fact it had nothing to do with practice, that is, with the conditions that existed in the only place where socialism in practice could be found at that time—the Soviet Union. Lange's theory was a considerable intellectual achievement, but it did not explain any reality because its premises were never based on existing conditions.

A similar explicitly normative approach characterizes the next important work on the theory of socialism, Lerner's *Economics of Control.*[6] In the Introduction to his book Lerner explicitly states that he is concerned with the principles of a system that does not exist but that can "reap the benefits of both capitalist economy and collectivist economy." He calls his system a controlled economy "*to contrast it with the actual world.*"[7]

Lerner's analysis, though much more elaborate, does not differ essentially from Lange's. Consequently, this approach to the economic theory of socialism has come to be known as the Lange-Lerner approach. After all

[3] V. Pareto, *Cours d'économie politique,* Vol. II (Lausanne: F. Rouge; Paris: Pichou, 1897), pp. 91 f, 364 ff.; and his *Manuel d'économie politique* (Paris: V. Giard & Brière, 1909), pp. 362 ff.; E. Barone, "Il ministero della produzione nello stato collettivista," *Giornale degli economisti,* 1908; English trans. in F. A. Hayek (ed.), *Collectivist Economic Planning* (London: Routledge and Kegan Paul, 1935), pp. 245–90.

[4] L. Mises, "Die Wirtschaftsrechnung im sozialistischen Gemeinwesen," *Archiv für Sozialwissenschaften,* Vol. XLVII (1920); English trans., pp. 87–130 in Hayek (ed.), *op. cit.*

[5] F. A. Hayek, "The Present State of the Debate," pp. 201–43 in Hayek (ed.), *op. cit.;* L. Robbins, *The Great Depression* (London: Macmillan & Co., 1934), p. 151; O. Lange, *On the Economic Theory of Socialism,* ed. B. E. Lippincott (Minneapolis University of Minnesota Press, 1938), pp. 57–142.

[6] A. P. Lerner, *The Economics of Control* (New York: Macmillan Co., 1944).

[7] *Ibid.,* p. 2 (italics mine).

the years that have passed since the works were published, the Lange-Lerner theory still enjoys the status of a recognized theory of the socialist economy.

There is no doubt that the time is ripe for some attempt at reconsideration. A theory of socialism should start from an analysis of the existing socialist systems.[8] It should, of course, be a positive theory, free from normative judgments. These are evident and even commonplace conditions, but they are not easy to fulfil. I shall try to keep as close as possible to the realities of socialist economies and not to indulge in building castles in the air. A strictly positive theory can be constructed, however, only when the rational core of the real system under consideration can be discovered. This rational element is not always easy to detect. In such cases the theory must acquire some normative features and suggest solutions compatible with the general rational pattern of the system. Thus, though I shall try hard to be "positive," I shall often be moving on the boundary between "positive" and "normative," trespassing now and then into the "normative."

It is my conviction that the analysis of socialist economies must lead to an economic theory of socialism very much different from the theory of capitalism as it exists at present. The differences between the institutional frameworks of the two systems are very great indeed, though they are sometimes obscured by a terminology which calls socialist institutions by their old capitalist names. As a result of these institutional differences, the systems must work in different ways. The forces leading toward equilibrium are different and the equilibrium positions must be different.

This approach is in striking contrast to that which employs a mock-perfect competition equilibrium as a model for a socialist economy's equilibrium. When confronted with reality, such an approach must seem very strange indeed to an observer not aware of the history of the problem.

II. THE FOUNDATIONS OF THE THEORY OF SOCIALISM

All modern societies have a common characteristic of which little account is taken in economic theory. It can be stated as follows: the population has two ways of achieving its economic ends, the direct and the indirect way, or the individual and the collective way. The individual way consists of actions undertaken by individuals within the framework of existing restraints resulting from institutional, technological, and market

[8] The term "socialism" is used throughout this article in the sense in which Pareto, Mises, and Lange used it. It means a system in which all the means of production are owned by the state. It is perhaps useful to state this explicitly because in the discussion of practical problems the socialist economies have come to be known as "centrally planned" or "soviet type." But we shall retain the old term which, besides being shorter, has the merit of being diametrically opposite to "capitalism." This will help us now and again to show the contrasts that exist between capitalism and socialism.

conditions. The simplest pattern of those actions is made up of actions directed at acquiring income and actions directed toward spending that income to acquire goods that satisfy wants. The collective way consists of inducing the state authority to take actions that will satisfy the wants of the population.

Not all the economic objectives of individuals can be realized by the individuals' actions. The economic objectives a person has as an earner of income and as a consumer may, in most cases, be achieved in a direct way. He will base his choices on his preference function and act on the market by selling his labor and buying consumer goods. But the economic objectives a person has as a member of a nation, class, party, or group connected with some sort of activity (peasant, scientist, etc.) and also a number of long term consumers' objectives can be achieved only by the indirect way.

If an individual wants the economy to grow at a faster rate, he may not be able to achieve this objective by saving more out of his income; the result may even be the opposite of his desire. If an individual wants the advancement of science, better working conditions, or cheaper public utilities, he cannot achieve these by individual action. He cannot vote for these objectives with his dollars but has to vote at the election to bring to power a government that would have this sort of policy. If he wants more butter and fewer guns, he can achieve this, not by spending more on butter, but only by overthrowing the government that is sponsoring armaments.

The influence the population may have on the state is exerted through political channels by various means through which public opinion makes itself heard—by elections and, in some circumstances, by revolution. The degree of sensitiveness of the state to the interests and aspirations of the population may be taken as a measure of the degree of democracy in the political system. But we must not fall into the error of believing that the population ever transmits to the state detailed prescriptions as to the activities the latter has to undertake. From what we know of political programs, election platforms, and revolutionary slogans, we must infer that only broad lines of economic policy are explicitly transmitted from the population to the state. The state authority, being aware of the needs and wishes of the population, determines the particular objectives of its economic activity and makes appropriate decisions.[9]

[9] An interesting and apparently similar classification of social choices is made in K. J. Arrow's *Social Choice and Individual Values* (New York: John Wiley & Sons, 1951), chap. i. Arrow divides the decisions into political (expressed by voting) and economic (making use of the market mechanism). He aims to construct "a procedure for passing from a set of known individual tastes to a pattern of social decision making" (p. 2); but in the sphere of political decision this endeavor is frustrated from the outset by the well-known "paradox of voting." He then proceeds to discuss the impact of individual decisions on social choice under the familiar assumptions of welfare economics. This approach is very different from that made in the present

When people use the direct way to achieve their economic ends, they make their own decisions and act accordingly. Those decisions reveal their scales of values, which can be represented by individual preference functions.

The same is true of the state. If it makes decisions, it must have some implicit scale of values, and these can be represented by a "state preference function."[10] As was explained above, the state preference function emanates in a very general way from the wishes of individuals, but it is determined by the state and is not any sort of total of individual preferences.

In the national economy there exist, therefore, two systems of valuation: the multiple system of individual preference functions and the single state preference function.

The important point to bear in mind is that these two systems of valuation are not mere theoretical models but do exist in actual fact. They exist in the sense that the decisions based on each of them are a reality. The preference functions may not be consciously plotted by the subjects that "have them," but they can be "revealed" by analysis of the decisions based on them.

Preference functions upon which actual decisions and actions are based may be called "effective preference functions." Only effective functions can be revealed, and only such functions can be recognized as legitimate instruments of economic analysis.

Therefore, it is meaningless to have objectives that can be achieved only by the state as variables of individual preference functions. They are certainly not weighed by the individual against other objectives, and *there is no way of revealing his preferences concerning them.* It is illegitimate to say that they are part of an individual preference function. They belong to

---

paper, where the political decision is assumed to consist in electing the kind of government that would correspond to individuals' general ideas but where the detailed aims of state policy are formulated by the government itself. How those state aims (we shall call them state preferences) are arrived at (brain trusts, committee bargaining, lobbying, etc.) is not for economists to investigate, just as we always ignore the problem of why the consumers' preferences are what they are.

[10] I used the concept of a state preference function in an article on the theory of economic planning published in 1937 ("Próba ogólnej teorii gospodarki planowej," *Ekonomista*, 1937, No. 4; 1938, No. 1). The concept as used now differs in many important respects from the old one.

A line of approach that may be considered similar to this concept may be found in an earlier article by H. Zassenhaus, "Über Die Ökonomische Theorie der Planwirtschaft," *Zeitschrift für National Ökonomie*, Vol. V, No. 4 (1934); English trans. "On the Theory of Economic Planning," in *International Economic Papers*, No. 6 (1956), pp. 88–107. Brilliant as it was, the contribution of Dr. Zassenhaus never got the recognition it deserved, and in a few years the Lange-Lerner approach prevailed as the recognized theory. An even earlier, but probably better-remembered, article by M. Dobb, "Economic Theory and the Problems of Socialist Economy" (*Economic Journal*, Vol. XLIII, No. 172 [December, 1933], pp. 588–98), can be looked upon as a plea for recognition that a state preference function exists, though the author never used that term. Again, this article has not had much influence on the subsequent development of the theory of socialism.

the state preference function; they enter the state's scale of values as their significance is weighed by the state against other objectives of the same kind. They can be revealed as part of the state preference function.

All this is true of any system, capitalist or socialist. It may be noted here that, though the concept of a dual preference system has not been developed in theory,[11] in the discussion of the practical economic problems of capitalism it is being increasingly taken for granted that the targets of economic policy do not result from the signals of the market but are determined by the government's pursuing economic aims adopted with a view toward the future.[12] If we speak of a "big-push" or the conditions for a "take-off," or of an "implanted economic development," we admit this fact and urge a policy which would bring real benefits to consumers but would ignore consumers' sovereignty.[13] It is not the "invisible hand" of the market mechanism but the more and more prominent hand of the state that guides the economy under contemporary capitalism.[14] The significance of the dual-preference approach for the theory of a capitalist economy will not be elaborated here.

While it has been possible (though more and more inadequate) to base the economic theory of capitalism on one preference system only and to take account of the state activities but occasionally, this sort of approach is inadmissible for socialism. There the state plays too important a role to be ignored.

The theory of a socialist economy must be built upon the concept of

---

[11] It must be noted, however, that such a system was mentioned by O. Lange in a short passage on p. 96 of his *Economic Theory* (*op. cit.*); but he dismissed it as "not very probable."

[12] An emphatic statement of the independence of state investment decisions from consumers' preferences may be found in P. N. Rosenstein-Rodan, "Programming in Theory and in Italian Practice," in *Investment Criteria and Economic Growth* (Cambridge, Mass.: Center for International Studies, Massachusetts Institute of Technology, 1955), p. 24.

[13] P. N. Rosenstein-Rodan, "Notes on the Theory of the 'Big Push,'" (Cambridge, Mass.: Center for International Studies, Massachusetts Institute of Technology, 1957); W. W. Rostow, "The Take-off into Self-sustained Growth," *Economic Journal*, 1956; A. Bonné, *Studies in Economic Development* (London: Routledge & Kegan Paul Ltd., 1957), chaps. xi, xii.

[14] An early recognition of the existence of economic aims of the state can be found, naturally enough, in writings on public finance (see E. Lindahl; *Die Gerechtingkeit der Besteuerung* [Lund: Gleerup, 1919]; and also Mauro Fasiani, "Der gegenwartige Stand der reinen Theorie der Finanzwissenschaft in Italien," *Zeitschrift für Nationalökonomie*, Vol. III [1931/32], 652–91; Vol. IV [1932/33], 79–107, 357–88).

A more recent and very explicit recognition of the important role played by the capitalist state today may be found in J. Tinbergen, *Economic Policy: Principles and Design* (Amsterdam: North-Holland Publishing Co., 1956), particularly chap. i.

Another interesting contribution to the problem of state preferences under capitalism is found in a mimeographed memorandum by Ragnar Frisch, "Numerical Determination of a Quadratic Preference Function for Use in Macroeconomic Programming" (Oslo: Universitet Socialøkonomiske Institut, 1957). Frisch suggests a method of plotting preference functions from data collected by interviewing prominent politicians about the policies to be pursued by the state.

the dual valuation system—on the state preference function and on the system of individual preference functions.[15] In a socialist economy it is necessary, therefore, to analyze two sets of decisions, those of the state and those of the individuals.

To determine the sphere of influence of state decisions as against that of individual decisions is the central institutional problem of a socialist state. But it is a problem which exists also under capitalism. In fact, the difference in the location of the boundary between those two spheres may serve as a definition of capitalism as against some intermediate system. In what follows we will, however, be concerned exclusively with socialism.

III. SOME RELATED CONCEPTS OF WELFARE ECONOMICS

Before we proceed any further, it may be useful to make a few remarks about some concepts used in welfare economics that bear some resemblance to our state preference function but, in fact, differ from it in many important respects.

The greatest affinity can be discovered between the state preference function and the welfare function defined in the most general way.[16] The state preference function may be considered to be a special case of the general welfare function. But the interest of welfare economics has moved in a different direction. No concept of the state preference function, as it is understood here, has been developed. The most generally used form of a welfare function is one in which the utilities of different persons are ordered according to some not specifically defined ethical criteria.[17] As variables of the welfare function we have individual utilities, which, in fact, are not known (unless fragments of them are revealed ex post facto by consumers' market behavior), and the shape of the function is determined by ethical convictions held by the observer or attributed by the observer to somebody else. This sort of function is very far removed from

---

[15] We therefore dismiss as not realistic a "dictatorial model" of a socialist economy where only the valuations of the state are valid, as mentioned, for example, by Lange (*op. cit.*, p. 90). This approach to the economics of socialism cannot be described as a generally recognized theory but has found its way into a number of textbooks, probably on account of its simplicity. The "dictatorial model" may be looked upon as a limiting special case in a theory of socialism conceived in a more general way.

[16] See A. Bergson, "A Reformulation of Certain Aspects of Welfare Economics," *Quarterly Journal of Economics*, Vol. LII, No. 1 (February, 1938), p. 312. In P. A. Samuelson's *Foundations of Economic Analysis* (Cambridge, Mass.: Harvard University Press, 1958), the welfare function is given the form $W = W(Z_1, Z_2, \ldots)$, where the Z's represent all possible variables," and the function characterizes "some ethical belief, that of a benevolent despot or a complete egotist or of all men of good will, the misanthrope, the state, race or group mind, God, etc." (p. 221).

[17] Such a function would take the form

$$W = F(U^1, U^2, U^3, \ldots),$$

as in A. Bergson's "Socialist Economics," in *A Survey of Contemporary Economics*, Vol. I (ed. Howard S. Ellis) (Homewood, Ill.: Richard D. Irwin, Inc., 1948), p. 418.

any reality; it cannot be revealed by anyone's activities and will be of no use in our analysis of the socialist economy.

Nor can much virtue be found, for the purposes of a theory of socialist economics, in the otherwise very interesting attempt to derive "community" or "social" indifference curves from the individual preference curves.[18] This sort of summing-up process is never performed in practice and can be conceived only under unrealistic assumptions. It is essentially utopian. This is, in fact, admitted by many, if not by all, of those examining this concept.[19]

The state preference function contains the scale of values of the state and so can be considered a special case of the general welfare function. But, first, this scale of values is the scale of the state, which actually has authority over the economy; it is not just any ethically derived scale. Second, it is concerned not with individual utilities but with measurable quantities existing in the national economy. Third, it is observable and can be "revealed" by the actions of the state. In brief, it is an effective function.

The state preference function is not deduced from individual preference functions. To someone accustomed to the traditional way of thinking in terms of consumers' sovereignty this may seem improper. But, as explained above, in some special (but not at all irrelevant) way the state preference function represents the wishes of consumers. What is most important, it is a fact: it exists and manifests itself in observable economic actions.

IV. THE STATE PREFERENCE FUNCTION

A satisfactory theory of the socialist economy must be able to explain how a socialist economy actually works. Such a theory is, of course, the ultimate aim, but what is attempted in this paper is the much more limited objective of making the main elements of the socialist economy subject to the tools of economic analysis. I shall, therefore, state the problems rather than solve them; I shall remain on a high level of abstraction and be concerned only with the most crucial problems. The first concept we must tackle is that of the state preference function. This concept is significant in either system but is fundamental to the theory of socialism;

---

[18] The earliest use of this technique is in T. Scitovsky, "A Reconsideration of the Theory of Tariffs," *Review of Economic Studies*, Vol. IX (1941–42), No. 2, pp. 89–110. The most important contribution to this problem is P. A. Samuelson's "Social Indifference Curves," *Quarterly Journal of Economics*, Vol. LXX, No. 1 (February, 1956), pp. 1–22.

[19] See, for example, Samuelson, "Social Indifference Curves," p. 15.

Tinbergen "doubts the relevance of the question whether social welfare functions can or cannot be derived from individual ones. . . . For the time being . . . the theory of economic policy would be better to take the policy-maker's welfare function as its starting point. But, no doubt, this has to be a temporary attitude only" (*op. cit.*, pp. 14–15). While I am in full agreement with the main line of Tinbergen's argument, I, of course, strongly disagree with the last sentence in the quotation.

and it ought to be expressed in such a way as to make possible the substitution of numerical data for its variables. Second, a framework must be provided for analyzing the interrelation between the state and individual preference functions. All the more detailed analysis (for which, it is hoped, the approach presented here will provide a basis) is left to some future studies.

The preference function of the state has the same formal features as does the individual preference function. Its independent variables represent the means by which the state achieves its aims. They must be expressed in some measurable way.[20] The simplest solution would be to express those variables in quantities of final goods or services available in the national economy for consumption, investment, or export. The variables so expressed we may call the "goods" of the state preference function. These "goods" will usually be aggregates, such as food, clothing, rolling stock, etc. This implies a further problem of disaggregating the totals into particular goods, which may be a rather intricate process but which for the time being we shall ignore.

The value of the function which the state maximizes may be taken to represent some sort of "state utility"; but it may also have another significance which I shall explain later.

The function may be represented by an indifference map, the curves of which will be convex to the origin (decreasing marginal rate of substitution). This is a familiar property of a preference function, which can be accepted as a property of the state function without raising any serious problems; but it is not a very illuminating property. The important problem is the shape of the function. Even a fragment of it would suffice, but no state so far has published a white or blue book containing its preference function. The preference function is implicit in the state's activities, but it is never stated explicitly. However, neither is the consumer's preference function, and that has not prevented economists from making it the basic concept of economic theory.

The consumer's preference function has to be revealed,[21] and so has the state preference function. The consumer's preference function is revealed through the consumer's market behavior. This is not an ideal way of discovering the preference function, but we have no better device. Its main defect is that the consumer's preference function is revealed only after he has acted on the market. The manifestation of the consumer's preferences in the form of demand is an "ex post" phenomenon.

With the state preference function we are in a better position. We have not only ex post facto manifestations of the function in the form of

[20] If, therefore, we consider such a state aim as "education," we have to make it measurable by expressing it by the number of classrooms in use or, better still, by the number of classroom-hours per month or year.

[21] P. A. Samuelson, "Consumption Theory in Terms of Revealed Preference," *Economica*, New Series, Vol. XV, No. 60 (November, 1948), pp. 243–51.

actually executed policies of the state but also what we may call "declared targets of policy," which are "ex ante." In a socialist state these targets are officially determined and published as a national economic plan.

A published plan is, of course, a "co-ordinated" one (a term from the parlance of planning commissions), and that means not only that the plan is feasible in terms of resources and techniques but also that all the resources and technical possibilities are to be used fully. A plan determines the "ex ante" equilibrium of the system.

If this is the case, the point of equilibrium must be on the production-possibility curve. The shape of the production-possibility curve, at least in the range where production is practical, must be assumed to be known. Consequently, if we have a point on the production-possibility curve, we have also the transformation rate at this point and in its immediate vicinity.

But a "co-ordinated" and approved plan implies also that the targets of the plan correspond to what the state considers most desirable. Therefore, the co-ordinates representing the targets determine a point which is not only on the production possibility curve but also at the point on the curve that the state considers best. In other words, that point is a point of equilibrium determined by the production possibilities and the preferences of the state. A state indifference curve can be drawn through that point. Its slope would, of course, be equal to the slope of the production-possibility curve.

The segment of the state preference function directly adjoining the equilibrium point would therefore be revealed. It is, of course, only a small segment of the function, but it gives us important information: the rate of substitution between or relative valuation of the two state "goods" in the neighborhood of the equilibrium point.

The procedure may be generalized and applied to many goods, in which case a whole system of rates of substitution will be revealed. These rates will be equal to the slopes of the indifference curves of the state preference function near the equilibrium points. They may also be looked upon as relative shadow prices implicit in the state's decisions about quantities. We may call these prices "state preference prices." They constitute a price system connected to and consistent with the plan targets expressed in physical quantities. In its policies the state should maintain this link between quantities and prices as a condition of consistency. In other words, state preference prices ought to be included in the state plan as an important supplementary chapter to the chapter containing quantities.[22]

---

[22] As things happen now in socialist states, the prices are not part of the national plans. And it may be taken for granted that, if the state-preference-price criteria were applied, some inconsistencies in the plans would be discovered. This is exactly one of the points at which we have to introduce some normative element into our analysis.

The state preference prices are relative prices, but there is nothing to prevent us from making them absolute by expressing them in any arbitrary unit we may choose. Once we do that, the sum total of values of all products (which is being maximized by the state) ceases to be some "state utility"—an ordinal concept—and becomes a value of national product expressed in whatever units we choose—a quantity measurable in cardinal numerals. To distinguish it from the national product as understood in the ordinary way, we may call it the "state-preference national product."

There is really nothing new or surprising in this. The state-preference national product is a purely conventional concept, and a similar measure could be constructed for any preference function. It is only when there are numerous individual preference functions with utilities having no common measure that this concept cannot be applied. With a single state preference function the state-preference national product is merely one way of evaluating the real national income. A problem that is insoluble if we look at it from the point of view of many individual preference functions is, of course, simple if we start from one function only.[23] And again this simplified approach, which is of no use under individualistic assumptions, may be useful for our analysis of a socialist society.

What we have done is to show how the state preference function is revealed by the data that are declared by the state. This is a realistic approach, because in practice the socialist state determines plan targets in physical quantities, and the rates of substitution which indicate the shape of its preference function are implicit and have to be revealed. But this is not the only procedure that could be used. Contrary to what is possible with consumers' preferences, the state might very well declare not the production targets but the shape of the function itself. By confronting the preference function with production possibilities, the planners might then determine the production targets. To a theoretical economist, such a procedure presumably is simpler and states the issues more clearly. But what the opinion of the practical planner would be is an open question. What is really important is to have target quantities of "goods" consistent with transformation rates and state preference prices, both elements being equally valid parts of the national plan. This alone would be a great improvement on the present system because it would require an internally consistent model of the whole interdependent national economy and, consequently, would necessitate concentration on the determinateness of the system. This is important because overdeterminateness is the curse of socialist economies. And note that it is not an overdeterminateness of the theoretical model, which can trouble only the armchair economist counting his equations, but an overdeterminateness in practice which leads to uninvited and mostly unpredictable consequences.[24]

---

[23] P. A. Samuelson, "Evaluation of Real National Income," *Oxford Economic Papers*, Vol. II, No. 1 (January, 1950), pp. 1–21.

[24] By "overdeterminateness in practice" I mean the overdeterminateness of the system of decisions taken by the state. These decisions determine the "ex ante"

This has been, of course, a very simplified presentation of the problem. For practical planning purposes we must make much more elaborate assumptions. What is intended here is only to show the lines along which this sort of problem can be attacked.

V. THE ZONES OF INFLUENCE IN SOCIALIST ECONOMY

So far I have concentrated on the state preference function. But the crucial problem of an economic theory of socialism is the interaction of the state and individual preferences.

If we take a short-term view, we may abstract from the influence the individual has on the state preference function through political channels and consider the state and individual preference functions to be independent of each other.

There may be areas in which state and individual preferences do not meet, that is, areas in which each unit is confronted with possibilities depending only on natural or technical conditions. But where they meet they constitute restraints for each other. Each of them (or, rather, the activities resulting from each of them) becomes a part of the environment restraining the actions resulting from the other's preferences. We must try, therefore, to determine the zone in which state preferences are supreme (the zone of state influence), the zone in which individual preferences are supreme (the zone of individual influence), and the zone in which state and individual preferences meet (the zone of dual influence). To determine which part of the national economy belongs to which zone means to define the nature of the economic system in question.

Capitalism once was, or was, at least, considered, a system in which the whole national economy belonged to the individual zone. But in present-day capitalism there is usually some state zone and a quite significant dual-influence zone.

At this point one more important difference between the two systems must be stated: Capitalism is a system in which the boundary lines between the zones as defined above are fairly stable. The reason is, of course, the greater rigidity of economic institutions under capitalism. The most important single cause of this rigidity is the link that exists in capitalism between private property and production. This link is in fact a basic feature of capitalism. When there is private property in production, the organization of the system cannot easily be changed without affecting private property rights. Indeed, any encroachments by the state on the economic life of the country are difficult. Capitalism has certainly changed

---

equilibrium which, in socialism, is an emphatically practical phenomenon, since the state's decisions lead to real actions. The socialist system, like any system, cannot be either overdetermined or underdetermined "ex post," but, if it is overdetermined "ex ante," it determines itself "ex post" in a way not desired or expected by the planners.

in the last hundred years—the state- and dual-influence zones have expanded, and the individual zone has contracted. But the change has been slow and painful; the economic theory of capitalism tacitly recognizes this fact by taking the institutional framework of capitalism for granted and not bothering much about examining the consequences of its changes.

Socialism may be defined as a system in which the national economy is divided between the state-and the dual-influence zones. No individual zone exists under full socialism. The boundary between the state- and the dual-influence zone, however, may be anywhere in the range between the limiting case in which the whole national economy is in the state zone and that in which the state zone is not much more extensive than in capitalism. This makes socialism a system of which many different variants may exist and in which the change from one variant to the other can be made fairly easily and promptly by nothing more than a governmental decision, since many institutional rigidities characteristic of capitalism do not exist under socialism.

In socialism institutional changes are a part of the operation of the system. Changes in the position of the boundary between state- and dual-influence zones may occur at any time and may sometimes be instantaneous. Institutional changes inside each zone are even easier;[25] institutional change may often take less time than changes in capital equipment. The theory must take account of this and look upon institutional changes as a particular class of available alternatives.

This sort of approach would permit an economic theory more general in nature than the traditional theory of capitalism. In such a theory capitalism would be considered as a small range of special cases in which the zone of state influence is fairly limited and the institutional setting is fairly rigid. Socialism would be represented by a much wider range of special cases at the opposite end of the scale where no zone of individual influence is allowed but where one case can easily be transformed into another. Intermediate systems, such as "the welfare state," or "people's democracies on the way to socialism," can be defined in a similar way.

I must now attempt a more detailed analysis of the zones of state, dual, and individual influence, and try to determine the nature of the boundary line between those zones. This will require a theoretical model, which must be a simplification of reality, but I shall try to keep it as close as possible to what happens in socialist economies.

The state zone is the part of the national economy in which the scales of values are the preferences of the state. No consumers' preferences enter into the picture. In socialism this situation exists as a rule in the investment-goods industries, where resources, capital equipment, and products are all owned by the state.

---

[25] For example, changes in the sizes of enterprises, which are of considerable importance but cannot be discussed here because of limited space.

In all branches producing consumer goods there is the possibility of a dual-influence zone, with the boundary of the state zone being drawn differently in different cases.

Let us start with the limiting case and assume that all the national economy belongs to the state zone; consumers' preferences have no significance. The only restraints are then natural resources and techniques. This is the familiar theoretical dictatorship model. It corresponds roughly to "war communism," a system that existed in Soviet Russia for a short time during the civil war, 1918–20.

The quantities of all goods produced and the distribution of them among the members of the population are determined by the state. In other words, there is a full rationing system. This sort of model is not realistic in present circumstances and of little use except as a limiting theoretical case of the institutional alternatives. We may describe this case as a case of "no market economy."

The next alternative would be a system in which consumer goods are sold in the market. In this market the state is the only supplier and determines all the quantities brought for sale. The consumers (as buyers) are free to buy as much or as little as they want. The state, being anxious to sell what is produced, will adjust the prices to consumer demand so as to have no unsold stocks. It may, therefore, be said that quantities are fixed by the state, but prices are determined by the consumer demand according to consumers' tastes.

The difference between this case and the previous one is that the distribution of consumer goods has been transferred from the state zone to the dual-influence zone or, preferably, that the boundary between the zones has been moved so as to leave the distribution of consumer goods in the dual-influence zone and permit a market for consumer goods to be established.

On that market, it must be noted, consumers' preferences (strictly, consumers' demands) influence prices and the distribution of goods only. The quantities of particular goods are *not* affected, nor are the resources used in their production, nor the distribution of resources among particular producing plants.

This is a very typical situation in present-day socialist economies—an equilibrium between supply and demand on the market for consumer goods is maintained by adjusting prices, whereas quantities produced are not affected by demand at all and are governed by the central plan. We may call this case a "first-degree market economy."[26]

The "second-degree market economy" exists when the next adjoining

---

[26] It might be possible to conceive a *first-degree market economy* in which prices are fixed by the state and quantities determined by consumers' preferences. This possibility of applying alternative instruments of economic policy seems to be of considerable theoretical interest. It is probable that it could be applied to higher degree market economies. In the present article only the simplest case is presented.

range of economic variables is transferred from the state- to the dual-influence zone. In other words, these variables are made to depend not only on state but also on consumers' preferences. This "adjoining range" includes the quantities produced of particular consumer goods, the quantities of resources (excluding new investments) used in their production, and the distribution of resources among particular plants.

This would leave unaffected by the change the aggregate quantity of consumer goods, the aggregate quantity of resources used in producing consumer goods, and the capital equipment employed in industries producing consumer goods. The second (unaffected) set of quantities being kept constant, the first set of quantities will be determined by adjusting production to consumers' demands and maximizing profits in the whole consumer-goods sector. The principle of maximization of profits would assure rational distribution of resources and the production of rational quantities of particular goods.

The second-degree market economy corresponds roughly to the system aimed at by the "decentralization reforms" and "model reconsiderations" which are at present taking place in the people's democracies.

The "third-degree market economy" exists when the determination of the pattern of new investments in plants producing consumer goods depends on the consumers' demands for finished products. This means that decisions concerning what sorts of investment are to be made and to which plants they should be assigned are transferred from the state- to the dual-influence zone. The aggregate quantities of produced consumer goods, of resources used, and of new investments remain in the state zone.

This simple classificatory system may be made more complicated in many ways; for example, the consumer-goods sector may be divided into a number of subsectors. But our aim here is simply to demonstrate how the interaction of state and consumers' preferences and their differing spheres of influence can be taken into account.

One more important observation might be added: As a result of the dual influence of the state and the consumers, the socialist economy will have two independent sets of prices, one coming from the state preference function and one from the consumers' preference functions. Both systems of prices are rational and "correct" in their particular way. The "state" prices will be applied to all dealings between state enterprises and will be used in all national accounting calculations. The "consumers' " prices will apply to sales by state enterprises to consumers. The coexistence of these two sets of prices must be a characteristic of a rationally managed socialist economy.[27]

---

[27] This opinion has a normative element in it. The necessity of two simultaneous systems of prices is not generally recognized. No clear, uniform principle for determining prices has so far been accepted in socialist countries.

VI. CONCLUSIONS

The aim of this article has been to lay a basis for a realistic theory of a socialist economy. It started from the fact that there are two sets of preference functions that are effective in a national economy: the preference functions of the population, which manifest themselves in purchases and sales in the market, and the state preference function, which is expressed by the economic plans and policies of the state. Both are necessary to express the economic interests and aspirations of the population. The population influences the state preference function through political channels. A perfect democracy might be defined as a system in which the state's preferences represent people's interests in an accurate way. The examination of the working of these political channels is, however, outside the scope of economics and must be left to political science. What the economist has to do is to take account of the observable fact that two systems of preference exist and are sources of decisions in every economy and to try to understand the results of their interaction. The existence of dual preference systems ought to be comprised in the economic theory of any system, but it is basic to the development of a theory of the socialist system. From these assumptions some fundamental propositions for the economic theory of socialism were derived.

The preferences of the state were examined in some detail. It was found that in a contemporary socialist state they exist in an implicit form but may be "revealed" by the declarations and activities of the state.

A method was suggested for attaching numerical values to the state preference system. It could be used to make the socialist system internally consistent and not overdetermined.

Once the concept of the state preference function was defined, its interaction with individual preference functions had to be explained. The possibility of various institutional arrangements was discussed and the principles of interaction stated. It was suggested that this might lead to a more general theory that would embrace both the theory of capitalism and the theory of socialism as special cases. To explain the interaction of state and individual preferences, the device of zoning the national economy was introduced, the zone of dual influence being the crucial one. It was noted that some sorts of market exist in that zone. Their properties differ considerably from those of capitalist markets.

All this has been a suggestion for a new approach to the economic theory of socialism. The theory itself still remains to be worked out.

It is possible to list some fundamental problems that ought to be examined first. The working of the markets under "zoning" conditions is, perhaps, the most important problem. Particular attention should be paid to the labor market, which also falls under the "zoning" system but was not discussed here. Then comes the problem of the socialist state enterprise, which has to take decentralized decisions consistent with the preferences of the state. Collective consumption, a feature of socialism, should be examined along with the problem of the markets. Then, of course, an analysis of growth must be initiated, since growth problems are crucial in every socialist system. The investigation of monetary problems may be considered less urgent, but would present ample scope for concepts differing widely from those used in capitalism.

Very much remains to be done. It is hoped that the approach suggested in this article will be of use in that work.

9. ON THE THEORY OF THE CENTRALLY ADMINISTERED ECONOMY: AN ANALYSIS OF THE GERMAN EXPERIMENT*

Walter Eucken

In this comprehensive article, Eucken analyzes in detail the problems and weaknesses of a centrally planned economy, as illustrated by the operation of the Nazi German economy. Almost all of his analysis, however, applies as well to centrally planned socialist economies, as the selections in Part III show.

Eucken explains how plans for the production and distribution of goods are made in the centrally administered economy. He stresses the many serious problems caused by the movement from economic calculation in value terms to planning and allocation in physical terms. In this connection, he points out how the central authorities relied for the fulfillment of their plans on the illegal activity and unreported inventories of individual firms. Eucken shows the essential differences between market economies and centrally administered economies in investment decisions, economic fluctuations, the distribution of income, and international trade. Thus, he concludes, any use of markets and prices to direct the economy necessarily curtails the power of the central administration to control it.

* Reprinted, with permission, from *Economica*, New Series, Vol. XV, No. 58 (May, 1948), pp. 79–100, and No. 59 (August, 1948), pp. 173–93. The article was translated from the German by T. W. Hutchinson. Walter Eucken was Professor of Economics at the University of Freiburg, Germany.

INTRODUCTION

1. AFTER 1936 the German economy came more and more under central direction and administration. This was not the result of a conscious effort of policy to create a new form of economic organization. It was rather a result produced accidentally. It was the full-employment policy which started the movement, and it was the implementation of this policy which led step by step towards a centrally administered economy ("Zentral-verwaltungswirtschaft").

In 1932–33 the full-employment policy began with public works, expansion of credit, a cheap money policy, and a pegging of the exchange rate. As this policy threatened to bring a sharp rise in prices, a general price-freeze was ordered in 1936. Germany—like many other countries since then—entered upon a period of "repressed inflation." Prices ceased to give expression to the scarcity of goods and services on the markets. This state of affairs gave rise to the creation of a central administrative apparatus to direct the economy, to supervise foreign trade, to allocate the most important raw materials such as coal, iron and cement, to weigh up priorities, distribute licences and so on. This was the beginning. With the growing danger of war, and with its actual outbreak, the measures of central administration and direction played an increasingly important role in the economy. It was necessary to concentrate productive resources on armaments and to force up the rate of investment. There was the growing pressure of an expanded but immobilized supply of money. So more and more branches of production, and even the distribution of labor supplies and consumers' goods, came under the orders of the central planning authorities.

It was not that the *whole* everyday economic life of the country was controlled by the central administration through the direction of labor, production orders, compulsory deliveries, rationing and so on. On the contrary, important markets remained free for a long time. Only in recent years did barter develop on a large scale, when the German people not only got their rations of bread, potatoes, or meat, from the central authorities, but tried to obtain food and other consumers' goods by barter, or grew vegetables and potatoes for themselves. Then different forms of economic organization were combined together. But since 1938 it was *one* of these forms which dominated, that of the centrally administered economy.

The following pages are concerned almost exclusively with this element in the German economic system ("Wirtschaftsordnung"), and not with the very important problems of money and barter which arose in the course of this interesting episode. An economic order in reality is always made up of a combination of different pure forms. We are only concerned here with one of these. A centrally administered economy is not to be confused with one where all property is collectively owned. Certainly, central administration and direction of an economy can be combined with collective ownership of property, as, for example, in Russia since 1928. But this combination is not necessary. The interesting point is that in Germany the means of production remained predominantly in private ownership, and farms and factories alike continued to belong mainly to private individuals and companies. But the private owners could only dispose over their means of production to a limited extent. There was widespread requisitioning of industrial stocks, which were only released for definite purposes consistent with the central plan. We can say, in fact, that for the economic process as a whole, it was not the plans and actions of individual businesses and households that were decisive, but the plans and orders of the central authorities.

2. What questions do we want to put about the German experiment? In our case, a question which has been much discussed, and which has shown itself to be a fruitful one: are the same economic "laws" valid in the centrally administered economy as in the exchange economy?

Economists have given two fundamentally different answers to this question. J. S. Mill spoke of "the very different laws" which held for the competitive as compared with the collectivist economy. Similarly also Dietzel.[1] In contrast with these "dualists," the "monists" hold that the economic processes of an exchange and of a collectivist economy—two concepts usually not at all precisely defined—are essentially similar. This was the view of Wieser, Pareto, and especially Barone. The point of view of these writers has been widely accepted, and on the whole the monists predominate.

Who is right? Is the fundamental logic of economic action really the same in the commercial as in the socialist society, as Schumpeter has recently held?[2] Or, are these two quite different worlds? This is much more than a purely academic question. In the economic life of this century both methods of direction are being applied, that of the exchange economy and that of the centrally administered economy. The history of our time offers for our analysis, as to our forefathers it did not, many experiments in the central administration of economic life. We are dealing with this one experiment. Can we understand the economic phenomena of the twentieth century if we approach them with a single unified theoretical apparatus created for the analysis of the exchange economy? Or is it necessary to work out a special theory of the centrally administered economy to do justice to economic reality?

---

[1] J. S. Mill, *Logic*, book 6, chap. 10, para. 3; H. Dietzel, *Theoretische Sozialökonomik* (1895), pp. 85 ff.

[2] Barone, in *Giornale degli Economisti*, 1908; Pareto, *Manuel*, pp. 362 ff.; and Schumpeter, *Capitalism, Socialism, and Democracy* (New York: Harper and Bros., 1942), chap. 16.

Wieser and Barone had no knowledge of such definite examples as we have. Of course, historical cases of a predominantly centrally administered economic order are numerous, for example those of Egypt or of the Incas. But economic processes in our modern industrial age are so much more complex and comprehensive, and the tasks of direction so much more difficult, that these older examples are of secondary interest. Economists today have material before them quite unknown to their predecessors.

Our analysis of the German experiment was undertaken just at the moment when this experiment was coming to its close. The direction of the economy by central administration broke down in 1946–47. Procedures and forms pertaining to monetary and barter economies, and to an economy of self-sufficient household units, began to spread. But this investigation is not a historical one; nor is it an obituary notice. Our aim rather is to get a grasp of the general principles which German experiences can teach. It is agreed that the direction of economic life by a central administration came about in Germany mainly for purposes of war. Frequently improvisations had to suffice, instead of the long-term planning possible in peace. What is simply a peculiarity of war conditions must not be attributed to the centrally administered economy.

I. THE ECONOMIC PROCESS AS A WHOLE

1. How a Central Administration Works

The study of the organization of an exchange economy begins with the procedures of individual firms or households, let us say, in a leather factory. It is ascertained that the firm bases its plans on price and cost calculations, that is, on the relation of the prices of the products to the prices of the factors of production. This is what is decisive in guiding production. In this way each firm controls, in its own sphere, a fraction of the economic process, and the process as a whole is controlled by means of prices.

The study of a firm in a centrally administered economic order—for example during the German experiment—leads to quite another conclusion. Our leather factory produces on the orders of the Leather Control Office. This "Control Office," "Department" or "Planning Branch" ("Fachabteilung" or "Planstellee") allocates raw hides and auxiliary materials. It gives the firm its instructions to produce, and disposes of the leather it produces. For knowledge as to how the plans are formed by which the economy is guided in a centrally administered system, we must go to these control offices. There were "Controls" for textiles, clothing, glass, pottery, iron and so on. How did this central direction work out?

In four stages:—

First, there was the collection of statistical material for which the

Controller would have at his disposal a Statistical Section. This primary importance of statistics is a characteristic of the centrally administered economy. The statisticians tried to assemble for the planning authorities all the important data necessary: thus, for example, equipment, storage capacity, the need for storage space, the needs for coal and electricity, the production and import of raw materials, the production and uses of, for example, leather, textiles or other raw materials and other products. From this statistical material a quantitative balance-sheet was obtained which put the supplies against the consumption for the preceding year, half year, or quarter.

The statistics had to follow precise orders with regard both to their collection and treatment. They formed the foundation for the planning itself which was the *second* stage of the process. This consisted of drawing up programs for requirements and supplies, and for the means by which the two were to be balanced.

It is an essential point that the figures planned for requirements had their source only partially in the demands of the higher authorities, who would be requiring for purposes of armaments, or investment in general, particular quantities of iron, machinery, leather, etc. Another part originated with other users ("Bedarfsträger"), that is, mostly other control offices. Thus for example, leather would be ordered by the Shoe Control, or the Machinery Control, while the Leather Control ordered tanning materials, oils, fats, coal and so forth from the control offices responsible. Requirements always came in to the particular planning branch or control office collectively, or in aggregates ("gebündelt"). It is important that at this very early stage in drawing up the plan, standardization of goods became a necessity. Determining the leather requirements, for example, of the Shoe Control was all the more difficult the greater the variety of types of shoe in production. Central planning requires standardization.

After the centrally administered economy had been working some time, the planning offices often used the figures for earlier planning periods, which could be ascertained with precision. The figures were intended for the *future* planned quantities, but were taken over without further scrutiny from previous plans. There was a danger here that the necessary consistency with the facts of the present position might be lacking. For this reason the central authorities higher up, for example in the Ministry of Economics, often had occasion to warn against the exuberance of the statisticians. For example, it was on one occasion explained that: "However much planning may require a statistical basis, it must never be forgotten that statistics can only relate to the past. The outward form which planning assumes, that is, balances of figures, is not the essence of planning, which is rather an active shaping of the future." Incidentally, the calculating of needs per head of the population was held of small significance, as it took no account of local and occupational differences.

With regard to supplies, the principal item apart from imports and drawing on stocks, was, of course, production. Here the principle was laid down that production had to be estimated on the basis of the narrowest bottleneck. For instance, equipment and raw materials might be ample, but if it was coal or labor that was in short supply, it was in accordance with *these* that plans had to be drawn up. As bottlenecks were constantly shifting, the basis of the plan had constantly to be altered. The real art of this sort of central planning lay in recognizing promptly where the bottleneck was to be expected next.

Over the balancing of requirements against supplies, long battles were necessary, and we shall be dealing with these repeatedly later on. The many single control offices fought for allocations of more coal, or transport, or labor. On the other side, the requirements of each "consuming" party, every one trying to get hold of as much leather, textiles or petrol as possible, had to be cut down. The attempt would be made first at the level of the individual Control Office, by lengthy negotiations, to get the different "consumers" to moderate their demands. But the higher authorities took a hand from the start. They did so, in the *first* place, by fixing grades of priority, and *secondly*, by giving the decision in cases of conflict.

As an instance for the fixing of priority rankings, the petrol arrangements may be taken. First, in November, 1941, it was ordered that petrol was to be used only for war purposes in the strict sense. Allocations were to be made on the basis of the following priorities:

1. For providing the population with food and fuel.
2. For clearing railway stations and docks.
3. For maintaining agricultural production.
4. For sanitary organization and the police.
5. For firms on important war work and for the building plans of the Plenipotentiary Authority for Special Problems of Chemical Production.
6. For providing for the armaments and other production decisive to the war effort.
7. For providing for the building plans of other industries decisive for the war effort.

For the valuing and directing of the stream of goods the grading of needs in this way was essential, and the individual control offices had to proceed accordingly. If no agreement was arrived at, let us say, as to how much coal the Leather Control should get, the Minister of Economics himself had to decide.

The results of this procedure were set down in a Budget or Balance Sheet ("Mengenbilanz"), for a quarter or half a year, or for a whole year, according to the peculiarities of each process of production. Here is an outline of one of these Budgets:

OUTLINE BUDGET

Supplies	*Consumption*
1. Home production	1. Home consumption (arranged according to uses)
2. Additions from occupied territories	2. Needs of occupied territories
3. Imports	3. Exports
1—3 Total of current supplies	1—3 Current consumption
4. From stocks	4. Additions to stocks
1—4 Total supplies	1—4 Total consumption

Under heading 1 on the right (home consumption), it would be set out in detail how much, say, leather, had been fixed for the armed forces, for agriculture, for machinery, for shoes, and so on.

That is what the plans of the centrally administered economy looked like. They consisted of a long series of interlocking budgets of one control authority after the other. The controls for coal, iron, electricity, petrol, leather, textiles, and so on, set out their budgets which together made up the plan as a whole. But the fitting together of the detailed programs was brought about through the general directions (e.g., priority rankings) of the higher authorities, and through their actual intervention in many particular cases. Thus, although the control officers carried out and worked out the programs, they were dependent on, and subordinate to, the ministeries and other central offices. That was how the planning process was unified.

The *third* stage was the issuing of production orders to individual firms. The production of the firms was fixed in terms of quantities for particular periods of time, and with regard to varieties and qualities. Requisitioned raw materials were released to the individual factories for their production, and orders for the disposal of the resulting product were issued. The very difficult task of working out production orders for individual firms was often carried out through industrial organizations like the "Reichsgruppe Industrie," cartels, associations, etc. Experts had to be used who were at the same time highly interested parties, and, similarly, organizations which were private pressure-groups. We shall be returning, also, to this subject.

Fourthly, and finally, there was the check-up on results. Firms were obliged continuously, either quarterly, monthly, or even daily, to report their stocks and production, and the control offices had continually to be checking that the actual figures and the "programmed" figures agreed. Shortfalls might be traceable either to particular firms, or to the non-arrival of allotted raw materials, or through labor being drawn off by other control offices, and so forth.

In any case, the heads of the control offices had to intervene. So the carrying out of the plans was accompanied by continual negotiations and running battles. In the end another factor would intervene in this checking up on the plans. The plans were naturally often being carried through months, or even a year, after their original working out. Meanwhile the data had altered, for instance, with regard to coal supplies. It was then necessary to revise the plans and production orders.

This was how the four interconnected stages proceeded and were continually repeated. Other centrally administered economies might proceed in a similar way or in a different way. What is the economic significance of this procedure?

2. The Directing Mechanism

Let us consider for a moment a small, closed, self-sufficient, household economy ("Eigenwirtschaft"), a community of thirty people, who produce for themselves everything they consume, and are under the authority of a single individual. The task of directing such an economy would be as follows: the director day by day has to decide how the factors of production shall be combined, where each worker is to work, who on the potato field, who in the forest, and what tools each shall have at his disposal. At the same time he has to decide as to the use of the land, buildings, livestock, and transport. He has to decide also the time-structure of production, that is, as to investment and savings. This is only possible if the director is clear the whole time as to the importance of different requirements, and how much each unit of the factors of production can contribute, in each different use, to satisfy the community's needs. All these valuations are interdependent. If, for example, the director decides to build a bridge, that is, to invest, then *all* values are altered. Each unit of the means of production, an hour's work on the potato field, or in the forest or the stables, gets a different relative significance and a general shifting may prove necessary.

Economic calculations run in three directions. The planner constantly examines how far the factors of production in their previous use and occupation have actually met the needs of the community. These cost calculations relating to the *past* are the basis of the plans for the *future.* Plans for the future are tentatively built up from past experience, the task being to meet *existing* scarcities, or those expected in the near or distant future. Economic calculation, therefore, is made up out of examination of the past and projection into the future, with attention to the present. Each individual unit of consumers' goods and means of production is allotted its niche in the economic cosmos by the plans of the directing authority.

With division of labor, and an economy of many millions of people, there is a corresponding task. But in this case the direction will not be set by calculations by the individual. Rather, the task will be to find *the form of organization for economic life best suited to a satisfactory direction of the economic process from the point of view of the needs of the community*.

The particular solution to the problem of direction which the centrally administered economy in Germany arrived at, had two essential characteristics. (1) Planning and direction were based on round aggregate valuations without individual values or calculations of marginal cost. (2) As economic calculation had no compelling force behind it, this method of direction was able to survive for a long time.

(1) (*a*) To take the first of these two points: the offices of the central administration worked with aggregate valuations derived from the calculations of the statisticians.

Who made these valuations? In the first place they were proposed by the sectional control offices. In our example, the Leather Control proposed to distribute leather among different users (e.g., the armed forces, footwear, industrial purposes), according to the users' own valuations. After negotiations with the "consumers," alterations would be made; that is, an attempt would be made to bring the valuations of the Leather Control into equilibrium with those of the "consuming" control offices. The dealings were always in mass quantities. Values were not given to single units but were calculated for total quantities, perhaps for five or eight thousand tons at a time. These aggregate valuations, and thereby the direction by the control office of the factors of production and of consumers' goods, were supported by the fixing of priority gradings by the higher central authorities which we have just referred to. But these priority grades were always ineffective. They were too crude, and the individual grades were made up of too many different kinds of needs. (For example, Grade three, "petrol for maintaining agricultural production.") Secondly, these gradings took insufficient account of the decreasing importance of particular types of need as they came to be satisfied. Finally, they took no account of the supply position with regard to complementary goods. A decree of the Central Planning Office of December, 1944, deals with this very clearly: "The problems of directing production by the crude process of priority grades become more and more difficult as scarcities increase. Unimportant production must not merely be slowed down, but stopped altogether. To fix an order of priority for important production in accordance simply with the nature of the product must lead to serious mistakes and misdirection, if the supply position of the consumer is not taken into account. The provision of single screws, which may be all that is needed to complete some agricultural machinery, may be much more important than supplying the same screws to a tank factory, which has a much higher priority, but which will need the screws only some months ahead. The various levels of need, in conditions of general shortage, cannot be dealt with by priority orders. Particularly with the present strain on all the means of production, all offices responsible for directing production must maintain a close scrutiny, to ensure that each item as it is produced is directed to the right destination. I lay it down that the time has come to enforce the principle: 'Planning instead of Priorities.' I decree that with effect from January 1st, 1945, all priority rankings lapse."

If particular sectional controls were unable to agree about aggregate values, the decision had to be made higher up by central authorities. This is clearly shown in a decree of 1942: "Every effort is to be made by the sectional controls, in agreement with the consuming organization, to fit requirements to productive possibilities. Only in exceptional cases, when a decision of this kind is not possible, may it be referred to the Ministry concerned. If the planning office and the consuming organization are not under the authority of the same Ministry, the decision must be made by a common superior authority."

No values could be reckoned in individual detailed quantities. Decisions had to be made daily about single tons of iron or copper, or about individual workers. Where and for what purpose were these factors to be used? What value had they in each of the many various possible uses? Where and how were they to be used for the maximum satisfaction of needs? These questions could not be answered by such round aggregate valuations. If there were 1,000 cbm. of wood to be disposed of, this would be distributed in round quantities for fuel, mining, artificial silk and so on, without any full consideration being possible with regard to particular qualities.

(*b*) Some sort of cost calculation did find a place in the set up. But this cost accounting was also of a "round" aggregate kind. When the Petrol or Leather Control made allocations to the different "consuming" parties or sectional controls, they were continually comparing the services and foregone services which petrol and leather in general rendered in different uses. Also, in cases of conflict, when the responsible Ministry was asked for a decision, say, as to how much leather was to go for shoes and how much for machinery, the decision was made on a general cost comparison. Costs were made after general considerations as to the aims of the economic system. It would be considered whether these general aims would be better served by using leather for workers' shoes or for machinery. The services rendered in one direction to the overall plan were weighed against those foregone in another direction. Thus, however generally and imprecisely, there was some consideration of cost questions.

Certainly any calculation of marginal costs was impossible: for example, in one province in 1945 there were 1,000 tons of iron to distribute. Iron was needed by all sorts of branches of the economy, by handworkers, engineering, textiles, railways, repair works and so on. How many tons should each particular branch of industry and each firm receive? Should the textile industry get 80 tons? Or more? Or less? A choice had to be made. Here also cost considerations were weighed up. The services iron could render in this use and that were compared. But the value of *single tons* used in one way or another could not be calculated. So values were reckoned in round aggregates, and distribution followed according to general estimates of this kind.

(*c*) As has been explained, a comparison of realized and planned figures would be made in order to compare actual production with that planned.

But there was no real economic accounting. The quantities set out in the plans were compared with the quantities actually used or produced by the firms. But whether the factors of production were used economically, whether, that is, the planned cost figures were rightly worked out or in need of amendment, could not be deduced by comparing the planned and the actually realized figures. A tile works for example would be allotted far more coal than it needed, and this would be corrected only many months later. If the figures of actual production agreed with those planned, then there were no grounds for any correction. This comparison of planned and actual figures afforded no possibility of approaching an optimum combination of factors by trial and error. And the control offices realized this.

(2) (*a*) *The compelling force of economic calculation:* The price system in an exchange economy is not merely a measure of scarcity or a calculating apparatus (the efficiency of which, incidentally, we are not concerned to judge here). The price system, rather, is a controlling mechanism of compelling force. If costs exceed returns, the discrepancy forces the firm in the long run to make a change or to close down. To put it in another way, if price relationships are such that the prices of the factors of production necessary for producing a good are higher than the price obtainable for this good, then there must be a change.

But in the centrally administered economy, valuations—themselves arrived at in a different way—play a different role. For example: during the war a silk-weaving factory was built at C. (Hanover). Even from rough "aggregate" valuations it was clear that this location was unsuitable, and that the Crefeld silk-weaving factories could produce much more cheaply. The consumption of iron, cement, machinery and labor for the new factory in C. was unnecessary and a wrong investment. This could have been ascertained even by a rough aggregate value-cost comparison. The factors of production could have served the needs of the plan better in a different use. Nevertheless the decision to build was carried out. Personal considerations turned the balance. In the exchange economy, the factory in C. would have been condemned as a failure. In the centrally administered economy, where there is no automatic process of selection, it could be built and kept working. For these overall valuations have no compelling force behind them. Economic science should pay more attention to this peculiarity of economic calculation in a centrally administered economy, for it exercises a significant influence on the way in which the economic process works out.

(*b*) How are these facts to be explained? How is it that in the centrally administered economy economic calculation exerts no decisive force? The purpose in calculating costs in a perfectly competitive system is well known from the textbooks. Costs show what values the factors of production could realize in an alternative use. All sorts of needs, effectively backed by the purchasing power of income-receivers, struggle for the versatile factors, and the decision is made by price-cost calculations, in which costs represent foregone utilities. Production *must* meet needs backed by purchasing power. This is the compelling "*must*" of economic calculation. Through the agency of cost calculation, it is effective needs which control the productive process. Certainly, in monopolistic or oligopolistic markets the directing power of the consumers is essentially prejudiced and weakened.

In the centrally administered economy, there is quite another relationship between needs and supplies. The tension between the two finds no effective expression in the markets. Demand and supply for iron, coal, and all other goods do not originate with different independent economic individuals, each with his own plans. Rather, the fixing of needs and the direction of production are in a single hand. The planning authorities consequently proceed by first fixing the requirements for coal, bread, houses, and so on, and then adjusting the productive process to these needs by their aggregate valuations and production orders. But they do not have to proceed like this. They can also proceed subsequently by altering the consumption side of the equation, which is then adjusted to the production side. Allocations of textile goods can suddenly be cut or the construction of a new factory halted. Consumers cannot control the central administration. All economic power is concentrated in the central administration, which is thus itself subject to no controlling mechanism.

Perhaps this may be regarded as a weak point in the centrally administered economy. In fact, it is only a weak point if the maximum satisfaction of needs is regarded as the purpose of production. The absence of any compelling force in value and cost estimates is at the same time a source of strength, for it makes full employment comparatively simple to bring about. We shall return later to this point at greater length. Furthermore, the political authority is able, in the centrally administered economy, to shape developments in economic life in accordance with its political objectives, regardless of cost calculations.

3. The Role of Prices

We shall study this question also from two points of view: (1) What role did prices play in Germany? and (2) What general lessons are to be derived from German experience?

(1) German economic policy was concerned as far as possible to control the economic process by indirect methods. Here, for example, is what an important decree had to say: "All planning must have the aim of exercising the maximum directive effective effect on the economy with the minimum of interference. Interventions are unnecessary so long as individual firms voluntarily cooperate in the policy laid down by the State, or where, from considerations of purely private self-interest, their actions correspond with the requirements of the nation." On this principle, an attempt was made to avoid all direct control over intermediate stages of

the productive process. The central control of weaving, for instance, made possible indirectly the control of spinning.

From the efforts of the central authorities to control the economic process indirectly, rather than by direct order, it was a short step to attempting the use of prices, and this attempt was actually made.

A. In order to be able to use prices as an instrument for controlling economic life, the Ministry of Economics and the Price Commissioner endeavored to unify and improve accounting and the calculations of their profits by private firms. Particularly as deliveries for the armed forces gained in importance, very precise instructions as to cost accounting were issued. The economic calculation of many German firms was markedly improved and unified at this time. At certain points too, prices were used with success to achieve a combination of the factors of production somewhat nearer to the optimum, for instance with regard to the production of munitions for which no former prices existed.

At first, in these cases, the costs of production of the individual firms were calculated, and prices fixed accordingly for each individual firm on the basis of its costs. Consequently, the firms had no interest in working economically, for profits were a percentage of costs, and were greater if costs were high than if they were low. Therefore, in 1940, to induce firms to produce economically, another system of calculating prices was introduced: on the delivery of the munitions a uniform price was paid, reckoned in accordance with the costs of an average enterprise. A stimulus was thus given to improved production methods in order to make profits. This procedure was later much refined.

Particular achievements of this kind do not alter the fact that the prices, as they existed, were inadequate for controlling economic life as a whole. The current prices expressed the scarcity relationships of the autumn of 1936. Any change had been prevented by the price freeze. If the plans of the central authorities had envisaged meeting a requirement equal approximately to the earlier demand, then the prices and price relationships would have remained serviceable longer. But the opposite was the case: public works, and investment for armaments purposes, brought about big discrepancies between the centrally planned needs and the earlier demand curves. The prices fixed for iron, coal, tiles and so forth, no longer expressed the relationship between needs and supplies as these were laid down in the plans of the central authorities. Calculations based on these prices for products and for the means of production could not command the factors of production to meet the needs of the plan; and profit and loss calculations and budgets gave no information as to whether the factors of production were being combined in the optimum way for the production of the goods as planned by the central authorities.

No improvement in the methods of calculation could get round this fact. The prices which the firms reckoned with in their books failed as an expression of scarcities, and so lost their controlling function.

B. This made a second question all the more important: would it not have been possible to fix prices afresh? The prices of 1936 were useless for the purpose of reducing the aggregate valuations of the central authorities to prices for particular quantities. But would it perhaps have been not impossible to do this by new prices? The existing prices represented a long obsolete system of data. Couldn't new prices be fixed which would have given the maximum support to the plans of the central administration?

Two methods were discussed in connection with this problem: (1) was it perhaps possible for higher authorities themselves to fix important prices afresh? Or (2), if this was not possible, could not the prices be refixed by a temporary application of the market mechanism?

To take a particular example in Germany, namely that of the price and use of copper-beechwood. Almost throughout the whole of the nineteenth century beechwood had been used only for fuel and charcoal. Owing to a series of discoveries in the last 50 years it found many new uses and gained considerably in importance. There was the discovery that the soaking of the wood with tar would turn beech logs into railway sleepers of high quality. The discovery of artificial drying and steaming methods led to beech being used on a wide scale for furniture and woodwork of many kinds. Many discoveries in the plywood industry again considerably extended the range of uses. Finally, there was the discovery which made beechwood a basic material for the production of cellulose and opened up a further field of consumption.

What would constitute a reasonable distribution of the continual supplies of beechwood between these almost unlimited uses if an optimum utilization was to be obtained? Without doubt, the pegged price of beechwood as compared with other timber prices, and with most other prices, was much too low. It had been kept at the same level since 1932. Would it not have been reasonable, by raising the price of beechwood, to ensure an efficient use of particular qualities and quantities?

The forestry authorities had several times examined the question as to whether a new and higher price for beechwood should be fixed, but the right price could not be discovered. The central forestry administration only knew that the current price for beechwood was too low. It was able to get a rough conception of the new value of beechwood and thus could make a rough aggregate valuation. But from this aggregate valuation no exact price per unit could be discovered. The new data and prices were far too imprecisely known to venture on such an experiment. A distinguished forestry specialist said at the time: "We do not know the value of beechwood; we only know that it is relatively high. How high, the market must decide later."

It may well be asked whether the market could not have decided then and there. That would have been to adopt our *second* method: to have left the prices of wood free for a time. Wouldn't then the right price for beechwood have resulted? But the prices of all the products of the consuming industries, of furniture, plywood, cellulose, mining, railways, and so on, were fixed. So were the prices of all the substitutes for beechwood. Thus, the prices of all the various products which made use of wood as a raw material gave no expression to the relationship between needs and supplies in the market for wood. In short, the partial freeing of the prices of a single group of goods would have been pointless. The interdependence of *all* markets and of the economic process as a whole, would have necessitated the freeing of *all* prices and the determining of the scarcities of *all* goods, in order thereby to establish them in the single case of beechwood.

Here we reach a more fundamental question. Why were not all prices free? *Wouldn't it then have been possible to determine relative scarcities by new price relationships, and thus reduce the new round aggregate valuations of the central authorities to individual prices?* Such a step, alone for reasons of monetary policy, was ruled out by the German government. The general freeing of prices would not merely have led to the development of new price relationships. The existing inflationary pressure would have led to a sharp rise in the general level of prices, to an appreciable fall in the value of money, to irrefutable wage claims, to obvious losses for savers, and to a rise in the cost of armaments. The tight hold on prices at their previous level, and the repression of inflation by pegging prices, became a dogmatically held principle of economic policy, as it has since become in other countries.

This negative answer in the German case does not dispose of the whole problem. Let it be supposed that there was no inflationary pressure, and that the arguments on monetary grounds against freeing prices had not held. Could not freely formed prices have replaced the aggregate valuations of the central authorities? For example: an armament firm receives 10 millions on account of deliveries, and pays 5 millions of this to its workers. If the workers had been allowed with this purchasing power to express freely their demands for consumption goods, for bread, meat, clothing, housing, and so on, they would of course have expressed their own valuations for consumption goods and not those of the central authorities. Prices would have expressed the valuations of the mass of consumers, not those of the central administration. The prices of bread, houses, clothing, and of all the factors of production responsible for these goods, would have conflicted with the carrying through of the plans of the central authorities. Prices would have expressed the plans of consumers and not the plans of the central administration. Above all, goods would have been drawn into consumption rather than investment uses, and a conflict would have arisen between the central plans and those of individual households and firms. Here we reach the basic question.

(2) Would it not perhaps have been possible to graft prices on to the controlling mechanism of the centrally administered economy in the following way? The central administration would have distributed con-

sumption goods by rationing, as well as fixing prices. With regard to consumption goods, demand and supply would have been equated by rationing. But with regard to the factors of production, there would have been no rationing. Entrepreneurs would have applied for these to the state authorities. The factors would have been priced, and then these prices adjusted according to the extent of demand. By this adjustment of prices would not demand and supply have been brought into equilibrium and would not thus exact cost calculations have been possible? In this way, the German authorities would have been proceeding in accordance with proposals outlined by, for example, O. Lange. Wouldn't it have been possible to follow out this proposal?

The position was that a constant struggle was taking place for the factors of production between the different control offices, planning departments, and ultimate users. To stick to our example, the representatives of agriculture fought to get leather for harness, those of industry for machinery, of the workers for shoes. Or iron was wanted for small craftsmen, for machinery, for transport and so forth. The quantities available were generally too small and didn't meet the demands of all the sectional controls and departments. The proposal we are discussing would have had these battles fought out through a pricing system. The distribution of suitable supplies of leather between individual uses would have been effected by prices.

This method of control was out of the question for the central administration, for it would have meant to some extent letting the control of the means of production—in this case leather or iron—out of its hands. When fixing prices and rations for food and also for manufactured goods, and in its investment program, the central administration could not know the amount of leather or iron that would be wanted by the different control authorities or the other requirements for such materials. These demands only appeared subsequently. If the allocation of the means of production had been left to the decision of the price-bids of the businesses and departments, then the results might have contradicted the plans of the central administration. For example, it might have happened that a relatively large quantity of leather would have been used for agricultural purposes, or for workers' shoes, which would have brought about an acute shortage of, say, driving belts for machinery, and thus jeopardized the production program of the central administration in other branches of industry. Therefore, the central administration cannot leave the direction, in any important respects, of such means of production to be decided through pricing, but must reserve the direction for itself, which was what happened in Germany.

As soon as the firms, or sectional controls, had been left free to determine their own demand independently, with the central administration confining itself to fixing prices in relation to scarcities, conflicts would have arisen between the plans of the central administration and the plans of the firms and controls. Such conflicts would have been resolved by orders from the central authorities, that is, by abandoning the price mechanism. This proposal, therefore, cannot be carried through in practice, even under the assumption of a suitable monetary policy. *Competition can be used to improve efficiency, but as a mechanism of direction for an important section of the economy it cannot be applied without the abdication of the central authority.*

4. Some Consequences

It is possible to understand the economic process in the centrally administered economy, now we have seen the place in this process of the central factors: these are, the plans and production orders of the central authorities arrived at by calculations of physical quantities to which "overall" aggregate valuations are assigned. The following features at once arrest the attention:

1. Central planning presupposes standardization and the fixing of norms and types for production. It is impossible for the planning authorities to take full account of the countless changing individual needs of consumers, to provide variety in clothes or shoes, to get these goods to those who want them most, and to adapt their plan to changing wants. Central orders are the easier to give, the more schematized are production and consumption.

The needs of *consumers* can easily be reduced to norms by rationing and allocations, and the influence of the infinite variety of individual preferences eliminated. "The experiences of the last seven years clearly demonstrate," wrote a textile expert in 1946, "that it was not only the deployment of industry for war purposes, but rather, the increasingly dominating role of the planning authorities that constantly tended to reduce the number of goods (raw materials or finished products) which the plans envisaged." Simplifying the *production* side was more difficult. The multitude of small and middle-sized firms in Germany had each their own different variety of demand for machines, spare parts, materials and so on, which it was very difficult for the planning authorities to weigh up and decide upon. In every way the small and middle-sized firms in their infinite variety are difficult to fit into central plans. Planning authorities can best carry out their tasks of valuation and direction with respect to mass-produced goods, which use a few standardized materials and a small number of processes. The comparatively standardized character of agricultural production explains why agriculture is easier to plan than industry.

Central administration of the economy has led not only to standardization but to a general preference for the largest scale for production when new factories are being built. The Volkswagen factory in Fallersleben is an example. The significant point here is that it is not only the size of the plant which affects the economic order. Much has been written about this in the literature of the subject, and it has been argued that the growing size of the plant must result either in monopoly or in a centralized economy. Sometimes this development has in fact taken place. But the causal connection runs also in the reverse direction. *According to the type of economic system, different optimum sizes of plants will be aimed at.* For example, in the centrally administered economy, a particularly large scale will be preferred or created such as would never have come into being otherwise. This is what happened in Germany. The preference for particularly large-scale units results from the special form which planning takes in the centrally administered economy. Over a period of years, under a centrally administered economic regime, the German economy took on quite another shape: the trend was all to standardization and large-scale units. But where this could not develop quickly enough—which of course was apt to happen—difficulties and disturbances were inevitable. For example, as a consequence of the numerous different types of motor car, it was very difficult for the central administration to keep the armed forces supplied with spare parts.

2. As we have seen, the programs were drawn up by the sectional controls. Each control was out to produce as much as possible, for each held its own line of production to be specially important. So the Leather Control would try to get hold of as much coal and transport as possible in order to step up leather production. Coal and transport facilities were needed by all the other sectional controls. The resulting struggle between the controls for the factors of production, and particularly for labor supplies, had, as we have seen, to be decided by orders from the center. But much time went by before the ministry or political authority responsible could be called in and give its decision. Meanwhile, each control would be using every means it could to procure factors of production or labor supplies. This collision between sectional controls was a characteristic of the centrally administered economy. A sort of group anarchy seemed to be inherent in the system. In spite of the intervention of the higher authorities, this "anarchic" tendency must be recognized if the apparatus of control is to be understood.

3. The centralized method of control also results in the leadership responsible for directing the economic process passing into quite other hands than those which wield it in a competitive economy. The business man disappears with the rise of a centrally administered economy, because his main function, that is, the meeting of consumers' needs and the discovery of possibilities for supplying them at a profit, disappears also. In his place, the technician moves into the key position both in the firms and in the planning offices. Friction in firms between the technical and the business side is a well-known phenomenon. In the centrally administered economy in Germany it was the technician who gained the supremacy. But along with the privileged technician the statistician took on an important role in the direction of planning, for the entire planning process was

based on statistics from the first proposals to the working out of budgets, and to the comparison of planned and actual figures.

This change in the nature of the leadership was no accident, but a direct result of the special method of control in the centrally administered economy, in which the tendency is increasingly to replace economic considerations by technical.

4. Finally we must ask whether any equilibrium emerges in the centrally administered economy.

Those of the planners who pondered this question were inclined to answer in the affirmative. They understood by "equilibrium" the balancing of the budget of physical quantities in their section of the economy, and they were concerned that this should finally be completely achieved. Extensive negotiations among the sectional controls, and finally decisions by the central authorities higher up, could, they thought, bring it about that, for example, the quantity of coal which the Leather Control used came to the same figure both in the balance sheet of the Coal Control and in that of the Leather Control: or that the quantities of leather goods, shoes, harness, and so on, which appeared in the balance sheets of different sections of industry and agriculture, corresponded with the quantities in the budget of the Leather Control. The plans then were held to "balance," and a quantitative equilibrium was held to have been attained.

Certainly this equilibrium, when it actually existed, was not an equilibrium in the economic sense. The question thus remains open whether an *economic* equilibrium can be said to emerge in the centrally administered economy, or whether any tendency to such an equilibrium exists.

This question is difficult to answer, because the concept of equilibrium in an exchange economy is not immediately applicable to a centrally administered economy. In the exchange economy, three different levels of equilibrium can be distinguished.

First, there is equilibrium for the individual household or firm. In the centrally administered economy, equilibrium for the household is not possible nor is it aimed at. Rather, it is a characteristic of the centrally administered economy that the household cannot actively press its demands, but is simply the passive recipient of quantities fixed in the aggregate "overall" allocations from the center. Hence the case can occur in a household of a scarcity of bread with a superfluity of tobacco. Thus the balancing of satisfactions or marginal utilities in accordance with Gossen's second law does not take place. This brings it about that households try to approach nearer to maximum satisfaction by means of exchange, that is by other procedures than those of the centrally administered economy. (Barone and many of his followers come to a different conclusion because they work with a model which is not that of a centrally administered economy. They assume that the individual income receiver gets a particular sum of money from the central authority which he can freely dispose of. Here the principle of Gossen's second law and of the equilibrium of the household would actually be fulfilled. But then the State would be surrendering the directing of the economy to consumers and would cease to direct it from the center.)

Partial equilibrium for the *individual firm* is also impossible in the centrally administered economy. It is impossible to speak of the marginal returns to capital for each kind of factor of production being equal, or of there being any "law" of, or even tendency to, equimarginal returns. For the individual firm only makes subsidiary decisions and has to fit in with the allocations of factors that come from the planning authorities.

Similarly, the concept of *partial equilibrium of individual markets* is not applicable in the centrally administered economy. With regard, for example, to accommodation in a town, if this is distributed not by demand and supply in the market, but by allocation, there can be no equilibrium in the sense of the commercial economy. There is no equating of two independent quantities, demand and supply, but the distribution of a supply fixed to correspond with the planned requirements of the central authorities.

If these two conceptions of equilibrium fail to apply to the centrally administered economy, must this also be so with regard to the *third* conception, that of *general* economic equilibrium? The question arises whether in the centralized economy the productive processes for all goods, that is, the proportions in which labor and the means of production are applied in each case, can be so fitted in with one another as to represent an optimum fulfillment of the requirements of the plan. In the centralized economy in Germany, these proportions were not realized. One bottleneck followed another. Often they accumulated simultaneously, and there was no mechanism for guiding the processes of production in the direction of equilibrium proportions. Aggregate valuations and calculations, which could not be essentially improved on by the grafting on of a price mechanism, did not suffice to bring about these adjustments. This fact, as remains to be shown, was of particular importance with regard to investment.

5. Supplementary Remarks

1. It was shown at the start that the study of an economic system predominantly of the centrally administered type, as in Germany, must turn away from the private households and firms and be focused rather on the planning authorities. That is where the mechanism of direction is to be found. But if one subsequently turns back to the firms and households it will be noticed that what goes on there does not correspond with the account given by the planners. This discrepancy was of essential importance for economic life in Germany—and indeed not only in Germany. Certainly the procedure in private firms was completely overshadowed by the plans of the central administration. But the firms had their own

subsidiary plans, and to understand German economic life in this period it is necessary to take account of this subsidiary private planning.

A shoe factory gets allocations of leather, coal and electric power, and in accordance with its orders, produces shoes of a particular quality. Often, particular materials would be lacking, say, spare parts for machines, or chemicals; or allocations of these would arrive late. In one way or another, there would be "disequilibrium." The firm helped itself by resorting to its own "black" stocks, or by purchase or exchange. Otherwise, production would have been impossible. The central plans often related only to the so-called "key" materials, while the others would be obtained privately. The planning authorities often reckoned with the firms helping themselves, or with their possessing their own unreported stocks, or with their making their own deals. In this way, the private plans of the firms supported and supplemented the centrally administered economy.

It is not correct that the black market always hindered the attainment of the central administration's targets. On the contrary: in modern industrial production, firms require too many different kinds of auxiliary materials and parts for the central authority to keep track of them all, in spite of the most far-reaching standardization. A factory making machinery, for example, had completed certain machines punctually as ordered. But they couldn't be dispatched because there were no nails for nailing down the cases. It actually happened that a manager waited for months with delivery until the nails were allocated. Other managers would not. Fearing the consequences of late delivery, they got themselves the nails by exchange. Such "illegal" actions were of daily occurrence, but in spite of their illegality they were an essential aid to the fulfillment of the "legal" plans. In other cases, such transgressions certainly were harmful.

2. We reach here an important general question: can such complicated processes of production as those of a modern industrial economy be directed alone by the methods of a central administration? If, conceivably, all exchange deals and all black markets were completely suppressed by the confiscation of all stocks, could a central administration direct the economy at all? In modern factories, dozens, even hundreds, of materials are used daily in changing quantities. Is it conceivable that all these raw materials, goods, spare parts, chemicals and so on could be allocated by the central authorities in the right qualities and at the right time? Wouldn't an attempt of this kind at a *total* direction of the central administration throughout the economic system be suicidal? Would the disproportionalities be kept within tolerable limits?

This question cannot be precisely answered on the basis of German experience. For in Germany the procuring of many materials, and even of labor supplies outside the official channels of the central administration, played an important role. Certainly from what could be observed, the conclusion followed that without the procurement of black supplies of the means of production and of labor, the productive process would have suffered severe disturbances in many of its branches and for considerable periods of time. What is unique about this phenomenon is not that one pure form of economic order—that of the centrally-administered economy—has to be supplemented by other forms. This is also the case with regard to other economic orders of society. The subsistence economies of small family groups directed by the head of the family are not usually found in their pure form. Usually certain goods, say, salt, or metals, are got by exchange, so that here too, though for quite other reasons, there is a mixture of different pure forms of economic order. In contrast to other mixed economies, supplementary arrangements outside the central plan are explicitly forbidden by the planning authorities and the State. This is not the case in other mixed economies. It is a peculiarity with widespread consequences. The functioning of a centrally administered economy and its methods of control presuppose—at any rate they did in Germany—private exchanges which were often undertaken against the special orders of the central authorities.

3. The following definite conclusions can be drawn. The economic planning of a central administration consists of the balancing of the physical budgets of the sectional controls, and out of that balance a certain statistical "equilibrium" emerges. But because aggregate economic calculations permit of only the roughest cost estimates, the central administration has no means of bringing about any sort of general economic equilibrium. Firms and households, within the framework of the central plans, attempt by exchange to realize as far as possible the principle of equimarginal returns and of individual equilibrium. Thus, by these subsidiary and independent plans and actions, firms and households approach more nearly an equilibrium than is possible by the methods of direction of the centrally administered economy alone.

II. THE ECONOMIC PROCESS IN ITS SEPARATE BRANCHES

1. Investment and Saving

1. The student of history will remark that where an economy is predominantly under the direction of a central administration, it is usual for an exceptionally large amount of investment to be undertaken. This was the case in Germany after 1936, in Russia after 1928, and in quite other societies, such as those of the Incas in 1500 and of ancient Egypt, and in many other examples. How is this historical fact to be explained?

One decisive element responsible cannot be dealt with by economic theory, since it lies quite beyond its range. This is the sociological fact that the leadership in such a community builds towns and roads, factories, railways, power stations, and so on, in order to strengthen its political power. The methods of centrally administered control may be introduced for the specific purpose of speeding up investment. This consideration played an important part in Germany in the thirties. A central administration is less concerned with the production of consumers' goods. It is particularly those branches of industry—like the iron and steel industry—which go to produce investment goods, which will be expanded. If this investment is successful in increasing political power, its effects on consumption will be disregarded. Political and economic authorities may not always be in the grip of this sort of striving, but it always plays a certain role.

The economist cannot explain why the central administration *wants* to force up the rate of investment, but he *can* answer the equally important question as to *how* it can enforce its will, since this depends on economic factors. In this respect, the apparatus of a centrally administered economy is of particular interest.

2. What are the differences in the processes of investment in a commercial economy and a centrally administered economy?

(*a*) A machine tool factory is being expanded. If this happens in the commercial economy, it is the plan of the entrepreneur which decides whether and how this project will be carried out. His plan will be based on existing and expected prices, that is, on the costs of the new construction and equipment, and on the expected prices for raw materials and the finished product. Here the length of the prospective period of amortization for the new equipment is decisive. With the data constantly changing as they do today, investments may often not be undertaken if the amortization is reckoned to take longer than three to five years.[3] In any case, economic calculation acts as something of a brake, by enforcing a definite selection between different projects, and it is a factor of some influence with regard to every investment or the purchase of every machine.

It is quite otherwise in the centrally administered economy, with its indecisive aggregate valuations. Whether a machinery factory was to be built or not was decided in Germany by the Ministry of Economics (later by the Ministry of Armaments Production). The Ministry examined and estimated whether a factory as a whole was useful to the total plan. But the Ministry could not compare the values invested in the new construction with the values this new construction would yield. The amortization period and the rate of interest were not taken into account. Neither acted as a brake. So huge investment projects were undertaken, stretching ahead for very long periods into the future. Only round aggregate comparisons were made of the uses rendered by the labor and other factors employed in this and competing directions. The checks on investment, effective in the commercial economy, are lacking in the centrally administered economy.

If a project was approved, the necessary labor supplies, cement, steel, and so on, were released and allocated by the Ministry, via the departmental "Controls," and the investment began. The banks were left with a

[3] Cf. F. Lutz, "The Interest Rate and Investment in a Dynamic Economy," *American Economic Review*, Vol. XXXV, No. 5 (December, 1945), p. 811.

quite subsidiary role, for it was not their granting of credit, but the central administration, which decided about the investment. Of necessity, the banks will have an insignificant place in a centrally administered economy. The fact that the banks later provided intermediate credits, and that it was through their agency that the machinery factory met its obligations, was of no essential importance, except for subsequent accounting. It was not the granting of credits that directed the labor supplies and means of production, but the orders of the central authorities. The purchase of securities, and saving out of incomes, were only of secondary significance (in so far as they represented a restriction on spending). The control of investment was not influenced by them. In short, the process of investment was very simple, and could not fail because of insufficient liquidity, or the state of the security market, or the threat of price changes.

(*b*) To understand the problem rightly, we must look more closely at the economic process as a whole.

A very simple example will show what investment implies. A peasant has harvested twenty units of wheat. Part of the wheat will go via the mill and the bakery to the final consumer, and part will be used for fodder or seed. This second part is "put back" (zurückversetzt), that is, it does not go by the shortest route to the consumer from its point in the productive process, but is used as a means of production in another process further removed from final consumption. This "keeping back" of goods is what is meant by capital investment.

Let us survey a whole economy—for example the Germany economy in 1939—and look at all the land, mines, railways, stocks of raw materials and labor supplies as they were at that moment. How should the economic process then have been directed *with regard to time?* Labor supplies and the physical means of production could have been directed to the greatest possible extent to new construction, expanding railways, roads, to the more intensive cultivation of the land, *away from* supplying goods for present consumption. Then goods would have been "put back," or there would have been investment on the maximum scale. Or the opposite could have occurred. Labor supplies and the means of production could have been concentrated as completely as possible for consumption in the present or in the immediate future, and machines, livestock, and so on consumed without replacement. The temporal direction of the economic process is decisive with regard to the supply of consumption goods and the extent of productive equipment. In reality, some course will be followed between the two extremes we have described.

How the decision is made will differ according to the structure of the economic order. If income receivers or consumers command the system, then the inter-temporal direction of the economy will depend on them and on their inter-temporal dispositions, including, that is, their savings. With perfect competition and an appropriate monetary system, voluntary restriction of consumption precedes investment.

If, however, the money supply may be expanded by credit creation, or under monopolistic conditions, investment can be planned ahead of saving and the restriction of consumption is forced upon certain groups of income receivers subsequently. To that extent, entrepreneurs and banks, rather than the consumers, decide the amount of investment. Even under these conditions the voice of the consumer can still make itself heard through the medium of voluntary savings, and prices and price expectations.

In the centrally administered economy, the consumer is dethroned. He cannot control the economic process. He can no longer, through the instrument of price changes, attract the factors of production or decide how much of them shall be set aside for investment. The central administration distributes consumers' goods, and it directs the factors to the production-goods industries, or rather, it decides the quantity of factors to be "put back" for these industries. Consumers cannot foil the administration in its plans, for it can do what is not possible in any form of exchange economy, that is, exclude *any* influence from the side of consumers on the economy, and thereby on the level of investment.

The special characteristics of the investment process in a centrally administered economy may now be distinguished and explained more precisely. They consist, *first,* in the ability to concentrate to the maximum on investment, labor supplies and the means of production; *secondly,* special difficulties arise with regard to the *proportions* of investments.

3. *How is a central administration able to concentrate labor supplies and means of production to such a high degree on investment?* How did this happen after 1938 with regard to the German armaments industry, and after 1945 in the Eastern Zone for reparations investment? Two facts were and are decisive:

(*a*) Without interference from consumers, factors of production can be directed to investment purposes in the manner described. Instead of producing textile goods for consumers, foodstuffs, or housing, they can be *ordered* to build roads, blast-furnaces, airplane factories, etc.

What are the limits to this re-direction, or to the quantity of investment? In the subsistence levels of the different categories of the population. If all the supplies of labor and the factors of production were used for building, machinery, and on production-goods—(that is, if all were "put back")—no consumption goods at all would be produced, the people would starve, and the investment plans could obviously never be completed. Evidently, the central administration cannot go so far. So particular quantities of the factors are devoted to producing food, clothing, etc., in order to keep in being the labor supplies necessary for reaching the investment targets.

This concept of the Subsistence Minimum is of great practical importance for the centrally administered economy, and is indispensable for understanding it theoretically. The Subsistence Minimum consists of the quantity of goods that must be distributed to the different categories of labor in order to preserve their efficiency. It differs according to the branch of production—(the lumberjack needs more pairs of shoes than the metal-worker)—and in accordance with the region, climate, and habits of the population. But the planning authorities must always take account of the Subsistence Minimum. If the miners are not getting this minimum, as detailed investigations in Germany have shown, coal production falls off.

It might be that this Subsistence Minimum is only of a temporary significance? It might be argued that this rate of investment would surely make possible in the future an improved supply of consumers' goods? This does not follow. So long as the chief aim of the central plans is the maximum expansion of investment, then the earlier investments in iron and steel works, power stations and the other production goods industries, serve principally to produce goods which are again applied to further investment. Strong historical forces work in this direction.

(*b*) There is a second reason for the rapid expansion of investment by the methods of a centrally administered economy.

The central administration can take over supplies of goods without giving anything equivalent in exchange. For example, the stocks of spinning or weaving firms, or of metals, can be requisitioned without compensation. This often happened in Germany. Certainly the firms were paid in money, but they could get no goods for this money. In this way, means of production were "saved" for investment. Often these firms used the vast balances of money in their possession for lending to the government. This procedure shows very plainly how the centrally administered economy is based not on exchange but on allocations.

Side by side with investment in some fields went a disinvestment or capital consumption in others. This consumption of capital was an essential aid to investment in other branches. German industry took on a curiously schizoid appearance. On the one side, there were firms with stocks falling and machinery deteriorating, and on the other new construction and the expansion of equipment. Even within the same firm these processes, partially of capital consumption and partially of increased investment, could be observed. In any case, by these methods the central administration was able to get more factors released for investment than would have been possible by the methods of an exchange economy. The essential point is not simply this re-direction of the means of production from consumption goods industries to investment, but that this re-direction took place uncompensated.

4. This is one aspect of the investment process in a centrally administered economy: its facility in rapid concentration of labor and means of production on particular investment programs. Now for another equally important aspect:

Every investment requires complementary investment. If, for example, in a small closed economy it is decided that a new cattle-shed be built, attention will be given to proportional increases in cattle, carts, fodder, etc. Otherwise the new cattle-shed will not be fully used, and the investment will be of no, or only a small, use. Even in this small closed economy there are difficult problems of valuation and planning in bringing about an expansion of the number of cattle, the fodder, and sheds, so that the different investments fit in and synchronize with one another.

In a modern economy with its complex organization and extensive division of labor, made up of millions of firms, the task is incomparably more difficult. This was apparent even in Germany. As we are aware, the centrally administered economy with its round aggregate valuations and statistical calculations, commands no mechanism of direction by which the proportions of goods produced are harmonized. Thus, for example, the investments in motor-roads in the middle thirties were much too large and in no suitable proportion to the expansion of petroleum production. On the other hand, investment in railways was neglected for a long period, and corresponded in no way with the increased transport requirements resulting from other investments.

It was clear that the central administration was in no position to bring about a balanced investment program.

5. In this respect, too, there are contradictory tendencies in the centrally administered economy.

Its peculiar propensity to invest can easily be asserted through its ability to limit the claims of current consumption, and to undertake extensive investment programs regardless of risk. At the same time it is characterized by one-sided disproportionate investments, with some branches of industry excessively expanded while others are unduly contracted.

These contradictory tendencies derive from the fact that a central administration can certainly step up investment quantitatively but cannot satisfactorily plan it qualitatively. If its complementary investments are lacking, the economic value of a single investment project is correspondingly reduced—for example, with regard to the cattle-shed in the private economy for which no complementary investments were undertaken. The economic value of the huge road construction was small. The economic quantity of investment, that is its value, depends on a balancing of investment projects or on their proportions.

For these reasons it is difficult to compare quantities of saving with quantities of investment. What is the quantity of investment? Economically, it can only be expressed through prices. Its level depends on the single investments being physically and temporally co-ordinated. The amount of labor and means of production used is not decisive, but rather the directions and proportions of the individual investments. The volume and value of investments are not identical—as the example of the motor roads demonstrates. Economically, estimates of savings and investments can only be estimates of values.

2. Fluctuations and Employment

1. Full employment can be brought about comparatively easily in the centrally administered economy, and there are no depressions and dismissals of workers. Why this should be so follows readily from what we have said above.

First, it is because investment on a relatively large scale is always taking place in the centrally administered economy. In the different types of exchange economy, as is well known, the cycle of depression and recovery is usually connected with fluctuations in investment. By avoiding any falling off in investment, depressions can be avoided also. In the centrally administered economy, one long process of investment follows another.

Secondly, there need be no unemployment because every worker can be taken on regardless of costs. In an exchange economy, workers are dismissed because there exists a measure of scarcity with regard to single units, that is with regard to efficiency units of labor, *and* because this measure of scarcity has a compelling force behind it. Workers are dismissed if the return resulting from their employment does not cover the costs. The central administration with its methods of round aggregate valuations cannot determine whether an individual worker at road-building is thereby producing goods of a value to cover the costs. Furthermore, even if it is estimated that the costs of employing several thousand workers on road constructions are not covered, the central administration does not have to cut the work short. In these conditions full employment is always attainable.

2. But this is only one side of the problem. The absence of depressions and unemployment and of checks to the expansion of investment, does not alter the fact that the economic process in a centrally administered economy can have no equilibrium. For this would have to mean that investments, for example, in mining, railway construction, or in the steel or shoe industries, would have to be co-ordinated in the right proportions. It is just this which is not possible. Because an acute coal shortage threatened coal production would be increased. But with more coal would come a shortage of railway wagons. This would be because there was insufficient investment in rolling-stock factories and because the repair shops were insufficient. Consequently, while there was more coal produced, its value would be relatively low, because the complementary goods would be lacking. One-sided expansion of particular lines of investment by the directing authorities at the center was constantly finding expression in such disproportionalities.

This lack of an equilibrium positon made itself felt in firms, or branches of industry, through sudden shortages of spare parts, raw materials, particular chemicals, or means of transport. The apparatus of production would be unduly expanded in some directions and unduly contracted in others. Finally, the efficiency of the apparatus in producing either capital or consumption goods would suffer.

3. Modern trade cycle theory must be extended to take account of these facts.

Economists have been concerned to describe and explain the upward and downward swings of boom and slump in exchange economies, and the sequence of events in the various markets for the factors of production and for consumption goods, capital, labor, and so forth. When we turn to economic societies of a predominantly centrally administered type, it is apparent that the cyclical phenomena just described are absent or else have a different significance: price fluctuations signify little or nothing, capital markets either do not exist or play a minor role; saving has another meaning, and interest almost none at all. There are none of the fluctuations of boom and depression so often described for the exchange economy.

Economists must not withdraw at this point, but widen the field of their investigations. If, in the past, they have studied the disproportionalities in economic development as these arise in a predominantly exchange economy, now they have to do the same for the type of economy dominated by a central administration. That is, not simply disequilibrating tendencies in the American economy of 1948 have to be investigated, but also the other kinds of disequilibria such as arise in the Russian economy. England's difficulties in 1947, which are those of an economy of a centrally administered type, must be studied just as much as the depression of 1929–32.

Certainly these disproportionalities are of quite another character, just because the processes of different types of economic system develop very differently. The theory of fluctuations becomes a theory of disproportionalities, or of divergencies from equilibrium, which may occur in the processes of different kinds of economic systems.

3. Production and Distribution

1. The distribution of the social product proceeds fundamentally differently in a centrally administered economy from the way in which it proceeds in a competitive economy. In the competitive economy, incomes are fixed mechanically. Prices for the factors of production are formed as part of the process of combining together capital, labor and the means of production. Production and distribution are bound up together as one procedure. It is the same fact seen from two different angles.

In the centrally administered economy, distribution and the fixing of incomes are in the hands of the central authorities. It is not the productive contribution as automatically worked out by the calculating mechanism of prices that is decisive, but the plans of the central authorities.

How do they decide?

Centralized economic plans, as we have seen, usually aim at a maximum of investment. This determines, pretty well of necessity, the distribution of income. Income receivers get neither so *little* that the maximum possible investment cannot be reached because of a falling off in the efficiency of labor, nor so *much* that it is more than will maintain efficiency. Either of these alternatives would mean withdrawing labor supplies and means of production for consumption purposes away from investment. So the various categories of labor get Subsistence Minima for food, clothing and housing. (In order to avoid confusion with the concept in Ricardo's chapter five, it should be emphasized that the Subsistence Minimum consists of the quantity of consumers' goods which the different types of labor must get in order to carry out a particular task.)

2. The Subsistence Minimum naturally cannot be fixed individually for each worker—an impossible task for the central administration relying on its round aggregate valuations. How many consumers' goods the particular individual needs to maintain a certain efficiency at his job cannot be determined by the planning authorities. So instead of individual decisions round allocations are decreed. Ration cards for food are graded by groups ("normal consumers," "heavy workers," "specially heavy workers").

In Germany attempts have also been made to raise productivity by bonuses for good performance, but this hardly alters the fundamental principle of distribution and the provision of consumers' goods. Such bonuses are simply a means of raising efficiency as far as possible within the framework of the fixed Subsistence Minima. No comparison of value is, or could be, made between the additional production resulting and the additional consumers' goods allocated. Competition, here also, is adopted by the centrally administered economy simply as a means of increasing production, not of deciding its direction.

This is how the workers, employees, and managers fare. It might be asked how the incomes of the leaders at the narrow apex of the pyramid are formed. The answer would have to be that the allocation of goods to this class was regarded as of the same importance as investment.

3. Barone and his followers have put forward the view on the relation between distribution and production that these can be separated by the central authority. The fixing of incomes does not have to follow the economic principles of the competitive economy, with shares fixed by an anonymous procedure. Men are to be freed from the economic mechanism, and the authorities can distribute shares according to other than economic principles, e.g., according to some ethical rule. First the distribution of consumers' goods, then production, would be adjusted to the right and just income levels.

The accuracy of this statement can be judged from the foregoing account.

(*a*) It is true that the process of distribution in the centrally administered economy is quite different from that under competition, because it is decided by central authorities and not by the price mechanism.

(*b*) It is true also that the level of income, for example, in return for eight hours' work, is not dependent on the productive contribution of the worker. This is the way in which production and distribution are made independent of one another. (Whether this independence is socially desirable is a serious issue of social policy.)

(*c*) But the relation between production and consumption is quite different, and this is what Barone and his followers fail to see. They assume that a central aim of the economic planners is to bring about as large and as fair a distribution of consumers' goods to the entire people as possible. They therefore assume that a fair distribution is decided on *first,* and *then* production is adjusted accordingly.

Whether this could be a central aim of policy need not be argued. Perhaps it could. But economic science has to investigate reality, and in reality the leadership of a centrally administered economy has as a main objective the forcing through of a maximum of investment. That was the case in Germany and in Russia too. The facts are that the total supplies of consumers' goods, and their distribution to individuals, are mainly determined by the investment programs. It is not what is considered the ethically right distributive shares which determine the direction of production. It is not incomes allotted in just proportions which govern production. On the contrary, the centrally determined production programs govern distribution, and these programs are determined by the striving after a maximum of investment.

It is not correct that the distribution of the social product can be completely separated from its production. Distribution is fitted into the production programs so as to promote maximum output. In consequence the processes of distribution in a centrally administered economy can be analyzed theoretically. In all cases where, as in Germany, production plans were directed at a maximum level of investment, distribution proceeded according to certain principles.

4. Monopoly and the Centrally Administered Economy

1. The transition to a centrally administered economy, under the impetus of the full employment policy, was made much easier in Germany by industrial concentration in combines and syndicates. Where, for example, firmly established syndicates existed, as in coal mining, and in the iron and steel, cement, and potash industries, the administration of the syndicates simply had to be changed into branches of the central authority. The syndicates took on legally the status of public bodies, and became compulsory. The pig-iron syndicate, for example, now *allocated* what previously it had sold centrally. The officials of the syndicates and their internal organization remained essentially the same. The combines also, as in the steel and chemical industries, proved to be easily adaptable to the structure of a centrally administered economy. The administrative apparatus of I.G. Farben was used as it stood, as the controlling instrument for parts of the chemical industry. Not that it had been originally designed

for that purpose, but it now fulfilled it admirably. Wherever syndicates and combines did not exist, as in the many sections of the engineering or paper industries, it was more difficult to build up the apparatus of the centrally administered economy. The central organization had first to be created, and the officials necessary were lacking.

The relationship between the combines and the central administration was still closer. The great partially monopolistic combine in the cigarette industry sold its cigarettes as branded goods at fixed prices to the final purchaser, and had made the whole trade completely dependent on it. It is only a short step from this partially monopolistic control of the market to the rationed allocations of cigarettes by the central administration, with the fixing of a margin for the distributor. In the centrally administered economy, not only does the influence of consumers disappear, but traders lose their independent directing function in the economic process. Here too, the combines and syndicates prepared the way. Moreover, it can be shown that the processes of economic calculation by the combines show similarities with those of the centrally administered economy. Already in combines difficulties arise over satisfactory cost accounting, and statistics play a more important part in economic calculation. The centrally administered economy is like a single huge combine comprising the whole economic life of the country.

This connection between private business and the central administration is even closer than we have so far described. Private pressure groups are not merely the pace-makers for the centrally administered economy. In the course of the experiment in Germany the private bodies and central administrative offices were closely interlocked. Power in the central administration lay partly with the heads of the combines and syndicates. This union of the central administration of the economy with private property was of key importance. It encouraged that tendency to "group anarchy" to which we referred.

The centrally administered economy has in this connection considerably increased industrial concentration, not merely with regard to the size of the technical unit as has already been mentioned. Industrial concentration does not consist so much in the growth of the size of the productive unit, but in the combining together of many units under unified leadership in trusts and syndicates. In the centrally administered economy these combinations were encouraged and furthered. In Germany many compulsory cartels and marketing agreements were organized, as, for example, in the milling industry as early as 1933. These associations and cartels were needed to control the industry. An important order of 1942 explains: "To carry through planning simply and efficiently, it is nearly always necessary to take over the individual organizations, the cartels, distributing agencies, rings and committees as well as the regional offices from which the individual firms get their orders." They became organs of the central planning authority. Moreover, it was simpler for the central authorities to negotiate with a few large units than with many small ones. For these reasons, private organizations exercised a powerful influence, while small competitors were at a disadvantage. The private and public bodies which wielded economic power were fused together.

2. Should then the centrally administered economy be correctly regarded as a case of monopoly, or of a conglomeration of monopolies?

This question is given an affirmative answer by some theoretical economists. If they were right, the German and Russian economic systems of, say, 1942, would be systems in which monopoly was predominant and the monopolies which existed for each branch of production were united in a total monopoly. The analysis of monopoly would thus "swallow up" the theory of the centrally administered economy.

Certainly, theoretical analysis revealed similarities in the two cases in their economic processes, as, for example, in fixing wages. Under conditions of monopsony the wage can of course be forced down well below the marginal productivity as when a single spinning mill provides the one demand for workers who offer their labor competitively. In a centrally administered economy, also, the workers are dependent not on the private owner of a spinning mill but on the central administration—in either case on a monopoly.

3. However, the essential difference between monopoly and the centrally administered economy is clear from this example. The position of the management of the spinning mill in the cases of monopsony is certainly very powerful, and the workers are dependent on it. But there is no obligation or compulsory national service as in the centrally administered economy, and consumers' goods are not allocated but can be bought on the market.

To summarize, there are no demand or supply and no markets in a centrally administered economy; nor is there exchange. This is replaced by allocations. In the centrally administered economy, there are no independent agents, with their own plans, meeting for economic exchange.

In the exchange economy, there are always at least two such units, even in the case of bilateral monopoly, as when the railway authority as monopsonist purchases carriages from the rolling-stock combine as monopolist. But as soon as rolling-stock production was taken under the direction of the central administration, the combine was no longer an independent agent with its own plan, but an instrument of the central administration which controlled also the state railways. Steel, labor and so on were allocated from the center for rolling-stock. The volume of production was not determined by markets or prices. There was certainly a plan for rolling-stock, but this plan was only partial and dependent.

Monopoly and the centrally administered economy are similar at many points, but they are two domains in which the economic process develops very differently. The characteristic of the centrally administered economy is that demand is decided by the same central authorities which direct production.

5. International Trade

1. In the exchange economy the decision as to which goods are to be traded internationally, on what terms and in what quantities, and how the flow of capital is to be directed, is made through the mechanism of the price systems of the countries concerned and the rates of exchange which purport to bring these systems of prices into equilibrium. In detail the procedure differs greatly in accordance with the form of the markets and the monetary systems. When monopolies, partial monopolies, or oligopolies are predominant, foreign trade is dependent on their strategy with regard to demand or supply, while this strategy will be absent under perfect competition. How does international trade proceed with regard to countries whose economies are directed by a central administration?

2. This single question contains a whole complex of others. For there are many different possible cases to be investigated. It might be that the central administration in country A is negotiating with the central administration of country B or with a single private monopoly organization, or with partial monopolies or oligopolies in B, or that competition ruled in B's markets. Foreign trade would proceed differently in each case, and differently also in accordance with the place of foreign trade in the total plan of A. The central administration may build its plans for foreign trade into the total plan from the start, or it may be concerned rather to plan on the basis of autarchy, with foreign trade only having the role of smoothing out disproportionalities as they occur. All these issues are of importance, and German experience has something to contribute to their answer.

Here we shall discuss one example which in fact seldom occurs, but which is of special interest for the analysis of the centrally administered economy, because it is an extreme case. In 1945 the territory of the German economy was split up into four zones, and within each of these zones into a number of "Länder," each with its own government, and each constituting a separate centrally administered economy. Out of one comprehensive economy there were now some dozen and a half. Orders previously valid for the whole of Germany ceased. Instead, trade between the zones began, that is, trade between a number of centrally administered economies. For example, a machinery works in South Baden was no longer allotted steel by a Reich authority, but the central government of South Baden had to get it in exchange from the central authorities of the British or American zone, for tobacco, sewing cotton, or carbide.

These exchanges differed from those usual in international trade, in that the partners to the exchange not only used the same currency, the mark, but that the same prices had been fixed for all goods and services. So that if "Land" A exchanged steel goods for potatoes with "Land" B, it would be on the basis of the same officially fixed prices for potatoes and steel, and certainly these prices played a peculiar role in the transaction.

3. What was the result of this experiment?

(*a*) Central administration of the economy necessarily requires a central direction of foreign trade. If merchants and industrialists in Land B had exchanged freely tobacco and textile goods, for steel or leather, on the basis of contracts with merchants in Land A, then both A and B would have had to give up the centralized planning of their internal economies. For steel, leather and textile goods would have been put outside the control of the central plans by this sort of foreign trade. Freedom of foreign trade and central administration of the economy cannot be reconciled. All attempts failed—even on the part of the Control Commission authorities—to bring about a greater freedom of exchange inside Germany without giving up the central administration of the economy.

(*b*) The central authorities with their round valuations tended to trade in quantities of standardized goods—coal, timber, or electricity. Even those Länder which would have been interested in exchanging more highly finished goods with other Länder, cut down this sort of trade while keeping up deliveries of standardized goods or even increasing them. A central administration is not in the position to distribute to consumers by means of exchange a variety of more highly finished industrial products; the adaptability and quick decisions necessary to exploit the fleeting opportunities of the market are lacking.

(*c*) What and how much was exported and imported did not depend on precise calculations, nor could the cost principle be given any precise validity. For example: Land A would be offered typewriters by Land B to a total price of forty thousand marks, and would ask for sewing cotton in exchange from B. The responsible authorities in B would now have to solve the valuation problem, *in spite of* the official fixed prices for both typewriters and thread being the same in the two Länder. For these prices no longer gave expression to the relative shortages of the goods. The officials in B would have to refuse to exchange the quantity of thread which cost forty thousand marks at these prices, for the one hundred and fifty typewriters at forty thousand marks. To correspond with the far higher value of thread, ten thousand marks worth only would be offered, and the balance of thirty thousand marks in paper money of little practical value. To arrive at precise valuations it would have been necessary to compare the uses of smaller quantities of the two goods. But the data were not available to determine exactly the value of one hundred and fifty or one hundred and forty typewriters as against that foregone in delivering each kilo of thread. The exchange was proposed on the basis of a rough estimate. The values of other goods would also have had to be estimated if the exchange was to be properly calculated; and it would have been necessary to work out whether exactly this quantity of thread should have been offered, or whether it would not have been better to have imported not typewriters but potatoes or wheat in exchange for the last fifty kilos, and if so in what quantities? Or, wouldn't it have been better to offer, at least in part, other goods and not thread, say, tobacco, medical instruments, or wine, also produced in this Land? The foreign trade authorities in B would have had to have known the values of all other goods, and of individual units of all other goods, to trade to the full advantage.

Those who have taken part in such negotiations must have sometimes wished that theoretical economists could have been present who believed that the problem was solved if a number of equations could be set out equal to the number of unknowns—equations which represent in the abstract the general interdependence of economic quantities but tell us nothing concrete. In such cases as we have been discussing the only possible course was to import or export certain goods on the basis of round aggregate estimates.

(*d*) To back up these estimates and the resulting transactions, the central authorities resorted to statistics. They tried to estimate statistically consumption per head of potatoes, butter, or coal, and then work out the necessary imports and the quantities available for export. But the figures showed only what quantities had been consumed *previously*, and were only of any use if the data had not changed. Since this often was the case, the statistical calculations were of little help.

(*e*) Owing to the great difficulties the central administrative authorities had in carrying through exchanges with other Länder, they sought the advice of expert circles in industry, agriculture, trade, etc. These experts were always interested parties, who in that way came to exercise political and economic power. So in this field also, economic pressure groups furthered their interests through the central administration.

4. Exchange between two Länder is not the same as in the case of bilateral monopoly.

In the case of bilateral monopoly, as is well known, there is no equilibrium though there are certain limiting factors, as Carl Menger in 1871 and Edgeworth, more precisely, in 1881, showed.[4] It might be assumed that the theoretical proposition that exchange relationships are not precisely determinate in the case of bilateral monopoly, though they can be brought within a determinable range, could be applied to exchange between two Länder with centrally administered economies. If, in fact, as in our case, Land A is a monopolist with regard to the supply of typewriters and B of thread, the requisite assumptions seem to be given for applying the theory of bilateral monopoly.

Such an application would be incorrect. The theory of bilateral monopoly starts from the assumption that the two monopolists know the value of their individual products and also the costs at which they are

---

[4] Cf. C. Menger, *Grundsätze der Volkswirtschaftslehre* (1871), p. 175 ff; Edgeworth, *Mathematical Physics* (1881). On the development of the theory of bilateral monopoly, see Stackelberg, *Marktform v. Gleichgewicht* (1934), p. 89 ff.

producing them. The central authorities do *not* know these values, and there are no determinable limits given within which the exchanges between two central administrations have to take place.

If an isolated autarchic economy A buys a certain quantity of barley from another such economy B and pays in wool, then the range for the price of barley in terms of wool is fixed by the valuations put upon these two goods by the authorities in A and B, who can fix them with precision. The foreign trade department of a centrally administered economy cannot. They are not in a position, relying on round aggregate valuations and statistical data, to value and compare precisely individual units of the two goods which depend on the data and values of individual units of all other goods in the economy. There is no precisely limited range for exchange relationships or "prices" in transactions between centrally administered economies, and there is no equilibrium of exchange.

III. CONCLUSION

1. Some Comparisons

It is now possible to return to our original question. In spite of great variations in the details, does the economic process in the centrally administered economy proceed in essentially the same way as in the exchange economy? Is the basic logic in the two cases the same?

1. In either case the aim is to provide for certain needs by combining means of production and labor supplies for productive purposes as in any form of economy.

Does the similarity hold at least with regard to the task the economic process has daily to solve?

The answer is no, only in appearances. In the exchange economy individuals are face to face, day in, day out, with the scarcities in food, clothing, etc., which they have to overcome by acting in one way or another. As they produce little for their own consumption, there are division of labor and exchange between a number of individual households and firms. No one is surveying the process as a whole. The requirements even of bread are expressed simply by, and for, each individual according to his purchasing power. It is the meeting of the scarcities as felt by the individual person or household which is the objective of the economic process in an economy controlled by competitive prices.

It is different in the centrally administered economy. Economizing there does not find its origin and purpose in the scarcities felt by the individual, since these never effectively assert themselves. The central administration and the planning authorities fix a total requirement for bread, meat, steel, etc., for a particular period of time, and in doing this leave out of account individual needs, valuations, and plans, on which individuals base their actions in the exchange economy. Individuals may strongly prefer their bread to be of wheat rather than of rye, but the central administration can simply substitute rye bread; similarly, individuals may voluntarily save very little, but centrally planned investment may be put much higher. The planned requirements of the central administration are what is decisive. If the central plans in the centrally administered economy are completely and successfully carried through, then the economic process has reached its objective, even if the needs of individuals are satisfied to a far smaller extent than they might be.

Scarcity means two quite different things in the centrally administered economy as compared with the exchange economy. The basic purpose of economizing is quite different.

2. Inevitably, the method by which the economy is controlled must be equally different.

In the exchange economy, it is the exchange relationships—that is the prices—which have to regulate the economic process, because it is with a view to exchange that firms and households make their plans. In the centrally administered economy, the plans of firms and households have lost their independent power. Therefore there can be no exchange, no markets, no direction by prices, even when prices are calculated. Prices can only have a completely subsidiary role. Instead of *exchanges,* there are *allocations* of raw materials, machinery, etc., to the firms, of jobs to workers, of consumers' goods to consumers. No such question ever can arise, for example, as to whether for an individual worker there is any correspondence to him between his particular work in a machinery works, and the rations of consumers' goods he receives, and whether these goods represent the same value as his productive contribution.

With exchange replaced by allocations, all other economic institutions and procedures change their character, even though they do not change their names. Cartels, co-operatives and trade unions become instruments of control, and no longer represent groups in the market. Labor exchanges are no longer intermediaries between demand and supply, but are the authorities for the central direction of labor supplies.

To believe in the possibility of grafting prices on to the mechanism of control in a centrally administered economy is to believe in a squaring of the circle. Either the central administration is directing labor and means of production by its allocation, or the multitude of households and firms are decisive in the economy, in which case prices are formed. If control is left to the price mechanism, the central administration abdicates economically, while if the central administration takes over control, prices lose their directing function.

3. The analysis of the German experiment shows the full extent of the differences arising from this fundamental contrast. In the centrally administered economy, saving, investment, distribution, international trade, etc., are quite different processes.

The centrally administered economy embodies the maximum possible concentration of economic power. The opposite is a system of complete competition in all markets, where the individual has virtually no power, apart from each man's infinitesimal influence on the economic process. An exchange economy, with monopolies, partial monopolies, or oligopolies, stands with regard to the distribution of economic power between these two extremes.

4. In economic orders of society where the method of centrally administered control predominates, the center of gravity shifts. Consumers and entrepreneurs are no longer in control, but the central administration. *First*, the meeting of individual consumers' needs recedes into the background, for the central administration is unable to find out what they are, and to weigh them up. It has to fix consumers' needs "overall" or "totally." *Secondly*, there are no exact cost calculations according to which production can be organized. *Finally*, such economies are as a rule dominated by the objective of a maximum of investment, and therefore aim at cutting consumption to the Subsistence Minimum. In fact, such an economy is not one directed to meeting consumers' needs. The basic principle of control is quite different.

Therefore, a special and different theory of the centrally administered economy is required and is possible.

2. Criticisms of Some Hypotheses

1. How did it come about that many economists failed to see the fundamental differences between the centrally administered economy and the exchange economy and therefore misconceived the nature of an essential part of economic reality? They believed that in both cases there was the same economic scarcity to be overcome. As perfect competition gave the optimum solution, the Ministry of Production in the centrally administered economy had to act as though perfect competition ruled. Only with regard to the distribution of the social product would there be a deviation from "economic" principles. The same economic categories—so Barone believed—such as price, wages, interest, profit, saving, would emerge, even though under other names. The principle of costs in both cases would control the economic process.

In fact, neither is the same thing, neither scarcity, nor the method of control, which works not through prices but through round aggregate valuations. The principle of cost cannot operate with regard to individual units, and has no compelling force behind it.

In economic orders of society in which the methods of control are those of a central administration, in contrast with the views of Barone and his followers, the same terminology may be in use as in the exchange economy ("price," "interest," etc.), *but these words mean something entirely different.* The terminology is being applied to categories of quite another form. In both types of economy, there are "farmers," "traders" and "banks" but their economic significance is fundamentally different, since they are instruments for carrying out central plans rather than themselves independent planning agents.

It would be scientifically convenient to have a single simple theoretical apparatus of universal applicability, irrespective of whether the British economy of 1900, the German economy of 1939 or that of Russia in 1948 is under discussion. But that is not practicable. The variety of forms realized in practice has to be taken into account, for they are decisive for the way in which the economic process works itself out.

2. Barone tried to show that for the collectivist economy also as many independent equations could be set out as are necessary mathematically to determine the unknowns. He believed that the solution of the equilibrium equations would in fact be possible, without himself showing how it could be done. The work of Taylor, Lange, Lerner and others followed this up. They asked how the indices of significance for the different individual goods could be determined under "socialism," and they believe they have found a simple effective method, that of trial and error. The calculating process of perfect competition was to be applied in a socialist order of society—"socialist" in the sense that property was to be collectively owned.

We have shown above that this possibility does not exist, partly for monetary reasons (because of the excess money) and partly for a more important reason, namely, that any use of the price mechanism for controlling the economic process sets a limit to the power of the central administration. There is a simple "either-or" alternative. *Either* the control is through prices, and therefore on the basis of the plans of households and firms, *or* it is based on the plans and valuations of a central authority. The two methods of control exclude one another.

It is no accident that even in contemporary economic orders of the centrally administered type—as, for example, in Germany—experiments on Barone's principles are not in fact attempted. Such theoretical analysis is not based on deduction from economic reality. Perhaps economists have been induced to formulate the problem in this unrealistic way because of their interest in politico-economic controversies. Our analysis here is not concerned with issues of economic policy. (At the same time it might be pointed out that the problem has its peculiarities even from the point of view of policy. Can an efficient and just competitive mechanism be created with collective ownership of the means of production? With regard to this question it might be remarked that the concentration of economic power brought about by collective ownership of the means of production renders it highly improbable that the all-powerful collective property owners would undertake the experiment of leaving the control of the economic process to competition, and that they would not rather themselves control the economy by central orders, that is through a central administration. From the point of view of the history of ideas it is of interest that the socialist movement which started from a criticism of competition at the beginning of the last century, is today itself proposing to establish a competitive mechanism.)

3. How can the theoretical problem be formulated to correspond with reality?

Modern theory deviates from reality in two directions. Often models are constructed *a priori* with no reference to economic reality, and the question is then asked as to how economic activity would proceed in such an *a priori* model. Such attempts are dangerous, because the builders of these models think that a question about reality is being answered, while the very form of the question, as they put it, excludes reality.

On the other hand, the analysis may start from crude imprecise concepts like "capitalism," "*laisser-faire*," or "socialism." Such terms as these fail to describe actual economic systems. We must beware of proceeding like the chemists in earlier centuries who made experiments without specifying precisely the conditions under which they were making them. Theoretical deductions are of little service when the conditions postulated are not clearly set out. "In the excitement of perfecting our instruments of analysis, we have tended to neglect a study of the framework which they assume" (L. C. Robbins). Models constructed *a priori* and imprecise "blanket" concepts like "capitalism," "socialism" and the like can be of little help in the investigation of economic reality.

How can we come by a more precise understanding of the forms in which the economic process really develops? By penetrating and investigating real businesses, households or planning authorities, and by examining each form of economy as it occurs. We shall then discover that in economic reality in the past and in the present, in spite of its variety, a limited series of pure forms has occurred and does occur, and that these are mixed together in different ways and different combinations. It is apparent that actual economic orders always represent some particular combination of pure forms. In Russia, for example, in the fourth decade of this century, the economy is by no means exclusively dominated by the central administration and its plans. Though this method predominates, side by side there exist elements of an exchange economy, there is also barter, and there are self-sufficient rural economies. All these forms of organization should be taken account of in a scientific analysis of the every-day economic process in Russia.

An analysis of the forms of economic reality should precede theoretical analysis. The actual forms of economic organization must be derived from economic reality, and these will then provide a basis for theoretical analysis. In this way it becomes possible to explain individual cases and bring out their significance for a knowledge of general principles—for example, the case of the German experiment from 1936 to 1947.

10. THE ROLE OF PLANNING IN SOCIALIST ECONOMY*

Oskar Lange

In this article, Oskar Lange discusses a centrally planned socialist economy, in contrast to the decentralized market socialist economy depicted in Selection No. 5 above. He believes that comprehensive planning and detailed control of the economy are justified in order to mobilize the economy to achieve important goals—such as a war effort, the elimination of traces of capitalism in the early days of socialism, and rapid industrialization. But, he contends, as a socialist economy develops and matures, it becomes both possible and necessary to introduce a large area of decentralized decision making into the economy.

Lange proposes that the central authorities continue to determine the basic proportions and directions of the economy, but give up detailed, day-to-day management of the economy by administrative orders. Instead, he envisions the central authorities achieving the results they desire by "economic means"—financial mechanisms and incentives which induce, rather than command, managers and households to do what the plan requires. Such "economic means" include market prices which equalize supply and demand and supplant administrative distribution of producer goods. In this way, Lange hopes to combine central control of the main features of economic development with a high degree of decentralization of detailed decision making.[1]

---

* Reprinted by permission from Oskar Lange, *The Political Economy of Socialism* (Publications on Social Change, No. 16) (The Hague: Institute of Social Studies, 1958), pp. 16–28.

[1] Lange's proposal has not, however, been adopted in Poland, for a number of

ECONOMIC planning, or, more precisely, the planning of economic development, is an essential feature of socialism. It expresses the fact that socialist economy does not develop in an elemental way but that its development is guided and directed by the conscious will of organized society. Planning is the means of subjecting the operation of economic laws and the economic development of society to the direction of human will.

The experience of the construction of socialism in various countries indicates that the establishment of planned economy is one of the first achievements of the socialist revolution. It precedes the full development of socialist relations of production, though it requires a certain minimum of such relations. In the transitional period, when non-socialist modes of production still play an important role, the economy becomes already subject to planned direction of its development. This is made possible by the existence in the economy of a large socialist sector which controls, as one frequently says, the "commanding outposts" of economic life. This is the minimum requirement of establishing planned economy.

Economic planning starts with the direct intervention of the state in economic relations. This intervention has for its objectives the liquidation of capitalist relations of production and the control of the non-socialist sectors of economy which still remain. The basis which makes control of the non-socialist sectors possible is the existence of a socialist sector, particularly that part of the socialist sector which is nationalized, and which controls the commanding outposts of the economy.

In this first, transitional phase the new revolutionary state is not neutral with regard to the various sectors of the economy. It consciously utilizes the nationalized socialist sector as an instrument of controlling the development of the whole economy. The means it utilizes consist of economic instruments which result from the existence of the nationalized sector comprising the decisive controlling part of the economy, and also of intervention by political force, i.e., non-economic force. In the first revolutionary period, intervention into economic processes by political force plays a decisive role.

In the first period of development of a socialist economy, both the planning of economic development and the day-to-day management of the socialist sector are highly centralized.

There may be some doubts of how far this represents a universal necessity. For instance, in Poland, we had some discussions whether such a period of highly centralized planning and management was a historical necessity or a great political mistake. Personally, I hold the view that it was a historical necessity.

---

complex political and economic reasons. These are lucidly discussed in John Michael Montias, *Central Planning in Poland* (New Haven: Yale University Press, 1962), chaps. 9, 10.

It seems to me that, first, the very process of the social revolution which liquidates one social system and establishes another requires centralized disposal of resources by the new revolutionary state, and consequently centralized management and planning. This holds, in my opinion, for any socialist revolution.

In under-developed countries, there is a further consideration. Socialist industrialization, and particularly very rapid industrialization, which was necessary in the first socialist countries, particularly in the Soviet Union, as a political requirement of national defense and of the solution of all kinds of political and social problems, due to backwardness, requires centralized disposal of resources. Thus, the very process of transformation of the social system and in addition, in under-developed countries, the need of rapid industrialization, impose the necessity of high centralization of planning and management.

The process of rapid industrialization requires such centralized disposal of resources for two reasons. First, it is necessary to concentrate all resources on certain objectives and avoid dissipation of resources on other objectives which would divert resources from the purpose of rapid industrialization. This is one of the reasons which leads to highly centralized planning and management and also to the allocation of resources by means of administrative establishment of priorities. The second reason why rapid industrialization demands centralized planning and management is the lack and weakness of industrial cadres. With the rapid growth of industry the cadres are new and inexperienced. Such old cadres which had some experience in management of industry and other economic activities are frequently politically alien to the socialist objectives. In consequence high centralization of managerial decisions becomes necessary.

Thus, the first period of planning and management in a socialist economy, at least according to our present experience, has always been characterized by administrative management and administrative allocation of resources on the basis of priorities centrally established. Economic incentives are in this period replaced by moral and political appeals to the workers, by appeals to their patriotism and socialist consciousness. This is, so to speak, a highly politicalized economy, both with regard to the means of planning and management and with regard to the incentives it utilizes.

I think that, essentially, it can be described as a *sui generis* war economy. Such methods of war economy are not peculiar to socialism because they are also used in capitalist countries in wartime. They were developed in the first and the second world wars. In capitalist countries, similar methods were used during the war, namely, concentration of all resources on one basic purpose, which is the production of war material, centralization of disposal of resources in order to avoid leakages of resources to what was considered non-essential utilization (everything which was not connected with the prosecution of the war). Allocation of resources by administrative decision according to administratively established priorities and wide scale use of political incentives to maintain the productivity and discipline of labor through patriotic appeals were characteristic of war economy. This was the case in all capitalist countries during the war.

It shows clearly that such methods of centralized planning and management are not peculiar to socialism, that they are rather certain techniques of war economy. The difficulty starts when these methods of war economy are identified with the essence of socialism and considered as being essential to socialism.

One of the methods of war economy, which most of the socialist countries used at one stage or another, was compulsory deliveries by peasants of part of their produce. Many comrades in my country feel rather upset by the present program of our government of abolishing such deliveries. They fear that this implies giving up some socialist principle. I usually answer them by asking whether they remember who in Poland first introduced compulsory deliveries by peasants. Such deliveries were first introduced during the first world war by the occupation army of Kaiser Wilhelm the Second, whom I do not think anybody regards as a champion of socialism. These methods cannot be considered as an essential aspect of socialism; they are simply methods of war economy necessary in a revolutionary period of transition.

The fate and history of these methods is a classical example of the dialectical character of the development of socialist society. Methods which are necessary and useful in the period of social revolution and of intensive industrialization become an obstacle to further economic progress when they are perpetuated beyond their historic justification. They become obstacles because they are characterized by lack of flexibility. They are rigid; they lead, therefore, to waste of resources resulting from this inflexibility; they require a wasteful bureaucratic apparatus and make it difficult to adjust production to the needs of the population. However, it seems that the greatest obstacle to further progress results from the lack of proper economic incentives in this bureaucratic centralistic type of management. This hampers proper economic utilization of resources, encourages waste, and also hinders technical progress.

Therefore, when the socialist society starts to overcome these centralistic, bureaucratic methods of administrative planning and management, it indicates, so to speak, that it is maturing. I would not want to make this a final definition of the period of transition. But I might say that substituting for the methods of administrative and centralized management new methods based on the utilization of economic laws indicates the end of the period of transition and the beginning of the functioning of an established socialist economy. I would not say that this is the only aspect of the problem of the period of transition, but it is certainly an important aspect of it.

The period of centralized planning and management, as I said, is the result partly of the necessities of the revolutionary transformation of society and, in under-developed countries, also of the needs of rapid industrialization. In studying this period, a certain important sociological factor has to be taken into account, which is the weakness of the working class in an under-developed country. It seems to me that it is on the basis of this weakness, under conditions of under-development, that the bureaucratic state machine gains great importance, and phenomena like the "cult of personality" develop. It, so to speak, in a way substitutes for the spontaneous activity of the working class.

But here again, the dialectics of the processes of construction of socialism becomes apparent. The centralistic methods are successful in achieving rapid industrialization and, as a consequence, cause a rapid growth of the working class. The working class grows in numbers as well as in consciousness and political maturity. Next to the growth of the working class, another important sociological element appears. This is the growth of a new socialist intelligentsia which largely comes from the ranks of the workers and peasants. When it becomes clear that the highly centralized administrative and bureaucratic methods of management create obstacles to further progress, a part of the political and state apparatus becomes convinced that a change of methods of administration and management is needed. Thus, new social forces mature which require and also make possible a change of these methods.

This precisely is the basic difference between the development of a socialist society and a society which is based on antagonistic class relations. There is no ruling class which may oppose these changes. There may be certain strata or groups which have a vested interest in the old methods and create obstacles, but these obstacles can never become of such importance as to make impossible the changes required by new historical circumstances.

This is very clear if you take, for instance, the experience of Poland, where the industrialization by means of centralized administrative planning and management has led to a great increase of the working class. Our working class is now more than three times what it was before the war. The working class has got experience in large industrial establishments. It was at first to a large extent of peasant origin and that, of course, weighed on its psychology. But that was only a transitional phase. Industrialization and the social revolution have created a new intelligentsia—largely coming from workers and peasants. All that led to a maturing of the forces of the new socialist society. In consequence, we got such a phenomenon as the great movement of workers' councils demanding self-government of workers in industry—the general demand to change the methods of management of the national economy. The party has accepted these demands of the people and given them organized expression.

Changes in the methods of planning and the management of the economy are taking place today in practically all socialist countries. Forms and contents are different, but all these changes imply a certain decentralization or deconcentration of management. I do not want to enter into a description of what is happening in the various socialist countries. I shall rather present to you what I personally believe is the proper formulation of the role and methods of planning in a socialist economy.

First, it must be stated that in a socialist society, planning of the economy is active planning. Some of the economists in Poland use the term "directive planning," but this term is ambiguous; therefore, I shall rather use the term "active planning." By this, I mean that planning does not consist only of coordination of the activities of various branches of the economy. It is something more: namely, it is an active determination of the main lines of development of the national economy. Otherwise, if planning were mere coordination, the development of socialist economy would be elemental; it would not really be directed by the will of organized society. If economic development is not to be elemental but is to be directed by organized society, then planning must be active economic planning.

Two problems arise with regard to active economic planning. First, what is its scope; what activities in the economy have to be planned? And second, what are the methods of securing the realization of the plan?

The active character of planning does not require that it go into each detail of economic life. We actually had a period in the socialist countries (perhaps with the exception of China, which started at a later level and profited by the experience of other socialist countries) when the output of even the least important commodity was planned. There was the famous joke in Poland—really, it was not a joke, but it was true—that the production of pickled cucumbers was in the national-economic plan. Another case, which again was not a joke but a fact, was that the State Planning Commission made a plan of the number of hares which were to be shot during the year by hunters. At the same time, you could not get, for instance, buttons or hairpins for ladies, simply because they had been forgotten in the plan.

Active planning and effective direction of the development of the economy are quite possible without planning such details. Even more, planning such details hampers really effective direction of the economy. Actually, I think it may be said that controlling such details had nothing to do with planning. It was a part of the high centralization of day-to-day management of the economy by means of administrative measures. This is a different thing than planning.

However, the plan which is to determine the development of the economy must include at least two things: first, the division of national income between accumulation and consumption; second, the distribution of investments among the different branches of the economy. The first determines the general rate of economic growth; the second determines the direction of the development.

Unless these two things are in the plan, there is no active guidance of the development of the economy. This is, therefore, the minimum requirement of the plan. In addition, it may or may not include the targets for the production of certain basic commodities, like basic raw materials, basic means of production, and so on. These are technical problems, not fundamental problems.

These are the fundamental aspects of the plan which determine the pace and the direction of development of the economy. In addition, economic planning must be concerned with coordination of the activities of the various branches of the economy—first of all, with coordination of the financial aspects of the plan and of its real aspects, in particular coordination of the total purchasing power at the disposal of the population and the amounts of consumer goods which are provided for distribution to individuals. The plan must also in some way and by some means be interested in the coordination of the output of the various branches of the national economy. Otherwise, the determination of the directions of development established by the plan may not be realized. If there is no proper coordination between the output of the various branches, investments may not be realized because the necessary investment goods are not produced. All kinds of bottlenecks appear and cause difficulties which may make it impossible to carry out the investment plan. So much for the content of the plan.

The second problem is that of the methods of securing the realization of the plan. Here, we have basically two possible methods. One consists of administrative orders and administrative allocation of resources. The various units in the socialist economy are ordered to do certain things—for instance, to produce so much of something. The resources which are necessary for that purpose, both material and financial, are allocated in an administrative way. This was the traditional method of realizing the plan in the past period. The second method consists in the use of what we call "economic means," namely, of setting up a system of incentives which induces people to do exactly the things which are required by the plan. It seems to me that in effective planning, both methods have to be used, though in different proportions.

Preference should be given to the use of economic means. Administrative methods should be limited to those fields where, for some reason or other, economic means are ineffective. Such situations, where economic means are not effective, always do exist. They exist, of course, particularly in periods of very great changes, because economic means are rather subtle instruments responding to "normal" changes in the situation and frequently breaking down when very fundamental or revolutionary changes are needed. In such cases the use of administrative means must be accepted. Even in a capitalist country, in situations of profound change, the state uses measures of administrative control, because the normal kind of economic means is not sufficient to provoke the responses which are necessary.

The fundamental decisions of the plan—the division of national income between accumulation and consumption and the basic direction of investments—are really of a political character, and the means of implementation must be partly administrative. The decision of the plan concerning the rate of accumulation is basically realized by administrative measures. Part of the national income produced is not paid out in the form of individual incomes; part of the profits of the socialist enterprises are held back by the state, and this is an administrative measure. So also are all forms of taxation of enterprises and individuals. The basic directions of investments—for instance, the decision to build an electric power plant—are usually not made as a reaction to market situations, but are made as basic decisions of economic policy, though in this case the realization of the decisions may make use of all kinds of economic instruments.

We may ask in what sense the economic plans must take account of economic laws. Even when the realization of the plan is achieved by administrative measures, the plan must observe the general economic laws concerning the proportions necessary in the process of production and reproduction. For instance, if the plan provides for an increase of the production of steel, it must provide for a certain additional output of coal which is needed to produce the additional steel. *Any* kind of planning has to take care of such objective kinds of relationships.

There are also other economic laws which must be observed by the plan. These are the laws which result from the operation of economic incentives under the circumstances created by the plan. The process of realization of the plan sets into motion definite economic incentives to which the people react in a certain way which can be calculated. Even in the period of administrative planning, certain economic incentives were operative, and their consequences had to be taken into account. In this period, however, economic means were only subsidiary in relation to administrative means. I would say that now the situation has to change in the sense that the economic means are the rule and administrative means become subsidiary to the economic means. Thus, the plan has to observe the laws of production and reproduction; and insofar as the realization is based on the use of economic means, i.e., the operation of economic laws, it also has to consider these laws.

By utilizing economic means, planning makes use of the automatic character of people's responses to given incentives. Thus, certain automatic processes in the economy are established. However, these automatic processes are not elemental. These two things should be distinguished. The difference is that in a socialist society, where the automatic processes are part of the method of realization of the plan, the conditions establishing incentives are set up by economic policy; whereas in capitalist society, these conditions develop in an elemental way. There is a basic difference: In one case (capitalism), the incentives develop in an elemental way and are not subject to conscious control of society; in the other case (socialism), they are consciously established by organized society in such a way as to produce the desired results. As Engels said: "The social causes set into motion will produce to an ever-increasing extent the results desired by man."

I shall illustrate this by an analogy. The capitalist economy may be compared to an old-fashioned balloon which is moved by the currents of the air in the direction in which the wind pushes it. Man has no control whatever over the direction in which the balloon is moving. The socialist economy in the period of realization of its plan by administrative measures can be compared to an old-fashioned airplane, in which the pilot with his hands moves the steering gear. By always attending to the steering gear, the pilot directs the plane in the direction he chooses; whenever the current of the air changes, he moves the gear in such a way as to keep in his chosen direction. Planning in which the realization is based on economic means I would compare to a modern plane which has an automatic steering mechanism. The pilot sets the mechanism in the direction in which he wants the plane to go, and the automatic mechanism keeps the plane in the desired direction. The pilot can read a book or a newspaper in the meantime, and the plane by itself keeps the desired direction. But it is not the direction where the wind pushes the plane, but the direction which the pilot has chosen—consciously chosen. It is the pilot who determines the direction of the plane; if he wishes, he can change the direction by re-setting the automatic mechanism.

If I were to carry the analogy to the end, I would say that the pilot must, of course, from time to time determine whether the automatic steering mechanism is working. As a rule, experience shows that when the wind is very strong, the automatic mechanism does not work, and the pilot has to take the steering gear in his hand and steer himself. When the wind again becomes quiet, he can once more let the automatic mechanism work. In sudden upsetting situations, administrative measures have to be used in managing a socialist economy.

The next problem is to what extent the decisions implied in the plan, (not their realization, but the decisions themselves) can be centralized, or can or even must be decentralized. The need for centralized decisions obviously results from the need for coordination. Such decisions as the basic direction of investments, since they also must be coordinated through the coordination of various branches of economy, must be centrally planned. Each plan must have centralistic elements. I would say that the basic decisions of the plan must be made centrally. In addition to that, the plan may have as subsidiary parts certain decentralized subsidiary plans, in order to secure the proper flexibility. There are two criteria which determine the decentralization which economic planning can or must have. One determines the possibility of decentralization and the other the necessity of decentralization.

Economic planning should be decentralized so far as it is possible to set up economic incentives such that the decisions of the decentralized units are the same as the decisions which would be made centrally. Second, economic planning *must* be decentralized in all cases where the central decision responds to a situation too late, because in such cases, unless there is decentralization, central planning becomes fictitious. What actually is obtained is an elemental development. It is important to notice that in all socialist countries, in the period of highly centralized planning and management, there were many elemental processes of this type.

For instance, in Poland in a certain period the elemental processes were so common that one could have asked whether a planned economy still existed. On the one hand, there was a plan; but on the other, the economy produced results in a very elemental way. The elemental character of this process was the result of two facts. One was the over-centralization of the plan. Before processes that took place in various branches of the economy came to the attention of the central authority, and before the central authority took action, irreversible things had already happened. The result was purely elemental. The other fact was the existence of "wrong" economic incentives. When the old moral and political incentives stopped working (they can only work for a certain period), it was discovered that all kinds of incentives were implicit in the plan of which the central authority was not aware and which hampered the realization of the plan.

Thus, it is a practical and important question to know how many of the decisions are made in the central economic plan, and how many decisions are delegated to lower economic units, e.g., enterprises or organizations of enterprises in the industry, etc. This is particularly important with regard to the investment plans. In Poland, for instance, we are now developing a scheme which provides central planning of what we call fundamental investments, for instance, building a new plant or substantially enlarging an existing plant. We give the enterprises the right to undertake the subsidiary investments autonomously, without asking anybody for approval.

The latter has proved to be necessary in order to assure greater flexibility of investment decisions. For instance, if the enterprise needs to put up funds for unforeseen repairs, or if it wants to buy machines to increase output quickly, or to make some technical improvement, it must have the power to do so. Our experience was that before it got the approval of the central authority to make the necessary investments, the whole situation was already different. Thus, the situation was utterly inflexible. The financial resources for such subsidiary investment would consist of a part of the amortization fund of the enterprise and of bank credits it could take up for the purpose of such investments. Investments of small enterprises are to be entirely financed by bank credits without appearing at all in the central economic plan.

Now, of course, one thing should be kept in mind. The fact that a part of that investment is financed by bank credits does subject them in an indirect way to central planning, because obviously the bank can refuse to give the credit. The bank acts on the basis of a certain general economic policy in deciding how much credit it is going to give, for what purpose it is going to give it, and on what conditions it will give it. These are indirect ways by which the central authority influences the subsidiary investments.

A similar economic problem, and a more acute one, exists with regard to the planning of production. In the former period, even the smallest product had to be in the central economic plan. Now, however, only the basic production of enterprises is in it. The enterprise has the right to undertake what is called subsidiary production, which is not in the plan. There is quite a discussion among Polish economists as to whether production should be in the economic plan. There are a few economists who think that production should not be in the economic plan at all, but that it should respond only to the economic incentives of the market. The practical solution which will probably be adopted in Poland will be to put in the central economic plan the output of certain basic commodities, like coal, steel, raw materials, certain means of production, and textiles of mass production, i.e., commodities of a particular significance for the national economy. As to the rest, the enterprises will have a plan of output in terms of its total net value without prescribing the detailed assortment. A shoe factory, for instance, will have a total value plan of output but be able to produce any assortment of men's shoes, ladies' shoes, and children's shoes, according to its own decision.

All these are problems of technique and not of principle. I think that the one essential thing in the socialist economy is that the plan has to be an active one which determines the pace and the direction of development of the national economy. The other things are really questions of technique, which may change under different conditions. There is, however, one more problem which I want to mention in this connection. This is an essential and not a technical thing—the plan must be based on correct economic accounting. Correct accounting of economic costs and economic benefits, and consequently a correct price system, are indispensable.

In a socialist economy, prices have two purposes: One is as a means of distribution, and the other as a means of economic accounting. Therefore, there are two principles which must be taken into account in the formation of prices. This requires a calculation, at least as we see it now in our work in Poland, of two kinds of prices, namely, market prices and accounting prices.

Unless distribution of consumers' goods is done by rationing, the market price must obviously be such as to establish equilibrium on the market, to equalize demand and supply. The same holds also for prices of the means of production when administrative allocation is removed and enterprises freely buy and sell their products. Market conditions determine the equilibrium prices which equalize demand and supply. The principle of determining the market prices is very simple. They simply must equalize demand and supply.

However, market prices are not sufficient. In addition, there must be calculated accounting prices, which reflect the social cost of production of the various products. The accounting prices, of course, may strongly differ from the market prices. In Poland, we propose now to calculate what we call the initial or normal prices, which would be the cost of production plus a profit, which serves to cover accumulation and the collective consumption of society. To these normal prices, we propose to add a (positive or negative) markup in order to obtain the market prices which equalize demand and supply. Then the (positive or negative) differences between the market prices and the normal prices would be an indicator for economic planning.

The indication for the next plan would be to increase output (by making the necessary investments) where the market price is high above the normal price, and to stop expansion or even diminish output where the market prices does not cover the normal price.

The great controversy at this moment among Polish economists is what cost should be included in the normal price: whether it should be average cost of the enterprises in a given industry or marginal cost. The majority of economists take the view that it should be marginal cost. Those who are in favor of average cost really consist of two groups: one is in principle in favor of average cost, and the other is in principle in favor of marginal cost but believes that this would in practice be a very difficult system of calculation and so takes average cost simply because the other solution, though theoretically better, is very difficult to realize in practice.

The proponents of marginal cost, of course, propose to use a practical approximation to marginal cost. The cost on the basis of which the normal price is to be calculated is the average variable cost of the group of enterprises which have the highest cost in the industry. The method proposed is to classify the enterprises in several groups (not too many, because it has to be practically easy), and then to take the group of enterprises which have the highest cost as the pilot group. It serves as the indicator. There is a reason for using average variable cost of the group. If we take just one enterprise, we may get a very unrepresentative figure. We want to have something which represents the real cost structure of the industry. Therefore, we take the average variable cost of the enterprises in that last group.

The argument in favor of marginal cost and of this procedure of practical interpretation of marginal cost is this: We have, for instance, electric power plants. Each plant produces at a different cost. Suppose we can save electric power. What is the diminution of cost to society? Obviously, when we save electric power, we still stop or diminish production not in the plants which have the lowest cost, but in the plants which have the highest cost. The cost in the latter plants represents the resources we save; it represents the saving to society. If we have to expand the output of electricity, the cost to society is the cost of operation of electric power plants which produce at the highest cost. Consequently, if changes in the use of electric power take place, the effect on the cost to society is determined in the most costly plants, and that change is marginal cost. We consider only variable cost in the highest cost plants, because the fixed cost is given and does not change in consequence of a change of utilization of electricity.

This is basically the system which a majority of Polish economists propose. To the marginal cost, there must be added something to cover all the fixed costs in the industry. This may be zero, because the larger profits of the enterprises which produce at lower cost may be sufficient for this purpose. If not, we must add something to marginal cost. Such additions would have everywhere to be proportional to the marginal cost so that the normal prices would be proportional to the marginal costs of the various products and cover the fixed cost.

The indicator for the plan would be whether the market price is higher or lower than this normal price, i.e., whether it socially pays to expand or reduce the output of a product. I have to add that this normal cost would also have to include a surcharge to cover capital accumulation and collective consumption, e.g., non-productive expenses of the state, etc. Such additions would have to be in the same proportion in all branches of the economy so as not to affect the proportions between the normal prices and marginal costs.

So much on this subject. It is clear that good and effective economic planning requires a development of economic science and that it must be based on scientific economic analysis. This is one of the basic differences between a socialist and a capitalist economy. In a capitalist economy, the economic processes are elemental; whereas under socialism, they can be directed on the basis of scientific knowledge of the needs and possibilities of the whole national economy.

PART III

Case Studies of Economic Systems

The case studies of economic systems which follow are living illustrations, respectively, of the theoretical models of capitalism, market socialism, and central planning analyzed in Part II of this book. These case studies show how the models' abstract principles of economic organization and control are applied in real economies. They reveal the compromises and adaptations required by cultural, historical, and geographical factors. And they demonstrate that actual economies are hybrids or mixtures of theoretical economic systems, rather than pure examples of them.

It is striking to note that all of these working economies combine—though in different proportions—private and public ownership of the means of production, consumers' and planners' sovereignty, and the decentralized market and central planning in resource allocation. The selections that follow explain and appraise the nature of, and reasons for, the specific combination of seeming alternatives which each of these living economies has chosen.

Regulated Capitalism

The Western regulated capitalist economies differ considerably in regard to the extent and nature of government economic planning and state intervention in economic life. The United States and France, discussed in the next two selections, are respectively among the countries with the least and the most government regulation of economic activity.

In the United States, the emphasis of the central government is on indirect intervention through aggregative monetary and fiscal measures to promote high employment and price stability, and on various expenditure programs to devote resources to public purposes and to redistribute income through transfer payments. Direct controls over private activity are relatively limited. Finally, there is no overall national economic plan, although various kinds of public and private planning do occur, as Selection No. 11 shows.

In France, in addition to indirect guidance of the economy through monetary and fiscal measures and various kinds of specific intervention, the government has attempted to steer the private economy by aggregative "indicative planning." Using national economic accounts and input-output tables, the government, in collaboration with representatives of business, agriculture, and trade unions, has attempted to draw up an agreed medium-term plan for the development of the economy. This plan, however, is only "indicative," not "imperative"—essentially a forecast, not a directive—and it is prepared only at the branch level, not covering individual private firms. By coordinating the production and investment programs of the different branches of the economy, the plan seeks to reduce uncertainty and risk for individual firms and to promise them a "balanced market" in which to acquire factors of production and sell output. Although firms still make their own decisions freely in the market, they do so with the benefit of knowledge about the intentions of the rest of the economy and the government's credit, tax, and price policies. Selection No. 12 analyzes and evaluates how France has tried to combine overall government planning with decentralized decision making.

11. ECONOMIC PLANNING IN THE UNITED STATES*

Gerhard Colm[1]

It is sometimes asserted that economic planning does not exist in, and is not compatible with, the U.S. economic system. This article identifies and explains four types of economic planning currently operating in the United States: business planning of production and investment; government planning for specific programs, such as the development of water resources; economic policy planning for stabilization; and planning of priorities in the use of national resources for such goals as national security, raising the living standards of low-income groups, etc. The author also discusses the principal techniques used in economic planning, including long-term projections using national income accounts, interindustry tables, surveys, and mathematical programming. Although there is no comprehensive national economic plan in the United States, the various partial plans, such as those of business, are drawn up in the light of more aggregative plans, such as the government's plans for stabilization and growth. Thus, there is considerable interdependence among the various planning efforts.

* Reprinted by permission from *Weltwirtschaftliches Archiv*, Band 92 (1964), Heft 1, pp. 31–54, with some omissions. Gerhard Colm is Chief Economist of the National Planning Association.

[1] In the preparation of this paper I had the assistance of several National Planning Association (NPA) colleagues, particularly of Sidney Sonenblum and Joel Darmstadter with respect to national economic projections, Louis Stern with respect to planning of water resource programs, Marshall Wood with respect to mathematical programming. I also made some use of the answers to a questionnaire by the International Congress of Administrative Sciences prepared in 1961 by Gerhard Colm, Harvey S. Perloff and Irving Fox. Even though this article is largely based on work done by the NPA, opinions expressed are those of the author.

I. IS THERE ECONOMIC PLANNING IN THE UNITED STATES?

If national economic planning is understood to mean a formal organization for directing the productive resources of the nation towards the highest priority national goals, then it is doubtful that one can speak of national economic planning in the United States. To a large extent the development and allocation of productive resources are directed by market signals—by the interplay of supply and demand. The decisions of individuals in their capacity as consumers, workers, and business managers are guided largely by such factors as prices and costs, profit and income expectations, new orders, opportunities offered. Yet it would be misleading to conclude that there is no economic planning in the United States. First, there is a great deal of *program planning* in federal, state, and local government—planning for specific programs involving substantial and recognized government responsibilities. Second, there is *business planning* in private enterprise. Third, there is *economic-policy planning*, that is, planning on the national level, not for directing, but at least for promoting the development and use of resources for recognized national objectives. Finally, economists in the United States are contributing greatly to the development of methods and quantitative economic analyses for planning—substantially ahead of the actual use of such methods in the United States.

Paradoxically, there persists a deep popular suspicion that planning is an instrument of communist or socialist countries which has no place in a free enterprise system; in fact, much of the practice in government and business and much of the thinking move in planning concepts. In any international survey of planning in the Western countries, one could not simply report "does not apply" for the United States.

This article will deal with the role planning plays, or might play, in what is basically a market economy. The topic lies on the borderline of existing and potential developments. Those who believe that planning has no real place and therefore no future in the market economy will dismiss as a fleeting aberration such rudimentary program, business, and economic-policy planning as there is in the United States. However, it will be regarded as a promising beginning by those who believe that in our age a market economy will be successful only if it is integrated with substantial elements of planning. I subscribe to the latter point of view and therefore place considerable emphasis on the budding planning efforts in the United States. The same events would be reported quite differently by those who, on the one hand, believe that these planning efforts are a mere blemish on an otherwise perfect market economy and should be dismissed as a fad; or those who, at the other extreme, believe that planning cannot be blended with, but would only supplant, the market system. This article tries to present observations on factual developments, but the way facts are emphasized and interpreted often depends to a large extent on the perspective in which the facts are observed.

II. PROGRAM PLANNING IN THE UNITED STATES

Certain functions required by modern society are not fulfilled exclusively by the working of the market-price system. Examples are national defense, education, transportation, and development of natural resources. Such programs have traditionally been insulated from the market operation: defense and education, from the early beginnings of the country; transportation, from the development of the highway, canal, and railroad system in the 19th century; and natural resources, from the time of the great conservation movement of the early 20th century.

The alternative to the allocation and management of resources by the price system is political determination implemented by budgetary and appropriations processes and regulatory procedures. Not every management of such a function by political means makes use of planning. Political decisions can be made and are made to some extent by response to pressure, by logrolling, or by sheer drifting. But even a political skeptic will agree that political decisions are not and should not be made merely on such grounds. Actually, an increasing degree of planning is used in the United States in the preparation and deliberation of public programs, in both the executive and the legislative branches of government.

Program planning requires the establishment of a specific goal which indicates in quantitative terms what is to be accomplished in a field within a given time, the effects which such an accomplishment would have on other areas, and a spelling out of the resources which are needed for reaching the goal. After a plan has been adopted, it is up to the government agency to organize the use of resources for accomplishing the goal efficiently. When we think of a specific project—say construction of a school or of a road—then it is obvious that efficient operation must be based on a plan. Even in our private affairs, we would not undertake a journey without first making a plan which indicates where we want to go and what means of transportation we want to use and within what time schedule. When we plan not only one particular unit of activity but some group of activities—e.g., education within a community or within a state or for the nation as a whole—planning becomes more complex, if only because more groups and jurisdictions become involved. A notable case of progress in program planning in recent years is the national defense field. Here, conditions were simplified because full responsibility rests with the federal government, even though the relative independence of the various services—Army, Navy and Air Force, and even certain subdivisions in these services—had to be considered. For most other government programs, program planning on the national level has to consider that responsibilities are frequently shared with federal, state and local governments as well as with private enterprises. Not only are both public and private activities directly involved in many of these functions, but they are always indirectly affected.

There are a number of important functions involving various levels of government and private enterprises—urban renewal, ground facilities for air transportation, outdoor recreation (e.g., the National Park System), training and retraining programs, and so on. Most of these functions have by necessity become matters of government concern because often their benefits are expected to accrue over a very long period of time, as in the case of outdoor recreational facilities, which have to be planned many decades in advance. Private investments depend on a relatively shorter payoff period and would not adequately take care of the future needs in these areas even if reasonable fees would be charged for the use of these public facilities. It is primarily the time factor which makes conservation of natural resources a matter of concern for the government. This also is an example of an area in which government at every level and government and private interests are interrelated.

In other cases, the investments have to be made well in anticipation of demand for use of facilities, and this often implies a higher risk than private enterprise can be expected to incur. In some cases, such as educational facilities or road construction, the activity cannot effectively be guided by market signals because it would be too cumbersome to charge prices, or it would not be desirable to make the service available only to those who are able and willing to pay the price. Again, in other cases, the benefit often accrues not only to those directly concerned but also to many other individuals or to the community as a whole, as, for instance, in programs for basic research involving large outlays for research equipment. Thus, there are for each of these functions different reasons or a combination of reasons why accomplishment of a task requires guidance by planning as well as by the signals of the market.

* * * *

III. BUSINESS PLANNING

Successful business operation has, of course, always involved advanced planning. Even to the present time, however, major emphasis has been put on short-term planning for marketing and production decisions. However, for the last two decades long-term investment planning in consideration of anticipated as well as current market size has become increasingly important.

Most of the larger corporations maintain special divisions charged with planning investments in new plant and equipment, as well as planning for manpower, research, production and diversification programs, inventory holdings, and other business operations. Even when these special planning units exist, it is often difficult to identify the locus of planning decisions in the business enterprise. Usually these units provide planning information and occasionally a tentative plan, while the decisions remain the prerogative of high-level management. Business has always been conducted by a mixture of "hunches" as to what line of production appears promising in the longer run and by observation of short-run market indicators. Planning is a kind of systematization of the hunches. The long-range plans are subject to annual, if not quarterly, revisions on the basis of market developments. Thus, planning and observation of the market supplement each other as guides to business management.

A variety of methods of planning are used by business from simple "common sense" techniques to sophisticated mathematical programming and operations research. Currently, the more sophisticated techniques are highly experimental, offering great promise for the future. Already, a number of successful applications have been achieved, particularly in the field of inventory control, product diversification policy, and short-term production decisions. Even so, the simpler approaches still dominate. The basic idea in such approaches can be illustrated with respect to steel. A long-term projection of the national economy is used as a bench mark to determine what the development of steel-consuming lines of production is likely to be. Here, attention is paid to the construction industry, automobile and other durable goods products, railway construction, and so on. Also considered are trends in substitution of other materials for steel as tastes and relative prices change, the effects of technology on steel consumption, and the impact of international competition. After the total demand for steel (or specific types of steel) has been projected, the steel company will establish a target of the share in the market which it will seek to obtain. This, then, will be the basis for establishing an expansion or modernization program. Occasionally, considerations of local market and supply characteristics will permit a determination of the regions in which added capacity should be located.

Management will, of course, not accept such determination of a plan without consideration of other facts, such as the availability of financial resources. Management also takes into consideration the degree of uncertainty and the possible harm done by basing decisions on either too optimistic or too pessimistic projections. A firm in a strong financial condition can risk the use of a more optimistic projection in order not to miss an opportunity. A firm in a weaker position will be more cautious in order to avoid bad investments which could have fatal consequences. In the case of business planning, as in the case of program planning, projections are needed outside the line of business of the particular corporation or outside the function under deliberation. There is no major line of business which is independent of economic developments as a whole, or which can afford to ignore the expectations of major customers and competitors, domestic and foreign. Thus, successful business planning must, by necessity, be concerned with national and international economic developments and the policies which affect such developments.

IV. ECONOMIC-POLICY PLANNING

The government's responsibility for promoting economic development is firmly rooted in American tradition since the days of Alexander Hamilton's program in support of manufacturing industries and Henry Clay's public improvement program to Roosevelt's New Deal. President Roosevelt established a National Resources Planning Board, which did fruitful work but did not succeed in setting up a coordinated planning mechanism for the government as a whole. It was abolished by the Congress in 1943. Only in the Employment Act of 1946 was established, by statute, a procedure for guiding economic and fiscal policies. This act created a Council of Economic Advisers in the Executive Office of the President and a Joint Economic Committee in the Congress, each with a professional staff. The legislation requires the President to transmit to the Congress at least once a year an Economic Report which should set forth (1) levels of employment, production, and purchasing power required to accomplish the purposes of the act; (2) estimates of employment, production, and purchasing power as they are likely to develop under existing legislation in the foreseeable future; (3) changes in legislation and policies required to influence economic development in the direction of the goals set forth under (1).

This law, which requires the setting up of a goal and a statement of the steps which are needed to accomplish the goal, represents, in my opinion, a mandate for planning. The law does not specify the period for which the statement is to be made, nor what details are required. At times the act has been interpreted simply as requiring qualitative statements, such as that employment should rise or prices be stabilized—which I believe is a misreading of the legislative intent. It is true that the language of the act as finally adopted was intentionally less specific than the original proposal made in 1945, because it was believed by the deliberating committees of the Congress that the exact method of estimation should not be frozen before experience had shown what kind of presentation would be feasible. This commendable caution does not deny the fact that the legislation did establish a planning mechanism for the guidance of economic, fiscal, and monetary policies of the government. It must be admitted, however, that today, 17 years after the adoption of the Employment Act, planning has not yet developed into a routine mechanism. Nevertheless, recommendations for economic and fiscal policies have been formulated in the executive branch and examined in the Congress on the basis of the concept prescribed by the Employment Act.

Even though no formal planning procedure has been developed, the advice given to the President by the Council of Economic Advisers has been based on the use of planning concepts. Thus, the recent proposal for tax reduction was based on (1) a projection of the increase in total production required to reduce unemployment to a tolerable level; (2) a computation which showed that under the continuation of existing policies unemployment was likely to rise—even in the near future; and (3) an estimate of the effect that a tax reduction, combined with some increase in government expenditure, would have on aggregate demand, business investments, and total production of goods and services. The recommendation is significant because it departs from popular concepts of "sound" fiscal policy and subordinates traditional budget rules to economic-policy planning.

Economic-policy planning is largely the province of the federal government. However, economic growth requires action as well in the nonfederal public sector, in the consumer sector, and in the business and labor sectors of the economy. Both program and business planning play an important role in the support of economic growth as well as being affected by overall national developments and expectations. In an economy of private enterprise a national economic policy depends on the possibility that business plans, to some extent, can anticipate general economic developments, as they are shaped both by the forces of the market and government policies.

So long as there are many unsatisfied needs to be served by the public sector, program planning will be an important channel by which economic-policy planning is implemented. However, many of the programs are not under the direct control of the federal government but are in the jurisdiction of state and local government and semipublic institutions. The federal government can exert a powerful influence on the state and local governments by such devices as grants-in-aid or guarantees of bonds issued by these governments or public authorities created for the performance of specific functions. However, economic-policy planning will inevitably result in some regions benefiting more than others and the planning devices must take this into account in order to encourage maximum cooperation from local groups. As the trend in program planning appears to be increasingly towards cooperation among various levels of government, economic-policy planning will undoubtedly be affected.

Economic-policy planning, as currently practiced, takes advantage of the fact that the consumer sector can best be influenced by taxes—particularly the individual income tax and certain excise taxes—which affect consumer disposable income. Experience seems to suggest, for instance, that a reduction in taxes imposed on the consumer, particularly in the middle and lower income brackets, results fairly promptly in additional spending of more than 90 percent of the tax relief. It is somewhat more difficult to reduce consumer spending by the imposition of additional taxes. The experience during the war showed that an increase in taxes often resulted in the demand for increases in wages and higher incomes, in which case policy objectives were not accomplished. Another device used for influencing consumer purchases is a change in terms for installment purchasing. In general, we are still so far from a saturation point of consumer desires so that, for the foreseeable future, it seems possible to increase consumer demand by tax reduction and other stimuli, while the level of living of certain low income groups can be increased through welfare, educational, and training programs and other *ad hoc* devices.

It appears more difficult to get business investments into line with a plan for economic growth under conditions of a free enterprise economy. Tax incentives may help, but only with varying effectiveness depending on the circumstances. Credit policy (e.g., through government controlled investment banks) may help in countries in which scarcity of capital is the main obstacle to economic development. In the American economy, availability of funds is generally not the most important limiting factor of business investments, so that increase in the availability of funds through tax relief or credit policy will not in all instances correspondingly increase the amount of investment. The tax reduction of the Revenue Act of 1962 gave business an investment tax credit; at the same time, the Treasury Department permitted a more liberal depreciation allowance. These factors probably were effective more as a motivational incentive than as a result of the actual increase in available funds.

There seem to be two other important factors which act as stimuli for business investments, besides the expected flow of funds and expected profit margins. One is the necessity to adopt new technology in the international and interindustry competitive struggle, and the other is the expectation of expanding markets. It has been shown earlier that it is one of the purposes of business planning properly to anticipate likely expansion of markets in various lines of production and services. Here, economic projections serve business planning. However, the relationship also works the other way round. Economic-policy planning becomes effective if business management uses the economic projections which indicate the opportunities for expansion and thereby help to bring business investments in line with the policy plan. This "announcement effect" of the plan on business investment decisions will work, however, only if business is convinced that the plan is realistic and particularly that the government will play its role in implementing policies for the promotion of economic growth.

This is the crucial element in what has been called "indicative" planning, particularly as it is practiced in France and Japan. There business representatives participate in the deliberation of long-term goals for various industries and in preparing estimates of investments needed to accomplish these goals. The people participating in the estimation and planning process are likely to follow the same reasoning in their own business decisions. To the extent that the business leaders who participate in the planning also influence the attitude of other businessmen in the same branch, the plan becomes self-enforcing. We do not have the same self-enforcing effect in the United States. An effort was made by the Council of Economic Advisers a few years ago to consult with leading business economists on investments needed to achieve a certain rate of growth. But there was skepticism that such a rate of growth would be accomplished and that the government would and could actually pursue the policies needed to promote it. Furthermore, the practice in France and Japan rests to a large extent on the fact that business is more tightly organized so that there are business representatives who can speak for their particular branch of industry and influence all major enterprises in that branch. Also, the degree of cartelization, or at least understanding, among the business enterprises permits a businessman to translate a goal for a line of production into the share for his own enterprise. In the United States, there is not the same degree of cooperation among enterprises in the same line of production, and businessmen would hesitate to enter any such collective considerations because of fear of violating antitrust laws. Nevertheless, the increasing use of economic projections as a bench mark for business investment decisions moves in the same directon as indicative planning. The announcement effect can operate in an economy of large, even though unrelated enterprises.

V. PRIORITY PLANNING

Program planning and business planning are concerned with the planning for certain programs or certain economic units. Economic-policy planning is concerned with the economy as a whole. Here a further distinction needs to be made. Economic-policy planning, in the recent past, has been concerned with the *performance goals* of the economy, that is, high employment, a desirable rate of growth, reasonable price stability and equilibrium in the balance of payments. For such goals the specific purposes for which productive resources are used can be ignored as long as they do not remain idle and as long as balance is attained between production for current consumption and future growth. However, in addition to the concern with this overall performance of the economy, there has developed a growing concern with questions of allocation of resources—with *achievement goals*, such as health, education, cultural objectives, national security, raising the standard of living of low-income groups, space exploration, and promotion of foreign economic and social development. These goals to some extent support each other; but to some extent they compete with each other for limited resources.

Planning for these achievement goals is an outgrowth of program planning as discussed above. There is a difference, however, in that we used the term "program planning" for public programs (even though public programs are often integrated with private activities), while achievement goals are conceived irrespective of whether they are in the public or the private domain. More important, program planning is focused on one program at a time—it is partial planning. Here, we are concerned with the allocation of all productive resources to the various national economic objectives.

Program planning, by necessity, becomes priority planning when programs become so large that expansion of one program has an effect on other programs so that their interrelationship must be considered. Priority planning also is an outgrowth of performance planning because we cannot be satisfied with establishing goals for high or full employment without raising the question of "employment for what?" One might say that priority planning represents a merger of program planning and economic-policy planning.

It is significant that there has been a growing concern in American life in recent decades with national objectives and with priorities among goals competing for the productive resources of the nation.

The planning of achievement goals is not meant to be accomplished by direct government allocation of all resources but by the conventional use of government expenditure policies, tax policies, and other vehicles of economic policies and their effect on the behavior of businessmen, workers, and consumers in general. Therefore, priority planning of achievement goals is not outside what we have called economic-policy planning, but approaches it from a broader perspective than that concerned solely with the performance goals of high employment, economic growth, and economic stability. We said before that in spite of the mandate of the Employment Act a regular procedure for long-term economic-policy planning has not yet been established in the United States. With respect to priority planning this deficiency applies even more, since the need is becoming more and more apparent while the development of procedures is at best rudimentary.

VI. PLANNING AND PROJECTIONS

Program, business, and economic-policy planning all require projections of economic activities and of resource availabilities. However, the types of projections required for these various planning purposes differ in terms of their detail and the manner in which they are used.

Program planning requires consideration of broad economic developments on a national or regional level. A water resource plan, for instance, whether regional or national, must be related to the anticipated water utilization by agriculture, industry, power, navigation, urban household consumption, and so on. Only the projection of the national economy as a whole can indicate the future development in these various sectors of the economy and the water needs that would result from them. Similarly, a road construction or air transportation program must be related to anticipated needs for transportation of various types, which again is related to the development of the economy as a whole. Training and retraining programs also must be related to anticipated demand for workers of various skills; that is, they must be related to changes in industrial composition, growth of technology, and regional development.

Thus, program planning requires a development of general economic projections which can serve as bench marks for setting goals for these specific functions. That is one reason why there has developed in the United States such a demand for long-term economic projections. The nature of such national economic projections which are being used as bench marks for functional planning will be discussed in a later section.

Business planning requires not only projections of board national and regional economic developments but also projections in considerable industrial and geographic detail. Such detail permits relating a specific enterprise's activity to future markets and developments in competing products.

The use of projections in business planning is believed to have greatly influenced, for instance, the very high rate of investment activities in 1957. It has indeed been claimed that in anticipation of future markets overinvestment occurred at that time because actual markets did not expand as promptly as was anticipated. The experience of overinvestment, or of the deficiency in the development of aggregate demand in subsequent years, has probably resulted in some temporary disillusionment about investment planning in anticipation of future markets. It is most likely, however, that business enterprises will continue to make increasing use of investment planning guided by the use of long-term projections. However, the more individualistic attitude of entrepreneurs may well preclude policy planning from having the degree of self-enforcement in America which it seems to have in countries such as France and Japan. There appears to be a great need in the United States to establish closer participation of business and labor in the planning process, in a way that will not conflict with United States antitrust policy.

Thus, overall economic projections are needed if only to provide bench marks for program and business planning. These projections will be most useful if they permit a breakdown by industries and regions. They are usually presented in the form of national economic accounts. The National Planning Association (NPA) publishes periodically 5- and 10-year projections in the form of national economic accounts with about 20 subdivisions. They have been widely used by business and government for bench mark purposes. Also, other research organizations (e.g., Stanford Research Institute) have engaged in occasional long-term national economic projections. The federal government has initiated the preparation of a 10-year growth model under the leadership of the Council of Economic Advisers, and with the cooperation especially of the Bureau of Labor

Statistics in the Department of Labor and the Office of Business Economics in the Department of Commerce. This projection will utilize a 1958 interindustry table, now in preparation.

Long-term economic projections which are used as bench marks for program or business planning are designed as an aid in estimating future demand or need for particular products or services. The great difficulty with such forecasts is that they imply not only strictly economic but also political forecasts. Obviously, the economic future will differ depending on foreign policy developments, such as continuation of the "cold war" and international tension, relaxation of tension with arms reduction, limited war, or even a nuclear disaster. An economic forecast can only make *assumptions* with respect to such international developments. To this extent, every economic projection is hypothetical in character. The projections used in the United States as bench marks for program and business planning make this hypothetical character of the forecast very clear to the users.

It is more difficult to deal with implications of economic projections for growth policies. The economic future is affected by policies designed to influence economic development. If there are indications that the economy, under existing policies, would have a low, sluggish rate of growth, it is a fair guess that the government will modify policies in order to promote a more satisfactory rate of growth. Thus, there is the paradoxical situation that prediction of a sluggish rate of growth and high unemployment under existing policy may lead to the prediction that these policies will be modified, which could result in an accelerated rate of growth. This would invalidate the primary prediction without refuting it. Actually, the hazard in forecasting public reaction to predicted economic developments may be called the "uncertainty principle" in economics.

Forecasting what action a government is likely to take is complicated by a variety of factors, such as possibly conflicting objectives, e.g., economic growth; high employment; equilibrium in the international balance of payments; popular pressure in one or another direction; conflicts between different parties in power in the executive and legislative branches of government; effectiveness of policies that have been adopted, and so on. In recognition of these difficulties, the NPA has always computed alternative projections assuming adoption of different economic policies. However, those who want to use projections as guideposts for their own business planning or for program planning cannot very well use alternatives, but need one estimate which they use for their own planning purpose. In response to this need, the NPA has developed a "judgment model" which incorporates the best judgment about likely government measures and their effectiveness. The term "judgment model" was selected as a warning to the users that this model does not represent an entirely objective observation of economic development but, in the final analysis, must incorporate also the judgment of individuals about likely political reaction to economic developments and likely economic effect of political measures.

Although a judgment model projection (with alternatives) is required for program and business planning, a "decision model" projection is needed for economic-policy planning. Basically, in accord with the requirement of the Employment Act and in accord with the requirement of logic, computation of the decision model requires three types of interrelated projections: First, that line of development representing a movement towards a desirable level of production and employment; second, the probable development implied by continuation of present legislation, policies, and business attitudes; and third (possibly with alternatives), the likely effect of proposed changes in legislation and policies, including their effect on consumer, labor, and business attitudes.

Basically, this set of three projections, which, for example, has been used in examining proposals for tax reduction and other policies in support of economic growth, makes up the decision model used for economic-policy planning purposes. It should be emphasized that decision model and judgment model projections can be based largely on the same statistical data and estimates. However, they serve different purposes and the data require adaptation to these different purposes. The decision model helps in suggesting policy goals and in the formulation of policies designed to promote achievement of these goals. Every kind of long-term economic projection implies the setting of goals and policies which will be adopted. For the judgment model, it is usually thought prudent to assume that there will be some slippage in the accomplishment of the goal. Any such assumption would be wholly inappropriate for the decision model.

The first step in constructing a decision model was described above as representing a projection of the American economy if the goals of high employment, price stability, equilibrium in the balance of payments, and so on are to be accomplished. Sometimes decision models are constructed as if the goal is given from the outside and the only task consists in determining the policies needed to accomplish this predetermined goal. In other words, a goal is assumed, and the policy instruments are variable. Under the conditions in the United States, however, we cannot assume that the goal is a predetermined datum. As a matter of fact, one purpose of the decision model must be to determine what kind of goal should be considered and proposed for adoption.

Let us assume, for instance, that somebody suggests a 6 percent sustainable rate of growth to be a desirable goal and estimates what policies are needed to achieve it. Assume we find that achieving such a rate of growth leads into bottlenecks and inflationary tendencies which require adoption of physical controls over the flow of materials and of price and wage controls, and so on. Such policies would not be acceptable to the American people under conditions short of a national emergency. Therefore we would try out goals which may be more modest but could be accomplished within the existing institutional framework.[2]

Actually, on the advice of the Council of Economic Advisers, the President has mentioned a goal of a sustainable rate of growth of better than 4 percent, presumably between 4 and 4.5 percent per year. It was believed that such a rate of growth could be accomplished without adoption of materials and other controls. It was also believed that such a goal would be compatible with the other concerns of government—particularly the objective of reasonable price stability and eventual equilibrium in the balance of payments.

The decision model presumably would be the tool for the formulation of fiscal, monetary and other economic policies needed in support of that rate of economic growth deemed desirable and feasible in the given political and social frame of reference. But, the fact that this tool has been used primarily for the formulation and appraisal of fiscal and monetary policies should not suggest that these are the only devices needed for accomplishing such a desirable rate of growth. Actually, a higher rate of growth may also have implications for quite a number of other economic policies—for instance, in the field of price-wage relationships, and with respect to programs which could actively support economic growth, such as urban development, transportation, research, education, training and so on. There is a growing recognition in the United States that support of economic growth requires an interrelated system of government measures, particularly since we are dealing here with growth under conditions of rapid technological change and, consequently, rapid change in the requirements for manpower skills. Planning for economic growth is a much more complex undertaking than implied in the older concept of a stabilization policy designed to mitigate the ups and downs of the business cycle.

VII. NATIONAL ACCOUNTS PROJECTIONS

The national budget has proved to be the most useful framework for the projections needed for program, business, and economic-policy planning. Not only are the data presented in a consistent manner so that economic interrelationships can be evaluated, but the accounts are sufficiently flexible to permit analyses at different levels of aggregation and to allow for the addition of further detail as the need appears.

The projections usually cover 5 and 10 years ahead, but should be renewed each year for a 5- and 10-year period. This conforms with most

[2] "Within the existing institutional framework" should not be interpreted in too narrow a sense. This phrase should permit evolution of institutions in adaptation to new tasks. Preparation of a decision model contains a political aspect. It will differ if undertaken for a conservative or progressive government.

business and economic-policy planning, which tends to have a 5-to-10-year planning horizon. Some program planning, however, requires much longer horizons when major facilities, such as highways and dams, are involved. The national accounts projections are easily adaptable to these longer intervals.

The NPA's *Economic Projection Series* illustrates the way in which this type of projection is made. Trends are analyzed in the supply factors (population, labor force, employment, hours, productivity) and demand factors (consumer expenditures, plant and equipment investment, residential construction, foreign trade, federal defense and nondefense expenditures, state-local expenditures) in the economy, bringing the two sides into balance by a series of feedbacks and successive approximations. The model is tested for consistency, not only in terms of historical trends but also in the interrelationships among such factors as changing industry productivity; industrial and occupational distribution of employment; composition of final demand expenditures; and industry gross output or industrial production indexes. Other key relationships which are examined in making the projections include: spending and saving patterns of consumers in different income brackets; trends in capital output and capital-labor ratios; household formation in relation to housing demand; the relationship of the tax structure to revenues at multiple levels of government. The data are drawn from the standard government sources, input-output studies, and other special studies, such as household expenditure surveys, government budget studies, and capital investment analyses.

In making the projections, past trends must usually be modified to account for sharp changes in technology and tastes which appear imminent and for shifts in economic policy which appear likely. The expected policy changes are the basis for the full employment judgment model projections previously mentioned. The national accounts model also shows alternative projections under differing assumptions about policy changes, productivity, allocation of final expenditures, and levels of national defense.

As the national accounts projections have developed, it has become clear that additional detail in terms of industrial and geographic distribution of output are useful to program, business, and economic-policy planning. Economic programming, because of the existence of interindustry information, offers the opportunity for obtaining detailed industry projections consistent with overall national accounts projections. Some experimentation with economic programming for specific regional projections has already taken place. However, currently the most useful projections of state and metropolitan area economic activity are derived as disaggregations of the national accounts projections. That is, projected nationwide totals of such indicators as population, labor force, income, and output are allocated among subnational areas in terms of likely migration trends in population and plant capacity. Program planning increasingly involves the participation of local governments; economic-policy planning is increasingly concerned with local developments which deviate from the national pattern; and business planning is involved with local market and plant location considerations. For these reasons, demand for regional projections is growing.

VIII. MATHEMATICAL PROGRAMMING FOR EMERGENCY PLANNING

I mentioned above that mathematical programming has been used increasingly as an aid in specific tasks of business planning. Some attempts also have been made to use mathematical programming for comprehensive economic planning. A major experiment in this area developed from the experience of World War II. During that period, it took the War Production Board many months to estimate whether a specific request of the military commanders for production of various weapons and other supplies was feasible, and only limited study could be made of the effect on civilian production and its relation to requirements. This type of planning—mobilization planning—necessarily embraced such a large part of the economy, with decisions in one area having such decisive effects on other sectors of the economy that the planning had to be very comprehensive.

In order to be better equipped for the tasks of evaluating mobilization and preparedness programs, the federal government initiated in 1948 the development of a detailed input-output table (based mostly on data from the 1947 and 1948 economic censuses). This table was to serve as the basis for projections which in turn would be used for testing the feasibility of mobilization and military production plans. Mathematical programming—computation of optimum use of available resources for stipulated objectives—was expected to give the answer. The system was not yet operational at the time of the Korean crisis in 1950, but experimental results were available by the end of 1952, using a somewhat simplified set of stipulations applied to a 200-sector table.

The governmentwide undertaking was discontinued with the change in administration in 1953. It was also realized that the mobilization task in the nuclear age would be basically different from that of World War II, so that a planning system developed on the basis of that experience and data referring essentially to 1947 would not be fully applicable. For several years after 1953, very little was done in this area under federal government sponsorship.

However, it was realized by experts in the agencies concerned with mobilization and civilian defense that such a computational system could be of value for tasks for which a country should be prepared in a nuclear age, but very little was done to develop it until 1958. At that time, it was decided to prepare a mathematical model for the implementation of these responsibilities. The Office of Emergency Planning in the Executive Office of the President contracted to the National Planning Association the responsibility for developing a computational system called PARM (Program Analysis for Resource Management), designed primarily for planning under conditions of a nuclear disaster. However, the computational system also could be used for guidance in evaluating a disarmament effort, in studying a cold war or peacetime economy, in tracing effects of major particular programs (such as a highway program or urban redevelopment), and other contingencies.

The system is designed for man-machine interaction; it does not pretend to answer what decisions should be made in a given situation, but rather tests the feasibility of initially stipulated programs. If the system test shows that resources would be overstrained by the stipulated programs, another test with modified program requirements would be made. If the test shows that important resources would be left idle, the decision maker would again modify his programs, perhaps by increasing the size or changing the composition of his initial stipulations.

The system in its present form is relatively disaggregated—including about 2,000 activities. For each of these activities, there are input factors which define its consumption of the principal products and services produced by other activities, per unit of activity performed. Each such input factor has an associated leadtime, defining the time of input relative to the time of output. Factors are also included for inputs needed for the creation of new production capacity for most activities. In most cases, the system itself will automatically indicate the need for the creation of new capacity and the appropriate input factor, whenever the demand for the output of an activity exceeds its capacity. These several sets of input factors are in part adapted from data developed under the earlier program, and in part based on new data from many sources, including the 1958 economic censuses.

The system also contains data on capacity and inventories for most activities, and is constrained to produce schedules consistent with the initial capacities and inventories. These latter data and many of the important control totals are kept up to date by use of current information or by extrapolation.

Somewhat detailed and rather sophisticated estimating techniques for developing final demand stipulations have been incorporated into the PARM system. For example, the personal consumption expenditure stipulations are developed by means of a series of nonlinear estimating equations which relate spending for specific goods and services to income distribution and family size.

The system is time-phased and looks into future requirements and possibilities before estimating production schedules for a given period. Schedules are computed on a high-speed electronic computer with large storage capacity, which performs several hundred million calculations in a few hours. Present estimate of the time needed for a complete passthrough of the model, including the application of all stipulations to the present level of aggregation, is about eight hours. Revised plans for a more highly disaggregated model are now in progress but take account of the coming availability of an even more efficient computer, with speeds many times greater than the one now being used.

The PARM system was described in some detail because it is a model most specifically designed as a man-machine tool for planning. There have been developed a number of other mathematical models in the United States which are primarily designed for short-run economic forecasting, but secondarily can also be used for the evaluation of changes in government programs and planning. I would like to mention among these mathematical models particularly a system of simultaneous equations worked out by a number of economists specializing in various fields of agriculture, consumption, foreign trade, housing, investment, money and finance, government, demography, etc. This model divides production into 32 sectors. It is like PARM a dynamic model. This model represents a cooperative effort originally under the sponsorship of the Social Science Research Council and currently "housed" and sponsored by the Brookings Institution. While several mathematical models have been used with various success for short-term economic forecasting, none of them has yet been used directly, as far as I know, for actual policy formulation in the United States.

IX. CONCLUDING REMARKS

The planning efforts in the United States surveyed in these pages give a picture of unintegrated efforts by government agencies concerned with specific programs, by thousands of private enterprises, by agencies of the federal government concerned with the economy as a whole, and by private research organizations. Actually, these various efforts have more mutual consistency than appears on the surface. Program and business planning are *partial* planning, but partial plans must be seen in the perspective of economic development as a whole. Economic policy planning is concerned with the economy as a whole, but economic policy cannot be effective unless it influences, at least indirectly, decisions on specific programs of government and investment decisions by business.

Thus, we have in the United States planning by a great variety of planning units and using a great variety of planning methods; nevertheless, we have considerable interdependence among these various planning efforts, unorganized and intangible as they may be. It is probable that the planning efforts within the federal government will, in time, be better implemented and coordinated; but it is not likely that in the near future business enterprises will use an official government projection as guide for their own investment planning, as is said to be done in France and Japan. For these countries, it might be said that an *économie concertée* is evolving. In the United States, however, many of the larger corporations will continue to prepare their own national and industry projections or will use projections prepared by private research organizations or by consultant firms. It is, therefore, a desirable development that the federal government has recently initiated a statistical economic growth project which in time will permit private research organizations and consultants to prepare improved projections tailored for the needs of business planning. This would be analogous to the long-standing practice of publishing official census data for use by private organizations in market analyses. The use of projections for business planning makes possible a dynamic market analysis, based not on data of the past but on reasonable expectations.

The type of planning which we described in its initial stage of development in the United States has some similarity with the planning in other Western countries. It is beginning to have a significant impact on the performance of the American economy and is likely to aid in the achievement of a desirable and less fluctuating rate of economic growth. Nevertheless, planning is and remains a tool for public and private operations. The best tool does not assure that a job will be well done. It all depends on the way this tool is used by government and private enterprise.

12. FRENCH PLANNING*

Charles P. Kindleberger[1]

The following selection traces the development of French planning and summarizes how the national plan has been prepared and implemented. It examines the problems of economic planning in France and evaluates the contribution of planning to economic growth. It concludes with an appraisal of the applicability of French planning in other countries.

THIS . . . paper concerns the history, description, delimitation, evaluation, and generality of French planning. Monosyllabically, it deals with what French planning has been, is, and is not; how well it works; and if it could work out of France. French planning is very much *au fait*, so that accounts of its development and present state abound. These aspects will be dealt with minimally. Primary interest attaches then to how planning differs from other aspects of economic policy, to what extent it has been responsible for the remarkable postwar growth of France, and whether it is capable of being transplanted to other jurisdictions.

THE DEVELOPMENT OF FRENCH PLANNING

The origins of French planning lie in the wartime preparation of French emergency needs for overseas assistance after liberation. With liberation achieved, the program was extended and a special department set up in the Ministry of National Economy. But the requirement of the French mission in Washington for a more systematic statement of govern-

---

* Reprinted by permission from *National Economic Planning,* ed. Max F. Millikan (Universities-National Bureau Committee for Economic Research, Special Conference Series, No. 19) (New York: National Bureau of Economic Research, 1967), pp. 279–97, with the omission of most of the source references and some other material. Charles P. Kindleberger is Professor of Economics at the Massachusetts Institute of Technology.

[1] I am grateful for detailed comments on an earlier draft by Michael Lipton, John Sheahan, and A. Van Nimmen.

mental intentions and requirements resulted in the consolidation of scattered agencies into a central General Planning Commissariat, in January, 1946, under the direction of the chief Washington negotiator, Jean Monnet. The first publication of the commissariat was written in English as well as in French, with the Congress in mind: *Statistical Review of the Economic and Financial Situation of France at the Beginning of 1946.* A year later, the first four-year plan, covering 1947–50, was adopted. With the change in United States aid from piecemeal to systematic, under the European Recovery Program, the First Plan was extended to 1952 to coincide with the coverage of the Marshall Plan.

The First Plan had a slogan, "Modernization or decadence," and chose to concentrate expansion on six "basic" sectors: coal, electricity, steel, cement, agricultural machinery, and transportation. At the time of the extension of the initial four-year period, two further industries were added: fuels and fertilizers. Coal, electricity, and railroad transport were nationalized and could be expanded from within. The others were fairly well concentrated and implicitly threatened with nationalization. In steel, capital for expansion was provided from counterpart funds and other government sources (as in other industries) but on condition of mergers. Government intervention was *ad hoc* in design and in implementation; the emphasis on expansion, modernization, efficiency, and modern management which characterized this intervention, however, was systematic.

The Second Plan, organized with a gap of one year, covered 1954–57, and rested on a more systematic basis in national accounting. The emphasis was still on expansion, but this was now extended from the eight sectors to the economy as a whole. The "basic sectors" of the First Plan were followed by the "basic actions" of the Second: research, improved productivity, marketing reform, assistance to equipment, and training, that is, programs to produce more, but under competitive conditions of quality and price. The threat of socialization had ended, and the Planning Commissariat was transformed into an agency for forecasting and economizing. Goals were laid down overall and by sectors, including housing. Most of these were overfulfilled, though not all (machine tools). But the expansive pressure led to price increases and balance-of-payments deficits. Exports grew steadily, but imports grew at a greater rate. The Pinay government chose growth rather than maintenance of reserves, which were allowed to run down virtually to zero by 1957.

The Third Plan ran from 1958 to 1961 and was addressed to growth and the correction of the balance of payments. The need to reduce costs was underlined by the prospective entry into force of the Common Market. The pressure for expansion was maintained, with an increase of 20 percent projected for the four years (manufacturing, 33 percent; exports, 70 percent). Restoration of the balance of payments was to be achieved in six years. The critical position in internal and external balance meant that the leadership in economic policy in France in 1958 was assumed by monetary and fiscal policy, in which the Planning Commissariat had little voice. Quasi devaluation occurred in the summer of 1957. The Fourth Republic ended in May, 1958, and with the entry into force of the Fifth came more effective authority in the monetary and fiscal field. The 5 percent rate of expansion sought by the plan gave way to a mere 1 percent. In December, 1958, the Rueff program provided for devaluation of the franc, a cutback of budgetary expenditure, and adjustment of the tax system. The balance of payments righted itself in nine months, rather than six years, and set the stage for a new advance. In 1960, an "interim plan" was adopted for the years 1960 and 1961, to make up for the slowdown of 1958 and 1959. The overall rate of increase was set at 5.5 percent per year (7.4 percent in industrial production). Rapid increases were achieved.

In the Fourth Plan, over the years 1962–65, the rate of expansion was again set at 5.5 percent a year, raised from the original experts' target of 5 percent. Whereas earlier plans had been called plans of modernization and equipment, this was one for economic and social development. The economic development involved the same prescription as before: expansion, full employment, maximum efficiency, and hence no reduction in working hours. The social side involved heightened pressure for housing and educational capital and attention to urban renewal. In addition, problems of regional balance were explicitly addressed in the plan, to push particularly those regions like Brittany and the Central Massif where industrialization has lagged.

The Fifth Plan, covering 1966–70—five years this time, rather than four—is still in process of formulation as this is written. Newspaper accounts indicate that the projected rate of growth is reduced from 5.5 percent a year to 5, to prevent overheating of the economy. In five years the increase in overall production would be 27 percent, that in private consumption 24 percent, in public expenditure 39 percent. Within the total of public expenditure, housing and military equipment outlays were projected at increases of 34 percent; schools, hospitals, telecommunications, roads and other public projects at 54 percent. M. Massé's[2] report called for an increase in autofinancing of private investment out of profits —from 60 to 70 percent; a maintenance of the work week; and an increase in the prices of public services to allow reductions in governmental subsidies.

THE PLANNING PROCESS

Descriptions of the methods of French planning have been provided in great detail. For our purposes it is sufficient to observe that a given plan begins with an overall macroeconomic rate of growth agreed between the

---

[2] [Pierre Massé is General Commissioner of the French Plan.—EDITOR.]

Planning Commissariat and the Treasury, the economic staffs of which overlap. The Planning Commissariat is divided into three horizontal divisions: Economics, Finance, and Regional, plus 10 vertical sections: Agriculture, Energy, Water, Transport, Industry, Fisheries and Artisans, Construction, Housing, Urban Development, Overseas Territories, and earlier, Algeria. The total permanent full-time staff is small, consisting of no more than 35 professionals, and 140 in all.

For the rest, the plans are elaborated by a series of commissions, which used to meet once for each plan, and now convene annually. The horizontal commissions were two for the Third Plan and five for the Fourth, dealing with General Economics and Finance, Manpower, Productivity, Research, and Regional plans. The vertical commissions have expanded from 7 in the First Plan, to 17 in the Third, and 22 in the Fourth: Agriculture, Agricultural and Food Industries, Artisans, Buildings and Public Works, Chemicals, Culture and Arts, Energy, Housing, Nonferrous Mines and Metals, Overseas Territories, Oil, Post Office and Telecommunications, Radio and Television, Sanitary and Social Equipment, School, University, and Sport Equipment, Fisheries, Steel, Trade, Transformation Industries, Transport, Tourism, and Urban Equipment. The commissions organize working parties to deal with specific problems as they see fit: Under the Fourth Plan that on Transformation Industries had 60 such parties. Some 3,000 persons served with commissions and working parties on the Fourth Plan.

In addition to the commissariat and the commissions, which actually set out the targets and means of their achievement, the plan is submitted to a number of consultative bodies; to the Economic and Social Council, which was provided for in the constitutions of the Fourth and Fifth republics and is made up of almost 200 representatives of various interest groups and intellectuals; and to the High Planning Council, composed of ministers of state and heads of various national bodies, such as the chamber of commerce, the employers' federation, the trade union groups, and so on. This numbers 60. The Economic and Social Council has an Investments and Planning Section which is now brought in early on the choice of the growth rate. Apart from the First and Third plans, which were adopted by administrative order, the plan is submitted to Parliament for ratification. In the Fourth Plan, the debate was a heated one and resulted both in some modification in favor of regional projects and agricultural interests and a change in the order of events. Submission to the National Assembly formerly took place at the last stage; the Fifth Plan, however, was submitted before it had been finally determined, to permit greater democratization in the planning process.

The planning begins, as noted, with an agreed overall rate of growth, chosen from among a series, such as 3, 4.5, 6 percent. After consultation with the Investment and Planning Section of the Economic and Social Council, a growth rate is adopted. At this stage, the government adds directives covering major objectives—balance-of-payments or regional equilibrium, for example—or education, housing, urban redevelopment, etc. The result is a government directive to the Planning Commissariat. Then the commissions within the commissariat go to work to prepare detailed and consistent targets by sectors and industries. Used in the process are national accounts for the final year of the plan estimated by the Services des Études Économiques et Financières (SEEF) of the Ministry of Finance, investment and labor requirements of the horizontal commissions, assisted by detailed industry studies of such organizations as BIPE (Bureau d'Information et des Prévisions Économiques), income elasticities of demand, as calculated by CREDOC (Centre des Recherches Économiques et de Documentations sur la Consommation), the input-output tables of INSEE (Institut National de Statistiques et Études Économiques). Forecasts are made for those elements in the process as are subject to no or only to limited control, such as exports, the prices of imports, the rate of technical progress, etc. End-year targets by sectors and industries are broken down and built up again by an iterative process to obtain consistency, shuttling back and forth between the horizontal and vertical commissions and working parties of the commissariat and the commissariat staff itself. Moving from the preliminary projections with their expression of political choices to the provisional targets for each sector which are to be debated by committees, and back to the writing of a coherent overall plan is a time-consuming one, using up in present practice a minimum of three years.

IMPLEMENTATION

A consistent plan does not ensure implementation, even though industry, agriculture, employers, and labor have been consulted in its design. French planning is indicative, rather than imperative, as is discussed below; that is, it shows the directions in which the economy ought to go, rather than providing specific targets for individual plants and firms. The mechanism for achieving the plan is usually said to be twofold; on the one hand, two-fifths of national income and half of gross investment, at the peaks, have been represented by the national government (public enterprises, 11 percent of net national product and 30–35 percent of gross investment); on the other, national savings flow to a considerable extent through government hands, taking into account the nationalization of the major commercial banks and insurance companies and the mobilization of savings deposits through the Caisse des Dépôts et Consignations (to make no mention of the Crédit Foncier and the Crédit Agricole). In addition, the counterpart funds developed by U.S. aid in the early days of the plan were invested by the government through specially created Caisses de Modernization. The private capital market functioned poorly; so firms wishing to expand were dependent upon reinvested profits (autofinancing as the French call it) and government allocations. In addition to these means of ensuring compliance, government policy more generally could be brought to bear on individual firms through the administration of price control, tax measures, and in some cases affecting especially foreign investors, licensing approval. In particular cases, a firm would enter into a quasi contract with the Ministry of Finance and the Ministry of Industry, an exchange of letters in which the firm would set out a statement of its intention to invest, and the ministries would express their approval and inform the firm of dispositions taken by them in its favor.

There is some doubt about these means of implementation, however. In the first place, nationalized industries, and even government departments, have not been wholly submissive to the plan. The *force de frappe*, or nuclear deterrent, of the French was not provided for in early versions of the Fourth Plan. The Planning Commissariat's opposition to the tunnel under Mont Blanc and preference for the cheaper Fréjus alternative under Mt. Cenis were overridden. Parliamentary acceptance of the plan does not guarantee voting the necessary credits in the field of public works, which have been considered too important to be fixed rigorously over extended periods of time.

Nor do the nationalized industries help that much. Some of them guard their autonomy better than firms in the private field. The threat of nationalization has been said to have been more potent than nationalization itself. Despite its dependence on the state for capital, Régie Renault, its director has asserted, is administered like a private enterprise, and even a French governmental publication, in calculating the proportions of public investment controlled by the state, "such as those for public works," excludes "certain nationalized enterprises in the competitive sector." The public corporations, especially in railroads, aviation, and electricity, have been among the leaders in increasing efficiency and improving technology. Unlike public corporations in many less developed countries, which have a weakness for wasteful investment programs, they have pioneered in the calculation of efficiency conditions for pricing and investment. To a certain extent, their calculations have become those of the plans. But it is a mistake to regard French planning as using nationalized industries to carry out its designs. Here, as in private industry, where it does not permit itself to be persuaded, it must persuade as much as command.

Even in the field of private business, the plan's powers declined somewhat between 1958 and the 1963–64 inflation with its profits squeeze. Autofinancing picked up and the private capital market as well. Whereas public funds and bank credits accounted for 61 percent of gross investment of the steel industry under the First Plan, the proportion fell to 11 percent under the Third. Control of the supply of capital worked effectively when the economy as a whole was expanded through demand inflation, investment was highly profitable, and savings were in short supply. With cost-push inflation, there may be some profit squeeze in some lines, which would increase the importance of capital availability in the hands of government, but reduce the incentive to expand; and where expansion is maintained at a high pace, with ploughed-back profits or access to foreign funds, as in automobiles, the Planning Commissariat is beginning to have doubts that expansion *à outrance* is an optimal policy.

The central fact of the implementation of French plans, as we shall see presently, is that it has not been doctrinaire.

THE NEED FOR FRENCH PLANNING

Justification for French planning has been found by different people in a number of aspects of the French economy: in ineffective macroeconomic policy; in the muddle of democracies with their permanent danger that government will express contradictory preferences; in the need for information on the part of French businessmen; in the failure of the price system; and in the need to convert businessmen from restrictionist to expansionist attitudes.

The notion that planning has been a substitute for adequate macroeconomic policy finds particular justification in international economic relations. With an overvalued exchange rate from 1950 or so to 1958, planning called for expansion of exports and was supported by a variety of devices: special access to credits, special provision of exchange to meet accessory expenses of exporting, credit insurance, insurance against changes in domestic prices, tax adjustments, advances for the purchase of raw materials, concessions on price controls, governmental agreements with industries including, among other aspects, remission of the value-added tax on exports, and the use of funds to advertise abroad. The adoption of a new exchange rate and a monetary and fiscal policy of restraint at the end of 1958 (aided by the end of the Algerian conflict) eliminates much of this Rube Goldberg disequilibrium mechanism. As already noted, the restoration of the balance of payments which the Third Plan thought would take six years was accomplished in nine months.

Outside foreign trade, however, the contention does not stand up. It is true that monetary and fiscal policy have not always been coordinated with planning; it is not clear how annual budgets could be made to conform to a four-year plan originating three years in advance of the initial plan year. But it is possible that planning created more problems for monetary and fiscal policy than the reverse. The rate of expansion in the Second Plan has been mentioned, and lately under the Fourth Plan the Pressure on the labor supply, on wages, and hence on prices has been so great as to call for the stabilization measures of the Treasury. An initial impression was that it was lucky that the Economic and Social Council had raised the sights of the Planning Commissariat from 5 to 5.5 percent growth per year, since the higher rate of expansion enabled the French economy to absorb the Europeans returning from Algeria in substantial numbers in 1962 and 1963. By 1963 it appeared that the Planning Commissariat had underestimated the labor requirements of the French economy, which was drawing increasing numbers of North Africans, Spaniards, Portuguese, and Italians, which the plan had not counted on, but was still reflecting sharply rising wages; or perhaps it has overestimated the fluidity of the French labor market and the readiness with which labor could be drawn from areas of excess population like Brittany.

That French government has a propensity to exhibit a muddle is well known and indeed the subject of a thick monograph written before the record of French postwar growth had been firmly established. The plan may, moreover, have gone some distance to clarify national objectives, for the public sector as well as for the private, even if the public sector did not always submit to the wishes of the Planning Commissariat. But planning is to be distinguished from *dirigisme* which prevailed in the interwar years—the steady interference of public decisions in response to day-to-day difficulties without systematic, long-term elicited aims. The interventions of the authorities are substantial and increasing, and forecasting at a minimum is needed to give them coherence and rationality.

But while government might perform in an incoherent and contradictory way in the absence of a plan, the real danger as seen by most French observers was in the failure of the price system. Sometimes it was thought that the price system produced the wrong amount, whether too much or too little capacity, as separate firms, making their own forecasts of global demand, followed independent investment programs. In the initial stages, it was thought that capital was scarce and that any investment in excess capacity would be a serious waste. Later, the fear was general among French economists that private enterprise and the price system tended to lead to underinvestment. This view was subsequently abandoned without modifying the basic distrust of anarchic competition. More recently, the European Economic Community and the French officials which have made representations to it have renewed the view that private pricing leads to excess investment and waste through unemployment. It is, of course, possible to reconcile these views with the position that the price system produces too little investment in noncompetitive industries—through a tacit mutual acceptance of inertia by existing firms——and too much in competitive. In these circumstances, planning calls simultaneously for more competition and less, with each therapy applied separately. It is hard to find an explicit statement of this point of view, but it may well be implicit in the contradictions that abound in writing on the subject.

Among those who believe that the price system fails to produce the right level of investment, the plan is regarded as market research or, sometimes, merely as information. The exigencies of the market and of capitalism demand an informed economy, and a discussed economy, though not a concerted economy. In a dynamic economy, large cost-reducing innovations must be based upon a view of the rate of growth. Uncertainty depresses investment.

The record of French planning, however, does not altogether confirm the view that private myopia will depress investment. The First Plan underestimated the growth of demand in electricity, which above other fields should lend itself to accurate forecasting. The Second, using improved methods, such as linear programming, was overly timid: Four-year targets were reached in two years. Concurrently, the Planning Commissariat tried to repress expansion in steel. The record of Charbonnage de France and of the European Coal and Steel Community in coal is one of overestimating demand and the need to expand capacity. In automobiles, the French Plan and the European Economic Community have both been bearish. Wickham states that planning is exhaustive market research, which supports rather than replaces the market mechanism, and thereby generally increases the inducement to invest, although it should probably dampen it in some sectors such as automobiles, steel, wheat, soap powders, shipbuilding, etc.[3]

This is a neuralgic issue, whether the planners replace or supplement the price system, and whether the information or market research provided by the plan increases or depresses the rate of investment which would otherwise obtain. Information removes uncertainty, but collusion removes it more thoroughly, either collusion with government, or with other firms. Simple forecasting—the "onlooker effect" as Frisch puts it[4]—is not enough. To achieve credibility, the forecasts must be confirmed. This encourages the quasi contract or tolerance of the cartel. It is the great virtue of French planning that it has left individual firms free to experiment, innovate, overexpand and underexpand by restricting its planning to indications rather than commands. Its further virtue is that it has failed to eliminate uncertainty in foreign trade, an area where market research and the provision of information function ineffectively. The uncertainty arising from the openness of the French economy has been a vital element in the success of planning.

If planning is not compensation for faulty monetary and fiscal policy, nor shadow-pricing required by the failure of the price system, nor coherence and rationality in governmental, multifarious, previously inchoate intervention, nor pure market research and the provision of information on demand, what is it? There is room for the possibility that French planning has not been immutable, and that its original essence, of which it retains a large measure, is "promotion," or "pressure for expan-

[3] S. P. Wickham, "French Planning: Retrospect and Prospect," *Review of Economics and Statistics*, Vol. XLV, No. 4 (November, 1963), pp. 335–47.

[4] Ragnar Frisch, "On the Need for Forecasting a Multilateral Balance of Payments," *American Economic Review*, Vol. XXXVII, No. 4 (September, 1947), pp. 535–51.

sion." In a previous comment on the subject, I suggested that: "Knowledge of income and industry projections and faith in the inevitability of expansion are communicated to firms at intra- and inter-industry meetings. This is perhaps the most powerful effect [of French planning], and one which has a faint resemblance to a revivalist prayer meeting."

This passage has been chided for its "faintly derisive tone," but it is interesting to note an echo of the same note in the most straightforward description of the plan, without a trace of irony: "People have to be convinced, one is tempted to say 'converted.' "[5] Later, the Planning Commissariat occasionally had fears that its pressure for expansion had overreached itself and that certain industries were going too far, threatening "overequipment," waste, and risks of underemployment.

The point to note is that French planning is not an exercise in programming or optimizing, but the provision of a flexible framework which is subject to change and adjustment on an *ad hoc* and empirical base. The standard cliché is that French planning is indicative, rather than imperative. Bauchet prefers the term "flexible" to "indicative."[6] Massé insists that it should be "active."[7] French economic thought is essentially interventionist, and this characteristic raises the most important issues for economic policy. When the French intervene among domestic firms in their own economy, it is of course their own concern. Readiness to act on a case-by-case basis affecting United States business in France poses larger international questions. But a still more important choice is required if the French attempt to export this interventionist-at-the-particular-level philosophy to the Common Market, or block progress on the Kennedy Round tariff reductions under GATT. There can be no doubt of the need to intervene in particular cases on occasion: the first request to GATT for an exception to the most-favored-nation clause came from the United States, which wanted to discriminate in favor of the Pacific trustee islands; President Kennedy intervened in the U.S. Steel price increase of May, 1962, and Secretary Anderson of the Treasury telephoned the Ford Motor Company to request them to postpone or halt the purchase of the minority shares of Ford of Dagenham in the autumn of 1960, backing down, however, when he learned that the arrangements had gone too far ahead to be called off. But here the rule is nondiscrimination, and particular intervention occurs only in exceptional cases.

French economic officials "reject the inhuman fatalism of 'laisser-faire, laisser-passer,' " and point out the need for "regulating the exercise of economic freedom." Objection was expressed in August, 1962 to the

---

[5] John Hackett and Anne-Marie Hackett, *Economic Planning in France* (Cambridge, Mass.: Harvard University Press, 1963), p. 368.

[6] Pierre Bauchet, *Economic Planning: The French Experience* (New York: Frederick A. Praeger, Inc., 1962), p. 24.

[7] Preface to François Perroux, *Le IVe Plan Français* (Paris: Presses Universitaires de France, 1962).

action of General Motors in closing down a Frigidaire plant in Gennevilliers and discharging 685 workers because of the competition of imported refrigerators from Italy, and to Remington Rand's action a month later in dismissing 800 workers at Caluire, near Lyons, as it concentrated its manufacture of portable typewriters in the Netherlands. Applications to invest in France by Chrysler (Simca), Libby, McNeill & Libby (canning), and General Electric (Machine Bull) were all granted, but only after discussion and adjustment of the business arrangements in the latter two cases. Other European countries, to be sure, are not above concern in these matters: viz., the Parliamentary clamor in Britain over the Ford purchase in 1960 and the Chrysler acquisition of a minority holding in Rootes in 1964, and the unsuccessful Italian intervention at the EEC to establish rules of competition for American automobile firms operating inside the Common Market. Automobiles present a most interesting case study for future observation of French planning, the Common Market, European Free Trade Association–EEC competition, and the treatment of American direct investment. It will be particularly a testing ground for the principles of customs union and nondiscrimination if the 13 or so major companies in Europe (4 each in Britain, France, and Germany, and 1 in Italy, to say nothing of the smaller companies in Britain, the Common Market, and EFTA) were to be reduced by competition to 3 or 4, as in the United States market—some of them, perhaps, the same in the two continents.

French justification of special attention to foreign investors is that their sources of capital lie outside the scope of the control of the plan, so that the major instrument of control of French firms, capital allocation, is inapplicable. This overstates the matter. In most direct investment, a great deal of the capital is acquired locally in any event. Moreover, as already noted, the effectiveness of the state's domination over the capital market has varied, declining considerably from its initial substantial height until it rose again under the recent profit squeeze. From this side of the Atlantic it appears that there is more concern for and attention to American firms seeking to establish operations or interests in France than for European firms. There seems to be a disposition on the part of French ministries to regard European competition as suitable in general because of the comparable size of the firms concerned, but American firms as requiring special attention because of their size and power. Case-by-case intervention is therefore justified as the rule, rather than the exception.

Rapid German economic growth ostensibly based on the operations of competitive markets has a substantial ingredient of intervention. This has taken the form largely of fiscal policy, though there are those who attribute an important influence to anticartel policy. (It is interesting, incidentally, to observe that French policy under the plan favored making bigger firms out of smaller, through mergers, especially in steel and under the First Plan, whereas German anticartel policy, at least under the Allied occupation, and to a degree later, made little ones out of big ones.) But there is this important distinction between intervention through fiscal policy and that through direct contact: The former still operates by means of the invisible hand; the latter, despite the insistence upon an indicative rather than an imperative plan, comes close to ordering. The Citroën plant in Rennes, the Usinor plant in Dunkirk, the electronics plant in Brest, and especially the allocation of quotas in oil come close on the domestic front to the same sort of intervention that seems to apply to United States firms.

It is in the international economic area that French planning faces its most serious dilemma, and one apart from income policy in which it is far from clear what the answer may be in theory and practice. Marjolin[8] and Massé[9] believe that the logic of planning requires its extension to the Common Market. "Arguments that are valid on a national scale are equally valid on the scale of a group of countries." "Planning, including programme planning, presupposes an economy whose relations with the outside world are limited or can be restricted, should the necessity arise." The Fourth Plan's success has been threatened in different ways by inflation at home and inflation in Italy. The Baumgartner-Pisani "plan" in agriculture, while it is tantalizingly vague on detail, appears to call for planning or programming of production and distribution in agricultural staples on a two-price system, one positive and high and the other zero, on a world basis. Staff members of the Food and Agriculture Organization are beginning to talk of worldwide "programming" for primary commodities, though in discussion this sometimes comes down to little more than better information, such as the commodity study groups have been providing.

* * * *

Against this is the view that competition from imports was vital in preventing planning by the planned from turning into a cartel. In steel, the resistance of small enterprises was "successfully attacked by the ingenious device of exposing the industry to international competition."[10] "Foreign competition has proved an essential spur to prevent agreed planning from facilitating the cartelization of the whole system."[11] In a closed economy there was the great risk that the common background of businessmen and government officials and the view of both that companies in the same business shared common interests to which antagonism and competition were foreign would cause targets for industries to become targets for firms, and planning to become an impediment rather than a spur to progress. Everything here depends on temperament. In the Japa-

[8] Robert Marjolin, "Do We Need a Plan for Europe?," *E. E. Bulletin*, July, 196?

[9] "French Economic Planning," *French Affairs*, December, 1961.

[10] John Sheahan, *Promotion and Control of Industry in Postwar France* (Cambridge, Mass.: Harvard University Press, 1963), p. 174.

[11] Wickham, *op. cit.*, p. 341.

nese 10-year plan of 1960, the announcement of the 1970 target of doubling industrial capacity led to serious inflation as each highly aggressive competitor responded to the news by doubling his capacity in a single year. In France, the danger as seen by Sheahan and Wickham is that the target for all would become the target for each, on a fixed-shares-of-the-market basis. The open economy thus either disrupts planning by introducing uncertainty into an area where the need is for market research, information, reduced uncertainty and risk, or prevents planning from turning industry static by requiring the individual firm to go beyond maintaining a share of the market and working to innovate, undertake extra investment, and to hold down costs and expand through price competition.

The French dilemma is illustrated by the fact that most officials come out strongly on both sides of the issue. Massé "readily concedes the tonic value of competition," but holds it is "essential to be able to recognize the dividing line between incentive and waste."[12] Wickham has the Common Market providing checks and balances on one page and making planning difficult on another.[13]

The other major dilemma is between planning and macroeconomic policy. It has already been mentioned that planning is not a substitute for adequate macroeconomic policy, except perhaps in the balance-of-payments area. Sound macroeconomic policy may contribute more to planning than contrariwise. The dilemma is this: If planning is to a large degree promotion, or body-English, to sell expansion, and if policing the planning works best in an overheated economy where the power to withhold capital is effective because of a profits squeeze, and mistakes in planning are eradicated by growth in demand, then planning means inflation. Inflation may be stalled off by extra increments of labor on which the planners did not count—*pieds-noirs*, Algerians, Portuguese, Italians, and Spanish, together with women out of the house, farm workers off the farm, and clerical labor out of the inefficient distribution sector. This is fortuitous. High rates of growth can be obtained in a dual economy, where the archiac sector shrinks as resources are transferred to the modern sector. But once the availability of incremental resources for the modern sector dries up, the rate of expansion must slow down, plan or no plan.

Maddison holds that French growth was the result of management of demand and had little or no relationship to planning.[14] In his system, demand is all. There can be no doubt but that the maintenance of high demand does encourage workers to leave the farm, or to come out of the household, and that to this extent, demand creates its own supply. It is also possible that planning straightened out some kinks in the supply curve.

[12] *Op. cit., French Affairs.*

[13] Wickham, *op. cit.*, pp. 341, 347.

[14] Angus Maddison, *Economic Growth in the West* (New York: Twentieth Century Fund, 1964), pp. 151–53.

But the contention of this paper is that French planners underestimated three aspects of overall supply, which largely canceled out: (1) the resistance of large pockets of domestic labor in regions like Brittany, among housewives, etc.; (2) the mobility of international labor from southern Europe and North Africa; and (3) the increases in productivity implicit in modernization and in the shrinkage of artisanry and small-scale peasant farming. The easy gains from the latter two sources of growth have now been harvested, however, and unless the wave of additions to the labor force from the postwar baby boom makes them good, macroeconomic pressure will find itself exerted against a rising marginal cost curve, instead of a surprisingly flat one.

In these circumstances, income policy is whistling up the wind, as the Dutch found out in 1963. The price system *may* shift the character of investment to greater labor saving, though there is no evidence that the French planners recognized what was happening in this respect in the 1950s, and reshaped their planning in this direction which the German market economy seems to have pursued of its own accord in response to changes. There is more and more talk of the need for planning income distribution, which is normally a function of factor pricing and macroeconomic policy, but little discussion of what may be involved. To plan high rates of growth and high profits, when the rate of innovation, though high, is autonomous and labor is limited is to overdetermine the system. It is well to say that you plan for no increase in leisure, but the Régie Renault will give an extra week's vacation, going from three to four, if a tight market gives labor the bargaining power. Labor's refusal to enter into the Planning Commissariat on a substantial scale, so as to preserve its freedom of action, is a symptom of the problem, rather than a cause.

EVALUATION

Is French planning a success? To ask the question is to pose another: By what criteria should it be judged? Wickham deliberately rejects the rate of growth and chooses instead stability of the growth rate, conformity of the results with targets, and investment productivity.[15] It is hard to see the basis for the first; moderate success on the second may reflect nothing more than that any plan tends to be self-confirming, without indicating whether any single plan is the best possible plan, or better than total absence of planning. Investment productivity is a function of the rate of technical progress, on the one hand, and of the efficiency of resource allocation, on the other. John Despres claims that the lower capital-output ratio in France than in Britain, with roughly the same rate of investment in each, is proof of more efficient allocation of resources

[15] *Op. cit.*, p. 344.

under planning because Britain and France presumably use the same industrial technology.[16] But this leaps too many steps. With identical allocation and identical technologies, Britain could have a higher capital-output ratio than France because of less efficient firms: There is evidence to suppose that in the nationalized industries such as railroads, coal, and possibly electricity, this has been the case. Or with firms of equal efficiency, and identical technologies, the British aggregate capital-output ratio could be higher because the composition of final investment demand was different. Or with labor relatively scarcer in Britain than in France, it is only normal to expect a higher capital-output ratio. More likely, in my judgment, the technologies have not been identical.

France started the postwar period with a large technological lag. This gap was closed, and French innovative capacity in many lines exceeded that of its neighbors, certainly of Britain. To what extent this change in productivity was a direct result of planning and of the activity of the horizontal Commission for Productivity, which was brought into the Planning Commissariat from the Productivity Agency, and to what extent it was an independent phenomenon can be debated. Certainly beginning with the Second, the various plans placed great stress on increasing productivity, including special productivity loans and special financing for the production of new products. But the case can be made that productivity increases bulked larger in the implementation than in the planning. Innovation is a consequence of technical virtuosity, which is unpredictable. It does not proceed at an even pace which can be projected. Planners can provide exhortation to technical progress and incentives, but they cannot summon it into being or claim credit for its time path. The French economy used its scarce resources with great efficiency —more efficiency than almost any other country in Western Europe in the postwar period—but whether this is owing to *ex ante* planning or empirical management is impossible to determine, with the latter favored by the record.

In short, it is easy to give French planning high marks for macrodynamic success, although the growth of the economy seems to have followed more an Abramovitz-Solow model of growth through technological progress than a Harrod-Domar model based on investment. The record on macrostability is so-so—despite Wickham's claim—with no serious setbacks, but with difficulties in the balance of payments and income distribution and with need for macroeconomic policy alongside and occasionally opposed to planning goals. On the microeconomic front, it is difficult or impossible to devise an adequate test: Bottlenecks were broken during the early days, but entrepreneurs ignored the plan's attempt to apply the brakes in some fields, and seem not, as yet, to have suffered from it. Perhaps it is enough to score the macrodynamic success.

---

[16] "Planning and French Economic Growth," unpublished honors thesis, Harvard College, March, 1963.

Planning and growth are associated, even if it be true that causality cannot be established, that growth without planning can be found in other contexts, and perhaps planning without growth. The final question poses itself: Are French planning and its success exportable?

CAN FRENCH INDICATIVE PLANNING BE APPLIED ELSEWHERE?

The success associated with French planning has established an enormous vogue for it. Belgium adopted planning on the French model in 1959. The establishment of the National Economic Development Council in Britain draws admittedly on the same inspiration. Chancellor Ludwig Erhard in establishing a four-year framework for the annual budget and creating a Council of Economic Advisers felt obliged to uphold "social market economy" and to insist that he was not "pandering to the politico-economical fashion as expressed in the term which by now has become almost a slogan, 'planification.' " One German who is now a member of the council, moreover, was prepared to contemplate that the major modifications of the German economic structure, for which he saw a need, would require planning to carry through. Organizations which had already embraced planning as doctrine were not slow in finding their beliefs confirmed. Perhaps the most persuasive voice lifted in its behalf was that of a Washington economic journalist who urged its application in the United States.[17]

There is no lack of disagreement. Bankers, businessmen, statesmen, and economists do not hesitate to point out that French planning is more French than planning: Where it abjures price and wage controls, import quotas, consumer rationing or government allocations of labor, materials, and capital, and involves a minimum of interference with private decision making in the economy, it may not be planning at all. Economists in the less developed countries who are inordinately impressed with indicative planning have not questioned whether the primary impetus for French growth did not arise from the backlog of technological advancement into an economy with highly developed skills and institutions, and have shown too little awareness of the tradition of centralization and close contact between government and business technicians in France. More generally, the French system may be seen as squarely in the mainstream of a tradition of cooperation between government and industry which goes back at least to the time of Colbert. In his presidential address to the American Economic Association, Mason concludes that French planning is irrelevant to the United States.[18]

But the relevance of French-type planning to the developed countries

---

[17] Bernard Nossiter, *The Mythmakers: An Essay on Power and Wealth* (Boston: Houghton Mifflin Co., 1964), chap. 8.

[18] Edward S. Mason, "Interests, Ideologies, and the Problem of Stability and Growth," *American Economic Review*, Vol. LIII, No. 1 (March, 1963), Part I, p. 12.

of the West which have competition, appetite for income, capacity for innovation and resource reallocation, and reasonably effective monetary and fiscal policies is perhaps not the issue. Where these ingredients of growth are not present, or only latent, some mechanism is needed to call them into being or into action, and planning is as good a mechanism as any other—perhaps better. Whether French-type planning can evoke growth in countries where the listed attributes are missing, as in the less developed countries, or have lost their cutting edge, as in Britain, is another question. The French economy in 1946, poised on the brink of resurgence, could use the stimulus of planning to great effect.

But planning is not the all-purpose weapon. However much it may have contributed to French growth, it has failed to cope with the problem of stability, or rising costs and prices, or income distribution, problems to which the United States must give heed along with growth. Moreover, growth seems to have made progress lately in the United States, as in Germany, though the circumstances of the two economies differ in important respects and it is dangerous to reach hard and fast conclusions. . . .

The important issue, to which reference has already been made, is the extent to which intervention in the economy occurs at the level of the firm, and with regard to the specific results of action rather than conformity to general rules of conduct. This is the old issue of "rules v. authority" in monetary policy. In the United States there will be economic bills of attainder, administrative rulings, appeals to public opinion, pressure, or even laws designed to produce a particular result in a particular situation. They will be exceptional under present circumstances. If indicative planning is adopted, the role of authority will perhaps not expand much, but the likelihood is that it would expand some. The extent of such intervention in France is greater now and likely to increase. When planning gives rise to growth which makes competition more feasible, we have the best of all possible worlds. Where planning is primarily intervention, the gain is less evident. It can be argued that intervention in France has been efficient economically. It can also be argued that it is becoming increasingly regrettable politically.

Market Socialism

Yugoslavia is the only true example of a market socialist economy which combines public ownership with decentralized resource allocation through markets and prices. As a result, the organization, operation, and performance of the Yugoslav economy are of great interest not only to economic theorists and students of comparative economic systems, but also to policy makers both inside and outside the Communist orbit. The Yugoslav experience has been followed closely in many newly independent, less developed countries committed to government ownership and entrepreneurship but aware of the enormous difficulties of comprehensive, detailed central planning. To these countries, the Yugoslav economy has appeared to offer a promising model which could be adapted to their own economic and cultural circumstances.

The contemporary Yugoslav economy both resembles and differs from the theoretical model of market socialism described in Part II above. Its similarities include (1) public ownership; (2) a combination of consumers' and planners' sovereignty; and (3) decentralized decision making by enterprises in response to market forces, instead of detailed planning and administrative orders in physical terms by the central authorities. At the same time, the Yugoslav economy differs from the Lange model of market socialism in several important respects: (1) Prices, with some exceptions, are ordinarily determined by market forces, rather than set centrally. (2) Enterprises do not follow the Lange rules for choosing outputs and inputs but instead attempt to maximize profits. (3) Investment funds are not rationed by an equilibrium interest rate. (4) Workers' councils play a major role in enterprise management.

Yugoslavia has devised its own answers to the problems, such as imperfect competition and managerial incentives, raised by the critics of the theoretical model of market socialism. It has also had to deal with problems of foreign trade and agricultural organization not considered in the theoretical writings on market socialism. The Yugoslav economy thus offers a unique and original example of market socialism, adapted to Yugoslavia's particular economic, political, and cultural conditions. The following articles explain and evaluate the evolution of the Yugoslav economic system and its current operation.

13. ECONOMICS OF SOCIALISM IN A DEVELOPED COUNTRY*

Rudolf Bićanić

Over the past 20 years, Yugoslavia's market socialist economy has evolved through several stages of progressive decentralization, culminating in a comprehensive economic reform in 1965 which is still being gradually implemented. In this selection, Bićanić traces the changes in various aspects of the Yugoslav economic system, including administrative control over the economy, property relations, the position of the enterprise, savings and investment, consumption, economic growth, stabilization, the price system, and the foreign sector. He then appraises the current economic reform, asserting that it is characterized by "four D's: Decentralization, Deétatization, Depoliticization, and Democratization." However, powerful interest groups oppose the reform for various reasons, and its success is by no means assured.

ECONOMIC REFORM IN YUGOSLAVIA

WHAT IS happening in the political and economic arena in Yugoslavia today should not be haughtily dismissed as the result of disruptive ideological disagreement among self-righteous Marxist factions. Nor is it a reflection of the evil influence of foreign propaganda, Communist or anti-Communist. Nor has it grown out of mischievous activity of reactionary forces eager to achieve the restoration of the old regime.

Some of the problems facing Yugoslavia are particular to Yugoslavia, and in them history and geography speak. But many of the most pressing

---

* Excerpted by special permission from *Foreign Affairs*, Vol. 44, No. 4 (July, 1966), pp. 633–50. Copyright 1966 by the Council on Foreign Relations, Inc., New York. Rudolf Bićanić was Professor of Economics in the Faculty of Law of the University of Zagreb.

are those which every community of nations is experiencing today in both East and West, problems of international regionalism or of supranational centralism. Other countries, too, face problems such as inflation versus stability; maximizing growth or the standard of living; authoritarian discipline as a convenience of the few or democratic self-government as the responsibility of the many. And there also are many other problems which are specifically socialist. All the complexities of the modern world are bound to take a special form in a multinational commonwealth of 20,000,000 people seeking to build socialism beyond the present level of $500 national income per head per year.

The casual observer is often puzzled. Only a few years ago Yugoslavia was presented as an example of a country with one of the highest growth rates in the world; now the foremost aim of economic policy is to reduce investment. For more than a decade the socialist economy struggled against bureaucratic command; now an administrative price freeze has had to be introduced. It was the first country in the world to initiate workers' management in factories and business enterprises and to abolish the wage system; now there is division about whether this means too much or too little democracy. The 1963 Constitution formally declared a one-party state; yet the top political leaders now emphatically demand that the economy be depoliticized. National problems were said to have been solved; and now the country is pregnant with increased tensions among the constituent nations, tensions newly created and socialist in origin. Efforts to find solutions to all these problems are now concentrated into two words: *The Reform.*

It has been said by highly responsible people that this Reform has very great significance, greater even than the introduction of workers' management which has so far been considered the most original contribution made by the Yugoslav brand of socialism. The new policy became possible only when a major political battle between those favoring centralist solutions and those in favor of self-government had cleared the way. First, in 1963, a new Constitution was adopted which confirmed the principles and enlarged the legal framework of self-government, further decentralized the country along federal lines and enhanced democracy within the socialist system. It took two years of inside discussions before the Constitution was adopted. Then, in 1964 at the Eighth Congress of the League of Communists, the same policy was restated in clear political terms, as issues became more polarized and clarified. Finally, in 1965, the federal parliament decided that the Reform should be carried out, which meant putting the third stage of socialist development into operation.

The immediate purpose of the Reform was to combat an increasing pace of inflation; to remove a deficit in the balance of payments; to get idle capacity in industry going; to reverse the increase in unemployment; to raise a standard of living so unfavorably low compared to neighboring countries in the West; and to find a form of government able to give the country a consistent economic policy. These short-term objectives were necessarily linked to some longer term measures of structural change in the economy such as: to overhaul the whole price system; to revise growth and investment policies; to put the productivity of the economy on an internationally competitive level; and to liberalize foreign trade in order to remove the structural causes of its continual deficit. The whole economic system introduced in 1954 had become obsolete, and the new Constitution of 1963 laid down new principles for the economic and political system, the main aim of which could be described as to base the whole economy and society on workers' management. Thus the Reform is an integration of short-term and long-term economic objectives and the implementation of the 1963 Constitution.

To make clear what this means we must review the development of the Yugoslav economic system in the two previous stages. First came administrative socialism of the Stalinist type from 1945 to 1952, inaugurated in the Constitution of January, 1946. This was followed by what was known as the "New System" of 1953 to 1964, given legal blessing in the constitutional reform law of 1953. The third stage was formulated in the new Constitution of 1963.

EVOLUTION OF THE YUGOSLAV ECONOMIC SYSTEM

The Mechanism of Social Control

In the Stalinist centralized type of economic system, government machinery was completely merged with party organization and business management into one monolithic system, run by authoritarian, centralized command through the medium of directives. That is, orders issued from those above to those below in the hierarchical system were not binding on those above, but had to be implemented without question by those below. This inefficient system blocked initiative from underneath and placed responsibility for numerous operational decisions—and mistakes—on top party leaders. It was finally discontinued at the end of 1952.

Under the decentralized New System the government apparatus was separated from business management and workers' management was introduced into business organizations, which were authorized to run current operations. In the government, the bureaucratic element was separated from the political party organization, and ultimately the position of the top party functionaries was separated from that of the head of the government. Ministries were abolished and only a small number of administrative state secretaries remained. Instead of being subordinated to ministries, the socialist enterprises formed their branch associations, federated into business chambers, to organize cooperation and represent their interests. Parliament, although consisting of Communist party members only, nevertheless became less and less a rubber stamp. In this tripartite ramification the position of the party organization was that of arbiter, without formal responsibility for running current affairs; this made criticism and even personal changes in government possible without directly engaging the authority of the party. In spite of this, however, the *de facto* influence of party officials remained great, and this led to a split between the real decision makers and those who had to bear the responsibility for implementing decisions.

The Reform emphasized the fight against government bureaucracy, which continued to wield great influence at all levels, notwithstanding the self-management legislation. Moreover, a further division in the mechanism of social control was taking place. The aim now was to depoliticize decision making in business management, not only in regard to current operations but also in the field of investment and with regard to branch size, location, and financing.[1]

The main criticism of the politically minded was that they pushed their special interests with no regard for economic optimums; interfered in the selection of top personnel of business enterprises, taking political reliability as a justification for promotion in spite of managerial incapacity; and put pressure on enterprises, demanding expenditure beyond what the law ordered for extra-economic funds and fiscal benefits. The federal authorities were not immune to criticism either.

Those who oppose depoliticization claim that it is a sign of the decomposition of Communist control. Its supporters claim it is a prerequisite of the increased division of social functions necessary in a developed society.

Property Relations

In the centralized system, all business organizations, industries, banking, transport, commerce, mining, building—everything except small-scale handicrafts employing up to five persons—became state property. A drive to nationalize agriculture also took place at an accelerated rate.

In the decentralized system, all nationalized property remained, but its character changed from state to "social" property, which meant that management was taken out of the hands of the state administration and (in 1950) given over to the workers' councils, whose power gradually increased. In 1959 nationalization of houses and building sites took place, but the forcible collectivization of peasant property was discontinued in 1953, and only purchase or economic cooperation was used to increase

---

[1] Tito said, "It is my opinion that we must absolutely discontinue the practice of political people deciding where and what should be built, and how much. This is something the enterprises and factories should decide. . . . The building of new factories will also be decided upon through the intermediary of the banks. But political factors should keep out. We political people can give only general lines of an investment policy; you must make the decisions." Vladimir Bakarić, President of the Assembly of the National Republic of Croatia, stated explicitly that, before the Reform, "Power in Yugoslavia was in the hands of quite a social segment ranging from party to leading business officials; all these lost their power when self-management was introduced in factories and enterprises."

further the socialist sector in agriculture. The basic fact was that, with the two exceptions of peasant holdings (limited to 10 hectares) and small handicrafts (limited to five workers), it was no longer possible to increase the size of the socialist sector by expropriation, but only by savings from the income produced by the workers themselves within the socialist sector.

The Reform faced the following situation: The rural exodus had increased more quickly than the effective demand for labor in the socialist sector, which led to considerable unemployment, a reduction in labor productivity, and an increase in the cost of housing and communal services in towns. Ever-increasing imports of food for the growing industrial population and for millions of foreign tourists increased the demand for agricultural products which the socialist agricultural sector and existing peasant production were not in a position to satisfy. Prices of agricultural products therefore rose and a change in the policy toward the unused capacity of peasant holdings became necessary. The growing tourist business argued in favor of further use of the private sector in the catering trade.

The Position of the Enterprise

Under administrative socialism, enterprises were totally smothered by state administration. All materials were supplied to them, prices and costs were determined by ministries, sales were transformed into allocation orders, all profits anticipated were paid into—and consequently all deficits covered by—the state budget. The enterprise became a technical unit of government administration.

In the decentralized system, socialist enterprises were free to operate their current activities according to their own decisions and at their own risk. They sold their products on the market, bought raw materials, decided on the employment of personnel, contracted loans and made their own annual plans. They had to cover costs by proceeds from the market, and shared the benefits with the social community (federation, republic, and commune). This sharing underwent several changes, from profit sharing to income sharing, until finally the wage system was abolished and instead the workers' councils were given the right to dispose of part of the income of the enterprise allocated to its funds, while another part of the income was allocated to the workers as their personal income. This distribution was, on an average, as follows: 60 percent of the income of the enterprise went to the social community, 27 percent to the workers, and 13 percent to the funds for self-financing. But investment resources remained centralized, and so did decisions regarding the founding of new enterprises—a matter left to the political authorities.

Under the Reform a much bigger share of the income was allocated to the enterprise—i.e., 70 percent for investment and workers' personal income. The fiscal burden on the enterprises was diminished: the income tax on enterprises was abolished; the capital tax was reduced from 6 to 4 percent of working capital; the turnover tax, hitherto paid by producers, was changed into a consumers' sales tax collected by the retail trade. The workers' councils were left to decide what proportions of the income at their disposal should go to the self-investment fund and to workers' personal income. Only 30 percent of the net income, instead of 60, was to be taken by the social community. This was to satisfy a long-standing complaint of the enterprises that those which had proved they were able to earn were punished by having their income taken away, while those incapable of making an income were rewarded by being given investment funds and subsidies from the central funds.

Whether enterprises are going concerns must be tested on the market. Prices are to be those of the world market, and enterprises which cannot stand such competition, with normal customs protection, will have to make efforts to do so, and reorganize, or close their doors. As many industrial enterprises were built on too small a scale and below minimum technological standards, and suffer from lagging production or incompetent management, this requirement of the Reform means a major structural change. No doubt the final responsibility will rest with the workers' councils, but a great deal of research, help and advice will be necessary; the workers' councils cannot be burdened with something which they are not capable of doing.

Savings and Investment Policy

In the system of administrative socialism all savings were incorporated into the overall state budget, and investment decisions were made by the top political bodies in the centralized plan.

The main innovation of the New System was the separation of investment funds from the state budget, i.e., the bulk of the investment savings was collected into a general investment fund by the central Investment Bank, which made microeconomic decisions regarding their distribution upon request of the individual enterprises, while macroeconomic decisions (how much for which sector and branch of industry) were made by the annual social plans. Thus some decision was shifted from the state bureaucracy to the bank bureaucracy, and the procedure became so complicated that in the end the decisions were guided by political factors.

As we have already said, the Reform demands that investment decisions be left to the enterprises. The free funds are concentrated and credits given by the banks on business principles. Therefore the General Investment Fund and other funds were discontinued in 1965, and their function taken over by the investment banks.

Consumption and the Standard of Living

The centralized system put standards of living and personal consumption on a very low level of priority. Administrative planning, low wages, moral stimulation rather than economic incentive for productivity, and a small span between the wages for skilled and unskilled labor—these were the main characteristics of the system. Only one exception must be emphasized: enlarged care for education and health, and an expansion of social insurance.

The decentralized system gave greater attention to consumption, which doubled from 1953 to 1963. Beginning in 1954, competition increased the choice and variety of goods, and this, plus the fact that imported goods were available, acted as a stimulus to employees to work more in order to be able to buy more. The stimulation of production by workers' management, income sharing, market economy and consumer credits also contributed to the increase in the consumption level. Changes took place among the consumers themselves. Over a million people shifted to towns and became urban consumers; a cultural revolution increased the level of education and stimulated new wants. The influx of foreign tourists and the large number of workers abroad (over 200,000) had their effect too.

The general line of policy was to stimulate production and productivity by higher incomes; this was counteracted from below by demands for equalization of income.

The Reform's main task was to link the level of living to that of productivity, and to raise both. These aspirations had to be suppressed temporarily because of the price increases of some agricultural products (meat, milk); the reduction of imports and forced exports of certain consumer goods; limitations on the disposable income in enterprises; and the pursuit of a deflationary policy. Compensation proposed by the Reform to offset income reduction had to be paid from the funds of the enterprises. All these measures intensified the problem of raising the level of consumption and increased pressure to carry out the Reform faster.

Economic Growth Policy

The centralized system had just one objective: to maximize investment while fixing an order of priority for the means of production over consumption, heavy industry over light, industry over agriculture. The rule was stiff: maximize growth at any cost, with no regard for optimization.

This obsession with growth continued in the decentralized stage of Yugoslav socialism. The rate of growth in the manufacturing industries was one of the highest in the world. Growth was still based on compulsory saving, with a threefold burden on existing fixed capital (i.e., on developed sectors): centralization of funds for depreciation, capital tax (6 percent) and the interest rate on long-term capital loans. The order of priorities, however, changed. After 1955, priority was given to those industries which could accumulate the greatest savings in the shortest time, mainly light and consumer goods industries. Decentralization of industries took place so that in each administrative district ("a little to everyone") industry had to accomplish a triple purpose: to create a working class or enlarge it; to provide fiscal income for the local administration; and to increase production. This led to the creation of a number of small and inefficient "political factories," built with credits provided from centralized funds—i.e., with other people's money. Thus the building of the "political factories" was the end result of the centralized investment fund. Had the investors had to do it from their own resources, they would have thought it over twice. Integration became the slogan of the next phase, but it, too, met with many obstacles, some subjective (i.e., resistance of the managers and local politicians). The merger of healthy and sick enterprises was often carried out for political reasons, regardless of reasons that were stronger.

The Reform demands that an end be put to this overall maximization of growth, and instead advances the principle of selective growth. Formerly the rate of industrial growth was 15 percent; the presently planned rates are between 7 and 10 percent, which is still very high. Many grandiose investment projects have been abandoned, and the whole federal investment commitment, which already centralized 80 percent of all available funds for the next five years, is being revised.

The Price System and Stabilization Policy

Low prices for capital goods, raw materials, and food; high prices (increased by the turnover tax) for consumer goods, both imposed by the central government—such was the main policy of prices and income during the first period. This meant a regime of fixed, low wages which in turn provided labor services of low productivity; and yet because labor was cheap there was little incentive to substitute for it capital of higher productivity. Technical improvement was a matter of autonomous decision, not induced by production costs. Thus in spite of heavy outlays for costly equipment and machines, often paid for with precious foreign currency, they frequently lay idle in sheds and fields because the system made them more expensive to use than labor.

In the decentralized system macroincome distribution was altered and market prices replaced fixed prices imposed by the government. Agricultural prices remained low and so did those of raw materials, semifinished goods, power, and transport. This was to stimulate industrialization and also to prevent abuse of the monopolistic position of these sectors. Other prices increased. The share of the gross national product taken for investment remained high (33.4 percent in 1964) and decisions to invest greatly surpassed the volume of production of investment goods, so that the prices of these increased 50 percent more than the general price index. Therefore, as early as 1957 limited price control was introduced. Inflationary pressure, caused by ever-increasing demand, had increased to such an extent by 1964 that galloping inflation threatened unless measures to stem it were taken and a stabilization policy introduced, curtailing, in the first place, investments.[2]

The Reform introduced a stabilization policy which explicitly deflated bank credits, reduced consumer credits, strengthened price control and severely curtailed spending (particularly on investment) at all levels of government—federal, republic, and communal.

Planning also had to be changed. The decentralized system had reversed central, authoritarian state planning and introduced combined macro–microeconomic planning by annual and five-year federal, republic, and communal social plans. The Reform abolished yearly social plans altogether, kept five-year plans as "moral and political commitments" and relied primarily on enterprise plans.

Foreign Trade and the Balance of Payments

From a complete state monopoly of foreign trade, the Yugoslav system moved to an open economy in three stages.

The centralized system was autarkic; it looked on foreign imports as a necessary evil to provide capital goods for which it had to pay with exports. The main interest was in amassing foreign currency; the domestic planned system of exchange of goods and of prices was considered completely divorced from the outside world. The decentralized system introduced first the commercial independence of enterprises on foreign markets. Foreign trading enterprises had to cover their expenses by their proceeds. At the same time, the volume of foreign trade began to increase rapidly. The idea that industrialization would make the country independent of foreign countries in the sense of less trade was seen to be erroneous; imports increased, not balanced by adequate exports. Multiple rates of exchange were introduced to cover the gap. But all these manipulated rates proved in the end to be ineffective and foreign debts increased rapidly.

Trading with Western countries was of vital interest for Yugoslav industries and for the food supply, to which the United States and other foreign aid and commercial credits, West and East, made significant contributions. The balance-of-payments deficit was to a great extent covered by foreign credits, international and commercial. Exports did not expand because of increased demand on the home market, lack of agricultural products, and the level of prices abroad which made it difficult for Yugoslav exporters to compete. The centralized accumulation of foreign currency did not stimulate increased exports.

The Reform introduced the following changes. First, the multiple exchange rate has been replaced by a uniform rate based on 1,250 dinars to the dollar. Reorganization will make possible trade based on world market

---

[2] In 1965 the effect of the Reform was to reduce the investment share in the GNP to 27.6 percent.

prices.[3] In foreign commerce, the main stress is now on liberalization. All quantitative restrictions will be removed. Customs duties, reduced from 23 to 11 percent, will remain as the chief form of domestic protection against foreign competition. A reserve fund of foreign currency will gradually have to be built up to $500,000,000 and then free convertibility will be introduced. In 1965, for the first time since 1945, Yugoslavia had an active balance of exports over imports. There was a satisfactory increase in invisible exports, especially from the tourist trade, the merchant fleet, and remittances of workers from abroad.

It has now been recognized that the main Yugoslav economic problems cannot be solved within the country. This means completely abandoning any idea of autarky and accepting a policy of long-term structural integration of the Yugoslav economy into the world division of labor, in place of merely short-term commercial operations. Instead of fear of competition, there will be a more self-confident policy of competitive interdependence which will pull the Yugoslav economy the hard but rewarding way toward progress.

EVALUATION OF THE REFORM

To sum up, the Reform intends to achieve far-reaching results indeed. Its aim is no less than to build a model of a socialist system for a developed country, one which will be able to stand the competition of other developed countries and progress on its own merits, without the constant tutelage of government machinery. This is to be achieved by a process of what I would call the four D's: Decentralization, De-étatization, Depoliticization and Democratization. The process has been begun within the framework of a Communist ideology and a one-party system, but it would not be objective to deny that it has an effectively liberalizing and progressively humanizing character.[4]

How might the Reform affect other socialist counties? Looking at the

[3] The use of world market prices for international trade among socialist countries is not a new one. The Eastern bloc took world prices as a basis for exchange. The difference between the Eastern and the Yugoslav system is that the former uses average prices of some past years while the latter takes actual world market prices. The Yugoslav Reform takes them as a measure for domestic prices as well, while other socialist countries stick to their domestic planned prices, each of them having a different structure from the others so that they cannot be brought under a common denominator.

[4] The concept greatly differs from that of the welfare state. The essence of the welfare state is to leave the production machine capitalist, with some marginal intervention in the public sector, and, by state taxation, to redistribute the income taken from the richer to the poorer consumers. The Reform in Yugoslavia denies this role of redistribution to the state (even to a socialist one) and endeavors to organize production on the basis of workers' self-management, in order to eliminate the roots of exploitation of man by man through income redistribution. It leaves decisions on income distribution to the workers who produce the income (on enterprise, local, regional, state, and international levels), but takes the world level of productivity as the objective measurement.

problem, one could say, with a considerable amount of bold generalization, that the European socialist countries are now entering the second stage, building a decentralized New System of the kind that Yugoslavia is just abandoning. The basic features of this process are: the reintroduction of market prices; gradual emancipation of the socialist business enterprises from the state administration; the introduction of commercial criteria into foreign trade; disbelief in the omniscient and infallible central planner; material stimulation of the workers' productivity. They still remain firm on certain principles: predominance of the political factor in economic decisions; priority of production over consumption; disbelief in workers' self-government; and belief that the process of de-étatization and democratization represents a danger for socialism.

The Reform in Yugoslavia is overcoming these past postulates of socialist policy. There are not many rational elements to aid one in forecasting how long it will take other socialist countries to gain the experience which Yugoslavia has paid for very dearly; but my guess would be that it will depend on the pace and level of their development, and on the pressure of technical progress due to international competition. The new Yugoslav model may provide some stimulating ideas to socialist and Communist parties in developed countries; and developing countries —particularly those which have decided to build socialism—may become aware of some pitfalls in developmental policies.

Yugoslavia's acceptance of a model of a developed country, after hitherto presenting its economic system as an example for underdeveloped countries, is a big step, one that would be likely to meet with opposition in any country, let alone in such a complicated multinational state as Yugoslavia.[5] Opposition to the Reform would logically be expected from those who are least developed, who have to work most and longest to cross the borderline and achieve the level of developed lands; from those who used to get more from the central moneybag than they put into it; and from those who gained more from their political influence than from their industrial skill. The greatest advocates of the Reform would be those who are most developed, who put more into the central bag than they got out of it, and whose economic strength was greater than their political influence.

These logical expectations correspond to reality. The first advocates of the Reform and the spearhead of it were the Slovene Communists. They were joined by the Croats, and the two now march together, and with them the Serbs of Croatia. The Reform's strongest opponents came from Serbia. The Communists from other republics took varied attitudes, feel-

---

[5] In the 1961 population census, 7,800,000 people declared themselves as Serbs (41.6 percent), 4,300,000 as Croats (23.4 percent), 1,600,000 as Slovenes (8.8 percent) and 1,046,000 as Macedonians (5.3 percent). The Montenegrins numbered 514,000 (2.8 percent), the Moslems 973,000 (5 percent), and those who declared themselves just Yugoslavs 317,000. The Albanians numbered 915,000 and the Hungarians 504,000.

ing probably not strong enough to compete with the larger Republics and expecting in the end to find their interests taken into account by either side.[6]

Yugoslavia has just reached the level of $500 annual income per head, which many economists consider to be the demarcation line between developed and undeveloped countries. So the model for underdeveloped societies would no longer work; it would pull the economy backward. The difference in the level of development in the 1960's shows that the average national income per head in the most advanced republic, Slovenia, amounted to $935; in Croatia it was some 20 percent more than the Yugoslav average of $605. In Serbia it was $480, Bosnia $348, Macedonia $339 and Montenegro $330. These differences, taken objectively, would not be of such economic importance if it were not for the following reason: The two most developed republics have crossed the threshold of development, while the others have not. This aggravates the psychological tension.

On the basis of this situation, there developed two opposite concepts, indeed two models of economic policy, both Marxist, both socialist; but one crystallized into an ideal type of a Communist recipe for an underdeveloped economy,[7] and the other into an ideal type for a developed socialist economic system.

Underdeveloped Model	*Developed Model*
Maximization of growth (no constraint)	Optimization of growth under constraint of profitableness
Autonomous investments decided by central planner	Induced investments decided by enterprises
Priority of production over consumption	Priority of consumption over production
Planned administrative prices	Market prices
Monocentric planning	Polycentric planning
Inflationary tendency	Deflationary tendency
National income redistribution by the state	National income redistribution by the producers themselves
Administrative direction of flow of goods, labor and capital	Flow of goods, labor and capital by economic interest
Autarky in foreign trade	Integration in the international division of labor

A second source of discontent arises from psychological attitudes, aspirations, and expectations, more than from objective conditions. In areas that are less developed there can easily arise an exaggerated sense of poverty, frustration and injustice, resulting in impatient demands for compensation from the federation in the form of grandiose projects of

[6] The Constitution of 1963 created a special federal fund to assist underdeveloped areas.

[7] Many of the articles in "Yugoslav Economists on Problems of a Socialist Economy," *Eastern European Economics*, Vol. II, Nos. 1–2 (Fall–Winter, 1963–64), express the views of this group of economists.

development. Among the more developed, on the other hand, a sense takes hold that they are giving much more than they are getting (exploitation), a fear that there will be a repetition of past oppression by the center, and —most sensitive of all—that their progress is being hampered by the less developed areas.

Now dress these collective and real interests in national symbols, put this new content into historical perspective, make it an emotional appeal for political action, and you have raised nationality feelings to a high state of tension. Socialism in Yugoslavia is not being built in a historical vacuum, and the federation consists of fully developed nations which have cultural individuality and rich political traditions. This was fully recognized in 1946 and reconfirmed in 1963 by all the constitutions of New Yugoslavia. These nations have a constitutional "right to self-determination, including the right to secession" (Constitution of 1963, Principles, I) as the Leninist formula goes, and this is a condition *sine qua non* of the existence of Yugoslavia.

* * * *

The national tensions which increased in all the nations of Yugoslavia to such an extent that they became a central problem, first economic and then political, were subject to analysis at the Eighth Congress of the Communist League. The line it took was that if there is a general phenomenon it must have a common cause. It found this cause in the system of bureaucratic centralism against which all the nations were reacting. In order to eliminate national tensions within the country, the first thing to do was to eliminate their common cause. Thus it was that the policy for reducing national conflict became closely linked to the policy of economic reform. The protagonists of the Reform are not provincial anarchists but stand above local nationalism; they are more "internationally minded" than the autarkic centralists. Their main idea is that the socialist economic integration of Yugoslavia is a long process which started in the liberation struggle of World War II but is not yet accomplished; indeed, that its development depends on the extent to which true socialist relations exist, and on the degree to which the policy inaugurated by the Eighth Congress will be carried out.

It is commonly agreed that the Reform is not progressing at a very satisfactory rate. One of the reasons may be that the federal government finds itself in a difficult position, struggling with the overt or covert resistance of the high bureaucracy which on one occasion discreetly puts on the brakes, at another pushes the reform measures to unrealizable and absurd lengths. The heated debates in the federal parliament, exclusively composed of Communists, where bills are passed with a majority of 4 or 6, show how far the process of liberalization has gone. On the other hand, they manifest the strength of the opposition to concrete reform.

One must remember that the Reform is divided into two kinds of measures. First, extensive central control was strengthened (price control, credit restrictions, rate of foreign currency exchange) in order to clear the field for the further liberalizing steps. But since some success was achieved in the first stage in relieving the immediate critical situation, a twofold reaction has now set in. This came to the fore in the meeting of the Central Committee in February–March, 1966. All participants were for the Reform; but some (mainly from Serbia) praised it and demanded that the first centralizing measures should be further pursued, while others (e.g., from Croatia) asked that more energetic measures be taken in pursuit of the main purpose of the Reform. In the complex tactics of the Reform—"to retreat in order to advance better"—some praised the retreat, others pressed for faster advance. Heed should be paid to the warnings of Boris Kraigher, the operational head of the Reform, that it may last for a long time, perhaps for a decade, and that the most difficult period, that of structural changes in the Yugoslav economy, is still ahead. Speeding up the Reform is of utmost importance. Failure of the Reform would deeply shake the faith of many people that Yugoslavia's problems can be solved by consent.

* * * *

14. PROBLEMS OF MARKET POWER AND PUBLIC POLICY IN YUGOSLAVIA*

Joel Dirlam

What decisions do worker-managed enterprises make regarding their output levels, price policy, and the distribution of revenue between personal income for the workers and reinvestment in the enterprise? How does a market socialist economy deal with the problems of imperfect competition which arise in a small, semideveloped country like Yugoslavia? How does the Yugoslav system try to reconcile autonomy for the enterprise with the interests of society as a whole?

These and other aspects of the Yugoslav firm, its behavior, and its regulation are examined in this selection, which is based on intensive research on the contemporary Yugoslav economy. Dirlam discusses in turn the nature and operations of the worker-managed firm, market structure in Yugoslav industry, the resulting problems of monopoly power and anticompetitive practices, and the measures taken to deal with them.

THE YUGOSLAV ECONOMY

THIS STATEMENT is primarily concerned with the degree of concentration in the Yugoslav economy, with competitive practices of business enterprises, and with public policy toward the problems of concentrated markets. In order to place the data and policy in proper perspective,

* Reprinted by permission from testimony before the Subcommittee on Antitrust and Monopoly, Committee on the Judiciary, U.S. Senate, 90th Cong., 2d sess., April 17, 1968, with the omission of most of the footnotes and statistical material. Joel Dirlam is Professor of Economics at the University of Rhode Island.

however, it is necessary to say something about the postwar development of the Yugoslav economy and the peculiar features of its system of industrial organization.

Although economic activity in 1967 stagnated, the overall rate of economic expansion in Yugoslavia during the years 1952–65 was 9 percent. The per capita rise in real income was 7.8 percent. This growth was accompanied by a shift of labor force out of agriculture and into manufacturing and services. In 1939 some 77 percent of the population was rural; in 1966 less than 50 percent. Another index of the remarkable transformation in the Yugoslav economy that has taken place since World War II is the change in exports from predominantly unprocessed products of agriculture and mines, to the highly diversified export pattern of 1966, when 36 percent of the value of exports consisted of manufactures. . . . The Yugoslav economy has, therefore, unquestionably moved out of the "underdeveloped" class to the developed and is heir to the difficulties that afflict the second, as compared with the first. This is not to deny that some areas suffer low income and high birth rates, and remain predominantly agricultural; but they are a regional, not a national problem.

The wide range of products currently turned out by the Yugoslav economy is traceable, in part, to the initial determination of the Communist party immediately after the close of World War II to imitate the Russians. The broad outlines of the program continued to be filled in even after the political split of 1948. While sober application of investment criteria might raise serious question today about the wisdom of attempting such a high level of fabrication in so many industrial fields, and indeed the Yugoslavs themselves have been engaged in a fundamental reassessment of their output pattern, the stability of their economy has undoubtedly been improved by the diversity of output.

While Yugoslavia was being industrialized, she was also moving from a centralized planning procedure that slavishly copies the Russians, down to their terminology, to a decentralized form of "indicative" planning that in many respects today seems less authoritarian than the French or British. The principle of centralized planning, in the sense of direction of output, investment, and pricing decisions by national ministries according to the requirements of a detailed plan, was abandoned in 1950–51. But it took time to dismantle the apparatus.

The principles of decentralization and self-sufficiency that were developed at the time of the political split from Russia have continued to command devoted support, and indeed they have been applied with what at times has appeared to be an excess of consistency. Not only are industrial and financial enterprises expected to be self-sufficient, but also scientific research institutes, higher education and the postal system. Each republic has at least one standard-gauge railroad system, and their policies are resolved in a council that sometimes fails to reach agreement on key issues such as selection of a standard type of electric locomotive. Hospitals and medical personnel are locally financed, and standards of care therefore tend to reflect differences in income levels. Not only is the Yugoslav economic system decentralized; power also appears to be diffused even at a decentralized level. Although they trust in market pressures to bring about the right decisions, the Yugoslavs have set up a large number of institutions that can influence the firm. A cartoon appearing in the leading Belgrade newspaper *Politika* in 1965 shows a meeting of the workers' council of a factory, with the local government council, the trade association, the chamber of commerce, and the union all occupying seats, while the managing committee of the factory and the workers' council hold chairs, asking plaintively, "Please, comrades, can you make a little room —we have to make some important decisions." By now, more than two years later, it is probable that at least the Communist party representatives and the local governments will have vacated their places.

In these moves toward a market socialism, the Yugoslavs led the other East European economies by at least 15 years, although the intellectual debt may not be adequately acknowledged. It is not improbable that the Yugoslav system will prove attractive to developing nations that are socialist, but not committed to the Russian or Chinese variants.

In this program, growth was given a much lower priority than achieving a better balanced use of resources. Much of the rapid expansion in preceding years had resulted from establishing new firms, and transferring labor from agriculture to industry; if borrowed funds (or gifts) for investment in fixed assets were to be made harder to obtain, and firms were to discharge redundant workers, growth rates would inevitably decline—as they have.

THE YUGOSLAV FIRM

In comparison with other East European countries, decentralization and reliance on the market have gone a long way. There are, in actuality, relatively few restrictions on the autonomy of the firm. To appreciate properly the causes and consequences of concentration, it is necessary to say something about how the firm is organized.

Organization

The key concept that describes the Yugoslav business firms, its powers, and its relations with other firms and the government is "self-management." Its property is not owned by the state but is held in trust by the firm for society. Only businesses with less than five employees are in the private sector, where private ownership of assets is allowed. The enterprise is not run by either local or federal government but by managers selected by workers in the firm. A workers' council, selected by the employees, in turn chooses a management committee, which roughly corresponds to the executive committee of a board of directors in a U.S. corporation. The general director, or manager of the firm, is chosen by a nominating committee, and the choice must be ratified by the workers' council. A representative of the local government sits on the committee to choose the general director. With this exception there is no provision for state intervention into the affairs of a solvent firm, although its financial reports go to the local government. If a firm under receivership does not prove profitable, it is liquidated.

Each enterprise adopts a set of bylaws that govern the details of responsibilities of management officials and committees. These include such matters as determining the relations among plants and divisions within the firm, the basis for income distribution, responsibility for making yearly and semiannual plans, provision for changing the director, approval of capital expenditures, and labor discipline. Certain key decisions, such as amalgamation with another enterprise, may require a referendum of all the employees.

Business firms may be launched or expanded in a variety of ways. According to the basic company law, enterprises can be formed by governmental units, trade associations, existing enterprises, or private citizens. Rade Koncar, for instance, which is one of the largest makers of electric equipment, started with the nucleus of a Siemens, Ltd., plant in Zagreb that had made small motors and transformers. The steel mill at Zenica, like other steel works, had been taken over by the government prior to World War II. Local governments have tended to finance light industries through direct grants or by using their influence (prior to 1965) in local banks. On occasion, individuals have pooled their assets and begun operations. Two engineers with $100 started a construction and design firm in Belgrade in 1962; four years later they were earning over $2 million and in the fall of 1967 caused something of a sensation by offering, with bank cooperation, to lend $5 million on a competitive basis to firms wanting to modernize or expand.

From the time when a new firm begins operations, it is independent even though its sponsors may have committed millions of dollars to its plant, as in the case of hydroelectric installations, railroads, or shipyards. The enterprise management and operations must conform to the enterprise law, which means the self-management procedure, including preservation of the assets as social property.

Although the Yugoslavs pay obeisance to the doctrine of enterprise independence, which is stressed in Article 6 of the Constitution and in Article 1 of the Basic Enterprise Law, they have established, and require all enterprises to join, a semigovernmental organization that enters into some phases of business affairs of the enterprises in an intimate way. This institution is called the Economic Chamber and is set up on federal, republic, and local levels. The Federal Economic Chamber in 1966 had 376 employees and included sections corresponding to industry groups.

The major administrative tasks with which the Chamber is formally charged by law are the allocation of foreign exchange quotas and supervision of producer-consumer agreements for price increases. But in addition it is in frequent contact with business firms through setting up study committees and holding meetings on current problems, or by participating in preparing proposals for legislative action.

It may be concluded that the primary function of the Chambers (other than the specific administrative duties) is to bring continuously to the attention of top management of enterprise the current economic goals developed by the Executive Economic Council. At the same time the Chamber does reflect views of business. It has urged, for instance, that the tax payment on equity be lowered and tariffs be increased.

Conflicts of Interest

In one respect, centralization still prevails. Enterprise accounts are kept according to a uniform accounting system, promulgated usually by the federal government, and the accounts are audited by a state service. Cash transactions between firms in the social sector are not allowed. The Yugoslav firm has been handicapped by an accounting system that has changed from year to year, but which has never resolved the central problem of a worker-managed industry. The emphasis in the Constitution, and in the Basic Enterprise Law, is on the right of workers to participate in the income of the enterprise on the basis of work done. They are not regarded as selling their labor power in the market. The income statement of a Yugoslav firm, therefore, fails to show wages as a cost; instead, after all expenses are deducted, the net income is divided between appropriations for personal income and for reinvestment. The leading economic weekly, *Ekonomska Politika,* has complained that no one knows what cost is and that Yugoslav firms go into the international market like Alice into Wonderland. The Yugoslavs are aware of the difficulties introduced by their continuing to follow Marxist accounting principles. Revisions of income accounting regulations have been drafted and have been discussed for many months. At least two versions of a new law regarding the calculation of personal income have been prepared, but neither seems to have sufficient support to be adopted. When the revision is finally adopted, some provision will be made for counting labor as a cost and taking it into account through inventory changes, before reaching net income.

Under present law, workers have a claim only to income arising from current output. Hence those employees shortly to be retired or contemplating job changes would have no incentive to vote for reinvestment of earnings. Yet the long-run interest of the firm might be damaged if its workers preferred to cut down on reinvestment and enjoy a higher level of consumption. If the workers were given some form of permanent claim on earnings of their enterprise, the conflict between their short-run interest and the long-term survival needs of the firm could be minimized. But this step would permit workers to enjoy an income from a source other than current work, which is contrary not only to the present constitution but Marxist principles. Nevertheless, the recent encouragement of investment by business firms in banks and by firms in joint ventures makes it possible for enterprises to get income from other firms through holding ownership rights. The next step may be to devise something equivalent to a common stock issue to workers voting for reinvestment, which they could retain as long as they remained with the firm and which would give them income additional to that they receive from current work performed.

Goals of the Firm

Nevertheless, powerful pressures influence the management of Yugoslav firms to make decisions in terms of a planning period of longer than a year, or the period within which workers might be employed without having contracts renewed. Circumstances in which workers can be dismissed are narrowly circumscribed. On the other hand, a worker who quits or is fired cannot easily get another job. The unemployment rate is high—at least 8 percent—not taking into account the several hundred thousand Yugoslavs working in Western Europe. Moreover, privileges such as housing, pensions, and other benefits associated with continuity in a job (although not including seniority privileges) might conceivably lead the workers' council to take into account in its pricing and reinvestment decisions the relative desirability of future as compared with present income.

Whatever may be the balance of costs and anticipated values weighed by the workers in the enterprise, their behavior since the reforms of 1965 seems to show that they are more concerned with present than future income. The proportion of enterprise income devoted to personal incomes, in spite of admonitions from the authorities to raise investment so as to promote modernization, was raised very substantially in 1965, 1966, and 1967. In 1965, incomes were raised about 24 percent to cover the increase in the cost of living.

Given these characteristics of the Yugoslav business firm, issuing from the perspectives and motivations of the participants in it, there is no reason to believe it will behave in a significantly different manner from a capitalist counterpart. In a market that is starved for goods, it will take advantage of the inelastic demand to raise prices and increase net income—whether it is paid out or reinvested. If the firm has what amounts to a national monopoly, like JAT (the only scheduled airline), or a regional monopoly, like Jugopetrol or INA in gasoline distribution, it clearly will have an incentive to restrict output so that the worker-participants enjoy larger incomes. There is much evidence to show that industries with a sufficient number of firms so that agreements are hard to obtain or enforce suffer from lower prices and lower incomes to workers, although failure of a few dominant firms to agree on profits-maximizing oligopolistic policies is not unknown. Intense price competition, particularly among Yugoslav exporters of canned meat and vegetables, is frequently condemned by the press. Excessive inventories of some products testify to import competition to which local firms have been too inflexible to respond.

MARKET STRUCTURE

The narrow market provided by the Yugoslav economy has inevitably resulted in a high level of concentration of production. The total number of industrial enterprises in 1967 approximated 2,500, including mining firms. There were, in addition, about 100,000 handicraft organizations.[1] Since there were, in 1963, approximately 5,441 establishments, the average enterprise (excluding handicrafts), therefore, has approximately 2.2 establishments.[2] In 1965 the largest 200 enterprises accounted for 60 percent of the total assets of industrial firms (excluding handicrafts) and the largest 122 for about 32 percent of the industrial employment, including handicrafts.

The largest 13 employers among 911 retail firms, or about 1.4 percent of the total, accounted in 1965 for over 10 percent of retail employment, and the largest 79, or 8.7 percent of the total number of firms, for 33.7 percent of retail employment. In the U.S. there are about 400 persons for every merchant wholesaler; in Yugoslavia, 20,000. Retailing in Yugoslavia (not counting handicrafts) is as concentrated as wholesaling.

Concentration was high in net product (reinvestment plus personal income and income taxes) of industrial and mining enterprises. In 1965 the largest 462 enterprises, or 18 percent (of the nonhandicraft firms), earned 69 percent of the total.

The concentration of manufacturing industries can also be measured in terms of shipments. According to the data developed for 1963, a high percentage of Yugoslav markets are highly concentrated. In 24.2 percent of the [103] market groups, roughly corresponding to 3-digit industries in the U.S., four firms or fewer shipped 100 percent of the value of output, and in 28.2 percent of market groups, four firms account for 75–99 percent of the output. In these extremely highly concentrated industries, however, are found only 15.2 percent of the enterprises, 36.1

[1] Handicraft units are quite numerous in some areas, particularly stone quarrying, meat slaughtering, milling, baking, miscellaneous food products, wine, spinning and weaving, footwear, wearing apparel, other textile products, sawmills, leather products except footwear, miscellaneous nonmetallic mineral products, metal products except machinery, electrical machinery and apparatus, and manufacturing industries not elsewhere classified.

[2] The number of units with less than four employees was subtracted from the total number of establishments.

percent of value added, and 27.3 percent of employment. Industries with more than 50 percent concentration ratios[3] made up 74.7 percent of the total number of market groups, 33.4 percent of the firms, 58.2 percent of value added, and 47.3 percent of employment. In the United States, based on 1963 census data, only 27 percent of the industries fall within the 50–100 percent concentration group.

Concentration ratios, while significant in assessing the probability of competitive behavior in a market, need to be supplemented by data on the absolute number of sellers. Information on the number of sellers of products conforming either to 4- or 5-digit classifications is available for Yugoslavia. More than three quarters of Yugoslav products, disregarding imports, are sold by 20 or fewer producers, and half of the products by 5 producers or fewer. Nor does there appear to be any trend towards a larger proportion of products sold by numerous producers.

* * * *

POLICY TOWARD MONOPOLY POWER AND ANTICOMPETITIVE PRACTICES

Economic Writing

Yugoslavs economists and politicians have given relatively little consideration to problems of monopoly, oligopoly, and imperfect competition, in spite of the trust that their system has placed in the market as a mechanism for bringing about conformity of behavior of the individual firm with social welfare. A paper by I. Drutter, published by the Economic Institute of Zagreb in 1964, is the only empirical survey of industrial concentration. In 1964, Dr. I. Lavrac argued that Yugoslav markets were too limited to permit competition, that either monopoly or monopolistic competition was inevitable, and that society should therefore exercise efficacious control.[4] Monopoly in marketing was briefly treated by Professor Vasic in a 1965 article, which lamented the absence of any detailed studies of the development of markets. In discussing the revision of the price control law in 1966, M. Todorvic, president of the Federal Executive Council, alluded to the high degree of monopoly in trade, which prevented prices from falling. A 1966 report on the general principles to govern price control legislation emphasized the importance of measures that would break down artificial market barriers. Direct regulation of prices, it was concluded, might be necessary where there was concentration of production, but in such circumstances agreements between producers and consumers to improve production and strengthen

[3] [That is, industries in which four firms accounted for 50 percent or more of total shipments.—Editor.]

[4] I. Lavrac, "Competition and Incentive in the Yugoslav System," in R. Stojanovic (ed.), *Yugoslav Economists on the Problems of a Socialist Economy* (New York: International Arts and Sciences Press, 1964), pp. 147–57.

stability could be adopted under supervision, to insure that cartelization and exploitation of monopoly did not take place. The report recognized that full convertibility of the dinar would greatly assist the relaxation of price controls, but this was not immediately possible. Protective tariffs were desirable only when the domestic industry could eventually compete in world markets.

It is remarkable that there have been no case studies either of industries or of the effects of price control or import limitation. Professor Sirotkovic's well-known book on Yugoslav planning mentions monopoly only in its preliminary discussion of capitalism. Other market discussions are largely theoretical, adopting the classifications that western economists have developed but making no attempt to apply them to Yugoslav markets.

Antitrust Legislation

Yugoslav law expresses antipathy to monopoly. Article 30 of the Constitution prohibits mergers or associations aimed at preventing free commerce of goods and services for the purpose of material advantages not based on work, or promoting other relations of inequality in business. The basic Law on Commodity Trade, adopted in 1967, in Article 52 forbids agreements among business enterprises which achieve a monopoly or other discriminatory (favored) situation on the market. Prohibited agreements specifically include market sharing, price fixing on internal markets, production limitation, or use of capacity, or other business activities resulting in limitation or prevention of free rivalry. Article 53 forbids speculation or activities resulting in shortages of goods on the market. "Unfair" competition is prohibited in Article 54. No precise definition of the term is given; it includes, generally, anything that damages other firms, consumers, or the economy. Deceptive labeling, packaging, or advertising practices are outlawed when they involve quality, quantity, or origin of a commodity or service.[5]

The Law on Commodity Trade also explicitly forbids activities by local governments that interrupt trade and set up local monopolies. The provisions countering this behavior are more extensive than those dealing with the monopolistic behavior of business firms, confirming the general belief that, at least as far as retail trade is concerned, the local governments have been following a policy of extreme protection.

Section 52 of the Law on Commodity Trade, however, explicitly permits price agreements and other understandings not contrary to law which contribute to increasing production and allocating work, or are for the purpose of specialization, or stabilizing the level or structure of prices, or improving the organization of trade and services, or broadening the line of products, or generally stabilizing trade.

---

[5] *Ekonomska Politika* noted two cases where unfair competition was charged. One involved use of a more attractive container for detergent, the other the use of "push money" to promote sale of television sets.

The enforcement of prohibitions against monopoly and unfair competition is entrusted to regional economic courts, set up under the Law of Economic Violations. The Economic Chambers also have a responsibility for preventing unfair competition and monopoly. Through their so-called "courts of honor" to be set up from members of the Chamber, regulations can be established setting forth good business practices and preventing the creation of monopoly. How the decisions of the "court of honor" are to be enforced is not clear, nor do I know what penalties can be imposed for violations. It is these courts, presumably, that are to decide whether an agreement tends toward creating a monopoly situation or contributes to increasing production.

I have come across no instance of an attack by the authorities on a monopoly under Section 52. Instances of price cutting have been challenged from time to time as "unfair competition." In February, 1967, a paper factory was accused by its competitors of selling printing paper at less than going market prices. In October, 1967, the export of corn was alleged to be unfavorably affected by "unfair" price cutting by some of the 30 exporting agencies.

Price Control

Price controls are administered by a Bureau of Price Control established under a law passed in 1962. In March, 1965, all industrial prices were frozen in an effort to check a cost-push inflation. Following a devaluation, the reform of July, 1965, administratively fixed specific price ceilings for about 90 percent of industrial products. As the economy became adjusted to the new price structure, many of the frozen prices were freed when the Price Control Bureau concluded that market conditions for the products concerned had stabilized and upward pressures were unlikely. Controls are presently exercised under a law passed in 1967 which, while laying down the principle that direct control of prices must be regarded as an exception to reliance on monetary and fiscal policy, establishes procedures for fixing ceilings, pricing new products, and raising controlled prices. Only when firms accounting for two thirds of the production *and* consumption of a given product reach an agreement, approved by their Economic Chamber, will the Bureau of Price Control approve an increase.

The Price Control Law, like the Law on Commodity Trade, expressly provides for agreements for fixing prices among horizontal competitors. Such agreements are not to violate Section 52 of the Law on Commodity Trade and they must be made public.

The law also relies on publicity to prevent price discrimination; there is an obligation to publish the prices of goods and services on the part of all enterprises. This is to prevent discrimination among buyers.

The price experience since the July, 1965, reform can be interpreted as demonstrating economic power at the retail level. Prices of industrial products after a moderate (about 2 percent) rise during 1966 leveled off in 1967. But the cost of living, as measured by retail prices, increased 6.9 percent in 1966 and about 7 percent in 1967, even though agricultural prices fell slightly. Retail margins were freed of controls during 1967 except for domestic commodities whose prices were controlled at the manufacturing level.

Business Associations

Yugoslav firms are permitted to join together in so-called business associations, which are permitted by statute to carry on cooperative activities ranging from providing information and standardization of products to joint marketing, allocation of production, and coordinating investment. Summaries of the powers of leading business associations indicate that some function much like our trade associations; others appear to have taken advantage of their statutory privilege to set up fairly detailed production requirements for their members. In these last cases the business association approaches a consolidation. It would not be safe, however, to accept the descriptions given by the association as a precise measure of the extent of their effective power over their membership. Members can withdraw; and agreements about specialization of output may not be easily enforced or renewed. Thus, the business association of railway equipment manufacturers is supposed to be concerned with adjusting production programs, purchasing capital goods, getting licenses, and selling the products. At a meeting of the association in November, 1967, however, there was a sharp division of opinion among the members, who were characterized as "a bunch of competitors," and no agreement was reached on specialization of output or price policy. Other associations appear to cover the production of so many different items that close coordination of production or other activities seems impossible. The 14 members of STANDARD, for instance, produce refrigerators, ranges, washing machines, dryers, dentists' equipment, and 25 other types of appliances.

The Basic Law on Business Associations provides that the contract among the members of the association cannot contain any clauses which are intended to limit the quantity of production or the use of capacity of the sellers, to exclude other economic enterprises from the market or share the market, or to fix selling prices on domestic markets. This provision is intended to prevent the possibility of a business association, or any kind of contractual business-technical relationship, creating a monopolistic situation on the market. There have been no serious attempts that I am aware of to examine the behavior of the business associations to determine whether they actually conform to this provision of the basic statute. Obviously there are possibilities for conflict between these prohibitions and the exercise of the powers that many of the business associations legally possess. For protection against monopoly Yugoslavs seem to depend more on self-restraint of the management of the business associations and on self-interest of the individual members than on outside intervention.

Import Limitations

Many industries have been hurt by imports resulting from trade liberalization after 1965. Higher imports have generated protectionist sentiments and, from all appearances, won some concessions that limit competition by imports in the domestic market. The automobile industry has been hard hit; imports for 11 months in 1967 were up 164 percent over the 1966 level. In December, 1967, the oil refinery at Bosanski Brod asked that tariffs on imported crude oil be eliminated, that the export of crude be forbidden, and that tariffs on equipment not made in Yugoslavia be abolished, while tariffs be increased on petroleum derivatives. The domestic tire industry complained in February, 1968, that "anarchistic imports" had created a difficult situation. Together with representatives of transport, agriculture, motor vehicles, importers, and the Federal Economic Chamber, estimates were to be made of the needs of the domestic market, on the basis of which the industry hoped to reach an agreement about import quotas. The domestic tractor industry urged that since its capacity is sufficient to satisfy the Yugoslav market for 1968, tractor imports simply led to piling up of inventories; a commission was set up by the Federal Economic Chamber and industry representatives to decide on the amount and kind of tractors to be imported for 1968. Domestic railway equipment manufacturers were successful in February, 1968, in having canceled an order by the Croatian Railways for 1,200 freight cars from Italy, because they could have been produced domestically. Representatives of the importers, on the other hand, alleged that their interests would be hurt if imports were controlled and argued that the domestic producers had a monopoly. Responding to complaints of manufacturers of colophene and turpentine, the Federal Economic Chamber arranged for these products to be shifted from the relatively free list of imports from bilateral trading partners to a more restricted category, with a tariff increase.

Perhaps the most important agreement on import limitation was that which applied to steel for the year 1968. Lengthy negotiations between the iron and steel producers and the metal fabricating industry, carried out by an interindustry steel committee, resulted in increases in the tariff on steel, with differential rates depending on whether imports were in excess of a quota. In return for the tariff increases, the domestic producers had to agree not to increase prices.[6]

The ability of the authorities to shift items from the completely liberalized list, which in 1967 accounted for about 25 percent of total imports, to other more restricted categories which are bought through a variety of

[6] The authorities apparently made no inquiry into the possibility of a bilateral oligopoly agreeing to squeeze the public.

exchange allocations stands as a threat to import competition. The exchange quotas under these restrictive arrangements are linked to specific quantities to be imported, and the domestic producers do their best to persuade the authorities that their inventory problems will be solved if imports are limited.

An amendment to the tariff law in March raised duties on 20 groups of items, including typewriters and electrical appliances. There are only two typewriter manufacturers in Yugoslavia, with a total output of 30,000 machines. Opinion was not unanimously favorable to the increase.[7] The adoption of an antidumping statute cannot be regarded as a threat to fair competition, although protectionist pressure undoubtedly inspired it.

MERGERS

Yugoslav authorities have encouraged mergers from time to time, but with more vigor since 1965. Their export difficulties and mounting international obligations have forced them to search for ways to improve productivity. Long-term supply contracts, technical cooperation, joint ventures, and direct combinations are advocated as means to achieve the desired end. Through the Economic Chambers and periodic pronouncements of political figures the virtues of "integracija" are set forth, for instance, in the Resolution on the Basis for Economic Policy in 1968, where the Economic Council of Parliament once more called attention to the necessity for furthering the process of integration.

There seems to have been little restraint exercised on the freedom of firms to move into those markets that showed promise of expansion. The authorities seem to have resisted the temptation to prevent entry by adopting some licensing provisions. One cannot be sure that these entries were mistaken, although newspaper stories emphasize the excess capacity and small output of the firms making the new products. In the fall of 1967, for example, nearly 20 firms were producing oil stoves. After reviewing the increase in inventories, both at the manufacturing and the retail level, of washing machines, stoves, and refrigerators, the moral was drawn that "autarky in production" ought to be replaced by cooperation, division of output, specialization, and adaptation of product mix to the needs of the market.

The number of Yugoslav business enterprises has fallen from 25,015 in 1959 to 14,232 in 1966, during which period there were 9,084 merged enterprises. For manufacturing, firms disappearing through merger in 1965 and 1966 constituted 5.9 percent of all firms; for all industry, 8.4 percent. By far the greater number of disappearances from 1959 to 1966

---

[7] A cartoon appearing the day after the increase showed a train ("industry") approaching a switch, with one track leading to "modernization" and to the horizon, the other terminating abruptly and labeled "increase in tariffs." The newspaper commented that the increase was justified as an emergency measure and not adequately discussed.

was accounted for by a reduction in the number of retailers, some 3,500 of which disappeared. From 1957 to 1966 the number of merchant wholesalers shrunk by 45 percent.

A majority vote of the workers is generally required to approve a merger, although the Basic Enterprise Law leaves the procedure to be decided by the bylaws. Mergers are sometimes turned down: In the summer of 1967 the workers of one shipyard voted down a consolidation with three others; they wanted to have the specialization and development programs decided before the merger. On other occasions, firms once merged have split. Newspapers carry frequent reference to "integracija" but it more often than not means a supply or technical cooperation contract rather than a merger.

EVALUATION OF YUGOSLAV ANTIMONOPOLY POLICY

There appear to be two contradictory tendencies at work in the Yugoslav markets. On the one hand, concentration is high, and the market power derived from it is strengthened by the agreements reached through the business associations for allocating and assigning production. Price control procedure in some ways can be manipulated to permit price increases even of products under control. Industry agreements supervised by the Economic Chambers can result in price increases if the Price Control Office approves. New products are priced with reference to similar items already on sale without approval of the Price Control Office, if information is submitted supporting the price.

Yet there are strong forces preventing the exertion of monopoly power on an appreciable scale. Fiscal policy has prevented inflationary pressures from government spending in the past two years; in fact, a surplus has been realized. Expansion of bank credit, which validated the investment and wage expenditures during the inflationary period prior to March, 1965, has been severely limited, and the money supply decreased in 1967. An unpopular credit crunch, accompanied by mounting unfinanced inventories, has kept inflation within tolerable limits.

Increasing freedom to import has also exerted pressure on producers to lower prices, or at least meet the import prices, and the reduction in tariffs carried through in 1965 has intensified competition. Products for which foreign exchange is freely available include raw materials, foodstuffs, spare parts, and some consumer goods, totaling about 25 percent of imports. Most consumer goods are imported by payment out of a global exchange quota fixed by the Federal Executive Council, which is allocated by the Economic Chamber according to agreement among the importers. If the importers are aggressive and efficient, they can be helpful in maintaining competitive markets.

In 1966, for instance, imports included 23,857 refrigerators, 26,712 vacuum cleaners, 51,633 transistor radios, 10,118 television receivers, and

4.3 million pairs of women's stockings. As a footnote to the stocking imports, the general director of one Yugoslav stocking factory was commended for his confidence in the face of competition. "He said he wasn't troubled; his quality was better than the imports, which lasted no more than a month." Nor did he use the occasion of the interview to complain publicly about unfavorable circumstances, high taxes, dumping, etc. "He says clearly—the plant has lowered the price of stockings."

The authorities apparently attempt to coordinate liberalization of imports with freeing domestic prices from controls. But this procedure can move no faster than the foreign exchange posture of the country permits. Limitations on important exports to Common Market countries seriously threaten the further liberalization of imports and thus the use of imports to check the power of domestic monopoly or oligopoly. The deliberate exposure of domestic producers to intense foreign competition has inevitably generated sentiment for protection.

In spite of the existence of numerous markets which are already oligopolistic, the authorities, as we have seen, are pushing for mergers to achieve cost savings, for example, by avoiding duplication or small runs in competing enterprises. This policy may be justified if present establishments are too small. Determining the relation between efficiency and the size of either a plant or a firm is no easy matter. Measured by one standard, such as number of employees, it would appear that in rather broadly defined industries Yugoslav plants tend, if anything, to be *larger* than U.S. plants. Other tests, however, would confirm the authorities' criticisms: The output per establishment in Yugoslavia of items such as automobiles, refrigerators, cement, tires, power transformers, and steel ingots (produced by open hearth) appears to be so low as to indicate that optimum economies of scale must be far from being realized. Deficiencies in the comparisons of plants by employment size are also indicated by the fact that the aggregate horsepower per 100 workers in the United States manufacturing was approximately four times as high in 1966 as in Yugoslav manufacturing. The respective amounts for the United States and Yugoslavia were 836 and 300 in fabricated metals; 4,373 and 500 in chemicals; 2,688 and 1,100 in paper; and 3,614 and 1,000 in primary metals.

Combining establishments with excess labor supply will not necessarily lead to greater efficiency, unless the redundant workers are let go. But this could be achieved without merger of firms. On the other hand, it is possible though not probable that the relatively low cost of labor in Yugoslavia might result in an optimum or efficient plant with more workers and less fixed capital than in the U.S. Data are not immediately available to resolve this question. The Yugoslavs themselves seemed to be arguing that the establishments were endowed with too much capital, because they were not using second and third shift operations.

There is no indication, however, that in their policies the authorities have surrendered to the narrow market interests of the enterprises, or that the firms themselves have really pressed for a general retreat from the principles laid down in the July, 1965, reforms. While growth has been sacrificed—industrial production in 1967 stagnated—there is general recognition that the rapid rates of expansion in earlier years had been achieved at the expense of both rational allocation of investment resources and the international reserve position of the country. It has required time for the enterprises to adapt themselves to a regime of financial rationality; in the long run a more flexible pricing policy will prevent the accumulation of excess inventories and achieve closer adaptation of quality to market needs.

The major need today is for an orderly system of financial accounting and statements which will make it possible for the Price Control Office to evaluate properly the prices of those firms which are not controlled in the public interest by import or domestic market competition.

Central Planning

The development of the Soviet Union, Eastern Europe, and Mainland China under Communism provides a rich historical catalog of experience in central planning. The following articles illuminate and compare different facets of this experience.

The first selection analyzes and evaluates the Soviet experience in central planning, which has served as the prototype for other Communist countries. The selection emphasizes Soviet experience in the central planning of industry. The second article examines closely the effort to apply central planning to agriculture, the sector of the economy commonly considered least appropriate for centralized planning and control. The third essay considers the operation and problems of the foreign trade sector of a centrally planned economy.

While the "classic" Soviet-type central planning model has some advantages for the "crash" mobilization of resources in a drive for rapid industrialization, it is much less suited to the efficient steady growth of a complex maturing economy. Thus, in recent years the European Communist countries have all embarked on economic reforms intended to "modernize" their economic organization, planning methods, and incentive systems. The article by John Michael Montias reviews and appraises these reform efforts. In Communist China, however, the traditional Soviet-type model of central planning is still applied, with limited success, as the last selection shows.

15. ECONOMIC PLANNING IN THE USSR*

R. W. Davies

The Soviet economic system has served as a prototype for other Communist countries, giving rise to the term "Soviet-type economy" in the literature of comparative economic systems. In this selection, Davies tells how a comprehensive scheme of central planning and administrative control was adopted, beginning in the late 1920's, to mobilize resources for rapid industrialization. He examines physical planning, financial planning, and the direction of the labor force, noting the advantages and disadvantages of the methods employed. The author then shows why this "mobilization" model is less suitable for the more "mature" contemporary Soviet economy and explains the resulting changes in resource allocation, economic organization, and planning techniques. He concludes with a discussion of the obstacles to further improvements in Soviet economic planning and management.

THE SOVIET PLANNING PROCESS FOR RAPID INDUSTRIALIZATION

An outline of the System

The Soviet government set itself the objective of a more rapid rate of industrialization, with a greater investment in capital-consuming industries and processes, than could be achieved within the framework of the

* Reprinted by permission. Originally published as "The Soviet Planning Process for Rapid Industrialization," *Economics of Planning*, Vol. 6 (1966), No. 1, pp. 53–67, and "Planning a Mature Economy in the USSR," *Economics of Planning*, Vol. 6 (1966), No. 2, pp. 138–52. R. W. Davies is Professor and Director of the Centre for Russian and East European Studies at the University of Birmingham, England.

market economy of the 1920's. The main objective was achieved, but with a much slower increase in living standards (consumer goods, agricultural output) than had been intended. To enforce its priorities, the Soviet government abandoned the major assumptions of its earlier policy:

1. A market relationship with the peasant was replaced by administrative or coercive control over his output. The centers of economic and political resistance in the rural commune were destroyed, and hundreds of thousands of *kulak* families were expelled from their home villages. Twenty-five million individual peasant farms were combined into 250,000 collective farms (*kolkhozy*), one or several to each village. The old boundaries and strips were destroyed, and most land and cattle were pooled and worked in common. Agricultural machinery was gradually made available from several thousand state-owned Machine and Tractor Stations (MTS). The *kolkhoz* was required to supply a substantial part of its output to the state collection agencies at low fixed prices in the form of compulsory deliveries. These supplies were then used by the state (*a*) to make available a minimum amount of foodstuffs to the growing urban population, and (*b*) for export. Exports of grain fell from 9 million tons in 1913 to 2 million tons in 1926–27 and 178 thousand tons in 1929; they rose (temporarily) to 4.8 million tons in 1930 and 5.1 million tons in 1931, and this increase was used to pay for imports of equipment and industrial materials. . . .

2. Inflation was permitted to develop: The wages of the expanding industrial and building labor force were partly met by increasing the flow of paper money. Prices began to rise, but the inflation was partly repressed through price control in both the producer goods market and the retail market (private shops and trading agencies were taken over by the state to facilitate this). For several years (1929–35) a rationing system was introduced in the towns, supplemented by state sales of goods above the ration at high prices. In this way, the available supply of consumer goods and foodstuffs was distributed over the old and the new urban population, and consumption per head in the towns was forced down. This was then an extreme form of the "regime of economy."

3. Within industry, the system of physical controls which had already existed during the 1920's was greatly extended. Prices were fixed, and there was no market for producer goods: Instead, materials and equipment were distributed to existing factories and new building sites through a system of priorities, which enabled new key factories to be built and bottlenecks in existing industries to be widened. The plan set targets for the output of major intermediate and final products, and the physical allocation system was designed to see these were reached.

To sum up these first three points: the policy of 1928–32 enabled a new allocation of GNP to be imposed on the economy. The discussions of the 1920's had assumed that savings would be made by the state within the framework of a dynamic equilibrium on the market between agriculture and industry. This placed a constraint on the proportion of GNP which could be invested, and on the allocation of that investment (investment in consumer goods industries would need to be sufficient to enable the output of consumer goods to increase at the rate required for equilibrium). Now this constraint was removed: Urban and rural living standards could be temporarily depressed, and physical controls used to divert resources to the establishment of new capital-intensive industries and techniques which gave no return during the construction period, and were relatively costly in the medium-term. This method of obtaining forced savings through physical controls resembled the wartime planning controls used in capitalist economies to shift resources towards the end product of the armament and maintenance of the large armed forces. In the Soviet case, the end product was the capital goods industries and the maintenance of the workers employed in building and operating them. But in both cases a shift in the allocation of resources which could not easily be achieved through manipulating the market mechanism was achieved through direct controls.

4. However, the system was not one simply of physical controls. Within a few years, the following features, stable over a long period, supplemented the system so far described:

a) Each peasant household was permitted to work a private plot, and to own its own cow and poultry. After obligations to the state had been met, the separate households and the *kolkhoz* as a unit were permitted to sell their produce on the free market ("collective farm market"), on which prices were reached by supply and demand. Here an important part of all marketed foodstuffs was bought and sold.

b) With some important exceptions, the employee was free to change his job. A market for labor existed, if a very imperfect one, and wage levels were formed partly in response to supply and demand. A corollary of this was that cost controls and profit-and-loss accounting were introduced in industry, to supplement the physical controls.

c) Rationing of consumer goods was abolished, and an attempt was made to balance supply and demand on the consumer market, as a whole and for individual goods, through fiscal measures, notably a purchase tax (the "turnover tax") differentiated according to commodity.

5. A large variety of unplanned and even illegal activities between firms supplemented and made feasible the rather crude controls of the central plan and must be considered as part of the logic of the system.

The Planning Process

We have so far established that Soviet plan controls may be divided schematically as in Figure 1. Each enterprise receives a set of output targets and input allocations with which to fulfill them; at the same time its monetary expenditures are controlled by financial or cost plans, which are less important to it than its output plan, but which come into operation if the pressure from above for higher output leads the enterprise to increase its money expenditures excessively.

FIGURE 1

PRINCIPAL PLANNING CONTROLS OVER INDUSTRIAL ACTIVITY

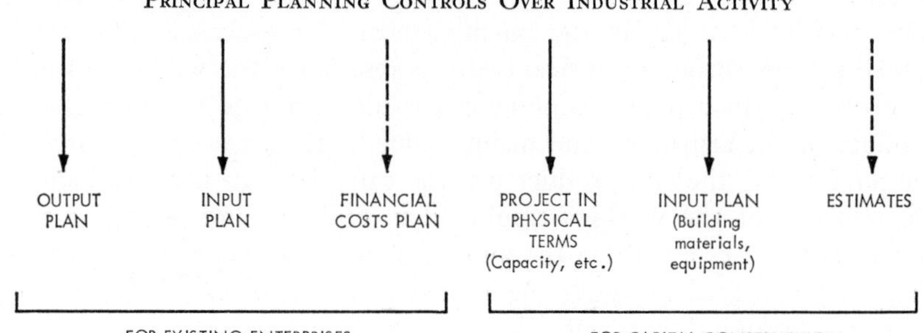

Disaggregation. A key problem for the central planners is to disaggregate their major decisions so that they will be enforced at the plant level and to aggregate information and proposals so as to be able satisfactorily to take into account the effect of their past and present decisions on different parts of the economy. In Soviet planning, this has normally been dealt with in the following ways:

1. Economic organization is adapted to handle this problem.

a) Factories are placed under the control of ministries or subministries, each of which is responsible for a particular group of products (e.g., iron and steel, motor vehicles). Each ministry is given very considerable control over its enterprises. The government is therefore to a considerable extent concerned only with handling transfers *between* industries.

b) Smaller factories producing low priority items are placed under the control of the government of one of the constituent republics, or under local authorities. In the past, the government tended not to bother with them, and to treat allocations to them as a residual.

c) Within the State Planning Committee (Gosplan), which is an advisory body to the government, and within each ministry or subministry, departmental organization mirrors the planning arrangements. In the iron and steel industry, for example, there are separate departments of the ministry responsible for sales of the industry's product, for supplies to the industry, for production plans of iron and steel works, and for capital construction. Within Gosplan, there are separate departments concerned with production, allocation, and construction. This is illustrated schematically in Figure 2.

FIGURE 2

CENTRAL ECONOMIC ADMINISTRATION

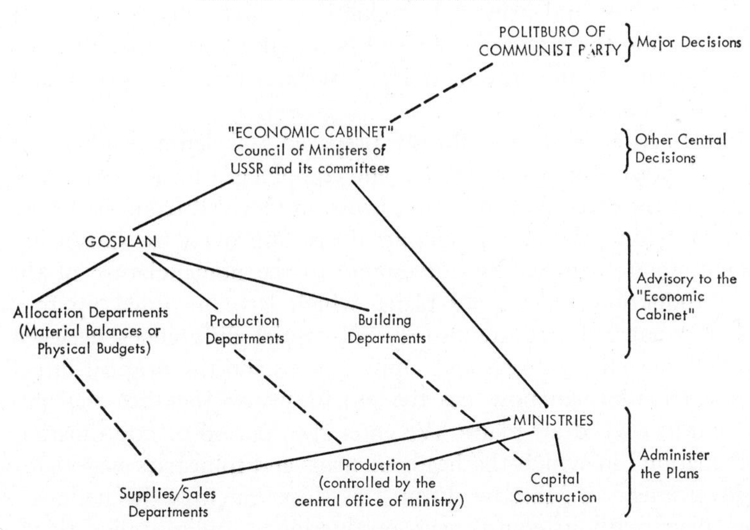

2. The time-horizon is divided so as to disaggregate. Five-year plans set broad rates of growth for GNP by sector of origin and end use, state output targets for important intermediate and final products, and list the location and intended capacity of all major construction projects. Annual plans (known as "operative" plans) handle the detailed application of these longer term plans in a particular year; quarterly and even monthly partial plans handle particular industries or aspects of planning.

3. Planning procedures are designed so as to enable more or less systematic aggregation and disaggregation. We give the procedure for the annual plan as an example:

FIGURE 3

PROCEDURE FOR ANNUAL PLANNING

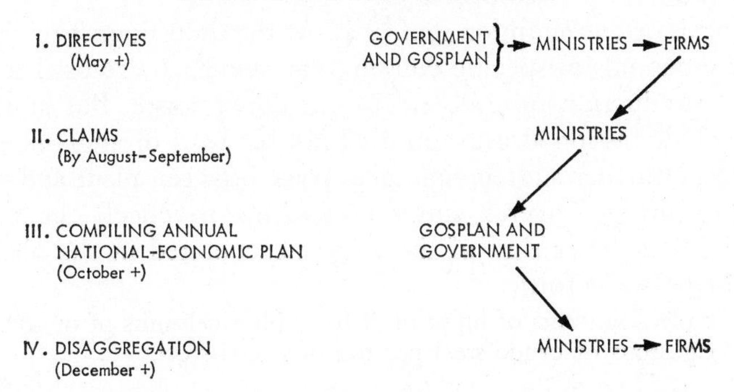

Stage I. Gosplan possesses a mass of data on past performance, and it or the government issues a statement about the principal economic magnitudes to be aimed at for the following year. These directives indicate the main proportions and principal production targets, the proposed investment allocation for each ministry, and proposals for the growth of output per man-year ("labor productivity," in Soviet terminology) and the reduction of costs.

Stage II. Ministries have already prepared a skeleton production program and set of claims for materials and equipment; this is now adjusted in the light of the directives and of information received from the firms. The forms on which claims are submitted are approved by Gosplan: The products itemized generally correspond to the nomenclature of the national production and supply plans, which have included up to 5,000 product groups. There are usually substantial differences between the ministries' output proposals and supply claims and the original directives.

Stage III. Gosplan now has the job of fitting together the ministry plans and its own draft plans: We enter the "period of coordination and reconciliation" in which the heads of firms and ministries negotiate with the government in Moscow. From this there emerges the national economic plan, with its constituent production, supplies (allocation) and investment plans. This whole negotiation is conducted in terms of, say, 30 times as many major indicators as were set out in the original directives.

Stage IV. The ministries now disaggregate the national economic plan to firm level.

4. These aggregation and disaggregation procedures are assisted by two important sets of what might be termed "control coefficients":

a) Output targets (or success indicators). The fulfillment of these has been the main driving motive of the Soviet firm and even ministry (managerial promotions and salaries tended to be related to success in fulfillment of output targets). Output targets were given for very broad groups of products at the national level, and they were supplemented by the sales departments of each ministry, whose disaggregation of the planned output target for a product group is supposed in theory to be binding on the firm. We return to the difficulties involved here later.

b) Norms or consumption standards. At the shop-floor level, hundreds of thousands of specific consumption standards are used to control the production process and to cut down waste. But at the plant level, discussion already proceeds on the basis of aggregated standards; a further aggregation takes place between plant and ministry. Gosplan uses overall input coefficients to check the claims of ministries, and many of these are incorporated in the plan. These may be of the form

x physical units of input of A for y physical units of output of B; e.g., tons of crude steel per ton of rolled steel.

or

x physical units of input of A for y value-units of output of B; e.g., tons of cement per 1 million rubles' building and assembly work.

Different consumption standards will be applied to different processes and even to different plants: these are probably quite reliable as a rough measure of efficiency and of reliability of claims, and a useful device for handling complex production activities centrally.

Coordination. The outline so far given of the planning process is unrealistic, for it assumes much smoother control than is possible in practice. Smooth planning has been vitiated by:

1. Uncertainty. Innovations, mistakes, and bottlenecks were not predicted with any accuracy; future proportions of coal and oil output, for example, were quite wrongly predicted even after World War II.

2. "Tight" planning. The plan was used as an instrument for forcing up production, and all targets were deliberately strained, all stocks minimized. This reinforced uncertainty and encouraged the emergence of unexpected bottlenecks. (In the early 1930's annual as well as five-year plan targets were sometimes wildly exaggerated.)

Moreover, we have so far been writing as if planning started from a clean sheet with each planning period. In fact, of course, planners work *at the margin.* Of a steel output of 12 million tons, as much as 10 million tons in an annual plan may be irrevocably committed to existing activities. Even in a five-year plan, possible shifts may be small: during the second five-year plan, for example, most capital investment was devoted to completing projects already started during the first plan or earlier.

The "coordination and reconciliation" activities undertaken by Gosplan in drawing up the annual plan are therefore limited by uncertainty, by the consequences of tight planning, and by existing commitments. Gosplan has two functions here. First, it seeks to balance programs by eliminating existing or potential bottlenecks due to the excess of demand over supply. To do this it follows a regular procedure and uses a list of priorities: thus it may cut cement supplies to housing in order to have enough to push through a crash program to complete a steel foundry needed to produce certain types of steel required by priority industries. Second, it tries to inject into departmental programs the priorities and investment programs favored by the government: thus it may increase cement supplies to the constructors of new chemical factories which are regarded as urgent.

In the coordination procedure, a great deal of use has been made by Gosplan of "material balances" or physical budgets, showing supplies and requirements for different product groups or types of equipment. These physical budgets were adjusted by the appropriate Gosplan through a fairly crude procedure of rule-of-thumb iteration. These were not input-output tables, for no technical coefficients had been calculated; sometimes a rough allowance was made for indirect outlays (e.g., of steel needed to make more machinery for motorcar factories if the output of motorcars was increased, as well as direct outlays of steel on the motorcars themselves). The procedure was therefore slow and inexact. At present, input-output tables and the traditional "material balances" are used side by side.

Financial Planning

1. Our account so far has been primarily concerned with physical planning. But as we have seen, a money flow corresponded to all the physical flows, and some of the money transactions in the system (e.g., wage payments, sales on the collective-farm market, sales on the retail market generally) were not accompanied by physical controls. Once the inflationary process had led to the initial reallocation of GNP in 1928–30, financial equilibrium was a subsidiary goal of the government. What was required was that money payments to the population (wage payments by the state, payments by the state to *kolkhozy* which were then distributed to their members, etc.) should not exceed the value of the supply of commodities available on the state-controlled market at fixed prices and on the collective-farm market at market prices. As outpayments by the state included the earnings of persons employed in the investment goods industries, in the social services, and in the armed forces, a gap existed between the cost-price of consumer goods (equal to the cost of wages in that sector and the materials, etc., it employed) and the total monetary demand.

This gap needed to be covered by taxation, and could be met in principle in one or all of three ways: (*a*) by direct taxation, (*b*) by allowing the profits of enterprises to rise and then taxing them, or (*c*) by an indirect tax: this could be an equiproportional markup on all goods, or imposed only on consumer goods.

a) Direct taxation has been of minor importance: there are no incomes uncontrolled by the state available to tax, and high income tax on state employees is regarded as undesirable.

b) Profits tax has been of some importance, but in the early stages the authorities feared that the monetary pressure on the retail market would lead to very high profits in the consumer goods industries (this pressure was not held back after 1935 by the rationing procedures which still operated in the case of producer goods).

c) The misnamed "turnover tax" therefore became the main source of tax: it is a markup on the wholesale price of consumer goods and the low delivery price of foodstuffs. The markup is differentiated by product for social reasons and to bring about a rough equality between the supply and the demand for each product. It was argued that a high level of tax on producer goods, which were mainly sold to the state, would only require the state to reimburse itself from a still higher tax rate on consumer goods.

Figure 4 illustrates the principal money flows in the system.

FIGURE 4

SOVIET FINANCIAL PLANNING: A SIMPLIFIED PICTURE (NOT TO SCALE)

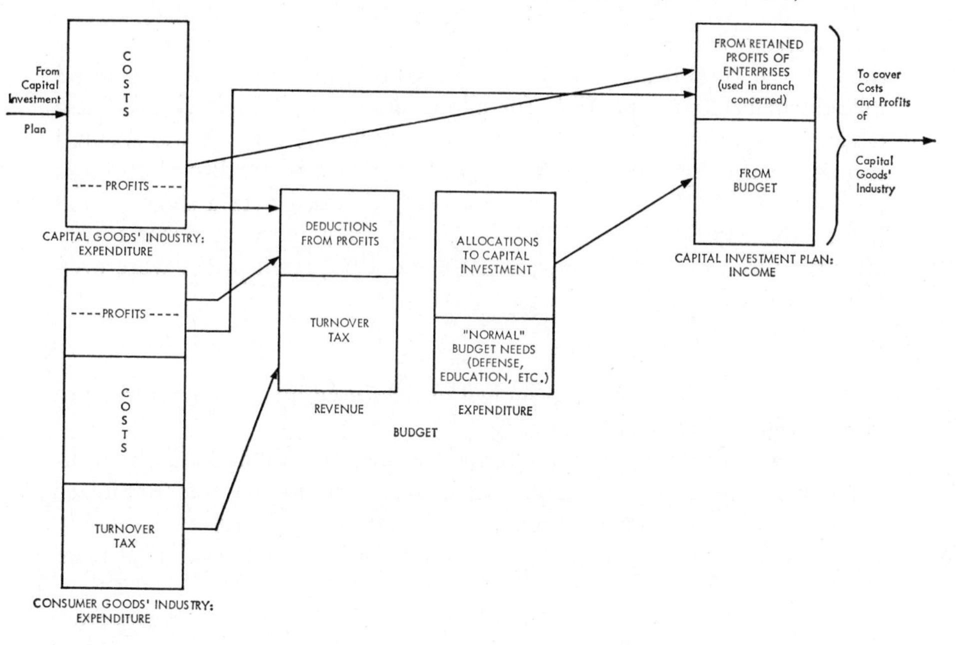

2. Prices in the producer and the consumer goods industries therefore had a common base; they were reached as follows:

a) costs of production, including wages, the cost of materials, overheads, a small allowance for depreciation, but no interest charge on capital;

b) a small markup for profits;

c) trade and transport costs.

To these was added in the case of consumer goods

d) turnover tax (differentiated by product)

to reach the retail price.

Profits are partly taxed, partly retained by the firm or industry; a high proportion of profits in excess of the plan is placed at the disposal of the firm in the "Director's Fund" (now the "Enterprise Fund").

It will be noted that the prices of producer goods are unresponsive to supply and demand, and could remain stable for many years. Each industry receives a price for its product equal to average costs for the industry plus a small margin for profit; but the industry itself can pay differential prices, offering high prices to high-cost firms and low prices to low-cost firms. However, prices include no systematic allowance for the varying richness of the capital stock of firms producing similar products. In practice, the rate of profit earned on different products varies enormously, owing to the hit-and-miss way in which prices were fixed.

3. Elaborate arrangements are made to control the flows of (*a*) short-term loans (for seasonal stocks, goods in transit, etc.), (*b*) wages, (*c*) allocations to investment (mainly financed by the budget), and (*d*) cash through the State Bank (responsible for working capital) and specialized investment banks (responsible for allocations to fixed capital). All these devices aimed at maintaining the financial equilibrium which was secured through balancing money incomes against money expenditures through the fiscal system. In the end, inflation was repressed over a short period before the World War II (1935–37) and in a more systematic way after the war (1948–). Between 1948 and 1953, retail prices were even substantially reduced.

Labor and Labor Controls

1. The following are the principal devices used by the government to control the urban labor force:

a) Once unemployment had been absorbed (by about 1932), recruitment of labor from the villages to the towns was organized systematically on contract with the collective farms.

b) Training and education of semiskilled, skilled, and technical manpower are systematically planned.

c) At various stages (particularly in the war and postwar years from 1940 to 1951), scarce grades or types of manpower were restricted in their movement or even subject to allocation.

2. In spite of these measures, labor was highly mobile, particularly in the early 1930's, and both central planners and factory managements utilize money wages to influence the allocation of labor—hence a form of labor market emerged, though recent studies of Soviet production functions have confirmed that it was highly imperfect:

a) The government approves national scales for different grades and types of labor in different areas, and adjusts these from time to time to take account of demand and supply; there is a high differential for skill.

b) There is an elaborate piece-rate and bonus system to encourage higher productivity.

c) Management can in practice manipulate bonuses and classifications to attract scarce kinds of labor.

3. Unskilled and even semiskilled labor are not basically a scarce factor of production (owing to the existence of a large stock of labor in the countryside). There has therefore been a recurrent tendency to substitute labor for capital.

4. The need for labor coupled with the pressure to fulfill the output plan encouraged management to overspend its allocation for wages and made for an inflationary situation. Control by the State Bank over wage

payments is the most important single element in maintaining wage stability.

5. Government control over trade unions has greatly assisted wage policy. The central wage bargaining process was very tenuous from 1929 onward. At the same time, a policy of cutting the rate for the job as techniques and organization improved was systematically enforced, so that money wages rose *less* rapidly than output per man.

6. But the government, as well as firmly controlling wage rates, also took responsibility for social conditions. Hours of work were restricted to seven to eight hours daily. Pensions, sickness and maternity benefits, holidays with pay, and welfare services (crèches, factory clubs, canteens), largely administered through the trade unions, were more generous than was the case in many Western countries at a similar stage of industrialization. These social benefits (particularly housing tied to the factory) were used to influence the movement of labor (high priority factories tended to have better facilities and housing; benefits were partly dependent on length of service at the particular factory).

Strengths and Weaknesses of the Soviet Planning System

No adequate "cost-benefit analysis" of the Soviet system or its constituent parts has yet been attempted. Here we simply list some of its principal achievements and failures:

Advantages

1. The system succeeded in enforcing allocation of a very high proportion of GNP to investment over a long period; within this allocation resources were concentrated on the growth-inducing producer goods industries, which were transformed from high-cost to low-cost industries. In general, it is possible with this kind of mechanism to enforce successfully high priority crash programs (e.g., the sputniks).

2. A high degree of centralization enabled the planners to inculcate the latest technology, imported from more advanced economies, into the whole economy at a rapid rate: project institutes, such as *Gipromez* (the State Institute for Projects of Iron and Steel Works), were able to plan large-scale technological advance for a whole industry on a national scale. For many major technological problems, the Soviet system of centralized research also carries great advantages at a more advanced stage of development (e.g., nuclear research).

3. Considerable economies of scale (including economies from standardization) and economies of effort are possible in nationally planned industries.

4. The output drive from above, characteristic of Soviet planning until recently, provides a powerful instrument for enforcing high capacity utilization, and for keeping management and men working at a high pace.

Disadvantages

1. The cost of concentrating resources on producer goods industries was very high. Thus the policy adopted towards the peasantry led to a drastic decline in peasant holdings of working livestock and forced the state in fact to reallocate unexpected resources to the agricultural equipment industry and hence to the high-grade steel industry. It also had a drastic long-term effect on peasant morale.

2. When the central planners make a *wrong* technological choice, the cost (because the policy is carried out on a national scale) is proportionately heavy; for example, there has been overinvestment in the coal industry and underinvestment in oil and chemicals.

3. When controls are highly centralized, initiative and innovation at the plant level are cramped. But decentralization of a system of administrative planning is difficult. If the success indicators are not very detailed, managements will produce what it is easier to produce rather than what is wanted. Control of quality through success indicators is very difficult. The sellers' market which was coupled with Soviet administrative planning reinforced these difficulties. At the same time it led to the tendency for each industrial ministry to become a self-contained "empire," carrying out wasteful backward integration in order to control its supplies. If advertising and inflated sales organizations are a high cost of modern capitalism, inflated supplies organizations were (and are) a high cost of Soviet central planning.

To sum up with an example: Central planning enabled the emergence of steel foundries and rolling mills, using home-manufactured equipment, which are technologically as good as those in the United States and are worked at a much higher capacity. It also produced a situation where Soviet bedsteads were the heaviest in the world (because planned in tons), were produced on too small a scale (because made under several ministries) and therefore costly, and owing to the sellers' market could be made of iron, when the consumer would have preferred something more modern.

This is a mere list of factors. Economists need to ask themselves: *how* costly and beneficial were these various factors? How far were the advantages and disadvantages of the system inextricably tied together? Could the Soviet strategy for rapid growth, or some features of it, be employed without the disadvantages? How many of the unsucessful features were due to the special conditions of Russia (including the difficult external and internal position of the government) and to the inexperience and imperfect knowledge of the people who made the system?

PLANNING A MATURE ECONOMY IN THE USSR

Economic Theory and the Soviet Economy

1. Traditional economic theory contrasts two types of system: the competitive or market system, with its "ideal type" of perfect competi-

tion, and "command economy," or "planning under a dictator." These are treated as two possible alternative methods of allocating resources.

a) The *market economy* is divided into competing units: a large number of individual consumers bargain with a large number of producers on the market. The goal of the producer is to maximize his profit; the goal of the consumer is to maximize his satisfaction. The resulting demand and supply are equated through price.

The decisions on the consumer market are reflected back into the factor market, where a similar bargaining process settles the distribution of incomes between factors and the distribution of the factors.

As a result, resources in such an economy are allocated "rationally," by which the economist means "in accordance with the desires of the consumers."

b) In the *command economy* (often referred to as "*planning under a dictator*"), final demand is determined not by individual consumers but by the decision of the central authority, as "dictator's preferences" or "planners' preferences" replace "consumers' preferences." The central authority also controls the allocation of all factors of production and the distribution of income. The system is completely centralized: its difficulty lies in the ability of the "dictator" to work out the "thousands of equations" involved in transforming his preferences into practical economic decisions.

2. How far does this theory provide an effective framework of analysis for contemporary capitalism and for Soviet planning?

a) The development of economic analysis in the past forty years has involved a number of realistic modifications of the original theory as applied to modern capitalism:

i) In many cases free entry into industries will be restricted and a state of imperfect competition will exist; at equilibrium, output may be lower and price higher than under perfect competition. However, economies of scale may make for lower costs in a highly organized oligopolistic industry: advantage and disadvantage must be carefully examined.

ii) While consumer *choice* exists, advertising, imperfect knowledge, and the power of initiative of the large firm mean that consumer *sovereignty* is quite restricted.

iii) The assumption of permanent equilibrium in the system is a microeconomic one. At the level of macroeconomics, supply does not create its own demand and hence the possibility of underemployment of factors exists. Macroeconomic equilibrium requires government intervention.

iv) The large government sector requires separate analysis. Nationalized industries produce as monopolies, but often with their "maximum profit" goal constrained; and as consumers they control a large part of the market for certain intermediate goods (e.g., an electricity board purchasing power-station equipment). The defense, education, and health departments of central and local governments are also large buyers and often act as oligopsonies. State fiscal and monetary and tariff policy regulates the market.

v) The view that firm's economic behavior can be understood solely in terms of aiming at maximum profit in response to market price is an insufficient one. Within the large firm, decisions will be taken administratively (through the hierarchy) or by a cooperative or bargaining process; and much interfirm behavior may also be explained in this way. Industry is not an infinite number of atoms responding to price, but a finite number of blocs: The bloc as a whole reacts to price, but also has dealings with other blocs which are to be explained in terms of organization theory rather than of the price mechanism; and bargaining and administrative processes help to explain economic behavior within each bloc.

However, even with these modifications the original theory retains much validity:

i) If firms do not always aim at maximizing their profits, they are concerned with making a satisfactory level of profits ("satisficing").

ii) There is consumer choice, and a market process also operates for intermediate goods and (partly) on the factor market.

iii) In spite of the considerable role of the government, a large segment of investment is still determined by the decisions of individual entrepreneurs (or entrepreneurial firms).

b) These developments of Western economic theory are of direct relevance to our understanding of the Soviet system:

i) Physical planning is not something unknown in capitalist economies. In the Soviet economy, relationships between firms are regulated by administrative and bargaining processes; in a competitive system they are largely regulated by the market. But analogies to all the administrative and bargaining processes described in the section on "the planning process" above may be found within the capitalist firm, and within the government sector (compare the process for making fiscal estimates in a market economy with the procedures for plan compilation in Soviet industry). The "thousands of equations" of Western economic theory are simplified by the existence of "administrative decentralization": subsystems of economic administrators share decision making with the Council of Ministers; and bargaining and pressure from lower units assist the decision-making process. Moreover, like decisions by private entrepreneurs, planners' decisions are made only "at the margin."

ii) Some important economic activity in the U.S.S.R. is to be explained in terms of a market mechanism, though most Soviet markets are highly imperfect. As we have seen, there is a partial market for labor, a fixed-price market for retail consumer goods, a free market for part of retail food sales; and various unofficial or illegal markets operate in practice.

Modern capitalist economies are imperfectly competitive and have important elements of administrative control; the Soviet economy is not entirely "planned from the center," and imperfect markets exist for certain purposes.

The Soviet Economy as a Special Case of Planned Economy

The Soviet planning system of the 1930's–1950's is not the only possible form of planned economy. In Soviet experience alone, at least two other forms of planning system have existed. In the period of *War Communism* (1918–20), industry was nationalized and industrial output was allocated physically. Owing to inflation the economy was virtually moneyless; labor was directly controlled, consumer goods were rationed and agricultural output subject to requisition. However, peasants continued to work their own land and no serious attempt was made to socialize agriculture. This system was the closest approach in principle to the "ideal form" of the command economy in the history of the Soviet system. In the period of the *New Economic Policy* (1921–29), as in present-day Poland, state ownership of industry was combined with private agriculture through a regulated market. The effectiveness of planning was constrained by the existence of the market, but central goals were to some extent enforced.

A considerable variety of forms of central planning is to be found in Eastern Europe.

The systematic study of forms of economic organization has so far been little developed. One may distinguish two basic ways of classification.

Ownership. A planned economy is unlikely to be one in which all economic activity is nationalized. It will be a "mixed economy," combining private ownership with state ownership and possibly embracing different forms of state ownership (very varied forms of public ownership have been experienced, incorporating different degrees of state, consumer, and workers' control). In this spectrum, the Soviet economy lies considerably toward the "state" end, particularly as far as industry is concerned. Nearly all industrial activity is nationalized, and since 1918 forms of syndicalism or "guild socialism" have been firmly rejected in favor of "one-man management" by administrators appointed by the state and liable to instant dismissal. The argument for this has always been in terms of economic efficiency and of the need to enforce a central state policy.

Allocation of Resources. Various forms of "market socialism" are in principle conceivable, and have been much discussed among economists (especially in Poland and Yugoslavia). To what extent can a scale of preferences (of planners or individual consumers or a combination of both) be put into effect through a market, on which state firms aim to maximize their profits in simulation of private enterprises? In a variation of this, suggested by Kornai and others, the state would use its regulatory powers only to counter inefficient decisions due to the existence of state monopolies. Prices in "market socialism" might be formed freely, or might be fixed by the planners, but would, of course, need to reflect the chosen preference-scale more or less exactly, as they would indicate to the producer what he should produce, and how he should allocate resources (including investment). In its extreme form, the economic behavior of "market socialism" ought not to differ from that of a private market economy.

The alternative approach is the one followed by the Soviet government: to allocate resources by direct physical controls, and to allow some degree of decentralization in decision making to other controllers at industry, region, or plant level.

Planning systems might be classified (*a*) by the relative strengths in them of the "market principle" and the "physical planning principle," (*b*) by the degree to which, within the market sector, the government regulates the market (imposes its preferences), and (*c*) by the degree to which decision making is decentralized within the physical planning sector.

We have not made any allowance for the *effectiveness* of controls. Should not the degree of planning be measured not only by the all-embracingness of the planners' goals and the detailedness of their controls but also by the extent to which the planners succeed in fulfilling their goals in the actual allocation of resources? For instance, War Communism was in principle a highly centralized system. But in practice central decisions were usually ineffective; illegal barter and local quasi markets tended to dominate economic life: what was the "real" economic system? Again, where was there more planning—in industry under War Communism, where detailed orders were not enforced, or in agriculture under the New Economic Policy, where indirect controls succeeded to some extent in moving agriculture in the direction desired by the central government? Further, good planners of course incorporate their knowledge of their objective possibilities into their goals: but is a planner whose goals are very limited, but successfully achieved, as "effective" as, say, the Soviet planners in 1929–31, who set quite impossible goals but did succeed in reallocating resources very drastically in the desired direction?

Planning A More Mature Economy

The basic allocation decisions and the planning process in the U.S.S.R. in 1928–53 probably had stronger "functional" elements than "dysfunctional" elements in the stage of moving the Soviet economy from a semiagrarian economy to an industrialized economy. But as the economy matured, the "dysfunctional" elements certainly became more prominent. The changed context may be summarized as follows:

1. Industrial output per head is now above the British level and moving towards the U.S. level for some important producer goods. The economy is vastly more complex than it was in the 1930's.

2. The Industrial Revolution has been accompanied by major social changes:

a) In 1928, two thirds of the population were illiterate; now, nearly everyone can read and write.

b) In 1928, some 3 million persons were employed in industrial labor; it is now (1965) over 25 millions.

c) In 1928, some 5 percent of the state-employed labor force (i.e., excluding peasants and collective farmers) had received professional or semiprofessional education; the figure now (1965) is about 15 percent.

3. The technological situation is different: as the economy becomes more mature, the amount of technological borrowing it can do tends to decline, and the amount of innovation required increases. This is reinforced by the long-term trend for labor to become a more scarce factor of production: the economy must increasingly come to rely on higher labor productivity and hence on more capital-intensive production (and/or on technical progress) rather than on increasing the industrial labor force.

In this new situation, changes in both allocation and organization are required. It is not easy to demonstrate that industrial efficiency is hampered by a relatively low standard of living (the Soviet average real wage is probably about a quarter that of the United States, but labor productivity may be over half the U.S. level). But in any case political and social pressures have dictated a shift in resources towards consumption. Such a shift requires a much greater output of food; and in agriculture it is very probable that the low return to the peasant for the output of the collective farm has held down productivity. And certainly as the economy has grown, the highly centralized planning structure has become less efficient and less workable.

Here we summarize the principal changes so far made in both respects since 1953.

Allocation of Resources

1. There has been a relative and absolute increase in the resources devoted to consumer goods (manufactures, manufactured foodstuffs). In the 1930's and in 1946–50, the output of producer goods increased much more rapidly than that of consumer goods; the gap is now much narrower.

2. A much higher proportion of total investment has been allocated to urban housing construction.

3. In 1953–58, the prices paid by the state for agricultural products

were very substantially increased; according to official figures, the money incomes of collective farms rose from 5 billion new rubles to 13.2 billion new rubles between 1953 and 1958. At the same time, the total annual investment in agriculture (state plus collective farm) increased from 2.1 to 5.1 billion new rubles. This double shift was accompanied by a rapid rise in agricultural output—by some 50 percent, according to official figures (i.e., a greater increase than in 1928 to 1953).

Between 1958 and 1965 agriculture tended to stagnate (even ignoring the bad harvest of 1963). Recent studies have shown that this stagnation has occurred simultaneously with a falling-off in peasant incomes and in the rate of growth of investment in agriculture. It seems likely that agricultural difficulties are at least in part due to the failure of the state to allocate a share of GNP to agriculture adequate enough to enable the goals of the planners to be achieved (organizational weaknesses may also have played a part).

4. There has been a significant shift in the distribution of income. The incomes of peasants tended (until 1958) to increase more rapidly than those of the urban population. Within the urban population, there has been a process of leveling up: the minimum wage has been increased, wage differentials have been narrowed, social benefits such as pensions have been substantially increased.

5. Nevertheless, the priorities have not been reversed. It seems certain, however the measurement is done, that a higher proportion of GNP is allocated to net investment than in the U.S., and that a higher proportion of this investment is allocated to the producer goods industries. As a result, the rate of industrial growth has remained high (7–9 percent a year), though less high than a decade ago.

Organization. Attempts to improve the working of Soviet planning have followed two main lines simultaneously: (1) improvements in central planning; (2) attempts to decentralize.

1. Improvements in central planning. Central decision making has undoubtedly tended to be more consistently thought out, and to become more logical and consistent.

Long-term technological decisions have been reconsidered, and a bold policy of technical change has been embarked upon. Thus oil has been given preference to coal, and the transfer of the railways to the diesel has been undertaken; this reverses previous policy. The development and manufacture of prefabricated reinforced concrete components and other building materials have been given preference over traditional materials like brick and timber. Plastics are being developed in preference to steel and other metals.

In the discussions about all these changes, most of which had previously been undertaken in capitalist economies in response to market criteria, there has been a great deal of emphasis on economic arguments.

The question of the appropriate criteria to use in making investment choices has been predominant here. Thinking has moved in the direction of adopting a single rate of return for the whole economy (the rate of return is, of course, the inverse of the so-called "recoupment period"): the standard formula now used is

$$\frac{I_1 - I_2}{C_2 - C_1} \leq R.P.$$

where I_1 and I_2 are the investment alternatives being compared and C_1 and C_2 are the costs of production in the two alternatives, and *R.P.* is the maximum permissible period in which the investment may be recouped. (This has tended to vary by industry, from 4–5 years in light industry, i.e., a rate of return of 20–25 percent, to 16–17 years in electric power, i.e., a rate of return of about 6 percent.)

The adoption of a standard rate for all industries would require the use of something like a cost-benefit analysis if the social welfare problem is to be taken into account; Soviet thought is moving cautiously in this direction.

A stumbling block to consistent macroeconomic decision making is the inconsistency of the prices in which goods are valued. Investment decisions, and indeed all multiproduct decisions, have to be discussed not in physical terms but in value terms. As we have seen, Soviet prices are an inadequate indicator of real costs: They do not include a capital charge (so capital-intensive production is relatively undervalued), they do not vary with the scarcity or abundance of the goods, the rent element for use of natural resources is inconsistent, and the price incorporates a profit markup which is more or less arbitrary. Rule-of-thumb adjustments are made by the central planners, but decisions are clumsy and often inaccurate.

A second line of approach to the improvement of central planning has been the attempt to improve knowledge at the center by use of mathematical methods. Technical coefficients have been worked out so that the consequences of alternative production policies may be taken into account more systematically; national and some regional input-output tables have been constructed (among the largest is the 438-sector matrix for planning purposes of 1964–65). The central planning of supplies and requirements seems still to be carried out by rule-of-thumb methods, but these are now supplemented by improved information. At the same time various methods of mathematical programming, such as the transportation algorithm, have been used to improve traffic flows (e.g., truck transport in Moscow, scheduling of Baltic steamers, timber and coal hauls), bringing savings of about 10 percent in costs for each problem.

2. Attempts at decentralization. Three major attempts have been made since 1953 to devolve some of the decision-making powers of the

central authorities. But these attempts have been conducted within the framework of the physical planning system, rather than representing an increase in the market sector of the economy.

a) 1954–56: "step-by-step" decentralization. The Gosplan–Council of Ministers central organization attempted to shed some of its powers by reducing the number of indicators in the national output, supply and capital investment plans; thus product groups, for which output targets were laid down, were made more aggregative. The intention was that each ministry, possessing more flexibility itself, would devolve some of its authority to its departments, which in turn would increase the decision-making powers of economic units.

The reform was on the whole unsuccessful. Ministries failed to pass down their powers to the factory; instead, they tended to use their increased authority to bind their own "empires" more closely together. At the same time, the reduction in the number of central output targets (success indicators) revealed clearly a dilemma inherent in administrative planning. The enterprise is required to maximize its output in terms of the output targets. If the targets are broad or loose, it will try to follow the "easiest" course within the target. If the target is merely for "tons of nails shorter than 2 inches" the factory will try to produce all 1$\frac{9}{10}$″ nails, because this is easiest. If it is for "numbers of nails," the factory will try to produce all ½″ nails. But if the plan is set in terms of ½″, 1″, 1½″ and 1$\frac{9}{10}$″ nails, there will be overcentralization. If the target is set in terms of gross value of output, the factory will maximize its use of materials and semifabs and minimize the net value it adds to each product (this has been dealt with by using a new indicator of "standard cost of work done to the product," but this has involved further—if smaller—difficulties).

b) 1957–65: regionalization. In 1957, industry was "regionalized": the industrial ministries were abolished, 104 regions were set up and all factories in each region were put under the regional economic committee. However, much of the central machinery was retained, particularly the sales organizations which control product mix: and gradually committees for each industry were reestablished, with research organizations attached. What emerged was a mixture of area-by-area and industry-by-industry control. This probably gave the factory manager greater effective power, if only because he no longer had one unambiguous boss; it also led to the breakup of the ministerial "empires" and a more effective consideration of regional factors in central decision making. But it also made economic administration very much more complicated.

c) September, 1965– : more authority to the factory. The reforms introduced by Kosygin contained two main elements. First of all, they abandoned the attempt at regional organization and returned to control by industrial ministries. More important, they made the first serious attempt to increase greatly the powers of the factory management. The most important measures are the following.

i) The importance of profits as a success indicator is intended to be greatly increased. Profits retained by factories are to be large and will be related to planned profit (if achieved) rather than actual profit so as to discourage firms from trying to keep their plan low. Bonuses to management and workers will be paid from and related to the amount of profit.

ii) Various measures are to be adopted to encourage the efficient use of capital investment.

iii) The powers of the factory management to determine the way in which it spends the total allocation for wages are greatly increased; the manager may divide up the total allocations as he wishes between classes of employee—he may, for instance, reduce the total number of persons employed in order to increase the portion of highly paid workers.

iv) The main global indicator of output is to be "actually marketed production" rather than "gross production"; it is hoped that this will force factories to produce goods for which there is a high demand.

However, the main physical indicators are retained, including both the plan of supplies in physical terms and the itemization of production items in physical terms in the national-economic plan; Kosygin merely expressed the hope that the degree of detail would be gradually reduced. The success of the reforms in moving away from administrative planning will depend on the extent to which a linear relationship can be established between the preferences of the planners and the profits earned by the factory; if such a linear relationship exists, and the factory aims at maximizing its profit, then the desired pattern of production will be achieved without administrative orders.

But the achievement of such a "linear relationship" requires a radical reform of the price system. The main suggestions for reform have been: make turnover tax into an equiproportional markup on the wholesale price (or value added) of all products; give higher profits for scarce products and negative profits for surplus products; include an interest charge on capital stock. But so far only the last of these proposals appears to be likely to be achieved in the near future.[1] The prices which the planners are to establish have not been worked out in detail, and even the method by which they could be reached is unclear. Kosygin has announced an impending price reform, but it seems unlikely to be a radical one.

---

[1] [Such a change was introduced in 1967.—EDITOR.]

Three things seem to block a major price reform: (1) Fear that an increase in market forces, or the use of profit as a "universal regulator" in a socialist economy, may diminish the control of the center over the allocation of resources; it is for this reason that proposals permitting a kind of "market socialism" to develop have been firmly rejected; (2) a feeling that profit will not be so powerful an incentive to managers to increase output as output targets in physical terms have been; and (3) inability (as yet) to arrive at the actual prices required.

The weakness of the reforms of the planning system we have so far discussed is, then, that they do not tackle the problem of *valuation* systematically or integrally. The reforms are essentially *ad hoc*. Thus all the proposals for improving the allocation of investment incorporate a required rate of return which is arrived at more or less empirically or even arbitrarily: The choice between investments is not consistently interwoven with long-term production planning. The result is likely to be that the approved pattern of planned investment is not entirely compatible with the approved production targets, so that adjustment by rule-of-thumb will still need to follow. Similarly even the most radical reforms proposed for short- and medium-term production and supply planning depend on the availability of a system of prices which systematically reflect the aims or preferences of the planners; prices must favor a production pattern which not merely widens present bottlenecks but also makes its contribution to the dynamic goals of the planners.

A far-reaching proposal such as Liberman's could worsen the operation of the system rather than assist it, if put into effect without an appropriate set of prices being available. This does not mean that the partial reforms which have been proposed or undertaken would not improve the operation of the present system. Waste and inconsistency have been reduced both by the use of better investment criteria and by the application of linear programming techniques to partial problems.

One general solution—much discussed and partly attempted in Poland and Yugoslavia—is for the required scale of prices to be reached by permitting state enterprises to compete on a market. The central planners would restrict themselves to controlling the general level of investment and to intervening in order to ensure that the market was as perfect as possible. The principal economic objection to this solution is that it would incorporate into the planned economy most of the disadvantages of modern capitalism, in a situation in which the imperfections of the market would be more considerable than in a privately owned economy.

Mathematical Methods. An increasingly influential school of Soviet economists holds that with the application of mathematical methods and the use of the computer the major dilemmas of central planning can be solved. Computers make it possible to examine the properties of a very large number of economic variables: With the aid of appropriately designed mathematical models, economic processes can be simulated on the computer so that plan variants can be tested for feasibility and consistency. The core of the method is that objective functions are set up which indicate what is to be maximized or minimized within a system of constraints. The functions yield a system of imputed values (efficiency prices or shadow prices); and these for the problem concerned are the consistent system of prices which, as we have seen, the nonmathematical proposals lacked.

Soviet mathematicians and mathematical economists believe that this technique can be applied to the planning of the entire economy. What is proposed is a "unified and automatized system of national economic planning and management" which would seek to optimize the achievement of goals set by the government. The economy would be divided for planning purposes into a number of blocs or subsystems (both by area and by sector); for each bloc an appropriate programming model would attempt to optimize subgoals consistent with and integrated with the overall national goals, which would in turn be incorporated in a macromodel for the economy as a whole. For each bloc, a set of shadow prices would emerge which would indicate its "best" economic behavior in the planning period. A measure of decentralization is inherent in the system: The elements in each subsystem would be free to move so as to optimize their subgoals within constraints obtained from the larger bloc of which the subsystem formed a part.

A requirement for the efficient working of the new system is the establishment of a consistent computerized system of information flows. All economic information (for instance, all inputs and outputs) will need to be classified by a unified system for the entire economy, so that data may be processed in forms suitable for feeding in to the planning models on which the system is to be based. A chain of computer stations is being established for assembling and processing economic information. (This is a long and arduous business; it is likely to take about 10 years.)

For the efficient operation of the system, actual economic forms need to be adapted as far as possible to the solutions found on the computer (inflexibilities in institutions and arrangements constitute constraints on optimization). In particular, actual prices, it is hoped, will be made to correspond more closely to the shadow prices obtained from the computations. This does not mean that all prices would necessarily need to be fixed by the state; actual market arrangements in a subsystem could be made consistent with the larger economic models (in principle, a private and uncontrolled sector could be incorporated as a stochastic element in the overall system).

If prices thus correspond to the preferences stated in the models, they would be appropriate for Liberman's proposal that profit should indicate to an economic unit how it should behave. But in the light of Western studies of the behavior of the private firm, it seems likely that the Soviet firm cannot be expected to behave as though maximizing profits were its sole goal; as part of the restructuring of planning, an appropriate system of incentives would be needed to ensure that decisions are executed.

So far we have spoken simpy of models which would optimize the achievement of government-fixed goals; we have evaded the problem of the preference functions which would convert those goals into meaningful quantities. At present, the goals of the Soviet government are stated in terms of a long series of targets for investment goods, intermediate goods, and final consumption goods. These targets, as we saw earlier, are reached both for five-year and for annual plans as the result of a long bargaining process and reflect both the need to overcome expected bottlenecks and the major investment projects and priorities which the government intends to encourage. To optimize the achievement of these targets (as is for example the aim in Hungary) is only to maximize the achievement of a network of decisions reached by a rule-of-thumb process. The alternative is to persuade the politicians to reformulate their goals in more general or more operational terms. A satisfactory outcome will obviously only be achieved as a result of a long and difficult dialogue between the politicians and the mathematically trained planners. One element in this dialogue must be a discussion on the extent to which the preference functions of the planning models should incorporate the preferences of the individual consumer. Some Soviet and East European economists would be prepared to go a very long way in the direction of consumer sovereignty; others have suggested that zones of state influence, individual influence and mixed influence would need to be determined. One considerable weakness of present Soviet discussions is that they have paid little attention to techniques such as cost-benefit analysis which are needed in order to bring social and other noneconomic factors more consistently into the considerations of planners and politicians: the rationale of economic policy making has not been carefully considered, and hence goals may remain inconsistent or ill-defined.

Conclusion

Few of the techniques of planning we have now been considering were available to the Soviet economist during the period of intensive industrialization; those which were available were worked out only in elementary form. In any case, the gap between the goals of the politicians and the assumptions of the economists was so great that little dialogue was possible. The politicians, and the politically minded economists, undertook the elaboration of their own system of planning and their own rule-of-thumb methods of quantifying their goals to make them operational. In doing this, they acquired a rich fund of valuable experience about the problems of development through central planning; the lessons from this experience, both successful and unsuccessful, could save resources in other economies where central planning is being used for development. Unfortunately, it is information about formal mechanisms for planning and financial control which has until now tended to be communicated from the Eastern bloc to the developing countries, rather than a realistic account of problems and achievements. For the developing countries, the further question exists: now that the new techniques for planning are available, can they be coupled with planning for a high rate of growth in conditions of rapid social change? If so, some of the successes of Soviet-type central planning may be achieved at less cost.

16. AN ORGANIZATIONAL MODEL OF COMMAND FARMING*

Jerzy F. Karcz

The agricultural sector in Communist centrally planned economies is characterized by "command farming," in which farms receive detailed, invariably ambitious, and often unrealistic quotas for deliveries to state procurement agencies, ordinarily at low prices. In this way, the state seeks to obtain agricultural production for urban consumption, industrial inputs, and perhaps export, at terms of trade unfavorable to the rural population. Collectivization and administrative interference in farm operations are among the methods used to enforce these difficult plan assignments, which are intended both to expand output and marketings and to make agriculture contribute to capital formation in industry. However, the unintended consequences of this approach include lack of specialization, labor shortages, low factor productivity, and stagnation of output.

In this article, Karcz analyzes these relationships in a formal organizational model based on his extensive studies of Soviet and East European agriculture. He explains why and how command farming emerged in the USSR, the extent to which it was adopted in Eastern Europe, how it operates, and what its weaknesses are.

 Jerzy F. Karcz is Professor of Economics at the University of California, Santa Barbara.

INTRODUCTION

As a friend of mine remarked privately, signs of "red agrarianism" could recently be observed on the East European scene as the socialist governments introduced a plethora of reforms designed to improve the performance of their agricultural sectors. In themselves, such policies are vivid testimony to the dissatisfaction with the performance of socialist agricultures.

"Red agrarianism" might or might not be too strong a term, but what we are unquestionably witnessing is a movement away from a particular set of institutions and mechanisms co-ordinating the economic activity within the agricultural sectors of command economies. It is in this latter sense that the term "command farming" is used here as a convenient shorthand expression, designed to describe a system first introduced in the USSR in the early thirties.

Socialist agriculture has been the subject of a very large research effort on the part of western specialists, and numerous analytical contributions have been made by the late Naum Jasny and Lazar Volin, as well as by Alec Nove, Nancy Nimitz, and others too numerous to mention here. Within the last few years, several economists have also constructed a number of abstract theoretical models, designed to describe the behavior of a co-operative enterprise (in some cases, indeed, the Soviet *kolkhoz*) on the basis of the usual restrictive assumptions. Simultaneously, the work of Gregory Grossman, Benjamin Ward, David Granick, and Robert W. Campbell has vastly increased our understanding of the working of the Soviet-type command economy (hereafter called only the "command economy").[1]

One method which appears to be particularly useful for a study of command farming is that used by Granick in his pioneering organizational model of Soviet industrial planning.[2] It is the great advantage of this method that it brings out clearly the interplay of various functional and dysfunctional aspects of Soviet industrial planning. This makes it possible to identify precisely the key relationships and to pinpoint those that

[1] Gregory Grossman, "Notes for a Theory of the Command Economy," *Soviet Studies*, Vol. XV, No. 2 (October, 1963), pp. 101–23; Benjamin Ward, "The Firm in Illyria: Market Syndicalism," *American Economic Review*, Vol. XLVIII, No. 4 (September, 1958), pp. 566–89; Benjamin Ward, *The Socialist Economy* (New York: Random House, 1967); Evsey D. Domar, "The Soviet Collective Farm as a Producer Cooperative," *American Economic Review*, Vol. LVI, No. 4 (September, 1966), Part 1, pp. 734–57; David Granick, "An Organizational Model of Soviet Industrial Planning," *Journal of Political Economy*, Vol. LXVII, No. 2 (April, 1959), pp. 109–30; David Granick, *Soviet Metal-Fabricating and Economic Development* (Madison: University of Wisconsin Press, 1966); Walter Y. Oi and Elizabeth M. Clayton, "A Peasant's View of a Soviet Collective Farm," *American Economic Review*, Vol. LVIII, No. 1 (March, 1968), pp. 37–59.

[2] Granick, *op. cit.*, *Journal of Political Economy*. A revised and enlarged version is found in Chapter 7 of his *Soviet Metal-Fabricating and Economic Development*.

are of special importance in assessing the impact of various reforms, including the "new economic systems."

Granick's analysis proceeds in terms of two conflicting models of the industrial sector, beginning with the fundamental (or command) model that has for prolonged periods of time dominated the subsidiary *khozraschet*[3] or market model. While the antinomy between market and command is relevant for the study of any sector of the command economy, it is the interplay between market and command mechanisms that is a characteristic feature of command farming. Consequently, we make no basic distinction between the two types of models, but attempt to incorporate both types of mechanisms into the single construct.

We follow Granick in many other respects as well. Thus, we use most of his key operating features, with only minor adjustments. Our objectives (O) are designed only as objectives for the agricultural sector, and they are viewed as emerging from certain key features of the Soviet environment (E). Within the latter, we specify separately only a few key features: others are aggregated for the sake of brevity within a catch-all category of "Peculiar Characteristics of the Command Economy" (E_4). Our mechanisms (M) are partly market and partly command. We also use a separate variable to describe the primary and auxiliary production units (PU), which are not necessary in Granick's model. Finally, our undesirable consequences (UC) are labelled as such primarily from the standpoint of their impact on the agricultural sector. Most of these consequences, however, are the result of certain economic phenomena operating spontaneously, or in an unplanned manner, subject to the constraints imposed by other operating features. The responses (R) are also those of the sector as a whole.

All of the other *caveats* listed by Granick (hybrid nature of the model, neglect of positive responses, etc.) also apply here. Finally, it seems in order to underline the fact that we do not address ourselves—except briefly in the final section—to the issue of alternative methods of agricultural organization within the context of rapid industrialization, although we believe that this kind of analysis provides additional insight into this important question.

THE EMERGENCE OF COMMAND FARMING

A schematic representation of command farming is shown in Figure 1, which closely follows Granick's presentation of his fundamental model. The specification of the various variables is best understood in terms of the peculiar background of command farming.

As Grossman has pointed out, "command economies do not arise spontaneously." Nor does command farming. The key feature (E_1) from this standpoint is the decision on the overall economic objective of

[3] [Literally, "economic calculation" or "economic accountability"—Editor.]

rapid growth, with priority given to heavy industry (it being understood that other sectors absorb the shocks). Scarcity of capital (E_2) combined

FIGURE 1

GRAPHIC REPRESENTATION OF COMMAND FARMING

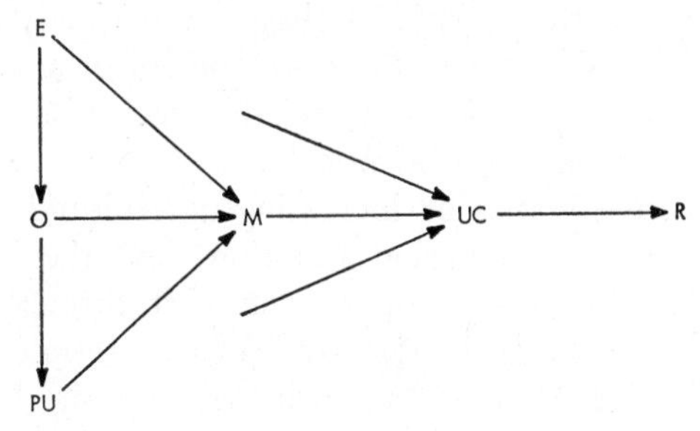

Each feature of the model is dependent on, or related to, that which is enclosed in parentheses underneath its specification.

Objectives (O)

O_1 Growing Marketings
O_2 Contribution of Agriculture to Capital Formation
O_3 Increase in Output through Changes in Technology and Production Functions
O_4 Collectivization of Agriculture
O_5 Rational Allocation of Resources

Production Units (PU)

PU_1 Collective Farm
PU_2 Household Plot
PU_3 State Farm
PU_4 Machine Tractor Station

Undesirable Consequences (UC)

UC_1 Failure to Specialize
(M_1, M_2, M_3, M_5)
UC_2 Capital Intensity
(O_4, PU_1, PU_2, E_4)
UC_3 Interdependence of Private and Socialized Sector
(PU_1, PU_2, PU_3, M_3)
UC_4 Impact on Labor Supply
(M_4, O_3)
UC_5 Uneven Farm Performance
(M_1, M_2, M_3, M_5)
UC_6 Faculty Indicators
(O_1, O_2, O_4, M_5)

Environment (E)

E_1 Industrialization at High Rate with Emphasis on Heavy Industry
E_2 Capital Scarcity
E_3 High Income Elasticities of Demand
E_4 Peculiar Characteristics of the Command Economy at Large

Mechanisms (M)

M_1 Procurement System
(O_1, O_2, O_4)
M_2 Agricultural Planning
(E_4, O_3, M_1)
M_3 Administrative Interference
(O_1, O_3, M_1, M_2)
M_4 Agricultural Incentives
(PU_1, PU_2, PU_3, O_2, M_5, M_6)
M_5 Farm Prices
(O_2, O_3, M_4)
M_6 Taxation
(O_2, M_4)
M_7 Credit
(O_5, M_4)

Responses (R)

R_1 Low Factor Productivity
R_2 Output Tends to Stagnate
R_3 Pressure for Reform

with the low rate of saving and the inability to attract foreign capital meant that reliance had to be placed exclusively on domestic capital formation. In turn, the high growth rate and rising incomes increased the demand for agricultural marketings to supply the rapidly growing urban population with food, light industry with agricultural raw materials, and the demand of the state for foreign exchange to finance imports of capital goods. Thus, the objectives of a high and rising volume of marketings (O_1) and the objective of a high saving ratio in the agricultural sector (O_2) follow directly from the environmental features of Soviet development. We may add at this point that these are perfectly valid contributions of the agricultural sector to the development of any growing economy (although their relative priority and the mechanisms through which they are achieved are not at all identical).

A related objective is that of increasing agricultural output through changes in agricultural production functions and the increase in new technology (O_3). This was to operate in part through economies of scale, and a by-product of this objective was the release of labor to industry. This objective is influenced primarily by the high rate of industrial growth (E_1), but is further accentuated by E_4, operating here as demand for labor on the part of industrial enterprises, searching for slack in order to maintain their ability to fulfill changing (or rising) production targets.

The introduction and maintenance of collectivization serve as the next objective (O_4). It has always been an ideologically appealing solution. To the extent that it could activate the economies of scale, it could also be thought of as a derived or secondary objective designed to assist in the performance of the objectives of greater farm output and marketings.

Collectivization of Soviet Agriculture

Recently, considerable light has been shed upon this subject by the researches of Professor Moshe Lewin.[4] At the time when the basic questions of the rate and the nature of industrialization were being debated and resolved, the Soviet agricultural sector consisted primarily of individual peasant households, which had just about completed the process of recovery from the ravages of foreign and domestic war (and, we may add, the policies of War Communism). It was simultaneously trying to adjust its production structure to the signals provided by changes in government price and fiscal policies. As I have shown elsewhere,[5] such policies during the years 1926–28 were not at all consistent with the objective of rapid industrialization. Failure to make the necessary adjustments in time led to the famous "grain procurement crisis" in the fall of 1927 that virtually eliminated exportable surpluses and threatened supply of the urban population and the whole fabric of the development plan.

Government response took the form of compulsory extraction (re-

---

[4] M. Lewin, "The Immediate Background of Soviet Collectivization," *Soviet Studies*, Vol. XVII, No. 2 (October, 1965), pp. 162–97, and *Russian Peasants and Soviet Power* (Evanston, Ill.: Northwestern University Press, 1968).

[5] Jerzy F. Karcz, "Thoughts on the Grain Problem," *Soviet Studies*, Vol. XVIII, No. 4 (April, 1967), pp. 399–434.

peated again a year later). These policies—a counterpart of the procurement methods under War Communism—proved effective enough (as they usually are in the short run). Their effectiveness appears to have persuaded Stalin and his supporters to adopt a policy of rapid collectivization, never envisaged in the First Five-Year Plan. In this sense, then, it is possible to view collectivization and the eventual emergence of command farming as being "so to speak pushed by the logic of events, with the transformation lubricated rather than propelled by ideological tenets."[6] But once the drive began, it became an objective in its own right, and the results had to be presented later in a favorable light in disregard of any inconvenient facts.

The collectivization which did occur was thus a function of the policy to increase state procurements (rather than total marketings) at any price and might be called properly a part of the policy of collecting "the agricultural surplus." It is not always recognized that this gave rise to some interesting policy developments in intersectoral relationships and an accompanying theoretical discussion.

On the practical level, so-called contract deliveries were used to implement objectives dealing with the volume of marketings and the contribution to capital formation. But the contracts also specified terms of trade as well as the various conditions of production (use of inputs, timing of operations, etc.). Of course, in this chaotic period the latter provisions were seldom carried out, but deliverable produce was collected, resulting frequently in deprivation of farms of seeding stock as well as a considerable part of consumption requirements. Efforts were made to reduce the use of money; cash advances to farmers were first limited, then in 1930 completely eliminated and replaced by advances in kind. Sales of consumer goods were tied to the delivery of products. It might be significant that at about this time the Commisariat of Trade was renamed that of Supply.

On a theoretical plane, several Soviet economists assumed that the end of the New Economic Policy and "the victory of socialism in the countryside" made possible a shift to an absolute command economy,[7] in which allocation of goods and services as well as of resources is carried out exclusively by orders. These developments were viewed as representing a significant step within the organized process of production towards the disappearance of distribution as a link between production and consumption. Market incentives in production were to be replaced by direct supply of producer as well as consumer goods to the ultimate user.

It would be premature to conclude that the directors of the system tried to introduce an absolute command economy within a given time period. Still, steps leading in that direction were being taken in agricul-

[6] Grossman, *op. cit.*, p. 107.

[7] Grossman's term. See also P. J. D. Wiles, *The Political Economy of Communism* (Cambridge, Mass.: Harvard University Press, 1962), pp. 67–68.

ture.[8] In any event, this policy was short-lived, and by mid-1932 there were many signs of retreat from such positions.

The major reason for the retreat lay in the distorted and overoptimistic view of the responses and motivation of households in the absolute command economy.[9] As is well known, Soviet collectivization was carried out in a rapid, brutal, though often haphazard manner. The erratic and discriminatory collection of procurement was accompanied by failure of the "supply" apparatus in the countryside. The extent of outward migration was without precedent: by 1932 agricultural employment declined by about 20 percent. Many were forced to leave, but many others must have left for the greater relative personal security in the city. Such as they were, the meager ration supplies might have seemed greater than the uncertainties of collectivization that often encompassed even the chicken and the cow.

Indeed, the year 1932, when many key decisions were made on the continuation of the general pattern of industrialization and the introduction of key features of command farming, was characterized by very mixed results. The Five-Year Plan was declared fulfilled and the industrialization program survived. But gross national product (in 1937 prices) declined below the level of 1931, and similar trends are shown by a reconstructed index of final industrial production. Agriculture seemed to be at the brink of disaster. Livestock holdings (which by one method of measurement accounted for about one-sixth of the 1928 capital stock) declined drastically. This was one factor responsible for the increase in grain marketings. Average farm marketings in 1928–32 were 7 percent below 1928, and per head of urban population the decline came to 25 percent; by 1932, the situation had worsened. Farm draft power declined by 28 percent. While sown area increased by 19 percent, the official index of output shows a decline of 14 percent, and a western calculation of agriculture's contribution to the national product indicates a decline of 28 percent.[10]

Since the system of command farming that did emerge represents a mixture of command and market mechanisms and incentives, it should be viewed as a compromise, designed to achieve a better compliance with the overall objectives of the state. Here we should emphasize the decision to continue the pattern of Soviet industrialization (E_1) and the

[8] Frequent complaints about violations of economic accountability in industry suggest something of this sort in that sector too, but there is always a shift to more direct controls in periods such as this.

[9] On this, see Ward, *The Socialist Economy*, p. 140.

[10] See the data in Richard Moorsteen and Raymond P. Powell, *The Soviet Capital Stock, 1928–1962* (New Haven, Conn.: Yale University Press, 1966), p. 361; Powell's essay in Abram Bergson and Simon Kuznets (eds.), *Economic Trends in the Soviet Union* (Cambridge, Mass.: Harvard University Press, 1963), p. 178; and Naum Jasny, *The Socialized Agriculture of the USSR* (Stanford, Calif.: Stanford University Press, 1949), p. 458.

related phenomenon of high income elasticities of expenditures (on food) (E_3). This is partly the result of the relative neglect of the production of consumer goods and services, and partly of the absence (or the insignificant size) of payments for medical care, housing, and education.

Chief Characteristics of Production Units

The most typical production unit has been the collective farm conforming to the provisions of the 1935 charter. Its most important characteristics are: production in accordance with the state plan of agricultural production and distribution of output according to the rules of the charter. Under this, the state has had a priority claim on part of the output (see below). Production expenses, tax and insurance payments, and allocations to investment funds all had to be met before remuneration of farm members, which was thus made a residual. The collective farm (PU_1) is hence a very special co-operative.

An important by-product of the collective farm is its private sector. This consists of household plots to which each member is entitled within prescribed limits and where a limited number of animals may be kept. In view of their importance, these plots are labelled here as a separate production unit (PU_2); as our model is intended to cover Eastern Europe, we include here also the farms of individual peasants. (As completely separate units, they are now important only in Yugoslavia and Poland.)

Like the collective, a state farm produces in accordance with the production plan, but it has always paid wages to its workers, and (unlike the collective) has always controlled directly all machinery used in production, particularly tractors. Our definition of state farm (PU_3) includes a variety of other similar production units.

The last production unit has been auxiliary in nature to the collective farm. Machine tractor stations (MTS's) (PU_4) concentrated all heavy machinery and much of the scarce trained labor in the early period of Soviet collectivization. In the USSR, they were abolished in 1958, when machinery was transferred to the collectives. They survive to a limited extent (service of financially weak collectives) in other socialist countries of Eastern Europe.

Introduction of Command Farming in Eastern Europe

The special production units of command farming (with the obvious exception of individual peasants) have been adopted in East European socialist countries in very special circumstances. The influence of environmental characteristics played a major role after the introduction of rapid industrialization plans. No East European country attempted to copy the exact pattern of Soviet collectivization, for reasons that were partly political and partly economic. After the seizure of power, all Communist governments conducted land reforms to eliminate privately owned large-scale holdings. These reforms tended to neutralize the political influence of large and powerful peasant parties, but they made it awkward to proceed immediately with massive collectivization. Moreover, large-scale disinvestment in livestock was one of the direct consequences of rapid Soviet collectivization. That cost could seemingly be avoided by gradual collectivization, and the Soviet experience with command farming during the thirties might have suggested that many if not most of the objectives could be fulfilled in a satisfactory manner by gradual collectivization.

Initial collectivization drives in Bulgaria and Yugoslavia occurred in the early postwar period, but the first major effort came in the latter country in 1948–49. At about the same time, collectivization campaigns began in other socialist countries. In general, several milder, intermediate forms of collectives (including, e.g., distribution of income in part in proportion to the contributed land and/or capital) were used, though the Soviet prototype remained the ultimate objective. Progress was decidedly uneven, as it was interrupted by numerous attempts to "decompress" command farming by increasing the effectiveness of market incentives. This was particularly true after 1953 within the framework of the "New Course" policies. In 1953, Yugoslav collectives were disbanded, and this also occurred in Poland in 1956. Though socialization of agriculture remains the ultimate formal goal in both countries, there has been no attempt to use outright compulsion to date. Elsewhere, however, the process of collectivization was eventually resumed. By 1965, in Eastern Europe the socialized sector of collective and state farms (but excluding household plots) included the following percentages of total arable land in each country: Bulgaria, 89; Czechoslovakia, 93; East Germany, 95; Hungary, 87; Poland, 14; Rumania, 87; and Yugoslavia, 15.[11]

Thus, the impact of command farming in Eastern Europe was not quite the same as in the USSR. In the former, the operation of command farming was linked for a considerable period of time to the introduction of collectivization. On the other hand, efforts to correct many of the undesirable consequences occurred more promptly. These two phenomena are, of course, interrelated. But all of the mechanisms, as well as the undesirable consequences, are to be found here as well.

Mechanisms of Command Farming

We now pass to the examination of the ways in which objectives of command farming have been implemented within the framework of the adopted production units. Our first three mechanisms are clearly of the command variety, but others represent a mixture of command and market elements, with the proportion varying at different stages of development and decompression.

The main key mechanism of command farming has been the system of

---

[11] U.S. Department of Agriculture, Economic Research Service, *The Europe and Soviet Union Agricultural Situation: Review of 1966 and Outlook for 1967* (Washington, D.C., 1967), p. 113.

state procurements of agricultural products. This is related first to the objective of increasing the volume of farm marketings (O_1) as well as to that of raising agriculture's contribution to capital formation (O_2). In both instances, reliance is placed on state rather than other procurement in order to concentrate the extracted produce—and savings—in the hands of the state for purposes of centrally determined distribution and final use. To the extent that individual peasant farming still operates, the system of procurements has also been used as a mechanism designed to accelerate the implementation of collectivization (O_4).

The chief characteristic of the procurement system is the use of compulsory delivery quotas. In the early period of industrialization (and until the early fifties in the case of the USSR), these deliveries were paid for at low, virtually nominal prices that remained unchanged in spite of the rapidly rising level of retail prices of industrial and other consumer goods. So long as MTS's existed as a main source of capital inputs in the collective farm sector, the system was supplemented by payments in kind by the farms for services rendered by these stations. In the early stages of command farming, a system of above-quota purchases (at considerably higher prices) was also introduced, with the objective of increasing the volume of output acquired by the state or other organizations. Because a typical Soviet or East European farm unit is a multi-product enterprise, the system was eventually extended to all the important farm products. Following the Soviet example, technical crops continued to be procured under the contract delivery system, but the environment in which delivery contracts were negotiated did not in any way eliminate the element of compulsion. Since premiums were paid for above-quota deliveries, a double price system also applied here. Prices paid in quota and above-quota deliveries were set centrally by the state.

The obligations to deliver were considered quite firm, and enforcement was assured through the provision that underfulfillment of quota deliveries increased the obligations in the succeeding years. In the USSR, the system also applied to individual household plots of the collective farmers until 1957.

The system of two types of deliveries was eventually abolished in the Soviet Union as well as all East European countries (with the exception of Poland, where compulsory deliveries still exist at very low rates). The obligation to sell a certain amount of output to the state continued to operate—though the number of quotas was somewhat reduced, particularly within the framework of the application of new economic systems to agriculture.[12]

Procurement quotas were at first determined centrally. Subsequently,

[12] See my "Some Aspects of New Economic Systems in Bulgaria and Czechoslovakia," in the forthcoming volume of proceedings of the Conference on the Agrarian Question in the Light of Communist and Non-Communist Experience, to be published by the University of Washington Press (W. A. Douglas Jackson, ed.).

the need to decentralize was felt in this area as well, and various local administrative agencies were given the right to vary the quotas within a given region. In the USSR, quotas were first imposed on planned sown areas or per head of livestock on hand. Since farms tried to avoid the tax involved in compulsory deliveries by attempting to avoid expansion of acreage or of herds, quotas were ultimately set on the "per hectare basis." This was also done in Eastern Europe in the postwar period.

The second key mechanism is that of agricultural planning (M_2). This is in part the manifestation of the centrally planned nature of the command economy as a whole (E_4), but it is also related to certain other objectives. To the extent that rapid changes were desired in the production structure (e.g., the expansion of cotton sowings in the USSR), the setting of direct output and sown area targets appeared to be advisable and may thus be related to our objective (O_3). Moreover, given the volume of procurement quotas, it also seemed preferable to make sure that what had to be delivered (at nominal prices) would, in fact, be first produced. Finally, the low professional qualifications of farm managers in the early stages of command farming may well have called for greater supervision by higher (and presumably more qualified) outside agencies.

The upshot was a great proliferation of targets of all kinds. These included area to be sown under particular crops, size and the composition of livestock herds, indicators of productivity, the use of equipment (primarily in state farms, where targets were set on the basis of technological efficiency), dates and quality indicators for the performance of certain operations, etc. The supply of many construction materials—other than those produced locally—was subject to allocation quotas, and overhead capital investment (such as irrigation facilities) was also planned centrally. Many indicators were at one time approved by the Council of Ministers itself.

The resulting administrative difficulties can only be branded as formidable, especially when planning of this sort was applied to individual peasant farms (as was at one time the case in East Germany and Czechoslovakia). Examples are often cited of instances when the procurement plans exceed output targets.

Beginning with the USSR in 1955 (the innovation spread rapidly throughout the bloc), this type of planning was abolished, and farms were formally allowed to plan their own output on the basis of firm procurement targets that continued to be assigned to individual farms. In practice, however, procurement planning of this type can be fully as effective as output planning, especially when procurement targets encompass such basic products as milk, meat, and grain. (Interviews with farm officials suggest that roughly 90 per cent of the structure of sowing can be determined by the joint impact of five or six procurement quotas. The number was usually greater.[13])

---

[13] This is explored at greater length in my paper cited in fn. 12.

It should be noted that certain key indicators were not planned for prolonged periods of time. Thus, no calculations were made of collective farm production costs until the early fifties. Given the existence of payments in kind and payment to labor out of residual income, such calculations would have been very difficult anyway. Given the high rate of taxation in kind through compulsory deliveries, they were moreover "outright embarrassing."[14] And it took roughly another decade (somewhat less in Bulgaria) before calculations of net income of collective farms became common.

The mechanism of agricultural planning is closely related to the third command mechanism of administrative interference (M_3). It is now readily apparent that most key decisions were made by administrative agencies which were not directly involved in farm operations. Many of these officials performed narrowly defined functions and sought to fulfill only their own particular goals. The interference of procurement officials into operational decision making was always considerable, and they seldom inquired into the long-range consequences of their decision for individual farms. In general, administrative officials entrusted with important decision-making powers were not given any incentives to increase the productivity of farm units.

The really significant interference came, of course, from the Party apparatus, particularly at the lowest administrative level. Their desires to enforce existing regulations, or to enhance the welfare of farms in their districts, was generally subordinated to that of gaining approval of their immediate (or the highest) superiors. It was also true that the task of discovering what the superiors were seeking to maximize at any one time was not always easy, in spite of the priority given to the objective of maximizing procurements and contributions to capital formation. This was particularly true in the Soviet Union, where major measures of farm policy were all too often implemented in the form of campaigns that often resulted in great reductions in both the production possibilities of farms and the individual welfare of farm members. Among the examples that could be mentioned are corn campaigns under Khrushchev, the extension of unirrigated cotton acreage into the Ukraine, sugar beets in Siberia, and the like.

Administrative interference at various levels has often been deplored, although the "right kind of involvement in farm affairs" has equally often been praised. Such formulations create a built-in incentive for violation of standing rules of the game, and we were not surprised to learn that practices of detailed output planning persisted for many years after 1955. The extent of such interference (to which there is no equivalent in industry) is perhaps best explained in terms of the relative ranking of agricultural objectives by various officials (with O_1 and O_3 being given a priority) and a desire to "improve" upon the functioning of the procurement sys-

[14] The expression was used by Nancy Nimitz.

tem and agricultural planning (M_1, M_2). A more fundamental reason could be found in the deep distrust of peasantry that dates back to the early years of Soviet power and to peasant resistance to collectivization (O_4).[15]

Given the existence of a free market for consumer goods (apart from periods of rationing), material incentives are in the main used to allocate labor. The nature of these incentives in state farms (PU_3) is straightforward enough, given the existence of guaranteed wages (supplemented by income of plots). In the collective farm sector (PU_1), however, the problem is much more complex. The farm itself, designed primarily as an instrument of forced saving (O_2), cannot serve as a provider of sufficient incentives to assure its members a reward that is adequate to assure a required supply of effort. Thus, the structure of incentives becomes particularly distorted. In the USSR during 1937, fully one-quarter of the total receipts from state procurements accrued to the producers of cotton. For less specialized farms, the household plot (PU_2) became the main source of income, particularly as the legalization of free market sales of farm products—at high prices (M_5)—offered a major opportunity to many to acquire cash. In the thirties, cash income from Soviet collectives never accounted for more than one-quarter of the total household money income from such distributions and sales on the collective farm market. More recently, the corresponding figure is approximately 50 percent. In Czechoslovakia, the share of total (cash and kind) income from the plot in total income of the collective farmer reached a peak of 43 percent, and declined to about 30 percent in 1966.

But the issue is more complex. The private plot economy depends to a very considerable extent on the provision of feed from the socialized sector (mainly through distribution in kind, but more recently also through sales at low prices). There was thus always *some* incentive to supply work to the socialized sector, but on several occasions command mechanisms (minimum number of days per year, restriction of plot size, etc.) were also employed to reinforce this tendency—which is somewhat weakened by the fact that periods of peak activity in the two sectors coincide.

Two more aspects of incentives deserve brief mention. One is the difficulty of retaining such qualified trained personnel as is available on farms; both the resistance to sufficient income differentials and the pull of the city are very hard to overcome. Again, especially in the Soviet Union, use has been made of administrative measures to keep the specialist on the farm.[16] The other refers to various attempts to stimulate participa-

---

[15] On this, see Alec Nove, "Incentives for Peasants and Administrators," in Roy D. Laird (ed.), *Soviet Agricultural and Peasant Affairs* (Lawrence: University of Kansas Press, 1963), pp. 51–68.

[16] Cf. the decree of April 24, 1962, translated in the *Current Digest of the Soviet Press,* Vol. XIV, No. 16 (May 16, 1962), pp. 16–17.

tion and to improve the quality of work through extensive use of premiums. This has an unfortunate tendency to introduce a considerable amount of uncertainty into the structure of rewards.[17]

Reference has already been made to the existence of a double price system in state procurements (until the reforms of 1958–60). If free market prices are included, a producing unit might have been faced with three different prices (M_5) for an identical product. As is explained in detail by Morris Bornstein,[18] the low delivery price served as an instrument of forced saving (O_2), while the above-quota price and the free market price were meant to provide incentives for greater supply of effort (M_4) and an increase in production (O_3). It was, however, the average realized price that influenced the total revenue of the collective farm and thus the cash incentives it could offer to members. As it turned out, even under the regime of strict output and procurement planning, average farm prices were not totally deprived of their allocational effect.

As we just noted, a single system of procurement prices is now the rule. Its introduction was beset by two distinct difficulties. First, because various governments (Soviet in 1958, Czechoslovak in 1959, Bulgarian in 1962) were apparently reluctant to give up the existing channels of capital accumulation, many price reforms were enacted under the constraint that allocation of resources to agriculture should not be altered. This, combined with the lack of any appropriate criteria for setting agricultural prices, failed to make production of many—primarily animal—products "profitable" (in the sense of covering production costs). Second, it also proved difficult to eliminate other distortions in the structure of procurement prices, such as the persistent undervaluation of grains.

Two other mechanisms deserve brief mention. One is agricultural taxation (M_6), functioning in the collective farm sector through the income tax on the collectives and in the private sector through a variety of what we can here call agricultural (at times straight land) taxes. The purpose of this taxation was to supplement the contribution of agriculture to domestic capital formation (O_2) exacted by the taxation in kind accomplished through the operation of the procurement and price systems. The second is agricultural credit (M_7), the use of which has varied a great deal from one country to another. It has been considerably greater in East European countries than in the Soviet Union, where advances from procurement organizations were relied upon to cover short-term needs for working capital, and where long-term credits were fairly insignificant in relation to internal financing.

---

[17] Karl-Eugen Wädekin, *Privatproduzenten in der sowjetischen Landwirtschaft* (Köln: Verlag Wissenschaft und Politik, 1967), pp. 121–34.

[18] Morris Bornstein, "The Soviet Price System," *American Economic Review*, Vol. LII, No. 1 (March, 1962), pp. 80–88.

UNDESIRABLE CONSEQUENCES

The first undesirable consequence from the standpoint of the agricultural sector has been its failure to specialize (UC_1). This is directly traceable to the operation of the procurement system (M_1) and agricultural planning (M_2), strengthened by administrative interference (M_3) and bolstered by the operation of farm prices (M_5).

One of the basic difficulties lay in the determination of the correct size of delivery quotas. As compulsory deliveries (including MTS payments) reached the level of about 90 percent of total sales—this was the case for grain in the early fifties in Poland and Czechoslovakia, and in the USSR almost throughout Stalin's reign—it proved impossible to avoid excessive assessments on many farms. This was aggravated by the tendency of quota-distributing agencies to "plan safely" for the fulfillment of regional quotas by allocating quotas to a larger number of farms than would be necessary under average harvest conditions. Since most products were subject to some sort of compulsory procurement, many advantages that could be realized from economies of scale were often dissipated. Worse yet, weak farms were often forced to deliver seed stocks of reasonable quality and later received seed grain of lower quality. On the other hand, more efficient farms were often assigned larger quotas (in a legal or illegal manner). Examples of "specialized farms" receiving quotas for 30 products were not at all uncommon.

While the procurement system did tend to freeze the structure of production at the existing level, it also stimulated production of certain types of produce in an artificial manner. In East European countries, larger and more efficient peasant farms were deprived of their own feed (this also occurred in the USSR), while weaker and less prepared farms were forced into livestock production, using feed purchased from the government at somewhat privileged prices. This kind of "pump priming" of grain often called for additional investments and resulted in high-cost production of animal products. The extent to which this was harmful is best revealed by the consideration that for all the countries of the socialist bloc, feed balances were insufficient to supply recommended feed rations. In 1964, feed requirements in Czechoslovakia were covered only to the extent of 85 percent in terms of grain units and 70 percent in terms of protein content. In 1962–64, the overall supply of Bulgarian collective farm animals with concentrated feed fell 30–35 percent short of requirements.

Quota-distribution procedures had yet another and equally adverse effect. Since no wheat quotas were usually set for mountainous areas, it suddenly became profitable to shift from rye to wheat production in spite of lower yields. The reason was that the total revenue from wheat sales (all at the higher above-quota prices) exceeded that from rye, which had a much lower average price because of the relatively high quotas for deliveries at the low quota-price. For the same reason, hog production (often on the basis of imported feed) tended to displace cattle in mountainous areas, and the production of sheep was drastically reduced in the non-black soil areas of the RSFSR.

The effect of detailed output planning on specialization (with the exception of a few specialized crops, such as cotton) tended to work in the same direction. In 1966–67, when output was planned only through procurement targets, every single farm I visited in Czechoslovakia would have introduced fairly drastic changes in its production structure in the absence of obligations to sell.

Command farming also turned out to be quite capital intensive (UC_2). This is in part related to collectivization (O_4) and the operation of the kind of production units that are used in command farming (PU_1, PU_2). As indicated earlier, initial farm power losses in the Soviet Union had first to be replaced by mechanized power; indeed, total agricultural capital stock in the USSR towards the end of the thirties was about the same as it had been in 1928. Collectivization also results in a high demand for structures, primarily to house the collectivized livestock. Many of these structures, however, contribute little to current production, and their impact on productivity is observable only with a considerable lag. At the same time, of course, investment in machinery is likely to be relatively lower, if—as can be expected—total allocations of capital to agriculture are limited by the demands of the other sectors of the economy.

In the Soviet case, the share of agriculture in total investment in the national economy during the prewar plan period was close to 15 percent (and never declined below 10 percent, even in wartime). Currently, it reached a peak of 22.5 percent in 1966–67. In 1953–63, Bulgaria placed about 28 percent of its gross investment in agriculture and forestry. The corresponding figures are 18 percent for Hungary and Rumania and 16 percent for Czechoslovakia.[19]

These consequences of the introduction of command farming reduce the *net* contribution of the agricultural sector to capital formation, and conflict with the stated (and legitimate) objective of agriculture's contribution to industrialization (O_2). At first glance, they may be interpreted as a once and for all expenditure, but the problem is more complex. For capital-output ratios in socialized agricultures have been rising very considerably in recent years.

This is partly the result of inefficient use of such capital inputs as are made available to individual production units. The Soviet experience with the operation of machine tractor stations is vivid testimony to this effect: the task of co-ordinating their activities with those of collective farms

---

[19] Maurice Ernst, "Commentary," in Jerzy F. Karcz (ed.), *Soviet and East European Agriculture* (Berkeley: University of California Press, 1967), p. 409.

could not be solved efficiently. State farms too, operating in a manner similar to that of state industrial enterprises with no explicit capital charges, tended to use this factor wastefully. In general, co-ordination of agricultural investments has been poor. This has been the case in the field of construction (in the early sixties, there was no housing for 20–25 percent of Bulgarian collective farm cows, calves, or sows). The ultimate impact of costly investments in irrigation facilities was frequently reduced because of failure to provide complementary drainage facilities. Finally, existing machinery stocks could not be used to capacity, given the shortage of spare parts and repair facilities that resulted from certain particular characteristics of the operation of command economy in industry (E_4).

The adopted system of incentives and farm prices characteristic of command farming (M_4, M_5), as well as the existence of its special production units (PU_1, PU_2, PU_3), resulted in a close interdependence of the private and the socialist sector in socialist agricultures, particularly in that of the USSR (UC_3). This is analyzed in great detail in an important book by Karl E. Wädekin.[20] We have already referred to the high contribution of household plot production to total incomes of collective farm members, and it is proper to say that they bore much of the burden of assuring a minimum—though not always adequate—supply of labor for the socialist sector. But this is not all. A special type of the division of labor also occurred in production of crops as well as animal products, with the private sector concentrating, e.g., on the production of potatoes and the socialized on that of grains, feed, and the technical crops. The main source of income from household plots was thus largely dependent upon supplies of feed from the socialized sector. In turn, the latter frequently acquired large numbers of young cattle from the private sector. Even today, the contribution of household plots to supplying the urban (and non-agricultural rural) population with foodstuffs is very considerable.

Private production on household plots, however, has always been suspect on ideological grounds. Various spontaneous attempts to limit the scope for private production in agriculture necessarily affected adversely total production as well. If—as happened in the USSR in 1959 through 1964—such limitations were applied on a national scale, these adverse effects were even more pronounced.

Command farming also affected adversely the composition, and in some instances the size, of the collective farm labor force (UC_4). This impact has varied substantially not only among the various countries of the European socialist bloc, but also regionally within a single country. Disparities of income levels for fairly comparable occupations, especially among the more trained and specialized agricultural workers, have been fairly high. These disparities were further reinforced by the usual "pull"

[20] Wädekin, *op. cit.*, chap. v.

of urban amenities, which proved particularly strong for those villagers with university or other specialized training. Obviously, incentives in agriculture (M_4) were a prime cause of this phenomenon. The situation was at times aggravated by attempts to link the size of professional reward to plan fulfillment (or the volume of production) and the resulting irregularity in *paid* (as opposed to planned) wages or rewards. All kinds of programs have been suggested to deal with this phenomenon, but no satisfactory solutions appear to be in sight. This is particularly inconsistent with the stated objectives of intensifying agricultural production, modernizing production methods, and introducing better technology (O_3).

In certain areas of the USSR, East Germany, and Czechoslovakia, the labor supply problem is much more severe. For here the flight from the land has operated with particular force and affected not only the supply of specialists but that of less qualified labor as well. The resulting age and sex structure of the farm labor force is particularly unsatisfactory. In the collective farm sector, the mobility of labor between farms is not very high. At present, it even appears that labor supplies might be inadequate precisely in some areas with major land improvement programs.

This problem is also related to another peculiar phenomenon (to which there is a counterpart in industry): the uneven performance of individual farm units (UC_5). Given the partly unplanned and often the random impact of the procurement system (M_1), and the uncertain influence of agricultural planning and administrative interference (M_2, M_3), it was often a matter of chance alone whether a given production unit found itself among the "leading" or among the "lagging" farms. These disparities were further reinforced by the impact of the system of farm prices (M_5). The number of such "lagging" farms is relatively large: in Hungary, 40 percent of collectives are currently classified in this category.[21] Elsewhere, their number has been diminished either by conversions to state farms or by mergers with more prosperous neighbors. Thus, command farming tended to promote the co-existence of a "subsistence" and a "commercial" sector in agriculture, a phenomenon that is also found in many market-oriented agricultural systems (including that of the United States).[22] To the extent that weak farms merely performed a function of social assistance in providing minimum living standards to individuals who could not be absorbed by other sectors of the economy, this would not be a serious problem. However, in some socialist countries this is no longer the case.

In the particular conditions of command farming, uneven farm performance gave rise to other undesirable phenomena. To some extent, it

[21] Fred E. Dohrs, "Incentives in Communist Agriculture: The Hungarian Models," *Slavic Review*, Vol. XXVII, No. 1 (March, 1968), p. 29.

[22] Cf. Wyn F. Owen, "The Double Development Squeeze on Agriculture," *American Economic Review*, Vol. LVI, No. 1 (March, 1966), p. 64.

contributed to the distortion of information by providing faulty signals to top decision makers (UC_6), perpetuating the impression that the existing income and performance disparities within the farming sector were due merely to managerial incompetence and testifying to the existence of large "internal reserves" (production potential) on weaker farms. But given the persistently high state demand for farm products and the absence of market mechanisms for the reallocation of factors of production within the sector, the state was unable to renounce its claims on a part of the output of these weak farms.

Over the years, we have therefore witnessed the emergence of special, but generally partial, programs to improve the condition and the production possibilities of weak farms. This gave rise to what socialist economists call the process of "secondary redistribution," under which resources initially extracted by the state through the system of farm prices or taxes are redirected to the weaker part of the agricultural sector. In practice, this amounts to the subsidization of weaker farms by their more fortunate counterparts, with adverse effects on incentives, internal capital formation, and the ability to obtain off-farm inputs. It is the opinion of most Czechoslovak economists that such assistance programs have not achieved their goals, but have contributed to the rise of production costs (or a slower rate of their reduction). This was particularly true when the assistance took the form of conversion to state farms, where production costs (except for Bulgaria and Rumania) have been considerably higher than those for the collective farm sector.

Moreover, the co-existence of two sectors in command farming further accentuated the already strong pressure for administrative interference and detailed planning of output and agro-technical measures. From what I have been able to observe on the spot, the effect of detailed supervision on incentives—one of the key factors involved—is often the opposite of what is required.

A special feature of command farming has been its tendency to generate faulty signals to various kinds of decision makers (UC_6). Priority of marketings and of the extraction of forced savings (O_1, O_2), the unfortunate tendency to stress the superiority of collectivized agriculture (O_4), and the political climate all combined to distort the flow of information available at various strata of authority.

At the level of the production unit, the chief casualty has been the collective farm, where meaningful cost calculations were prohibited for a considerable period of time, and where the structure of production was largely—if not completely—determined by many planning indicators imposed from above. Collective farm management was further forced to strike an uneasy balance between the provision of minimum incentives (in cash or in kind) to farm members and the fulfillment of procurement quotas or other success indicators. If the former were not forthcoming, there would be an adverse impact on labor supply. If the latter were not fulfilled, reprimands, other punishment, and dismissal would follow. There thus appeared a natural search for some slack and an all too frequent necessity to violate *some* regulation. But this only increased the scope of administrative interference (M_3), and further reduced the scope for autonomous decision making. On balance, however, the tendency was to emphasize short-term results to the detriment of long-run trends in productivity. Given the high rate of turnover in the administrative and the Party apparatus, the same tendency also operated in various "above-enterprise" agencies.

Although an unbelievably large amount of statistical reporting took place, emphasis was primarily placed on series that indicated satisfactory performance of socialist agriculture. While the indicator of "gross cash revenue" was used to represent overall results of collective farm activity, it eventually became clear (in both Czechoslovakia and the USSR) that it misrepresented trends in total gross output of that sector. Similarly, allocations of cash to "indivisible funds" were often used as an indicator of internal accumulation in collectives. Recent Czechoslovak data show that this series differed markedly from trends in the more meaningful series on internal accumulation of cash and kind, which moved in the opposite direction from allocations to indivisible funds after 1959. Finally, the official series seriously understates the share of agriculture in the national product. Whether or not this tendency toward misleading statistics affected major policy decisions at the highest level in all countries must still remain conjectural. But a claim has been made in Czechoslovakia that it did delay a shift of resources to agriculture for about three years prior to 1964. Under the circumstances, it is likely that the top decision makers were at least partly misled by their own statistical agencies.

The overall impact of the mechanisms and the undesirable consequences of command farming are clear enough: the agricultural sector as a whole appears to operate far short of its production possibilities frontier. Its first response then is that of low joint factor productivity (R_1), a conclusion substantiated by such calculations as are presently available for the USSR during the thirties and for Czechoslovakia in the postwar period.[23]

This does not necessarily mean that the imposition of command farming cannot lead to an increase in output. As is well known, Soviet farm output during the thirties recovered rapidly from the low reached in 1932–33. But as the rate of growth of marketings outstripped that of output, and as trends in farm income became less favorable towards the end of the decade, output began to stagnate. A similar tendency appeared in the USSR towards the end of the postwar recovery period (1949–52),

[23] D. Gale Johnson's, Douglas Diamond's, Gregor Lazarcik's, and my own.

and in virtually all East European countries by 1953. It would then appear that the tendency of output to stagnate (apart from recovery from unusual troughs) is a second response (R_2) under command farming.

It should be noted the emergence of R_2 probably went unnoticed in the USSR (exception must be made for such economists as V. G. Venzher) in the particular political climate of the Great Purge and the approach of World War II. In general, little attention has been devoted there to the study of the *total* impact of command farming on the performance of the agricultural sector. (For reasons that cannot be explored here, economic model-building in socialist countries is only a recent development.) It is thus likely that the full effect of command farming was not really recognized for a considerable period of time. This is why a Polish economist, in discussing the application of the procurement system, could say with justification that practitioners of command farming often find themselves in the position of the sorcerer's apprentice.

The tendency of output to stagnate and other undesirable consequences do generate a pressure for systemic reform (R_3), and recent history of communist agricultures provides ample evidence to that effect. However, the complex interrelationships that we have discussed above, as well as the impact of partial reforms introduced in the USSR and Eastern Europe, do suggest that the responsiveness of command farming to partial reforms is sluggish. For example, in the Soviet case in 1958–64, there was improvement of incentives without a corresponding increase in input supplies, and greater formal farm autonomy accompanied by rising procurement goals and restrictions on the private sector.

Recently, the decompression of command farming has taken the form of "new economic systems" in agriculture, accompanied by corresponding reforms (of varying degree of novelty) in the industrial sectors of the economy. Most of these reforms center on many key variables in our model. They stress greater farm autonomy in decision making, reduce the number (or the size) of procurement quotas, emphasize the allocative function of prices (by introducing many reforms that clearly point in the right direction), increase the importance and improve the conditions of bank credit, and attempt to use taxation rather than prices to achieve the desired inter-sectoral transfer of resources. Much attention has also been given to the improvement of incentives by raising the level of remuneration on the collective farms (USSR, Bulgaria, Czechoslovakia), or introducing various share-cropping practices within the collective farm sector (Hungary). Finally, efforts are being made to provide numerous agricultural services that have hitherto been sadly neglected, as well as to improve the volume and the conditions of the supply of off-farm inputs.

It is still too early to say whether these efforts will succeed without further institutional and policy reforms (and the outlook does not seem too bright in the aftermath of the invasion of Czechoslovakia). We ought to point out, however, that balance-of-payments considerations, as well as continuing growth of state demand for farm products, suggest that great attention should be paid to the impact of recent changes in agricultural planning practices as well as of administrative interference. In times of stress, the tendency has always been to apply these mechanisms with greater strength, and there are many subtle ways in which farm operations may be influenced by outside organizations.

CONCLUSION

A brief concluding statement is in order on the overall effectiveness of command farming within the context of economic development as such. Soviet experience, as well as that of some East European countries with relatively abundant availability of labor, suggests that command farming, or similar policies, might be used to assist the development of the economy in the early stage of rapid industrialization. The great danger lies in the fact that command farming, as such, tends to provide signals for turning points in economic policy only with a considerable delay and in a distorted manner. There is, of course, no guarantee that these signals will be interpreted correctly or that they will lead to the implementation of proper policies that deal simultaneously with a wide range of variables. Given the high capital intensity of command farming, which reduces considerably the contribution of agriculture to domestic capital formation, and its adverse or at best dubious productivity trends, it would seem appropriate to explore alternative institutional arrangements and agricultural systems.

In the light of the above, command farming does not appear to be an appropriate agricultural system for accelerating the rate of growth of an economy (such as the Czech) which is not characterized by relative abundance of labor.

Nor is it likely to be a satisfactory arrangement for countries that cannot afford to give first priority to increasing marketings because of the initially low level of per capita production. As is suggested by the experience of Mainland China with its own version of command farming, emphasis must be placed on raising productivity. In turn, the Japanese experience indicates that alternatives to command farming may yield superior results both for the economy as a whole and for its agricultural sector.

17. FOREIGN TRADE BEHAVIOR OF CENTRALLY PLANNED ECONOMIES*

Franklyn D. Holzman[1]

The foreign trade of centrally planned economies differs from that of market-oriented economies in a number of important ways, as a result of the nature of the centrally planned economic system. Typically, the foreign trade of such an economy is characterized by a high degree of autarky, inconvertibility, bilateralism, and discrimination—which in turn are attributable to such features of the economy as physical planning, ambitious targets, irrational price structures, disequilibrium exchange rates, and state trading.

In this comprehensive article, Holzman systematically analyzes how and why centrally planned economies conduct their foreign trade, and the resulting problems of inconvertibility, bilateralism, discrimination, dumping, and the inapplicability of most-favored-nation tariff treatment. He concludes by examining possible solutions to some of these problems.

* Reprinted by permission from *Industrialization in Two Systems: Essays in Honor of Alexander Gerschenkron*, ed. Henry Rosovsky (New York: John Wiley & Sons, Inc., 1966), pp. 237–65, with the omission of some footnotes and more technical portions. Franklyn D. Holzman is Professor of Economics at Tufts University.

[1] Many ideas for this paper developed while I was a consultant to the United Nations in 1963. My ideas were clarified in discussion there with Sidney Dell, Rudolph Nötel, Nita Watts, Stein Rossen, Juri Ryska, and Valery Naborov. I am also indebted to Joseph Berliner, Richard Caves, Herbert Levine, Charles Kindleberger, Egon Neuberger, and Raymond Vernon for comments on an early draft. The views reflected in the paper are my own and should not necessarily be attributed to any of the above individuals or organizations with which they are connected. Finally, I am indebted for financial assistance to the American Council of Learned Societies.

THE EARLIEST comprehensive and still relevant analysis of foreign trade in a centrally planned economy (CPE) can be found in Alexander Gerschenkron's *Economic Relations with the U.S.S.R.*[2] In large part, the present paper constitutes an extension of his work.

Traditionally, the foreign trade behavior of centrally planned economies has been characterized by a notoriously high degree of autarky, currency inconvertibility, bilateralism, and discrimination. Although these phenomena occur also in trade among capitalist nations, they do not constitute its "normal" features. Not only are the capitalist deviations from uncontrolled trade of lesser significance, but the issues they raise often differ from those raised by East European trade controls. This is primarily because of the impress on the foreign trade mechanism of certain unique characteristics of the centrally planned economies.

An attempt will be made in this paper to show the effects of central planning on foreign trade practices. In Section I the special characteristics of centrally planned economies that influence their foreign trade will be briefly described. Next, in Section II, it will be shown how they, together with some other relevant factors, affect foreign trade behavior. Finally, a few suggestions, emerging from the analysis, for amelioration of trade within the basic framework of central planning will be outlined in Section III.

I. CHARACTERISTICS OF CENTRALLY PLANNED ECONOMIES

We outline below certain characteristics of centrally planned economies which affect their foreign trade behavior. Some of these characteristics (and the foreign trade behavior resulting) should not be viewed as absolutely necessary to central planning, nor are they present to the same degree in each of the centrally planned economies. They are included because they have been relevant in most East European nations until the present time.

"IRRATIONAL" INTERNAL COST AND PRICE STRUCTURES AND DISEQUILIBRIUM EXCHANGE RATES

The prevalence of "irrational" costs and prices in the centrally planned economies is almost universally acknowledged and needs little elaboration. Basically, these are the result of: (*a*) extensive use of differential sales taxes and subsidies to implement certain internal policies;[3] (*b*) the Marxist failure fully to account in the cost structure for rent, interest, and depreciation; and (*c*) insensitivity of prices to supply-demand forces.

[2] This brief monograph was published in New York in 1945 by the Committee on International Economic Policy in cooperation with the Carnegie Endowment for International Peace.

[3] Such as, for example, a high rate of investment and military expenditures (large sales tax), or encouragement of new types of capital equipment (subsidies).

Another well-known feature of these economies is the prevalence of disequilibrium exchange rates. Those, of course, are of negligible practical importance anyway, because of the direct controls used to plan and implement foreign trade.[4]

Autarky

The desire for self-sufficiency in those commodities produced at a comparative disadvantage motivates all nations to some extent, thereby reducing the possible volume of world trade. The nations with centrally planned economies appear to be more strongly motivated in this direction than capitalist economies, for the following well-known reasons. First, because of the complicated input-output interrelationships among intermediate products, most of which are directly allocated, central planners try to avoid heavy dependence of the domestic economy on foreign supplies and, thus, to insulate it from the vagaries, both imaginary and real, of the world market.[5] Second, all nations endeavor to achieve a certain degree of self-sufficiency for reasons of military security—to diminish the risks of economic warfare. Owing to this universal desire, countries where all industry is nationalized are likely to reduce trade to a greater extent than those in which a large part of economic activity is in private hands.[6,7] Under capitalism, competition exists naturally and protection requires an explicit act by the government; under central planning as it is presently practiced, protection is the rule unless the government makes an explicit decision to allow imports to replace domestic production. Third, the autarkic bias of centrally planned economies may possibly be enhanced by their irrational price systems; in fact, it is often

---

[4] Whether exchange rates are in equilibrium is of little importance, of course, given the prevalence of irrational prices. Under the latter condition, unrestricted trade at the equilibrium exchange rate cannot be relied upon to benefit the domestic economy (see below).

[5] This view is not restricted, in the centrally planned economies, only to international trade but has its counterparts in domestic trade. In the Soviet Union, for example, one of the major reasons for the 1957 reorganization was the fact that the ministries and enterprises developed autarkic policies which led to excessive cross-hauling (within ministries) and an inordinately low level of subcontracting by enterprises. After the reorganization, regional autarky (*mestnichestvo*) was adopted by individual *sovnarkhozy* [regional economic councils] and created similar problems. The reasons for the local exhibitions of autarkic behavior are somewhat different from that at the international level. Lack of dependability in the former case is due primarily to difficulties with the internal direct-allocation supply system and to the managerial incentive system.

[6] This factor operates to curtail Eastern trade with the West much more than intrabloc trade. Along these same lines might be mentioned the desire of many nations to industrialize at any cost rather than submit to comparative advantage even when long-run comparative advantage suggests less industrialization. Rumania is a case in point.

[7] The strategic controls imposed by Western nations on trade with the East also contribute somewhat to the low level of East-West trade, although much less so now than in the past decade.

very difficult for the planners to decide what they should trade. These are serious impediments to trade.

State Trading

It has been said that ". . . economic planning of the type practiced in Russia is not feasible without the use of a foreign trade monopoly. . . ." [8] Whatever the reasons, foreign trade is nationalized in the centrally planned economies and is usually conducted by combines which function as agents of the state. This has at least three major consequences for foreign trade behavior.

First, among the Eastern nations, foreign trade is conducted primarily to obtain essential imports. Exports are considered not as an end in themselves but as a means to finance the necessary imports.[9] This view of the foreign trade process seems natural enough since the CPE nations, typically pursuing overfull employment policies (see below) can hardly be interested in mere employment effects of exports. If, notwithstanding this, some of the CPE nations have led intensive export promotion campaigns, it was because of the balance-of-payment pressures generated by rapid growth (see below), that is, ultimately, to pay for rising imports. In the West, the level of exports is just as (if not more) important a goal as the level of imports. Some individual traders export, others import, with gains to the economy, presumably reflected in private profits, in either case.

Second, the centrally planned economies take a barter-type approach to foreign trade and view exports and imports as interdependent. Profitability is assessed primarily with respect to overall "terms of trade" rather than on the basis of profit on each individual transaction. This is a consequence of the import orientation of trade (above) as well as of "irrational" internal prices, and of the predisposition, inherited from internal planning, to operate in categories of physical allocations.

Third, because foreign trade is run by a state monopoly, tariffs are basically redundant; trade is controlled by implicit import and export quotas. The decisions to trade are made directly by the government, often without the mediation of price comparisons. In the absence of such explicit decisions, trade will not take place, a reaction equivalent to that achieved by employing prohibitive quotas. By comparison, in capitalist nations profitable opportunities for trade may be pursued unless the

---

[8] Alexander Gerschenkron, *Economic Relations with the U.S.S.R.* (New York: Committee on International Economic Policy, 1945), p. 18. It should be noted that the character of the state trading could be substantially changed if internal planning practices were "liberalized."

[9] "Russia exports solely in order to obtain the wherewithal for payments for imports. In this sense, she is likely to live up to the classical doctrine of foreign trade and to reject the tenets of mercantilism. This, no doubt, sounds paradoxical, but is undeniable. From the Russian point of view exports are a loss and not a gain." (*Ibid.*, p. 47.)

government makes an explicit decision to the contrary. Such decisions may be implemented by tariffs, quotas, or exchange controls.

Overfull Employment Planning

An important aspect of the centrally planned economies has been their tendency, not unlike that of capitalist nations during wartime, to over-commitment of resources. The resulting excess demand by consumers for final products and by enterprises for factors and intermediate products expresses itself as either open or repressed inflation. Moreover, the strained plans lead to sellers' markets and to a relative lack of concern for the quality of output,[10] including goods for export. Although overfull employment planning is presently less pervasive than it was in earlier years, it still persists.

Quantity Targeting

Generally, enterprises have as their major goals output targets stated in physical or value terms rather than in other so-called success indicators such as profits, cost reduction, and so forth. This, together with the fact that most intermediate products are directly allocated, reinforces the tendency noted just above for management to be less concerned with "quality" than it otherwise might.

Rapid Economic Growth

Rapid economic growth is the overriding goal of the centrally planned economies, one in which they have achieved signal successes. The process of growth usually, though not always, generates import requirements more naturally and easily than exportable items.

Method of Balances

Supply and demand for most intermediate products are balanced quantitatively by direct controls—in the East European nations. This procedure, known as the "method of balances," is used because central allocation rather than the market performs the task of distributing essential industrial supplies.

This concludes the brief survey of various characteristics of centrally planned economies which have an impact on foreign trade behavior. Some (the first three) are more important for our purposes than others, but they are all included for completeness.

II. FOREIGN TRADE BEHAVIOR

We turn now to foreign trade behavior. The most important and interesting are the related problems of inconvertibility and bilateralism,

---

[10] Quality here refers to all characteristics of a commodity, including delivery.

which will be treated first. Others, discussed below, have to do with discrimination, most-favored-nation (MFN) clauses, monopoly power, and dumping.

INCONVERTIBILITY

Currency convertibility in its commonly used meaning refers to the right or possibility of the holder of a currency to exchange it for gold or for "hard" currencies. Limitations are placed on convertibility when a currency is in excess supply on foreign exchange markets or, what amounts to the same, when other currencies or gold are in excess demand by the holders of the currency in question. Among capitalist nations such limitations on convertibility are likely to be put in force if a currency is overvalued, owing to inflation or to more fundamental structural factors. With overvaluation, there is a tendency for imports to exceed exports. Usually, nonresidents are allowed to convert current earnings of the currency in question into their own currencies; balance is maintained by restricting imports, that is, by placing limits on convertibility for residents.[11]

Why are the currencies of the centrally planned economies, say, the ruble, inconvertible? Before the revaluations of 1961 most, if not all, East European currencies were overvalued. Overvaluation, although a sufficient condition for inconvertibility under capitalism, is neither necessary nor relevant, given the foreign trade institutions and practices of the centrally planned economies. So long as internal prices are disorderly and world prices are used as the basis for trade, and the composition and volume of trade are determined by direct controls and administered by a foreign trade monopoly, the exchange rate remains merely an accounting device. Its changes have no effect on trade. Thus, for instance, the substantial devaluations of April, 1936, and January, 1961, both of which brought the ruble into rough equilibrium in a purchasing power parity sense,[12] had no discernible impact on the volume, composition, or manner in which Soviet trade is conducted.

---

[11] Under extreme circumstances, nonresidents may be denied convertibility into their own currencies, particularly on capital account. Whether nonresidents are allowed to transfer the currency in question to residents of third countries depends on the degree of overvaluation with respect to all other currencies. Usually, conversion is allowed into "softer" but not into "harder" currencies or into gold. At present, any bloc currency is probably equally "soft," relative to the major Western currencies, since general convertibility prevails in the West. On the other hand, my guess is that some bloc currencies are less desirable than others in intrabloc trade although "which" and "by how much" are impossible to say under the present institutional arrangements.

[12] By this we mean that the foreign trade prices (that is, world prices) of goods exported and imported are, on the average, approximately equal to the domestic prices of the same goods at the given exchange rate. Given the controls which exist over Soviet trade, this appears to be the only operational definition of exchange rate equilibrium which is possible. Equilibrium, under this definition, may deviate substantially from "true" equilibrium, of course.

Currency inconvertibility in centrally planned economies is in part a reaction to balance-of-payment pressures and the lack of sufficient foreign exchange reserves. Yet, although these factors (related to rapid growth, overfull employment planning, inadaptability of exports, and repressed inflation) might partly justify the prohibition against converting domestic currency into foreign exchange by residents, they can hardly be adduced to explain the existing convertibility restrictions on nonresidents. Typically, the Soviet bloc laws do not permit nonresidents to convert domestic currencies into foreign exchange or gold, nor do they even allow them to accumulate such currencies.[13] These extreme legal restrictions on convertibility (to be explained below) obviously reduce the demand for bloc currencies. Their effect, additionally weakening the international financial standing of the bloc nations, has been superimposed on other factors discouraging the potential nonresident demand for bloc currencies. Clearly, even if foreigners were allowed to accumulate rubles, for example, their demand for Soviet currency would be blunted by circumstances always present under central planning.

First, there would be the considerable uncertainty on the part of nonresidents regarding the possibility of purchasing goods with bloc currencies. Nonresidents are quite limited in the scope of possible purchases from the East European nations, not because the latter do not have a large fund of exportables but because most commodity flows are directly planned and it is difficult to buy items not earmarked for export (implicit trade controls). That is to say, within the existing system of allocation, foreign holders of, say, rubles, are not allowed much, if any, opportunity to compete for goods with Soviet enterprises and domestic consumers. Their difficulties might be additionally increased by the fact that trade negotiations are usually conducted with special foreign trade organizations subordinate to the foreign trade monopoly rather than directly with producing or distributing enterprises. This substantial limitation on purchases by nonresidents is aptly called by Oscar Altman "commodity inconvertibility," in contrast with "currency inconvertibility."[14]

Second, uncertainty generated by inaccessibility of bloc exportables is compounded by the irrationality of internal pricing and the overvalued exchange rates which make it difficult to determine in advance of negotiations the prices at which goods may be bought or sold. The foreign trade

---

[13] Exceptions to this rule occur in the use of temporary imbalances in bilaterally balanced trade relationships as well as according to provisions in some bilateral agreements for payment in gold or convertible currency if imbalances exceed prescribed limits for a period of time.

[14] Oscar Altman, "Russian Gold and The Ruble," *International Monetary Fund Staff Papers*, Vol. 7, No. 3 (April, 1960), pp. 430–31. Note that "commodity convertibility" essentially means absence of restrictions on exports. The term "free trade" on the other hand is typically used to denote absence of restrictions on imports, though in theory it encompasses exports as well.

prices, therefore, usually deviate considerably from domestic prices and are, as a "first approximation," based on "world prices." Although this practice largely eliminates the overvaluation problem and may, additionally, reduce somewhat the uncertainty (due to irrational internal prices) in the case of simple standardized commodities, the prices of complex products remain quite conjectural. Finally, uncertainty as to the "value" of a ruble is still further increased by factors mentioned above concerning the quality, delivery, and general unadaptability of exports to foreign markets.[15] To sum up, from the point of view of nonresidents, bloc currencies are not only inconvertible in the usual sense, but also undesirable because of the substantial uncertainties regarding their exchangeability for goods.

Owing to the significance and uniqueness of "commodity inconvertibility" of bloc currencies, it is impossible to explain its existence and implementation without discussing the foreign trade monopolies of centrally planned economies.

First, and most important, since central planning is implemented primarily by direct allocation of resources, the planners deem it necessary to insulate the flows of products from external disruption. This is accomplished by the foreign trade monopoly by prohibition of foreign-held ruble balances and by inconvertibility of rubles into other currencies as well as commodities.

Second, when internal prices are not "rational" as indicators of the relative values of goods to the planners or in terms of some measure of "real costs" (for reasons discussed earlier), free trade (commodity convertibility) cannot be allowed (nor can the foreign trade monopoly be dispensed with) because it would lead to a pattern of trade disadvantageous to the centrally planned economies and productive of large gains for their Western trading partners.

* * * *

Let us sum up these conclusions in another way. Given the irrationality of internal prices, resident convertibility (free imports) cannot be allowed because it will lead to large-scale importation of commodities which have relatively high prices but which, in fact, may be more cheaply produced at home (for example, many consumers' goods). On the other hand, strict controls over exports, discouraging potential ruble holdings by foreigners, must be maintained lest nonresidents compete in domestic markets for goods which, owing to subsidies or some other costing quirk, have a low price but, in fact, are expensive to produce. Nonresident "free" expenditure within the bloc countries cannot be allowed, because it may involve losses to their domestic economies. As noted earlier, the bloc nations do not grant convertibility rights to nonresidents except in the special in-

[15] One might also mention here that Western governmental controls and consumers' resistance to imports from the bloc countries have similar effects on the "value" of their currencies.

stance when the swing credit limits of a bilateral agreement are exceeded. Moreover, foreigners are usually prohibited from accumulating bloc currencies, whether within or outside the centrally planned economies. The only exception to this prohibition is that made for temporary imbalances within the rigid framework of bilateral trade agreements. Presumably, this is because the availability of bloc currencies to outsiders might lead to large discounts in world currency markets, something the East European planners undoubtedly wish to avoid.[16]

In the case of Western nations with inconvertible currencies, nonresidents are encouraged to hold, or spend, the "inconvertible" currency—the problem is that they don't want to. The centrally planned economies are in the peculiar position of being unable to try to boost their exports, thereby improving the position of their currency, by allowing nonresidents freely to import from them.[17]

---

[16] It might be argued that the bloc nations could avoid the pricing uncertainty problem by pricing net of sales taxes and subsidies *or* that they could circumvent the internal price problem by simply agreeing to buy or sell freely at world prices. Although it is true that the pricing predicament is somewhat overstated by the consumer-producer goods dichotomy in the text, it is also true that sales taxes and subsidies are not the only reasons for irrational prices in the bloc countries (see Section I). If it were, the bloc countries would undoubtedly have solved by this time the intrabloc pricing problem and would no longer have to rely on the embarrassing solution of using world prices in their trade. The many articles which have been published in the East European journals on how to choose commodities for foreign trade are a tribute to the intractability of the problem. A recent Soviet source makes the following commentary: "Wholesale prices, as is known, do not reflect with adequate completeness and precision the socially-necessary labor outlays for the manufacture of goods. Prices of means of production are mainly below value while the prices of many consumer goods are above value. Moreover, the prices of goods within each of these departments also diverge from their value. Thus, numerically-equal outlays of social labor are expressed in different prices. The use of such wholesale prices in internal trade leads to a certain violation of the equivalence of exchange. *That is why, in our opinion, the internal wholesale prices now in force cannot be utilized for forming a new system of prices in trade between the socialist countries* (italics in original). Otherwise the prices of the world socialist market would have the same shortcomings as the internal wholesale prices and would not reflect the outlays of socially necessary labor. In view of the fact that the composition of exports and imports of countries is not the same, trade at such prices would bring about an unjustified redistribution of the national income. States in which the share of goods with prices below value is higher for exports than for imports would turn over part of their national income to countries with a bigger share of exports at prices above value."

As for world prices, they are at present clearly an uneasy expedient. For one thing, there are few, if any, homogeneous commodities. In addition, even in those instances in which commodities appear to be virtually homogeneous, it turns out that different prices are quoted from place to place and from month to month. The concept "world price" is largely an abstraction for the purpose at hand. Finally, even if there were "world prices," they would not always be relevant for pricing bloc products because of the differing comparative advantage (supply-demand) conditions within and without the bloc.

[17] The problem of freeing trade and establishing convertibility with disequilibrium prices is the foreign trade counterpart of the internal problem of decentralizing and using the profit motive without rationalizing the price structure.

BILATERALISM

The percentage of bilaterally conducted trade is higher in the centrally planned economies than in either the Western industrial or the developing nations. Moreover, it is higher now than it used to be in the same economies during the 1930's when they were still in the capitalist orbit. Intrabloc trade is more bilateral than East-West trade. Institutionally, the high degree of bilateralism is accomplished by means of annual and long-term trade and payment agreements which attempt, within limits and after taking account of credits, to keep trade between the two participating countries in balance over the period in question. These agreements are implemented, of course, by direct governmental controls over the level and composition of imports and exports.

The centrally planned economies recognize the advantages of multilateralism and have even taken some tentative steps toward increasing its scope in intrabloc transactions. Why, despite that very recognition, bilateralism is still so strongly adhered to can be attributed to currency inconvertibility and the factors behind it discussed above. Since no nation is willing to hold balances in rubles, *levs*, and so forth, payments of the centrally planned economies must be balanced insofar as they are unable to produce gold or develop export surpluses with convertible currency nations.

A second factor leading to bilateralism is the tendency among bloc countries to strive for overall payments balance (especially among themselves), and therefore, erroneously, for bilateral balance (see below). The main reason for the attempt to achieve overall balance has to do with the already discussed view that exports are not an end in themselves but simply a means of financing imports. To the extent that trade policy is guided by such considerations, there is a tendency to strive for an overall payments balance, in the first place, there is no strong incentive to develop an overall export surplus. Next, imports are confined by controls to the amount which can be financed currently through exports, previous policies of not developing export surpluses having produced no large foreign exchange reserves. Consequently, like all nations under balance-of-payments pressures (owing to rapid growth, difficulties in adapting to export markets, and so forth), centrally planned economies resort to the utlimate adjustment of payments by limiting imports to the level of possible exports.

Now, the necessity or desire to achieve overall balance does not logically require bilateral balancing by nation. Among capitalist nations, however, it has been observed that nations with export marketing problems sometimes resort to bilateral balancing agreements to absorb each other's second-line exportables. The propensity to do so is much stronger among the planned economies. In fact, it is difficult to see how a substantial degree of multilateralism could be achieved by these economies, simultaneously with the desired overall balance. The twin objectives are accomplished imperfectly under capitalism via the automatic operation of price, income, and capital flow adjustment mechanisms that do not function under central planning. The easiest way to achieve overall balance in the latter case is undoubtedly by planning for a high degree of bilateral balance.

Envision the difficulty of planned multilateralism with overall balance. Suppose country A trades with B, C, and D. Overall balance can be achieved by relatively simple balancing with each nation. This is not to say that bilateral balancing is easy, for it undoubtedly requires considerable negotiation and, on the part of one or both partners, either some uneconomic trading or the foregoing of some profitable trading. On the other hand, suppose A runs a surplus with B. This means that A (B) goes into negotiations with C and D requiring a net deficit (surplus) equal to the surplus (deficit) with B (A). But there may be no particular reason why C and D should want to run surpluses with A exactly to offset deficits with B. Under planning, where prices are misleading and only the relatively few goods specifically earmarked for export or import can be traded, nations may be loathe to accept a surplus (deficit) with another nation because of the subsequent difficulty of buying (selling) more than can be sold to (bought from) third countries. This, in effect, is equivalent to a situation in which the various inconvertible currencies have different values to different holders. If interest conflicts occur along these lines, there is no economic adjustment mechanism to resolve them. An administrative reconciliation, if any, would undoubtedly involve a substantial reduction of profitable trade and/or addition of unprofitable trade. The problems are likely multiplied as the number of nations in the system increases. (In a system with economic adjustment mechanisms, the problems would probably be lessened as the number of nations increased.)

A third factor encouraging bilateralism is the opportunity that bilateral agreements offer the economically stronger nations (often, in this context, the nation least dependent on the trade in question) to improve the terms of trade. This possibility may motivate the Soviet Union, at least, to trade bilaterally with its smaller partners.

Fourth, the tendency toward bilateral balancing in foreign trade may be strengthened by carryover from the general use of an analogous technique, the "method of balances," in internal commodity planning.

Finally, some of the nonbloc nations with which the centrally planned economies trade prefer bilateral arrangements because of balance-of-payments problems. Even if a centrally planned economy were prepared to trade on a multilateral basis, it would be forced into bilateral trade by such trading partners.

Foreign Trade Discrimination

A basic objective of the Western trading community has been to achieve trade without discrimination. In the foreign trade usage discrimination means that one not buy in the lowest—or sell in the highest—price markets.[18] To the extent that restrictions (tariffs, quotas) are applied to trade, the objective is to have them applied equally to all nations, that is, in a nondiscriminatory manner. Foreign trade discrimination may be motivated by either economic or political factors; discussion will proceed from the former to the latter.

Inconvertibility and bilateralism have almost inevitably involved the introduction of apparently discriminatory controls by capitalist nations; the situation is similar in the case of the centrally planned economies. Western nations discriminate against their trade partners *via* exchange controls and explicit commodity and/or country import quotas. The centrally planned economies achieve the same results by implicit controls which are the outcome of implementing planning decisions regarding the volume, content, and direction of trade.

Among Western nations, where inconvertibility has often been due to overvaluation, serious questions have been raised whether those apparently discriminatory practices observed have in fact really constituted true discrimination.[19] Suppose, as was the case after World War II, that the British pound was overvalued with respect to the U.S. dollar, but not with respect to the Greek drachma. Suppose also that, at going exchange rates, Greek tobacco was more expensive than American tobacco. If the British bought Greek rather than American tobacco, they could be accused, under current conventions, of not buying in the cheapest market, hence of discriminating. It could be argued, however, that if one takes into account the overvaluation of pound and drachma vis-à-vis dollar, Greek tobacco is actually cheaper to the British than American tobacco, and that the apparent discrimination is an illusion resulting from the maintenance of unrealistic pegged exchange rates. It could also be argued that adherence to the ideal of nondiscriminatory application of quotas and exchange controls under these circumstances would unduly and unfairly reduce the volume trade.

Can discrimination by the centrally planned economies be rationalized on similar grounds? The answer is a hesitant yes, hesitant because the reason is somewhat different. As we have seen, inconvertibility of bloc currencies cannot substantively be attributed to overvaluation in a "purchasing power parity" sense. In fact, by adopting world prices as a first approximation in their foreign trade negotiations, the CPE's are in effect adopting implicit exchange rates which are, in the purchasing power parity sense, "equilibrium" rates.

On the other hand, however, one could interpret the various uncertain-

---

[18] The term price is taken here to include all commercial considerations. In contrast with foreign trade discrimination, monopolistic price discrimination means using market power to buy cheaper and sell dearer than the competitive price. See this writer's "Discrimination in International Trade," *American Economic Review*, Vol. XXXIX, No. 6 (December, 1949), pp. 1234–44.

[19] That is, not buying in the cheapest and selling in the dearest markets.

ties, mentioned earlier, which are responsible for inconvertibility, as indications of a discounted value of currency. Presumably, there is some discount rate at which foreigners would be willing to hold rubles, *levs*, and so forth, if allowed to.[20] Or, more realistically, one might say there is a price (interest rate, terms of trade) at which foreigners could be prevailed upon to adapt themselves to large-scale, bilaterally balanced trade with bloc nations. The extensive trade of the centrally planned economies with each other at the expense of trade with nonbloc nations, then, may be attributed in part at least, not to discrimination but to the unwillingness of nonbloc nations to adapt themselves, without a charge, to large-scale trade with the centrally planned economies, under the CPE ground rules. To the extent that there is trade between West and East, it is conducted largely according to the former's ground rules—multilaterally, with imbalances settled in convertible currencies or gold.[21]

The extraordinarily large amount of foreign trade discrimination which does exist between East and West[22] is ascribable not primarily to the economic factors just discussed but to politically strategic factors. Both the centrally planned and the Western nations are guilty of politically motivated trade discrimination. Important special instruments of such discrimination are: (*a*) the controls by the United States and COCOM nations over so-called strategic exports to the centrally planned economies as well as (*b*) the strong preferences[23] for direct intrabloc trade among the centrally planned economies. The chances for growth of political discrimination are greater in the centrally planned economies than in the Western nations because of nationalization of trade resulting in closer interconnection between political and economic decisions. The interconnection is inevitably less intimate where the conduct of trade is largely in the hands of private enterprise. Finally, it is worth noting that if discrimination results from the formation of preferential trade areas and customs unions in the West, it usually takes the form of differential tariffs.

---

[20] There may not be an exchange rate which would eliminate the currency discounts—that is, reduce the interest rate in question to zero—since the discount is not entirely due to overvaluation.

[21] If bloc exchange rates were operational, rather than merely accounting devices, then because of the discount on bloc currencies, prices in intrabloc trade would tend to be higher than prices in East-West or West-West trade. In fact, as we have seen, bloc trade is conducted at world prices regardless of the exchange rate, and under these circumstances, the potential discount on bloc currencies cannot easily be isolated statistically. The actual statistical picture shows bloc exports to the West at lower prices and imports from the West at higher prices than those prevailing in intrabloc trade. This is believed the result largely of Western discrimination against and controls over trade with the East. See this writer's articles in the *Review of Economics and Statistics*, Vol. XLIV, No. 2 (May, 1962) and No. 4 (November, 1962); and in *Soviet Studies*, Vol. XVII, No. 1 (July, 1965).

[22] The evidence for this is that today's intrabloc trade amounts to almost three fourths of the trade of these nations (Eastern Europe), whereas their mutual trade amounted to only about one fourth of the total before World War II.

[23] These have substantially weakened in the past few years.

The CPE's, on the other hand, implement their "customs union" by implicit quotas. Whereas it is possible for outsiders, if they can surmount tariff barriers, to buy or sell within a Western customs union, it is much more difficult for the outsider, regardless of cost-advantage or need, to break into the planned intrabloc trade.

MFN Clause Tariff Problems[24]

The nations of Eastern Europe customarily request MFN treatment on tariffs in their trade with the West. In return, they purport to reciprocate in ways described in Section III below. The usefulness of such reciprocal guarantees has been questioned in the West ever since the late 1920's when the U.S.S.R. revived its trade with Europe. The question is of considerable importance today because so much of the increase in world trade and reduction in trade discrimination comes about through the mutual lowering of tariff barriers in which the MFN clause plays an obvious role.

The basic difficulty faced by the CPE nations in adapting to the MFN clause on tariffs is quite obvious. Whereas in the West the mutual cutting of tariffs provides a free market price criterion of the appropriate change in volume and distribution of trade, in the centrally planned economies the decisions (*a*) to import or not to import and (*b*) from whom to import,[25] are made quantitatively by quotas that are implicit in the planning process. It is well known that sensitivity to price is in this case much lower than in capitalist countries. It is also worth noting that regardless of the level of tariff, in a centrally planned economy,[26] imported commodities are ordinarily sold at the same price as comparable domestically produced goods. Differences between the "import price plus cost of distribution plus tariff" and the price of the comparable domestically produced goods are equalized by offsetting taxes or subsidies. When the planners have finally decided to import a commodity, tariffs have no impact on final domestic price—nor is the domestic price necessarily affected (in the short run, at least) by the decision to increase through imports the availability of a commodity. Last, but not least, import decisions continue to be largely "quantitative"; tariffs cannot be allowed to assume their usual market functions so long as exchange rates are in disequilibrium and the relationship between internal prices and costs of production is distorted.

---

[24] The effect of the most-favored-nation clause is to place on the conceding state the obligation to grant to the nationals and goods of the beneficiary state, either in general or in certain specified respects, the treatment accorded or in future to be accorded to the nationals and goods of the state receiving most favorable treatment in the territory of the conceding state.

[25] The decision "from whom to import" is probably less centralized than the one dealing with "what and how much to import" in bloc trade with the West. The foreign trade combines are often told to buy or sell such and such commodities but are left to themselves to seek the best market.

[26] Not all of the centrally planned economies have, or have had, tariffs.

During the past few years, the Soviet Union and Hungary have introduced new double-column tariffs with the clear purpose of providing bargaining weapons against discriminatory treatment by EEC and EFTA. Those nations which do not grant the Soviet Union and Hungary MFN treatment will pay duties according to the higher of the two tariff schedules, all others according to the lower. The foreign trade combines presumably will have an incentive to shift their purchases to countries which receive the lower schedule of duties, because both their profits and the premiums based on these profits are reduced by imports from the higher tariff countries.[27] It may appear that granting MFN status under these double-column tariffs is equivalent to granting MFN status under free market conditions, but in fact it is not. First, it is unlikely that the extensive planned bilateral intrabloc trade would be disrupted or altered for small price differentials, which may develop in favor of Western nations as a result of granting the latter MFN status. Second, for reasons already mentioned, the lowering of a tariff would have no effect on the decisions "how much" and "what" to import—that is, competition with domestic suppliers would not be allowed. The only possible effect of the new system, then, would be to redistribute trade among a nation's Western trading partners.

Monopoly Power

The conduct of trade by state organizations inevitably introduces elements of monopoly power into foreign trade. Monopolistic market power is, of course, often exercised by capitalist trade concerns, for example, those connected with petroleum and aluminum. The major objection to monopoly power in international trade is that it may lead to an unequal distribution of the gains from trade. This consequence of monopoly power has usually been accepted by the market economies as an undesirable, but natural and inevitable concomitant of trade conducted by private enterprise. Objections raised with respect to state trading reflect the conviction that state traders have much more power to drive a hard bargain than private monopolists. This, however, is not necessarily true. As in the case of private traders, the power of the state trader is determined by his share in the world market, the importance of the commodity in his domestic market, etc.—that is, it depends on the assorted relevant "elasticities." In the case of wheat, for instance, the state trader may have relatively little power, in the case of aluminum, relatively much—and in either commodity, possibly neither more nor less power than a private trader.

---

[27] That is to say, ". . . profits are calculated on the basis of the value of their deliveries of imported goods to domestic distributing, etc., enterprises at the uniform domestic price of those goods *minus* the foreign exchange cost of their imports together with any duty payable on them. . . ." (United Nations, Economic Commission for Europe, *Economic Bulletin for Europe*, Vol. 14 [1962], No. 1, p. 53).

In bilateral agreements between East and West, the bargaining power of the East is strengthened by another institutional factor already mentioned. The CPE's are more interested in imports than exports—the latter are viewed as a necessary evil. On the other hand, Western nations are just as interested in maintaining the level of exports. This has led to temporary and unplanned surpluses of West with East during the course of bilateral agreements. Under these circumstances, the burden of achieving balance largely falls on the Western nation which does not want to extend credit.[28] This may involve accepting in payment goods which are of lower priority and higher price than are available elsewhere in the world market.

Dumping: Definition and Identification

Dumping is usually defined as selling abroad at a lower price than at home. When the commodity is not sold domestically and therefore has no home price, "domestic cost of production" or "export price in third markets" are sometimes substituted. The Soviet Union has been accused of dumping in Western markets a number of times, first in the early 1930's, particularly in regard to grain, and again more recently in regard to aluminum, tin, glass, and so forth.[29] That the Soviet Union and other state traders have the power to dump[30] is unquestioned. Whether the above criteria of dumping are proper for a centrally planned economy (of the sort described above) is a more difficult question.[31]

First, to the extent that the currencies of the centrally planned economies have been or are substantially overvalued by official exchange rates, comparison of domestic and export prices is a misleading criterion of dumping. Under these circumstances, exports must be nominally subsidized. The nominal losses on exports are matched, of course, by larger nominal profits on imports.

Second, as noted above, relative domestic prices in the centrally planned economies reflect subsidies and sales taxes introduced to satisfy domestic fiscal and other requirements. Here again, comparison of domestic and export prices is a misleading criterion of dumping even when exchange rates are not overvalued.

Third, the centrally planned economies, following the labor theory of value, have a different concept of "cost of production" from that of the West. This makes the use of "cost" an imperfect substitute for "price" in

---

[28] The provision in many of these bilateral agreements for payment in gold or convertible currency in case the imbalance persists or exceeds certain limits prevents this factor from assuming larger proportions than it otherwise would.

[29] The East European nations have been forced to sell fairly systematically below world prices in Western markets in the postwar period because of real or imagined inferiority of Eastern goods, for political reasons, and so forth.

[30] That is to say, they have sufficient monopoly power to separate the various markets in which they sell as well as to prevent the reimport of goods. They can also easily subsidize losses on dumping out of the general treasury.

[31] For an excellent discussion of dumping, see Gerschenkron, *op. cit.*, pp. 45 ff.

assessing dumping. The problem can be exemplified by commodities like petroleum whose "cost" does not include the quantitatively important categories of rent and interest. Yet, a fairly strong case can be made, in connection with dumping, for accepting the labor theory view of "cost" prevalent in the East. To begin with, when all commodities are so valued, the resulting generally lower price level is compensated for by the commensurately higher value of the equilibrium exchange rate. Next, the configuration of relative prices that emerges from this kind of cost accounting may be treated in the same category as the differences in relative prices which exist between nations as a consequence of different preference structures. Like differences in consumers' tastes, the permanent and basic differences in ways of evaluating "cost" may be accepted as parameters of the world trading system.

Fourth, and in many ways most difficult to deal with, is the fact that export and import decisions are not independent of each other as in capitalist economies; instead, state monopolies view exports as payment for imports.[32] The connection is especially close in bilateral agreements.[33] Thus, for example, a state trader who sold a commodity at one half of domestic cost could hardly be accused of "true" dumping, if the foreign exchange earned were used to import goods purchased at one third of domestic cost. A nominal financial loss on exports would be in this case more than offset by the financial gain on imports.[34]

Although this approach may seem fair from the point of view of the CPE's, it fails to take account of the rationale behind antidumping legislation.[35] A major purpose of antidumping legislation is to prevent the disruption of domestic markets and loss of domestic production facilities as a result of what might be termed unfair competition. If one's markets and production facilities are lost in (fair) competition with a truly lower cost producer, one can expect, in return, assured imports at lower prices. If, however, a foreign supplier sells below domestic price because of temporary surplus or in an attempt to break into a market, the low price is not likely to be maintained and the disruptive effect is without compensating benefits. CPE exports offered at a loss in order to reap a large profit on imports would seem to fall into the second category; they would not necessarily reflect a stable comparative advantage position. They are, therefore, potentially "disruptive" and should not be allowed.

---

[32] On this point Gerschenkron (*op. cit.*, p. 46) writes: ". . . What on the face of it looked like a case of dumping reveals itself on closer scrutiny as a normal application of the principles of international specialization. . . ."

[33] However, in my view, it would probably not be possible to link specific exports and imports.

[34] It is this view of the trade process which has enabled the centrally planned economies to maintain overvalued exchange rates and still engage in a reasonable volume of trade.

[35] The centrally planned economies would, of course, welcome Western dumping. Their major foreign trade objective is to get as good terms of trade as possible, and they have no fear of market disruption.

Finally, systematic data on the prices, taxes, and subsidies to commodities exported by the centrally planned economies are not easily available. Consequently, an evaluation of dumping charges is difficult, if not impossible, regardless of the criterion used.

III. POSSIBLE SOLUTIONS TO MAJOR PROBLEMS

We have concluded our survey of the impact of central planning, as it is practiced in Eastern Europe, on foreign trade behavior. Clearly, national economic planning has some inconvenient and costly consequences for the bloc nations in the foreign trade area. We will now consider briefly what, if anything, might be done *without* fundamental change in the central planning system to alleviate some of the difficulties relating to inconvertibility and MFN clauses.

Inconvertibility and Bilateralism

Inconvertibility and bilateralism are probably the knottiest problems facing the Eastern nations. They, themselves, have been actively concerned for many years over the disadvantages of their rigidly bilateral trading system. The most recent evidence of this concern is the establishment of the International Bank for Economic Cooperation, which at present devotes its efforts to setting in motion a type of payments union for multilateral clearings (to be discussed below).

Can the planned economies eliminate inconvertibility without substantially changing their planning system? If the analysis presented above is correct, they cannot. Until their price systems are rationalized and especially until central allocation of resources is less rigidly adhered to, commodity inconvertibility will remain a fact. Furthermore, their currencies will remain essentially inconvertible into foreign exchange. This is in striking contrast to the situation of capitalist nations. There pure overvaluations (due to differential inflation) may be simply eliminated by devaluation, and deeper seated disequilibria (due to shifts in international supply or demand, wartime destruction, etc.) can usually be either "worked-off" or adapted to over time, given the application of a proper assortment of policies including devaluation.

Yet, although full convertibility, particularly "commodity" convertibility, may be infeasible, it may still be possible to achieve partial "currency" convertibility or transferability as well as to reduce the rigidity of bilateral clearings. Three proposals are considered, the last of which is currently being tried by Comecon.

1. Partial "currency" convertibility[36] might be achieved if the centrally planned economies were willing: (*a*) to let nonresidents hold their currencies in the event of deficits; (*b*) to guarantee the value of these holdings against devaluation vis-à-vis convertible currencies or gold; and

[36] This proposal is an elaboration of a suggestion made by Altman, *op. cit.*, pp. 430–31.

(*c*) to pay interest on such funds at a rate which would overcome the reluctance to hold them generated by the uncertainties mentioned earlier.[37] The advantage of establishing "currency" convertibility along these lines would be that it permits a considerable multilateralization of trade. Deficits and surpluses not only become possible but can be offset against each other through trading of currencies. Even if deficits and surpluses are not "cleared," extension of short-term credit automatically takes place, of course, though presumably at a relatively high cost.

The clear disadvantages of this system, if it is to operate in both intrabloc and East-West trade, are twofold. First, and possibly of overwhelming importance, is the fact that bloc currencies would undoubtedly sell at a substantial discount relative to Western currencies and gold. For prestige reasons, this might seem unacceptable to some of the bloc nations. Secondly, the need to pay high interest rates on currency balances held by Westerners would reduce if not eliminate the profitability of East-West trade. Under these circumstances, the bloc nations might feel impelled to retreat to the present system of running import surpluses only when these can be financed out of stocks of convertible currency, gold, or formal loans.[38]

In intrabloc trade, where bilateralism creates great difficulties, the first objection noted above would become immaterial,[39] and the second would be of much lesser importance. The greatest difficulty would appear to be the problem of getting a group of nations committed to Marxist economic doctrines to agree to such a program and to allow it to operate with a sufficient degree of flexibility. Clearly, without such flexibility the discounts and premiums on the various currencies in question could not properly reflect their changing values in intrabloc trade. However, if some flexibility were achieved, the way would be opened to multilateral clearings. Furthermore, the system would have a built-in mechanism to discourage nations from running deficits to obtain from others involuntary credits—the greater the deficit, the higher the discount rate, since other nations become less eager to hold one's currency.

There is some similarity between this system and the swing-credit bilateral clearing presently in use in intrabloc trade. At present, a nation

---

[37] Presumably the high discount rate will not only encourage nonresidents to hold bloc currencies per se, but will discourage them from converting to hard currencies or gold. The possibility of converting to hard currencies or gold would lower the discount rate at which nonresidents would be willing to hold the bloc currencies. Whether or not it would be possible to get nonresidents to hold bloc currencies without convertibility rights is problematical. The required discount rate would certainly be very high.

[38] For psychological and institutional as well as economic reasons, formal loans repayable in convertible currency would undoubtedly be made at lower nominal rates of interest than would be required to get nonresidents to hold one's currency on an informal basis.

[39] Undoubtedly, exchange relationships to Western convertible currencies would develop or be established; but since they would operate only within the bloc, they could be limited to reasonable amounts.

running a deficit (unplanned) that exceeds prescribed limits is required to pay the excess in gold or convertible currency. Since gold and convertible currency are at a premium, this is equivalent to paying a charge or interest rate for running a deficit with another nation. The important advantages of the above proposal over the existing system are two: For one thing, the various bloc currencies could be exchanged for each other, thereby multilateralizing clearings and facilitating the development of a short-term credit mechanism. In contrast, at present, incentives are designed to ensure bilateral balancing. Moreover, the value of each nation's currency (the interest one must pay on balances outstanding) would depend not on its various *bilateral* balances outstanding but on its *overall* surplus or deficit.[40]

2. If currency convertibility cannot be achieved along the line suggested above, it might still be possible to sidestep the inconvertibility problem but nevertheless achieve an increase in multilateral clearings. This could be done if the planned economies were in the position to build up substantial reserves of convertible currencies, reserves large enough to finance any normal deficits which might result from trading multilaterally with all nations in a position to do so.[41] Admittedly, in practice this may be quite difficult. The addition to reserves needed for extension of multilateral transactions is probably small in comparison with bloc nations' national product and trade volume, perhaps on the scale of two to three billion dollars. Yet, even this relatively minor increase may well prove infeasible in the immediate future. The Eastern nations have recently been soliciting credits from the West—this is hardly the climate in which to expect them to develop export surpluses. It may be especially difficult, if not impossible, to develop the necessary surpluses in Western markets where gold and hard currencies would be obtained.

Furthermore, the system could work for any length of time only if the centrally planned economies, having accumulated the appropriate amount of reserves, would succeed in maintaining them. This means that an overall balance of payments must be achieved with all nations by each bloc member or, given a convertible currency pool within the bloc, by the bloc as a whole with the West. Such a discipline may be difficult to achieve in view of the factors mentioned at the beginning of this paper. Historical experience gives support to doubt since there probably has been a substantial net outflow of (decline in) reserves from the bloc, particularly from the U.S.S.R., over the past decade.

Last, one may question whether the Eastern nations would be willing to develop deficits with each other if these were to be paid in convertible currencies and gold. Why not use the funds to buy in the West? Again,

[40] In this respect, the solution envisaged above is similar to that of the old European Payments Union (EPU). Another similarity is that under the EPU, the percentage of gold and dollars required in settlement of deficits increased as the deficit increased. Under our proposal, presumably the interest rate on outstanding balances would increase as the overall deficit increased.

[41] Even now the CPE nations trade fairly multilaterally with many Western nations on the basis of convertible currencies and gold.

to keep hard currency reserves in the bloc would require the sort of discipline noted under the previous point. The real difficulty here lies in the lack of incentive in bilateral transactions for bloc nations freely to incur deficits with each other that would be financed with highly valued convertible currency.

3. The new bloc clearing arrangement[42] mentioned above is somewhat less ambitious financially than either of the two preceding proposals. In effect, it provides that all intrabloc transactions take place through the Bank and be accounted for (paid for) in so-called transferable rubles. Payment in transferable rubles means that a surplus with one nation can be used to pay off a deficit with another. To ensure that no nation will take advantage of the system to obtain involuntary short-term credits, the agreement specifies that each participant must balance its account in transferable rubles over the calendar year. According to a newspaper report, this is to be accomplished by following up the original bilateral trade negotiations with multilateral negotiations in which the net surpluses and deficits would be offset against each other by additional commodity exchanges.

The system appears simple; will it work? It seems obvious that if it does work, that is, if multilateral clearing takes place and all accounts are balanced at the end of each year, success should be attributed not to the clearing arrangement per se, but to the negotiations which prearrange the balance. It may well be argued that, given the negotiating mechanism, the transferable rubles are totally unnecessary, except perhaps as a psychological fillip to the proceedings. The new value and usefulness of nonresident holdings of national currencies will arise from multilateral negotiations; the transferable ruble system simply accounts ex post for what has already been determined.[43]

If one grants the peripheral significance of transferable rubles, the real workability of the system will be seen to depend on the success of the bilateral-multilateral negotiation in achieving balance and improving the volume and distribution of trade. The achievement of overall balance may be no simple matter in the absence of economic adjusting mechanisms or incentive devices,[44] and in view of the fact that the position of a net

[42] Eventually the Bank established to implement the clearing arrangement will, in addition to performing clearing operations, provide short-term credits for trade among the contracting parties and perhaps finance longer term projects in which two or more nations are interested.

[43] If the transferable rubles have any functions at all, they would seem to be connected with credit creation and with the possibilities that the prearranged balances will not be realized. In either instance, it would seem more useful to use transferable rubles than national currencies.

[44] Such as having to: pay a net overall debt in convertible currency or gold; or pay a high interest rate on debts in transferable currency; or change prices of goods imported and exported (devaluation). The EPU increased the percentage of gold and convertible currency required in payment of overall debt as the size of the debt increased, to discourage persistent deficits.

debtor tends to strengthen a nation's ability to force undesirable goods on others. The effect of the system on the volume and distribution of trade is difficult to assess. On a priori grounds, one would think that there must be many latent trilateral and multilateral trading possibilities to be revealed under the new system, possibilities which, if realized, could improve the distribution of trade. However, we know little about the bases upon which foreign trade decisions are made; improvements, if any, may be small. Much will depend, for example, on the degree to which intrabloc surpluses and deficits form "closed" or "open" circuits after initial negotiations.[45]

If a large percentage of the aggregate surplus-deficit forms an "open" circuit, then aggregate balance will only be achievable at the price of further trade (bilateral balancing) between the net creditors and net debtors; this may be considerably less advantageous to either or both than bilateral balancing was to individual bloc nations under the old system, and certainly less advantageous than a hard currency settlement.

Much will also depend on the fashion in which nations, no longer committed to bilateral balance, determine their bilateral export-import cutoffs. If bloc nations, freed from the necessity of bilateral balancing, evaluate their cutoffs not only in terms of domestic opportunity costs but vis-à-vis Western markets as well, a reduction in intrabloc trade could result.

It seems highly probable in view of the difficulties in achieving overall balance that, in fact, the bloc nations will be largely unwilling to run surpluses or deficits with each other in the initial bilateral negotiations. In other words, not much multilateralization of trade will take place, for the reasons discussed under the second heading in Section II, above.

To sum up, the prospect of *substantial* gains arising out of the new clearing mechanism appears slim in the absence of better bases for making foreign trade decisions and in the absence of an economic, as opposed to administrative, balancing or equilibrating device. Therefore, it is not surprising that the Poles reportedly have already asked for a replacement of transferable rubles by convertible currencies. This suggests that at least one of the contractual parties to the new agreement is opting for a system outlined in the second proposal above.

The problem of "commodity inconvertibility" deserves a few final remarks too. There seem to be at least two ways in which its seriousness might eventually be reduced. First, it is apparent, particularly in the case of the U.S.S.R., that the pace of overfull employment planning has slowed down and that persistent shortages, sellers' markets, and so forth are now

---

[45] A closed circuit is that circumstance when A owes B, B owes C, and C owes A. If the amounts owed are equal, deficits cancel out. In an open circuit A owes B, B owes C, and C owes D. Here B and C achieve balance but A ends up owing D. The open circuit exists when other currencies in question are not equally "soft" or "inconvertible," a likely possibility under the circumstances.

somewhat less of a problem than in the past. If this trend continues and if inventories gradually become larger relative to flows of goods, it may eventually become possible to relax the restrictions on export. Nonresidents may eventually be allowed to buy commodities more freely without fear of disrupting planning. Second, the usual reasons adduced for autarky do not hold strongly in the case of consumer's goods. Extensive and relatively unrestricted trade in consumers' goods would not threaten the integrity of planning because consumers' goods are final outputs, not inputs. Furthermore, since most consumers' goods are highly substitutable (in comparison with inputs, especially in the short run), interruptions in supplies of particular items need cause little loss in household satisfaction. Moreover, the military importance of most types of consumers' goods is low and there is no need on these grounds to seek self-sufficiency.

MFN Reciprocity

Before World War II, the Soviet Union (presumably) reciprocated MFN status by agreeing to increase its imports (and exports). Although this expedient satisfied a number of the Soviet trading partners, it deviates in several respects from the ideal. First, the bilateral guaranteed expansion of trade and pricing arrangements are almost certainly not equivalent to what they would be under a mutual reduction in tariffs.[46] Second, in theory a mutual bilateral lowering of tariffs should increase trade between the participants as a result of both trade creation (competition with domestic suppliers) and trade diversion. In fact, there is nothing in these agreements to ensure such results, and it may be that a preponderance of the bilateral increase of trade is at the expense of other nations. This fosters bilateralism and is contrary to the "equal treatment" and antidiscriminatory spirit of MFN clauses.[47] The third point is related to the above, that is, once MFN is in effect, the Western partner has no way of knowing whether the Eastern partner has actually increased access to its markets to third nations, an access which should be extended equally to the Western nation in question, as a privilege of MFN status.

These objections can largely be met in practice, if not in theory. In answer to the first objection it can be argued simply that if the guaranteed

---

[46] Precise equivalence is unknowable. There are at least two respects in which equivalence would not be achieved. First, the centrally planned economies have a much wider range of choice in buying and selling a given quantum of goods than have the free market economies. Second, as is well known, there is not equal access to technical know-how for East and West; the Eastern nations incur a large, implicit import surplus along these lines, for which they make no proper payment.

[47] "When we recognize that the most-favored-nation clause does not serve its purpose in trade relations with a foreign trade monopoly, and have introduced quantitative stipulations into trade agreements, we have still not established equality of trading opportunity. We have merely provided for a certain volume of trade . . . there is no reason to assume that quantitative regulations embodied in agreements concluded between pairs of countries would provide for equality of trading opportunity." Gerschenkron, *op. cit.*, p. 29.

expansion of trade and pricing arrangements are not satisfactory to the Western trading partner, it need not grant MFN status. Presumably this is a negotiable matter.

The third objection could be met by including in the bilateral MFN agreement a stipulation that the Eastern nation's imports from its Western trading partner are to increase as rapidly as the Eastern nation's trade as a whole.[48] The Eastern nation would only be allowed to deviate from this formula if it could show that: (*a*) its increased trade resulted from granting MFN status to third nations or (*b*) that it had shifted its trade to third countries on strictly commercial grounds.

The second objection is more difficult to handle under traditional bilateral MFN negotiating procedures. It is important to note, however, that to the extent that trade expansion develops on "strictly commercial grounds," as noted above, the seriousness of the second objection will gradually be reduced. A more complicated but also more substantive approach to our second objection was originally proposed by Alexander Gerschenkron for U.S.S.R.–West trade[49] and has since been expanded by a number of writers to include all East-West trade. According to this, to reduce the discrimination and bilateralism automatically involved in bilateral MFN treaties, the latter should be multilateralized and concluded by the U.S.S.R. (or all Comecon nations simultaneously) with, perhaps, the NATO nations or the EEC. Under such an arrangement the Eastern commitments to expand trade would be in terms of a global quota for all nations entitled to MFN status. At the same time, the distribution of trade would be determined by commercial considerations. The implementation of such a proposal might be cumbersome, but probably no more cumbersome than the tariff-reducing negotiations which now regularly take place under GATT.

[48] If bloc preferential treatment is to be taken into account, the last eight words should read: "as the Eastern nation's trade with the West."

[49] Gerschenkron, *op. cit.*, pp. 37 ff.

18. EAST EUROPEAN ECONOMIC REFORMS*

John Michael Montias

In recent years, the East European countries (with the exception of Albania) have embarked on economic reforms which seek to increase efficiency and growth by reducing detailed central planning in physical terms, relying more on financial measures and incentives to guide enterprise decisions, and, in some cases, grouping enterprises into associations or trusts. However, there is great diversity among the various countries in the scope, nature, intensity, timing, and pace of reform.

In this selection, Montias explains the reasons for the reforms and identifies the principal similarities and differences in the reform programs of the various countries. He then analyzes the factors likely to determine the success or failure of reform, emphasizing problems of price formation and monopoly.

INSTITUTIONAL REFORMS designed to transform an entire economic system are so complex and so difficult to comprehend in their entirety that they offer unlimited scope for more or less gratuitous speculation. One may easily draw up plausible conjectures about the motives for the reforms of the East European economic systems or criticize this or that illogical aspect of their construction. It is more difficult, if it is possible at all, to answer the fundamental questions one would like to pose about their eventual effects. Can they be expected to increase the efficiency of the

* Reprinted by permission from testimony before the Subcommittee on Antitrust and Monopoly, Committee on the Judiciary, U.S. Senate, 90th Cong., 2d sess., April 17, 1968. Some footnotes are omitted. John Michael Montias is Professor of Economics at Yale University.

socialist economies, either in their static allocation or in their growth-generating capabilities? Are they systematic enough to take hold, as they did in Yugoslavia, or will they be neutralized and rendered ineffectual by centrifugal counterforces in the same manner as previous half-hearted attempts at changes in the system that were limited to a partial remolding of the command economy? I cannot answer these pivotal questions, but I hope that my remarks will narrow down the area where possible answers might lie.

BACKGROUND

Much can be learned about the reasons for the present reforms and about the factors likely to condition their success or failure from a study of the evolution of the East European economic systems.

There is evidence that the highest authorities in the more developed countries of the area began to recognize the disadvantages of overcentralization almost as soon as replicas of the Soviet planning system were set up and began to function in the late 1940's and early 1950's in their respective economies. They found from experience that it was inefficient to try to centralize the operational management of the economy in any detail. As early as 1952, the Czechoslovak Planning Commission issued instructions to ministries, central administrations, and enterprises with the aim of carrying out a simultaneous "decentralization of national economic planning and of economic management." Only the methodology for drawing up plans at lower levels and the stipulation of "basic targets" were to remain centralized. A similar although more tentative attempt to delegate planning and executive functions to lower organs—mainly to the ministries—occurred in Poland in 1953–54. More far-reaching moves in the same direction were made in Poland, Czechoslovakia, and East Germany in 1958–59. While the early efforts at breaking the bureaucratic logjam in the central coordinating organs fell far short, both in their scope and in their internal coherence, of more recent attempts, both the earlier and the later reforms were meant to fulfill the same broad purpose: to enable the central coordinating authorities to concentrate on essential tasks—particularly on maintaining an overall sectoral balance in the course of rapid development—by freeing their personnel from work required to reconcile the supply and demand for a myriad of commodities and from the exigencies of detailed surveillance and control of plan execution.

It need hardly be stressed that the formal institutional arrangements of an economic system may not reflect its real mode of operation and may give a false image of the real extent of central control over producers' decisions. In the usual state of a command economy, the congestion of communication channels between the center and producing enterprises and the inability of the center to take certain decisions in time to affect the operations of the enterprise force producers to exercise their own initiative. The central planners must reconcile themselves at all times to a certain degree of *de facto* decentralization. The cumulative effect of decisions escaping central direction may even on occasion cause important lapses from plan fulfillment and seriously thwart the planners' will. Thus the nominal delegation of decision-making authority to lower organs may only express the recognition of an existing state of affairs. Decentralization will only impair the coordination of the supply and demand for individual materials and items of equipment, to the extent that the center previously did coordinate input and output decisions for these goods. In the same vein it may be argued that a more systematic balancing of aggregate inputs and outputs by the Planning Commission, accompanied by the devolution of coordinating decisions for individual commodities onto lower organs, even if these organs entertain an imperfect view of the overall market, may be an improvement over ritualistic but ineffective attempts at meshing the supply and output plans for thousands of individual items. The reforms attempted in Eastern Europe in the 1950's failed in the sense that overcentralization persisted or recurred in spite of the ostensible delegation of planning and executive authority to ministries and to still lower organs of the state apparatus. The reasons for this retrogression are instructive in the light of current developments.

The first and most obvious explanation is that entrenched bureaucrats resisted the delegation of decision-making powers and undermined the reforms. This argument is not fully convincing for, up to the late 1950's, none of the reforms could be said to have seriously disturbed the vested interests of the planning or managerial bureaucracy. Executive titles were reassigned; responsibilities were shifted; nevertheless, politically loyal bureaucrats with experience in planning and high-level management stood an excellent chance of keeping their jobs in the administration or of finding an equivalent niche if their old posts were abolished. Upper-level functionaries, may, however, have impeded the reforms by their unwillingness or inability to change their style of work, in particular by maintaining their petty tutelage over enterprises instead of encouraging managers to exercise their own initiative in matters that did not seriously affect state interests.

To find a more satisfactory explanation for the failure of the early reforms, we must look deeper into the nature of a command economy and consider the impact of a partial decentralization of decision making on these systems. The East European economies were partitioned along functional lines according to sectors—industrial, transportation, and so forth—whose main criterion of success was the volume of their output or, if they produced a service, the value of their activity at centrally fixed prices. Each sector claimed as much capital and labor and as much of the materials and services produced by other sectors or imported from abroad as it could, since the more inputs were made available to producers in the sector the greater the output they were capable of turning out. The chief organ responsible for dividing up scarce resources and assigning them to competing uses according to the priorities laid down by the Communist Party was the Central Planning Commission. When, in the course of institutional reforms, ministries were assigned certain planning and executive functions formerly exercised by the Planning Commission, they made their decisions from the narrow viewpoint of their sector, instead of defending nationwide interests. In the end, intersectoral conflicts had to be resolved by the Planning Commission. Since input and output decisions in any modern economy tend to be highly interdependent, conflicts of interests among enterprises belonging to different sectors were the rule rather than the exception; and central authorities were deluged with appeals which had to be resolved expeditiously, if not efficiently, if the economy was to move forward with a minimum of disruption toward established goals. It should be noted, incidentally, that intersectoral conflicts tended to be more acute when development plans were excessively ambitious and resources were grossly inadequate to fulfill them, for the disproportions inherent in the plans had to be corrected on an *ad hoc* basis by the Planning Commission. In such situations, there was hardly any chance at all that spontaneous coordination between representatives of the various sectors could supplant the need for coordination from above during the period when the plans were ostensibly being carried out. In sum, the failure of the system was in its inability to substitute indirect inducements for direct commands, so as to cause enterprises to moderate their appetite for additional resources.

Given the type of price system in effect at the time, one may wonder whether any incentive scheme could have been devised that would have harmonized sectoral interests with central policy. The prices of goods traded among socialized enterprises, far from equating supply and demand and from expressing the relative scarcities of the goods to which they were attached, diverged significantly from production costs for reasons that had more to do with administrative inertia than with the state of their demand. As revisions of wholesale price levels were made only every three to five years and average wages tended to creep upward despite central controls, the production costs of goods exhibiting lower-than-average gains in labor productivity had every opportunity to rise above their established prices.

Indeed, the occasional revisions of centrally administered prices were not coordinated in any way with the partial reforms in the system that were promulgated prior to the 1960's. Under these circumstances, attempts to substitute macroeconomic directives—limits on costs, approved wage bills, gross output targets, sales quotas—for targets expressed in physical terms and for centrally ordained rations foundered on the conflicts of interests I have already described: enterprises complying with the letter of the directives rather than with their spirit disrupted the intersectoral flow of output and upset microeconomic proportions by biasing the assortment of their output or the makeup of their orders for inputs. They did this, of course, with a view to swelling their profits, adding to the value of their production, or otherwise qualifying for the bonuses awarded to managers on the basis of one or more of the success criteria established by higher authorities.

CURRENT REFORMS

We may now consider whether the economic reforms presently being carried out in the Soviet Union and in Eastern Europe are well enough designed and go sufficiently far to check the centripetal tendencies that nullified previous efforts in this direction. Whether a particular reform will take root depends largely on the nature of the price system and of the incentive schemes that will be instituted, for these two institutional parameters will determine the extent to which the planners will be able to use prices, as well as monetary and fiscal policy, to guide managers to decisions compatible with centrally established goals, instead of setting targets for individual commodities and of rationing out materials and equipment to producers.

With the exception of Yugoslavia, which has recently taken further steps toward the liberalization of its socialized economy, the countries of Eastern Europe have all retained important elements of the command economy in their reformed systems. Administrative rationing of key resources and centralized price setting for basic producer goods are still in evidence from Vladivostok to Prague. The amalgamation of enterprises into very large units monopolizing production in each subsector—a common feature of all the reforms—has practically eliminated competition as a source of efficiency. It is extremely unlikely under these conditions that the central planners will be able to mobilize and channel the initiative of plant managers—operating under the tutelage of enterprise directors and of the heads of sectoral administrators—precisely toward the goals mapped out by party authorities. The reforms may nonetheless bring about a net improvement if enterprises under the influence of these decentralized inducements happen to choose inputs and outputs acceptable to the central decision makers even though the resulting pattern of allocation may diverge from that which was initially expected or planned for by these authorities. The latter, by abstaining from administrative interference with producers' decisions, by resisting centripetal tendencies, and by pressing for further consolidation of the decentralized institutions created by the reforms, will reveal their preference for the new patterns of inputs and outputs, and, more broadly, for the overall performance characteristics of the institutionally renovated economy. It is this ultimate ratification by high officials in the Communist party and in the government which previous reforms never received.

After these general considerations, it may be in order to list the chief common features and differences among the reforms, as they are contemplated or actually being put into effect at the present time in Bulgaria, Czechoslovakia, East Germany, Hungary, Poland, Romania, and Russia. This descriptive listing, it should be noted, is confined to the industrial sector, and, within that sector, to socialized enterprises. (Except in Poland where experiments are going on with the leasing of state property to private operators in certain retail services, including gas stations, the reforms hitherto do not offer substantially wider scope to private enterprise.)

Similarities among Countries

The common features are these:

1. The chief coordinating organs—the Planning Commission, the Ministry of Finance, and the Ministry of Foreign Trade—will resort to financial inducements to guide socialized enterprises to desired goals and will restrict the scope of target setting and of physical quotas for materials, capital investments, and imports.

2. Enterprises will be given more autonomy in drafting their plans and in the course of plan execution with respect to the volume and composition of their output and their finances. They will have more choice in the selection of their suppliers (in the case of wholesale and retail establishments) and of their contractors and subcontractors (in the case of producing enterprises). Contracts between enterprises will no longer merely ratify and fill in the decisions of superior authorities as to who should supply whom with what. The financial independence of enterprises will be enhanced by permitting them to retain an appreciably larger part of their profits than in the past.

3. In industry, enterprises are to be organized in "associations" or "sectoral directorates" exclusively responsible for the management and development of a specified range of industrial production.

4. The national bank and the specialized investment and trade banks, wherever they lead a separate existence, will exert greater influence over enterprises via the extension of short-term credits to cover a large part of their working capital and long-term credits to finance a substantial share of their long-term investments. The banks will discriminate in the allocation of short- and long-term credit according to the ability of enterprises to repay loans (although the criterion of social return, if it differs from the criterion of profitability for the enterprise, is still expected to dominate credit allocation).

5. Prices of producer goods are to be revised—if one of the periodic revisions has not recently taken place—with a view to making them conform more closely to "socially necessary costs." (Although complete information is lacking on details of price formation, in certain countries, including Bulgaria and Romania, a general tendency to interpret "socially necessary costs" more flexibly—for example to include capital charges and

rents—may be discerned.) The need to revise prices more frequently in line with changing costs and demand conditions is recognized everywhere, but the practical conclusions that will be drawn from this consideration are likely to differ from country to country.

Differences among Countries

The main differences are these:

1. In only two countries (Czechoslovakia and Hungary) will enterprises and associations be allowed to set prices for any significant proportion of output for standardized producer goods (as distinguished from goods produced on special orders). In Hungary, where "free prices" for producer goods are slated to comprise a much larger share of total sales than in Czechoslovakia, 28 percent of sales for domestically produced raw materials and 85 percent for processed goods (including all timber and paper goods and all construction projects) will be free of direct price controls.

2. Bonuses to management hinge on the fulfillment of profit plans in Poland and East Germany; on profit and sales plans in the Soviet Union; on "gross income," equivalent to value added, in Czechoslovakia; on total profits irrespective of plan in Hungary; and on the growth of labor productivity and profits in Bulgaria.[1] In Romania bonuses will undoubtedly be tied to plan fulfillment, but it is not yet apparent whether the link will be to profits or to some other "indicator."

3. The number of binding directives issued to enterprises by ministries and other authorities varies from country to country. In Czechoslovakia and Hungary where the changes introduced are the most profound, binding directives will, wherever possible, be abolished, although some physical targets are retained in the yearly plans and a number of scarce materials are still on the ration list. But the wage bill, at least in Czechoslovakia and Hungary, will not be directly set by the center: It will be indirectly influenced by progressive taxes on wages, which will discourage the excessive disbursement of profits for this purpose. In the Soviet Union, as well as in most of the remaining countries, the wage bill will still be subject to direct control.

4. The degree to which investments will be decentralized and in particular will be initiated and financed by enterprises from their own funds supplemented by bank loans differs significantly from country to country. It is interesting that the Czechoslovak authorities, mindful of their adverse experience of the late 1950's when investments were too rapidly "decon-

---

[1] The size of the bonus depends on the growth in labor productivity, but the bonus is financed from plan profits. Note that labor productivity is defined as the ratio of the enterprise's gross output to its labor force and that incentives thus still hinge indirectly on gross output, which includes the value of materials processed. This type of bonus, which induces the squandering of material inputs, has now been rejected in the majority of East European countries.

trolled" and inflationary pressures were released, adopted a fairly conservative policy in this regard, although they are likely to give enterprises more leeway in investment policy than the less developed nations of the area, which are still bent on marshaling the greatest possible financial resources for the construction of new factories.

5. Some reforms, including the Hungarian, call for the delegation to the enterprise of certain import and export decisions and for the right of the enterprise to retain a part of its foreign-currency earnings. In Bulgaria, extra allotments of foreign currency can be obtained only if an enterprise's exports exceed plan. In Czechoslovakia, which has suffered an acute shortage of convertible foreign currency in recent years, the provisions in this regard are less liberal; nevertheless, a few very large exporting enterprises like the Škoda Works in Pilsen will be brought closer to their foreign markets by the creation of special foreign-trade enterprises operating in the framework of the same industrial association as the producing enterprise.

6. In the Soviet Union, Bulgaria, and East Germany the reforms were introduced piecemeal, starting with "experimenting enterprises," and were gradually extended to cover the bulk of industrial output. In the other countries the reforms were put into effect in all industrial enterprises simultaneously.

Since the reforms everywhere in Eastern Europe are open-ended in character and undergoing constant modification in the light of experience, there is no reason to believe that the similarities and differences I have listed will continue to prevail. There can be no question, however, that the Communist leaders of Czechoslovakia and Hungary have so far endorsed a more profound institutional transformation than other East European states. Perhaps the most radical departure from the previous system they have ratified consists in giving free scope to producer goods' prices for an appreciable number of commodities and in severing managerial incentives from plan fulfillment. There is still some hesitation on the subject among Communist officials and among economists in these two countries, but the moment cannot be far off when decisions of enterprises based on considerations of profitability will be held valid, even if they cause deviations from approved plans. At the other end of the scale, the Romanian government has been the most tardy in scheduling systematic changes and the most guarded in framing reforms when it finally decided to do so late in 1967. If one were to grade the remaining countries according to the intensity of the reforms being carried out (all lying between the extremes already listed), East Germany and Bulgaria would come out slightly ahead of the Soviet Union and Poland.

Timing and Scope of Reform

Our sample of experimenting economies is too small to account convincingly for the intensity of a country's reforms by its level of development or other special circumstances. Nevertheless, several factors seem to have influenced the timing and the scope of the reforms.

In general, the economies that are high on the intensity scale are relatively highly developed, export manufactures on a large scale, and have grown at relatively slow rates since the beginning of the 1960's.[2]

East Germany stands lower on this scale than we should expect, since it fulfills all three of the above conditions; but it may be supposed that its extraordinarily repressive dictatorship works against economic liberalization, which could easily spill over into the political arena. Walter Ulbricht's unwillingness to tolerate the kind of free-for-all discussion about the best "model" for a socialist system that has blossomed out in Hungary and Czechoslovakia since 1963 may also have retarded the adoption of more radical measures.

While a high level of development and economic dependence on the export of manufactures are to some extent correlated in Eastern Europe, it is at least suggestive that Hungary and Bulgaria are both more intensively engaged in exports of manufactures than one would expect from the level of development they have achieved and are also more committed to reform than Poland and Romania, which may be taken as their respective counterparts in development.[3]

It is easier to find convincing reasons why levels of development and of manufactured exports should be related to the intensity of reforms than to establish the statistical relation among these variables. The gist of the argument is that a centralized system of the Soviet type is a suitable vehicle for "extensive growth"—a rapid expansion of industrial output accomplished by dint of massive injections of labor and capital, using mainly established techniques—but that it is not capable of maintaining smooth and rapid "intensive growth" at a later stage of development based on technical progress, improved organization, product development, and new combinations of inputs capable of yielding increases in output with only moderate net additions to total inputs. If this argument is accepted, it will be at least as evident that a system where production is determined by

---

[2] From 1961 to 1965, the year-to-year increase in national income, according to official estimates, averaged about 2 percent in Czechoslovakia and East Germany, 4–5 percent in Hungary, a little over 6 percent in Bulgaria, Poland and the Soviet Union, and 9 percent in Romania.

[3] In 1965 Hungary exported per capita a value of $81 of manufactured goods (not including foodstuffs); Bulgaria, $56; Poland, $34, and Romania, $16.5. Yet, according to Hungarian estimates, the national income per capita of Hungary was more or less on the same level as that of Poland and only 20 percent larger than that of Romania. In 1964 Bulgaria's national income was estimated to be $470 per capita as against $498 in Poland and $423 in Romania. Note also that Czechoslovakia, with a national income per head less than twice as great as Romania's, exported more than seven times as much per capita in manufactured goods. (Exports of manufactures were computed from official trade statistics converted at the official exchange rate, a procedure yielding meaningful results inasmuch as the trade of Comecon countries is carried on at "foreign-exchange prices" approximating prices prevailing in world trade.)

central authorities vested with the responsibility for distributing the capital and the materials required by enterprises to fulfill their output targets hardly provides a proper environment for exporters of manufactured goods competing on world markets for orders depending crucially on the quality, servicing, and technology of their products. The situation in the Comecon Market, which was isolated for many years from the competition of manufacturers in capitalist economies, has changed radically in the past decade. The Czechs and the East Germans must now supply technologically advanced capital goods to win orders from their less developed customers in the Soviet area if they wish to meet the competition of Western suppliers. Exporters must have a considerable degree of financial and organizational autonomy to develop products that will preserve or widen their markets, both in Eastern and in Western Europe. What makes this competitive struggle so crucial is that the more developed countries of Eastern Europe are highly vulnerable to fluctuations in the world demand for their manufactures, due to the hypertrophied expansion of their heavy industry: lacking the raw materials basis for their industrial complex and suffering from a shortage of domestically produced farm products, they must increase their exports of manufactures at least as fast as their industry grows in order to pay for their imports of materials and foodstuffs.

It would be an error to infer from the conjectured need for more thorough reforms in the highly developed East European economies that the institutional changes will be more successful wherever they happen to be more systematic and more profound. For there are also greater obstacles to success in a country like Czechoslovakia than in Bulgaria or Romania. To extent that most prices, even where the reforms are most far-reaching, will be linked to past production costs reflecting an inefficient state of affairs, they will not offer a reliable guide to determine which production lines should be curbed and which developed, which factories should be closed down and which expanded. But even if it turned out that prices did emit the right signals, it is doubtful whether the painful structural changes to which they would point would be systematically undertaken. In 15 to 20 years of extensive development, hundreds of inefficient plants have mushroomed forth in Czechoslovakia, especially in rural, less developed areas, which can only prosper as long as their inefficiency is concealed behind the more or less profitable operations of the multiple-plant, monopolistic enterprises to which they are subordinate. The elimination of inefficient units would create temporary pockets of unemployment with undesirable social and political side effects. (Whatever the demerits of the old system, it had the advantage in the eyes of workers of protecting them from this liability.) These structural problems are less acute in countries such as Poland, Bulgaria, and Romania, industrial late comers where the introduction of borrowed technologies has been so rapid that obsolete productive capacity built up in earlier years contributes only a relatively small share of industrial output.

The paramount importance of prices correctly reflecting relative scarcities—or at least coming closer to this norm than prereform prices—is that this will make it possible to calculate meaningful costs and returns and thus provide an *impersonal measure of efficiency*, which had so far been absent. Anyone today may, with some justice, deny that an enterprise should be wound up or a product line discontinued because none of the indicators at hand provides totally convincing evidence of the inefficiency of these operations. Costs are so distorted by subsidized raw material prices, by deviations from opportunity cost in foreign trade, and by the absence or the inadequate levels of capital charges that no firm conclusions about the inefficiency of a given operation can be inferred from them. An incontrovertible measure of efficiency would equip "rationalizers" of production with a weapon that, while it might not be proof against political lobbying by threatened interests, would permit them to offer a good deal more resistance against arbitrary interference than in the recent past.

THE ORGANIZATION OF INDUSTRY IN THE CONTEXT OF THE REFORMS

The trend in Eastern Europe since the late 1950's has been toward the merger of small enterprises and especially toward the creation of powerful associations reminiscent of cartels or holding companies.[4] Integration is generally proceeding along horizontal lines in Eastern Europe, except in Hungary and East Germany where at least some enterprises have been integrated vertically—from raw materials to finished products.

The planners in authority are counting on a number of distinct advantages from the consolidation of enterprises and from their association in sectoral directorates with a monopoly of planning and production for a range of products in each industry. First they hope to facilitate the coordination of individual inputs and outputs within the broader framework of the consolidated balances for groups of commodities prepared by the Planning Commission. The schema the authorities have in mind would require the procurement organization attached to each association to communicate its requirements for materials and capital goods, within the aggregate limit imposed by the plan directives, to the sales organizations of the associations capable of supplying them with these inputs. Negotiations between suppliers and their customers would go on until every enterprise had fully committed its output and had contracted for sufficient supplies to produce this output in the desired assortment.

The advocates of mergers and associations do not explain why lateral liaison should work in the present setup when all previous attempts to

[4] The most recent reforms in Czechoslovakia, for example, merged 1,371 old into 713 new industrial enterprises. These enterprises are grouped into 85 "productive economic units" with wide-ranging powers over their "subjects."

bring it about failed in the past. The obstacle to spontaneous coordination lay, and still lies, in the mutual interdependency of production programs: No producing plant can specify its inputs until its output-mix has been pinned down, but its own output-mix depends on the demands from enterprises that directly or indirectly supply it with material inputs. Several revisions of the contracts between suppliers and their clients, at a considerable cost in time wasted and energy, would be required to achieve anything like consistency in the production programs of all plants.

Second, the designers of the reforms believe that research and development can best be carried on within very large enterprises or by agencies whose management will be close enough to the production problems of an industrial sector to guide research toward concrete and relevant objectives but which will have a wide enough *vue d'ensemble* to avoid the duplication of R.&D. efforts typical of more fragmented organizations. Similar considerations about the need for ensuring close ties between producers and their foreign clients and suppliers militated in favor of the type of monopolistic organization that was generally adopted in Eastern Europe.

The Czech and Slovak writers who have given a good deal of attention of late to issues of market organization have thrown up a number of objections to the "monopolistic management" of production sectors. First and foremost, those among them who favor the creation of a full-fledged socialist market economy deplore the elimination of competition. They argue that initiative and drive, which were stifled under the old system, can only be recaptured in a competitive climate. A second point that is often made is that the monopoly management of a production sector (corresponding to a given range of goods) tends to perpetuate the old bureaucratic procedures for allocating materials and capital goods—especially the mechanical distribution of the quotas of rationed materials available to the sector on the basis of "standard" shares for each region and for every enterprise within a region, thereby "embalming" the negative features of the old system. Third, the monopoly position of an enterprise or of a group of enterprises distorts the nature and direction of technical progress, especially if the prices of the outputs are set by a centralized agency. For it has been observed, at least under present Czechoslovak conditions, that R.&D. efforts are biased toward innovations capable of raising output and cutting costs in preference to those that might improve the quality of the product or the range of choice open to consumers. Finally, and most obvious of all, a sales monopoly in a line of products invites open price increases wherever prices are free to move and covert increases where they are not.

There has also been increased recognition among Czechoslovak economists that the net effect of the positive and negative elements of monopoly management may differ appreciably from one sector or product line to the other. The trouble, according to some analysts, is that organizational forms are cut from a single pattern by central authorities, ignoring the need for differentiation. Eugene Löbl, the eminent Slovak economist and intellectual leader, argues that there is a natural symbiosis between large and small firms, the latter subcontracting for the former or filling the interstices of market demand that the giants cannot easily satisfy. Small independent enterprises are more "resonant" to market signals than large; they make more efficient use of market information.

Granted that a mixed solution is optimal, with a few very large enterprises carrying on most of the R.&D. and many small independent units adjusting flexibly to market demand, how should such a state be brought about? Are the system managers located in Prague or Budapest capable of working out an optimal scheme of organization and then of decreeing its adoption? Or should they encourage the spontaneous formation of enterprises—by merger, spin-off, or the creation of new ventures—until some sort of institutional equilibrium will have been reached?[5] In short, does decentralization of the decision-making process, which so far has only been extended to the choice of inputs and outputs within bounds set by the center, require the decentralization of organizational forms as well?

These far-reaching questions open up a host of related problems about the role of the center as arbiter or regulator of independent enterprises, about short- and long-run managerial incentives and their relation to profit maximization over a variable horizon, about the incidence of risk and the responsibility of managers to society—matters which as far as I know have not been thought through by the economists crusading for more profound reforms. But the fact that they have been raised at all and that the reforms in most East European countries, including the Soviet Union, are considered open-ended, augurs well for the future evolution of economic institutions in these socialist states.

[5] So far the central authorities in the Soviet Union and in the East European countries under discussion have retained the exclusive power to create, to merge, and to wind up enterprises. In Yugoslavia, by contrast, there has been a substantial delegation of organizational powers to republics, communes, and even to existing enterprises.

19. PLANNING, MANAGEMENT, AND ECONOMIC DEVELOPMENT IN COMMUNIST CHINA*

Yuan-li Wu

This analysis of central planning in Mainland China shows how the Chinese Communists closely copied the Soviet model of comprehensive central planning and detailed administrative control, and how they experienced the same problems encountered earlier in the Soviet Union. Wu describes the scope of the national economic plan and how it is formulated and implemented. He explains a number of the reasons for "discrepancies between plan and reality," including basing detailed plans on inadequate or inaccurate information, inexperience of the planning staff, defects in the planning procedure, the managerial incentive system, and methods of adjustment to underfulfillments and overfulfillments during the implementation of the plan. Wu concludes with a summary of the main features of the Chinese economic model and the chief factors constraining Mainland China's future economic development under this model.

---

* Reprinted by permission from *An Economic Profile of Mainland China* (Studies Prepared for the Joint Economic Committee, 90th Cong., 1st sess.) (Washington, D.C.: U.S. Government Printing Office, 1967), Vol. 1, pp. 99–119, with the omission of the source references and some of the footnotes. Yuan-li Wu is Professor of Economics at the University of San Francisco.

INTRODUCTION

UNTIL THE COLLAPSE of the Great Leap Forward in 1960, Communist Chinese leaders frequently pointed to the reportedly high rate of China's economic growth, particularly that of the industrial sector, as evidence of the superiority of the Chinese model of economic planning. The Chinese experience was held up as a suitable example for other less developed countries in Asia, Africa, and even Latin America that desire rapid industrialization to emulate. While China's economic troubles in the early 1960's made the Chinese claim appear irrelevant, the successful Chinese nuclear tests since 1964 have again raised the issue of Communist China's economic potential under her system of planning and management. A reevaluation of the system is needed in order to determine both its performance in the past and its inherent properties which may bear upon the course of Communist China's future economic development.

The First Five-Year Plan covered the period of 1953–57. The Second Five-Year Plan (1958–62) coincided with the Great Leap, which ended ignominiously in 1960 although official reports would indicate that many of the production targets of the plan had already been reached by then. Officially, the period from 1961 through 1965 was designated as one of readjustment and consolidation, while it actually consisted of a major depression spanning approximately from the latter part of 1960 through the first half of 1962, followed by gradual recovery. The Third Five-Year Plan is scheduled for 1966–70. Thus there are two complete five-year plan periods from which we may expect to derive at least some tentative conclusions.

In the following pages we shall first examine what the national economic plan consists of and how it is formulated. The central focus in the first section will be the content of the plan, the structure of the government agencies involved in its formulation, implementation, and evaluation, and the manner in which crucial decisions are supposed to be reached and carried out.

The discussion will, however, deal with planning in the abstract. Reality and the plan do not necessarily coincide. Nor is reality always accurately perceived. These discrepancies occur for a variety of reasons. A historical one consists of the chronological development of the apparatus and of the data base needed in planning. During the entire Communist period from 1949 to date, as we shall see, partial rather than comprehensive planning has been the rule. But there are a number of other important reasons.

Discrepancies between planned development in theory and actual events often arise because the information on which the plan is based does not correspond to reality. A second reason is the possibility that while a plan may be initially quite realistic, it is changed after its initial formulation. Still a third reason is disregard of the rules and instructions in practice even though officially the plan remains in force. Such deviations in practice may take place at different levels of the enterprises and agencies in charge of plan implementation. Section II of this paper will be devoted to a discussion of these and other factors accounting for the discrepancies.

Because of the relatively short period during which economic planning has prevailed, information on the behavior of Communist Chinese planners and managers can be deduced only with considerable uncertainty as to its future relevance. But even on the basis of the limited time period for which data are available, it is possible to discern certain elements that seem to constitute a pattern. The possibility that these elements may continue to be effective lies in the apparently ideological and political roots of the behavior they portray. Discussion of this "behavioral pattern" is contained in Section III.

If the analysis is correct with respect to the behavioral pattern, we should be able to project one or more alternative courses of economic development for Communist China in the foreseeable future. The final section of this paper attempts to set forth some of the key variables involved. To a degree both the factors inherent in the behavioral pattern and those which are characteristic of the Chinese economic structure at its present stage of development can be discerned. While prognosis may be difficult, the interested observer can at least know what particular events and tendencies to watch.

I. THE NATIONAL ECONOMIC PLAN AND ITS FORMULATION AND IMPLEMENTATION

The Scope of the Plan

The national economic plan which theoretically governs all Chinese economic activities is composed of a set of component plans that provide the basis of achieving balance between the supply and demand of materials, labor, and financing, both nationally and on the regional level. At the national level, plans for the materials and labor balances rest on still other partial plans which may be conveniently subdivided into 12 categories or aspects as enumerated below; the regional plans are essentially the same as the national plan. The student of Soviet economic planning will not fail to note the essential similarity of the Soviet and Chinese planning systems, which is not surprising.

1. Industrial production.
2. Agricultural production.
3. Transportation.
4. Labor and employment.
5. Allocation of materials.

6. Commodity flow.
7. Projects of capital construction.
8. Social, cultural, and welfare undertakings (including public utilities, housing, health, and cultural and educational activities under which are included the training of the Communist party activists).
9. Foreign trade.
10. Technological development.
11. Production costs.
12. Commodity prices.

Of the 12 sectoral or partial plans, items 1, 2, and 3 deal with the output plans of individual sectors for which production targets, quota allocations to individual enterprises, and methods of production and technical norms are given. Items 4 and 5 are concerned with the allocation of labor and material inputs consistent with the preceding production and transportation plans. Item 6 deals principally with the distribution of final products for consumption. Items 7 and 8 are concerned respectively both with the allocation of resources to investment and collective consumption as end uses and with their specific commodity and project contents. The foreign trade plan deals with commodity trade and other balance-of-payments items involving foreign exchange. The technological plan has for its purpose the preparation of programs to provide Communist China with the latest scientific and technological information, including information from abroad. The cost plan specifies standard costs, as well as targets of cost reduction and projected changes in labor productivity and money wages. It is closely related to the plan of commodity prices; together they are instrumental in regulating the accumulation of capital—inasmuch as profit from state enterprises is a major source of government revenue—and in encouraging increase in efficiency in production. The cost plan serves therefore not only as an important part of the national plan in resource allocation, but, supplemented by technical targets in the other plans, it also provides guidelines for the management of individual enterprises so that decisions and operations at the enterprise level would contribute to the fulfillment of the national plan as a whole.

At the national level, the financial plan consists of four parts: the consolidated State budget; the credit and cash plans of the banking system; the financial plans of the ministries and their subordinate organs, enterprises and communes; and the estimated receipts and expenditures of government agencies and enterprises outside the regular budget. Government control of incomes and expenditures under this set of plans is an indispensable tool in regulating the allocation of resources between consumption and investment and in maintaining price stability. Very rigorous control over the supply of money in the hands of the public, first instituted in 1950, was a major measure in combating the hyperinflation that was not completely suppressed until 1951. An effort has been made to maintain the same degree of "cash control" since then although performance has not always been up to par, especially during the early sixties and, to a lesser extent, in 1956.

Plan and Management in the Individual Enterprise

At the operational level, the nature of the annual plan of the individual enterprise is aptly described by its title, i.e., the "plan of production, technique, and finance." In general, it includes within a section on production the quantitative and qualitative specifications of products, technical coefficients, the degree of utilization of equipment, and production schedules. In the part dealing with labor, the production plan specifies both manpower and work quotas, together with working hours, wage rates, personnel classifications, and labor welfare provisions. A separate part deals with the supply of raw materials, rates of their consumption, supply schedules and sources, and working capital requirements. Another part is concerned with the maintenance and repair of equipment and specifies schedules for major repairs and periodic inspections. A final component of the production plan deals with unit costs and the allowability of various costs in the "economic accounting" of the enterprise.

Parallel to the above production plan are three other parts dealing respectively with the sale and distribution of products, the technological requirements and improvements envisaged for the particular enterprise, and the financial receipts and expenditures of the enterprise corresponding to its level of activities and the specified cost coefficients. A series of statistical tables and budgetary schedules accompany these plans and form the basis upon which performance of the enterprise is scrutinized by the disbursing agents and auditors in the banking system.

The management of an enterprise is instructed to observe the targets and standards laid down in these detailed plans after they have been approved by the state economic commission. As an independent "economic accounting unit" the enterprise is required to deliver a planned profit calculated over costs, which do not, however, take interest charges into full account, with reward and punishment tied to the level of performance. In theory, the management of an enterprise is encouraged to overfulfill any part of the plan provided the other parts are not adversely affected. In practice, because of possible inconsistency between individual planned targets, the plan of an enterprise does not necessarily offer an unequivocal guide to operation.

The Apparatus of Data Collection, Planning and Plan Implementation

The national economic plan and its many components are formulated and implemented by a complex and ponderous set of government agencies. These may be described under the following headings:

1. *Information Gathering.* Data for planning are supplied by the State Bureau of Statistics. Established in 1952, the Bureau developed during the

subsequent four years a network of 160 offices and one-quarter million statistical reporting units at different levels of government. The number was expanded further during the Great Leap Forward.

2. *Planning.* Until May, 1956, the responsibility for formulating both the long-term and the annual economic plans was lodged in the State Planning Commission, also established in 1952. In 1956, a new State Economic Commission was put in charge of the annual economic plan. Individual departments within the two Commissions are responsible for the component plans. A separate State Construction Commission also existed from 1954 to 1958, when it was incorporated into the State Planning Commission. A State Capital Construction Commission, which maintained a parallel existence for three years from 1958 and was responsible for long-term investment projects, was incorporated into the State Planning Commission in 1961. In 1965 it was again separated from the State Planning Commission.

3. *Control of Inputs.* Several agencies supervise the allocation of labor and materials. Allocation of labor is in the hands of the Ministry of Labor and, in the case of penal and forced labor, the Ministry of Public Security. A Bureau of Foreign Experts and the education ministries also form an integral part of the mechanism regulating labor supply. A bureau for allocating the supply of materials was first established in 1956 and, after incorporation into the State Economic Commission during 1958–63, was in the latter year again put under the direct control of the State Council, where it has remained.

4. *Production.* An integral part of the apparatus of plan formulation consists of the "production" or "industrial branch" ministries, which oversee the operation of the various government enterprises in their respective commodity groups. At the national level, the number of these ministries increased from 12 in 1952 to 24 in 1956 and 25 in 1965, reflecting a process of broadening of coverage within the plan, regrouping for administrative purposes, and increasing specialization as a result of industrial development. As of the beginning of 1965, following the first session of the Third National People's Congress, the 25 such production ministries were in charge of—

1. Textiles.
2. Light industries (two ministries numbered first and second).
3. Chemicals.
4. Construction engineering.
5. Building materials.
6. Machine manufacturing (eight ministries numbered first through eighth), including the manufacture of various categories of arms, both nuclear and conventional).
7. Petroleum.
8. Coal.
9. Agriculture.

10. State farms and land reclamation.
11. Marine products.
12. Forestry.
13. Water conservation and electric power.
14. Railroads.
15. Communications.
16. Post and telecommunications.
17. Ocean transport.

The Capital Construction Commission noted earlier, which oversees plant construction and the installation of machines and equipment, may also be regarded as a component of the executive and production control apparatus.

5. *Trade and Distribution.* The domestic distribution channels are under the control of the Ministries of Food and Commerce and indirectly influenced by the Ministry of Foreign Trade. The operational end is handled by 22 domestic state trading corporations, some with affiliates in Hong Kong, and 10 specialized export-import corporations, supplemented by an external transport company and a ship-leasing concern.

6. *Financial Administration.* For the formulation and administration of the financial plans, the aid of several agencies and financial institutions is enlisted. These include the Ministry of Finance and the People's Bank of China, and, under their supervision, several specialized banks, a foreign exchange bank, a state insurance company, investment companies established to attract overseas Chinese investors, a large number of credit cooperatives, and a commission overseeing commodity prices.[1] The principal function of these institutions is to regulate consumption expenditure in relation to savings, to provide finance for the planned expenditures required by the production plans, to preclude unauthorized disbursements and interagency credit arrangements not provided for in the production plans, and to maintain control over costs through financial checks.

7. *Technological Change.* Another group of institutions which have begun to play an increasingly important role in Chinese economic development in recent years is headed by the Scientific and Technological Commission. Established in 1958, the Commission coordinates all scientific and technological programs of the many research institutes under the ministries, the universities and the Academy of Sciences. Its work in enhancing the degree of independence of Communist China in science and technology is a *sine qua non* of economic autarky.

Plan Formulation

In theory, plans are formulated by the planning agencies on the basis of data supplied by the State Statistical Bureau; they are then entrusted to

[1] The Communist Bank of China, which is the foreign exchange bank, is to be distinguished from the original Bank of China still operating under Nationalist Chinese control. The position of the overseas Chinese investment companies since the initiation of the Red Guards movement is not clear.

the operating agencies for implementation. If all plans were realistic and faithfully carried out, the course of Chinese economic development would depend entirely upon the substantive nature of the plan as exemplified by the bill of goods included in final demand and the manner in which they are selected and incorporated into the national economic plan.

Schematically, the process of plan formulation begins with the issue of "control figures" by the State Economic Commission to the central government ministries and provincial governments for transmission to the enterprises and agencies under their respective jurisdictions. The "control figures" consist of a set of production targets, input and cost coefficients, and other relevant indicators of performance described under the component plans for the enterprises to follow. Some adjustments of the initial control figures may be made at this time. Operational plans, including both targets and requirements, are then formulated by the individual enterprises and submitted to higher levels. Before 1959, the individual plans were integrated by industrial branches at the level of the national ministry. Beginning with the 1959 annual plan, they were also to be integrated at the provincial or regional (for autonomous regions) level.[2] Both the industrial branch plans and the territorial plans are then reviewed by the State Economic Commission for revision and integration into a plan of material and labor balances. The revised control figures are then reissued as targets for the individual operating agencies and enterprises.

As mentioned elsewhere, the manner in which the initial control figures are selected has never been fully explained. We can deduce, however, at least some of the principal considerations which enter into the selection of some of the output targets. These include (1) minimum requirements of the population in the case of some basic consumer products; (2) full capacity output in industries where demand is far from being satisfied and shortage of equipment or other inputs constitutes a bottleneck; (3) maximum output of certain goods where the availability of imported material is a constraint; (4) material requirements of investment projects selected for their role in offsetting certain sectoral imbalances or in programs negotiated under foreign aid arrangements; (5) for some commodities, outputs that are somewhat larger than those of the preceding period; (6) in the case of some intermediate products, input requirements based on the above choices of final products; and (7) choices that are based on defense and other noneconomic considerations.

Of the above factors not the least important are the political preferences of the Chinese Communist Party (CCP), which has within the party structure separate departments in charge of the affairs of (1) agriculture and forestry, (2) industry and communications, and (3) finance and trade. Some of the initial "control figures" issued by the State

[2] The decentralization plan of 1959 followed closely the Soviet decentralization program instituted earlier. There has been very little information about its fate since then.

Economic Commission doubtless originate from the CCP central committee. In the ultimate analysis, decisions on the really important priorities, therefore, rest with the Communist party. Since August, 1965, each of the three corresponding economic administrative offices under the state council has added a political department, which has further strengthened the role of purely political decisions and of political supervision of the economic administrators.

II. SOURCES OF DISCREPANCY BETWEEN PLAN AND REALITY

Poor Planning and Institutional and Management Problems

The preceding section has described the structure of the national economic plan which theoretically provides for (1) intersectoral balance within an input-output matrix, (2) correspondence between the plan in real terms and its counterpart in terms of monetary flows, and (3) the steady growth of the entire system at predetermined rates. Actual experience since 1953, when the First Five-Year Plan made its official debut, has, however, demonstrated both the recurrent emergence of sectoral disequilibrium at various levels and, since 1958, when the Second Five-Year Plan was ushered in by a Great Leap Forward, failure to achieve steady growth. There are many reasons why the idealized path of planned progress and actual experience do not coincide. One simple explanation is that some of the plans have been poorly conceived either as a result of the planning procedure and system used or in consequence of the inexperience and technical inadequacy of the planning staff. For the first four years of the First Five-Year Plan, both types of shortcomings apparently prevailed.

In September, 1956, when Communist China was about to embark upon the last phase of the 1953–57 Plan, the chairman of the State Planning Commission, Li Fu-ch'un, offered a candid appraisal of the Commission's performance. He noted that the Commission was at the time responsible both for long-term planning and for the formulation of the annual plan and that, during a part of the time under review, it was also responsible for the administration of certain industries and capital investment undertakings. Thus, burdened by the chores of routine administration and the incessant drafting and revision of plans, it was unable to pay sufficient attention to the collection and appraisal of data, consideration of long-term national interests, and the determination of specific facts in detail. Inadequate attention to detail and to local conditions was also in part the result of a practice forced upon the central government ministries and the provincial authorities, as reported in a Hong Kong study, because of their lack of time to prepare more realistic plans. Instead of waiting for the information contained in the plans prepared by the individual enterprises under their jurisdiction on the basis of "control figures" transmitted through their hands, as the proper procedure requires, the ministerial (i.e., industrial branch) and provincial authorities often made their decisions without the benefit of the operational plans of the basic units. Therefore, greater damage was done by inexperienced and/or unknowledgeable members of the planning staff than might otherwise have occurred. Furthermore, according to Li, the Commission also suffered from undue concentration of decision making and the consequent lack of flexibility to respond to new information received and to novel conditions. It was not possible, therefore, to arrive at intersectoral balance and to maintain it at all levels and in all regions. In short, there was incomplete, incorrect, inflexible, and shortsighted planning.

A no less simple reason accounting for discrepancy between the plan and actual performance is the fact that plans are sometimes disregarded. In the agricultural sector especially, the farmers in collective farms during 1956–57 and in communes since 1958 may not always have followed a predetermined course according to plan. Organizationally, with the exception of the greater part of 1958 and 1959, the government authorities have never been in full control of agricultural production. This situation has apparently continued during the years of agricultural recovery from the ravages of the Great Leap since 1962, as evidenced by the continuation of debate on the scope of government control of agricultural production in the communes. The point at issue is whether government control should be limited to requisition of output through planned purchases and the agricultural tax or whether production should be carried out under a unified plan even though the fulfillment of the detailed plans might be supervised at the local level. There were plainly people who held opposite views on this matter up to the eve of the Third Five-Year Plan in 1965. The continued presence of collective ownership in the communes, as opposed to state ownership which was originally intended in 1958–59 when the communes were first introduced, has contributed to this difficulty.

In the nonagricultural sectors, state ownership and full control were not complete until 1956. Even after 1956, it may not always have been possible to observe all aspects of the national economic plan and of the "control figures" because of possible conflicts among different targets issued to the managements of individual enterprises which have been encouraged to overfulfill some of the targets. In general, both management and workers are encouraged to overfulfill production targets. Periodic interplant or interenterprise contests and campaigns to emulate national production record holders may play havoc to production costs. Where costs are noninclusive through the omission of interest charges on fixed capital, the result may be the most uneconomical use of certain scarce resources. The failure of the Great Leap was at least partly brought about by the emergence of bottlenecks in labor supply and transportation, especially at times of peak demand, such as the harvest season. Deteriorations in quality, again notable during the Great Leap, resulting, for instance, in the excessive output of coal and ores with above normal impurities, were also responsible for the emergence of some of the bottlenecks. Where emphasis on breaking output records is persistent, the management may choose to produce more of those products for which the targets can be more readily exceeded regardless of the demand. There have also been reports on such matters as misuse of short-term working capital in long-term investment, inclusion in cost of items which represent a part of the profit reserved for the enterprises, and general preoccupation with indicators rather than the substance of performance. Regionalism has also acted as a disruptive factor to the national balance of input and output, while centralized balance of demand and supply at the ministerial level has often had the effect of creating unnecessary demand on the nation's transport capacity.

One can identify additional specific causes which can give rise to discrepancies between plans and reality and which have been operative during different periods up to this writing. In particular, the following principal factors can be enumerated.

First, the national economic plan may be based upon information which is inaccurate. Second, even when the data used in initial planning correctly reflect reality, actual performance may result in either overfulfillment or underfulfillment of the initial plan. Such a result may lead to changes in subsequent plans or, if anticipated early, even to changes during the same planning period. Furthermore, there is the possibility that changes are made in a plan independently of any anticipated underfulfillment or overfulfillment. Where many such changes are made, especially if they are in the same direction, such as the successive upward revision of targets, the likelihood of divergence from reality increases. If this situation is a general one, the entire plan may be incapable of realization. If only some economic sectors are affected, the final result may depend upon how plans in other sectors are adjusted in response to the exigencies. Third, plans may not be fulfilled because of exogenous shocks suffered by the economic system, or they may be overfulfilled because of unexpected "windfalls."

Reasons for Inaccurate or Inadequate Information Available to Chinese Planners

There are good reasons to believe that Chinese planners have employed incorrect or inadequate information in their economic planning. In the first place, the coverage of the statistics collected has not been complete or consistent. Since the State Statistical Bureau was not established until October, 1952, one would expect that a complete set of procedures for reporting and processing data could not be fully developed until quite some time after that date, even if full coverage of all the units that should report had been possible from the very beginning. Actually, not all of the private enterprises were nationalized or brought under joint operation with the government until the end of 1956, when the First Five-Year Plan had nearly run its course. In regard to statistics on trade and distribution, the organization of cooperatives through mergers and the formation of large associations of entire trades were also not completed until 1956. The same situation applied to the many handicraft work shops which accounted for a large proportion of the manufacturing sector of the economy. It would seem to be axiomatic that the coverage of statistical reporting, as well as the accuracy of the reports, tends to suffer as the number of reporting units increases and the individual size of each unit decreases. This situation would seem to have prevailed before 1956 when the socialization of the industrial and trade sectors had not yet been fully carried out. It was also true in the case of agricultural statistics. According to Li Fu-ch'un in September, 1956, "The State Planning Commission has in the past paid more attention to the state industrial enterprises of the Central Government, while inadequate attention has been given to industrial enterprises under the local governments, as well as agriculture, commerce, and cultural and educational undertakings." This imbalance in emphasis not only betrayed a general preference to develop a few large industrial enterprises, but acted as both a cause and an effect of inadequate information on the neglected sectors.

As will be noted later, one particular effect of incomplete statistical coverage may have been an underestimate of stocks on hand during the first years of the First Five-Year Plan. This may have happened outside of a few principal commodities for which a more complete record may have been available. However, even in the case of ferrous, nonferrous, and scrap metals, as well as timber, all of which are important in construction and investment projects, inventory taking at some of the principal centers was apparently not done until the end of 1954, thus effectively precluding any use of the findings even in the 1955 national economic plan. During the years since 1958, the complete collapse of the statistical reporting system as an aftermath of the Great Leap has again brought the question of coverage to the fore.

The shortcomings of incomplete coverage have been compounded by the inaccuracy of such statistics as can be collected. An example of inaccurate statistical reporting at the midpoint of the First Five-Year Plan may be found in a 1955 report by a deputy director of the State Statistical Bureau discussing the problem in 1954. In a survey of statistics from Liaoning Province, where the organization of statistical work had begun at an earlier date than in the country as a whole, there were 14,321 cases of erroneous reporting from the 232 national and local government industrial enterprises whose statistics were examined. Of these, 708 presented major problems, while cases of deliberate falsification numbered 476 or 3 percent of the total reports. The situation in other areas was probably worse.

Inaccuracy has characterized even statistics where coverage should not be a major problem. It stems from several different causes. The use of inadequately trained and inexperienced reporters, particularly because of the very large number of statistical reports required at all levels of administration, reflects the dilution of staff and the inevitable deterioration of quality. This effort has been felt not only in the collection of raw statistical data but also in their processing at later stages. A notable instance of gross inaccuracy was the erroneous estimate of food grain production in 1958, which first gave the total at 375 million metric tons, equivalent to a 100 percent increase over the reported output of 1957. In 1959, the figure was revised to 250 million tons, which was still a sizable overestimate according to some students of the problem. The error in 1958 was only a particularly notorious example of the possibly consistent inaccuracy exhibited by food grain production estimates during the first years of the First Five-Year Plan. Other examples of exaggerated reporting to which inexperience and lack of training on the part of the reporting agents contributed could be found in statistics of industrial production during the Great Leap, for instance, in the production of coal and steel.

Changes in definitions and concepts used in the statistical reports which are inevitable in a developing reporting system may have been responsible for some of the inaccurate reports. Such a development was probably involved in 1956 with respect to the definition of "unit area yield" and the method of estimating total output based on yield. The use of imprecise categories in report forms which lend themselves to diverse interpretations has of course the effect of compounding the confusion.

The preceding discussion has indicated how errors may be made involuntarily as a result of the incompetence of the reporting agents and the circumstances that add to their confusion. In addition, there is the possibility of collusion between the agents collecting statistics and their sources of data. Refugees from Mainland China have mentioned the practice of suppressing reports of deaths in order for the families of the deceased to receive larger food rations. Such practices would affect the size of the registered population especially in years of food shortage, such as 1960–62. On the other hand, some Western demographers have argued that the 1963 Chinese census contained underreporting.

Another source of inaccuracy and confusion, especially during the period before the development of relatively complete statistical systems by the State Bureau of Statistics, consists of the existence of reports on generally the same economic activities but using different concepts and dissimilar categories. Such duplication and conflict occur when more than one government agency is involved in reporting on the same set of facts, a practice which tends to be aggravated by the continual shifts of jurisdiction over different industries, the multiplication of the industrial ministries, and frequent mergers of agencies which have characterized the evolving administrative structure of the Communist government.

To the above we must add inherent bias as a source of inaccuracy. Beginning in the latter part of the First Five-Year Plan, overvaluation of new products at prices reflecting pilot costs has probably been a source of overestimate of production in the industrial sector.

Biased reporting is virtually inevitable when politics "takes command" as it did during the Great Leap. Under this slogan, statistical reports were to serve the express purpose of fanning enthusiasm and exhorting the population to greater productive effort. In practice, this meant that samples with an upward bias were often reported without qualification, which partly accounted for the very high productivity data recorded. The inaccuracy of statistics during 1958–60 attributable to this factor may be regarded, however, as an extreme case of a general predilection toward overoptimistic reports because of the assignment of production targets and work quotas to individual enterprises and work units and their employment in measuring performance. The pressure to report good results is equaled only by that of accepting them as accurate.

An entirely different category of inadequate information for planning purposes lies in the time lag between the availability of new data and their effective communication to the planners. In the first place, the collection and transmission of data may be delayed by the lack of automatic data processing equipment and the successive administrative levels at which relevant data must first be assembled. Even when prime data are transmitted both directly to the Bureau of Statistics and simultaneously to the successive higher levels of government under a "double tracking system," errors and discrepancies cannot be entirely avoided.

Although theoretically the national economic plan and the state budget both begin operating from the first of the year, the date of their final adoption has varied a great deal in the past. In 1953 and 1958, the two documents were finally approved in February; in 1956 and 1960, the date shifted to March-April; in 1954 and 1957, it was not until midyear before these basic plans were adopted. The delays in the formulation of the final national economic plan in the years mentioned may have been partly due to uncertainty about the data base. Clearly, operation during the months before the adoption of the plan could not be based on comprehensive planning and sectoral balance using final returns and targets.

According to a recent review of the subject, while computers have been employed in solving specific technological and economic problems —within the latter category, particularly in linear programming problems of transportation and location—statistics and other aspects of information, organization, and retrieval have apparently not received much attention in the development of computer use. Partly, the short time available between the date when data required for economic planning can become available and the date when the plan embodying the same information must begin to be implemented may be a result of the production process rather than inefficiency in data processing. In particular, information on the main fall harvest may be unavailable to the planners before plans for sowing and other preparations for the next planting must be firmly drawn up. In double rice crop areas, the second crop is harvested in October–November, while the early rice crop has to be planted in February–March of the following year. Thus, plans for the early rice planting may have to be made without full information on the size of the preceding rice crop. Where the production process is a continuous one, the problem is, of course, inherent. But because of the important role of agricultural production both in export and in the manufacture of consumer products and the scale problem in agricultural reporting, this shortcoming is perhaps more serious that it is in other economic sectors. Given this situation, the planners must resort to estimates rather than verified results of the preceding period. We are therefore again confonted with the questions of reliability of estimates and of possibly inherent biases.

A Summary

To recapitulate, during the period of the First Five-Year Plan, Chinese planners were probably without comprehensive nonagricultural data; such agricultural and nonagricultural data that were available were probably inaccurate, with an upward bias in the rate of growth of grain production, a possible underestimate of inventory for the earlier years, and an upward bias in industrial production and its rate of growth. For the first three years of the Second Five-Year Plan, statistical data available to the planners suffered especially from inaccurate reporting; political bias, deterioration in the statistical reporting system, and dilution of trained reporting staff as a result of an explosion of the volume of work led to gross exaggerations. For the entire period of eight years (1953–60) the reporting system suffered from lack of means for the rapid and accurate processing and organization of statistical and other information. Thus all the data that might have been available could not be used by the planners in good time. One must therefore conclude that during the years when planning was ostensibly carried out on a relatively systematic basis, the Chinese planners were actually without any firm data base for realistic planning. The data available to them had a distinct tendency to induce unwarranted optimism and to exaggerate the degree of success.

III. THE INDICATED BEHAVIOR OF CHINESE PLANNERS

Pattern of Response to Plan Overfulfillment or Underfulfillment

The preceding discussion has dwelt upon some of the reasons why plans are often unrealistic and why actual development may be erroneously reported and/or interpreted. We turn now to the question of how Chinese planners react to their own perception of success or failure in the implementation of plans apart from the correctness of the perception per se. Inasmuch as the observable behavior of Chinese planners has been limited to a relatively small number of years and information available is limited, the following discussion must be viewed as highly tentative. However, it is possible to detect certain indications of behavior which reflect the ideological and political background and outlook of Communist Chinese planners and which may, therefore, be regarded as more than random occurrences.

First, if performance appears lagging as a given plan is being carried out, a speedup is likely in the latter part of the same plan period. This means that speedups are probable in the second half of the year during an annual plan and in the last years of a five-year plan. Both observations appeared to be true during 1953–57.

Second, the above-mentioned pattern is reinforced by impatience on the part of the Communist Chinese leaders and their constant desire to overfulfill plans.

Third, during a given plan period, if the plan is believed to be overfulfilled, the planned rate of growth for the next period is likely to be set at a higher level than that of the present period. A higher planned rate is likely to accompany a greater degree of overfulfillment, and vice versa. During the First Five-Year Plan, the relationship between the planned and the realized rates of growth in modern industry followed this pattern with the exception of 1955–56. The realized rate of growth in 1955 was only 1 percent above the planned rate, while the planned rate of growth in 1956 was 21 percent higher than that of 1955.

It is possible for the first type of behavior to dominate the third type when the two are in conflict, as it did in 1956. On the other hand, it is conceivable for the third type of behavior to be dominant, in which case poor performance would lead to a lower planned rate in the following period, or even to a downward revision of the plan during the same period. In general, because of the inherent desire to speed up and to fulfill planned targets, one would expect dominance of the third type of behavior (when it points to a slowdown or retrenchment) over the first to be exceptional. Exceptions are afforded either when confidence has already been severely shaken or when the original optimistic perception is shown to be wrong. The latter seems to have been the case in 1959.

During the first half of 1959, for example, the fulfillment of production plans lagged behind in the industrial sector. Of 33 principal categories of industrial products, 19 saw the fulfillment of upward of 40 percent of the annual plan while, in the remaining 14, less than 40 percent fulfillment was reported. These figures contrasted significantly with the usual semiannual plan fulfillment of 47 to 48 percent in the value of industrial output during the first six months of an annual plan. As reported in August, 1959, by Chou En-lai, a downward revision of the annual targets for the year was ordered although the revised targets were still generally higher than the perceived realized levels of the preceding year. The lagging plan fulfillment during this period was a direct reflection of the unrealistic targets originally set for the year, while the initial setting of such high targets was a response on the part of the planners to the unusually large upsurge of production and plan overfulfillment reported, though not actually realized, in 1958. Chou explained the discrepancy between the initial 1959 plan and reality in the following terms:

> There were certain shortcomings and errors made in the course of drawing up and implementing the 1959 national economic plan and during the upsurge of the Great Leap Forward; the main ones were that production targets were set rather too high, the projected scale of capital construction was bigger than it should be, and the increase in the numbers of workers and staff a bit excessive. Our departments in charge of planning and economic affairs are not yet adept at the work of coordination and maintaining a balance under the conditions of a big leap forward in the national economic plan.

If comparison is made between the planned rates of growth in the First and Second Five-Year Plans, the sharp rise of expectations in 1958 was again illustrative of the third type of behavior.

Fourth, when an underfulfillment of plans is perceived, the planners are likely to be reluctant to take immediate cognizance of the fact for political as well as ideological reasons. Politically, the Communist leadership, like all totalitarian regimes, still clings to infallibility. Ideologically, it is difficult for such leaders to be persuaded that their dialectics could contain basic errors. Downward revisions of plans are not precluded as a result, but they are likely to be delayed. The net result, therefore, is likely to be overcompensation when adjustments are finally made while earlier adjustments might have brought about more moderate changes. This case was well illustrated by the directive in late 1961 ordering the curtailment of investment and other activities.

Adjustment to Bottlenecks

If we ignore all cases of deliberate disregard of the plan and of incompetent planning, we are left with discrepancies between actual performance and planned development of the economy which should be explained by (1) the effort to live up to the plan or to overfulfill it and (2) exogenous shocks suffered by the economic system. Mention has been made earlier of the common practice to speed up production and other activities in the second half of the plan period in order to fulfill or overfulfill the plan because of lagging performance during the first half, as well as the tendency to speed up the planned rate of progress when plan fulfillment or overfulfillment is perceived, rightly or wrongly. Both developments of this nature and exogenous shocks administered to the system, such as a major flood or drought or the sudden withdrawal of Soviet specialists and blueprints from China in mid-1960, would create bottlenecks in various sectors of the economy. The question then boils down to the effect of those measures which the planners are likely to take in order to resolve the immediate bottlenecks. Is it possible for overfulfillment of the plan in one sector to lead to underfulfillment in another? Could the net effect be a reduction of total output or at least a slowing down of the rate of growth?

The first and almost instinctive reaction to any shortage which may threaten plan fulfillment or overfulfillment, whatever may be its cause, is to call for economy and a reduction of the inputs required per unit of output. The admonition to increase unit productivity and lower cost can, however, lead to undesirable effects on the production of goods hitherto unaffected because of the noninclusiveness of the cost concept employed and the tendency to use more of those inputs which are not included in the cost. This is notably the case in regard to the employment of fixed capital. Since the degree of plan fulfillment is measured by certain indicators, such as the physical output quota, the management of an enterprise, when hard pressed, is liable to concentrate on one index of success at the expense of another. Underlying such behavior are both the very human tendency to pursue symbols of success rather than its substance, a tendency which is particularly fostered in any large organization or bureaucracy, and the Communist ideology which discourages the use of any meaningful criterion for the economic allocation of investment. The latter doctrinaire attitude is reflected in the expression, often employed in Communist Chinese circles, to the effect that "even if the meat in a stew should disintegrate (through overcooking) it would stay in the pot," by which is meant that no loss would be incurred in production, whatever may be its apparent cost, because in the absence of the exploiting class, all the fruit of labor now belongs to the people. What the people do not at first receive in one form, they will receive eventually in another.

Some economists in Communist China are well aware of the fallacy of this Chinese version of the "goulash principle," as may be seen in a very outspoken article by Sun Yeh-fang, former Director of the Economic Research Institute of the Academy of Sciences, who questioned the paradoxical attitude of not paying heed to the effectiveness of using capital, the embodiment of their own blood and sweat, by the working people, although the unenlightened capitalists used to care for such matters a great deal. But many leaders and cadres of the Yenan tradition do not seem to be able to appreciate such ideas of economic revisionism.

In order to expand production or to alleviate a severe shortage, a frequently employed technique is to make the objective the central theme of a mass movement, which will generate its own momentum, and, in so doing, often create new shortages in other sectors of the economy. The mass approach which was exemplified in Communist China's notorious drive for steel and grain during the Great Leap, as well as in many other production campaigns, is derived from two traditions: that of making crash efforts in military combat during the period of the revolutionary war before 1949 and that of relying on the power and "wisdom" of the masses which Mao Tse-tung has learned to manage so well in political struggles of the past.

Still other measures of adjustment in the face of specific bottlenecks have been (1) withdrawal from inventory, which was said to have been resorted to widely early in 1956, and (2) reallocation of the scarce resources at the expense of categories of demand that enjoy lower priorities, a practice which has been frequently employed.

Withdrawal from stock held in reserve when the original stock is not large has the effect of increasing the vulnerability of future production to new bottlenecks. This effect was well recognized in discussion in China. During 1955–56 and again during 1959, power, transport, and material shortages were met by allotting less to industries of lesser importance. Among the latter were included the light industries and direct demand for consumption. In short, the consumer goods industries and even light industries which do not necessarily serve the consumers may be given short shrift. Not only could such adjustments lead to a direct decline of production in sectors previously not affected by the events which have necessitated the adjustments, but the lower priority given to the consumer may have far-reaching deleterious effects on labor productivity. Should there be a general decline of labor productivity, or even a decline in some sector(s) supplies from which are used by the majority of other sectors, a decline in total output—not just one in the growth rate—could very well occur. Such was probably the case when serious bottlenecks arose in 1959–60 about the time of the upper turning point which marked the end of the Great Leap and the beginning of the Great Depression of the Communist period.

Still another course of adjustment is the employment of substitutes for products or inputs that are in short supply. The extent to which this measure can be effectively adopted depends upon the availability of unemployed resources at the time and the degree of substitutability between inputs, whether unemployed or employed, and their intersectoral transferability. Until 1956, considerable leeway in unemployed labor probably existed although the reserve capacity of other unemployed factors, especially industrial equipment, was very limited. By the time the First Five-Year Plan ended, Chinese production was approaching the boundary set by available resources, and further growth would have to rely upon new investments, expansion of the labor force, and improvements in technology. In fact, this was probably one of the principal reasons for the introduction of the small industry movement and the reorganization of labor in the communes as a part of the Great Leap program.

The unlimited substitutability of certain inputs for others that are in short supply cannot be readily assumed, especially where specialized equipment and industrial raw materials used in certain production processes are concerned. The very limited substitutability of unskilled labor, made available in the communes, for capital equipment was aptly demonstrated by the failure of the backyard furnace movement, which has been given recognition by the discontinuation of the drive and emphasis on quality and technological innovation during the 1960's. It is quite possible, therefore, that the level of productive investment in Communist China may not be determined by the availability of savings or the extent to which private consumption can be curtailed. Rather, it may be subject to a ceiling imposed by the availability of imported equipment which, in the absence of Western credit, now that large Soviet credit is unlikely, is a function of the capacity to export. The latter constraint may be much more stringent than the former, and as long as this condition is unchanged, adjustments to sectoral shortages by substitution would be strictly limited. The economists may find here a classical case in which inflexibility in factor supply becomes a serious obstacle to steady growth.

IV. PLANNING AND THE CHINESE DEVELOPMENTAL MODEL

From the preceding discussion it appears that comprehensive economic planning of the type described in theory at the beginning of this paper did not exist during the first three to four years of the First Five-Year Plan. The requisite data for planning were not fully available, nor was the apparatus of planning and plan implementation fully operative. However, real growth was registered during this period, although the perceived rate of growth was exaggerated. Sectoral shortages also developed during this period, but they were met without too great difficulty because of the existence of unemployed labor and accumulated stocks. This state of under-full-employment came to an end by the time the First Five-Year Plan had about run its full course. The period of growth coincided with one in which there was no comprehensive economic planning.

However, partly because of the exaggerated growth under the First Five-Year Plan as perceived by the planners, an increase in the planned rate of growth was ordered at a time when the boundary of production possibility had just been reached. These circumstances resulted in serious discrepancies between the planned growth of the economy and its actual performance, and in the face of drastic adjustments, the Chinese planning model for balanced and rapid growth proved to be unequal to the test. Thus, we are brought to the perhaps unexpected conclusion that Communist China does not really have any past experience in successful development under a *comprehensive* national economic plan which she can bring to bear upon the formulation and implementation of the Third Five-Year Plan that officially began in 1966. The previous two five-year plans do not offer her a reliable model that she can safely repeat. This is not to say that there has not been any planning experience or that errors of the past could not be avoided if the behavior of the planners and, even more important, of the political leaders, were modified. Nor does it mean that Communist China cannot attain certain high priority goals, such as the development of nuclear weapons.

On the basis of the behavioral pattern we have drawn, together with some of the technical relationships which appear to prevail at this stage of Chinese economic development, it is possible to describe the Chinese economic model in terms of a few propositions:

Proposition 1. Communist China's leadership is anxious to see the Chinese economy develop and, in particular, industrialize as rapidly as possible. For this reason they have been, and continue to be, prepared to depress consumption in order to maximize the rate of investment. During the period of economic expansion up to 1960, there was a tendency to accelerate the investment rate. In the future, one should expect the rate of investment to remain at a high level, so that the minimum level of consumption deemed necessary by the leaders will constitute a theoretical upper bound to the planned rate of investment.

Proposition 2. Past experience shows, however, that apart from certain types of labor-intensive investments, such as water conservation work, building of unpaved roads, etc., productive investment may be effectively limited by the supply of machines and, in particular, by the availability of imported materials and equipment for which there is no domestic substitute. Thus, for some time to come, at least a portion of the total investment that can contribute effectively to economic growth may be subjected to a far more stringent constraint than the availability of savings.

Proposition 3. The limit imposed on certain investments by the available supply of factors is but a reflection of the general lack of flexibility in factor supply and the limited maneuverability of the Chinese economy to meet sectoral shortages through substitution. Past experience again shows that labor is not universally useful as a substitute for capital and that even when it can act as a substitute, serious differences in product quality may develop. Consequently, it is essential for the Chinese economy to maintain a reasonable input-output balance between sectors if steady growth is desired.

Proposition 4. The past behavior of Chinese planners and managers suggests that sectoral imbalance is likely to emerge as a result of exhortations to overfulfill plans and the limited outlook of the managers in their eagerness to fulfill and exceed certain output targets. This threat to balanced growth is enhanced if the planners deem the record of their planning in the immediate past to be successful because of the impatience inherent in their behavior. The same threat may also be heightened by exogenous shocks administered to the system. In the past, such shocks have originated essentially, if not solely, from the political policies and ideological attitudes of the Communist leadership. The political origin of the Sino-Soviet dispute is a case in point.

Proposition 5. While Chinese planners are conscious of the need to maintain a minimum living standard and to see per capita consumption improve, whenever sectoral shortages occur resources are likely to be diverted from the production of consumer goods. The puritanical and austere modes of life which the Communist leaders have advocated as appropriate to the continuing revolution have contributed to a general reluctance to employ material incentives in lieu of ideological exhortations.

Proposition 6. Because of the relatively low level of per capita consumption in existence, labor productivity is likely to be adversely affected if the supply of consumer goods is sharply curtailed as a result of adjustments to meet sectoral shortages. This occurred toward the end of the Great Leap and, though probably to a much lesser degree, in 1956.

Proposition 7. In the past, Communist China's leaders have frequently employed mass organizations and political campaigns involving very large numbers of persons in attempts to complete certain tasks. This method, in which the leaders have placed great faith as a result of their personal political experience and Communist ideology, has often led to secondary economic disruptions when it is employed to relieve sectoral shortages, such as the use of harvest workers for flood control or steel and fertilizer production.

Proposition 8. Because of inaccurate statistical reporting, delays in communication, and reluctance to admit failure, an effective downward adjustment of the planned rate of growth to restore imbalance may be delayed. Consequently, as was the case in 1961–1962, the downward adjustment may result in overcompensation, converting a retrenchment to a decline.

Proposition 9. Since 1958, and especially since the withdrawal of Soviet specialists in 1960, the inflexibility of the economy with respect to specific factor supplies has become a major concern of Communist China's leaders. Its solution constitutes a primary objective of China's present-day applied research in science and engineering under the direction of the Scientific and Technological Commission. The successful nuclear detonations have demonstrated Communist China's independent technical capability in a rather limited sphere. Increased flexibility in factor supply and intersectoral substitutability could result from an uninterrupted major scientific effort on a broader scale.

The above model of the Chinese economy is one in which renewed expansion under the Third Five-Year Plan could well lead to an initial period of expansion followed by a downturn. However, even if the cyclical pattern repeats itself, it is entirely possible that the fluctuations would be "damped" if statistical reporting is improved, the response time shortened, and, above all, the behavior of the planners restrained. The last point leads to the following questions:

First, will the Chinese planners be less impatient? Perhaps a more appropriate question would be whether the Communist political leaders can afford to be more patient. Second, is it doctrinally possible for Communist China's leaders to permit material incentives to play a greater role and to continue to give consumption a higher place in their scale of priorities beyond the recovery period of 1962–65? Third, will Communist China maintain an educational and scientific policy that would provide the necessary professional manpower to put the country on a technologically independent basis and to give the economy more flexibility through technical innovation? Lastly, will the Communist leaders pursue domestic and foreign policies that would avoid giving serious shocks to the smooth operation of the economic system?

At this writing, Communist China is in a political flux. The Red Guards movement and internal purges which are carried on under the euphemistic banner of "cultural revolution" and the questionable hold of Mao Tse-tung and his potential successors on the country would seem to indicate certain trends, which, if continued, are more likely to repeat the unhappy experience of the past than to chart out a course of steadier growth under a realistic national economic plan. Some would say that the answers to all four questions raised in the preceding paragraph have already been given in the negative. Thus far, however, the outward political phenomenon of great instability could well turn out to be a political struggle from which a new leadership would emerge. It would be too early to postulate the behavior of the new leaders, not only in their capacity as the immediate replacements of Mao, but in the more distant post-Mao period, until their identities and policies can be established beyond a doubt.

However, should the Chinese planners learn their lessons well and balanced growth follow, the national economic plan as we have described would still not guarantee that the scale of priorities adopted will reflect in any sense the true preferences of the population. For this to happen the plan would have to be predicated upon an effective and meaningful pricing system as the Soviet Union has virtually admitted. Such a development is ruled out for the time being in Communist China inasmuch as it is considered utterly "revisionist."

PART IV

Selected Aspects of Economic Systems

Rather than analyzing or illustrating particular economic systems, as in Parts II and III respectively, the selections that follow compare different economic systems from several standpoints. The first article compares enterprise management in the United States and Soviet economies. The following three selections are concerned with the crucial question of the best economic system for the development of an underdeveloped country. The last two articles investigate the proposition that different economic systems are "converging," that is, becoming more alike.

Management

In every economic system, enterprise management has important functions of planning, coordination, administration, control, and supervision. However, the scope and character of these functions—management's responsibilities and powers—vary with the nature of the economic system.

In a capitalist market economy, management is free to adjust both outputs and inputs in pursuit of profits. In Lange's theoretical model of market socialism, managers are instructed to choose input combinations and output levels which lead to the most economical production of the socially optimal output, regardless of whether profits or losses result. In Yugoslav market socialism, however, enterprises follow the capitalist approach of adjusting outputs and inputs in pursuit of profit. In contrast, in a centrally administered economy, management's task is to fulfill the detailed plan fixed for the enterprise by the central authorities. Managers are expected to produce the scheduled output with the authorized inputs. The profit resulting from the sale of output is likely to be of subordinate importance. Thus, both management's assignment and its freedom to accomplish it vary with the economic system in which it operates. At the same time, it is interesting to note that essentially the same incentives—job security, promotion, and, especially, salary and bonuses—motivate management in all of these economic systems.

The following selection, comparing managerial incentives and decision making in the U.S. and Soviet economies, illustrates these points.

20. MANAGERIAL INCENTIVES AND DECISION MAKING: A COMPARISON OF THE UNITED STATES AND THE SOVIET UNION*

Joseph S. Berliner

Berliner points out the major differences and similarities between the U.S. and Soviet economies in managerial incentives and decision making. Since American managers operate in a much different economic environment, their problems and therefore their practices differ from those of Soviet managers. But in those aspects of economic life in which the two economies are somewhat alike, American and Soviet managers behave in much the same way.

The assignments, powers, and problems of enterprise managers differ notably in the two economies. In the U.S. firm, profit is the main criterion of managerial performance. The Soviet manager, on the other hand, is expected to achieve (or surpass) a number of plan targets which are sometimes mutually exclusive. In the sellers' market of the Soviet economy, managers are usually more concerned with the acquisition of inputs than with the disposition of output. The opposite is true in the U.S. economy, where the biggest problem of management under normal conditions is marketing, rather than purchasing. Thus, the energy spent by the Soviet

* Reprinted, with permission, from *Comparisons of the United States and Soviet Economies* (Papers Submitted by Panelists Appearing before the Subcommittee on Economic Statistics, Joint Economic Committee, 86th Cong., 1st sess.) (Washington, D.C.: U.S. Government Printing Office, 1959), Part I, pp. 349–76. Joseph S. Berliner is Professor of Economics at Brandeis University.

firm on obtaining materials is devoted by the American firm to selling and advertising.

At the same time, the two economies rely on essentially similar incentives to motivate managers toward whatever is defined as good performance. In both economies there are conflicts of interest between the owners of the enterprise and the hired professional managers who run it. And in both countries managers may engage in various illegal or evasive practices when they believe their interests conflict with existing laws and regulations.

THE REWARDS in income and prestige in the United States and Soviet economies are such that a larger proportion of the best young people in the U.S.S.R. turn to careers in heavy industry, science, and higher education, whereas in the United States a larger proportion of the best talent flows into such fields as heavy or light (consumer goods) industry, finance, commerce and trade, law, medicine, etc. Higher education, particularly technical, is more of a prerequisite for the attainment of a top business career in the Soviet Union than in the United States.

The principal managerial incentive in Soviet industry is the bonus paid for overfulfillment of plan targets. The incentive system is successful in the sense that it elicits a high level of managerial effort and performance. But it has the unintended consequence of causing managers to engage in a wide variety of practices that are contrary to the interests of the state. Managers systematically conceal their true production capacity from the planners, produce unplanned types of products, and falsify the volume and quality of production. In the procurement of materials and supplies they tend to order larger quantities than they need, hoard scarce materials, and employ unauthorized special agents who use influence and gifts to ease management's procurement problems. The incentive system causes managers to shy away from innovations that upset the smooth working of the firm.

Since American managers operate in a different economic environment, their problems and therefore their practices differ from those of Soviet managers. But in those aspects of economic life in which the U.S. economy approximates the operating conditions of the Soviet economy, American managers develop forms of behavior similar to those of Soviet managers. The separation of management and ownership characteristic of the modern corporation leads to conflicts of interest between managers and stockholder-owners, and management's pursuit of its own interest leads to activities similar to those of the Soviet manager striving to defend his interests against those of the owner-state. The spread of legislation constricting the freedom of operation of the American firm leads to the evasion of laws and regulations characteristic of the Soviet economy, though on a larger scale there. Finally, under wartime conditions the burgeoning of government controls and the dominant role of the government as customer alters the operating conditions of the U.S. economy in such ways that it closely approximates some of the normal operating conditions of the Soviet economy. The change is accompanied by black-market operations, hoarding, quality deterioration, and the use of influence, practices which are normal in the peacetime Soviet economy.

MANAGERIAL INCENTIVES AND RECRUITMENT

The most important decision a manager has to make is made before he ever becomes a manager; namely, the decision to prepare for a managerial career. The factors influencing this decision are of vital importance for our industrial society. Imagine the consequences if no one aspired to become a manager, or if young people chose management only as a last resort, or if other careers were so attractive that management got only the last pickings of each year's crop of youngsters. It might therefore be appropriate to begin with some reflections on the incentives that the United States and the U.S.S.R. offer their young people to choose a managerial career rather than some other.

The factors motivating young people to choose one or another occupation are probably not vastly different in the two countries. Family tradition is often decisive; many a youngster chooses a career simply because he wishes to be like his father (or mother). Special talents such as those of the artist, or early conceived deep interests, like the boy who must be a scientist, account for the career choices of some others. But most teenagers have no clear idea of what they would like to be. It is with respect to these youths that it is most interesting to speculate upon the incentive-pulls that the two systems offer for the choice of one career or another.

Education and Career Choice

The role of higher education in career choice is different in the two nations. Higher education is very much more of a prerequisite for the prestigeful and high income occupations in the U.S.S.R. than in the United States. To be sure, the person with a high school education or less has an increasingly difficult time entering the managerial ladder of the large American corporation. But in such fields as trade, commerce, construction and in small business in general, the opportunities are still vast for a financially successful career. College, and education in general, is not of decisive importance. And the brute fact is that a college diploma can always be obtained somewhere in the United States, with very little effort or ability, by just about anyone who can pay the tuition and write a semiliterate paragraph. Those who don't aspire to a managerial position or who fail to make the grade can, as workingmen, nevertheless enjoy a standard of living that is the envy of the world. The point is that the young American who is not inclined toward academic work need not feel that he is out of the competition for our society's best rewards.

This is not true in the U.S.S.R. A number of conversations with young Soviet people have convinced me that to be a "worker" is something devoutly to be shunned by most young people who have reached the high school level. There are at least two reasons for this attitude, which seems so anomalous in a "worker's state." The first is the enormously high prestige that Russian (and European) culture has always placed upon the "intelligent," the learned man, the man who works with his mind instead of his hands. The Soviet regime has striven hard to make manual labor respectable, and it undoubtedly has succeeded in endowing the worker with a social position relatively much higher than before the revolution. But the young person who has reached the educational level at which he can choose between being a worker or an "intelligent" would, other things being equal, choose the latter without question.

Other things are not equal, however. In particular, the income possibilities of a worker are far smaller than those of a college graduate, and this is the second reason for the desperate, and sometimes pathetic, drive for a higher education. Of course, a person must have reached the high school level before he can even begin to think about choosing between the career of a worker or an "intelligent." The steady annual expansion in the high school population has had the effect of presenting ever-increasing numbers of young people with the choice, and few of them would freely choose to be workers. If the expansion of the school population had continued, giving more and more young people the opportunity to avoid being workers, it would have raised serious problems for the recruitment of the labor force. The radical reform of the educational system by Khrushchev was undoubtedly motivated, in part, by the wish to avoid that problem.

Thus, the undesirability of a career as a worker has intensified the desire for higher education. Add to this the fact that there is no private enterprise, no small business in which a man could pull himself out of a worker's status and reach a position of prestige and income comparable to the self-made American businessman. I do not wish to state that the door is completely closed. By dint of hard work, ability, and certain other qualities, a Soviet citizen without the college diploma can from time to time rise to an important position in some economic hierarchy. But his chances are about as good as those of an equivalent person in a progressive American corporation. And the young person evaluating the importance of higher education understands this.

Finally, the Russian teenager who decides he has to get a college diploma has very few easy ways out. He can't buy his way into college, as the American student can if he has the money. There are no private colleges that can set whatever standards they wish. To be sure there are instances of bribery or influence, but they are certainly the exception. If the Soviet student wants a college diploma very badly, he has to work hard to gain admission and to be graduated. The very intensity of the drive for education, and the competition of many applicants for the limited number of admissions, permits the high schools and colleges to maintain high standards of performance. Moreover the colleges are financially independent of student tuitions: not only are there no tuitions but most of the students earn stipends. The consequence is that the typical Soviet student works harder and has to meet higher standards of performance than the typical American student. The standards are different in the two countries, of course, because of differences in the philosophy of education. But there is no doubt that study is a much more serious business for the young Soviet student than for the American.

One final note on education and incentives. The quality of the managerial (and technical) manpower of a nation depends on the proportion of the population comprising the pool from which the managers are drawn. That is, if half the population were for some reason excluded from the pool, the quality of the managers would be lower than if the whole population comprised the pool. Both nations suffer in this respect from the fact that rural educational facilities are poorer than urban, which reduces the pool of the potential college group. Since the Soviet rural population is larger percentagewise than that of the United States, and since their rural educational facilities are probably relatively worse than ours, they suffer more than we from this loss. But there are other ways in which our pool is curtailed more than the Soviet. First is the fact that the private cost of education keeps a substantial portion of our talented young people in the lower income groups out of college. I admit that this fact puzzles me. With our network of free state universities and with a fairly abundant scholarship program, I don't fully understand why any competent student who really desired it could not get a college education. It is my impression, however, that systematic studies generally show that we are losing an unfortunate number of young people to higher education for financial reasons. If this is so, we are worse off than the Soviets in this respect, for their education is absolutely free, and most students of any merit earn stipends besides. Lower income young Soviet people may nevertheless be unable to go off to college if the family needs their earnings. A young Soviet woman told me, in reply to my question, that this was why she never went on to college. She is not a very good illustration of my point, however, for she went on to say that she really wasn't very smart anyhow.

The second group that is largely lost from America's pool of potential managerial manpower is the Negro and some other racial minorities. It may well be that the proportion of college graduates among some of the

Soviet national minorities is smaller than for the Slavic nationalities; I have seen no data on this. But I would doubt that their loss from racial discrimination is as large as ours.

The third and largest group lost from our pool comprises exactly half our population—the female half. Sex discrimination certainly exists in the Soviet economy, probably more in management than in science and technology. But undoubtedly the female population enlarges the pool of technical and managerial manpower much more in the U.S.S.R. than in the United States. The difference in the role of women in the two countries must, I think, enter into the balance I am trying to strike, but it is not a subject on which I would recommend that your committee consider writing corrective legislation. For one thing it is not perfectly clear which way sex discrimination works in the United States. Women discriminate against working about as much as jobs discriminate against women.

Let me summarize briefly this discussion of the relationship of education to career choice. Education, and particularly higher education, is more important in the U.S.S.R. than in the United States as the gateway to a prestigeful and highly remunerative career. Competition is keener for higher education, the cost of education to the individual is less, and the standards of admission and performance are higher in the U.S.S.R. Both nations lose part of the potential pool of managerial talent, the U.S.S.R. because of its large rural population, the United States because of financial burdens and racial and sex discrimination.

Competition among Careers

How does a managerial career compare with the attractiveness of other careers in the two nations? The young American not dedicated to some particular field, but motivated by a roughly equal desire for prestige and money, might select some field such as law, medicine, business, or engineering. He would decidedly not go into education or science. An equivalent young Soviet person would make a somewhat different choice. He would certainly not select law, which has been assigned a most humble role in Soviet society. Nor would he select medicine, for while the prestige is high, the income is low. On the other hand, higher education or science would be an excellent choice. The very title of "Professor" or "Scientific worker" would assure him one of the highest places of honor in the society. And an outstanding career in either of those fields would assure him an income ranking in the upper 10 percent or perhaps even 5 percent (data are hard to come by) of the population. The difference in the economic and social position of the scientist and teacher in the two countries is of fundamental importance in the matter of career recruitment.

The American who decides to choose a career in the business world has a much wider range of choice than his Soviet counterpart. A great variety of fields offer roughly equivalent rewards in prestige and incomes: advertising, accounting, finance, commerce, trade, sales, light manufacturing, heavy industry. Of all these fields, it is only the latter that would exert a great pull on the young Soviet person. For 40 years the government and party have hammered home the central role of heavy industry, children are instilled with an admiration of technology, and heavy industry has been endowed with an aura of glamour that exceeds even our American fascination with technology. The ideological cards are stacked, in varying degree, against all other branches of the economy. In keeping with the ideology, the prestige and income possibilities in heavy industry are decidedly greater than in the other branches.

Not only will the student be attracted to heavy industry, but he is likely to choose engineering as his path of entry into whatever branch of heavy industry he selects. He would be attracted to engineering for the educational reasons discussed above. Engineering is, moreover, the most direct line of approach to a managerial career.

The Soviet engineering graduate will find his first job opportunities rather different from those of his American counterpart. If he is at the top of his class, the best offers will come from the research institutes, with top starting salaries and opportunities for graduate work. The poorer students will find lower paying jobs in industry. In the United States the situation is quite the reverse. The most successful students will be snapped up by recruiters from the large corporations, with the best starting salary offers. Some of the top students will, to be sure, spurn the attractive job offers and go on to further graduate work, but I suspect that many of those who go immediately into graduate work are the men who didn't get the good job offers. To be sure, many of the top American students who join the corporations are put immediately into research and development, but as many of them will be working on new passenger car or dishwasher design as will be working on electronic development and automation technique. The Soviet researcher is more likely to be working on the latter than the former.

The young Soviet engineer who goes into industry starts at the bottom of the managerial ladder, as chief of a production shop, or the design or maintenance departments of the enterprise. As new job opportunities develop, he faces the choice of continuing in direct production or taking one of the staff jobs in the enterprise, such as the planning department. If he stays in production proper, his career path may lead to chief engineer of an enterprise or to one of the higher economic agencies. If he moves into staff work, his career may lead to the directorship of an enterprise or of one of the higher organs. Either career leads to the pinnacle of Soviet management.

The paths that are least likely to lead to top management are finance or sales. I would guess the proportion of top management in the United States who started in such fields as finance and sales is much larger than in the U.S.S.R. There are no "colleges of business administration" in the Soviet

Union. The ambitious youngster who wants to work for the top of the Soviet business world studies engineering, not personnel and marketing.

Summarizing, industry in the United States has to compete with a wide variety of other branches of economic activity for its share of the best potential managerial talent. In the U.S.S.R. the values and the rewards are concentrated in relatively fewer fields, and industry is far more attractive than most others. Science and higher education, which scarcely compete with industry in the United States, are strong competitors of industry in the U.S.S.R. Among the various branches of industry, in the United States the light and consumer goods industries compete very effectively for both managerial and engineering talent. In the U.S.S.R. light and consumer goods industries are much less attractive than heavy industry. And finally the nature of industrial recruitment is such that technical education is much more important as part of the training of a would-be manager in the U.S.S.R. than in the United States.

My conclusion is that heavy industry, science and higher education attract, by and large, a better and more competent crop of young people in the U.S.S.R. than in the United States. Moreover, the competition for education is keener in the U.S.S.R., so that they get a more rigorously trained (trained in different ways, to be sure) corps of managerial, engineering, scientific and university personnel. On the other hand, such branches of the economy as sales, advertising, finance, trade and commerce, light industry, and law attract a much more competent group of people in the United States than in the U.S.S.R. Most of the outstanding people in these fields in the United States would, if they were Soviet citizens, have enjoyed successful careers in heavy industry, science, technology, or higher education. There is, after all, nothing startling in this conclusion. It is but another way of saying that each society gets what it pays for.

MANAGERIAL INCENTIVES AND DECISION MAKING

Material Incentives

The incentives that attract people into management are not necessarily the same incentives that motivate managers to do their jobs and do them well. What are the goals of the manager? What are the considerations that impel him to make one decision rather than the other?

The moving force of our economic system is the pursuit of private gain. The worker chooses the higher paying job, the businessman accepts the more profitable contract, the investor buys the higher interest security. The usual exceptions must of course be made; the laws must be obeyed, public opinion may sometimes require that one decision be made rather than another, people make wrong decisions, a short-run loss may be accepted for a longer term gain. But by and large—"other things being equal," as the economist likes to say—it is private gain that determines economic decision.

The Soviets have at various times experimented with other forms of incentive, for it did not at first seem quite appropriate that a Socialist economy should stress private gain. But practicality won out over dogma, and private gain has for the last 25 years been the keystone of the managerial incentive system. To be sure, we still find references to various social incentives such as Communist enthusiasm. But we are also reminded that while enthusiasm is well and good, communism, as Lenin used to say, must be built "not directly on enthusiasm but with the aid of enthusiasm born out of the great revolution; [communism must be built] on private interest, on personal incentive, on businesslike accounting." Moreover, the incentive of private gain will be with us for a long time. According to the eminent labor economist E. Manevich, it will not disappear until the day of general overabundance arrives, until the differences between country and city are eliminated, and until the differences between mental and manual labor vanish. We are safe in saying that for the next several decades at least, private gain will be the central economic inventive in both economic systems.

The form that material incentives take is of some importance. For the American businessman it is clearly profit. If you ask why did he take on this contract rather than that, why did he order this machine rather than that, why did he ship by truck rather than train, the answer would normally be, "because it's cheaper that way," or what comes to the same thing, "because he would make more money that way."

For the private businessman managing his own business, profit is clearly the guide to his actions. But most American business is not managed in this way. The men who actually run the firm are salaried managers, hired by the stockholders' representative body, the board of directors. The profit of the business does not belong to the manager but to the stockholder-owners. The fact is that the private interest of the manager need not necessarily coincide with that of the stockholder. In order to bring the manager's private interest into closer coincidence with that of the owners, most corporations have instituted some kind of bonus system, on the assumption that if the manager has a direct stake in the profit of the enterprise, his decisions are more likely to be those that will earn more profit.

In fashioning an incentive system for its managers, the Soviet government faced a problem similar to that of the American corporation. For all Soviet enterprises are run by salaried managers. If the Soviet manager's income consisted solely of his salary, it was conceivable that his private interest would not coincide at all points with the interest of the government. Accordingly a considerable variety of supplementary bonuses are available to the managerial staff. The bonuses are designed to motivate managers to make those decisions that the government considers to be in its own interest.

* * * *

But incentive for what? This is surely the crucial question. For we can readily imagine an incentive which was extremely successful in motivating action, but action of an undesirable kind. The test of an incentive is therefore not only its motivating power, but the extent to which it leads to the desired kind of decision.

Before proceeding to the relationship of incentives to decision making, let me clarify the sense in which I use the term incentive. By incentive I mean that consideration which explains why one decision was made rather than another. If a young person decides to find employment in the electrical machinery industry rather than in the furniture industry, the difference in basic salaries in the two industries may well have been the decisive consideration. In this case salary is the effective incentive. But once in the job, the salary does not vary according to whether one operating decision is made rather than another. When the manager decides to put one order into production ahead of another, or to substitute one material for another, it is not his salary he is thinking about. It is usually the size of the month's bonus that will depend on the decision taken. It is in this sense that the bonus is the principal incentive in the operational decisions of the Soviet enterprise.

Production Decisions

Two generations ago people debated the question of whether a Socialist economy could possibly work. History removed that question from the agenda. The last generation changed the question to whether the Soviet economy could work at all efficiently. That question has also been answered. These hearings would not otherwise be taking place. My discussion takes for granted that the Soviet economy is reasonably efficient and that the question at issue is how efficient.

There is little doubt that the system of managerial incentives, broadly viewed, has created a corps of managers dedicated to their work and responsive to the production demands made upon them. Like their American counterparts, they are deeply involved in their work, they worry about production quotas, they demand results from their labor force. As hired managers, they are aware that if their performance is not satisfactory, there are always other persons spoiling for a chance at their jobs. I have no way of knowing whether the intensity of managerial life is greater in the U.S.S.R. than in the United States; in both countries there are variations from industry to industry. But there are two reasons why industrial life probably proceeds at a faster tempo in the U.S.S.R. than here. The first is that the absence of free trade unions makes it difficult for workers to resist pressure for intense operation. The second is that industry is under constant exhortation from government and party for ever-increasing levels of production.

But the question as indicated above is not whether management is motivated to work hard. It is rather whether the incentive system motivates them to do what the state wishes them to do; whether, in other words, they get as much mileage out of their effort as they might get.

One of the most interesting conclusions of the study of Soviet managerial incentives is that the bonus system is directly responsible for motivating management to make a variety of decisions contrary to the intent and the interests of the state. The decisions to be described go far back in the history of the Soviet economy and have resisted countless efforts by the government to eliminate them. Most of them have survived the great organizational changes in industrial organization of the past several years. They are clearly deeply rooted in the soil of Soviet economic organization.

First, consider the matter of the reporting of information. In a planned economy it is vital that the central planners have as accurate information as possible about the productive capacity of enterprises. The bonus system, however, acts as a prevailing motivation for managers to understate their real production capacity. The reason is that the most important of the bonuses available to managers depends on the extent to which the production target of the enterprise is overfulfilled. If the manager honestly reports his full production capacity, and if for some reason something goes wrong in the course of the month, then he and his staff will lose that month's bonus. It is safer therefore to report a smaller capacity than really exists, in order that the production target will be kept low enough to allow for emergencies. The Russians call this "insurance" or "security." The consequence is that the planners can never be sure that their plans are based on accurate figures. The government is aware of the problem: "This is fully understandable," writes a Soviet economist, "because the lower the plan, the greater the opportunity to fulfill and overfulfill it. . . ."

Because the higher state agencies cannot trust management's reporting of its productive capacity, various techniques have been fashioned for setting targets high enough to force the firms to operate as close as possible to capacity. One of these techniques is the arbitrary increase of targets over last year's production. As a prominent state planning commission economist put it, "they take as the base magnitude the level of production achieved during the preceding period and raise it by some percentage or other." Sometimes this technique helps flush out the manager's "hidden reserves," but in other cases the arbitrary increase in targets leads to impossibly high tasks. Indeed, the spirit of planning is reflected in the systematic use of high targets as a device for keeping managers working at as fast a tempo as possible. In the past targets have been set so high (deliberately, one suspects) that one third of all enterprises failed to fulfill their annual plans. . . . The intense pace of plant operation has its distinct advantage from the state's point of view: it elicits from management a high level of effort that might not be forthcoming if the plans were set at a more modest level. But the price paid by the state is the manager's effort to defend his enterprise by concealing his full capacity.

When the target has been set, the manager's bonus depends on the success with which he fulfills it. Most of the firm's production does indeed follow the lines laid down in the plan. But when the end of the month rolls around and, as often happens, production is far short of meeting the month's target, then managers turn to a host of time-tested techniques of meeting—or seeming to meet—the targets. In certain types of production, such as metals, the target is expressed in tons; in such cases the manager might order his shops to curtail the production of relatively lightweight products (special and quality metals) and to throw more men and materials into the production of the heavier products. In textile production we read that the practice of setting targets in "running meters" (that is, in measures of length, without regard to width) causes managers to overproduce narrow-width cloth and underproduce broad width. In firms with a considerable variety of products, the production targets are expressed in value units—so many millions of rubles of production. In such cases managers tend to overproduce those products that have high fixed prices (all prices are fixed): they may deliberately use more expensive materials in order to drive up the value of production. These are some of an endless variety of ways in which managers "violate the planned assortment of production"—to use the official expression of disapproval.

How widespread are these practices? We really don't know. From time to time individual managers are publicly excoriated for such practices, and figures are published to show how widely the planned assortment of production had been departed from. But these may well be extreme cases, and it would be unwise to generalize from them. Occasionally, however, the results of special studies are published, and they give us some idea of the magnitude of the problem. The state planning commission recently released the results of a survey of the production practices of 63 enterprises. Of the total production by these enterprises in excess of the plan targets, only 43 percent consisted of the basic products normally produced by them; 26.5 percent consisted of "products not included in the plan when it was originally confirmed," 20 percent consisted of "other production," and 7 percent consisted not of finished products but of an increase in semifabricated parts and goods-in-process. While these data are not precisely in the form in which we would want them, they do provide a good indication of managers' tendency to produce those products that are best from their own enterprises' point of view, rather than those products that the state would most wish to have produced.

Two other consequences of the bonus system (and the pressure of high targets) should be noted. One is the simple falsification of reported production. "Thus, for example," we read in a Soviet article, "if the plan is fulfilled 99 percent, the managerial and engineering personnel receive no bonus. But if the enterprise fulfills the plan 100 percent, they receive bonuses of from 15 to 37 percent of their salary." Quite a lot of money hinges on that last percentage of production, and it is no wonder that management may succumb to the temptation to "fudge" the report a bit in order to earn the bonus. Again, the techniques of covering up for falsely reported production are myriad. To cite only one, production is "borrowed" from next month. That is, production that is expected to occur next month is reported as having been produced this month. If things go well next month, the "borrowed" output is "repaid"; if not the manager may get into trouble.

More serious than falsification, however, is the deterioration of the quality of production. The poor quality of much of Soviet consumer goods production is well known. In other types of production the danger of detection is greater, and quality standards are less readily violated. But the explanation of management's tendency to shave on quality is the same: the high production targets are so often not attainable, and the manager wants to keep his job. Much of the quality shaving is of a kind that is not easily detected: fewer stitches in the garment, fewer screws in the piece, greener lumber in the building, more impurities in the metal. But if the pressure is keen enough, more extreme forms of quality deterioration will be adopted.

Summarizing, the bonus system is an effective device for eliciting a high level of managerial effort, but in the context of excessively high production targets, it induces management to make certain types of decisions that are contrary to the intent of the state. The production of unplanned products, the concealment of production capacity, the falsification of reports and the deterioration of quality are the unintended consequences of the system of managerial incentives.

Procurement Decisions

The high level of production targets is but half the problem facing the Soviet manager. The other half is the perpetual shortage of materials and supplies. In order to get the greatest possible production from the available stocks of materials and supplies, the state employs a variety of devices to minimize the use of materials in production and inventory. Undoubtedly these devices have served to control wasteful use of resources, and they have also helped channel the flow of resources in the direction most desired by the state. But they have been self-defeating to some extent for they have forced managers to make certain kinds of decisions which frustrate the intent of the state.

The core of the matter is that managers simply don't trust the planning system to provide them with the supplies and materials they need in the right quantity and quality, and at the right time. . . . For all important materials the manager must still obtain an allocation order from his home office, which must in turn get the allocation order from the republican or all-union planning commission.

Thus, we still read of the "existing complicated system of obtaining allocation orders, under which every enterprise must submit detailed requisitions to Moscow a long time before the new planning quarter is to begin." Because plans are not always finally set at the time the planning period is to begin, enterprises sometimes start with "advance allocations," that is, temporary allotments of resources designed to keep them operating until the final allocation orders are available. . . . Perhaps even more serious than the complex supply planning system is the large percentage of enterprises that regularly fail to fulfill their plans, or fulfill them by producing the wrong products or substandard products. Since the production of these enterprises constitutes the planned supplies of other enterprises, the supplies of the latter are delayed or simply not available. Perhaps enough has been said to explain why "managers of enterprises did not have confidence in the possibility of getting their materials on time and having them delivered to the factory by the supply depot's trucks."

What does the manager do to make sure he gets his supplies? Just as he "secures" his production plan by attempting to conceal the existence of some production capacity, so he "secures" the flow of supplies in various ways. He overorders, in the hope that if he doesn't get all he ordered, he may at least get as much as he needs. He also orders excessively large amounts of some supplies in order to be able to buy directly from the producer, instead of having to go through the maze of jobbing depots. A survey of 15 Moscow enterprises showed a 10.4 percent overordering of metals for just this reason. Sometimes management's boldest efforts to obtain supplies are unsuccessful: ". . . over 300,000 construction workers undergo work stoppages daily because of the absence of materials at the workplace." In other cases their padded requisitions are accepted and they receive more than they need of some materials. The consequence is the piling up of hoards of supplies of all kinds, one of the most enduring problems of Soviet industrial organization. The government has waged a long-standing war against hoarding. One of the weapons by which it attempts to hold hoarding within bounds is through the use of quotas of working capital; that is, for its annual production program the enterprise is allowed to keep on hand at any one time no more than so many tons of coal, so many board feet of lumber, so many rubles worth of inventory. These quotas must be negotiated between enterprise and government, and the enterprise's interest demands that they be set as high as possible. The mutual attempt at outguessing the other leads to a familiar bureaucratic game: ". . . enterprises try to 'justify' and obtain as large quotas of working capital as possible. The financial agencies, aware of this, strive on the other hand to reduce the quotas of working capital." This kind of planning is hardly calculated to lead to the establishment of the optimal quotas. It is more likely that some quotas will be too large and some too small.

The most interesting of the techniques used by managers to "secure" their supply of materials is the employment of special supply expediters called *tolkachi*, or "pushers." The table of organization does not provide for this occupation, yet so great is the need that firms manage somehow to employ these people. The chief job of the expediter is to make sure that his enterprise gets the materials it needs and when it needs them. Accordingly he spends most of his time on the road, visiting his enterprise's suppliers, handing out little gifts here and there to assure that his orders are well handled, picking up supplies of one kind or another that his firm may be able to use or trade for other goods. Much of their activity is associated with the black market, that is, obtaining materials for which no allocation order has been issued. This may be done either by wrangling an allocation order out of a reluctant government official by one means or another, or persuading an approachable enterprise official to sell him the things he needs without an allocation order.

Some *tolkachi* take up permanent residence in the city in which the chief suppliers are located, and only occasionally return to their home firms for consultations. To keep the record clean, they are carried on the books as "senior buyer," or "supply agent." If they are known to be particularly adept at their jobs, they may be asked by other firms to represent them. Nothing is known of their incomes, but there is no doubt that they earn many times their base pay. And they fully earn it, both because of the vital nature of their work, and because the risks they take make them vulnerable to prosecution.

How widespread is the use of these expediters? Again, we catch only occasional hints of their prevalence. The most recent outburst against them reports that the number of *tolkachi* who annually visit the typical large enterprise runs into the thousands, and their expenses into hundreds of thousands of rubles. These, however, are only the reported expenses. More often than not their expenses are not reported as such but are concealed under such rubrics as "exchange of technical information," or "contract negotiations." Our latest informant, who is a senior investigator for the State Control Commission of the U.S.S.R., is of the opinion that despite continued official criticisms of the use of expediters, their number has actually been increasing. One of the reasons he adduces is interesting. In 1956, along with a wave of measures designed to give more freedom to plant managers, an order was issued relieving managers of the need to report in detail on all minor expenditures. Travel expenditures were among the items exempted. The measure had the unintended effect of encouraging the increased use of expediters.

The economic effect of the use of expediters is difficult to assess. There is no doubt that they are of vital importance to individual enterprises, but from the national point of view much of their activity involves merely the transfer to one fortunate enterprise of resources that otherwise would have gone to another. Since the higher priority enterprises have less need for expediters, the chances are that the net effect of their activity is to cause more resources to flow to lower priority enterprises at the expense of higher priority ones. On the credit side, however, their wide knowledge of sources of supply, of who has what to sell, is of some importance, and they do arrange for the movement of supplies that otherwise would have lain idle in one plant while another had need for it. In short, the expediter possesses a certain kind of knowledge that may be as important to economic organization as the knowledge of the engineer or the machinist. The planning system is able to direct the bulk of the nation's resources with reasonable effectiveness, but substantial quantities of materials and equipment elude the main stream of planning. How to get these resources back into the system is a problem that has exercised Soviet economists for a long time.[1]

In summary, the incentives that motivate managers to strive for the fulfillment of their production targets are the same incentives that motivate them to evade the regulations of the planning system. Because of the tightness of the supply system, which is deliberately engineered by the state, managers are compelled to defend their enterprises' position by overordering supplies, by hoarding materials and equipment, and by employing expediters whose function it is to keep the enterprise supplied with materials at all costs, legal or otherwise. The very planning system that serves to channel most of the nation's resources in directions desired by the state, serves also to misdirect a substantial volume of resources toward uses that are contrary to the wishes of the state.

Investment Decisions

If one were to ask what feature of the Soviet economic system accounts most of all for the rapid rate of growth, the answer would undoubtedly be the high rate of capital formation. The question at issue is whether it is as high as it might be, other things being equal. An examination of the system of managerial incentives will provide part, though by no means all, of the answer to this central question.

Management has a direct interest in obtaining new capital. It adds to productive capacity, and it is good for the record to show steady increases in production. Moreover fixed capital is provided to the enterprise as a free grant by the state, with no interest charge. The problem, therefore, has not been one of inducing management to accept more machines; it has rather been one of dissuading management from ordering too many machines. Far back in Soviet economic history one can find expressions of

[1] Recently there have been numerous suggestions that enterprises and economic regions publish catalogs of the commodities they produce and the surplus materials and equipment they would like to sell. The expediters are rather like walking catalogs.

the problem similar to that recently uttered by Khrushchev in connection with the dissolution of the agricultural machine-tractor stations:

The machine-tractor stations accept any machine whether they need it or not. They don't grow flax, but they take flax-growing equipment. They don't grow cabbage, but they take cabbage-planting machines. Consequently many machines are not used for years and hundreds of millions of rubles worth of state resources are frozen.

The reason enterprises accept any piece of equipment they can get their hands on is similar to that discussed above in connection with materials hoarding. One can never tell when he may need just that kind of machine and not be able to obtain it. If one has a chance to get it now, order it by all means. It may come in handy some day for trading in return for something one might be able to use more readily. And above all, there is no charge for holding the equipment; there is no interest payment, and if the machine is not used there is no depreciation charge either. Hence there is everything to gain and nothing to lose by holding on to as much machinery and equipment as one can obtain.

How to induce managers to take a less cavalier view of capital has been a long-standing concern of economists. They look with some nostalgia at the effectiveness of the profit motive under capitalism in this respect. An eminent Soviet economist put it this way recently:

In order to increase his profit as much as possible, the capitalist strives to use his equipment to the fullest extent possible, and in no case will he buy a machine that he doesn't need at the moment, since every surplus machine slows down the turnover of his capital and reduces his profit. For the same reason he strives to keep his inventories down to the very minimum and to market his finished products as quickly as possible.

Recent economic literature contains a number of suggestions of ways in which Soviet managers might be induced to order only that amount of capital needed for production purposes. One of the more interesting is a proposal advanced by the author quoted above. He suggests that profit be calculated not as a ratio to total production cost (as has always been done), but as a ratio to value of invested capital. In this way the enterprise with too much idle capital will show a lower rate of profit, and profit is one the principal indicators of overall performance. The suggestion is interesting because it proposes that return on capital be used as a criterion of performance, a rather "bourgeois" notion. It should not, however, be thought that the proposal envisages reliance on the "profit motive" as we know it. Profit is an important indicator of the efficiency of plant operation, but the firm does not "own" its profit, although it shares in the profit in a minor way. As a personal incentive, profit is relatively unimportant in Soviet industry, certainly by comparison with the bonus.[2]

[2] [As a result of Soviet recognition of these problems, reforms were adopted in 1965 under which interest is now charged on the enterprise's capital, profitability is calculated in relation to capital, and the enterprise retains a larger share of its profits.—EDITOR.]

If the incentive system motivates managers to overorder and hoard equipment, the situation is quite the reverse with respect to technological innovation. Concern over managerial resistance to innovation is of long standing, but it has come to the fore in recent years in connection with increased emphasis on automation and modernization of plant and equipment. The reasons for managers' tendency to drag their feet in introducing new products or production techniques are well understood by Soviet economists:

> The explanation is, first of all, that the introduction of new technology involves certain risks and requires a considerable expenditure of time; secondly, after new technology has been introduced, more difficult plan targets are set and consequently there is less opportunity for fulfilling them and receiving bonuses.

When a manager has a well-running plant, when the workers have learned their jobs and have become experienced in using the existing equipment, he is reluctant to upset the cart by trying something new. A new production line means trouble. Production bugs have to be eliminated, workers have to be retrained, time is lost, and spoilage is high. The chances are that plans will be underfulfilled and the precious bonuses lost, particularly in view of the tendency for plan targets to be raised to the rated capacity of the new equipment. It is courting disaster to try new things. If the old machines are wearing out, it is safer to repair or even rebuild them rather than introduce the more complicated new models. Outlays on the rebuilding of old machines often exceed the price of a new modern machine.

There is another reason why managers shy away from innovation. Even if the potential gains from new technology are great, it usually takes a number of years before they are realized. But it is Soviet policy to shift managers around from plant to plant every few years. Therefore managers have a strictly short-run point of view. Why take on all the headaches of introducing a new line when one is not likely to be around to enjoy whatever benefits may eventually accrue? Capital investment policy is by its very nature a matter of long-term planning, and therefore does not commend itself to the short-run horizon of management.

How does the state combat managerial resistance to innovation? One technique is direct pressure. Pressure exerted on and by their own superiors explains much of the innovation that does occur. Enterprise managers may drag their feet for a long time, but when the direct order comes down that the new automatic line must be installed in the next six months, it is eventually acted upon. Pressure is also exerted through the Communist party; if the party officials in the enterprise are under direct orders from Moscow that automation must be accelerated, they are in a position to force the manager to move faster than he otherwise might. Such pressures are important, although it must be noted in passing that both the manager's bosses and the local party people often try to shield the enterprise from such pressures. They are as dependent for their careers upon successful plan fulfillment as are the plant managers themselves.

Direct orders from above are one way of getting management to innovate. But innovation would proceed more rapidly if managers could be made to wish to innovate, instead of waiting until they are forced into it. The literature of the past few years is full of suggestions on how this can be accomplished. It is suggested, for example, that attractively high prices be set on new machines, in order to stimulate the producers of those machines to put them into production more rapidly. While this measure might ease the financial strain on the innovating firm, it will not remove the risk that the production plan may be sacrificed. And production is much more vital to the success of the enterprise than finance.

More to the point are the suggestions that the bonus system be employed as an incentive for innovation. Soviet economists seem to have enormous confidence in bonuses as a device for getting management to wish to do what the state wishes them to do. But how to adapt the bonus system to this purpose is more difficult. In the course of years a variety of special bonuses have been introduced for one purpose or another, in addition to the major bonus that comes from fulfillment of the production plan. There are special bonuses available for economizing certain critical materials, for reducing the volume of goods in process, for conserving fuel, for increasing labor productivity, for keeping the plant clean, for reducing the volume of spoilage, for operating the plant without stoppages, for winning "socialist competitions," and many others.[3]

This dilution of the bonus system may actually weaken its power as an incentive. If the special bonuses are small, they will not be very effective. If they are large they may detract effort from what is, after all, the main objective of the state: fulfillment of the production plan. For it is interesting to note the evidence that the relative size of the bonus for this or that special purpose often determines the manager's decision to concentrate on this or that objective. There are two types of innovation: relatively small measures such as organizational improvements or inexpensive alterations, and the more dramatic large-scale changes in production techniques. The former are included in the overall enterprise plan each year, under the name of the plan of organizational and technical measures (Orgtekhplan). It happens that there are certain bonuses available for the design and introduction of the large-scale innovations, but none for the fulfillment of the Orgtekhplan. The consequence is that research and managerial personnel concentrate on the large items and pay little attention to the small ones, even though the latter could result in great savings with relatively little cost and effort. Thus the very potency of the bonus as an incentive militates against its use for too many special purposes which may compete with each other.

[3] Not all these types of bonus are available to the director himself, but they are available to different groups of managerial personnel.

To conclude this discussion, the unreliability of the supply system and the absence of a charge for the use of capital motivate management to order more fixed capital than they need and to hoard machines and equipment. This tendency deflects a certain amount of currently produced capital goods from being put directly into production in their best uses. On the other hand, the incentive system discourages management from taking the risks associated with innovation. Direct orders from above lead to a substantial volume of innovation, and in many cases management may consider certain forms of innovation to be to their interest. The provision of special bonuses for innovation, if they were large enough to compete with the production plan bonus, might help provide an incentive for innovation, and much of the current discussion in the Soviet Union seems to point to this as the next phase.

SOME COMPARATIVE OBSERVATIONS

The preceding section has shown that Soviet managers are motivated to make a variety of decisions that are contrary to the interest of the state. Since the state's interest is paramount in the Soviet scheme of things, we may properly conclude that the incentive and decision-making system is "relatively inefficient," or "less than perfectly efficient." Let me caution the reader once more against inferring from this that Soviet managers do not do a good job. They do. There is no doubt that their system works well. If I have chosen to concentrate on the "pathology" of Soviet management, the purpose was not to create the impression of ineffectiveness, but to illuminate the gap that every economy shows between the actual and the ideal.

A comparison of Soviet and American management will help drive the point home. No one doubts that American management does a good job. But it would be fatuous to allege that it operates with perfect efficiency. An exploration of the inevitable gap between the actual and the ideal in the case of American management will help to place the corresponding gap in the U.S.S.R. in proper perspective.

A comparison of Soviet and American management is difficult for a curious reason; namely, we don't know enough about the more intimate aspects of American managerial practice. A moment's thought will make the reason clear. The American firm is a private enterprise in the full sense of the word. Its internal affairs are no one's business but its own. No one has the right to pry except with special cause. To be sure, the laws of the land have, over the years, required enterprises to disclose more and more of their private affairs to public and governmental perusal. But large sectors of the enterprise's internal operations are protected from the eyes of curious outsiders.

One of the most striking differences in the conduct of American and Soviet management is precisely in this matter of privacy. The Soviet enterprise is a public enterprise in the fullest sense of the word. It has no right to conceal its operations from any officially recognized agent of the state. And a great range of such agents have been deliberately endowed by the state with the obligation of keeping close watch on management and disclosing any irregularities or sources of inefficiency that come to their attention. These agents include the "home office" of the firm (the ministry), the state bank, the local governmental body, the central government's State Control Commission, the Finance Department (the tax collector), the local Communist party boss and his staff, the party secretary of the enterprise itself, and indeed just about anyone in the enterprise who enjoys the extracurricular activity of attending meetings to discuss the affairs of the enterprise (the *aktiv*).

If we can imagine an American business executive suddenly placed in charge of a Soviet firm, it is this public character of the enterprise which above all would drive him to distraction. It means that any government official can at any time demand to examine any aspect of the firm's operations he wishes to, that at any time he can be called on the carpet by the local party boss to explain a charge made by an irate customer, that any member of his staff (perhaps bucking for his job) can write a letter to *Pravda* exposing him for having made an irregular deal on some supplies, that any scatterbrained worker who wants to "get his picture in the papers" can rise at a public meeting that the director is obliged to attend and compel the director to explain why he hasn't yet installed the new assembly line. The point is that the result of this authorized prying often finds its way into the published Soviet economic and political literature, which gives us an insight into the more intimate operations of the Soviet firm that we cannot have in the case of the American firm. But in view of this committee's expressed interest in comparisons of the United States and Soviet economies, I have attempted certain comparisons below which appear to be highly suggestive.

Managers and Owners

The original form of modern business organization was the small firm in which the owner was also the manager. The owner-manager was responsible to no one but himself for his business decisions, and his interest as manager could not conflict with his interest as owner. The development of the modern giant corporation, however, had led to that separation of management and ownership first elaborated in the work of Berle and Means.[4] Under the new conditions the private interests of the hired managers (and the controlling group) need no longer coincide at all points with the interests of the stockholder-owners. This is precisely the relationship between the hired Soviet manager and the owner-state.

Berle and Means concluded from their study that "the controlling

[4] Adolph A. Berle, Jr., and Gardiner C. Means, *The Modern Corporation and Private Property* (New York: The Macmillan Co., 1945).

group, even if they own a large block of stock, can serve their own pockets better by profiting at the expense of the company than by making profits for it."[5] This is precisely what Soviet managers do when they produce unplanned commodities that are advantageous to their firms but not to the state, when they overorder and hoard commodities, and when they resist innovation. Because of the differences between the two economic systems, we should expect that the precise forms that the owner-manager conflict takes would be different in the U.S.S.R. and the United States. In the United States they are to be found in such decisions as the awarding of subcontracts, the accounting of profit in such way as to benefit the claims of the controlling group, the awarding of bonuses and other benefits to management, and in dividend payment policy. As in the Soviet enterprise, the accountant is of crucial importance in handling the books of the enterprise in such ways as make the best possible case for the manager; it is he, for example, who figures out the best way to distract the state's attention from the large expenditures on *tolkachi*. The accounting techniques are, of course, different in the United States; they involve "the charging or the failure to deduct depreciation; charging to capital expenses which properly should be charged against income account; including nonrecurrent profits as income though their real place is in surplus; and the creation of 'hidden reserves.' "[6]

A major difference between the Soviet firm and the American firm is that in the last analysis profit remains the criterion of managerial performance in the latter, whereas the Soviet manager is evaluated by a number of criteria that are sometimes mutually exclusive. Both systems have attempted to bring managerial interests into harmony with owner interests by some sort of profit-sharing system. In the Soviet case, it is clear that profit plays a very minor role, compared with bonuses, as a managerial incentive. In the United States the manager shares directly in profit to a very limited extent, and often follows other goals in his decisions. "The executive not infrequently tends to look upon the stockholders as outsiders whose complaints and demand for dividends are necessary evils . . ." concluded one American student of management.[7] In like fashion the Soviet manager often begins to feel like the "boss" and resents the intrusion into "his" affairs of the state, which after all is the owner. I have described above some of the ways in which the Soviet manager promotes the interest of "his" enterprise by means contrary to the interests of the owner-state. In the American corporation the forms are somewhat different. ". . . profits are reinvested in the business for the sake of bigness and to protect the company, and the interests of the stockholders may be given second place to the business leader's conception of what is best for

[5] *Ibid.*, p. 122.

[6] *Ibid.*, pp. 202–3, 335.

[7] Robert A. Gordon, *Business Leadership in the Large Corporation* (Washington, D.C.: The Brookings Institution, 1945), p. 309.

the firm itself." Executives manifest a "general unwillingness to liquidate unsuccessful enterprises" and thus put themselves out of jobs, however consistent liquidation might be with the interests of the stockholders.[8] The dramatic growth of corporate self-financing in recent years has strengthened the power of management to expand their own enterprises without having to go through the "test of the marketplace" for capital.

It was observed earlier that the desire for "security" and for what the Russians call a "quiet life" motivates a wide variety of managerial decisions such as concealing production capacity and resisting technological innovation that might rock the boat. Students of American management have also noted the change from the adventurous business tycoons of earlier days to a more professionalized managerial climate in which "greater emphasis is placed on education, training, and a scientific approach, and less on rugged, venturesome, and frequently heedless individualism. The desire for security seems to have increased, and the concomitant of a growing emphasis on security is a diminishing desire for adventure for its own sake."[9] There is indeed a remarkable parallel to this development in the change in the character of Soviet managers. There would have been a great affinity between the industrial empire builders of 19th-century America and the Soviet directors of the first two decades of the Soviet regime. Those directors were often men of little education who came out of the romantic conflict of revolution, who dreamed great dreams of building an industrial nation and who created an ethos of bold plans and adventurous undertakings. The old Commissar of Heavy Industry, Sergei Ordzhonikidze, would have understood the spirit of the ironmonger, Andrew Carnegie, and the man who built the great ZIL automotive works (now named after him) had the drives and the dreams of the bicycle mechanic, Henry Ford.

Time, and Stalin's purges, removed most of those old-timers and their place has now been taken by Soviet-educated young men born not of revolution but of bureaucracy. Organizations seem to develop "organization men" types, whether the organization happens to be communist or capitalist. An American reporter visiting with a group of Communist intellectuals reports that one of them had badgered him with questions about David Riesman's book, *The Lonely Crowd.* "The Communist had read Riesman's book and has been fascinated by it—not, he said, because of its application to life in the United States but because of what he maintained was its extraordinary relevance to the present conditions of life in the Soviet Union."[10] It is not, on reflection, very surprising that the job of running an industrial bureaucracy should place a common stamp on men of otherwise different backgrounds. The same would probably apply to the running of a large city or a large university.

[8] *Ibid.*, p. 309.

[9] *Ibid.*, p. 311.

[10] *The New Yorker,* April 6, 1955, p. 52.

Managers and the Laws

We have found that the Soviet manager is often compelled to evade regulations or even break laws. Part of the explanation is simply that there are so many laws. If a Chicago manufacturer fails to ship an order to a New York firm, and ships it instead to another Chicago firm, he has nothing to fear but the ire of the New York firm. But if a Kiev manufacturer fails to ship an order to a Moscow firm and ships it instead to another Kiev firm, he has injured a state enterprise and is subject to administrative action, a fine, or even criminal prosecution. If an American firm sells a substandard generator, he may lose money or his business. But if a Soviet firm sells a substandard generator, the director may go to prison. Thus, even if Soviet managers acted exactly as American managers do, we should expect to find more illegal or evasive activity in the Soviet Union than in the United States.

With the growing complexity of our society, more and more legislation is enacted to protect the public from potential abuses. With the growth of such legislation, managers find their activities more and more circumscribed by laws and regulations. The Soviet manager apparently treats such legislation rather lightly when it conflicts with the interests of his firm (and his career and pocketbook). How does American management react when confronted by a spreading web of restrictive legislation?

It is not easy to find out very much about American managerial practice in this respect. Unlike the Soviet press, which throws its pages open to reports of the irregular activities of managers in order to warn others, the American press is likely to shy away from this kind of reporting. Moreover the private nature of American business keeps this sort of activity from coming to light as easily as it might in Soviet industry. Nor is it the sort of thing that businessmen are inclined to talk about very readily. If it is true that a businessman would more readily be interviewed on his private sex life than on his private business activity, then we should require the late Dr. Kinsey to help provide the answers to the extent of unlawful or quasi-lawful business activity.

Prof. E. H. Sutherland, the eminent American criminologist and sociologist, made a bold attempt to investigate the phenomenon he refers to as "white-collar crime." His study is based on the decisions of a limited number of courts and administrative commissions against the 70 largest industrial-type corporations in the country. In the period 1935 to 1944 these 70 corporations were convicted 585 times for such practices as restraint of trade, misrepresentation in advertising, patent and copyright infringements, unfair labor practices, granting of rebates, and a few others.[11] The average was 8.5 convictions per corporation. These data provide some idea of the extensiveness of such practices but they clearly under-

[11] Edwin H. Sutherland, *White Collar Crime* (New York: Dryden, 1949), p. 26.

state the magnitude for a variety of technical reasons. Sutherland's conclusion is that "a great deal of scattered and unorganized material indicates that white collar crimes are very prevalent."[12]

The point I wish to make is that when American management finds itself in a position approximating that of Soviet management it tends to react in ways similar to those of its Soviet counterparts. Sutherland's unique study notes many aspects of American managerial practice that are astonishingly similar to those one might find in the literature on Soviet management. "These crimes are not discreet and inadvertent violations of technical regulations. They are deliberate and have a relatively consistent unity."[13] It is in precisely this way that the Soviet manager deliberately misappropriates earmarked funds or decides to shave on the quality of production. There is evidence that the Soviet manager, aware of the fact that "everybody does it" and that the investigating agencies have restricted budgets, counts on the law of averages (and his own superior shrewdness) to get away with it. So a member of the Federal Trade Commission wrote that "about the only thing that keeps a businessman off the wrong end of a Federal indictment or administrative agency's complaint is the fact that, under the hit-or-miss methods of prosecution, the law of averages hasn't made him a partner to a suit," and "Samuel Insull is reported to have remarked during his trial that he had only done what all other businessmen were doing."[14]

Similarities in managerial practice are paralleled by similarities in attitude to such violations, and toward the administrative agencies enforcing the laws and regulations. The Soviet manager does not think it is "wrong" to use influence to obtain materials unlawfully, or to fudge his reports to the government. Success is the important thing, and if you are successful you can get away with all sorts of violations. There is evidence that the Soviet manager feels contemptuous of government planners and of party hacks who try to tell him how to run his business but who themselves had "never met a payroll." Sutherland's picture of American management's attitudes contains strains of the same kind.

> The businessman who violates the laws which are designed to regulate business does not customarily lose status among his business associates. Although a few members of the industry may think less of him, others admire him. . . . Businessmen customarily regard government personnel as politicians and bureaucrats, and the persons authorized to investigate business practices as "snoopers."[15]

In the first section of this paper, it was pointed out that a managerial career carries a great deal of prestige in the Soviet Union and attracts a large number of the better students. These youngsters have been raised in

[12] *Ibid.*, p. 10.
[13] *Ibid.*, p. 217.
[14] *Ibid.*, p. 218.
[15] *Ibid.*, p. 220.

Soviet schools and have absorbed the incessant propaganda of the Communist regime. Many of them enter industry as green novices fresh from school, filled with high ideals about building the socialist fatherland and working for the common welfare. One wonders about the process by which the naive, idealistic young Komsomol member is transformed into the hard-headed manager who knows all the angles for survival in the Soviet business world. Numerous incidents such as the following provide a key to the answer. A young Soviet chemist had been assigned to the quality control department of his enterprise. He was quite pleased with himself when his test showed that a sample of production, which had previously been declared acceptable by his laboratory chief, turned out to contain an excess of phosphorus. He reported the "error" and expected to get a bonus for it. Instead, his boss obtained a new sample, gave it to an outside chemist for analysis, and submitted a report showing that the batch of production was acceptable after all. The young chemist protested, was transferred to another shop, and was finally fired on trumped-up charges.

What happens to such young people? Some never quite get the point and remain ordinary engineers in the plants. Others learn to adapt themselves after a few buffetings and, when they decide to play the game according to the real ground rules, begin to rise in the managerial hierarchy.

It is interesting to note that Sutherland's interviews with American businessmen turned up accounts rather similar to that narrated above. His explanation of the process by which the naive American youngster is initiated into the business of selling used cars, settling insurance claims, covering up irregularities in clients' accounts—indeed, toning down the results of chemical analysis—helps explain the process of transformation of the young Komsomol member:

> In many cases he is ordered by the manager to do things which he regards as unethical or illegal, while in other cases he learns from others who have the same rank as his own how they make a success. He learns specific techniques of violating the law, together with definitions of situations in which those techniques may be used. Also he develops a general ideology. This ideology grows in part out of the specific practices and is in the nature of generalization from concrete experiences, but in part it is transmitted as a generalization by phrases such as "we are not in business for our health," "business is business," and "no business was ever built on the beatitudes." These generalizations . . . assist the neophyte in business to accept the illegal practices and provide rationalizations for them.[16]

Summarizing, the economic world in which the Soviet manager operates compels him to engage in a variety of illegal or evasive practices. Since the Soviet business world is enmeshed in a much greater web of laws and regulations than the American, the Soviet manager finds his interest in

---

[16] *Ibid.*, p. 240.

conflict with the laws and regulations more often than his American counterpart. But when American managers' interests conflict with the laws, they too are prepared to take the chance of violating them. Both American and Soviet managers justify their actions by an attitude of contempt for governmental controls and investigating personnel, and by a hardheaded view that "business is business" and "everybody does it." Young people in both systems who wish to achieve managerial prominence have to learn to play the game according to the rules or disqualify themselves from the tough competition for the top.

Managers and Overfull Employment

Many of the peculiarities of Soviet management spring from the fact that the economic system works under conditions of perpetual overfull employment. By "overfull" employment I mean a condition in which there are not merely as many jobs as employables (as under full employment), but the demand for labor far exceeds the available supply. The same applies to other factors of production: materials, equipment, and commodities in general are demanded in far greater volume than the current rates of production. The ability of the Soviet government to maintain, through the planning system, a condition of permanent overfull employment is one of the greatest economic assets of the regime. We err when we interpret evidence of shortages in the Soviet economy as signs of economic weakness; they are rather indications that the economic engine is racing with the throttle wide open.

But just as an engine does not work at its maximum efficiency when it is working at its maximum capacity, so the Soviet economy pays a certain price for the advantages of overfull employment. It is the perpetual shortages of supplies that account in large measure for the losses due to overordering and hoarding. The hunger for goods by both firms and consumers encourages the deterioration of quality. The "sea of ink" associated with materials allocations, price fixing, priorities, and all the rigamarole of a controlled economy nurtures the spread of the *tolkach* and the use of influence for personal gain.

The normally functioning American economy does not confront our managers with this kind of problem. Hoarding makes no sense when materials are in adequate supply. Competition and consumer resistance force the quality of production up to standard. The role of influence is narrowly circumscribed when the bureaucratic machinery of government controls is removed. The biggest problem of American managers under normal conditions is marketing, not purchasing. The energy spent by the Soviet firm on obtaining materials is spent by the American firm on selling and advertising.

Thus, the major differences between the practice of American and Soviet management are to be ascribed to the differences in the economic environment. The interesting question is, How do American managers behave when placed in an environment that approximates that of the Soviet manager? The obvious test case is war. During World War II the national emergency forced us into a state of overfull employment. Along with this came the total immersion of government into economic life, with a great burgeoning of materials allocation, price fixing, cost-plus contracting, and a prevailing shortage of supplies.

It is interesting to note that the rate of growth of production during the war rose to levels rivaling the current rates of Soviet economic growth. The implication of this fact is important; it means that there is no magic in the Soviet economic system. Our economy could grow as rapidly as the Soviet economy does if our people would consent to being pushed around as totally as the Soviet people are.

But like the Soviet economy, we paid for our high rate of production in various forms of waste. One of the first consequences of the introduction of materials controls was the rise of the black market. The only full-scale study of the black market, to my knowledge, confirmed what many people felt to be the case at the time:

> During the war at least a million cases of black market violations were dealt with by the Government. Illegal profits ran into billions of dollars. Business interests and Government vied with one another in estimating the seriousness of the black market; business estimates, curiously, often being higher than those of the Government. Such extensive conniving in the black market in illegal prices and rationed commodities took place among so many businessmen, ordinary criminals, and even the average citizen that serious questions might be raised as to the moral fiber of the American people.[17]

To understand the position of the Soviet manager, we must realize that the American black market flourished at a time when the nation was fighting for its life and public indignation acted as a restraint. But if the economic controls that led to violations could not be justified by a national emergency, they would be thought of as just irritating obstacles, as so many hurdles that the resourceful manager must overcome as part of the risks of the game. There is good evidence that the Soviet manager takes just this amoral attitude toward economic controls, and it is therefore quite understandable that the evasion of controls would be more widespread.

The high quality of American production in normal times is a byword in international markets. But the effect on the economy of shortages was similar to that in the Soviet economy. One of the techniques used by Soviet managers is to represent lower quality merchandise as of higher quality, and to sell it at the higher price. In the United States during the war—

---

[17] Marshall B. Clinard, *The Black Market* (New York: Rinehart & Co., Inc., 1952), p. vii.

upgrading was one of the most difficult violations to detect, particularly where no professional investigator was available who could appraise the grade or where there were no State or Federal grades stamped on the commodity.[18]

The reports of government investigators read like some of the indignant letters of complaint we read in the Soviet press; men's shorts made of cheesecloth, water-resistant baby's pants which permit a third of a glass of water to leak through after one laundering—

if you pick up a board by both ends without breaking it in the middle, it's No. 1 Select—

testified an American businessman.[19]

One of the features of Soviet managerial life which helps protect the manager is the feeling of "mutual support" among various officials whose fortunes depend on the success of the enterprise. The Communist party secretary doesn't report the manipulations of a successful director because the party benefits from the success of the enterprise; the people in the "home office" (the Ministry) are reluctant to fire a director who violates the laws in order to get the materials his plant needs, for while the next director may be more law-abiding, he may not succeed in fulfilling his plan. This tendency to maintain a solid front against authority is a source of great irritation to the government, which periodically inveighs against it but has not been able to eradicate it. A similar sense of common front prevailed among groups of businessmen.

Nothing better illustrates the degree of organization and consensus among businessmen than their reluctance to testify against each other. . . . Some businessmen felt that the trade would disapprove of behavior that might undermine the solid front against the Government as well as interfere with supplies.[20]

One of the major differences in the position of management in the two countries is the nature of the penalty for failure. Under ordinary conditions the unsuccessful manager loses his job. But the Soviet manager faces many more situations in which the action necessary to get the job done carries with it the threat of criminal action. Indeed, whenever the Soviet government has found some managerial practice too damaging to its interests and too intractable to the normal sanctions, it has turned to the criminal courts. Immediately after the death of Stalin the punishment for economic transgressions was relaxed, but the new regime has not been able to continue operating without the courts. One of the severest economic problems following the decentralization of industry was the tendency toward "localism": that is, each economic region tended to favor the plants in its "own" region, and would discriminate against plants in other regions. When all exhortation failed, the government had to turn to the

[18] *Ibid.*, p. 224.

[19] *Ibid.*, p. 45.

[20] *Ibid.*, pp. 306–7.

law. Today, a manager who fails to honor the orders of plants outside his own region is subject to "administrative action, fines, or even criminal punishment."

Financial penalties, such as fines, have rarely proved successful as restraints on Soviet managerial behavior. American managers seem to have reacted the same way to the fines imposed for black-market violations. "They don't hurt anybody." "It just comes out of profits, like a tax." "They make so much money on the black market they can afford to pay steep fines." But imprisonment was another matter. "Jail is the only way; nobody wants to go to jail." "A jail sentence is dishonorable; it jeopardizes the reputation." This would not be quite the same in the case of the Soviet manager. At least during Stalin's lifetime some of the best people served their time in jail, and it definitely did not destroy their reputation among their neighbors; although the neighbors might be wary of associating with them. One has the impression that large numbers of Soviet managers feel the chances are fair that some day they will do their stretch, hopefully for a minor transgression.

The wartime economy of shortages injects the government into business life not only as an agency of control but also as the largest customer of many firms. In the Soviet case we have noted the importance of the *tolkach*, the expediter, the peddler of influence. We might note in passing that the economic system of Nazi Germany, in which government had also assumed a dominant role, also gave rise to this chap. The Germans called him the "contact man." As described by an American student of the German economy:

> To influence the powerful agencies of control, however, he [the German businessman] has good use for what might suitably be called a private relations department. Under the Nazi system of control of business by an absolute government, the contact man, or graft, or both, take the place of the public relations executive.
>
> The contact man is primarily a political figure. His job is to pull wires. He knows the influential members of the all-pervading Nazi Party in a position to bring pressure successfully to bear upon the men in charge of controlling agencies. . . . Two types of contact man are known to be used: one is an independent agent whom the businessman hires, or attempts to hire, whenever necessary; the other is carried on the payroll of the business in a more or less permanent capacity.[21]

The words might well have been written about the Soviet economy. In that sector of the U.S. economy in which government plays a dominant role as customer, the symbols of the mink coat or Dixon-Yates, depending upon one's political persuasion, come to mind. "Washington," wrote Senator Paul Douglas, "is indeed full of lawyers and 'representatives' whose primary commodity is 'influence.' "[22] The techniques of the Amer-

[21] L. Hamburger, *How Nazi Germany Has Controlled Business* (Washington, D.C.: The Brookings Institution, 1943), pp. 94–95.

[22] Paul H. Douglas, *Ethics in Government* (Cambridge, Mass.: Harvard University Press, 1952), p. 56.

ican influence-peddler differ little from those of his colleagues in the Soviet or Nazi economy. Gifts and *quid pro quo* favors are standard among Soviet *tolkachi.* Another way in which Soviet enterprises manage to exert influence is to have one of "their" men placed in other organizations that can be of use, rather like the unusually high employability in industry of retired military personnel. During the war the problem was particularly acute because of our government's desperate need for skilled managerial personnel, many of whom were on loan from corporations with which the government placed contracts. But the use of influence is not confined to government-business relations, as Senator Douglas pointed out in his critical defense of the ethics of government personnel:

> As a matter of fact, the abuses which have been exposed and properly denounced in the field of Government are quite widespread practices in private business. Thus the "padding" of expense accounts is so common that they are often referred to as "swindle sheets." Purchasing agents and buyers frequently exact toll from those who seek to sell them, and their Christmas presents and other perquisites appreciably increase their income. Business managers and directors think nothing of awarding contracts, insurance, and underwriting privileges on the basis of friendship and relationship rather than the quality and prices of the goods and services supplied. All this is taken as a matter of course in private business, although it obviously increases costs and intercepts gains which should go to stockholders and consumers.[23]

While gifts, payoffs, and bribery play their role in the Soviet scheme of things, the subtler and much more pervasive technique of influence is known as "blat." To have good blat with someone means that one has an "in"; one can always count on him for a favor because of friendship or family ties or some other relationship of confidence. Blat may be used to obtain everything from a new apartment to a carload of coal. The prominent British observer, Edward Crankshaw, has called blat the most significant word in contemporary Russia.[24] The way in which the American equivalent of blat is cultivated is described in one final quotation from Senator Douglas:

> Today the corruption of public officials by private interests takes a more subtle form. The enticer does not generally pay money directly to the public representative. He tries instead by a series of favors to put the public official under such feeling of personal obligation that the latter gradually loses his sense of mission to the public and comes to feel that his first loyalties are to his private benefactors and patrons. What happens is a gradual shifting of a man's loyalties from the community to those who have been doing him favors. His final decisions are, therefore, made in response to private friendships and loyalties rather than to the public good.[25]

Summarizing, many of the differences between Soviet and United States managerial behavior spring from differences in the economic cli-

---

[23] *Ibid.*, p. 25.

[24] *New York Times Magazine,* June 3, 1951, p. 35.

[25] Douglas, *op. cit.*, p. 44.

mate in which they operate. The stress on quality and appearance, the drive for innovation and technological development, and the interest in cost reduction reflect the force of competition and the buyer's market. Such similarities as have been observed in managerial behavior spring from features of the economic environment that are common to the two systems, such as large-scale organization and the intrusion of government into the economy. Under wartime conditions our economy takes on more of the features of normal Soviet economic life, and the consequence is that our managers adopt more of the normal practices of Soviet management.

Economic Development

There is no single economic system best for the economic development of every underdeveloped country. One would hardly expect the same economic system to be equally appropriate for feudal, peasant, and proletarian societies; more or less industrialized economies; heavily and thinly populated areas; tropical and temperate regions; etc. Nor can a country simply adopt a particular economic system in operation elsewhere. Instead, each underdeveloped nation must choose—from economic theory and the experience of other economies—the combination of economic institutions and instruments best suited to its stage of development, resource endowment, cultural and social traditions, and development objectives.

The study of comparative economic systems helps in this choice by showing the features, advantages, and disadvantages of various economic systems in theory and in practice. The three selections which follow analyze different economic systems as engines of economic development. They suggest combinations of government and private activity, of centralization and decentralization, and of planning and market forces which can promote economic development. The first emphasizes the role of the state in economic growth. The next presents the case for the market as a vehicle for economic development. The last shows how government planning and private decision making can work together for economic development.

21. INDIVIDUALISM AND THE ROLE OF THE STATE IN ECONOMIC GROWTH*

Alexander Eckstein

In this essay Alexander Eckstein analyzes the circumstances in which the state may be expected to play an important role in economic development. He then examines the activities in which the state is likely to engage and their effect upon individual choice and decentralized decision making in economic life.

I

ECONOMIC growth can be viewed as a broadening of the range of alternatives open to society. Clearly, technological and resource constraints are likely to be so compelling and overriding in primitive or underdeveloped economies as to leave comparatively little scope for the exercise of choice—either individual or social. On the other hand, the situation is quite different—at least in degree—at more advanced stages of economic development. At these stages, one of the principal manifestations of this broadening in the range of alternatives is precisely the greater opportunity to exercise choice over the form in which choices in the economy become institutionalized. This, in turn, requires a delineation of the spheres of public vs. private choice and a determination of the relative weight of each sphere.

One of the aspects of individualism, and possibly the one most relevant for our purposes, is the scope for individual choice and decentralized decision making in the economic sphere. In a preponderantly free enterprise market economy the institutionalization of these ingredients of individualism is more or less automatically assured. This does not, however, mean that this sytsem necessarily assures equal scope for the exercise of choice on the part of all individuals in the economic system, or that it

* Reprinted from *Economic Development and Cultural Change*, Vol. VI, No. 2 (January, 1958), pp. 81–87, by permission of The University of Chicago Press. Alexander Eckstein is Professor of Economics at The University of Michigan.

provides a greater scope for individual choice than an alternative system might. In contrast to preponderantly free enterprise market systems, in economies in which the public sector looms quite large, the scope for individual choice and decision making may be more a function of the political rather than the economic system. Thus the mechanism through which economic policy is formulated and the role of the ballot box in economic policy formulation become major conditioning factors.

In essence, what this suggests is that there is a potentially positive correlation between individualism and economic development. The extent to which this potential is translated into reality will depend upon the role played by individual choice and initiative in resource allocation, regardless of whether the choices and decisions are in fact arrived at primarily within the confines of the economic or political process. With this context in mind, let us attempt to spell out some of the factors and variables that are likely to condition the role the state may be expected or forced to play in the process of economic growth and its impact upon the position of the individual.

II

In analyzing the role of the state in the process of economic growth, the following elements may be considered as essential:

1. *The hierarchy of objectives, goals, and ends of economic development*—This necessarily involves an examination of both the qualitative and quantitative aspects, that is, the character, range, and variety of the ends sought as well as the level to be attained. The interplay of these dimensions of content, range, and level will be one of the principal factors defining the ambitiousness of the particular economic development program. In respect to content, several broad categories of objectives or motivations may be cited, for instance, those revolving around nationalism and those related to a striving for rising standards of living. In a sense, these might be considered as ultimate ends which need to be, and are in fact, broken down into a series of derived and possibly more concrete goals. Thus, at the stage when these objectives are disaggregated and sorted out as to the ranges and levels involved, they inevitably tend to become competitive rather than complementary entities in the sense that under *ceteris paribus* assumptions, the wider the range, the lower will have to be the level, and *vice versa.*
2. *The time horizon in economic development*—This entails a definition of the rate at which the goals are to be attained. In a sense, it is but another aspect of the hierarchy of objectives, since rapid or leisurely growth may be an explicitly stated end in and of itself.
3. *The means available* for attaining—at the desired rate—the content, range, and level of ends explicitly or implicitly formulated. Here one would have to consider such variables as resource and factor endowments and the state of the arts prevailing in the particular economy.
4. *The structure and character of institutions: social, economic, and political*—This is possibly the most complex of all the categories listed here.

The considerations most relevant for our purposes revolve around the rigidity of the institutional framework, its capacity to generate, absorb, and adapt itself to economic change and to the disruptive forces of industrialization. This would mean investigating factors such as the prevailing value system, class structure, social mobility, contractual and legal arrangements, degree and character of urbanization, land tenure system, degree of commercialization and monetization, character and structure of state organization, structure of political power, etc. However, analysis of these variables is greatly complicated by virtue of the fact that some of them are rather intangible, while their particular chemical mix—that is, the nature of combinations and interaction between the different institutional factors—and the reaction produced may be quite unpredictable. In effect, it is much easier to provide *ex post facto* rationalizations or explanations as to why and in what ways certain types of institutional structure were more conductive to industrialization than others, than to assess *ex ante* the height and the tensile strength of institutional barriers and their resistance to economic development.

5. *The relative backwardness of the economy*—From an economic point of view, relative backwardness—and the emphasis should be on relative—involves certain advantages and disadvantages. The disadvantages lie principally in the field of foreign trade, while the so called "advantages of backwardness" may be found in the realm of technology. Thus industrially advanced countries enjoy certain competitive advantages in world markets, and particularly in the markets of the underdeveloped areas themselves. This in and of itself can under certain conditions become a major handicap in the industrialization of backward countries. On the other hand, as Professor Gerschenkron has pointed out, one of the essential ingredients of relative backwardness is a gap in the levels of technology used and applied. Therefore the backward country can reap large potential gains by importing advanced technology from abroad and thus, in effect, make a technological leap from comparatively primitive to highly advanced levels.

   At this point another aspect of relative backwardness may be usefully introduced, namely the gap in material welfare or standards of living, and the gap in national power produced by differences in levels of industrialization. All three of these gaps—in consumption, technology, and power—could be viewed as different aspects of a "demonstration effect" through which the gulf between a potential and actual state is forcefully brought home. Characteristically, it is in this shape that the pressure for industrialization of backward countries is manifested. Once the disequilibrating and innovating forces of modernization, industrialization, and urbanization have been introduced on an appreciable scale,[1] one could say that, *ceteris paribus*, the greater the relative backwardness, the more acute will tend to be the "tension" arising from this chasm between the potential and the actual, and thus the greater will be the pressure for industrialization.

Given the five categories of elements and variables considered above, we are now in a position to state our hypothesis concerning the conditions

[1] This scale effect is, of course, both crucial and indeterminate, in the sense that what will be the operationally significant range will inevitably vary from country to country, depending upon size, institutional framework, etc.

under which the state will tend to play a greater or lesser role in the process of economic growth. On this basis then one could say that:

a) The greater the range of ends and the higher the level of attainment sought;
b) the shorter the time horizon within which the ends are to be attained, that is, the more rapid the rate of economic growth desired;
c) the more unfavorable the factor and resource endowments;
d) the greater the institutional barriers to economic change and industrialization; and
e) the more backward the economy in relative terms

the greater will tend to be the urge, push, and pressure for massive state intervention and initiative in the process of industrialization, and at the same time, the greater will be the need for such intervention if a breakthrough, rather than a breakdown, is to be attained.

III

Assuming that the state is compelled to make a major commitment on behalf of industrialization, what types of measures may the state be expected to adopt and what effect may these have upon the position of the individual, or more specifically, upon the individual choice and decentralized decision making in the economic sphere? From this point of view, a sharp distinction needs to be made between the elements and the degree of state power applied in the process of economic growth.

In analyzing the qualitative aspects of state intervention affecting the economic sphere, one could perhaps distinguish between five categories of action: provision of social overhead, provision of economic overhead, application of direct and indirect levers and controls, government operation of enterprises extending beyond the overhead sectors, and central planning.

Provision of social overhead might entail maintenance of law and order in the society; provision and enforcement of legal and contractual obligations; supply of educational, health, and social welfare facilities; assumption of military and defense functions, etc. In effect, these are categories of action which to the extent that they are provided at all, are usually furnished by public rather than private agencies.

Provision of economic overhead may involve the institution of central banking and of monetary and fiscal facilities, the development of a highway and railroad network and of other public utilities.

Application of direct or indirect levers and controls may be based on a wide variety of measures, such as introduction of tariffs, railroad rate discrimination, tax privileges and other types of subsidies, rationing of goods and of credit, price controls, etc.

Government operation of enterprises extending beyond the overhead sectors may range from management of some industries, or a few firms in different industries, to public ownership of all means of production.

Central planning may involve more or less total concentration of economic decision making in the hands of a national planning board.

Admittedly, this fivefold classification is arbitrary, and the line of demarcation between the different categories is quite blurred. Yet, in terms of their effect upon the exercise of individual choice and initiative, they present qualitatively rather significant differences. Thus, most of the items in the first two categories belong to what, in industrializing societies at least, are usually considered as the minimal and essential functions of a state. In contrast, centralized and comprehensive planning combined with total government operation of the economy may be regarded as maximum functions. One of the key questions that needs to be posed in this context is which one, or which combination, of categories will the state use to promote economic development? Whichever means it uses, how massively, to what degree, and with what intensity will it apply its power to the provision of these different categories? Moreover, how will particular kinds and degrees of state intervention affect factor supply, particularly the supply of capital and entrepreneurship?

It may turn out that the more massively and rapidly the state provides what can be considered its minimum functions, the less may be the pressure or the need for it to provide the maximum functions. Therefore, the reliance upon maxima may in effect be a function of past and current failure to provide the minima. In these terms, then, one could say that a necessary precondition for the broadening of opportunities for the exercise of individual choice, individual initiative, and the growth of individual values in underdeveloped countries, launched on a development program, is a high degree and rapid application of state power for the supply of social and economic overhead, combined with partial controls and planning as circumstances may demand them.

Theoretically one could, of course, visualize a system in which amidst public ownership of the means of production, national planning, and resource allocation was—within wide limits—based upon the operation of free consumer choice and consumer autonomy. Realistically, however, it would be extremely difficult to build sufficient checks and balances into such a Lange-like model to prevent it from slipping into a totalitarian mold. On the other hand, this is much less true in the case of partial planning and partial government operation of enterprises, which in many situations is needed to reinforce the provision of social and economic overheads, if comprehensive government planning and management is to be avoided.

The failure of the state in the minimum fields tends to be more or less directly reflected in capital formation and the growth of entrepreneurship. Thus, in many traditional societies, accumulations of merchant and other forms of capital tend to be dissipated because of: (*a*) the absence of adequate and contractual arrangements to protect these holdings from the more or less arbitrary ravages of officialdom, and (*b*) the failure of the state to institute a social security system, so that old age assistance, poor relief, and similar functions must be privately assumed through the family and kinship system. At the same time, condition (*a*) tends to reinforce the economic risks of various types of business and industrial investments. Moreover, the same condition further encourages the flow of capital into land investment, which in an environment of acute population pressure and agrarian value orientation, represents one of the safest and most profitable forms of holding. However, from the standpoint of the economy, this is merely a transfer payment, ultimately representing a leakage of investment into consumption. In effect, then, this is a milieu in which the state—through sins of commission and omission—tends to undercut actual and potential sources of capital accumulation, while at the same time making its contribution to the narrowing of business opportunities. Under these conditions the scarcities of entrepreneurial and technical talent tend to be further intensified through the neglect of education facilities. Moreover, to the extent that some education is provided, its orientation is frequently inhospitable to the growth of scientific and technical knowledge.

Viewed in these terms, perhaps one of the most important contributions the pre-industrial European city made to the industrialization of the continent was that it provided a legally and more or less militarily protected haven for the accumulation and conservation of capital, and for its investment in fields that were eminently productive from a point of view of economic development.

Amidst such circumstances, the formidable barriers to modernization and industrialization are likely to be perpetuated, while economic, social, and political tensions mount under the impact of innovating influences ushered in—as a rule—through foreign contact. Unless some means are found for alleviating these tensions through a process of change and adaptation, the potentially explosive forces in society may be expected to burst forth, sweeping away the old order, capturing the state, and using it as a total and far-reaching instrument for mounting an industrial revolution.

On this basis, one could argue that if India, for instance, wishes to avoid a totalitarian path to industrialization, her current plans and efforts do not provide for enough, rather than for too much, state intervention. Thus the large gap in the financial resources available for the implementation of the Second Five Year Plan may be a symptom of the inability and the reluctance of the Indian state to mobilize the means adequate for the implementation of the ends sought. But, even more fundamentally, perhaps, the inadequacy of the government efforts to spread adult education—both basic and technical education—rapidly, may be an important factor in inhibiting the attainment of certain economic objectives, while at the same time it serves to reinforce the great gulf between the small elite and the rural masses—a factor representing marked potential dangers in the political realm.

To sum up this phase of my argument, it may perhaps be useful to attempt to work with the concept of an "optimum level and pattern of state intervention" parallelling other optima—e.g., the optimum propensity to consume—incorporated in different types of economic and social science models. For our present purposes, this optimum would have to be defined in relation to two broad sets of objectives, i.e., striving for rising standards of living combined with an increase and/or preservation of the scope for the exercise of individual choice and initiative. The definition would also have to take account of the specific circumstances in each case, particularly in relation to the qualitative and quantitative aspects of state intervention, and to the variables listed in Section II above.

IV

We have discussed thus far the role the state may need to play in the process of economic growth without any reference to the character of the state and its capacity to perform the tasks required of it. Historically, however, particularly in the underdeveloped countries, the state—and the social structure on which it was based—was one of the very agencies hampering economic development. The same conditions that create the need for massive state intervention, in one form or another, also tend to breed a type of state which is singularly unequipped to intervene effectively on behalf of economic development. That is, economic backwardness is usually associated with political and other forms of backwardness.

Thus in China, for instance, the state has played a passive to actively negative role *vis-à-vis* the economy. The very concept of economic change and economic dynamism was alien to such a society with the nexus between economic growth and national power and/or welfare only very dimly understood, if perceived at all. The function of the economy was a largely static one, being charged with the primary task of supporting the ruling elite. Therefore, the state assumed very few responsibilities in the economy, beyond assuring that it would provide a stable, continuing, and adequate source of revenue for the imperial household and the gentry-bureaucracy.

The continuing failure of the traditional Chinese state to respond to the challenge of modernization, the institutional rigidities permeating the traditional social structure, the incapacity and unwillingness of the ruling classes to come to terms with change, their inability to understand the character of the innovating influences and to follow a policy of enlightened self-interest, have all served to retard the process of industrialization for so long that cumulative tensions of such explosive proportions were generated that they could no longer be contained, while at the same time perhaps nothing short of such an explosive force could have broken the shackles of the old order and swept away the barriers to economic growth. The violent eruption of the Chinese economy into what seems to bear the earmarks of an industrial revolution under totalitarian control can thus be viewed as an illustration of a resort to maximum solutions in the face of repeated and continued failure of the old state to perform and furnish the minimal functions referred to in the preceding section.

This course of development contrasts sharply with that experienced in Japan, where the breakdown of the old order accelerated by innovating influences produced a realignment of elites. The new elite, which bore some continuity with the old, then set out very deliberately to use the state as an instrument for modernization and industrialization. In doing this, the state from the outset paid major attention to developing rapidly the social and economic overhead sectors and to provide a general framework within which all types of enterprises, private and public, large and small, would grow. The state in effect conceived its role as initiator and promoter of the development process, leaving much of the execution to private enterprise.

While this is not intended to suggest that the Japanese experience can necessarily be duplicated in other countries, and in different circumstances, it is worthwhile to note that the state was able to perform this kind of a role amidst conditions which *ex ante* would have seemed exceptionally unfavorable. Not only were factor and resource endowments poor—in many respects poorer, perhaps not only absolutely but relatively, than those of some major underdeveloped areas today—but institutional barriers were formidable too.

However, an analysis of the conditions under which the state would or would not be *capable* of performing the functions required of it would be beyond the scope of this paper. Rather, I have tried to confine myself more specifically to a spelling out of the conditions under which and the ways in which the state may be *required* to assume a large role in initiating and promoting economic development without jeopardizing the growth of opportunities for the exercise of individual choice and initiative in the economic sphere.

22. PLANNING AND THE MARKET IN ECONOMIC DEVELOPMENT*

Harry G. Johnson

In this article Harry G. Johnson discusses the use of the market mechanism as an instrument of economic development. He suggests several reasons why the role of the market has frequently been neglected in economic development theory and policy. Johnson examines the functions of the market and its advantages and disadvantages in the context of economic development. He concludes that the market is a relatively cheap and efficient instrument despite its shortcomings. He therefore recommends that government development planning improve and strengthen the market system.

Economic development is a field of study in which economists have only recently begun to specialize, and in which consequently there is as yet no settled body of economic doctrine. I must therefore begin with the warning that what I am about to present is not the agreed view of a representative group of economists, but rather my own opinions. Though I have drawn on the literature of development and of economic theory in forming these opinions, I cannot say that the results constitute an authoritative statement of the present position of economics.

The fundamental causes of economic growth are not a subject with which economists have dealt much in the past, and they are not a subject with which economists can claim to be qualified by training and technique to deal now. My subject is not, however, the causes of economic development, but planning and the market in economic development; this involves the theory of markets, and on that subject economists by profession have a

*Reprinted, with permission, from *Pakistan Economic Journal,* Vol. VIII, No. 2 (June, 1958), pp. 44–55. Harry G. Johnson is Professor of Economics at the University of Chicago and the London School of Economics.

great deal to say. Indeed, from the time of Adam Smith, the theory of markets has been the core of economics as a social science.

It is true that the full ramifications of the market as an instrument of social and economic organization were not appreciated from the start by the classical economists. The English classical economists understood the functions of commodity markets; but they did not link the theory of distribution to the pricing process. The integration of the theory of factor prices with the theory of commodity markets was left to J. B. Say, and later Walras and Marshall, to work out. But the relation between the market and economic development lay at the center of the foundations laid by Adam Smith. Smith was concerned with economic development, and at the heart of his work was the market, determining the extent of specialization and division of labor and the limits to increasing productivity.

In recent times, there has been a retreat both in economic theory and in economic policy from the nineteenth-century ideal of the unfettered market as a principle of economic organization. But the economic pros and cons of this retreat have been fully debated, and the economist consequently has a great deal to say about the relative merits of the market as contrasted with other methods of economic organization, and the circumstances appropriate to each.

The subject of planning and the market in economic development is, therefore, one which falls definitely within the field of the economist. Before I go on to discuss it, I must define more precisely what I mean by it. "Planning and the market" may be interpreted in two different ways. First, it may refer to the contrast between direction of the economy by Government and the policy of *laissez-faire*. This is not my subject, though in a wider philosophical and historical context it offers much to discuss. For example, though *laissez-faire* and direction are often regarded as opposites, if one looks to the history of economic development one finds (as Professor Easterbrook has shown[1]) that economic development is almost invariably a process in which planning and direction on the one hand and freedom of enterprise on the other play their part, and are mixed. There is almost no case in which economic development has been entirely planned or entirely unplanned. The usual pattern is one of some framework of control by Government, within which the entrepreneur provides his services—a mixture of bureaucracy and enterprise, in which bureaucracy takes care of the major risks of development and enterprise faces and overcomes the minor ones. Another relevant point that Easterbrook makes is that an economy which succeeds in finding a formula for

[1] Professor Easterbrook's analysis was presented in the Marshall Lectures at Cambridge University in the spring of 1956. Unfortunately these lectures have not been published, but some of the ideas are available in W. T. Easterbrook, "Long Period Comparative Study: Some Historical Cases," *Journal of Economic History*, Vol. XVII, No. 4 (December, 1957), pp. 571–95.

growth tends to repeat that pattern after it has become inappropriate. For example, Britain has gone on trying to work the internationally-orientated pattern of her nineteenth-century development; Russia has been very successful in developing heavy industry but has not yet solved the problem of agriculture.

The alternative interpretation takes planning, in the sense of a general direction of the economy, as an established principle, and considers the market as an alternative to other and more direct means of detailed control. Given the general framework of economic planning, there is still a choice between two alternative methods of looking after the details. One is by direct detailed planning by a central authority, the other is by leaving the working out of details as far as possible to the operation of the market. (There is a third alternative, in which the Government is itself the entrepreneur and investor, which I shall consider later.)

This alternative interpretation is the one I shall be using: I shall discuss the question of the market mechanism as against detailed planning as an instrument of economic development. I should like to make it clear from the start that I am going to make a strong case for the market, as the preferable instrument of economic development, on two main grounds. The first is that the achievement of the desired results by control methods is likely to be especially difficult and inefficient in an underdeveloped economy; at this point I should like to remind you that a large part of Adam Smith's argument for *laissez-faire* was the inefficiency and corruption he saw in the Governments of his time. The second is that the remedies for the main fault which can be found with the use of the market mechanism, its undesirable social effects, are luxuries which underdeveloped countries cannot afford to indulge in if they are really serious about attaining a high rate of development. In particular, there is likely to be a conflict between rapid growth and an equitable distribution of income; and a poor country anxious to develop would probably be well advised not to worry too much about the distribution of income.

I am going to make a fairly strong case for the market, because the market figures relatively little in the literature of economic development, and the theoretical analysis which economics has developed in relation to markets is often overlooked or disregarded. Before getting down to business on the subject of markets, I should like to explore a little the question why, in the theory and policy of "economic development," so little scope is usually allowed to the operation of market forces. There have been, I think, three main groups of factors at work.

In the first place, there seems to be in human societies a set of social and psychological factors favoring intervention in the market. In this connection it is important to remember that the free market as commonly understood is essentially a characteristic of the nineteenth century—before then, and since, the common feature of economic organization has been intervention in the market. What are these factors? One of them, I believe, is the impatience of idealists and would-be reformers with the working of the market, and their desire to take direct action to improve things, according to their criteria of improvement: this attitude reflects the intellectual arrogance typical of reformers. The attitude is reinforced by the fact that the defects of market organization seem obvious to anyone, or can be made to seem so, whereas the socio-economic functions of the market are obscure and difficult to appreciate. The discovery of these functions was indeed the great achievement of the classical economists, and constitutes the only claim that economics has to the status of a science. The obscurity of the market's functions makes it easy, also, to confuse opposition to unattractive features of the free enterprise system which express themselves through the market, such as inequality of income and wealth, with opposition to the market as a mechanism of organization.

Opposition to and dislike of the market for the reasons I have just discussed is frequently allied with a positive belief in the desirability of Government intervention in the market, and a faith in the disinterestedness and effectiveness of such intervention. Belief in the desirability of Government intervention in the western world is associated with the spread of socialist ideas, and in its modern form can be traced back to Benthamite utilitarianism; elsewhere, it can probably be associated with the nature of the State as the dispenser of justice in primitive economies. Belief in the efficiency and disinterestedness of Governmental intervention is associated with the growth of the modern career civil service, with its standards of incorruptibility, particularly in Britain and countries influenced by the British example. (This explains why the belief is less prevalent in the United States than in other English speaking countries.) It is, in my opinion, an important question for underdeveloped countries whether their civil services are of the caliber required to administer the kinds of social and economic programs adopted in the advanced economies.

Opposition to the market as a means of economic organization is also inherent in the characteristics of an established and functioning civil service. One of these characteristics, a corollary of the standards of administrative efficiency and "public service," is a natural propensity to regulate. A good civil service, or a bad one, is rarely prepared to decide that non-intervention is the best policy; and to the bureaucratic mind the functioning of the price system as a regulator appears mere disorder and chaos. Another characteristic is an antipathy towards entrepreneurship; the entrepreneur is an agent of change, and as such disturbs the orderliness of the economy and makes it more difficult to regulate. This is not, of course, a universally valid generalization: civil services have, at times, played important entrepreneurial roles themselves, though usually under the pressure of political events. One special feature of the generally anti-entrepreneurial attitude of civil servants, noted by P. T. Bauer in his studies of West African trade,[2] is specially relevant to underdeveloped economies. This is the antipathy of the British-trained type of civil servant, literate and "responsible," to the semi-literate and socially unacceptable type of individual who possesses the knack of making money by trading—the small-scale entrepreneur on whose activities economic development from a low level may well depend.

These characteristics of civil services are important in considering the uses and limitations of control methods in economic development. The economist, or any other intelligent man, can easily think up ways in which market processes could be improved on by means of controls, assuming that he administers them himself and has infinite time in which to do so. But would the conclusion in favor of controls be the same if it were accepted that their administration had to be entrusted to a "responsible" civil servant of the British type, let alone a civil service with a less ingrained tradition of honesty and disinterestedness?

A third factor antithetical to the market has been the character of modern economics itself, as applied to economic planning. Modern economics has been strongly influenced by the theoretical revolutions of the 1930's, which were inimical to competition and the market. On the one hand, both the theory of monopolistic competition and the new welfare economics have been excessively concerned with criticisms of the efficiency of the market mechanism, criticisms formulated from a static viewpoint not obviously relevant to growth problems. On the other hand, the Keynesian revolution fostered aggregative thinking to the neglect of older ideas of substitutability in production and consumption (which in turn have receded into the limbo of mathematical economics); and the habit of aggregative thinking has to some extent been reinforced by the modern emphasis on statistical verification which has necessarily postulated simplicity of economic relationships.

In addition to these theoretical developments, development economics has been strongly influenced by the nature of the major problems with which economics was concerned before it turned to "development," namely mass unemployment and war finance, which inculcated the habit of thinking about economic structure as given, and of applying other criteria than consumers' choice. Two features of war-time economic planning are frequently overlooked in the attempt to carry over its concepts and techniques to peacetime planning. In the first place, the battery of controls applied in war-time rested very heavily on a strong appeal to patriotism. The application of similar techniques might be possible in an underdeveloped country which could mobilize and concentrate all the instruments of communication and propaganda on the single aim of devel-

[2] P. T. Bauer, *West African Trade: A Study of Competition, Oligopoly and Monopoly in a Changing Economy* (Cambridge: Cambridge University Press, 1954), especially chaps. 11, 12, pp. 145–71.

opment; but the capacity of most countries to do this is doubtful, especially as development presents no single dramatic objective comparable to victory. Secondly, in spite of the propaganda and the patriotic appeal, war-time economic policy in most countries ran into serious difficulties with the resurgence of the market in the form of black markets of various kinds, shop shortages, incentive problems, and so on.

I have been discussing various reasons why thinking about economic development has been inimical to, or neglectful of, market considerations. I now want to recapitulate briefly the various economic functions of the market and the price system as a method of economic organization. I shall be brief, as the argument is a familiar one.

In the first place, the market rations supplies of consumer goods among consumers; this rationing is governed by the willingness of consumers to pay, and provided the distribution of income is acceptable it is a socially efficient process. Secondly, the market directs the allocation of production between commodities, according to the criterion of maximum profit, which, on the same assumption, corresponds to social usefulness. Thirdly, the market allocates the different factors of production among their various uses, according to the criterion of maximizing their incomes. Fourthly, it governs the relative quantities of specific types of labor and capital equipment made available. Fifthly, it distributes income between the factors of production and therefore between individuals. Thus it solves all the economic problems of allocation of scarce means between alternative ends.

These are static functions; but the market also serves in various ways to provide incentives to economic growth. Thus the availability of goods through the market stimulates the consumer to seek to increase his income; and access to the market provides an opportunity for inventors of new goods and technical improvements to profit from their exploitation. Moreover, the market serves particularly to provide an incentive to the accumulation of capital of all kinds: first to the accumulation of personal capital in the form of trained skill, since such skill earns a higher reward; and second to the accumulation of material capital, since such capital earns an income.

The argument, then, is that a properly functioning market system would tend to stimulate both economic efficiency and economic growth. And it is important to note that the market does this automatically, while it requires no big administrative apparatus, no central decision making, and very little policing other than the provision of a legal system for the enforcement of contracts.

All this sounds very impressive; but it is clearly not the whole of the story. What, then, are the objections to the market, how serious are they, and what should be done about them in the context of economic development? I shall discuss these questions in some detail. But first I shall state briefly the central theme of my discussion. It is that in many cases the objections to the market can be overcome by reforming specific markets, so as to bring them closer to the ideal type of market; and that to overcome other objections to the market may be very expensive and may not prove to be worthwhile—in other words, the defects of the market mechanism may on balance be more tolerable than they look at first sight.

Now, what are the objections to the market? They can, I think, be classified into two main types. One type of objection is that the market does not perform its functions properly. The other type of objection is that the results produced by the functioning of the market are undesirable in themselves.

I begin with the first type of objection, that the market does not perform its function properly. Here it is useful to draw a distinction between two quite different sorts of cases—those in which the market operates imperfectly, and those in which a perfectly functioning market would not produce the best results.

Imperfect operation of the market in an underdeveloped country may be attributable to ignorance, in the sense of lack of familiarity with market mechanisms and of awareness of relevant information, or to the prevalence of other modes of behavior than the rational maximization of returns from effort. In the first case, the appropriate Governmental policy would seem to me to be, not to assume from the market the responsibility for allocative decisions, but to disseminate the knowledge and information required to make the market work efficiently and provide the education required to use it. The second case implies a more fundamental obstacle, not only to the use of the market but also to economic development itself, and suggests that successful economic development requires a basic change in social psychology. To my mind, it raises a serious question of fact. Is it really true that people in underdeveloped countries are strangers to the idea of maximizing gains? The idea that they are is very common in the literature and policy-making of economic development; one of its manifestations is the implicit assumption that both supplies and demands are completely price-inelastic. I am very sceptical about this, partly because of Bauer's work and partly because at least some of the actions of Governments in underdeveloped areas presuppose that even the poorest producers are susceptible to price incentives. I personally do not think one is justified in assuming as a general proposition that ignorance and illiteracy necessarily imply that men are not interested in making money. If it is true, there will be serious difficulties in the way of economic development; but again, the appropriate Governmental policy would seem to be to educate the people in the practice of rational economic behavior.

Even if the market functions perfectly, it will not produce the best possible results by its own criteria if there is a difference between social and private benefit or cost. This type of case may be particularly relevant to economic development; it includes the case of increasing returns to scale, and can be extended to include the possibility that technical progress or capital accumulation tend to proceed more rapidly in industry than in agriculture. But it raises an immediate question of fact—whether divergences between social and private benefit or cost are numerous and important or not. This is an important question, but one on which we do not know very much for certain. The theory of increasing returns is logically intriguing, but the influence of increasing returns still has to be disentangled from that of technical progress in historical growth. Again, it is a fact that few advanced countries are not industrial; but this by itself does not establish the wisdom of a policy of forced industrialization in an underdeveloped country. Aside from the question of fact, the existence of divergences between social and private returns does not necessarily indicate a need for the Government to replace the market mechanism; instead, the operation of the market can be perfected by the use of appropriate taxes and subsidies to offset any divergences between social and private returns.

I now turn to the second type of objection to the market, the point of which is not that the market does not work in the way it should, but that the results produced are undesirable in themselves. Here, I think, there are two major objections to the market. The first is that the income distribution produced by the market is unjust and socially undesirable. The distribution of income through the market depends on the wealth and talents of different individuals, and on their individual skill in seeing a profitable opportunity of employing their money or labor. If they make a wise or lucky choice, they may obtain a much higher income. The objection is that this method of determining the distribution of income is not just. But if you attempt to intervene in the distribution of income, you immediately encounter the problem that such intervention interferes with the efficiency of the market system. If people are not allowed to enjoy the income they could obtain by their decisions, their decisions in turn will be affected, and the efficiency of the system will be impaired. There is, therefore, a conflict between economic efficiency and social justice. The extent and importance of this conflict is likely to vary according to the state of economic development. The more advanced a country is, the more likely are its citizens to have consciences about the distribution of income, and to accept the high taxation necessary to correct it without disastrously altering their behavior; and on the other hand, the higher the level of income reached, the less serious will be any slowing down of the rate of growth brought about by redistribution policies. An advanced country can afford to sacrifice some growth for the sake of social justice. But the cost of greater equality may be great to any economy at a low level of economic development that wishes to grow rapidly, particularly as it is evident that historically the great bursts of economic growth have been associated with the prospect and the result of big windfall gains; it would therefore seem unwise for a country anxious to enjoy rapid growth to insist too strongly on policies aimed at ensuring economic equality and a just income distribution. I should add that the problem may not be in fact as serious as I have made it out to be, since in the course of time rapid growth tends in various ways to promote a more equal distribution of wealth.

At this point I should like to digress on a special aspect of the conflict between the market principle and considerations of social justice, which appears in some underdeveloped countries, the conflict created by opposition on moral grounds to the payment and receipt of interest. Now the view that interest is a bad thing is economically nonsensical (unless it is merely a terminological dispute) until the economy has reached a stage at which no more capital can usefully be employed. I am not here referring to the administrative difficulties of removing interest from the economy, but to the economic principle involved. The problem of underdeveloped countries centers around the scarcity of capital. If capital is scare, there should be both an incentive to the accumulation of it by saving, and a device for rationing supplies of it among alternative uses. These are the functions of interest. If you "abolish interest" in the sense of forcing interest to be called by some other name, as was the practice in the Middle Ages, the result will merely be inconvenience; but if you abolish interest in the economic sense, the result will be the loss of the economic services performed by interest. On the one hand, the amount of private saving will be reduced and its allocation to investment distorted by the restriction of investment to activities over which the saver has personal control. On the other hand, insofar as there is a pool of investment funds (created, say, by taxation or monetary expansion, or made available by foreign aid), some method will have to be found for rationing it out among competing claims if it is to be used efficiently. This problem has in fact arisen in Russia, where the engineers and planners who assess investment projects have had to work out concepts which amount to the rate of interest, to fill the gap created by the refusal of Marxian dogma to recognize that capital has a scarcity value and is productive.

The same sort of argument makes it seem undesirable for the Governments of underdeveloped countries to use their monetary policy to favor themselves with low rates of interest. Governments now often enjoy the privilege of paying a rate of interest of 2½ or 3 per cent; this encourages them to think, and to plan, as if capital were easily available. There seems no reason why Governments should enjoy low rates of interest when capital is scarce; on the contrary, it promotes wasteful investment and also, for reasons explained below, tends in the long run to promote inequality of income distribution.

I have been discussing the objection to the results of the market system on the grounds that it produces an undesirable distribution of income. A second objection of the same sort is that the free market will not produce as high a rate of growth as is desirable. I think there is a strong case for this objection, because people's actions in regard to saving and investment depend very much on their guesses about the future. Now people are likely to know their own current requirements better than the Government. But the requirements of the future have to be looked at not from the individual or family point of view or that of the nation as a collection of individuals, but from the point of view of the ongoing society. The needs of society in the future, many economists agree, tend to be underprovided for by the free market.

Even if the conclusion that state action is desirable to raise the rate of growth is accepted, this conclusion nevertheless does not carry with it a number of corollaries which are often attached to it. In particular, it does not necessarily imply that the state ought to undertake development saving and investment itself. Private enterprise may be more efficient than the Government in constructing and operating enterprises, so that the best policy may be to stimulate private enterprise by tax concessions, subsidies, and the provision of cheap credit. Similarly, it may be preferable to stimulate private saving by offering high interest rates, rather than by forcing savings into the hands of the state by taxation or inflation. One argument against a policy of low interest rates and forced saving is that it may in the long run contribute to the inequality of income distribution. The reason is that the poor or small savers are mainly confined to low-yielding fixed-interest investments, directly or indirectly in Government debt, because these are safe and easily available, whereas the larger savers can invest their money in higher-yielding stocks and shares or directly in profitable enterprises. There is, therefore, an opportunity here for Government both to stimulate saving for development and to improve the distribution of income.

There is another reason for being wary of the proposition that the state should undertake development investment itself—the danger that if the Government undertakes investment itself, especially if its administrators are not too clear on their objectives, the result will be the creation of vested industrial interests inimical to further development, and resistant to technical change.

To summarize the foregoing argument from the point of view of development policy, it seems to me that much of development planning could usefully be devoted to the improvement and strengthening of the market system. This does not imply the acceptance of all the results of *laissez-faire*, especially with respect to the rate of growth; but there are reasons for thinking that too much emphasis on a fair or ethical distribution of income can be an obstacle to rapid growth.

The argument I have presented has been concerned mainly with one side of the case for the market. The other side concerns the costs and difficulties of controls, in terms of the manpower costs of the administration they require, and their effects in creating profit opportunities which bring windfall gains to some members of the community and create incentives to evasion which in turn require policing of the controls. I have touched on that side of the argument sufficiently frequently to make it unnecessary to elaborate on it further.

Instead, I shall comment briefly on international markets in relation to economic development, since so far I have been implicitly concerned with internal markets. Economic development planning inevitably has a strong autarkic bias, by reason both of its motivation and of the limitation of the scope of control to the national economy. Nevertheless, international trade can play an important part in stimulating and facilitating the development process. Access to foreign markets for exports can permit an economy with a limited domestic market to exploit economies of scale, and the potentiality of such exports can serve as a powerful attraction for foreign capital and enterprise. Similarly, the capacity to import provided by exports can give a developing economy immediate access to the products of advanced technology, without obliging it to go through the long and perhaps costly process of developing domestic production facilities. Economic nationalism and excessive fear of the risks of international trade, by fostering aversion to exploiting the advantages of the international market, can therefore retard economic development unnecessarily.

One further comment on the international aspects of the market and economic development seems to me worth making. Discussion of the international side of development has been mostly concerned with commodity trade and commercial policy. But in fact one of the most important ways in which the world market system is imperfect is with respect to the international mobility of capital and labor. The problem of international capital movements has received a fair amount of attention, labor mobility and immobility much less. Now, the process of economic development in the past, especially in the nineteenth century, was characterized by vast movements, not only of capital, but also of labor, about the world. The mass movement of labor between countries has now been more or less shut off by the growth of nationalism. I believe it is important to recognize this restriction on international competition, and its implications for programs of economic development. It means—looking at the world economy as a whole—that the solution to the problem of maximizing world output cannot be approached directly, by bringing labor, capital, technology, and natural resources together at the most efficient location; instead, the other productive factors have to be brought to the labor. To a large extent, "the economic development of underdeveloped countries" is a second-best policy,[3] in which gifts of capital and technical training by advanced to underdeveloped countries are a compensation for the unwillingness of the former to consider the alternative way of improving the labor to resources

[3] See J. E. Meade, *The Theory of International Economic Policy*, Volume II: *Trade and Welfare* (London: Oxford University Press, 1955), and R. G. Lipsey and Kelvin Lancaster, "The General Theory of Second Best," *Review of Economic Studies*, Vol. XXIV (1956–57), No. 1, pp. 11–33.

ratio, movement of the labor to the resources. The fact that development is a second-best policy in this respect may impose severe limitations on its efficiency and rapidity.

To conclude, I have been concerned with the role of the market in economic development; and I have aimed at stressing the economic functions of the market, in automatically taking decisions about various kinds of allocations of economic resources, and the place in economic development programs of improvements in market organization and methods. I have been advocating, not a policy of *laissez-faire*, but recognition of the market as an administrative instrument that is relatively cheap to operate and may therefore be efficient in spite of objectionable features of its operations. The general assumption on which I have been arguing is that economic development is a process of co-operation between the state and private enterprise, and that the problem is to devise the best possible mixture.

23. PUBLIC PLANNING AND PRIVATE DECISION MAKING IN ECONOMIC AND SOCIAL DEVELOPMENT*

Gerhard Colm and Theodore Geiger

The authors show that every development plan—even in a highly centralized economy—involves some combination of direct implementation through government action, and indirect implementation through government guidance of the actions of individual decision makers. The success of the development effort therefore depends on the country's ability to work out a coordinated relationship between government and private plans and activities. The authors discuss the nature of the planning process in less developed countries and the appropriate roles for the government and private sectors in an economic development program. They then explain the various techniques for harmonizing public planning and private decision making with each other and with the goals of the national development effort.

REGARDLESS of its name, every modern form of economic system combines some measure of public planning with some latitude for private decision making. Even in the freest of market economies, the government's own expenditures are planned in accordance with annual requirements and with the anticipated longer-range needs for those services considered

---

* Reprinted, with permission, from *Organization, Planning, and Programming for Economic Development* (United States Papers Prepared for the United Nations Conference on the Application of Science and Technology for the Benefit of the Less Developed Areas) (Washington, D.C.: U.S. Government Printing Office, 1962), pp. 15–27. Gerhard Colm is Chief Economist and Theodore Geiger is Chief of International Studies of the National Planning Association.

appropriate for it to provide, and many large private enterprises plan their investment and market development programs for five or ten years ahead. Even in the most centralized socialist economies, the planning and administering authorities must take into account the probable responses of individuals and of local institutions to central government directives regarding production, consumption, saving, and investment. Hence, the task of harmonizing public and private decision making confronts every modern economic system, though in different forms and in different degrees.

The less developed countries of Latin America, Asia, and Africa are in the process of working out reconciliations of public and private decision-making which are relevant to the character of their economies, consistent with their social values, and more or less effective in achieving their chosen goals. The variation is very wide, ranging from such countries as Mexico, Brazil, and Argentina, in which private decision making in the free market plays the major role, to countries like Niger and Chad, in which the modern sector of the economy consists of a few government-owned or foreign-owned enterprises of various kinds. In consequence, it is impossible to discuss public and private decision making in a way which is equally valid for all less developed countries. While our aim is to present some guidelines and suggestions, the analysis which follows is necessarily cast in the form of a generalized discussion of the subject and is not to be construed as descriptive of any particular country.

FUNCTIONS OF GOVERNMENT PLANNING AND PRIVATE DECISION MAKING IN LESS DEVELOPED COUNTRIES

To a greater or lesser degree, the countries of Latin America, Asia and Africa are faced with common difficulties in seeking to accelerate their economic and social advancement. Among the problems relevant to the subject of this paper are: (*a*) the inadequacy of the existing infrastructure (transportation and communication, energy, and power facilities, etc.) and social capital (education, health, and housing facilities, etc.), (*b*) the shortage of investment capital, (*c*) the limited supply of managerial and technical skills, (*d*) the inadequate incentives and institutions for stimulating productive investment and increasing productivity, and (*e*) the heavy dependence upon foreign trade and external aid for obtaining the capital funds and the capital goods required for economic and social development. In such circumstances, governments have had to assume responsibility for discharging three types of functions in order to insure that economic and social development would actually occur in their countries.

The first function is that of national development planning. Broadly speaking, this function consists of defining the goals of the national development effort, estimating and mobilizing the necessary domestic and foreign resources of money and skills, and allocating or guiding them to those specific uses which seem likely to make the greatest contributions to achieving the national goals. This function may be carried out by explicit preparation of a long-range national development plan, as has been done in India and Pakistan, and is now beginning in several Latin American countries. Or, it may be done implicitly and unsystematically, as was customary in many less developed countries until recently. Today, most countries have recognized that, to be effective, national development planning must be carried on in a deliberate and systematic way.

The second function of government in economic and social development is to initiate those investments and manage those activities which comprise the public sector of the economy. In every economic system, there are certain essential services which only governments can perform (national defense, maintenance of law and order, etc.). In addition, there are certain types of investments which are so large or so pervasive in their importance to the economy as a whole that it is necessary or desirable for the government to undertake them. These generally include certain kinds of infrastructural and social overhead capital.

However, the public sector may cover a much broader range of economic activities either by deliberate preference, as in socialist countries, or because there are no practical or acceptable alternative ways of conducting them. For example, in some less developed countries, significant accumulations of capital exist in private hands, but these are often not invested in ways which directly and immediately contribute to economic growth. Traditional habits or present uncertainties may cause such private funds to flow into real estate, commodity transactions, money-lending, and other activities promising quick or large returns, which may eventually result in luxury consumption or investment abroad, usually in Western Europe or the United States. In other countries, there is no private capital or private sector of the economy in the modern sense of the term. In default of government initiative, too few private entrepreneurs would come forward to take advantage of such economic opportunities as may exist. Hence, for a variety of different reasons, the governments of many less developed countries not only invest in essential services and infrastructure but also establish and operate, at least initially, some or all of the new economic activities that are envisaged under the national development plan.

The third function of government in economic and social development is to stimulate, guide, and assist private initiative and activities so that they contribute to achievement of the national development goals. Virtually all the less developed countries are explicitly or implicitly committed to a significant measure of private economic decision-making as an essential complement to the economic functions of the central government. This results not only from deliberate choosing of the social values served by decentralized, nongovernmental decision making in economic life. Paradoxically, it is necessitated by the same scarcities of capital and skills as have impelled governments to assume the national development planning function and the entrepreneurial and managerial functions comprised in the public sector of the economy. In most less developed countries, neither the governments nor the ruling political parties possess the trained supervisory personnel, the technical skills, and the funds necessary to replace all significant privately conducted activities by central planning and government operation of the economy. Determination of the output and consumption of certain types of activities and products—especially those in services and consumer goods industries—seem to defy the detailed directives of central planners. Moreover, there are always potential sources of capital, talents, and initiative that are unavailable to governments, particularly when they operate by compulsion, but which can be stimulated to manifest themselves voluntarily by appropriate incentives and encouragements. The less developed a country, the less it can afford to neglect the potential resources that could be activated only voluntarily and in decentralized, nongovernmental forms.

In addition, the more numerous and detailed the entrepreneurial and managerial decisions that have to be made by the central government authorities, the slower, more cumbersome, and less flexible the operation of the economy becomes. Most less developed countries have found that the market mechanism is a much less wasteful way of making many kinds of economic decisions and for getting many kinds of economic tasks accomplished. A system of centralized direction of production, investment, and consumption is also susceptible to political pressures and the ponderous inflexibility of bureaucratic control. Some of the socialist countries have recognized this deficiency of a large, centralized public sector, and have tried to solve their problems by decentralizing many economic decisions and activities, and providing market-type incentives and pressures for guiding them. Yugoslavia is the leading example of such a country.

Also, many less developed countries have concluded that there are substantial benefits to be derived from attracting responsible private investment from the more developed countries. Continuing, well-conducted enterprises established by foreign companies and businessmen in less developed countries significantly increase the amount of capital available for productive investment; disseminate much needed managerial and technical skills among the local population; and create opportunities for—and often provide financial and technical assistance to—indigenous enterprises to get started as suppliers of the materials, components, and services required for their own operations.

There is a wide variety of different ways by which the government carries out its third function of stimulating and channelling private economic initiative and activity. (See section on "Government Policies in Support of Private Investment.") Thus, it is able to select the particular combination of policy measures that seems best adapted to achieving national development goals in socially acceptable ways.

The question, then, which each less developed country must answer for itself is which economic decisions and activities can best be undertaken by the government and which by private institutions and individuals. This choice is sometimes deliberate, but more often it grows out of the historical background and existing socio-political structure of the country.

THE PARTICIPANTS IN PUBLIC PLANNING AND PRIVATE DECISION MAKING

In order to clarify the interplay between public planning and private decision making, the actors or participants have to be defined.

In the Public Sector

Though we usually speak of the government, it must be remembered that the term covers a multitude of ministries, departments, and agencies, each engaged in planning its own activities. These include not only the several ministries or departments of the central government, but also those of provincial and local governments, as well as quasi-governmental agencies, such as social security funds, central banks, development banks and corporations, port authorities, railroad administrations, public utilities, highway commissions, government-owned and managed manufacturing enterprises, and so on. The planning of each of these governmental institutions has a greater or lesser effect on consumers, workers, and private enterprises. Each of these units of government is interested in specific policies and often subject to pressures from various groups in the population.

The multitude of activities and effects of the various parts and levels of government can themselves be planned only if there is some central planning agency which coordinates and directs planning for the government as a whole. Such a body is, in effect, responsible for the national development plan, as distinct from the different sectoral, functional, and regional programs, which deal in greater detail with the separable parts of the national economy.

The central planning agency has different locations in various countries. In some, it is located under the jurisdiction of one of the ministries (economics or finance); in others, it is organized as a ministry of its own; and in still others, it is an agency under the jurisdiction of a planning council in the office of the country's Chief Executive. National development planning is not a separate activity isolated from the other functions of government. Like budget-making, it is intimately related to all functions. Therefore, it can be effectively carried out only if, regardless of the location of the planning agency, it has the full backing of the country's Chief Executive, who is responsible for all official policies. This dependence on the highest governmental authority is best symbolized when the national development planning function is performed by an agency in the office of the Chief Executive, or the Prime Minister, and when he is directly involved in the planning process as head of a planning council.

Generally, the sectoral and functional programs contained in the national development plan can best be prepared and implemented in a decentralized manner by the individual ministries, departments, and agencies concerned. However, in some less developed countries with a scarcity of government planning personnel, the central agency may have to take on the additional functions of guiding the programing activities and training the programing personnel of the individual governmental and quasi-governmental agencies of the central administration and of provincial and local authorities.

In the Private Sector

While the participants in the public sector can be readily identified as units of the central and local governments, there is no simple way of defining the many different kinds of non-governmental enterprises and activities that play significant roles in national development efforts. A definition by enumeration will be clearer than a definition by characterization.

In some less developed countries, non-governmental activities in commerce and industry may take the form of corporate enterprises similar to the business corporations of the United States and Western Europe. In many other less developed countries, the most important commercial, industrial, and financial activities in the private sector are individual and family proprietorships, like those that predominated in the highly industrialized nations at earlier stages of their development. However, in most parts of Africa, Asia, and Latin America, the numerically largest portion of private economic activity is in agriculture and takes the form of large estates and of small peasant farms, the latter producing either cash crops, or subsistence crops, or a mixture of both.

In recent years, other forms of non-governmental economic activity have been established in less developed countries and have been assuming increasing importance. These include producers and marketing cooperatives, predominantly in agriculture; credit unions and other types of cooperative saving and lending institutions; productive enterprises financed or managed by trade unions, political parties, kinship groups, etc.; and similar institutions. In addition, there are various kinds of local community projects and village organizations. Though many of them may be officially sponsored or government financed, their operations largely depend upon the voluntary initiative and labor of their members, and they may be properly classified as part of the private sector.

Less numerous, but economically more significant, are various forms of joint government/private ventures, involving the participation of local entrepreneurs, and often of foreign companies, which contribute capital and managerial and technical "know-how." When, as is most often the case, the private participants in such joint enterprises are responsible for management, these activities, too, may be considered part of the private sector.

These many and diverse forms of private economic activity play different roles in the national development effort through people's decisions regarding what and when they will produce, consume, save, and invest. In the traditional forms of private economic activity (e.g., peasant farming, latifundia, moneylending, shopkeeping, etc.) these decisions tend to be based upon short-run calculations and on the assumption of static economic conditions, not of dynamic growth. Indeed, by definition, the less developed and more traditionalist a country, the more private economic activities will be of a subsistence nature in agriculture and characterized by a static outlook in commerce, banking, and industry. If these traditionalist and static enterprises are to contribute more effectively to economic growth, their motivation and decision-making have to be reoriented toward the prospects for future expansion and growth. One essential element in bringing about such a dynamic transformation is to enlist the active participation of the numerous, smaller types of private enterprises in the national planning effort.

Generally, it is only the larger, more modern, and more productive private enterprises, including the subsidiaries of North American and West European companies, that are oriented toward longer-term growth expectations. Some follow the practice, increasingly prevalent in the developed countries, of undertaking their own long-range planning of investment and market development within the framework of the national development plan. Such private planning plays a most important role in ensuring that the private sector will make the fullest possible contribution to achieving the goals of the national development effort.

THE CHARACTER OF PLANNING IN LESS DEVELOPED COUNTRIES

The publication of a plan is merely one stage in national development planning. The process as a whole consists not only of preparing the plan, but also of debating and adopting it, implementing it, and then comparing actual performance with the plan and revising it periodically on the basis of experience.

A national development plan always should have a long-range perspective covering general goals for at least ten years ahead, and more details of specific objectives for an intermediate period of four or five years. It should be an operational tool, closely related to the annual government budget, particularly for the short-run period of the next year or two. Operational shorter-term and perspective longer-term planning should be in fluid interrelationship, particularly through the "feed-back" effect made possible by effective progress reporting and evaluation, and periodic revisions.

In an economy in which private decision making plays the major role, the national development plan establishes goals for social and economic development; determines the programs in the public sector; presents forecasts of agricultural, industrial, and commercial investments in the private sector; and estimates the international transactions needed to realize the objectives. These estimates of investments in the private sector and of international transactions are of a different character and significance from the detailed investment programs prepared for the public sector.

In the public sector, the government can determine the specific programs needed and can then direct the execution of these programs. However, even in the public sector, there is an important qualification. These programs are financed either by voluntary private savings and taxation, or by forced savings of various kinds, such as inflation, restriction of consumption, compulsory labor, etc. While the programs are determined in part on the basis of estimates of the productive facilities, manpower, and skills needed to achieve the national development objectives, the expected growth in turn is the most important factor determining the financial resources which will become available.

In the private sector there is the additional task of estimating the likelihood that private domestic and foreign decision makers will in fact engage in the activities postulated by the plan. In addition, it is important to know the amounts and kinds of consumption which would be compatible with the national development goals and with the public programs subject to government direction. For this purpose, the plan has to contain consistent relationships among investments in public undertakings (infrastructure); in social capital (education, health, housing); in directly productive enterprises (public and private); and among government and private savings, consumption, and the other major components of the national domestic and external accounts. For the private sector, the estimates have not only to be consistent with the public sector and with the plan as a whole; they must also be realistic—that is, they must represent realistic forecasts of consumer actions, personal and private institutional savings, etc.

The government can influence consumption by price, tax, wage, and other policies and by a number of other devices discussed in the next section. For the determination of these policies, the plan has to serve as a guide. Thus, the estimates of the sectors in the economy which are not under direct government control commonly consist of forecasts of actions of private decision-makers as they are likely to behave under the influence of government policies specifically designed to affect their behavior. The realism of the forecast depends in part on the degree of influence the government can and intends to exert over the behavior of the private sector.

The uncertainty is inevitably greater with regard to the estimates of international transactions embodied in the plan. A country that depends largely on exports of a few primary products traded on world markets can usually exert little influence on the prices and quantities of these exports.

Hence, this item in the plan will always be purely a forecast, and it must be treated as independently given data. In contrast, other variables in the plan are subject to a greater or lesser degree of direct or indirect control (e.g. imports), and can be so adjusted as to be compatible with the independent factors. Because forecasts of the more or less independent factors may turn out to be erroneous and because these factors themselves cannot be significantly influenced by government policies, it is always prudent to provide contingency measures for adjustment in the other, controllable sectors in case adverse developments occur; for example, if export earnings are less than expected.

In forecasting investments in the private sector, an important distinction needs to be made between what may be called "strategic" investments and "collateral" investments. The former relate to increases in capacity in key industries which are essential for the fulfillment of other parts of the plan. These private investments are often projected on the basis of actual negotiations between the planning agency and the private enterprises concerned. As to the collateral investments, they may be estimated on the basis of surveys of the intentions of private enterprises, taking into account the fact that new investment opportunities arise with expanding markets. Thus, the collateral investment decisions will generally be made automatically as the economy expands in the course of economic development. Inclusion of a projection of collateral investment in the plan is necessary in order to estimate the total demand for funds and the total increase in productive capacity which are likely to be forthcoming. These estimates are, however, less firm than those for the strategic investments and are subject to a considerable margin of error.

It has not been possible in the short space available to indicate more than a few of the many ways in which goal setting, program determination, forecasting, and choice of implementation policies interact with one another in the complex process of planning for economic and social development. The essential role which the forecasting, or projection, of the main components of the national accounts and balance of payments plays in the planning process is not always sufficiently recognized. Conversely, it is sometimes denied that any process which relies so heavily upon forecasting can legitimately be called planning. Those who hold this view maintain that national development planning is only possible if the government has, and is willing to use, the power of directly determining all significant decisions in the economy concerning production, consumption, saving, and investment.

Such a narrow definition of planning is neither accurate nor useful. It is not accurate because all national economic plans, even those of the most centralized and authoritarian socialist countries, contain an important element of forecasting the probable future behavior of individuals and organizations. The level and composition of consumer demand as specified in the plans of centralized socialist economies are essentially estimates of the likely behavior of consumers under certain conditions fixed by the government, rather than directives that will inevitably be obeyed, or which could be exactly enforced. The production goals fixed by central socialist planners, particularly in agriculture, contain a large measure of uncertainty—and to that extent are forecasts—because they are based upon assumptions about the effects on productivity not only of the weather and other natural phenomena but, more importantly, of the attitudes and motivations of farmers and other producers. The external transactions posited in the plans of socialist economies also contain a large element of forecasting. Their inability to control the behavior of world markets and of other governments is one reason why these countries strive to minimize their dependence upon imports—especially from noncommunist economies—despite the higher costs often involved in such autarkic policies.

Indeed, planners of all ideological persuasions have to recognize the fact that governments have only a limited capacity to influence or offset the effects of certain developments, such as a drop in the world prices of primary products, natural catastrophes, the initiative and conscientiousness of the individual citizen, and the variability of producer and consumer responses. Also, a country cannot enjoy the advantages of vigorous innovation and enterprise without giving the managers of private and public enterprises a high degree of freedom from bureaucratic regulations and political interference. However, no country pursuing a determined policy of social and economic development could expect that all required adjustments in the plan would be made only in the public sector. A successful economic and social development plan depends on the ability to work out a constructive relationship between government planning and private decision making, particularly with respect to strategic investments.

TECHNIQUES FOR HARMONIZING PUBLIC PLANNING AND PRIVATE DECISION MAKING

For each country, the major elements in its national development plan can be ranged from those which are most independent of control, such as foreign trade and the weather, to those which are susceptible of control by the government, such as public expenditure programs. In between, are the many factors in which private decision-making predominates but is subject to more or less influence by government policies. Thus, every plan implies some combination of direct implementation through government action, and indirect implementation through the guidance provided by government policies and by the planning process itself for the actions of private decision makers.

While public and private economic activities should be conducive to realization of the goals of the national development effort, they do not always have this character. In the public sector, governments may not make the necessary decisions or may not carry them out effectively, for a variety of political and social reasons. Similarly, the results of private decision making may not always contribute to economic and social advancement, and in some cases may be counter to it, again for a variety of reasons. Insofar as the causes are accessible to remedial action—and this is not always possible at any given stage of a country's political and social evolution—there is a variety of techniques for harmonizing public planning and private decision making with one another and with the goals of the national development effort.

The Announcement Effect of the Plan

A national economic development plan will generally specify the amounts of investments in the different branches of industry in the private sector which are consistent with the other elements of the plan and are required for the increase in production posited as a goal for a future year. The problem is to maximize the probability that private decision makers will actually undertake the investments proposed in the plan.

A major factor working toward this result is what has been called the "announcement effect" of the plan. If the managers of private enterprises are convinced that the government is determined to execute the programs and actions required of it in the public sector and, hence, that there is a good chance that the development goals could be achieved, then the plan for the private sector represents not only what is required of private enterprises but also reveals the opportunities for expansion likely to occur in various industries. In effect, it becomes a matter of self-interest on the part of entrepreneurs to increase productive capacity in line with the opportunities highlighted in the plan. This result depends, of course, on the conviction that the plan is feasible and that the government and other private decision makers will play their respective roles. Success breeds success, and the "announcement effect" can be a continuing one rather than a one-time event.

It is particularly important for the success of the "announcement effect" that the investments be made which provide the transportation and energy facilities and other elements of infrastructure required for expansion of the private sector. Public educational and training programs, and housing for additions to the work force, are often required for labor mobility and industrial expansion. Confidence in the plan can also be strengthened if representatives of private enterprises are consulted in the planning process so that they have a sense of participation and have an opportunity to explain the kinds, locations, and timing of the infrastructure and social capital investments they believe are needed for the success of their own efforts. Such private participation in national development planning is discussed below.

Government Policies in Support of Private Investments

Important as it can be, the announcement effect of the plan is not sufficient by itself to induce the required investments by the private sector.

Assuming that the reasons for the lag are not primarily deficiences in infrastructure or social capital, they are usually caused by a lack of capital available to the private sector; by absence of the required technology, skills, or manpower; or by attitudes and motivations which are not conducive to increased investment or increased productivity. There is a variety of government policies which can help to fill these gaps, and provide incentives and pressures for more productively oriented behavior by private individuals and organizations.

Fiscal and monetary policies of various kinds are important means by which governments can support the private sector. The government's budgetary policy has a major influence on the activities of the private sector through the size and timing of a surplus or deficit. Special tax benefits can be provided for stimulating productive investments, and differential rates may be used to discourage traditional kinds of investments which make little or no direct contribution to the national development goals. In providing such tax incentives, however, care must be taken to prevent possible misuse of them as tax "loopholes." Sometimes, the entire tax system needs to be reformed in order to ensure that all groups in the population contribute equitably to the national development effort.

Through its ability to influence long- and short-term interest rates, the government can ease the shortage of investment or operating capital available to the private sector from the commercial banks and other private lending institutions. More important in many less developed countries than interest rate policy are the ways in which the government exercises direct control over credit availability, investment licensing, construction permits, rationing of capital obtained as foreign aid, etc.

Governmental policies relating to prices and wages can help to maintain the profitability of efficient enterprises within a framework of reasonable price stability. In addition, price policies for public enterprises can be designed which will improve the performance and prospects of private enterprises. Import and foreign-exchange policies can help the private sector to obtain the quantities and kinds of capital goods, materials and components, and operating supplies which can only be purchased abroad; and they can also provide protection against foreign competition for "infant" industries.

Agricultural policy is particularly important in less developed countries, for the agricultural sector often provides the major source of domestic savings for investments in infrastructure, social capital, and new industries; of the foreign-exchange earnings needed to import capital goods; of labor for new factories and service trades; of food to feed the growing population of the towns; and perhaps also of some of the raw materials required for manufacturing. The capacity of the agricultural sector to fulfill these functions exercises a major influence on the development of industry and other new activities. Hence, it is generally necessary to undertake extensive and continuing programs of technical assistance and vocational training in the countryside; to provide adequate credit facilities for agricultural improvement; to encourage the development of producers' and marketing cooperatives and other new forms of cooperation among small farmers; to build farm-to-market roads, irrigation systems, and other installations; and to institute other measures required to increase agricultural productivity. In some countries, basic reform of the whole agrarian system is required before agriculture can begin to play its proper role in the national development effort.

Often, however, more direct measures of specific assistance to the private sector are needed. Development banks—sometimes operating through industrial development corporations—serve as important instruments for extending loans, and in some cases equity capital, to enterprises wishing to expand, or to new ventures which lack the financial resources required for investment in accordance with the plan. Government subsidies have also been used, either in the form of low-interest loans or of outright grants to cover the initial deficits of new enterprises, public and private. Whether institutionalized in development banks and corporations or administered by regular government agencies (e.g. ministries of finance or industry), such government loans and grants form an important link between the public planning process, on the one hand, and the decisions of private enterprises, on the other. Their effectiveness is increased when development banks and corporations provide not only funds but also managerial advice, particularly to new enterprises.

A major contribution to the development of the private sector is made by government policies and measures for mobilizing external resources of funds, commodities, and technical assistance, and making them available by various devices to private enterprises. These external resources may take the form of aid from international organizations and the governments of other countries, or they may be obtained through private foreign investment and the nonprofit activities of educational, research, and philanthropic institutions, trade unions, cooperative societies, and other voluntary private groups in the developed countries.

There is also a regulatory or restrictive group of government policies, in addition to the measures of positive stimulation and assistance just outlined. It may sometimes happen that enterprises will invest faster than envisaged in the plan in order to gain an advantage over competitors or for other reasons. This may be beneficial except where, as in countries with a basic shortage of capital, it may divert resources from higher priority purposes. In such cases, funds for financing "excess" expansion may have to be restricted.

Alternatively, it more often happens that, despite the government's incentives and subsidies, traditionally oriented enterprises—indigenous and foreign—may not invest in the expansion or modernization of their facilities, which may play a strategic role in achieving the objectives of the plan. In this case, new entrepreneurs may be encouraged by the government, or it may itself have to make and initially operate the investments which the private sector is unwilling or unable to undertake.

Other types of limitations on the freedom of action of the private sector imposed by governments include the regulation of the monopolistic and restrictive practices of private—and sometimes public—enterprises, the protection of labor and consumers, the maintenance of public health and safety, and the elimination of other activities and conditions considered socially undesirable.

Governments have to consider not only the impact of restrictive or compulsory measures on the specific enterprises that have provoked them but also the broader effects on attitudes and motivations in the private sector as a whole, as well as the implications for achievement of the national development plan. Since inconsistencies between the objectives of the plan and private decisions are bound to arise from time to time, it is essential that machinery be provided for resolving those conflicts that are of strategic importance in a manner which is just to the individual enterprises involved and is in the best interest of the national development effort as a whole.

In this brief space, it has been possible only to list the main kinds of policy instruments at the disposal of governments for stimulating the private sector to grow and to contribute as effectively as possible to the national development effort and for harmonizing private activities with those of public authorities. In many ways, this is the crucial portion of the strategy of economic and social development. Selecting the proper combination of policy measures and direct subsidy programs is an exceedingly difficult task in most less developed countries not only because of the scarcity of the required financial resources and administrative skills but, more fundamentally, because of social and political obstacles. As already explained, national economic projections or forecasts are most useful tools for helping governments to determine the particular combination of public policies and programs needed to assist the private sector to perform its functions more effectively. But, whether these policies and programs will actually be carried out depends upon the willingness and ability of the government to overcome the political and social resistances to change, the weaknesses in its administrative capabilities, the resentment of influential special interest groups, and sometimes even the apathy of the people themselves. However, all of these difficulties can be significantly eased to the extent to which the private sector and the people generally become voluntary participants and partners in the national development effort.

Private Planning and Participation in Public Planning

The harmonization of public planning and private decision making is not a one-sided process involving only policy choices and actions by the government. It also requires appropriate measures by private decision makers.

In order to contribute most effectively to the national development effort, private enterprises need to engage in their own long-range planning, particularly of their investments in plant and equipment. It is desirable for large enterprises of all types to calculate the productive capacity, manpower, import, and financial resources they are likely to require during the planning period. These private plans should then be made available on a confidential basis to the government planning agency and revised periodically. This applies particularly to what we have called strategic investments in the private sector. Mention has already been made of the desirability of meetings between government planners and the managers of such strategic private enterprises. These negotiations are important not only to ensure consistency in the requirements of the public and private sectors but also to foster constructive attitudes on both sides and mutual understanding.

If the private sector is to make the greatest possible contribution to the national development effort, the many different kinds of private decision makers, large and small, have to be permitted and encouraged to participate actively in the public planning process so that they can acquire a sense of voluntary commitment to achieving the objectives of the national development plan. One method used in a number of countries is for the planning agency to establish advisory committees composed of representatives of industries, the farmers, the trade unions, and other significant private groups. In addition to such direct participation of the private sector in the planning process, each country will, of course, officially review and legally adopt its national development plan in accordance with its constitutional and political procedures.

Ultimately, the success of a national development plan depends upon the basic attitude toward it. To the extent that both public planners and private decision makers recognize that the planning process is a tool, not an end in itself, the task of harmonizing public planning and private decision making will be less difficult in practice and more fruitful in results. Successful fulfillment of this task will make a most important contribution to social and economic progress within a framework of democratically developing institutions.

Convergence of Economic Systems

Are Western capitalist market economies and Communist centrally planned economies becoming more alike? Some economists believe this is so because of concurrent trends toward greater state intervention in the regulated capitalist economies and toward greater decentralization in the centrally planned economies. Others question whether these tendencies are marked enough to justify a conclusion as strong as "convergence." The following articles present two views of the evidence for convergence.

24. DO COMMUNIST AND FREE ECONOMIES SHOW A CONVERGING PATTERN?*

Jan Tinbergen

In this essay, Jan Tinbergen points out how changes in Communist centrally planned economies and in Western capitalist market economies have tended to reduce the differences between them. However, he stresses, these differences are still very striking. Tinbergen discusses the important problems currently facing each type of economy. He then indicates how the possible solutions to their respective problems may further narrow the differences between the two types of economies. He concludes by stating his belief that there is for each country an "optimum" economic system which combines elements of capitalism and socialism and the market and planning.

It should be noted that some economists would disagree with certain aspects of Tinbergen's analysis. For example, they would question the statement (2, vii) that Communist countries have given up the idea that each country should have its own heavy industry, and the implication (4, v) that workers effectively participate in enterprise management in Communist centrally planned economies (a category which excludes Yugoslavia).

---

* Reprinted by permission from *Soviet Studies*, Vol. XII, No. 4 (April, 1961), pp. 333–41. Jan Tinbergen is Professor of Economics and Development Planning at the Netherlands School of Economics.

1. WE ARE witnessing today the coexistence of two radically different economic systems, the "communist" and the "free" economies (according to western terminology) or the "socialist" and "capitalist" systems (according to the eastern vocabulary). The various names given to them are far from precise. Perhaps the most imprecise thing about them is the suggestion that each of these systems represents something well-defined and hence invariant. Reality shows both to be in permanent change. Analysis of the nature of this change can prove quite fascinating. This essay proposes to show that the changes are in many respects converging movements. As will be seen, our essay is a very brief sketch only, trying to indicate a few main tendencies and not going into any detail, or, for that matter, into differences between the communist countries.

The main forces behind the changes may be brought under two broad headings. On the one hand each system is learning from experience and trying to overcome some of its own weaknesses. On the other hand the systems begin to influence each other more and more. While in the beginning the communist system was not taken seriously by the free system this has changed to a considerable extent. The communist system has been interested in some "capitalist" achievements from its very start. Now it is not so much imitating some of the western methods as learning economics from its own experience.

2. Some of the major changes which have occurred in the communist system since the Russian revolution will very briefly be summarized in this section:

(i) For a short while it was thought that specialized management was superfluous and that "the workers" could take care of this activity. It was soon learned that specialization is more efficient with regard to management. In fact, the traditional principle of resistance to specialization in all forms is becoming increasingly less prevalent.

(ii) For a short while an attempt was made to equalize incomes in a drastic way. The well-known consequences of such equalization by decree forced the regime to introduce a wage system which makes wages largely dependent on productivity. Strangely enough, this was then labelled "socialist wage policy."

(iii) For some time planning was done in terms of physical quantities and not in terms of money values. Gradually the use of money as a common denominator penetrated into the planning system and the significance of prices and costs was more and more recognized.

(iv) For a long time interest was considered an unnecessary concept as a consequence of the elimination of private ownership of capital goods. Gradually it was discovered that the elimination of interest as a form of private income does not mean that it should also be disregarded as a cost element.

(v) Rationing was abolished a few years after the Second World War and free consumer choice accepted as a proper institution. Gradually some more emphasis was given to consumption as the purpose of production.

(vi) Mathematical methods of planning, considered as "capitalist" for a long period, were recently recognized to be objective and helpful and are now widely discussed and applied.

(vii) A profound change is under way in the concepts of international trade, not only between communist countries but also between communist and free economies. The idea that each country should have its own heavy industry is no longer adhered to.

3. The so-called free economies have also undergone thorough changes, which will now be summed up.

(i) The public sector nowadays is considerably larger than it was in the nineteenth century. Especially in western Europe public utilities are publicly owned; railways and tramways, coal mines, steel works, insurance companies and banks are often in the public sector.

(ii) The amount of taxes levied in western economies, often in the neighborhood of one quarter of national income, means that taxes are among the important regulators of economic activity. In addition a considerable portion of the nation's savings is made in the public sector.

(iii) Free competition has been limited in many ways as a natural consequence of some technical forces (high fixed costs of production). It has also been voluntarily restricted by such movements as the drive for standardization.

(iv) Partly as a consequence of (iii) governments have limited the freedom of entrepreneurs by anti-trust laws.

(v) Access to education has been given gradually to an increasing portion of the population, often by providing education without charge. Moreover, education has been made compulsory up to a certain age.

(vi) Market forces have been eliminated or modified in some particularly unstable markets, especially in agriculture and in some cases even international commodity agreements have been concluded.

(vii) Planning has gradually been given an increasingly important role, both in big private enterprises and in the design of national economic policy.

(viii) Deliberate development policies have been in existence for a long time. In the nineteenth century already, transportation facilities were often created with public help. At present a whole range of measures, from tax facilities to government investments in infrastructure as well as in manufacturing industry proper, are applied to further the development of remote areas or poor regions.

(ix) Some forms of price and wage control as a direct means to prevent inflation have been used recently in a few "free" economies.

4. Several of the changes recorded above are in fact bringing the communist and the free economies closer together. This cannot be said,

however, to mean that the differences are already small. There are very large differences still. But the process has not stopped. Both types of economies are facing many problems. They will have to move further. In this section we try to give a picture of the most striking differences still in existence and in the subsequent sections of the most important problems to be solved in both types of economies.

(i) The most striking difference is, of course, the size of the public sector. It should not be forgotten, however, that the power of the private sector in western countries is not commensurate with its formal size. In many indirect ways western societies have reduced this power. For example, taxes take away almost half of the profits. Of the remainder, a large part is invested and only a small part paid out as dividends. Western as well as communist economies are to a large extent dominated by managers. In the west, shareholders are no longer powerful. Social legislation in many respects also restricts the freedom of action of private entrepreneurs. So do a number of regulations with regard to quality control, pollution of water and air, building activity, town and country planning and so on.

(ii) Another important difference is the degree of freedom in production decisions. Factory managers in the west have much more freedom in this respect than managers in communist countries where a still very large number of items is planned centrally.

(iii) Accordingly, there is a considerable difference in the degree of detail in which the future course of the economy is planned in communist countries and in "free" economies. This refers to production as well as, e.g., to foreign trade.

(iv) Prices are controlled centrally in the communist countries to a much higher degree than in western countries, where, as a rule, only a few agricultural prices are under direct control. Here again, however, western countries use more indirect means of influencing prices. Among these, competition is the main institutional means, but import duties and monetary policies and (in Holland) wage control and price control of some other items are supplementary instruments.

(v) Industrial democracy is very different in the two types of countries. In the west only some beginnings have been made with codetermination of workers or their organizations in some social issues. In the communist world workers are given opportunities to participate in the discussions about the economic plans of the enterprise and about the use of a portion of the enterprise surplus.

(vi) Education constitutes another subject in which there is still considerable difference. In the "free" countries a certain portion of the potential students of secondary and university training cannot receive the education they need for lack of financial means. The portion is declining, however, as a consequence of several types of financial help, which in some countries enable as much as half of the student body to carry on their studies.

(vii) The differences in the level of savings are recently less striking between such countries as the continental European countries and the communist countries than they were before. Savings of about 20% of national income are now no exception in these western countries; Japan is saving nearly 30%. The United States and the United Kingdom, however, save considerably less.[1]

(viii) Regarding the principles of the international division of labor and the priorities of investment projects the differences between east and west are rapidly disappearing.

5. Corresponding to these problems the communist countries may have to face the following issues:

(i) A major problem seems to be the question of whether or not a gain in efficiency will result from making a large number of small enterprises in essence "private" enterprises by some sort of lease or concession system. If one tries to imagine the volume of administration now usual, say, in shops, it must be a burden on general efficiency.

(ii) A second major problem seems to be whether or not more freedom in production decisions can be given to managers. With rising real incomes citizens of the communist countries will require a finer pattern of qualities and assortment which it is hardly possible to plan centrally. Those closest to the market can probably best judge the needs. There does not seem to be any danger of the central authorities losing control over general economic development as a consequence of granting this type of freedom for the individual manager.

(iii) One also wonders whether or not the number of items planned centrally should be diminished in order to relieve the central planning agencies of a heavy burden which appears to have relatively unimportant qualifications in terms of increments in national wellbeing produced. The same may well apply to international trade planning.

(iv) The next question communist countries might put to themselves relates to price fixing. What harm is there in permitting prices to move as a consequence of relative shortages or abundances and letting them contribute to restore equilibrium? Is not such a method in fact quicker than a mere adaptation in production programs or stocks? Prices will have to move anyhow as a consequence of technical progress and changes in crops. It remains an open question whether the changes should be permitted to individual sellers or only to central authorities. In other words, there seems to be a choice here where the answer is not so clear beforehand and where there is an element of discretion.

(v) A very fundamental question, going far beyond economic institu-

[1] One may comment that probably the U.S. and the U.K. are the most mature economies among the western countries. Interestingly enough, however, continental Europe used to have the same low savings rate as the U.K. and the U.S. for a long time, but after 1950 showed a remarkable increase.

tions, is of course the one about a possible widening of democracy in our sense. It is not within the scope of this essay to make any speculations on this important subject.

6. Certainly the "free" economies also have to face questions.

(i) Has the public sector the correct size? In the United States important commentators have made the point that it is too small in that country and that recently some public tasks have been neglected.

Even if in European countries the question does not seem to be a controversial issue, the related question of how further to restrict the privileges of some forms of private income or capital still is one under discussion. There is an interesting argument about the possibility of restricting consumption financed out of capital gains, introduced by Nicholas Kaldor's book on an expenditure tax. Possible restrictions on the income paid to directors are discussed and the case for higher inheritance taxes has not been decided upon. The impression of a certain stagnation in the reforms in this field is due not so much to general satisfaction about the present state of affairs as it is to the fact that progressive political parties are re-thinking their programs.

(ii) There is not much debate in western countries about restricting the freedom of decisions of managers about their production programs. Rather there is an increasing interest on the side of management for general economic forecasts and market analysis to help them in their decisions.

(iii) Accordingly the case for some more planning is a living issue in the west. One government after the other feels it has to do something in this field. The most recent example is Belgium, with a possibility for Germany to follow. In Asian countries planning is generally accepted; only the methods differ. The borderline European and Asian country, Turkey, has just established a planning agency. Latin American countries are one after the other engaging in some planning. There is a wide variation in the degree of detail planned and the time has come to discuss in a more precise way which degree of detail is the most appropriate. The outcome of such a discussion may also have its value for the communist countries.

(iv) Price formation is an issue of discussion in the west mainly when the general price level is at stake: should not governments have more instruments to counteract inflationary price rises, especially of the cost-push type? The existing situation is unsatisfactory. The use of only monetary and financial means contains the danger of creating unemployment before the price level goes down. Wage control as an indirect means of controlling prices is not accepted. International integration in order to strengthen competition may give some help in small countries, but does not solve the problem for larger countries. It may therefore be that after all some new form of price setting is necessary.

(v) There is a continued pressure in western countries to facilitate the access to education for larger groups of the population. Some of the proposals are going into the direction of the communist solution, namely to pay a wage to the student. Other proposals are more traditional.

(vi) Industrial democracy is an unsolved question too. The attempts so far made in Western Europe differ from country to country. None is very satisfactory.

7. The picture given shows that communist as well as "free" countries have to solve some problems and that there may be further tendencies to a converging movement. This is true particularly for the main question about the degree of decentralization in production decisions and planning. It is to some extent also true for the process of price formation. It is less clear with regard to the formal side of property, but a distinction between formal property and the real situation must be made. As already observed, both the income from property and the freedom of decision with regard to its use have been strongly reduced in the west and the process may continue.

It is interesting to add a more theoretical analysis to the factual description already attempted. What does economic science have to tell us about the probability of a further convergency of the organization patterns? It is evident that economic science can only tell us something about the subject in so far as economic forces will determine the movements. Clearly in the past other than economic forces have been at work. Nevertheless, would it be denied that economic considerations are important both to communists and, let us say, to Americans?

The chapter of economic science we may first consult is welfare economics. In principle, it tells us about the conditions which the optimum pattern of organization of society has to fulfill. Its contents have long been considered a defense of the free enterprise system, but wrongly so. It is true that welfare economics show that uniform prices (i.e., absence of price discrimination) are among the conditions for maximum welfare. But these can be established just as well by a system of government-controlled pricing as by competitive markets.

Another proposition of welfare economics is that prices should be equal to marginal costs. This statement implies that for the activities characterized by high fixed costs and technical surplus capacity private enterprise cannot be the system leading to maximum welfare, unless two-part pricing be applied for these activities.[2] Even in the case where all enterprises in these branches of activity would apply two-part pricing the question might arise whether or not a more efficient administration of this system could be obtained if these enterprises were combined. This combination, in turn, in order not to degenerate into a super-monopoly should be in

[2] J. Tinbergen, "The Theory of the Optimum Regime," *Selected Papers* (Amsterdam: North Holland Publishing Co., 1959), p. 264.

public hands. Socialization may be the best solution therefore for all the activities concerned.

Similar remarks are valid with regard to activities showing external effects. It can be shown, on the basis of welfare economics, that activities of this kind should be carried out by integrated units; integrated, that is, with the producers or consumers whose wellbeing is affected by the external effects. Socialization may again be a solution.

In concrete terms, the most important activities falling under these two categories are about the same as those already socialized in Western European countries, namely public utilities, rail and air transportation, highway construction and education. Possibly also steel and coal should be added and perhaps other types of transportation.

A further subject relevant to welfare economics is taxes. Two principles are important: first, that there must be some form of income redistribution and second, that income tax is not the optimal way of doing so. The redistribution taxes should approach as much as possible the lump-sum type, i.e., the type not taxing marginal income. Wealth taxes are perhaps the nearest example we know today.

All this points to the desirability of some sort of a mixed system, as far as property is concerned, and to a tax system which may hit personal wealth more than it now does in the west. It also points in the direction of admitting more decentralization with regard to the activities showing constant or increasing costs, i.e., generally for industries where small units are justified, as the communist countries may discover in the future.

8. Reference to another chapter (or chapters) of economics may be needed, in order to answer the following questions. What element of truth is there in the contention sometimes made that there is no optimum in the middle, but rather a tendency for optima to be at the extremes?

This opinion is sometimes illustrated by the argument that "once you start to deviate from market price formation you have to regulate more and more until the whole economy is regulated." Is this illustration relevant to our subject and would it, in a general way, disprove the assumption of an optimum somewhere halfway? The alleged tendency to divergency rather than convergency can no doubt be observed in some cases of war economy regulations. If you start rationing and price control in some markets you will soon find it necessary to regulate other markets too. The argument does not necessarily apply to other types of intervention, however. An interesting example to the contrary can be found in business cycle policy. Here it is generally accepted that if you regulate the total flow of demand by appropriate instruments—e.g., financial and monetary policy—you may then leave most markets to themselves. You can, in addition, select a few markets showing characteristics of instability, which may be controlled without the necessity for controlling other markets.

Those to be controlled are the ones showing long production lags or a long life of the products.

In the same manner the ownership of the means of production is not characterized as such by a tendency to spread. In Western Europe there exists a public sector of a certain size which has maintained itself for years without making it necessary to expand it rapidly in order to preserve some equilibrium. If in the U.S.S.R. private business has virtually vanished it is because it was discriminated against on ideological grounds and, in the initial period, for reasons of political power.

In the case of planning a similar position can be maintained. Planning the main elements of the economy does not necessarily imply the need for detailed planning.

It cannot be argued therefore that there is an inherent tendency for economic regimes to move to the extremes. Our theoretical reconnaissance therefore seems to support rather than to undermine the views derived from observation. No doubt the optimum organization of the economy will differ from country to country and from period to period. It is also hardly conceivable that we will soon be able to indicate precisely where the optimum lies, or even to say whether "east and west" will actually "meet" in their attempts to find the "welfare summit."

9. This essay may be concluded with a few remarks about the "non-committed" countries, that is non-committed to one of the two economic systems at the extremes. Being underdeveloped countries at the same time, they still have a significant number of feudal elements. They are less subject to preconceived ideas about the economic system. If the state sector plays an important role in some of them it is because the necessary initiative was first taken in this rather than in the private sector (Turkey, India).

This group of countries is now facing some very urgent economic needs, partly as a consequence of increasing contacts with the outside world, partly because they have only recently become independent states. The most pressing need is the one for a higher level of production. Another need is to live under a system of stabler prices. Several secondary aims of policy can be derived from these primary ones, such as the full use of resources, an increase in investment levels and a diversification of their production pattern.

Because of the presence, in today's world, of the two major systems the underdeveloped countries are looking to both in order to learn from them. They are above all interested in rapid growth and less in such issues as parliamentary democracy, since they have hardly ever had it. The communist example impresses them greatly. Planning is in high esteem. State initiative does take up part of the tasks neglected by private initiative. The willingness to interfere with price formation is understandable since they are often depending on typical unstable markets. Conditions seem favorable in these countries to try to combine the best elements from communism and free enterprise. These countries therefore may become the experimental ground for economic regimes.

They may, as they sometimes do in technical matters, skip one phase in their development and at once aim at the best solution. They should try to. And we may follow with particular interest the pattern of society that is emerging.

25. THE CONVERGENCE OF WESTERN AND COMMUNIST ECONOMIC SYSTEMS: A CRITICAL ESTIMATE*

Jan S. Prybyla

This critical appraisal of the convergence thesis first distinguishes "convergence" from "coexistence." It then carefully analyzes four principal tenets of the convergence thesis—three involving changes in the Communist centrally planned economies and one relating to the Western market-oriented economies. Prybyla concludes that while there is some evidence for convergence in regard to consumption and the combination of planning and market elements, many fundamental differences between the two types of systems will remain.

IN ITS broadest rendering the thesis of convergence states that the social, economic, and political systems of the West and of the communist world show a trend toward the attenuation or elimination of the basic differences which separate them. According to this view the socioeconomic and political systems of Communism and the West tend to converge over time. A corollary is usually drawn to the effect that convergence will lead to a lessening of international tensions and thus remove the danger of mutual nuclear annihilation. Clearly this is an intriguing view which deserves close scrutiny, critical appraisal, and a more careful formulation than it has so far received.

Unfortunately such a broad statement of the problem, while ultimately the only valid one, is not easily handled. Hence the various components of the problem are usually dealt with separately. Of these, changes in the

* Reprinted by permission from *Russian Review,* Vol. 23, No. 1 (January, 1964), pp. 3–17, with the omission of some footnotes. Jan S. Prybyla is Professor of Economics at Pennsylvania State University.

Western and communist economic systems lend themselves most readily to quantification and tend, therefore, to be most often used both to support and decry the convergence argument. Also on occasion the geographical coverage is limited to the United States and Western Europe on the one hand, and to the Soviet Union and its East European allies on the other. It is in this restricted sense that the convergence thesis is examined here.[1]

Even within this much narrower compass the difficulties are formidable. There is, first of all, the problem of the diversity of economic systems; there is also the considerable element of conjecture involved in the projection of past and present trends into the future. There is danger in abstracting economic trends in the communist world from communist political evolution, and there are pitfalls awaiting anyone who attempts to disentangle long-range trends from the still inadequate network of Communist data.

CONVERGENCE V. COEXISTENCE

Convergence must be carefully distinguished from coexistence. In a sense convergence is the Western counterpart of the essentially Soviet coexistence thesis. Both convergence and coexistence are dynamic approaches to economic phenomena as against the conservative (Chinese and Goldwaterian) positions which maintain that the nature of capitalism and communism never changes. While both convergence and coexistence are based on the assumption of evolutionary change, there is marked disagreement on the nature and direction of change.

The ideological starting point of the coexistence argument is the Marxian theorem of capitalism's inevitable travel down the path of internal contradictions toward eventual transformation into socialism, and the swift progress of socialist economies toward a communist state of abundance and equity. The distinctive feature of the coexistence thesis is the shift of emphasis from the inequities, weaknesses, and final disintegration of capitalism considered *in vacuo* to the *comparative* performance of capitalist and Soviet-type socialist economies. The confrontation contrasts socialist economic stability with capitalist business cycles and unemployment, and stresses comparative growth rates, per capita levels of industrial output, and other selected quantitative criteria of economic performance. In short, coexistence—insofar as it is not fraudulent semantics—is convergence through the eventual recognition of the superiority of socialism

[1] "Western Europe" as used in this paper is a political rather than a geographical concept. It means "non-communist Europe" and includes such geographically eastern countries as Greece and Turkey. However, the concept is mainly relevant to the more industrialized countries of noncommunist Europe. The term "communist economic systems" is used to describe the whole spectrum of Soviet-inspired, socialist, command economies in Eastern Europe. The term "Western economic systems" covers noncommunist economies from Sweden to the United States.

over capitalism; it is convergence on Communist terms. Coexistence is in essence a theological view couched in economic vocabulary: "right" (communism) triumphs over "evil" (capitalism) by virtue of its own inherent strength and powers of attraction without recourse to global war. It is the theology of a more successful society which has much to lose in open conflict, seeking a way out of anachronistic rigidities without loss of the inspirational impetus which ideology furnishes. The fact that the coexistence thesis is better known and easier to spot than the convergence argument reflects in part the traditional need of communist societies to verbalize historical trends.

Convergence, on the other hand, when properly formulated is free of normative affiliation. It analyzes developmental trends in Western and communist economies without the aid or hindrance of a philosophical apparatus that ascribes to history the power of linear programming. It is essentially analytical and pragmatic. It detects the emergence within the two broad types of economic systems of similar arrangements that have less to do with any preconceived normative notions of capitalism and communism than with the effective solution of problems posed by increasingly complex, mathematized, engineering-oriented facts. It traces the growth of a common core of rationality in economics which is neither communist nor capitalist but which rests rather on the need to quantify, to define with precision, and to draw conclusions that are practicable.

ARGUMENTS FOR CONVERGENCE

Now to examine some of the major tenets of the convergence thesis. The treatment is necessarily brief and its main purpose is to provide for more exhaustive analyses.

Disaffiliation

It is argued that at least some of the forces which in the past operated in the direction of divergence between the Western and communist economies are currently on the wane, paradoxically by reason of the fact that communist economic systems have by now established a "safe" distance from their parent capitalist stem, that they no longer are or imagine themselves to be "encircled" by hostile, superior powers, that they are going concerns more interested in improving their performance than in stressing those features, however crude, which distinguish them from their mother system. As a result there is less need to experiment with spectacular innovations such as drastic income leveling, job selection and educational policies geared to proletarian origin, disdain for the division of labor as a capitalist prejudice, physical planning and disregard for opportunity costs, commune-type agricultural organization, autarkic proclivities, and so forth. The implication here is that the end of what may be termed *the process of disaffiliation* means a more sophisticated approach to facile doctrinal slogans and a waning of revolutionary fervor. This line of reasoning is usually buttressed with persuasive examples drawn from the current Soviet-Chinese dispute.

A somewhat similar development is allegedly observable in the West. Western attitude to the communist economies is said to have passed through three stages: (1) a stage at which the very practicability of communism as an economic category was seriously questioned; (2) a stage at which this practicability was admitted on the basis of rather eloquent evidence, but it was doubted whether communist economies could function at all efficiently; (3) a stage at which (2) tends to be answered in the affirmative, but the question is *how* efficiently?

The disaffiliation argument deals with comparative attitudes. It concludes that these are becoming ruled more by reason and technological constraint than by fear and emotion. A parallel is sometimes drawn with the gradual erosion of the crusading spirit of Christianity. While the ideal of the one Shepherd and one flock is on the books, it tends to be prompted by means other than those once employed by Richard Coeur de Lion.

The weakness of the disaffiliation argument is that it tries to do too much with a highly volatile raw material. Also, the connection between the completion of the process of breaking away and convergence is rather flimsy. It could conceivably be argued that the very distance traveled by the communist economies and their success in many fields may lead to a hardening of positions into which so much history had gone. Moreover, a number of the policy objectives spelled out in the (1961) Program of the Communist party of the Soviet Union point away from convergence. Certainly, communist experimenting with new forms of economic organization and novel social processes is no less distinctive and revolutionary than in the past. Thus, the loss of revolutionary fervor implied in the disaffiliation argument is questionable. The revolution is continuing although in different forms. It takes place in the yearly transfer of millions of peasants from agriculture to industry, in the training of vast masses of people, in the gradual internalization by the people of a milder but very real totalitarian structure of government, in the emergence of comrades' courts, citizens' militia, and other "public" organizations for the suppression of individualism, in the development of the Soviet "wild East" and the exportation of communist methods and strategies of economic growth in the guise of Soviet, Czech, and East German steel mills and dams. The disaffiliation argument seems to confuse revolutionary nonsense (conspicuous differentiation) with revolutionary content. It is true that the Russians have over the years shed much revolutionary nonsense. But this does not mean a parallel lessening of revolutionary go. The enthusiastic reception reserved for Fidel Castro by the young people of Leningrad elicited from a British observer that

> . . . the outburst of youthful enthusiasm is also a reminder for (Khrushchev) as well as for outsiders, that no Soviet leader can quite forget the

revolutionary origins and aspirations of his country. They represent an emotional factor that must be reckoned with even in cold calculations.

Maturity

A more rigorous version of the disaffiliation argument is found in the view that as the communist economies mature, *i.e.*, as they catch up with the more advanced economies of the West in production, productivity, real wages, per capita income, etc., they will be faced with complex problems of growth and allocative efficiency the solutions to which will tend to be more similar to those adopted in the West than the more primitive, largely administrative and political methods used in the past. What is involved here is convergence through the narrowing of the developmental gap and the gradual disappearance of institutions characteristic of the take-off stage. The argument ascribes much of the tension between the communist and Western economic systems to their different levels of development and to the distinctive patterns of behavior characteristic of those levels. It regards Stalinism as a particularly brutal but not unusual stage in the process of economic growth and recalls in this connection the far from rosy conditions of early capitalist development. It thinks of Stalin as a socialist super-Scrooge who one day will be followed by smoother organization men not unlike those who today from the Kremlins of Madison Avenue persuade the American consumer that what he gets is really what he wants. For an explanation of the particularly violent and obnoxious aspects of Soviet economic history in the thirties and forties, the argument appeals to Asiatic cultural influences and the disaffiliation view discussed above. When propounded by modern-day Soviet-type socialists such as Professor Oskar Lange, the explanation runs mostly in terms of "historical necessity," although it is admitted that the Poles, at least, think that it might have been a great political mistake.

This *maturity argument* begins with the proposition that in its beginnings a socialist system of the Soviet type is faced with a twofold task: economic breakthrough and a radical sociopolitical transformation of the framework of society. Setting up of a new socioeconomic and political order tends to assume disproportionate importance and manifests itself in severe centralization of planning and management and the politicalization of economics. Experience shows that this initial step succeeds both in deeply transforming the socioeconomic structure of society and in chalking up impressive rates of growth. The latter are largely a function of the political regime's concentration on a few high-priority, industrial objectives. The result is a lopsided, quick growth with vast areas of allocative inefficiency. As the process continues, the number of priority claimants to resources goes up sharply. The chronic overcommitment of resources raises problems of alternative costs and points to a need for meaningful allocative principles, criteria of planners' preferences that would take into account relative resource scarcities, scarcity as distinct from control pricing, and the circumscribing of political voluntarism in economic decision making. All this inevitably leads to a close look at some of the more dogmatic, inspirational, but allocatively useless Marxian tenets, and perhaps eventually to the adoption of a less rigid, less metaphysical, more "economic" theory of resource use. The net result seems to be the rise of market socialism of the Yugoslav type in which political dictatorship is combined with advanced decentralization of economic decision making and the operation of a system of scarcity prices over broad areas of the economy. The reason that Yugoslavia has moved into this position well before the other communist economies is ascribed to the fact that President Tito found it strategically and geographically practicable not to wait for the sluggish evolution of Soviet thought on these matters.

It is interesting to recall that the market mechanism (whether or not modified by governmental intervention and oligopolistic industrial structures) fits in well with a variety of political systems. It is by no means the exclusive property of political democracy as currently understood in the West. The market mechanism is a kind of dictator that rewards and punishes those operating within its laws. Western governments are relieved by it of much unpopular and distasteful activity; with justification they are able to shift the blame for a great deal of potentially explosive economic hardship onto the individual's relationship with an impersonal force, the more since this relationship is said to reflect consumer sovereignty. The incorporation of a modified form of the market mechanism into communist economic systems may not only make these economies perform more efficiently, but may also remove from the political directorate some of the trappings of coercive totalitarianism associated with administrative management of the economy.

There are some indications that portions of the maturity argument are valid and that the abandonment by communist countries of war-economy methods of management and planning may mean convergence. It is interesting to see that what was once regarded as a question of principle (e.g., central determination of the scope of a production plan) is now looked upon as a question of technique. If the switch makes for better technique, it erodes the principle. This is in essence what is meant by the gradual shift in the direction of an economic rationality common to both East and West. The search for theoretical guides to the achievement of an optimum allocation of resources that would maximize output in terms of planned product mix and preference schedules is actively pursued in the communist world at the intellectual level. Until now party-dominated policy has only marginally taken note of the debate. As will be shown below, Western economic theory and policy have during this time been involved in excursions into state planning and into the meshing of long-range growth objectives for the economy as a whole with short-term individual decision making. The aim is to resolve a latent conflict between the narrowly private enterprise point of view and a social point of view.

In this conflict the state tends to assume an increasingly important and determining role. There does seem, therefore, to be a *prima facie* case for the tendency of the two systems to meet somewhere halfway on the related questions of growth, stability, and efficiency.

Consumption

The thesis of convergence frequently makes use of the *consumption argument.* In its most popular version the argument of consumption states that a fat Russian is a harmless Russian. What is meant is not only that rising consumption standards in the communist world will efface the more glaring and superficial differences between the underfed (in terms of quality), shoddily clad, and underhoused Russian, and the overfed, well-dressed, air-conditioned American, but also that high consumption somehow generates a keen interest in self-improvement and is prejudicial to the ascetic, other-minded, future-oriented faith on which communist societies have traditionally been based. There is implicit in this argument a linking of high-consumption economy with what the Russians call "private property mentality," and a subsidiary connection between the latter and a less bitter, more cheerful, and eager outlook on the world.

In the decade of the fifties, per capita consumption in the Soviet Union just about doubled. Without any significant shift in resources away from heavy industry and other priority sectors, a 5 percent annual per capita increase in consumption is feasible in the years to come. As of now, urban living standards in the U.S.S.R. can be broadly compared with those of Japan and Italy (excluding the north), and with the situation in Britain in the late forties and early fifties. There are, of course, many differences of detail. Thus if fashion and variety are ignored, the volume of clothing purchases in Russia and the United States is just about equal. The Americans have about 83 times as many automobiles per head as the Russians, but the Russians are ahead in second best durables such as motor bikes and sewing machines; the Americans have over four times as much housing space per head as the Soviets (and of incomparably better quality), twice as many radio sets and shoes. The Russians are ahead in movie attendance and in starchy foods.

The current Soviet plans foresee a substantial development of the service sector over the next twenty years. Personal services in all communist economies are still underdeveloped in volume and extremely vexing in quality. A persistent sellers' market in most consumer goods and services makes life under communism reminiscent of the darker days of wartime England. However, even in these neglected areas improvement is discernible. In 1955 transport and trade services generated only 27.8 percent of the Soviet gross national product as compared with 57.8 percent in the United States (1960), 47.5 percent in Japan (1960), and 39.8 percent in Italy (1960). In spite of improvements in recent years, much remains to be done.

The convergence through consumption argument is summed up by a correspondent of the London *Economist:*

> . . . although the communist system has not brought as big an advance in consumption standards for the Soviet people as it or any other sensible system could have done, the stage of eventual breakthrough to a tolerably affluent urban society—with which the West might find it cosier to live—could be near.

Few economists in the West would quarrel with the conclusion that communist living standards are on the rise. The validity of the connection which the argument tries to establish between a tolerably affluent urban society and cosier international living may, however, be doubted. Hitler's Germany and prewar Japan were, after all, tolerably affluent societies in the sense of urban consumer welfare. To directly link levels of affluence to political aggressiveness or the lack of it is dangerous and probably inaccurate. All that can safely be said is that there will be some convergence of overall living standards. However, it the Soviet party program is in earnest, the future development of consumption in the U.S.S.R. (and probably in other countries of the communist world as well) will concentrate on communal consumption (free public transportation rather than private automobiles, communal catering rather than the family dinner), while the area of individual consumption will be strictly circumscribed. Affluence may thus take on a qualitatively different meaning under Communism than in the West. It may mean greater opportunities for organized togetherness in goods and services without any appreciable increase in the private enjoyment of goods individually owned. This view is only partly attenuated by the reflections below concerning socialization trends in the West.

Socialization

So far the thesis of convergence has stressed the communist side of things. The general impression was that the onus of convergence was on the communist systems in terms of attitudes, decentralization, theoretical refinement, and consumer participation. The *argument of socialization* shifts the emphasis to the behavioral patterns of Western economies. It is argued under this heading that one of the most significant trends in Western economies in recent decades has been the steady growth of the governmental sector and the gradual emergence of the state as an active participant, and in some countries the determining factor, in the economic process. This has been visibly so in Western Europe and less obviously but nonetheless significantly so in the United States.

Government spending on goods and services in the United States has risen from 9.4 percent of the gross national product in 1900 (on the basis of 1962 prices) to 21.2 percent in 1962. If transfer payments such as interest, subsidies and welfare benefits are added, it can be said that governmental influence is keenly felt in more than one quarter of the economy. In contrast to Western Europe, defense is an important channel through which this influence comes to be exerted in the United States. In 1900 the governmental sector in the United States employed a mere 4.9 percent of the labor force; by 1962 over 16 percent of the labor force held government jobs at the federal, state, and local levels. In all Western countries the socially undesirable effects of the market are corrected by heavy progressive taxation and transfer payments. In sum, a free but carefully watched market is in most instances combined with vigorous state measures of social welfare. In Western Europe, moreover, the state is a heavy investor in the economy although the actual technique of investment varies from country to country.

The actual influence of the public sector on the economy in the United States and elsewhere tends to be understated by figures of the kind cited above. In fact, the government in the United States controls the prices of goods and services in at least half the economy. The manner in which this is done is less formal, less institutionalized than in Western Europe, but no less real. Direct administrative control is exercised over the prices of communications and public utilities, transport, energy and over a wide range of the products of agriculture. Occasional governmental pressure is used to correct prices in key industries of the private sector (e.g., steel), and direct influence is exerted through the manipulation of government stockpiles of key raw materials, and through the use of quotas and other devices (e.g., oil, cane sugar). Government contracts in the defense industries spill over into the most remote corners of the economy. The Federal Reserve Board through its open market operations, discount rate policy, and legal reserve requirements affects the credit conditions in the country and indirectly the climate of investment activity. The use of these and other weapons by the government has risen sharply over the years, and there is strong pressure for their extension into areas in which the private sector fails to perform functions for which, perhaps, it had never been intended (e.g., social security, health insurance). Unlike some Western European countries such as France, the United States has not yet ventured into direct government planning for economic growth, but in view of the disappointing growth performance of the period 1933–61 the possibility of a shift in this direction cannot be discounted. The growth of the role of the state in the economy of Western countries is not due exclusively to successive wars. It is as much the result of a growing desire for social equality, opportunity, and security which the regular commercial network very frequently fails to bring about. It is also the result of the recognition of the state's responsibilities for economic stability and long-range growth. An interesting by-product of these developments is the tendency for power to shift from the legislative to the executive organs of the state. Economic policy requires for effectiveness quick and sometimes daily responses which a deliberative assembly fails to provide.

The argument of convergence through the gradual socialization of the

West is not without strength. However, it has to be very carefully formulated. Thus, before asserting that the state sector in the West is gradually coming to wield economic powers not unlike those held by the state in communist countries, it would be wise to examine carefully the nature of the concept of the state in the West and under communism. It remains nevertheless true that, for example, the avoidance of a serious slump in the Western economies over the last two decades for which the state has in no small measure been responsible is a step in the direction of the communist standards of a cycleless economy.

CONCLUSIONS

Two tentative conclusions seem to emerge from this brief discussion of the convergence thesis in its four aspects of disaffiliation, maturity, consumption, and socialization.

Superficially the Western and Communist economic systems do indeed show signs of convergence. A steel mill in Pittsburgh is run in much the same way as a steel mill in Krasnoyarsk. In overall levels of technology, consumption, scientific achievement, there is convergence. There is also a community of training which is needed to sustain and raise those levels of technology, consumption, and scientific achievement. The more extreme attitudes which for many years differentiated East and West are beginning to give way to more subtle and sophisticated ones. More and more the stress is on processes rather than on disjointed events, on the variety of techniques of running an economy rather than on unchangeable principles. There seems to be in both the Communist and Western camps a willingness to experiment with different techniques so long as the results are satisfactory from the standpoint of resource allocation and welfare.

On the other hand the basic differences between the two systems remain formidable. Many of these fundamental differences are outside the rather narrow confines of economics: they concern the place of the individual in society and the extent to which individual subjective valuations are allowed to influence the course of events. They deal with the nature of the state power and the effectiveness of the channels of communication between the individual citizen and the state. In short, convergence to be fully meaningful must concern itself with much more than economic processes. Such considerations are important in evaluating the growing socialization of the Western economies and the repeated attempts at decentralization and the use of a limited market within the communist world.

Yet even within the narrow scope of economics the developments of the last 20 years do not always point in the direction of convergence. High consumption, for instance, may mean very different things depending on the balance between individual and communal consumption. The same is true of the freedom of occupational choice and of the mechanism by which the bill of goods is made up. In short, economic convergence is not as simple a matter as it is often taken to be, nor is it the ultimately determining factor. The Western and Communist economies show in this respect a number of conflicting trends which do not, as of now, add up to a clear-cut convergence thesis.